Lecture Notes in Computer Science   13274

Formal Methods

Subline of Lectures Notes in Computer Science

More information about this series at https://link.springer.com/bookseries/558

Maurice H. ter Beek · Rosemary Monahan (Eds.)

Integrated Formal Methods

17th International Conference, IFM 2022
Lugano, Switzerland, June 7–10, 2022
Proceedings

 Springer

Editors
Maurice H. ter Beek ⓘ
ISTI-CNR
Pisa, Italy

Rosemary Monahan ⓘ
Maynooth University
Maynooth, Ireland

ISSN 0302-9743   ISSN 1611-3349   (electronic)
Lecture Notes in Computer Science
ISBN 978-3-031-07726-5   ISBN 978-3-031-07727-2   (eBook)
https://doi.org/10.1007/978-3-031-07727-2

This Springer imprint is published by the registered company Springer Nature Switzerland AG
The registered company address is: Gewerbestrasse 11, 6330 Cham, Switzerland

Preface

This volume contains the papers presented at the 17th International Conference on integrated Formal Methods (iFM 2022) held in beautiful Lugano, Switzerland, and hosted by the Software Institute of the Università della Svizzera italiana (USI). These proceedings also contain seven papers selected by the Program Committee of the PhD Symposium (PhD-iFM 2022) chaired by Marie Farrell and João F. Ferreira.

In recent years, we have witnessed a proliferation of approaches that integrate several modeling, verification, and simulation techniques, facilitating more versatile and efficient analysis of software-intensive systems. These approaches provide powerful support for the analysis of different functional and non-functional properties of the systems, and the complex interaction of components of different nature, as well as validation of diverse aspects of system behavior. The iFM conference series is a forum for discussing recent research advances in the development of integrated approaches to formal modeling and analysis. The conference series covers all aspects of the design of integrated techniques, including language design, verification and validation, automated tool support, and the use of such techniques in software engineering practice.

iFM 2022 solicited high-quality papers reporting research results and/or experience reports related to the overall theme of formal methods integration. The Program Committee (PC) originally received a total of 53 abstract submissions, which eventually resulted in 46 paper submissions from authors in 24 different countries spread over all six continents: 40 regular papers, five short papers, and one journal-first paper submission. Each submission went through a rigorous review process according to which all papers were reviewed by three PC members, with the help of many external reviewers, followed by a short yet intense discussion phase. The decision to accept or reject a paper was based not only on the review reports and scores but also, and in particular, on these in-depth discussions. In the end, the PC of iFM 2022 selected 16 papers for presentation during the conference and inclusion in these proceedings: 14 regular papers, one short paper, and one journal-first paper. This amounts to an overall acceptance rate of 34.8% (35% for regular papers and 20% for short papers). The PC of PhD-iFM 2022 received eight submissions and selected seven papers for presentation during the conference and inclusion in these proceedings.

To credit the effort of tool developers, this edition of iFM introduced for the first time EAPLS artifact badging. The Artifact Evaluation Committee, chaired by Alessio Ferrari and Marie-Christine Jakobs, received seven submissions and worked hard to run often complex tools and long experiments. All artifacts achieved the available and the functional badge, while two artifacts of particularly good quality were awarded the functional and reusable badge.

The conference featured keynotes by Yamine Aït Ameur (Toulouse INP and IRIT-CNRS, France), Roderick Bloem (Graz University of Technology, Austria), and—as a joint keynote speaker of iFM 2022 and PhD-iFM 2022—Louise Dennis (University of Manchester, UK). We hereby heartily thank these invited speakers.

We are grateful to all involved in iFM 2022. In particular, all PC members and external reviewers for their accurate and timely reviewing, all authors for their submissions, and all attendees for their participation. We also thank all chairs and committees (Journal First Track, Artifact Evaluation Committee, and PhD Symposium), itemized on the following pages, and the excellent local organization and finance and publicity teams chaired by Carlo A. Furia.

We are very grateful to the organizations which sponsored the conference: The Hasler Foundation, Springer, and the European Association for Programming Languages and Systems (EAPLS).

Finally, we thank Springer for publishing these proceedings in their FM subline, and for facilitating the EAPLS artifact badges on the papers, and we kindly acknowledge the support from EasyChair in assisting us in managing the complete process from submissions through these proceedings to the program.

We hope you enjoyed the conference!

April 2022

Maurice H. ter Beek
Rosemary Monahan

Organization

General Chair

Carlo A. Furia   Università della Svizzera italiana, Switzerland

Program Committee Chairs

Maurice H. ter Beek   ISTI–CNR, Italy
Rosemary Monahan   Maynooth University, Ireland

Journal First Track Chairs

Ferruccio Damiani   University of Turin, Italy
Marieke Huisman   University of Twente, The Netherlands

Artifact Evaluation Committee Chairs

Alessio Ferrari   ISTI–CNR, Italy
Marie-Christine Jakobs   Technical University of Darmstadt, Germany

PhD Symposium Chairs

Marie Farrell   Maynooth University, Ireland
João F. Ferreira   University of Lisbon, Portugal

Program Committee

Erika Ábrahám   RWTH Aachen University, Germany
Yamine Aït Ameur   Toulouse INP and IRIT-CNRS, France
Petra van den Bos   University of Twente, The Netherlands
Giovanna Broccia   ISTI–CNR, Italy
Ana Cavalcanti   University of York, UK
Ivana Černá   Masaryk University, Czech Republic
Louise A. Dennis   University of Manchester, UK
John Derrick   University of Sheffield, UK
Brijesh Dongol   University of Surrey, UK
Einar Broch Johnsen   University of Oslo, Norway
Rajeev Joshi   Amazon Web Services, USA
Nikolai Kosmatov   CEA List, France
Michael Leuschel   University of Düsseldorf, Germany
Alberto Lluch Lafuente   Technical University of Denmark, Denmark
Matt Luckcuck   Maynooth University, Ireland

Anamaria Martins Moreira	Federal University of Rio de Janeiro, Brazil
Dominique Méry	Loria and University of Lorraine, France
Stephan Merz	Inria Nancy and Loria, France
Luigia Petre	Åbo Akademi University, Finland
André Platzer	Carnegie Mellon University, USA
Jaco van de Pol	Aarhus University, Denmark
Kostis Sagonas	Uppsala University, Sweden
Gerhard Schellhorn	University of Augsburg, Germany
Emil Sekerinski	McMaster University, Canada
Marjan Sirjani	Mälardalen University, Sweden
Volker Stolz	Western Norway University of Applied Sciences, Norway
Silvia Lizeth Tapia Tarifa	University of Oslo, Norway
Helen Treharne	University of Surrey, UK
Elena Troubitsyna	Åbo Akademi University, Finland
Frits W. Vaandrager	Radboud University, The Netherlands
Andrea Vandin	Sant'Anna School of Advanced Studies, Italy
Heike Wehrheim	University of Oldenburg, Germany
Anton Wijs	Eindhoven University of Technology, The Netherlands
Kirsten Winter	University of Queensland, Australia
Burkhart Wolff	Université Paris-Saclay, France
Naijun Zhan	Chinese Academy of Sciences, China

Artifact Evaluation Committee

Cedric Richter	University of Oldenburg, Germany
Pedro Ribeiro	University of York, UK
Felix Pauck	Paderborn University, Germany
Emilio Incerto	IMT School for Advanced Studies Lucca, Italy
Virgile Robles	CEA List, France
Yannic Noller	National University of Singapore, Singapore
Davide Basile	ISTI–CNR, Italy
Martin Tappler	Graz University of Technology, Austria
Bishoksan Kafle	University of Melbourne, Australia
Mathias Fleury	University of Freiburg, Germany
Danilo Pianini	University of Bologna, Italy
Sharar Ahmadi	University of Surrey, UK

PhD Symposium Program Committee

Wolfgang Ahrendt	Chalmers University of Technology, Sweden
Clare Dixon	University of Manchester, UK
Angelo Ferrando	University of Genova, Italy
Ivan Perez	National Institute of Aerospace and NASA, USA
Alexandra Mendes	University of Porto and INESC TEC, Portugal

Maike Schwammberger   University of Oldenburg, Germany
Graeme Smith   University of Queensland, Australia

Steering Committee

Erika Ábrahám   RWTH Aachen University, Germany
Wolfgang Ahrendt   Chalmers University of Technology, Sweden
Ferruccio Damiani   University of Turin, Italy
John Derrick   University of Sheffield, UK
Carlo A. Furia   Università della Svizzera italiana, Switzerland
Marieke Huisman   University of Twente, The Netherlands
Einar Broch Johnsen   University of Oslo, Norway
Luigia Petre   Åbo Akademi University, Finland
Nadia Polikarpova   University of California, San Diego, USA
Steve Schneider   University of Surrey, UK
Emil Sekerinski   McMaster University, Canada
Silvia Lizeth Tapia Tarifa   University of Oslo, Norway
Helen Treharne   University of Surrey, UK
Heike Wehrheim   University of Oldenburg, Germany
Kirsten Winter   University of Queensland, Australia

Local Organizers

Mohammad Rezaalipour   Università della Svizzera italiana, Switzerland
Diego Marcilio   Università della Svizzera italiana, Switzerland
Elisa Larghi   Università della Svizzera italiana, Switzerland
Roberto Minelli   Università della Svizzera italiana, Switzerland

Additional Reviewers

Sara Abbaspour Asadollah   Constantin Catalin Dragan   Violet Ka I Pun
Ole Jørgen Abusdal   Jannik Dunkelau   Cedric Richter
Sharar Ahmadi   Mamoun Filali-Amine   Justus Sagemüller
Christian Attiogbe   Paul Fiterău-Brostean   Joshua Schmidt
Boutheina Bannour   Predrag Filipovikj   Arnab Sharma
Chinmayi Prabhu   Aditi Kabra   William Simmons
   Baramashetru   Eduard Kamburjan   Marek Trtík
Nikola Benes   Paul Kobialka   Fabian Vu
Lionel Blatter   Stefan Marksteiner   Shuling Wang
Jean-Paul Bodeveix   Hugo Musso Gualandi   Simon Wimmer
Zheng Cheng   Muhammad Osama   Hao Wu
Sadegh Dalvandi   Felix Pauck   Tengshun Yang
Crystal Chang Din   Valentin Perrelle   Bohua Zhan

Side Channel Secure Software
(Abstract of Invited Talk)

Roderick Bloem ⓘ

University of Technology, Austria
roderick.bloem@iaik.tugraz.at

Abstract. We will present a method to analyze masked hardware or masked software for vulnerability to power side channel attacks. Masking is a technique to hide secrets by duplication and addition of randomness. We use the Fourier expansion of Boolean functions to find correlations between variables and secrets and we present an abstraction-refinement technique that reduces the search for correlations to the satisfiability of a formula in propositional logic. This technique allows us to find leaks in industrial-size circuits, while taking detailed timing aspects such as glitching into account.

Formal methods to analyze the power side channel security of software often take a simplistic view of the side-channel leakage that is incurred during a software execution. We take a detailed look at how software executes on a real processor, and specifically on the IBEX RISC-V CPU. Using our verification tool, we find vulnerabilities that are surprising on first glance. We present both modifications to harden a CPU against leaks and guidelines for writing software that can be proven not to leak any further information.

References

1. Bloem, R., Gros, H., Iusupov, R., Könighofer, B., Mangard, S., Winter, J.: Formal verification of masked hardware implementations in the presence of glitches. In: Nielsen, J.B., Rijmen, V. (eds.) EUROCRYPT 2018. LNCS, vol. 10821, pp. 321–353. Springer (2018). https://doi.org/10.1007/978-3-319-78375-8 11
2. Gigerl, B., Hadzic, V., Primas, R., Mangard, S., Bloem, R.: Coco: co-design and co-verification of masked software implementations on CPUs. In: Bailey, M., Greenstadt, R. (eds.) 30th USENIX Security Symposium (USENIX Security 2021), August 11–13, 2021, pp. 1469–1468. USENIX Association (2021). https: //www.usenix.org/conference/usenixsecurity21/presentation/gigerl
3. Hadzic, V., Bloem, R.: CocoAlma: a versatile masking verifier. In: Proceedings of the 21st Conference on Formal Methods in Computer Aided Design (FMCAD 2021), New Haven, CT, USA, October 19–22, 2021, pp. 1–10. IEEE (2021). https://doi.org/10.34727/2021/isbn.978-3-85448-046-4 9 , https://ieeexplore.ieee.org/document/9617707/

Contents

Probability

Learning and Synthesis

Security

Static Analysis and Testing

PhD Symposium Presentations

Invited Presentations

Verifying Autonomous Systems

Louise A. Dennis$^{(\boxtimes)}$ (iD)

University of Manchester, Manchester, UK
`louise.dennis@manchester.ac.uk`

Abstract. This paper focuses on the work of the Autonomy and Verification Network (https://autonomy-and-verification.github.io). In particular it will look at the use of model-checking to verify the choices made by a cognitive agent in control of decision making within an autonomous system. It will consider the assumptions that need to be made about the environment in which the agent operates in order to perform that verification and how those assumptions can be validated via runtime monitoring. Lastly it will consider how compositional techniques can be used to combine the agent verification with verification of other components within the autonomous system.

Keywords: Verification · Autonomous systems · Model-checking · Runtime verification

1 Introduction

Autonomous systems are increasingly being used for a range of tasks from exploring dangerous environments, to assistance in our homes. If autonomous systems are to be deployed in such situations then their safety assurance (and certification) must be considered seriously.

Many people are seeking to leverage the power of machine learning to directly link inputs and outputs in a variety of autonomous systems via a statistical model. This paper examines an alternative, more modular, approach in which the decision making component of the system is constructed in a way that makes it amenable to formal verification. This approach necessitates an integrated approach to the verification of the whole autonomous system – both in terms of validating assumptions about the way the environment external to the system behaves and in terms of compositional verification of the various modules within the system.

2 A Cognitive Agent Decision Maker

Our decision making component is a cognitive agent programmed using the Beliefs-Desires-Intentions (BDI) programming paradigm.

At its most general, an *agent* is an abstract concept that represents an *autonomous* computational entity that makes its own decisions [39]. A general

Supported by organization x.

M. H. ter Beek and R. Monahan (Eds.): IFM 2022, LNCS 13274, pp. 3–17, 2022.
https://doi.org/10.1007/978-3-031-07727-2_1

agent is simply the encapsulation of some computational component within a larger system. However, in many settings we desire something more transparent, where the reasons for choices can be inspected and analysed.

Cognitive agents [7,33,40] enable this kind of reasoning. We often describe a cognitive agent's *beliefs* and *goals*, which in turn determine the agent's *intentions*. Such agents make decisions about what action to perform, given their current beliefs, goals and intentions. This view of cognitive agents is encapsulated within the Beliefs-Desires-Intentions (BDI) model [32–34]. Beliefs represent the agent's (possibly incomplete, possibly incorrect) information about itself, other agents, and its environment, desires represent the agent's long-term goals while intentions represent the goals that the agent is actively pursuing.

There are *many* different agent programming languages and agent platforms based, at least in part, on the BDI approach [5,11,23,29,35]. Agents programmed in these languages commonly contain a set of *beliefs*, a set of *goals*, and a set of *plans*. Plans determine how an agent acts based on its beliefs and goals and form the basis for the selection of actions. As a result of executing a plan, the beliefs and goals of an agent may change and actions may be executed.

We consider agent architectures for autonomous systems in which a cognitive agent decision maker is supported by other components such as, image classifiers, sophisticated motion planning systems with statistical techniques for simultaneous localisation and mapping, planners and schedulers for determining when and in what order tasks should be performed, and health monitoring processes to determine if all the system components are functioning as they should. The agent decision-maker coordinates information and control between these systems.

3   Verifying Autonomous Choices

The starting point of our approach is the use *formal verification* in the form of model-checking [10] (specifically, in our case, *program model-checking* [37]) for the cognitive agent.

Formal verification is the process of assessing whether a formal specification is satisfied on a formal description of a system. For a specific logical property, φ, there are many different approaches to this [6,12,21]. Model-checking takes a model of the system in question (or, in the case of program model-checking the implemented system itself), defining all the possible executions, and then checks a logical property against this model. Model-checking is therefore limited by our ability to characterise and feasibly explore all such executions.

The properties we verify are based on the *choices* the agent makes, given the information that is available to it. This is feasible since, while the space of possibilities covered by, for instance, the continuous dynamics of a robotic system is huge (and potentially infinite), the high-level decision-making within the agent typically involves reasoning within a discrete state space. The agent rarely, if ever, bases its choices directly on the *exact* values of sensors, etc. It might base its decision on values reaching a certain threshold, but relies on other parts of the system to alert it to this, and such alerts are typically binary valued (either the threshold has been reached or it has not). We assume this information is transmitted to the agent in the form of *environmental predicates* which the agent then treats as beliefs.

A very simple example of this is shown in Fig. 1. In this the agent decision maker uses two simple plans to choose whether to stop or follow a path. When it makes the choice it sends a command to an external control system (which can stop or execute path following behaviour). Information from sensors has been processed into two possible environmental predicates, obstacle or path. A property we might wish to verify here is

if the agent believes there is an obstacle then it will try to stop.

With only two predicates and this very simple behaviour we only need to explore four execution traces to see if the property is correct. The correctness will depend on the priority of the two plans. If their priority is incorrect then, in the case where the system detects both an obstacle and a path, it will follow the path rather than stopping. Errors of this kind, where priorities (or behaviour) are not correctly specified for situations where multiple events are taking place are typical of the errors we detect with our approach.

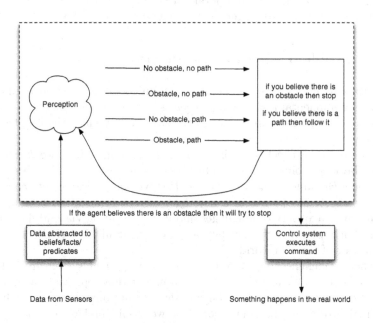

Fig. 1. Verifying a simple agent decision maker

3.1   The MCAPL Framework

We use the MCAPL framework [13,16] in our work, which provides a route to the formal verification of cognitive agents and agent-based autonomous systems using program model-checking. The MCAPL framework has two main sub-components: the AIL-toolkit for implementing interpreters for BDI agent programming languages in Java and the AJPF model checker.

Agent JPF (AJPF) is a customisation of Java PathFinder (JPF) that is optimised for AIL-based language interpreters. JPF is an explicit-state open source model checker for Java programs [28,38][1]. Agents programmed in languages that are implemented using the AIL-toolkit can thus be model checked in AJPF. Furthermore if they run in an environment programmed in Java, then the whole agent system can be model checked.

AJPF comes with a property specification for stating properties about BDI agent programs. This language is propositional linear temporal logic (PLTL), extended with specific modalities for checking the contents of the agent's belief base (**B**), goal base (**G**), actions taken (**A**) and intentions (**I**). This property specification language is described in [16]. As well as the modalities for beliefs etc., the property specification language supports the standard logical connectives ($\wedge$, $\vee$, $\neg$, $\implies$) and the temporal operators, $\square$ (where $\square p$ means that p is always true) and $\lozenge$ (where $\lozenge p$ means that p will eventually be true).

4   The Problem with Environments

In order to prove meaningful properties about our cognitive agent we need to consider the environmental predicates it receives from its environment and, importantly, sequences of these predicates as the situation in which the agent is operating evolves.

When we model check a decision-making agent in AJPF we *have to* use a purely Java environment to supply these predicates since JPF restricts us to the model-checking of Java programs. However in general agents controlling autonomous systems operate in a heterogenous environment with components programmed in a variety of languages and communicating via middleware such as the Robot Operating System [30] and behaviour ulitmately determined by the behaviour of the real world.

So when model-checking an autonomous hybrid agent system in AJPF we have to construct a Java *verification environment* that represents a simulation of some 'real' environment. We can encode assumptions about the behaviour of the 'real' world in this simulation, but we would prefer to minimize such assumptions. For much of our autonomous systems work we try to have minimal assumptions where on any given run of the program in the simulated environment, the environment asserts or retracts the environmental predicates that the agent receives on an entirely random basis. This means that we do not attempt to model assumptions about the effects an agent's actions may have on the

---

[1] https://github.com/javapathfinder.

world, or assumptions about the sequence in which perceptions may appear to the agent. When model checking, the random behaviour of the verification environment causes the search tree to branch and the model checker to explore all environmental possibilities [15].

We call this most simple verification environment, where environmental predicates arrive at random, an *unstructured abstraction* of the world, as it makes no specific assumptions about the world behaviour and deals only with the possible incoming perceptions that the system may react to. Unstructured abstractions obviously lead to significant state space explosion so we have explored a number of ways to structure these abstractions in order to improve the efficiency of model checking, for example specifying that some predicates never appear at the same time. These *structured abstractions* of the world are grounded on assumptions that help prune the possible perceptions and hence control state space explosion.

What if these environmental assumptions turn out to be wrong?

Consider a simple intelligent cruise control programmed as a cognitive agent. This cruise control can perceive the environmental predicates `safe`, meaning it is safe to accelerate, `at_speed_limit`, meaning that the vehicle has reached its speed limit, `driver_brakes` and `driver_accelerates`, meaning that the driver is braking/accelerating. In order to formally verify the behaviour of the cruise control agent in an unstructured environment we would explore the behaviour for all subsets of {`safe`, `at_speed_limit`, `driver_brakes`, `driver_accelerates`} each time the vehicle takes an action. The generation of each subset causes the search space to branch so that, ultimately, all possible combinations, in all possible sequences of action are explored.

We would like to control the state space exploration by making assumptions about the environment. In the case of the cruise control, for instance, we might suggest that a car can never both brake and accelerate at the same time: subsets of environmental predicates containing both `driver_brakes` and `driver_accelerates` should not be supplied to the agent during verification, as they do not correspond to situations that we believe likely in the actual environment. However, since this introduces additional assumptions about environmental combinations it is important that we provide a mechanism for checking whether these assumptions are ever violated.

Runtime Verification. We use a technology called *runtime verification* [17, 36] to monitor the environment that one of our autonomous systems finds itself in and check that this environment conforms to the assumptions used during verification. Our methodology is to verify the behaviour of the program using a structured abstraction prior to deployment – we refer to this as *static verification*. Then, during testing and after deployment, we continually check that the environment behaves as we expect. If it does not then the *runtime monitor* issues a violation signal. We do not discuss what should happen when a violation is detected but options include logging the violation for later analysis, handing over control to a human operator, or entering some fail-safe mode.

We can generate a verification environment for use by AJPF from a *trace expression*. Trace expressions are a specification formalism specifically designed for runtime verification and constrain the ways in which a stream of events may occur. The semantics of trace expressions is presented in [2]. A Prolog implementation exists which allows a system's developers to use trace expressions for runtime verification by automatically building a trace expression-driven monitor able to both observe events taking place and check their compliance with the expression. If the observed event is allowed in the current state – which is represented by a trace expression itself – it is consumed and a transition function generates a new trace expression representing the updated current state. If, on observing an event, no transition can be performed, the event is not allowed. In this situation an error is "thrown" by the monitor.

A trace expression specifying a verification environment can therefore be used in the actual *execution* environment to check that the real world behaves as the (structured) abstraction assumes. Essentially the verification environment represents a model of the real world and a runtime monitor can be used to check that the real world is behaving according to the model.

Figure 2 provides an overview of this system. A trace expression is used to generate a Java verification environment which is then used to verify an agent in AJPF (the dotted box on the right of the figure). Once this verification is successfully completed, the verified agent is used with an *abstraction engine* that converts sensor data into environmental predicates. This is shown in the dotted box on the left of the figure.

If, at any point, the monitor observes an inconsistent event we can conclude that the real world is not behaving according to the assumptions used in the model during verification.

Verification Results. We created trace expressions representing the property that the driver of a car only accelerates when it is safe to do so, and that the driver never presses both the brake and acceleration pedals at the same time.

From this trace expression we were able to generate a verification environment for the cruise control agent and compare it with performance on an unstructured abstraction. We chose to verify the property:

$$\Box(\mathbf{B}_{car}\ \mathsf{safe} \implies \Box(\Diamond(\mathbf{B}_{car}\ \mathsf{safe} \lor \mathbf{B}_{car}\ \mathsf{braking}))) \tag{1}$$

It is always the case that if the car believes it is safe (at some point) then it is always the case that eventually the car believes it is safe or the car believes it braking.

We needed the initial $\mathbf{B}_{car}$ safe in order to exclude those runs in which the car never believes it is safe since the braking behaviour is only triggered when the belief *safe* is removed.

When model checked using a typical hand-constructed unstructured abstraction, verification takes 4,906 states and 32:17 min to verify. Using the structured

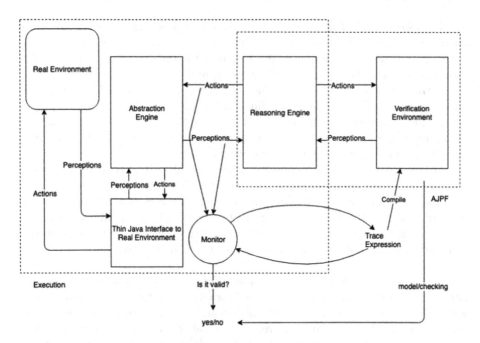

Fig. 2. General view of the runtime monitoring framework from [14]

abstraction generated from the trace expression the property took 8:22 min to prove using 1,677 states – this has more than halved the time and the state space.

As discussed, the structured abstraction may not reflect reality. In the original cruise control program the software could override the human driver if they attempted to accelerate in an unsafe situation. We removed this restriction. Now we had a version of the program that *was incorrect* with respect to our property in the unstructured environment model but remained correct in the structured environment model. We were then able to run our program in a motorway simulation contained in the MCAPL distribution where the "driver" could accelerate whenever they liked – the runtime monitor correctly detected the violation of the environment assumption and flagged up a warning.

Full details of the use of runtime verification with structured abstractions of environments can be found in [20].

5 Compositional Verification

We now look beyond our agent decision-maker to see how we can derive properties about the behaviour of an autonomous system of which the agent decision-maker is only one part. To motivate this we will discuss the verification of a vehicle platooning system (reported in [26]) and an autonomous search and rescue rover.

Vehicle Platooning. The automotive industry is working on what are variously called *road trains, car convoys,* or *vehicle platoons.* Here, each vehicle autonomously follows the one in front of it, with the lead vehicle in the platoon/convoy/train being controlled by a human driver.

In these platoons, vehicle-to-vehicle (V2V) communication is used at the continuous control system level to adjust each vehicle's position in the lanes and the spacing between the vehicles. V2V is also used at higher levels, for example to communicate joining and leaving requests to the platoon's lead vehicle. It is these leaving and joining requests that we consider here.

We assume that this lead vehicle serves two roles. It is controlled directly by a human driver but it also acts as the central decision-making component in platoon operations such as leaving and joining protocols. Therefore there is a software agent in the lead vehicle, in all the other vehicles in the platoon and in any vehicle wishing to join the platoon. These software agents control the enactment of the protocols for joining and leaving the platoon.

Search and Rescue Rover. Consider an autonomous rover deployed in a disaster situation. The autonomous rover has two types of sensor: the vision sensor is used for navigation around the area while an infrared sensor detects sources of heat that might indicate an injured or trapped person. There is a route planner that works with the vision system to provide obstacle free routes to target locations and a battery monitoring system that monitors the power level of the rover. Finally there are two cognitive agents: a goal reasoning agent which takes input from the sensors to select target locations for searching or recharging and a plan execution agent that selects and executes route plans based on battery level information and may send recharge instructions to the goal reasoning agent[2].

5.1   Module Level vs. System Level Properties

Vehicle Platoons. We implemented the reasoning needed to follow the leaving and joining protocols for a platoon as a cognitive agent and were able to verify properties of these agents such as:

> *If a vehicle has a goal to join a platoon but never believes it has received confirmation from the leader, then it never initiates joining the platoon.*

However we are also interested in properties of the global system, for instance we might wish to know that

> *If an agent ever receives a joining agreement from the leader, then the cars in the platoon at the joining location have created enough space for the new car to join.*

---

[2] Code for these two agents can be found in the `src/examples/eass/composi`
`tional/rescue` directory of the MCAPL distribution.

In AJPF's property specification language this would involve both beliefs of the joining agent (that it has received an agreement) and actions of the agents in the specified places in the platoon (that space has opened up). We could, of course, verify each agent separately – for instance that the leader never *sends* an agreement message unless it believes that a space has opened but this fails to really tell us system behaviour. We also have a second problem. While it is all very well to verify that *eventually* an appropriate message is sent or an appropriate action is performed sometimes we require timing constraints on this – particularly in an environment such as a motorway where vehicles are moving at speed. So we are interested in properties like:

> *Given assumptions about the time taken for a vehicle to move to the correct spacing, to move to the correct place adjacent to the platoon and to change lane and for messages to be delivered then the time the required required for a completed join maneuver is within desired bounds*

AJPF's property specification language simply cannot express these properties.

Therefore we opted to use a different approach to verify global properties of the system. In this approach the agent is represented as a more simple automata with many implementation details and edge cases associated with handling unexpected environment behaviour, such as receiving unrequested agreements, removed. This simple automata is then combined with automata representing other vehicles and communication to verify timing properties using the UPPAAL model-checking tool [3,4]. Meanwhile we use AJPF to prove desired properties of the agent implementation.

Search and Rescue Rover. In the case of the Search and Rescue rover we are interested in verifying system level properties such as:

> *If the rover needs to recharge, it will execute actions to move to the charger location.*

This requires, at a minimum, formal guarantees about the behaviour of both agents and the route planning system, and ideally would also involve some analysis of the behaviour of the battery monitor.

In this case we can break this down into properties we want to hold of the individual system components and then combine these. For instance, we want to establish a couple of properties for the plan execution agent, namely:

> *If the plan execution agent believes the battery to be low and the current goal is not the charge position then it will send a recharge message to the goal agent.*

> *If the plan execution agent believes the current goal is the charge position and has a plan to get there then it will instruct the control system to follow the route to the charge position.*

We want to establish that the goal agent has the property:

If the goal agent believes a recharge is needed then it will set the target location to be the charge position.

The route-planner is not a BDI agent, but we can model the algorithm it uses and prove properties of that using Event-B [1]. For instance our route planner outputs a set of routes $\mathcal{R}$ as a sequence of waypoints, $w_0, \ldots, w_n$ so we established:

The current target location appears as a waypoint in all routes suggested by the route planner.

We then need a mechanism to combine these proofs.

5.2   Combining Results

In both our case studies we generated a number of formal verification results using different formalisms and technologies. The challenge is then to combine these into a system level result.

The Platoon. For our platooning system, we established properties both of the agents controlling the individual vehicles involved in the platoon with details of the communication and control behaviour abstracted away in an unstructured verification environment and timing properties of the system behaviour with details of the agent behaviour abstracted away.

For simplicity, we assume that our system S consists of just two agents/vehicles and our verification works has given us the following:

- V_1 and V_2: timed automata representing the vehicle control used to verify properties in UPPAAL.
- V_1' and V_2': untimed abstractions of V_1 and V_2 represented in an unstructured verification environment in AJPF.
- A_1 and A_2: BDI agent implementations used to verify properties in AJPF.
- A_1' and A_2': abstractions of A_1 and A_2 with BDI elements removed used to verify properties in UPPAAL.
- *Comms12* is a timed automaton representing the inter-vehicle communications used to verify properties in UPPAAL.
- *Comms12'* is an untimed abstraction of *Comms12* represented in an unstructured verification environment in AJPF.

We use $\parallel$ to represent the parallel combination of these automata into a system S. So $V_i' \parallel A_i \parallel$ *Comms12'* represents a system used to prove a property about agent, A_i, in AJPF, while $V_1 \parallel A_1' \parallel$ *Comms12* $\parallel A_2' \parallel V_2$ is a system consisting of two agent abstractions and timed automata used to prove a property about interactions of the agents in UPPAAL. In [26] we prove that individual proofs about these systems containing abstractions can be conjoined into a single theorem about the system, $S = V_1 \parallel A_1 \parallel$ *Comms12* $\parallel A_2 \parallel V_2$.

We applied this to our platooning system. In AJPF we proved proved:

If a vehicle with a goal of joining the platoon never believes it has received confirmation from the leader, then it never initiates joining to the platoon.

While, in UPPAAL, we proved:

If an agent ever receives a joining agreement from the leader, then the preceding agent has increased its space to its front agent.

So the combined system has the property:

If a vehicle never believes it has received confirmation from the leader, then it never initiates joining to the platoon **and** *if an agent ever receives a joining agreement from the leader, then the preceding agent has increased its space to its front agent.*

Indicating that an agent never initiates joining the platoon unless the preceding agent has increased its space to it front agent.

Search and Rescue Rover. In the platooning example, our combined property was expressed in a mixture of logics as used by the individual verification tools. For the search and rescue rover example we sought to place this kind of combination within a framework based on the concept of *contracts*.

For this system we specify contracts for each module, in the form of assumptions and guarantees and show, using first order logic, that these contracts imply the system properties. The verifications of individual modules allow us to argue that the module fulfils its contact.

Contracts in First-Order Logic. We assume that our system consists of a set of modules, $\mathcal{M}$, and a signature, Σ, of variables.

For a given module, $C \in \mathcal{M}$, we specify its input modules, $\mathcal{I}_C \subseteq \mathcal{M}$, updates, $\mathcal{U}_C \subseteq \Sigma$, assumption, $\mathcal{A}_C : \Sigma \to Bool$ and guarantee, $\mathcal{G}_C : \Sigma \to Bool$. Taken together $\langle \mathcal{I}_C, \mathcal{U}_C, \mathcal{A}_C, \mathcal{G}_C \rangle$ form a *contract* for the module.

We use the notation $C^\uparrow$ to indicate that a C emits some output and $C^\downarrow$ to indicate that C receives an input.

We assume that all modules, C, obey the following:

$$\forall \phi, \overline{x} \cdot \overline{x} \subseteq \Sigma \backslash \mathcal{U}_C \wedge \mathcal{A}_C \wedge C^\downarrow \wedge \phi(\overline{x}) \Rightarrow \Diamond(\mathcal{G}_C \wedge C^\uparrow \wedge \phi(\overline{x})) \tag{2}$$

Intuitively, this states that if, at some point, C receives an input and its assumption holds then eventually it emits an output and its guarantee holds. Moreover, for any formula, ϕ, which does not involve any of C's update variables then, if ϕ holds when C recieves the input, ϕ also holds when C emits the output – i.e., ϕ is unaffected by the execution of C.

We have a second assumption that explains how inputs and outputs between two modules, C_1 and C_2, connect:

$$C_1^\uparrow \wedge C_1 \in \mathcal{I}_{C_2} \to C_2^\downarrow \tag{3}$$

Intuitively this states that if C_1 emits an output and is connected to the input of C_2, then C_2 recieves an input.

We use these two rules to reason about our system.

Module Contracts. As an example module contract, the contract for the goal reasoning agent was:

Inputs. $\mathcal{I}_G$: $\{V, H, E\}$
Updates. $\mathcal{U}_G$: g
Assumption. $\mathcal{A}_G$: $\top$
Guarantee. $\mathcal{G}_G$: $(g \neq chargePos \Rightarrow$
$(\exists h \cdot h \in \mathbb{N} \wedge (g, h) \in GoalSet \wedge (\forall p, h_1 \cdot (p, h_1) \in GoalSet \Rightarrow h \geq h_1)))$
$\wedge (recharge \iff g = chargePos)$

The goal reasoning agent's inputs are the outputs of the Vision system V, the heat sensor, H and the plan execution agent, E. It updates the target goal, g. It has no assumptions ($\top$) and guarantees that:

1. If the target goal, g, (which it updates) is not the charge position then $(g, h) \in GoalSet$ for some heat signal, h, and for all other positions in the GoalSet the heat for that position is lower than h.
2. If a recharge is needed then g is the charge position

Does the Goal Reasoning Agent Meet its Contract? We proved, using AJPF, that if the goal reasoning agent believed a recharge was required then it would set the goal to be the charging position. We also proved that if recharge was not required it would select the position with the highest heat signature. Note, however, we proved this for specific assumed positions (with these assumptions embedded in a verification environment), rather than the general properties stated in the contract.

Using our contracts we proved:

If at any point all plans sent to the plan execution agent by the planner module are longer than available battery power, then eventually the current plan will contain the charging position as the goal or there is no route to the charging position

$$\Box(\mathcal{G}_P \wedge (\forall p \cdot p \in PlanSet \to length(p) > b - t) \wedge E^{\downarrow}) \implies \qquad (4)$$
$$\Diamond((g = chargePos \wedge g \in plan) \vee PlanSet \neq \varnothing))$$

using the two rules (3) and (2).

In a series of works [8,9,18] we have considered a number of variations on this example, as well as different kinds of contracts and sets of rules for reasoning about them.

6   Conclusion

This paper has focused on work performed by members of the Autonomy and Verification Network. In particular we have focused on the use of the MCAPL framework for verifying decision-making agents in autonomous systems [15,16], the use of runtime verification to check that environments behave as assumed by abstractions [19,20] and techniques for combining heterogenous verifications of different components or aspects of an autonomous system [8,9,18,26].

Our approach is built upon constructing verifiable autonomous systems by locating key high-level decisions in a declarative component based upon the BDI-model of agency.

AJPF is not the only tool aimed at enabling the verification of autonomous systems. Tools are being developed for analysing the behaviour of image classifiers [25], reasoning about control systems [22], programming planning systems with defined formal properties [27] and validating both the models used by planning systems [31] and the plans produced [24]. This is why the work on compositional verification is so critical. To truly verify an autonomous system we need to consider all the software components that make up the system, verify each of them with the appropriate tools and then combine those verifications together.

Data Access Statement. The MCAPL framework, including most of the examples in this paper, is available on github, https://github.com/mcapl/mcapl, and archived at Zenodo, https://zenodo.org/record/5720861. The only example not available with the framework is the platooning example which can be found at https://github.com/VerifiableAutonomy/AgentPlatooning.

Acknowledgements. This work has been supported by EPSRC, through Model-Checking Agent Programming Languages (EP/D052548), Engineering Autonomous Space Software (EP/F037201/1), Reconfigurable Autonomy (EP/J011770), Verifiable Autonomy (EP/L024845/1), Robotics and AI for Nuclear (EP/R026084/1), Future AI and Robotics for Space (EP/R026092/1), and the Trustworthy Autonomous Systems Verifiability Node (EP/V026801/1). Thanks are due to Rafael C. Cardoso, Marie Farrell, Angelo Ferrando, Michael Fisher, Maryam Kamali and Matthew Luckcuck for much of the work presented in this paper.

References

1. Abrial, J.R.: Modeling in Event-B. Cambridge University Press, London (2010)
2. Ancona, D., Ferrando, A., Mascardi, V.: Comparing trace expressions and linear temporal logic for runtime verification. In: Ábrahám, E., Bonsangue, M., Johnsen, E.B. (eds.) Theory and Practice of Formal Methods. LNCS, vol. 9660, pp. 47–64. Springer, Cham (2016). https://doi.org/10.1007/978-3-319-30734-3_6
3. Behrmann, G., David, A., Larsen, K.G.: A tutorial on UPPAAL. In: Bernardo, M., Corradini, F. (eds.) SFM-RT 2004. LNCS, vol. 3185, pp. 200–236. Springer, Heidelberg (2004). https://doi.org/10.1007/978-3-540-30080-9_7

4. Bengtsson, J., Larsen, K., Larsson, F., Pettersson, P., Yi, W.: UPPAAL — a tool suite for automatic verification of real-time systems. In: Alur, R., Henzinger, T.A., Sontag, E.D. (eds.) HS 1995. LNCS, vol. 1066, pp. 232–243. Springer, Heidelberg (1996). https://doi.org/10.1007/BFb0020949

5. Bordini, R.H., Hübner, J.F., Wooldridge, M.: Programming Multi-agent Systems in AgentSpeak Using Jason. John Wiley & Sons, Chichester (2007)

6. Boyer, R.S., Strother Moore, J. (eds.): The Correctness Problem in Computer Science. Academic Press, New York (1981)

7. Bratman, M.E.: Intentions, Plans, and Practical Reason. Harvard University Press, Cambridge (1987)

8. Cardoso, R.C., Dennis, L.A., Farrell, M., Fisher, M., Luckcuck, M.: Towards compositional verification for modular robotic systems. In: Proceedings 2nd International Workshop on Formal Methods for Autonomous Systems (FMAS 2020) (2020)

9. Cardoso, R.C., Farrell, M., Luckcuck, M., Ferrando, A., Fisher, M.: Heterogeneous verification of an autonomous curiosity rover. In: Proc. 12th International NASA Formal Methods Symposium (NFM). LNCS, vol. 12229, pp. 353–360. Springer, Cham (2020). https://doi.org/10.1007/978-3-030-55754-6

10. Clarke, E.M., Grumberg, O., Peled, D.: Model Checking. MIT Press, Cambridge (1999)

11. Dastani, M., van Birna Riemsdijk, M., Meyer, J.-J.C.: Programming multi-agent systems in 3APL. In: Bordini, R.H., Dastani, M., Dix, J., El Fallah Seghrouchni, A. (eds.) Multi-Agent Programming. MSASSO, vol. 15, pp. 39–67. Springer, Boston, MA (2005). https://doi.org/10.1007/0-387-26350-0_2

12. DeMillo, R.A., Lipton, R.J., Perlis, A.: Social processes and proofs of theorems of programs. ACM Commun. 22(5), 271–280 (1979)

13. Dennis, L.A.: The mcapl framework including the agent infrastructure layer and agent Java Pathfinder. J. Open Source Softw. 3(24) (2018)

14. Dennis, L., Fisher, M.: Verifiable autonomy and responsible robotics. In: Software Engineering for Robotics, pp. 189–217. Springer, Cham (2021). https://doi.org/10.1007/978-3-030-66494-7_7

15. Dennis, L.A., Fisher, M., Lincoln, N.K., Lisitsa, A., Veres, S.M.: Practical Verification of decision-making in agent-based autonomous systems. Autom. Softw. Eng. 23(3), 305–359 (2016). https://doi.org/10.1007/s10515-014-0168-9

16. Dennis, L.A., Fisher, M., Webster, M., Bordini, R.H.: Model checking agent programming languages. Autom. Softw. Eng. 19(1), 5–63 (2012)

17. Falcone, Y., Havelund, K., Reger, G.: A Tutorial on runtime verification. In: Engineering Dependable Software Systems, pp. 141–175. IOS Press, Amsterdam (2013)

18. Farrell, M., et al.: Modular verification of autonomous space robotics (2019)

19. Ferrando, A., Dennis, L.A., Ancona, D., Fisher, M., Mascardi, V.: Verifying and validating autonomous systems: towards an integrated approach. In: Colombo, C., Leucker, M. (eds.) RV 2018. LNCS, vol. 11237, pp. 263–281. Springer, Cham (2018). https://doi.org/10.1007/978-3-030-03769-7_15

20. Ferrando, A., Dennis, L.A., Cardoso, R.C., Fisher, M., Ancona, D., Mascardi, V.: Toward a holistic approach to verification and validation of autonomous cognitive systems. ACM Trans. Softw. Eng. Methodol. 30(4), 43:1–43:43 (2021). https://doi.org/10.1145/3447246

21. Fetzer, J.H.: Program verification: the very idea. ACM Commun. 31(9), 1048–1063 (1988)

22. Garoche, P.L.: Formal Verification of Control System Software. Princeton University Press (2019), http://www.jstor.org/stable/j.ctv80cd4v

23. Hindriks, K.V.: Programming rational agents in GOAL. In: El Fallah Seghrouchni, A., Dix, J., Dastani, M., Bordini, R.H. (eds.) Multi-Agent Programming, pp. 119–157. Springer, Boston, MA (2009). https://doi.org/10.1007/978-0-387-89299-3_4
24. Howey, R., Long, D., Fox, M.: VAL: Automatic plan validation, continuous effects and mixed initiative planning using PDDL. In: Proceedings of the ICTAI, pp. 294–301 (2004). https://doi.org/10.1109/ICTAI.2004.120
25. Huang, X., et al.: A survey of safety and trustworthiness of deep neural networks: verification, testing, adversarial attack and defence, and interpretability. Comput. Sci. Rev. **37**, 100270 (2020). https://doi.org/10.1016/j.cosrev.2020.100270, http://www.sciencedirect.com/science/article/pii/S1574013719302527
26. Kamali, M., Dennis, L.A., McAree, O., Fisher, M., Veres, S.M.: Formal verification of autonomous vehicle platooning. Sci. Comput. Program. **148**, 88–106 (2017). http://arxiv.org/abs/1602.01718
27. Lacerda, B., Faruq, F., Parker, D., Hawes, N.: Probabilistic planning with formal performance guarantees for mobile service robots. Int. J. Robot. Res. **38**(9) (2019). https://doi.org/10.1177/0278364919856695
28. Mehlitz, P.C., Rungta, N., Visser, W.: A hands-on Java PathFinder tutorial. In: Proceedings of the 35th International Conference on Software Engineering (ICSE), pp. 1493–1495. IEEE/ACM (2013). http://dl.acm.org/citation.cfm?id=2486788
29. Pokahr, A., Braubach, L., Lamersdorf, W.: Jadex: a BDI reasoning engine. In: Bordini, R.H., Dastani, M., Dix, J., El Fallah Seghrouchni, A. (eds.) Multi-Agent Programming. MSASSO, vol. 15, pp. 149–174. Springer, Boston, MA (2005). https://doi.org/10.1007/0-387-26350-0_6
30. Quigley, M., et al.: ROS: an open-source robot operating system. In: Proceedings of the ICRA Workshop on Open Source Software (2009)
31. Raimondi, F., Pecheur, C., Brat, G.: PDVer, a tool to verify PDDL planning domains. In: Proceedings of the ICAPS 2009 (2009). http://lvl.info.ucl.ac.be/Publications/PDVerAToolToVerifyPDDLPlanningDomains
32. Rao, A.S., Georgeff, M.P.: Modeling agents within a BDI-architecture. In: Proceedings of the 2nd International Conference Principles of Knowledge Representation and Reasoning (KR&R), pp. 473–484. Morgan Kaufmann (1991)
33. Rao, A.S., Georgeff, M.P.: An abstract architecture for rational agents. In: Proceedings of the International Conference Knowledge Representation and Reasoning (KR&R), pp. 439–449. Morgan Kaufmann (1992)
34. Rao, A.S., Georgeff, M.P.: BDI agents: from theory to practice. In: Proceedings of the 1st International Conference on Multi-Agent Systems (ICMAS), pp. 312–319. San Francisco, USA (1995)
35. Rao, A.S.: AgentSpeak(L): BDI agents speak out in a logical computable language. In: Van de Velde, W., Perram, J.W. (eds.) MAAMAW 1996. LNCS, vol. 1038, pp. 42–55. Springer, Heidelberg (1996). https://doi.org/10.1007/BFb0031845
36. Rosu, G., Havelund, K.: Rewriting-based techniques for runtime verification. Autom. Softw. Eng. **12**(2), 151–197 (2005)
37. Visser, W., Havelund, K., Brat, G.P., Park, S., Lerda, F.: Model checking programs. Automat. Softw. Eng. **10**(2), 203–232 (2003)
38. Visser, W., Mehlitz, P.C.: Model Checking Programs with Java PathFinder. In: Proceedings 12th International SPIN Workshop. LNCS, vol. 3639, p. 27. Springer, Cham (2005)
39. Wooldridge, M.: An Introduction to Multiagent Systems. John Wiley & Sons, Chichester (2002)
40. Wooldridge, M., Rao, A. (eds.): Foundations of Rational Agency. Kluwer Academic Publishers, Applied Logic Series (1999)

Empowering the Event-B Method Using External Theories

Yamine Aït-Ameur[1]([✉]), Guillaume Dupont[1], Ismail Mendil[1],
Dominique Méry[2], Marc Pantel[1], Peter Rivière[1], and Neeraj K. Singh[1]

[1] INPT-ENSEEIHT/IRIT, University of Toulouse, Toulouse, France
{yamine,guillaume.dupont,ismail.mendil,marc.pantel,
peter.riviere,nsingh}@enseeiht.fr
[2] LORIA, Université de Lorraine and Telecom Nancy, Nancy, France
dominique.mery@loria.fr

Abstract. Event-B offers a rigorous state-based framework for designing critical systems. Models describe state changes (transitions), and invariant preservation is ensured by inductive proofs over execution traces. In a correct model, such changes transform safe states into safe states, effectively defining a partial function, whose domain prevents ill-defined state changes. Moreover, a state can be formalised as a complex data type, and as such it is accompanied by operators whose correct use is ensured by well-definedness (WD) conditions (partial functions).

This paper proposes to define transitions explicitly as partial functions in an Event-B theory. WD conditions associated to these functions prevent ill-defined transitions in a more effective way than usual Event-B events. We advocate that these WD conditions are sufficient to define transitions that preserve (inductive) invariants and safety properties, thus providing easier and reusable proof methods for model invariant preservation. We rely on the finite automata example to illustrate our approach.

Keywords: State-based methods · Invariants preservation · Partial definitions and well-definedness · Safety · Event-B

1 Introduction

Our proposal stems from the following two extensive research observations:

First, formal state-based methods have demonstrated their ability to model complex systems and reason about them to establish properties reflecting the modelled requirements. In particular, they have proven to be effective in ensuring system safety through the verification of invariant properties. This ensures that each reachable state of the modelled system fulfills these invariants, i.e. the system state is always in a safe region and never leaves it. In general, invariants verification is based on an induction principle over traces of transition systems, i.e. invariants hold in the initial state and if they hold in any state, then they hold in the next state (deterministic) or next states (non-deterministic). The proof is carried out on the formalised model using the associated proof system.

M. H. ter Beek and R. Monahan (Eds.): IFM 2022, LNCS 13274, pp. 18–35, 2022.
https://doi.org/10.1007/978-3-031-07727-2_2

Second, the modelling of complex systems in system engineering relies on domain knowledge that is shared and reused in system models. It contains definitions as well as domain-specific properties. In general, this domain knowledge is formalised as theories with data types, operators, axioms and theorems proved using the associated proof system, *independently* of the designed models. In these theories, a Well-Definedness (WD) condition is associated to each operator expressing the constraints to be fulfilled for its application (partial function). The theories are used to type concepts in system models, to manipulate them with operators, and finally to establish system specific properties with the help of the axioms and theorems issued from these theories.

Our Claim. From our observations, we claim that it is possible to exploit externally defined theories and rely on the associated WD conditions to establish system properties, in particular, safety ones. *The idea consists in formalising state changes (transitions) explicitly as partial function expressed by operators defined in external theories.* The WD conditions associated with each theory operator when discharged as proof obligations (PO) prevent ill-defined transitions.

Objective of this Work. In the presence of theories that axiomatise domain specific data types, our approach defines another modelling and proof technique for invariant preservation in Event-B [2]. It relies on the use of automatically generated WD proof obligations associated with operators coded as partial functions, to circumscribe the states of the system under design to a given safety domain.

Organisation of the Paper. Next section discusses invariant and WD proof obligations with respect to related work. Section 3 overviews the Event-B concepts needed for our approach. Section 4 describes the formalism of *finite automata*, used to illustrate our approach and Sect. 5 shows their formalisation as an Event-B model. Section 6 presents our approach, and its correctness is justified in Sect. 7. Section 8 shows its application on finite automata. Last, a conclusion and future research directions are presented in Sect. 9.

2   Invariants and Well-Definedness (WD)

State-based methods are characterised by the explicit definition of a state, usually characterised by variables as well as a set of actions that modify them. These actions rely on the generalised assignment operation based on the *"becomes such that"* before-after predicate (for deterministic and non deterministic assignments) introduced, in particular, by the seminal work of [1,9,11,14]. This operation defines a state transition and it is encapsulated in ASM rules [7], substitutions or events in B and Event-B [2], Hoare triples [14], Guarded Commands (GCL) [9], operations in RSL [13] and VDM [17], actions in TLA$^+$ [18], schemas in Z [26] and so on. All these methods provide a proof obligation (PO) generation mechanism that generates proof goals submitted to the underlying method's proof system. These ones are involved in the description and verification of invariants defining safety properties resulting from requirements.

Invariants. The before-after predicate (BAP) allows to observe the state of a system and state changes in traces describing system behaviours. Inductive-based reasoning defined on such traces establishes properties, in particular invariant preservation. Informally, it states that if a property holds for the initial state and that, for any transition, this property holds before and after this transition, then it holds for every state of the system.

Without loss of generality, let us consider an Event-B guarded event: WHEN $G(x)$ THEN $x :\mid BAP(x, x')$ END. x is a state variable, $G(x)$ a guard (predicate) and $BAP(x, x')$ a BAP relating before x and after x' state variable values. Under $A(s, c)$ axiomatisation of sets and constants definitions, the invariant $I(x)$ preservation PO for such event is $A(s, c) \wedge G(x) \wedge BAP(x, x') \wedge I(x) \Longrightarrow I(x')$. This PO shall be proved **for each** event of the model.

Well-Definedness (WD). According to [4], Well-Definedness describes the *circumstances under which it is possible to introduce new term symbols by means of conditional definitions in a formal theory as if the definitions in question were unconditional, thus recovering completely the right to subsequently eliminate these symbols without bothering about the validity of such an elimination.* It avoids describing ill-defined operators, formulas, axioms, theorems, and invariants.

In Event-B, each formula is associated to well-definedness POs [19] that ensure that the formula is well-defined and that two-valued logic can be used. A WD predicate $WD(f)$ is associated with each formula f. This predicate is defined inductively on the structure of f. For example, if we consider a and b being two integers, P and Q two predicates, f of type $\mathbb{P}(D \times R)$, the following WD definitions can be written as $WD(a \div b) \equiv WD(a) \wedge WD(b) \wedge b \neq 0$, $WD(P \wedge Q) \equiv WD(P) \wedge (P \Rightarrow WD(Q))$, $WD(P \vee Q) \equiv WD(P) \wedge (P \vee WD(Q))$ or $WD(f(a)) \equiv WD(f) \wedge WD(a) \wedge a \in \mathrm{dom}(f) \wedge f \in D \nrightarrow R$ where $\nrightarrow$ denotes a partial function. Once the WD POs are proved, they are added as hypotheses in the proofs of the other POs [2].

Invariants and WD. When reporting an error in a proof by J-P. Verjus, A. J. M. van Gasteren and G. Tel [12] identified the concepts of "always-true" and "invariant". In Event-B, "always-true" is expressed using theorems on variables, while "invariant" is expressed as inductive invariants. In addition, invariant properties shall be expressive enough to derive safety properties. Our approach is illustrated on Event-B. We consider a state change as a transformation function on state variables. As this function is partial, it is associated with WD conditions.

Handling WD conditions and partial functions ($\nrightarrow$) definitions in proofs and proof systems is not new. The paper of C.B. Jones [15] clearly highlights the importance of dealing with such definitions. In formal proof systems, it has been addressed in different manners using two-valued and three-valued logic (with weak and strong equality), subset types, denotational approaches, type-correct conditions of total functions, etc. [4, 5, 16, 19, 23, 24, 27].

Our Proposal. Our research focuses on state-based modelling with Event-B but may be transferred to other state-based methods. We view a state change (transition) as a partial function $Trans : State \nrightarrow \mathbb{P}(State)$ (or $Trans : State \nrightarrow State$ for a deterministic system). Here, $State$ denotes the Cartesian product of the type of each state variable. As an invariant must restrict state changes to safe states, this function can be seen as a partial function, *well-defined* on the set of safe states $Safe_{St}$ as $Trans_{Inv} : Safe_{St} \nrightarrow \mathbb{P}(State)$. To preserve the invariant, one has to prove that: $\mathbf{ran}(Trans_{Inv}) \subseteq \mathbb{P}(Safe_{St})$.

Based on the definition of such function, our proposal consists in describing an alternative approach to Event-B invariant preservation based on the definition, in an Event-B theory, of a data type T describing a *State* with a set of well-founded operators (well-defined partial functions). An operator $Op(x_1 : T_1, x_2 : T_2, \ldots, x_n : T_n)$ with n arguments returns an expression of type T and is associated to a logical condition of the form $WD(x_1, x_2, \ldots, x_n)$ stating that $x_1, x_2, \ldots, x_n \in \mathbf{dom}(Op)$. Each operator describes safe state changes according to a given *reusable* property *independently* of any model. Below, we show how this approach works for Event-B models.

3   Overview of Event-B

Event-B [2] is a *correct-by-construction* method based on set theory and first order logic (FOL). It relies on an expressive state-based modelling language where a set of events models state changes.

3.1   Contexts and Machines (Tables 1b and 1c)

Table 1. Global structure of Event-B Theories, Contexts and Machines

Theory	Context	Machine
THEORY Th	**CONTEXT** Ctx	**MACHINE** M
IMPORT Th1, ...	**SETS** s	**SEES** Ctx
TYPE PARAMETERS E, F, ...	**CONSTANTS** c	**VARIABLES** x
DATATYPES	**AXIOMS** A	**INVARIANTS** $I(x)$
Type1$(E, ...)$	**THEOREMS** T_{ctx}	**THEOREMS** $T_{mch}(x)$
constructors	**END**	**VARIANT** $V(x)$
cstr1$(p_1: T_1, ...)$		**EVENTS**
OPERATORS		**EVENT** evt
Op1 <nature> $(p_1: T_1, ...)$		**ANY** α
well−definedness $WD(p_1, ...)$		**WHERE** $G(x, \alpha)$
direct definition D_1		**THEN**
AXIOMATIC DEFINITIONS		$x :\mid BAP(\alpha, x, x')$
TYPES A_1, ...		**END**
OPERATORS		...
AOp2 <nature> $(p_1: T_1, ...): T_r$		**END**
well−definedness $WD(p_1, ...)$		
AXIOMS A_1, ...		
THEOREMS T_1, ...		
END		
(a)	(b)	(c)

A `Context` component describes the static properties of a model. It introduces the definitions, axioms and theorems needed to describe the required concepts using *carrier sets* s, *constants* c, *axioms* A and *theorems* T_{ctx}. A `Machine` describes the model behaviour as a transition system. A set of guarded events is used to modify a set of state variables using Before-After Predicates (BAP) to record state changes. Machines are made of *variables* x, *invariants* $I(x)$, *theorems* $T_{mch}(x)$, *variants* $V(x)$ and *events* evt (possibly guarded by G and/or parameterized by α).

Refinements. Refinement (not used in this paper) decomposes a *machine* into a less abstract one with more design decisions (refined states and events) moving from an abstract level to a less abstract one (simulation relationship). Gluing invariants relating abstract and concrete variables ensure property preservation. We do not give more details on refinement as the approach we propose applies to any Event-B machine being either a root machine or a refinement machine.

Proof Obligations (PO) and Property Verification. Table 2 provides a set of automatically generated POs to guarantee Event-B machines consistency.

Table 2. Relevant proof obligations

(1)	Ctx Theorems (ThmCtx)	$A(s, c) \Rightarrow T_{ctx}$ (For contexts)
(2)	Mch Theorems (ThmMch)	$A(s, c) \wedge I(x) \Rightarrow T_{mch}(x)$ (For machines)
(3)	Initialisation (Init)	$A(s, c) \wedge G(\alpha) \wedge BAP(\alpha, x') \Rightarrow I(x')$
(4)	Invariant preservation (Inv)	$A(s, c) \wedge I(x) \wedge G(x, \alpha) \wedge BAP(x, \alpha, x') \Rightarrow I(x')$
(4)	Event feasibility (Fis)	$A(s, c) \wedge I(x) \wedge G(x, \alpha) \Rightarrow \exists x' \cdot BAP(x, \alpha, x')$
(5)	Variant progress (Var)	$A(s, c) \wedge I(x) \wedge G(x, \alpha) \wedge BAP(x, \alpha, x') \Rightarrow V(x') < V(x)$

Core Well-definedness (WD). In addition, WD POs are associated to all Event-B built-in operators of the Event-B modelling language. Once proved, these WD conditions are used as hypotheses to prove further proof obligations.

3.2 Event-B Extensions with Theories

In order to handle more complex and abstract concepts beyond set theory and first-order logic, an Event-B extension for supporting externally defined mathematical objects has been proposed in [3,8]. This extension offers the capability to introduce new data types by defining new types, operators, theorems and associated rewrite and inference rules, all bundled in so-called *theories*. Close to proof assistants like Coq [6], Isabelle/HOL [23] or PVS [24], this capability is convenient to model *concepts unavailable in core Event-B*, using data types.

Theory description (See Table 1a). Theories define and make available new data types, operators and theorems. Data types (**DATATYPES** clause) are associated to *constructors*, i.e. operators to build inhabitant of the defined type. These ones may be inductive. A theory may define various *operators* further used in Event-B expressions. They may be FOL *predicates*, or *expressions* producing actual values (<nature> tag). Operator application can be used in other Event-B theories, contexts and/or machines. They *enrich the modelling language* as they occur in the definition of axioms, theorems, invariants, guards, assignments, etc.

Operators may be defined explicitly in the DIRECT DEFINITION clause (case of a constructive definition), or defined axiomatically in the AXIOMATIC DEFINITIONS clause (a set of axioms). Last, a theory defines a set of axioms (AXIOMS clause), completing the definitions, and theorems (THEOREMS clause). Theorems are proved from the definitions and axioms. Many theories have been defined for sequences, lists, groups, reals, differential equations, etc.

Well-Definedness (WD) in Theories. An important feature provided by Event-B theories is the possibility to define *Well-Definedness* (WD) conditions. Each defined operator (thus partially defined) is associated to a condition ensuring its correct definition. When it is applied (in the theory or in an Event-B machine or context), this WD condition generates a proof obligation requiring to establish that this condition holds, i.e. the use of the operator is correct. The theory developer defines these WD conditions for the partially defined operators. All the WD POs and theorems are proved using the Event-B proof system.

Event-B Proof System and its IDE Rodin. Rodin[1] is an open source IDE for modelling in Event-B. It offers resources for model editing, automatic PO generation, project management, refinement and proof, model checking, model animation and code generation. Event-B's theories extension is available under the form of a plug-in. Theories are tightly integrated in the proof process. Depending on their definition (direct or axiomatic), operator definitions are expanded either using their direct definition (if available) or by enriching the set of axioms (hypotheses in proof sequents) using their axiomatic definition. Theorems may be imported as hypotheses and, like other theorems, they may be used in proofs. Many provers like first-order logic, or SMT solvers, are plugged to Rodin as well.

4 An Illustrative Case Study

We illustrate our approach for invariant preservation by using *finite automata* as a running example. We define finite automata using a set of operators, and consider the *deterministic* property as an invariant property we wish to study. Finite automata are modelled as labelled state transitions systems (LTS). A set of operators are defined on LTS together with a logical property formalising the *deterministic* property.

A $\mathcal{L}ts \in \mathcal{LTS}$ is defined as a tuple $\mathcal{L}ts = (s_0, S, \Sigma, \rightarrow)$ where $s_0 \in S$ is an initial state belonging to the set of states S, Σ an alphabet and $\rightarrow \subseteq S \times \Sigma \times S$ is a transition relation. $\epsilon \in \Sigma$ denotes the empty label.

In order to keep the paper in reasonable length, we focus on two operators: *PrefixedUnion* (Fig. 1d) builds the union of two $\mathcal{L}ts$, each of which is prefixed by discriminating labels ll and rl and linked to a new initial state, and *PrefixedMerge* (Fig. 1c) merges two $\mathcal{L}ts$ using an intermediate label l. We require that each operation preserves the deterministic property of $\mathcal{L}ts$: if the $\mathcal{L}ts$ fed into these operators are deterministic, then so are their output.

---

[1] Rodin Integrated Development Environment http://www.event-b.org/index.html.

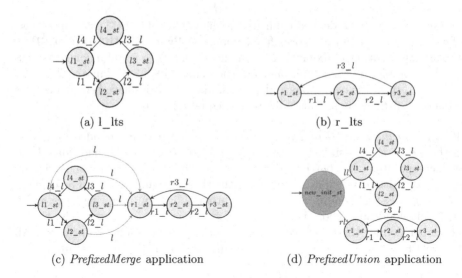

(a) l_lts

(b) r_lts

(c) *PrefixedMerge* application

(d) *PrefixedUnion* application

Fig. 1. Examples of LTS operators applications

Remark. It is worth noticing that finite automata are our objects of study, and should not be confused with the state-based semantics of Event-B expressed as transition systems.

Next Steps. Below, we present two Event-B developments: a classical one (Sect. 5) relying on inductive proofs of the invariant using core Event-B and a second one (Sect. 8), corresponding to the proposed approach relying on the use of externally defined Event-B theories and on WD conditions. This enables us to compare both modelling approaches by highlighting the differences between the usual Event-B approach with invariant preservation, and the use of WD conditions.

5   Invariant Preservation: Core Event-B

Modelling finite automata in Event-B follows the classical development process of defining the **context** axiomatising the concepts required to model these automata and the **machine** modelling transformations on them through a set of **events** while ensuring **invariants** (here, determinism) are preserved.

As the purpose of the paper is to show that invariant preservation can be guaranteed using theories and associated WD conditions, only extracts of the model based on the classical approach using Event-B are shown.

An Event-B Context for LTS Definition. The Ltsbasic context of Listing 1 is a set of axioms defining LTS constructs. They introduce a *ConsLts* constructor (**axm5** bijection ↣) and accessors to handle any $Lts \in \mathcal{LTS}$. Last, **axm8** defines a specific LTS, namely *InitLts*, that will be used in the machine for initialisation.

```
CONTEXT      Ltsbasic
SETS     S Σ 𝓛𝒯𝒮
CONSTANTS   init    transition    state    UsedAlphabet   ε ConsLts init_state
AXIOMS
    axm1 :  init ∈ LTS → ℙ(S)
    axm2 :  transition ∈ LTS → ℙ(S × Σ × S)
    axm3 :  state ∈ LTS → ℙ(S)
    axm4 :  UsedAlphabet ∈ LTS → ℙ(Σ)
    axm5 :  ConsLts ∈ (ℙ(S) × ℙ(Σ) × ℙ(S × Σ × S)) ↠ LTS
    axm6 :  ∀lts, init_st, tr, s, a · lts = ConsLts(init_st ↦ s ↦ a ↦ tr) ⇔
                init(lts) = init_st ∧ transition(lts) = tr ∧ state(lts) = s ∧ UsedAlphabet(lts) = a
    axm7 :  ε ∈ Σ ∧ init_state ∈ S
    axm8 :  InitLts = ConsLts({init_state} ↦ {init_state} ↦ ∅ ↦ ∅)
END
```

Listing 1. Basic $\mathcal{L}ts$ constructs.

An Event-B Machine to Manuipulate LTS. The objective is to define a set of transformations formalised by events to build a deterministic automaton. The idea is to use a trace of events leading to a deterministic LTS. For this purpose, we use a correct-by-construction method relying on a set of events to build deterministic LTS, preserving the invariant stating LTS determinism.

```
MACHINE      ltsDeterm
SEES     Ltsbasic
VARIABLES    lts
INVARIANTS
    inv1 :  lts ∈ LTS
    inv2 :  init(lts) ≠ ∅// Init state exists
    inv3 :  state(lts) = init(lts) ∪ dom(dom(transition(lts))) ∪ ran(transition(lts))//states
    inv4 :  UsedAlphabet(lts) = ran(dom(transition(lts)))  // well built Used Alphabet
    inv5 :  ∃i · init(lts) = {i}// Unique initial state
    inv6 :  ε ∉ ran(dom(transition(lts)))// No ε transition
    inv7 :  transition(lts) ∈ S × Σ ↛ S// Deterministic transition (function)
```

Listing 2. $\mathcal{L}ts$ determinism invariants.

Listing 2 shows the list of invariants stating that an LTS is deterministic. `inv2-4` define constraints on the states and labels while `inv5-7` define determinism with single initial state, absence of ϵ label and finally the transition relation is a function (single image ↠).

```
EVENTS
    INITIALISATION  ≘
    THEN
        act1 :  lts := InitLts
    END
    PrefixedMergeEvt  ≘
    ANY    l_lts , r_lts , l , l_init_st , r_init_st , l_st ,  r_st , l_UsedAlpha , r_UsedAlpha
    WHERE
        grd1 :       l_lts ∈ LTS ∧ r_lts ∈ LTS ∧ l ∈ Σ
        grd2−3 :    init(l_lts) = {l_init_st} ∧ init(r_lts) = {r_init_st}
        grd4−5 :    l_st = ({l_init_st} ∪ dom(dom(transition(l_lts))) ∪ ran(transition(l_lts)))∧
                     r_st = ({r_init_st} ∪ dom(dom(transition(r_lts))) ∪ ran(transition(r_lts)))
        grd6−7 :    l_UsedAlpha = ran(dom(transition(l_lts))) ∧ r_UsedAlpha = ran(...)
        grd8 :       (l_st ∩ r_st) = ∅
        grd9−10 :   l ∉ ran(dom(transition(l_lts))) ∧ l ≠ ε
        grd11−12 :  ε ∉ r_UsedAlpha ∧ ε ∉ l_UsedAlpha
        grd13−14 :  transition(r_lts) ∈ S × Σ ↛ S ∧ transition(l_lts) ∈ S × Σ ↛ S
    THEN
```

```
   act1 :   lts := ConsLts(
                {l_init_st} ↦ l_st ∪ r_st ↦
                (l_UsedAlpha ∪ r_UsedAlpha ∪ {l}) ↦
                (transition(l_lts) ∪ transition(r_lts) ∪ {s · s ∈ l_st | s ↦ l ↦ r_init_st}))
   END
   PrefixedUnionEvt ≙ ...
        . . .
END
```

Listing 3. Model events building a deterministic $\mathcal{L}ts$.

Listing 3 shows the set of events building a LTS (Fig. 1). Due to space constraints, only the *PrefixedMergeEvt* event is shown. It is parameterised by two LTS (left *l_lts* and right *r_lts*) and a connecting label *l*. It is guarded by conditions ensuring that *l_lts* and *r_lts* are well-built and that $l \neq \epsilon$ (**grd1-14**). Action `act1` builds the resulting LTS by updating the state variable *lts*.

In this approach, it is necessary to describe the invariants ensuring that the state variable defines a deterministic LTS so that the invariant preservation PO (4 of Table 2) is discharged.

Although the studied example is well-known and simple, writing these invariants may be a difficult task for the system designer.

6   Data Type Theory-Based Invariant Preservation

The invariant-preservation approach of Sect. 5 relies on an inductive proof where invariants and state variables are directly modelled by the designer using Event-B set theory and its type system (which can be seen as a weak typing system compared to proof assistants like Coq or Isabelle/HOL).

In this approach, the designer describes explicitly safe states, invariants and mandatory guards in the models. The designer has to prove invariant preservation POs for each event. Moreover, this invariant has to be written and proven in further developments, so reusability is compromised. It is possible to design models of systems which exploit externally defined theories to type system features and to manipulate these features using the operators associated to these types *defined as partial functions*. When these operators are used, the WD conditions, associated with them, generate POs on the system design model.

We claim that it is possible to use these WDs to enforce invariants and therefore ensure the safety requirements of the system being designed. In the context of state-based formal methods, this claim is based on the view of invariants as conditions for *well-defined partial functions/transformations*, defined in external theories, with system state type corresponding to one parameter of each of these functions. In addition, the proofs performed on the theory side, achieved once and for all, are reused in system design models verification.

Three main steps are identified. The first one (**Step 1**) is to produce, once and for all, the relevant theories formalising the data types and operators used in the models. The second step (**Step 2**) requires to instantiate the defined theories for the specific types used by the model. Finally, the third step (**Step 3**) uses the defined types and operators for typing and manipulating the state variables.

6.1   An Event-B Datatype Based Domain-Specific Theory (Step 1)

Theories conforming to the template of Listing 4 are built and *proved once and for all*. These theories provide generic and parameterised data types, with operators (partial functions) associated to WD conditions and relevant theorems.

```
THEORY    Theo
TYPE PARAMETERS      ArgsTypes
DATA TYPES
    T(ArgsTypes)
    Cons(args : ArgsTypes)
OPERATORS
    Op₁   <Predicate>  (el : T(ArgsType), args : ArgsTypes)
        well−definedness condition  WD_Op1(args)
        direct definition  Op_Exp1(el, args)

        . . .

    Opₙ  <Predicate>  (el : T(ArgsTypes), args : ArgsTypes)  . . .
        well−definedness condition  WD_Opn(args)
        direct definition  Op_Expn(el, args)
    Properties  <Predicate>  (el : T(ArgsTypes))
        direct definition    properties(el)
THEOREMS
    ThmTheoOp₁ :  ∀x, args · x ∈ T(ArgsTypes) ∧ args ∈ ArgsTypes∧
            WD_Op1(args) ∧ Op1(x, args)  ⇒  Properties(x)

        . . .

    ThmTheoOpₙ :  ∀x, args · x ∈ T(ArgsTypes) ∧ args ∈ ArgsTypes∧
            WD_Opn(args) ∧ Opn(x, args)  ⇒  Properties(x)
```

Listing 4. Data type theory template

Listing 4 shows a template of theory where the data type T is built from type parameters *ArgsType* and a set of predicate operators Op_i defining relations between concepts of type T and other parameters. *These predicates are used in a model to define before-after predicates* as one of their type parameters $T(ArgsTypes)$ corresponds to the type of the model state.

The predicate *Properties* is defined to capture properties on data of type $T(ArgsTypes)$. It formalises requirements and many of them can be defined.

Last, the central theorems $ThmTheoOp_i$ state that, for each operator Op_i, if its *WD* condition holds then its application implies properties expressed on any element x of type $T(ArgsTypes)$ using the predicate *Properties*. *It can be used to check invariant preservation*. It is worth noticing that these theorems encode a *structural induction principle*. It is proved *once and for all, independently of any model behaviour description*. Additional theorems, for other properties, characterising the defined data type may be expressed.

6.2   An Event-B Instantiation Context (Step 2)

The theory of Sect. 6.1 is generic. Next step instantiates it with the specific objects of interest, i.e. state manipulated by the Event-B machine.

The context Ctx of Listing 5 instantiates the theory of Listing 4. Type synthesis and matching of Event-B is used to instantiate the generic data type T with sets s as data type $T(s)$. Then constants and axioms are defined classically.

Here again, the important theorems $ThmTheoOp_i$ $Inst$ are introduced. They instantiate the generic theorems $ThmTheoOp_i$. As the generic theorems $ThmTheoOp_i$ are already proved, the proofs of these theorems are trivial provided that type checking succeeds. These theorems are

CONTEXT	Ctx
SETS	s
CONSTANTS	c
AXIOMS ...	
THEOREMS	

$\quad$ **ThmTheoOp$_1$Inst**: $\forall x, args \cdot x \in T(s) \land args \in s \land$
$\qquad$ **WD_Op$_1$**$(args) \land$ **Op$_1$**$(x, args) \Rightarrow$ **Properties**(x)
$\quad$ ...
$\quad$ **ThmTheoOp$_n$Inst**: $\forall x, args \cdot x \in T(s) \land args \in s \land$
$\qquad$ **WD_Op$_n$**$(args) \land$ **Op$_n$**$(x, args) \Rightarrow$
$\qquad\quad$ **Properties**(x)

Listing 5. Context instantiation.

the reduction of the polymorphic type of the theory to the concrete type of the model, here the set s.

6.3 A Domain-Specific Event-B Machine (Step 3)

At this level, a machine template that exploits the defined theory and the instantiated context is built. Listing 6 depicts an Event-B machine with a single state variable x of type $T(s)$ by typing invariant $TypingInv$. Then, a set of events Evt_i, including the initialisation event[2], possibly parameterised, manipulate state variable x. Action act1 of each event uses operators of the theory in the before-after predicate (BAP) for state variables changes.

MACHINE	$Machine$
SEES	Ctx
VARIABLES	x
INVARIANTS	

$\quad$ $TypingInv$ $\quad:\quad$ $x \in T(s)$
$\quad$ $AllowedOper$ $\quad:\quad$ $\exists args \cdot args \in s \land ($ **WD_Op$_1$**$(args) \land$ **Op$_1$**$(x, args)) \lor$
$\qquad\qquad\qquad\qquad\qquad\qquad ($ **WD_Op$_n$**$(args) \land$ **Op$_n$**$(x, args) \lor \dots)$

THEOREMS
$\quad$ $SafThm$ $\quad:\quad$ **Properties**(x)
EVENTS
$\quad$ $Evt_1 \;\hat{=}\;$ $\qquad\qquad$ ... $\qquad\qquad\qquad$ $Evtn \;\hat{=}\;$
$\qquad$ **ANY** α $\qquad\qquad\qquad\qquad\qquad\qquad$ **ANY** α
$\qquad$ **WHEN** $\qquad\qquad\qquad\qquad\qquad\qquad\quad$ **WHEN**
$\qquad\quad$ $grd1$ $\;:\;$ $\alpha \in s \land$ **WD_Op$_1$**(α) $\qquad\quad$ $grd1$ $\;:\;$ $\alpha \in s \land$ **WD_Op$_n$**(α)
$\qquad$ **THEN** $\qquad\qquad\qquad\qquad\qquad\qquad\quad$ **THEN**
$\qquad\quad$ $act1$ $\;:\;$ $x :|$ **Op$_1$**(x', α) $\qquad\qquad\quad$ $act1$ $\;:\;$ $x :|$ **Op$_n$**(x', α)
$\qquad$ **END** $\qquad\qquad\qquad\qquad\qquad\qquad\quad$ **END**
END

Listing 6. An Event-B machine with domain-specific properties

A useful consequence of the use of operators as before-after predicates of events, is the identification of event guards. Indeed, operators application is only possible if their WD conditions in the guards hold.

Two main properties are formalised. First, invariant $AllowedOper$ expresses that state variable x is only handled using the operators of the theory when their WD hold; this is *crucial* in the method as it excludes any other type of event from altering x (completeness). Second, theorem $SafThm$ captures that the properties $Properties$ hold. According to the $ThmMch$ PO (Table 2), this

---

[2] For the initialisation event, the guard does not involve state variables.

theorem results from invariants *TypingInv* and *AllowedOper*, together with the axioms and theories of the context *Ctx*.

7   The Proof Process

We have presented a revisited model relying on a data-type-based approach, similar to proof assistants like Coq or Isabelle/HOL, in which a data type and a set of operators are defined to manipulate system states through their type. Then, we have encoded, in the invariant clause, the typing (*TypingInv*) and constraints (*AllowedOper*) corresponding to closure and well-foundedness of operators to strongly type the state variable with respect to the needed operators. Doing so, we embed a stronger type system than Event-B provides. Last, as invariant guarantees typing, safety property *SafThm* can be proved deductively.

Unlike the invariant-based approach of Sect. 5, this approach offers a systematic way to prove invariant preservation. Indeed, proving *SafThm* is straightforward, it is a direct use of the instantiated theorems *ThmTheoOpInst* proved in the context as an instantiation of the generic theorems *ThmTheoOp* of the theory using the modus-ponens proof rule ($\Rightarrow$-elimination rule). Concretely, the proof effort is concentrated on the *reusable* proof *once and for all* of *ThmTheoOp$_i$*. Other POs are straightforward: *AllowedOper* consists in identifying which allowed operator is used in the disjunction, and *SafThm* is proven deductively using *ThmTheoOp$_i$Inst* for each allowed operator.

The correctness of this approach consists in establishing that any property P proven true in this approach can be proven true in the classical, invariant-based approach. Concretely, correctness is captured by the *ThmTheo $\Rightarrow$ PO_Inv* meta-theorem. We have formalised the proof of this theorem in the Coq [6] proof assistant.

Finally, the approach presented here is similar to encapsulation and application programming interfaces available in programming languages with modules. The *Theo* theory offers a set of generic operators used by models (interface) and the *AllowedOper* invariant encodes encapsulation as the defined state variable is manipulated with the theory-based operators of its type only.

8   Revisited Event-B Models for LTS

Back to the case study of deterministic finite automata (Sect. 5), we describe how the proposed approach is applied. We follow the steps identified in Sect. 6.

8.1   A Data Type for LTS (Step 1)

```
THEORY
  TYPE PARAMETERS  S ,  L
  DATA TYPES
    𝓛𝓣𝓢(S, L)
    ConsLts(init : ℙ(S), state : ℙ(S),
      alphabet : ℙ(L),
      transition : ℙ(S × L × S), eps : L)
```

Listing 7. A theory of 𝓛ts: data-type and constructor.

Listings 7, 8 and 9 describe the theory of 𝓛𝓣𝓢 that we have formalised.

Listing 7 describes a theory of LTS defining a data type 𝓛𝓣𝓢(S, L) where S and L are types for states and labels, respectively. A constructor ConsLts is defined together with accessors to retrieve LTS components (init, state, alphabet, transition and ε).

```
OPERATORS
  UniqueLabelTransition <predicate> ...
  InitUnique <predicate> ...
  NoEpsTransition <predicate> ...
  GetUniqueInit ...
  WellBuilt <predicate> (lts : 𝓛𝓣𝓢(S, L))
    direct definition
      init(lts) ≠ ∅ ∧ alphabet(lts) = ran(dom(transition(lts)))∧
      state(lts) = init(lts) ∪ dom(dom(transition(lts))) ∪ ran(transition(lts))
  IsDeter <predicate> (lts : 𝓛𝓣𝓢(S, L))
    direct definition
      WellBuilt(lts) ∧ InitUnique(lts) ∧ NoEpsTransition(lts) ∧ UniqueLabelTransition(lts)

  Wd_ConsLtsDeter <predicate> ...
  ConsLtsDeter <predicate> ...
  ConsSingleStateLts <predicate> ...
  Wd_PrefixedUnion <predicate> ...
  PrefixedUnion <predicate> ...
  Wd_PrefixedUnionDeter <predicate> ...
  PrefixedUnionDeter <predicate> ...
  Wd_PrefixedMerge <predicate> (l_lts : 𝓛𝓣𝓢(S, L), l : L, r_lts : 𝓛𝓣𝓢(S, L))
    direct definition
      InitUnique(r_lts) ∧ state(l_lts) ∩ state(r_lts) = ∅ ∧ eps(l_lts) = eps(r_lts)
  PrefixedMerge <predicate> (
      lts : 𝓛𝓣𝓢(S, L), l_lts : 𝓛𝓣𝓢(S, L), l : L, r_lts : 𝓛𝓣𝓢(S, L))
    well−definedness  Wd_PrefixedMerge(l_lts, l, r_lts)
    direct definition
      lts = ConsLts
      (init(l_lts), state(l_lts) ∪ state(r_lts), alphabet(l_lts) ∪ alphabet(r_lts) ∪ {l},
      transition(l_lts) ∪ transition(r_lts)∪
        {s, init_r_lts · s ∈ state(l_lts) ∧ init_r_lts = GetUniqueInit(r_lts) |
          s ↦ l ↦ init_r_lts}, eps(l_lts))
  Wd_PrefixedMergeDeter <predicate> (l_lts : 𝓛𝓣𝓢(S, L), l : L, r_lts : 𝓛𝓣𝓢(S, L))
    direct definition
      IsDeter(r_lts) ∧ isDeter(l_lts) ∧ state(l_lts) ∩ state(r_lts) = ∅∧
      eps(l_lts) = eps(r_lts) ∧ l ∉ alphabet(l_lts) ∧ l ≠ eps(l_lts)
  PrefixedMergeDeter <predicate> (
      lts : 𝓛𝓣𝓢(S, L), l_lts : 𝓛𝓣𝓢(S, L), l : L, r_lts : 𝓛𝓣𝓢(S, L))
    well−definedness  Wd_PrefixedMergeDeter(l_lts, l, r_lts)
    direct definition
      PrefixedMerge(lts, l_lts, l, r_lts)
```

Listing 8. A theory of 𝓛ts: operators, WD conditions and theorems.

Listing 8 shows a subset of operators associated with the 𝓛𝓣𝓢(S, L) data type. In particular, we show the *PrefixedMerge* and *PrefixedUnion* operators, used in the development of our example (Sect. 5). Each operator is associated to a relevant WD conditions for excluding wrong arguments (partial function).

General operators for $\mathcal{LTS}$ are defined: *WellBuilt*, stating that an LTS is correctly built from the constructor using the defined acessors, *IsDeter* asserting that a LTS is deterministic, other operators required to manipulate LTS, such as *UniqueLabelTransition*, *InitUnique*, *NoEpsTranstion*, etc. and other operators required for our case study:

- *ConsLtsDeter*, a derived constructor for deterministic LTS. It restricts the constructor *ConsLts* of $\mathcal{LTS}(S, L)$ with a WD condition *Wd_ConsLtsDeter* to build deterministic LTS only;
- *consSingleStateLts*, a specific operator, used for initialisation, building a LTS with a single state;
- *PrefixedUnion* and *PrefixedMerge* applied to not necessarily deterministic LTS with *Wd_PrefixedUnion* and *Wd_PrefixedMerge* WD conditions;
- deterministic union (*PrefixedUnionDeter*) and merge (*PrefixedMergeDeter*) build deterministic LTS. Their WD conditions (*Wd_PrefixedUnionDeter* and *Wd_PrefixedMergeDeter* respectively) express, in particular, that both l_lts and r_lts parameters shall be deterministic;

Note that each operator outputs the lts parameter from two input parameters l_lts and r_lts. This definition style defines a transformation allowing to write Event-B before-after predicates.

This theory does not **guarantee** that the produced LTS are deterministic if the operators are not applied in the appropriate manner.

```
THEOREMS
  thm1-5 :  ...
  ThmTheoConsOneSt :  ∀lts, new_init_st, ε · lts ∈ 𝓛𝓣𝓢(S, L) ∧ ε ∈ L ∧ new_init_st ∈ S∧
              ConsSingleStateLts(lts, new_init_st, ε)  ⇒  IsDeter(lts)
  ThmTheoUnion : ∀lts, l_lts, r_lts, ll, rl, new_init_st·
              l_lts ∈ 𝓛𝓣𝓢(S, L) ∧ r_lts ∈ 𝓛𝓣𝓢(S, L) ∧ ll ↦ rl ∈ L × L ∧ new_init_st ∈ S∧
              Wd_PrefixedUnionDeter(new_init_st, ll, rl, l_lts, r_lts)∧
                  PrefixedUnionDeter(lts, new_init_st, ll, rl, l_lts, r_lts) ⇒ IsDeter(lts)
  ThmTheoMerge :  ∀lts, l_lts, r_lts, l·
              l_lts ∈ 𝓛𝓣𝓢(S, L) ∧ r_lts ∈ 𝓛𝓣𝓢(S, L) ∧ l ∈ L ∧ eps(l_lts) = eps(r_lts)∧
              Wd_PrefixedMergeDeter(l_lts, l, r_lts)∧
                  PrefixedMergeDeter(lts, l_lts, l, r_lts) ⇒ IsDeter(lts)
END
```

Listing 9. A theory of LTS: operators, WD conditions and theorems.

The remaining part of the defined theory (Listing 9) contains a set of theorems useful to prove model properties that use the defined types.

In particular, the proven theorems *ThmTheoOp* state that all the operators manipulating deterministic LTS (by the WD condition as hypotheses) produce deterministic automata. Thus, starting with a deterministic automaton, the correct application of any number of operators will always produce a deterministic automaton. As mentioned in Sect. 6.1, these theorems encode structural induction. They guarantee that LTS are effectively deterministic.

8.2 An Instanciation Context for LTS (Step 2)

Next step, following Sect. 6.2, leads to an Event-B context describing specific LTS through theory instantiation. It is obtained by instantiating theory type parameters S and L with *States* and Σ, respectively.

```
CONTEXT      CtxLts
SETS         States    Σ
CONSTANTS    init_state      ε
AXIOMS
    axm1:  init_state ↦ ε ∈ States × Σ // Initialisation
THEOREMS
    ThmTheoConsOneStInst:  ∀lts, new_init_st, ε · lts ∈ LTS(States, Σ)∧
        ε ∈ Σ ∧ new_init_st ∈ States∧
                ConsSingleStateLts(lts, new_init_st, ε) ⇒ IsDeter(lts)
    ThmTheoUnionInst:  ∀lts, l_lts, r_lts, ll, rl, new_init_st · l_lts ∈ LTS(States, Σ)∧
        r_lts ∈ LTS(States, Σ) ∧ ll ↦ rl ∈ Σ × Σ ∧ new_init_st ∈ States∧
            Wd_PrefixedUnionDeter(new_init_st, ll, rl, l_lts, r_lts)∧
                PrefixedUnionDeter(lts, new_init_st, ll, rl, l_lts, r_lts) ⇒ IsDeter(lts)
    ThmTheoMergeInst:  ∀lts, l_lts, r_lts, l · l_lts ∈ LTS(States, Σ) ∧ r_lts ∈ LTS(States, Σ)∧
        l ∈ Σ ∧ eps(l_lts) = eps(r_lts)∧
            Wd_PrefixedMergeDeter(l_lts, l, r_lts)∧
                PrefixedMergeDeter(lts, l_lts, l, r_lts) ⇒ IsDeter(lts)
END
```

Listing 10. An instantiated context of LTS.

Useful constants are defined and typed in axiom **axm1**. Theorem *ThmTheoInst* corresponding to the instantiation of the generic theorem *ThmTheo* is also described. Its proof is straightforward by instantiation of the hypotheses.

8.3 A Data Type Specific Machine for LTS (Step 3)

Last step, corresponding to Sect. 6.3, describes an Event-B machine in Listing 11 that is equivalent to the Event-B machine of Listing 3.

```
MACHINE MachineLts
SEES     CtxLts

VARIABLES    lts

INVARIANTS
    TypingInv:  lts ∈ LTS(S, L)
    AllowedOper:  ∃l_lts, r_lts, ll, rl, l, new_init_st, eps·
        l_lts ∈ LTS(S, L) ∧ r_lts ∈ LTS(S, L) ∧ l ↦ ll ↦ rl ∈ L × L × L∧
        new_init_st ∈ S ∧ eps ∈ L ∧ (
        consOneStateLts(lts, new_init_st, eps)∨
        (Wd_PrefixedUnionDeter(new_init_st, ll, rl, l_lts, r_lts)∧
            PrefixedUnionDeter(lts, new_init_st, ll, rl, l_lts, r_lts))∨
        (Wd_PrefixedMergeDeter(l_lts, l, r_lts)∧
            PrefixedMergeDeter(lts, l_lts, l, r_lts))  )

THEOREMS
    SafThm:  IsDeter(lts)
EVENTS
    INITIALISATION  ≙
    THEN
        act1:  lts :| ConsSingleStateLts(lts', init_state, ε)
    END
    PrefixedMergeEvt  ≙
    ANY    l_lts,  r_lts,  l
```

```
WHERE
    grd1 :   l_lts ↦ r_lts ↦ l ∈ LTS(S, L) × LTS(S, L) × L
    grd2 :   Wd_PrefixedMergeDeter(l_lts, l, r_lts)
THEN
    act1 :   lts :| PrefixedMergeDeter(lts', l_lts, l, r_lts)
END
PrefixedUnionEvt ≙ ...
    ...
END
```

Listing 11. A Machine of LTS with a type state variable.

The *MachineLts* of Listing 11 describes a single state variable *lts* and two invariants. The first one *TypingInv* types the state variable *lts* with the data type of the instantiated theory.

The second invariant *AllowedOper* states that, once initialised with *ConsSingleStateLts* operator, the *lts* variable can be manipulated with *PrefixedMerge* and *PrefixedUnion* operators only. None of the other operators are allowed to manipulate the state variables (closure and well-foundedness). The *SafThm* theorem states that the *lts* state transition system is deterministic. Finally, the events that manipulate the state variables are defined, they implement machine state changes.

8.4   Proof Process

The development presented in this section is a reformulation of the one presented in Sect. 5. However, the mechanism of proof of invariants provided by these two developments differs. In this development, the proofs are eased thanks to the WD conditions associated with each operator and used as guards, together with the proved theorem instantiated in the context. All of the proofs follow and reuse the proof schema shown in Sect. 7.

9   Conclusion

In this paper, we have presented an alternative approach for checking invariants and thus safety properties in the Event-B state-based formal method. In the same spirit as proof assistants like Coq or Isabelle/HOL, this approach relies on the extension of Event-B with typing that enforces the checking of conditions related to partial functions using well-definedness (WD) conditions. It consists in encapsulating data types and allowing behavioural models to manipulate typed state variables within events using a subset of operators as long as their WD conditions are met. Furthermore, we demonstrated that it is possible to satisfy invariant preservation proof obligations by using theorems expressed at the data type level and instantiated at the model level.

The defined approach combines algebraically defined data types and their useful properties expressed as WD conditions and theorems (Event-B theories) with behavioural models based on state-transitions systems expressed as a set of state changes using guarded events (Event-B machines). This approach complements the invariant-based approach by enabling inductive proofs at the machine level, or proof of the structural induction principle on the data type theory side. The designer can choose the most appropriate one depending on the difficulty of the modelling and proving activities.

Finally, the proposed approach has been implemented in many different cases: data types, operators and relevant properties (WD and theorems) have been defined for hybrid systems [10] (mathematical extension with a data type for differential equations), interactive critical systems [20–22] (a domain model with a data type for aircraft cockpits widgets) and Event-B models analysis [25] (Event-B reflexive meta-model with a data type for Event-B states and events).

In the future, we plan to integrate the proposed approach into a refinement chain. On the theory side, we intend to describe refinement of data types so that gluing invariants can be proved using the proposed approach. Studying liveness properties by introducing variants is also targeted. Last, we intend to develop a Rodin plug-in to automate the whole approach.

References

1. Abrial, J.: The B-book - Assigning Programs to Meanings. Cambridge University Press, Cambridge (1996)
2. Abrial, J.R.: Modeling in Event-B: System and Software Engineering. Cambridge University Press, Cambridge (2010)
3. Abrial, J.R., Butler, M., Hallerstede, S., Leuschel, M., Schmalz, M., Voisin, L.: Proposals for mathematical extensions for Event-B. Technical report (2009). http://deploy-eprints.ecs.soton.ac.uk/216/
4. Abrial, J.-R., Mussat, L.: On using conditional definitions in formal theories. In: Bert, D., Bowen, J.P., Henson, M.C., Robinson, K. (eds.) ZB 2002. LNCS, vol. 2272, pp. 242–269. Springer, Heidelberg (2002). https://doi.org/10.1007/3-540-45648-1_13
5. Barringer, H., Cheng, J.H., Jones, C.B.: A logic covering undefinedness in program proofs. Acta Inform. **21**, 251–269 (1984)
6. Bertot, Y., Castran, P.: Interactive Theorem Proving and Program Development: Coq'Art The Calculus of Inductive Constructions, 1st edn. Springer Publishing Company Incorporated, Heidelberg (2010). https://doi.org/10.1007/978-3-662-07964-5
7. Börger, E., Stärk, R.F.: Abstract State Machines. A Method for High-Level System Design and Analysis. Springer, Heidelberg (2003). https://doi.org/10.1007/978-3-642-18216-7
8. Butler, M.J., Maamria, I.: Practical theory extension in Event-B. In: Theories of Programming and Formal Methods - Essays Dedicated to Jifeng He on the Occasion of His 70th Birthday, pp. 67–81 (2013)
9. Dijkstra, E.W.: Guarded commands, nondeterminacy and formal derivation of programs. Commun. ACM **18**(8), 453–457 (1975)
10. Dupont, G., Aït-Ameur, Y., Singh, N.K., Pantel, M.: Event-B hybridation: a proof and refinement-based framework for modelling hybrid systems. ACM Trans. Embed. Comput. Syst. **20**(4), 1–37 (2021)
11. Floyd, R.W.: Assigning meanings to programs. In: Proceedings of Symposium in Applied Mathematics - Mathematical Aspects of Computer Science, vol. 19, pp. 19–32 (1967)

12. van Gasteren, A.J.M., Tel, G.: Comments on "on the proof of a distributed algorithm": always-true is not invariant. Inf. Process. Lett. **35**(6), 277–279 (1990)
13. George, C.: The RAISE specification language a tutorial. In: Prehn, S., Toetenel, H. (eds.) VDM 1991. LNCS, vol. 552, pp. 238–319. Springer, Heidelberg (1991). https://doi.org/10.1007/BFb0019998
14. Hoare, C.A.R.: An axiomatic basis for computer programming. Commun. ACM **12**(10), 576–580 (1969)
15. Jones, C.B.: Partial functions and logics: a warning. Inf. Process. Lett. **54**(2), 65–67 (1995)
16. Jones, C.B., Middelburg, C.A.: A typed logic of partial functions reconstructed classically. Acta Inform. **31**(5), 399–430 (1994)
17. Jones, C.B.: Systematic Software Development Using VDM. Prentice Hall International Series in Computer Science, Prentice Hall, Hoboken (1986)
18. Lamport, L.: Specifying Systems. The TLA+ Language and Tools for Hardware and Software Engineers. Addison-Wesley, Boston (2002)
19. Leuschel, M.: Fast and effective well-definedness checking. In: Dongol, B., Troubitsyna, E. (eds.) IFM 2020. LNCS, vol. 12546, pp. 63–81. Springer, Cham (2020). https://doi.org/10.1007/978-3-030-63461-2_4
20. Mendil, I., Singh, N.K., Aït-Ameur, Y., Méry, D., Palanque, P.: An integrated framework for the formal analysis of critical interactive systems. In: Liu, Y., Ma, S.P., Chen, S., Sun, J. (eds.) The 27th Asia-Pacific Software Engineering Conference, June Sun, p. 10. IEEE, Singapore, Singapore, December 2020
21. Mendil, I., Aït-Ameur, Y., Singh, N.K., Méry, D., Palanque, P.: Leveraging Event-B theories for handling domain knowledge in design models. In: Qin, S., Woodcock, J., Zhang, W. (eds.) SETTA 2021. LNCS, vol. 13071, pp. 40–58. Springer, Cham (2021). https://doi.org/10.1007/978-3-030-91265-9_3
22. Mendil, I., Aït-Ameur, Y., Singh, N.K., Méry, D., Palanque, P.: Standard conformance-by-construction with Event-B. In: Lluch Lafuente, A., Mavridou, A. (eds.) Formal Methods for Industrial Critical Systems, pp. 126–146. Springer International Publishing, Cham (2021)
23. Nipkow, T., Wenzel, M., Paulson, L.C.: Isabelle/HOL. A Proof Assistant for Higher-Order Logic. LNCS, vol. 2283. Springer, Heidelberg (2002). https://doi.org/10.1007/3-540-45949-9
24. Owre, S., Rushby, J.M., Shankar, N.: PVS: a prototype verification system. In: Kapur, D. (ed.) CADE 1992. LNCS, vol. 607, pp. 748–752. Springer, Heidelberg (1992). https://doi.org/10.1007/3-540-55602-8_217
25. Riviere, P.: Formal meta engineering Event-B: extension and reasoning the *EB4EB* framework. In: Raschke, A., Méry, D. (eds.) ABZ 2021. LNCS, vol. 12709, pp. 153–157. Springer, Cham (2021). https://doi.org/10.1007/978-3-030-77543-8_15
26. Spivey, J.M.: Z Notation - A Reference Manual, 2 edn. Prentice Hall International Series in Computer Science, Prentice Hall, Hoboken (1992)
27. Stoddart, B., Dunne, S., Galloway, A.: Undefined expressions and logic in Z and B. Formal Methods Syst. Des. **15**(3), 201–215 (1999)

Cooperative and Relational Verification

Journal-First: Formal Modelling and Runtime Verification of Autonomous Grasping for Active Debris Removal

Marie Farrell[1(✉)], Nikos Mavrakis[2], Angelo Ferrando[3], Clare Dixon[4], and Yang Gao[5]

[1] Department of Computer Science and Hamilton Institute, Maynooth University, Maynooth, Ireland
marie.farrell@mu.ie

[2] Department of Electronic Engineering, University of York, York, UK

[3] Department of Computer Science, University of Genova, Genova, Italy

[4] Department of Computer Science, University of Manchester, Manchester, UK

[5] STAR-Lab, Surrey Space Centre, University of Surrey, Guildford, UK

Abstract. Verifying that autonomous space robotic software behaves correctly is crucial, particularly since such software is often mission-critical, that is, a software failure can lead to mission failure. In this paper, we describe the process that we used to verify the autonomous grasp generation and capturing operation of a spent rocket stage in space. This paper summarises a publication by the same authors in the journal Frontiers in Robotics and AI (2022) which harnesses multiple formal and non-formal methods to verify an autonomous grasping system.

1 Introduction

Active Debris Removal refers to the removal of debris, such as spent rocket stages, from orbit. Current approaches include the use of autonomous robots which are equipped with an arm to capture this kind of debris [10]. Identifying a suitable grasping point on the target surface and ensuring a stable grasp is a crucial function in systems that are deployed for active debris removal.

This paper summarises our work in [4] which describes our approach to verifying a pre-existing system for autonomous grasping [10] for active debris removal in space. To begin, the system was modelled using the Architecture Analysis and Design Language (AADL) [5] to extract a modular system design, and requirements were formalised using the Formal Requirements Elicitation Tool (FRET) [7]. The Dafny program verifier [8] was used to formally model and verify system components against their requirements for the grasp generation algorithm.

From the FRET requirements and Dafny conditions, we synthesised runtime monitors using ROSMonitoring [6] to provide runtime assurances for the

This work was supported by grants EP/R026092 (FAIR-SPACE) and EP/R026084 (RAIN) through UKRI/EPSRC under the Industrial Strategy Challenge Fund (ISCF) for Robotics and AI Hubs in Extreme and Hazardous Environments.

© Springer Nature Switzerland AG 2022
M. H. ter Beek and R. Monahan (Eds.): IFM 2022, LNCS 13274, pp. 39–44, 2022.
https://doi.org/10.1007/978-3-031-07727-2_3

system. We also described our experimentation and analysis of the testbed and the associated simulation (shown in Fig. 1). We provided a detailed discussion of our approach noting how the modularity of this particular autonomous system simplified the usually complex task of verifying a system post-development.

Previous work argues that heterogeneous verification [1] and integrated formal methods [2] are especially useful in autonomous robotics. Our work in [4] illustrates this for an autonomous grasping system, and provides contributions that are relevant for formal methods developers, particularly those interested in integrating multiple tools as well as testing/simulation results. A first version of the Dafny model that we used for verification was presented in [3] and was refactored in [4]. We note that [4] is not a simple extension of [3], rather it provides a detailed approach to verification where our modified Dafny model provides a piece of the verification evidence. The next section summarises the verification approaches and tools that were leveraged in [4] and the results obtained, and discusses specific aspects of our approach.

2 Summary

In [4], we described our use of non-formal (AADL, simulation, physical experiments) and formal (FRET, Dafny and ROSMonitoring) tools for the analysis of a previously developed autonomous debris grasping system. This section summarises the benefits that each approach offered, the resulting gaps in the requirements that were identified and our approach to post-implementation verification.

2.1 Verification Approaches

We briefly summarise the non-formal and formal verification approaches that were used in our case study.

AADL: We started by creating an AADL model of the system. This largely served as a reference point while we distilled the system into its component elements (both hardware and software). We refactored our original method to divide off the functions of `imagepreprocessing` and `findoptimalgrasp`. These components were originally encoded as a single entity in our algorithm, to more easily facilitate runtime monitoring for the system. This refactoring supported the use of runtime monitors and the definition of detailed requirements for each of these components. Using the AADL model (Fig. 1 in [4]) to define the system's requirements was advantageous since it allowed us to focus on certain components of the system when specifying requirements. It also served as a point of reference for the variable and component names that were used in natural-language requirements.

FRET: We used FRET to elicit and formalise our requirements (20 in total, shown in Table 1 of [4]). We had previously [3], identified three requirements specific to the software itself. However, in [4], we adopted a much broader view of the system which allowed us to identify and formalise many more requirements.

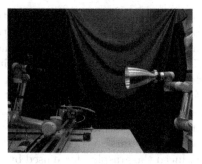

Fig. 1. Simulation setup (left) and physical testbed for experimentation (right). The autonomous robotic arm on the left of each image must grasp the debris, in this case an apogee kick motor (`AKM`) shown on the right of each image [4].

Our goal was to utilise formal methods, specifically Dafny and ROSMonitoring, to verify our system. The intermediate FRET representation was desirable as it more closely resembled formal properties than their natural-language description. FRET can export CoCoSpec verification code [11] but we did not use it for this case study because it required Simulink-based tools, and our system was built using ROS in Python. Instead, we based our Dafny verification and runtime monitor generation on the requirements in FRET and the corresponding FRET-generated LTL semantics.

Dafny: We had previously developed a Dafny model of the `imagepreprocessing` and `findoptimalgrasp` components [3]. These were merged in the original Dafny model and, similar to the implementation, we refactored this Dafny model to fit the AADL model with minimal impact on the model's verification. This restructuring necessitated the addition of some specification structures for the `imagepreprocessing` component's auxiliary functions, but this was relatively straightforward. Overall we were able to discharge all of the Dafny proof obligations automatically using version 2.3 of Dafny in version 1.48 of Visual Studio Code on Ubuntu 18.04.

ROSMonitoring: For a subset of the FRET requirements, we created a catalog of runtime monitors using ROSMonitoring. Dafny was used to verify some of these requirements. However, the majority of the monitors were focused on those requirements that would be difficult to verify in a static verification tool like Dafny. It is worth noting that our use of FRET made the task of designing these monitors much easier because it gave a succinct semantics for each requirement. To check that the requirements were met, we ran these monitors offline (using log files) for both the simulation and the real system. We also emphasised that, due to the uniqueness of the autonomous grasping system, precise requirements for specific components could not be provided without an implementation.

Simulations and Physical Experiments: As shown in Fig. 1, we developed a simulation, using the V-REP simulator [13], and a physical testbed debris capturing scenario. The capturing scenario included a chasing spacecraft (service vehicle

SV) equipped with a 6-DOF robotic manipulator, a 2-fingered gripper and a depth sensor for point cloud extraction. The captured target was an apogee kick motor (AKM), modeled after the Thiokol STAR 13b family of rocket stages [12]. The arm generated a grasping point on the target nozzle, moved the gripper towards the grasping point, executed the grasping, and pulled the target back for a specified distance. The monitors that we developed were applied to both the simulation and real (physical) testbed. We conducted an experiment which intentionally injected a fault into the system to demonstrate the effectiveness of the monitors in identifying violations of the requirements. Specifically, we reduced the grasping force used by the gripper to grasp the target. As expected, the applied force could not hold the target because it slipped through the gripper fingers during the pulling phase, and the SV lost contact with the TGT. This fault was correctly identified by our runtime monitors.

2.2   Gaps in the Requirements

The construction of monitors helped us to detect gaps in the requirements. In particular, when we applied the monitors to the physical testbed (Fig. 1), the monitors for two requirements returned a 'violated' verdict. Hardware limitations were primarily to blame. The initial criterion indicated the pulling range to be 0.3 cm–0.5 cm for requirement R1.9 (Table 1 in [4]).

"R1.9: *The total pulling distance shall be between 0.3 and 0.5 m.*"

Although possible in simulation, it was not feasible in the practical system due to the robotic arm's limitations (safety mode enforced a shorter pulling range). We were able to better understand the hardware constraints as a result of this, and we adjusted the pulling range in the requirement. Similar issues occurred with requirement R2.3 (Table 1 in [4]) relating to the grasping force. As before, whilst the requirement was satisfied in simulation it was not in the testbed due to hardware restrictions.

"R2.3: *The SVG shall apply a force of 180N once contact has been made with the TGT.*"

There were three requirements (R1.1, R1.2 and R1.7, Table 1, [4]) that we did not formally verify or monitor. Of these, two were verified by construction on the testbed and the third via physical tests. It is important to recognise that requirements for autonomous robotic systems will contain elements that cannot be formally verified so other, non-formal, methods must be used in such cases. Specifically, R1.1 was verified by construction on the test bed where we physically placed the camera 0.5m away from the TGT.

"R1.1: *The Camera of the SV shall be positioned at least 0.5 m from the TGT.*"

With respect to R1.2, we didn't impose an initial velocity on the TGT in either the simulation or the testbed so this requirement was met by design. However, if this system were to be deployed then we would have to encode a way of determining whether the TGT was indeed motionless and potentially synthesise a monitor for this.

"*R1.2: The TGT shall be motionless before contact with the SVA.*"

Finally, R1.7 was verified via physical testing and visual examination. We intend to investigate whether it would be possible to develop a runtime monitor for this property as future work.

"*R1.7: Controller shall execute a joint trajectory to reach the BGP.*"

2.3 Post-implementation Verification

The typical development approach is linear, with the system architecture developed, requirements elicited/formalised, formal models of system components verified, monitors generated, and finally the system is implemented. However, it is often the case that system verification is forgotten about until the development is almost finished. This makes verification more challenging, especially as the complexity of the system grows [9]. Our situation was in the latter category: the system was nearly complete when we attempted to verify it.

Despite the normal challenges that such an approach brings, we were able to reverse engineer our verification method. Notably, the structure of our system was not overly simple, but its functionality was not overly complicated, and we were willing to make minor adjustments to the software to expedite the verification step. While it is always preferable to create the system with verification in mind from the start, having an implementation to evaluate against was also beneficial from a verification standpoint. We could query the system when defining the requirements to uncover exceptional circumstances where the requirements were broken, and hence revise the requirements and accompanying formal models. In a sense, both the implementation and verification artefacts were used to inform each other. The degree of modularity in the system would be the most important component in expanding this method to a more complicated system. It is evident from this research that the more modular a system is, the easier it is to analyse and verify with heterogeneous or integrated verification methods.

3   Conclusions and Future Work

Our paper [4], presented a case study which illustrates how distinct verification techniques can be used at various stages of the development process to verify an autonomous grasping system. We used AADL, FRET, Dafny and ROS-Monitoring alongside simulation and physical system tests to verify that the system behaved correctly. These verification approaches were not tightly integrated in the sense that there were no automatic translations between them.

However, the results from each stage and method provided input for the next. This demonstrates that even a loosely integrated approach to verification using distinct methods can be beneficial. Our work in [4] bolsters the argument that, for complex systems such as autonomous robotics, a combination of formal and non-formal methods is useful [2,9]. This is acheived via a detailed case study.

References

1. Cardoso, R.C., Farrell, M., Luckcuck, M., Ferrando, A., Fisher, M.: Heterogeneous verification of an autonomous curiosity rover. In: Lee, R., Jha, S., Mavridou, A., Giannakopoulou, D. (eds.) NFM 2020. LNCS, vol. 12229, pp. 353–360. Springer, Cham (2020). https://doi.org/10.1007/978-3-030-55754-6_20
2. Farrell, M., Luckcuck, M., Fisher, M.: Robotics and integrated formal methods: necessity meets opportunity. In: Furia, C.A., Winter, K. (eds.) IFM 2018. LNCS, vol. 11023, pp. 161–171. Springer, Cham (2018). https://doi.org/10.1007/978-3-319-98938-9_10
3. Farrell, M., Mavrakis, N., Dixon, C., Gao, Y.: Formal verification of an autonomous grasping algorithm. In: International Symposium on Artificial Intelligence, Robotics and Automation in Space. ESA (2020)
4. Farrell, M., Mavrakis, N., Ferrando, A., Dixon, C., Gao, Y.: Formal modelling and runtime verification of autonomous grasping for active debris removal. Front. Robot. AI (2022). https://doi.org/10.3389/frobt.2021.639282
5. Feiler, P.H., Gluch, D.P., Hudak, J.J.: The architecture analysis & design language (AADL): An introduction. Technical report, Carnegie-Mellon University, Pittsburgh, PA Software Engineering Institute (2006)
6. Ferrando, A., Cardoso, R.C., Fisher, M., Ancona, D., Franceschini, L., Mascardi, V.: ROSMonitoring: a runtime verification framework for ROS. In: Mohammad, A., Dong, X., Russo, M. (eds.) TAROS 2020. LNCS (LNAI), vol. 12228, pp. 387–399. Springer, Cham (2020). https://doi.org/10.1007/978-3-030-63486-5_40
7. Giannakopoulou, D., Pressburger, T., Mavridou, A., Schumann, J.: Automated formalization of structured natural language requirements. Inf. Softw. Technol. **137**, 106590 (2021)
8. Leino, K.R.M.: Dafny: an automatic program verifier for functional correctness. In: Clarke, E.M., Voronkov, A. (eds.) LPAR 2010. LNCS (LNAI), vol. 6355, pp. 348–370. Springer, Heidelberg (2010). https://doi.org/10.1007/978-3-642-17511-4_20
9. Luckcuck, M., Farrell, M., Dennis, L.A., Dixon, C., Fisher, M.: Formal specification and verification of autonomous robotic systems: a survey. ACM Comput. Surv. (CSUR) **52**(5), 1–41 (2019)
10. Mavrakis, N., Gao, Y.: Visually guided robot grasping of a spacecraft's apogee kick motor. In: Symposium on Advanced Space Technologies in Robotics and Automation (2019)
11. Mavridou, A., Bourbouh, H., Garoche, P.L., Hejase, M.: Evaluation of the FRET and CoCoSim tools on the ten Lockheed Martin cyber-physical challenge problems. Technical report, TM-2019-220374, NASA (2019)
12. Orbital ATK, I.: ATK space propulsion products catalog (2016)
13. Rohmer, E., Singh, S.P., Freese, M.: V-REP: a versatile and scalable robot simulation framework. In: International Conference on Intelligent Robots and Systems, pp. 1321–1326. IEEE (2013)

Formal Specification and Verification of JDK's Identity Hash Map Implementation

Martin de Boer[1]($\boxtimes$), Stijn de Gouw[1], Jonas Klamroth[2], Christian Jung[3],
Mattias Ulbrich[3], and Alexander Weigl[3]

[1] Open University, Heerlen, The Netherlands
[2] FZI Research Center for Information Technology, Karlsruhe, Germany
[3] Karlsruhe Institute of Technology, Karlsruhe, Germany

Abstract. Hash maps are a common and important data structure in efficient algorithm implementations. Despite their wide-spread use, real-world implementations are not regularly verified.

In this paper, we present the first case study of the `IdentityHashMap` class in the Java JDK. We specified its behavior using the Java Modeling Language (JML) and proved correctness for the main insertion and lookup methods with KeY, a semi-interactive theorem prover for JML-annotated Java programs. Furthermore, we report how unit testing and bounded model checking can be leveraged to find a suitable specification more quickly. We also investigated where the bottlenecks in the verification of hash maps lie for KeY by comparing required automatic proof effort for different hash map implementations and draw conclusions for the choice of hash map implementations regarding their verifiability.

Keywords: Real-world case study · Deductive program verification · Java Modeling Language · Verified hash map · Verified data structure · Cooperative verification

1 Introduction

Maps are versatile data structures and a common foundation for important algorithms as they provide a simple modifiable association between two objects: the key and a value. A hash map realizes this association with a (constant time) hash function, which maps a key to a memory location in the managed memory space. Thus, the typical operations, i.e., lookup, update and deletion of associations, achieve a constant run-time on average.

To optimize their performance, hash maps require complex memory layout and collision resolution strategies. The memory layout describes where and how associations are stored. The collision strategy handles the location resolution when the memory location is already occupied by a different key with the same hash. Further, an implementation needs to decide when and how a restructuring

© Springer Nature Switzerland AG 2022
M. H. ter Beek and R. Monahan (Eds.): IFM 2022, LNCS 13274, pp. 45–62, 2022.
https://doi.org/10.1007/978-3-031-07727-2_4

of the memory layout is necessary to maintain the performance over time because the addition and removal of association leads to fragmentation.

In this paper, we present the specification and verification of the Identity-HashMap class of the Java SDK as it appears in the latest update of JDK7 and newer JDK versions (up to JDK17)[1]. To our knowledge, this is the first case study, which formally verifies a real-world hash map implementation from a mainstream programming language library. In particular, it is part of the Java Collections Framework, which is one of the most widely used libraries. We formally specify the behavior of the implementation using the Java Modeling Language JML. The case study with all artifacts is available at [5]. We show how we combined various JML-based tools (OpenJML, JJBMC, and KeY) together to exploit their strengths and avoid the weaknesses. In detail, we firstly used JUnit tests with generated runtime assertion and JJBMC [2] to quickly prove contracts and strengthened the specification, OpenJML [7] to automatically prove contracts, and finally KeY [1] to provide preciseness by the cost of performance and required user interaction. Finally, we were able to prove 15 methods of the class with KeY.

Furthermore, we describe how various implementation choices of hash maps affect the verification performance with KeY. For this, we re-implemented commonly used hash map concepts in Java and specified them with JML.

Related Work. The hash map/table data structure of a linked list has been studied mainly in terms of pseudo code of an idealized mathematical abstraction, see [15] for an Eiffel version and [16] for an OCaml version. Hiep et al. [10] and Knüppel et al. [11] investigate correctness of some other classes of the Collections framework using KeY, the latter mainly as a "stepping stone towards a case study for future research". In [4], the authors specify and verify the Dual Pivot Quicksort algorithm (part of the default sorting implementation for primitive types) in Java.

2   Preliminaries

The Java Modeling Language (JML) [13] is a behavioral interface specification language [9] for Java programs according to the of design-by-contract paradigm [14]. Listing 1 shows an excerpt of the specification for the hash map method get; the full specification is covered in detail in Sect. 4. JML annotations are enclosed in comments beginning with /*@ or //@. The listing contains a *method contract* (lines 5–10) covering the *normal behavior case* in which an exception must not be thrown. The requires and ensures clauses specify the pre- and postcondition respectively; the framing condition is given in the assignable clause which lists the heap locations modifiable by the method. The special keyword \nothing indicates that no existing heap location must be modified, but new objects may be allocated. \strictly_nothing specifies that the heap must not be modified at all. Multiple contracts for a method are separated with the keyword also. JML also supports *class invariants* (line 3) which need to be established

---

[1] http://hg.openjdk.java.net/jdk7u/jdk7u/jdk/file/4dd5e486620d/src/share/classes/java/util/IdentityHashMap.java.

```
 1   class IdentityHashMap {
 2     private /*@ nullable */ Object[] table;
 3     //@ public invariant table != null;
 4
 5     /*@ public normal_behavior
 6       @   requires (\exists \bigint i; 0 <= i < table.length/(\bigint)2;
 7       @            table[i*2] == maskNull(key));
 8       @   ensures  (\exists \bigint i; 0 <= i < table.length/(\bigint)2;
 9       @            table[i*2] == maskNull(key) && \result == table[i*2+1]);
10       @   assignable \nothing;
11       @ also public normal_behavior ...
12       @*/
13     public /*@ nullable */ Object get(/*@ nullable */ Object key) {
14       Object k = maskNull(key); Object[] tab = table;
15       int len = tab.length, i = hash(k, len);
16
17       //@ ghost \bigint hash = i;
18       /*@ // Index i is always an even value within the array bounds
19         @ maintaining 0 <= i < len && i % (\bigint)2 == 0;
20         @ maintaining ...
21         @ decreasing hash > i ? hash - i : hash + len - i;
22         @ assignable \strictly_nothing;
23         @*/
24       while (true) {
25         Object item = tab[i];
26         if (item == k)      return tab[i+1];
27         if (item == null)   return null;
28         i = nextKeyIndex(i, len);
29       }
30     }
31   }
```

Listing 1. The lookup method `get` of class `IdentityHashMap` as an introductory example of JML specifications.

before and after every method invocation. To conduct inductive proofs for loops, these can be annotated with *loop specifications* (lines 19–22). The *loop invariants* (**maintains**) must hold when the loop is reached and after every iteration. In the example, the variable i is specified to remain in range between 0 and len and is always even. The *loop variant* expression (**decreasing**) computes to a natural number which must be strictly decreased in every loop iteration. The **assignable** clause specifies the heap locations all loop iterations are allowed to change. JML extends the Java expression language by first-order logic constructs like existential (**\exists**) and universal quantification (**\forall**). Also, the construct (**\num_of int x**; *G*; *C*) is relevant for the case study. It counts the number of values for x such that the guard *G* and the condition *C* are satisfied. For instance, (**\num_of int i**; 0<=i<a.length; a[i] !=null) returns the number of non-null elements in array a. The identifier **\result** refers to the method's return value in postconditions, and the expression **\old**(*E*) evaluates the expression *E* in the pre-state of the method invocation. JML **ghost** variables (line 17) behave like local Java variables during verification, but are not available at runtime and must therefore not have an impact on the effects and result of the method they are declared in. The special primitive JML value type **\bigint**

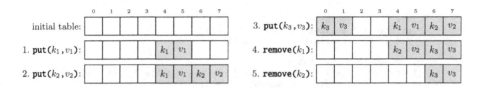

Fig. 1. Memory layout of the `table` array with length $N = 8$, $h_i = \text{hash}(k_i, N)$ for hashes $h_1 = 4$, $h_2 = 4$, and $h_3 = 6$.

refers to the mathematical integers $\mathbb{Z}$.[2] Finally, JML adds a few modifiers to the language like **nullable** which specifies that a field, method argument or return value may be **null**. Without the modifier, the value must not be **null** and, in the case of arrays, must not contain **null** values.

JML specifications can be used in different formal analyses, ranging from formal documentation, test case generation, runtime assertion checking to deductive verification. This paper will focus on the deductive verification of JML-annotated programs using two tools implementing different deductive JML verification approaches: KeY and JJBMC.

KeY is a theorem prover for JML-annotated Java programs that supports automatic and interactive verification. KeY encodes method contracts as proof obligations in dynamic logic, a program logic similar to the weakest precondition calculus or Hoare logic. The programs inside the dynamic logic formulas are resolved by applying a series of inference rules, thus symbolically executing the code and hence producing the weakest preconditions in first order logic. Further inference rules are applied to discharge these resulting obligations. KeY possesses a powerful automatic strategy that can prove most obligations fully automatically. In case of more sophisticated heavyweight specifications (like the ones in the present hash map case study), the user can apply inference rules interactively to guide the proof.

The tool JJBMC [2] on the other hand combines modular deductive verification with bounded model checking. It translates JML specifications to Java statements using additional assumptions and assertions. The enriched Java sources are then submitted to the state-of-the-art Java bounded model checker JBMC [8]. In Sect. 5.1 we will report how the combination of bounded verification with modular concepts inside JJBMC helped engineering the specifications.

3 The Verification Subject: JDK's IdentityHashMap

The `IdentityHashMap` is a hash table implementation of the interface `java.-util.Map` of the Java Collections Framework. Figure 2 shows an overview of the class. Like any `Map`, it implements a modifiable mapping between keys and

---

[2] At various places in the specifications, explicit casts like `(\bigint)2` have been added. These force the semantics of surrounding arithmetic operations to be in $\mathbb{Z}$ (rather than in 32-bit `int` with overflows) which simplifies the verification considerably.

values, s. t. every key k_i is associated with exactly one value v_i. In the Identity-HashMap, two keys k_1 and k_2 are considered equal if and only if $k_1 = k_2$ (equality by reference, see Listing 1 line 26 and Listing 4 line 33). In contrast, the equality of keys in HashMap is defined by the equals method).

The IdentityHashMap stores the key-value entries sequentially in a one-dimensional array (private field table). The class relies on the built-in function System.identityHashCode(o) which returns a hash code for the object o. The hash is the first candidate spot in table to lookup the entry, or locating a free spot to store the entry.

IdentityHashMap
-table : Object[]
-size : int
-modCount : int
+IdentityHashMap()
+IdentityHashMap(int)
+get(Object): Object
+containsKey(Object): boolean
+containsValue(Object): boolean
-containsMapping(Object, Object): boolean
+put(Object, Object): Object
-resize(int newCapacity): boolean
+remove(Object key): Object

Fig. 2. Excerpt of the IdentityHashMap class.

When an entry (k_1, v_1) is added (put(k_1, v_1), cf. Listing 4), a hash $h_1 \in \{0, 2, 4, \ldots, [2]N-2\}$ is calculated based on the hash of the key k_1 and the length N of the table (line 28). The key k_1 is then stored in table at the (even) index h_1, and the value v_1 is stored adjacently at (odd) index $h_1 + 1$ (line 40). Item 1. in Fig. 1 shows the case where an entry is added to an empty map. In case k_1 was already present in the table, it would not be inserted a second time (this would break uniqueness), but its associated value would be overwritten with v_1. While keys are unique, there is no guarantee that their *hash values* are. Collisions might occur: the calculated index in table can be already occupied by an entry with a different key. The new entry is then stored at the next free position in table (item 2. in Fig. 1, where (k_2, v_2) is stored at index 6, while its hash h_2 is 4). If that index idx is taken as well, the next even index $idx' = idx + 2 \mod N$ is calculated by nextKeyIndex and tried, until a free spot is found (item 3. in Fig. 1). This ensures that there is no gap (empty slots) between the calculated index and the actual index of a key. This collision resolution strategy is called *linear probing* [12]. Section 6.1 discusses other strategies. IdentityHashMap supports using the null value as a key. To distinguish the null key from an empty slot in the table, a constant object reference, NULL_KEY, is used in place of null.

The get(k) (Listing 1) method retrieves the value for a given key k. It searches the table with the same process that we described above for insertion: start at the hash of k (line 15+25) and move to the next key slot (two spots further, modulo N, see line 28) until k is found (line 26). The search also terminates when an empty element in the array is encountered: this means there is no entry with key k (line 27). To ensure termination, it is thus crucial that the array at all times contains at least one empty slot.

We do not discuss removing an entry (method remove) in detail, but only note that table needs to be rearranged as if the entry had never been added in the first place, so that remove introduces no gaps between the calculated and actual index of a key. For an example, see last items in Fig. 1.

4 Specification and Verification of the IdentityHashMap

We now discuss the specification and verification of core parts of the Identity-HashMap. The full case study comprises several hundred lines of source code and specifications and over 1.4 million proof steps (Table 1). An exhaustive exposition is therefore clearly not feasible. Instead, we focus on the core methods and highlight several of the main proof obligations and their proofs in this section.

Particularly with case studies of such a large size, it can be challenging, but is crucial, to make and keep the formal specifications manageable and understandable. Developers of the specification must quickly see which properties were formalized already and which remain to be fixed or added (if they turn out to be flawed during analysis). During the proof, one must understand the specifications sufficiently well to use them in proving the verification conditions. Clients of the IdentityHashMap should be able to use the class solely on the basis of the specifications (without looking at particular implementation details). To facilitate understandability, our specifications include comments in natural language that explain what the formal property expresses.

Some of the core properties maintained by the class invariant are for example that the table contains at least one empty spot (so that lookup methods terminate) (line 18 in Listing 2) and that all spots between the hash value and the actual index (including the wrap-around behavior as described in Sect. 3) in the table are occupied (lines 24 and 34) in Listing 2).

One could use the pure hash method from the Java code in the class invariant to refer to the hash of an object. But this can be inconvenient for the proof process: the hash method body must then be executed to derive that heap modifications do not alter hashes of existing objects (and that the result is deterministic, etc.). We simplify this by introducing a new mathematical (deterministic) function dl_genHash that does not rely on the heap to refer to an object hash and adding a postcondition to hash that its return value is dl_genHash. Let us now discuss some of the main proof obligations that arise in the verification of this class.

Termination of get(..). Listing 3 shows the specification of the loop in the get method. This loop also appears (in slightly different forms) in many other core methods of the hash map: the three contains* methods, put, and remove. The main goal of this loop is to search for a given key. As the loop guard is *true*, the loop only terminates if a return statement is encountered. Intuitively, if the given key is not present, the loop eventually hits the empty spot in the table, which the class invariant ensures to exist. If the key *is* present, eventually the condition item == k becomes *true*.

```
1   /*@ public invariant table != null &&
2   @    MINIMUM_CAPACITY * (\bigint)2 <= table.length  && // 4
3   @    MAXIMUM_CAPACITY * (\bigint)2 >= table.length; // 2^29
4   @
5   @ public invariant // Non-empty keys are unique
6   @    (\forall \bigint i; 0 <= i && i < table.length / (\bigint)2;
7   @      (\forall \bigint j;
8   @        i <= j && j < table.length / (\bigint)2;
9   @        (table[2*i] != null && table[2*i] == table[2*j]) ==> i==j));
10  @
11  @ public invariant // Size == number of non-empty keys
12  @    size == (\num_of \bigint i; 0 <= i < table.length / (\bigint)2;
13  @                                table[2*i] != null);
14  @
15  @ public invariant // Table length is always an even number
16  @    table.length % (\bigint)2 == 0;
17  @
18  @ // Table must have at least one empty key-element to prevent
19  @ // infinite loops when a key is not present.
20  @ public invariant
21  @    (\exists \bigint i;  0 <= i < table.length / (\bigint)2;
22  @      table[2*i] == null);
23  @
24  @ // There are no gaps between a key's hashed index and its actual
25  @ // index (if the key is at a higher index than the hash code)
26  @ public invariant
27  @    (\forall \bigint i; 0 <= i < table.length / (\bigint)2;
28  @      table[2*i] != null &&
29  @      2*i > \dl_genHash(table[2*i], table.length) ==>
30  @      (\forall \bigint j;
31  @        \dl_genHash(table[2*i], table.length) / (\bigint)2 <= j < i;
32  @        table[2*j] != null));
33  @
34  @ // There are no gaps between a key's hashed index and its actual
35  @ // index (if the key is at a lower index than the hash code)
36  @ public invariant
37  @    (\forall \bigint i;  0 <= i < table.length / (\bigint)2;
38  @      table[2*i] != null &&
39  @      2*i < \dl_genHash(table[2*i], table.length) ==>
40  @      (\forall \bigint j; \dl_genHash(table[2*i], table.length)
41  @              <= 2*j < table.length || 0 <= 2*j < 2*i;
42  @      table[2 * j] != null)); @*/
```

Listing 2. Excerpt of the class invariant.

We now prove termination formally, using the variant in the **decreasing** clause (line 21 in Listing 1). Suppose the loop invariant and the loop guard hold at the start of a loop iteration. If a **return** statement is hit in the iteration, then clearly the loop terminates promptly. Otherwise, we must show that the variant has decreased at the end of the iteration (with an updated value of i), but remains non-negative. The following cases (where i is the value at the start of the iteration) may be encountered in this order during the execution of the loop:

- If $hash \le i < len - 2$ then the updated value of i is $i + 2$, so clearly the value of the variant has decreased from $hash + len - i$ to $hash + len - (i+2)$ and remains non-negative (as $hash \ge 0$ and $i < len - 2$.)
- If $i = len - 2$ then the new value of i is 0, so the variant decreases from $hash + len - (len - 2) = hash + 2$ to $hash$ (and $hash \ge 0$).
- If $0 \le i < hash - 2$, the updated value of i is $i + 2$ and the variant decreases from $hash - i$ to $hash - (i + 2)$ and so remains positive.

```
1    /*@ // Index i is always an even value within the array bounds
2     @ maintaining
3     @   i >= 0 && i < len && i % (\bigint)2 == 0;
4     @
5     @ // Suppose i > hash. This can only be the case when no key k
6     @ // and no null is present at an even index of tab in the
7     @ // interval [hash..i-2].
8     @ maintaining
9     @   i > hash ==>
10    @      (\forall \bigint n; hash <= (2*n) < i;
11    @         tab[2*n] != k && tab[2*n] != null);
12    @
13    @ // Suppose i < hash. This can only be the case when no key k
14    @ // and no null is present at an even index of tab in the
15    @ // intervals [0..i-2] and [hash..len-2].
16    @ maintaining
17    @   i < hash ==>
18    @      (\forall \bigint n; hash <= (2*n) < len;
19    @         tab[2*n] != k && tab[2*n] != null) &&
20    @      (\forall \bigint m; 0 <= (2*m) < i;
21    @         tab[2*m] != k && tab[2*m] != null);
22    @
23    @ decreasing hash > i ? hash - i : hash + len - i;
24    @ assignable \strictly_nothing; @*/
```

Listing 3. Loop specification of the loop in the get method and the inner loop of the put method.

– If $i = \mathsf{hash} - 2$ then the loop invariant implies that all slots for keys in the tab array in the intervals $[0, \mathsf{hash} - 2]$ and $[\mathsf{hash}, \mathsf{len} - 2]$ are not equal to k, the key that we searched for, and non-null (in other words, all keys except the one at $i = \mathsf{hash} - 2$). If $\mathsf{tab}[\mathsf{hash} - 2] = k$ then clearly the return statement on line 26 is hit. Otherwise, since the assignable clause states that the heap is not modified by the loop, we know the class invariant holds, which implies there must be an empty key slot in the array. This must be $\mathsf{tab}[\mathsf{hash} - 2] = \mathsf{null}$ since all other key slots were non-null. In this case, the return statement on line 27 is hit and the loop terminates.

put(..) Inner Loop Assignable Clause. The assignable clause (Listing 3) is peculiar: the code has an assignment to an array element (which is not dead code), yet the clause states that no locations are modified. This is due to the meaning of loop specifications: they must hold whenever the loop guard is checked. This however is not the case after leaving the loop by a return statement. Therefore in our case the assignable clause does not have to hold for the loop iteration in which the return statement is reached, and this is the case whenever the assignment that modifies the **table** is reached.

This strong assignable clause is very useful to prove the remainder of the method: all facts true before the loop (this may include the class invariant) are still valid and can be exploited after the inner loop!

put(..) Satisfies Contract and Preserves Class Inv. We distinguish three scenarios with respect to the **put** method and wrote a contract for each of them. A so-called exceptional contract for the case that the hash map is full (it has reached max capacity): in that case the map is not modified and an exception is thrown. Another contract for the case that the map already contains the given key: then the corresponding value is updated. And a contract for the case where the table does not contain the given key yet so that the new key/value pair must be added. We shall focus on the proof of this last contract and discuss the main reasoning to show formally that, assuming the class invariant and precondition hold initially, **put** preserves the class invariant and satisfies the postconditions of this contract. This is the proof obligation that must be proven at line 41.

Consider the postcondition on line 10 of Listing 4, about the preservation of old entries. The table is modified at table[i] and table[i + 1] which are **null**, as per the loop guard. So clearly, none of the entries that were already present are overwritten. In particular, in the case where the **table** is not resized, the old entries are at exactly the same index as at the beginning of the method. If the table *was* resized, the postcondition in the contract of **resize** (not shown) guarantees that they are present. The second main postcondition on line 18 is easy to establish: it says that there exists an index in the new table at which the new entry is stored. At line 41 we know that i is that index.

Next, we focus on two of the class invariants. The invariants that there are no gaps (key indices with a **null**) between the hash of any key and its actual index in the table (lines 24 and 34) are satisfied for the new entry: this follows from the invariant of the inner loop in put, Listing 3 lines 7 and 15. For old entries, these properties remain true, because the method only overwrites a **null** entry, so it does not introduce new gaps. Hence, if there previously was no gap between an old key's hash and its index, then certainly there is not one after inserting the new key either.

Finally, we discuss the invariant that the map maintains at least one empty spot in **table** (line 18). The main challenge here is that table[i] was previously **null** (i.e. it was an empty spot) and is now overwritten with the key object, so is there guaranteed to be an empty spot *elsewhere*? Note that the capacity of the table, i.e. the number of entries that can be stored, is **len**/2 since every entry (key and value) occupies two indices. If the old size is smaller than $\mathtt{len}/2 - 1$, where **len** is the new length of the **table**, we can establish the desired property from the previous class invariant: as the size is the number of non-null entries (line 11) there must have been at least two empty spots. We now show that the old size is indeed smaller than $\mathtt{len} - 1$ whenever we reach the **return**-statement on line 41. The if-statement prior to it must then have been false (otherwise control jumps back to the beginning of the outer loop with the **continue** statement). Hence, one of the following two cases is true:

- If $\mathtt{s} + (\mathtt{s} \ll 1) > \mathtt{len}$ (where s is the new **size**) then **resize** must return *false*. This happens when the table length was at the maximum capacity already (so **resize** does not allocate a new table; it is a no-op) and the current size is less than that capacity - 1. If the size is equal to the max capacity - 1, **resize** (and **put**) throw an exception so the table is not modified.
- Otherwise $\mathtt{s} + (\mathtt{s} \ll 1) > \mathtt{len}$ is false. Simplifying the left shift to 2s yields $2\mathtt{s} + \mathtt{s} > \mathtt{len}$. If $\mathtt{s} \leq 3$, at most six array indices in the table are used, but the table length is at least eight (line 2, where MINIMUM_CAPACITY = 4). So there

must be an empty spot. If s > 2 then 2s + s ≤ len implies 2s + 2 < len. Some arithmetic reasoning about inequalities then suffices to establish the desired s < len/2 − 1.

```
 1   /*@ also private exceptional_behavior ...
 2     @ also ... // The key is already present in the table
 3     @ also public normal_behavior // The key is not present in the table
 4     @   requires size < MAXIMUM_CAPACITY - 1;
 5     @   requires !(\exists \bigint i; 0 <= i < table.length/(\bigint)2;
 6     @                            table[i*2] == maskNull(key));
 7     @   assignable size, table[*], modCount, table;
 8     @   ensures size == \old(size) + 1 && modCount != \old(modCount)
 9     @           && \result == null;
10     @   ensures // After execution, all old keys are still present
11     @           // and all old values are still present
12     @      (\forall \bigint i;
13     @         0 <= i < \old(table.length)/(\bigint)2;
14     @         (\exists \bigint j;
15     @            0 <= j < table.length/(\bigint)2;
16     @            (\old(table[i*2]) == table[j*2]) &&
17     @            \old(table[i*2+1]) == table[j*2+1]));
18     @   ensures // After execution, the table contains the new key
19     @           // associated with the new value
20     @      (\exists \bigint i;
21     @         0 <= i < table.length/(\bigint)2;
22     @         table[i*2] == maskNull(key) && table[i*2+1] == value); @*/
23   public /*@ nullable @*/ Object put(/*@ nullable @*/ Object key,
24                           /*@ nullable @*/ Object value) {
25     final Object k = maskNull(key);
26     retryAfterResize: for (;;) {
27       final Object[] tab = table; final int len = tab.length;
28       int i = hash(k, len);
29       //@ ghost \bigint hash = i;
30       /*@ // Loop invariant: see Listing 3 @*/
31       for (Object item; (item = tab[i]) != null;
32            i = nextKeyIndex(i, len)) {
33         if (item == k) {
34           java.lang.Object oldValue = tab[i+1];
35           tab[i+1] = value; return oldValue; } }
36       final int s = size + 1;
37       // Use optimized form of 3*s. Next capacity is len, 2*capacity
38       if (s + (s << 1) > len && resize(len))
39         continue retryAfterResize;
40       modCount++; tab[i] = k; tab[i + 1] = value;
41       size = s; return null; } }
```

Listing 4. The put method, including specifications.

4.1   Mechanic Proof

We specified 15 methods of the IdentityHashMap and verified in KeY that they satisfy their contracts and preserve the class invariant: the default constructor with accompanying **capacity** and **init** methods (responsible for establishing the class invariant initially), the observers isEmpty, maskNull, nextKeyIndex, size, unmaskNull, the lookup methods containsKey, containsMapping, contains-Value, get and mutators clear, put and the private resize method. Table 1 summarizes the main statistics. The observer methods all have short proofs (<1,000 steps) and no interactive steps. All lookup methods have similar statistics: around 50k steps per contract. KeY's support for user interaction was crucial

Table 1. Lines of code, lines of specification, and KeY statistics per method

Method	Steps	Br.	IS	SE	QI	OC	LI	MR	PO	JML	LOC
Def.constructor	7,724	56	86	66	101	1	0	0	1	10	3
clear	17,588	78	0	115	79	0	1	0	1	19	7
containsMapping	55,611	146	8	484	458	6	1	0	1	17	14
put	973,404	4,088	1,655	2,221	1,564	26	4	2	3	70	24
resize	223,357	340	487	491	270	3	2	0	4	125	29
other	172,307	438	115	846	1,243	14	4	0	13	113	59
Totals	1,449,991	5,146	2,351	4,223	3,715	50	12	2	23	354	136

Br.: Number of branches in the proof tree, **IS**: Interactive Steps (number of interactively (manually) applied rules), **SE**: Symbolic Execution steps, **QI**: Quantifier Instantiations, **OC**: Operation Contract applications, **LI**: Loop Invariant applications, **MR**: Merge Rule applications, **PO**: Proof Obligations (contracts) for the method, **JML**: lines of JML spec. (KeY only, not counting empty and comment lines), **LOC**: Lines Of Code (Java code not counting empty and comment lines).

and used extensively to introduce intermediate lemmas and find suitable quantifier instantiations in the proofs of the most complex methods: put and resize.

The IdentityHashMap uses features for performance that complicate reasoning, such as continue jumps in loops, bit shifts and exploiting integer overflows. To match the intricate Java semantics, we took special care to analyze the source code nearly verbatim. We stripped generics with an automated plug-in of the KeY tool suite. The total effort of the case study amounts to roughly five person months (800 h). The largest part of this consists of developing the formal specifications. This required many iterations of partial (failed) verification attempts with KeY and other analysis techniques (see Sect. 5.1) that led to corrections or additions to the specifications. With complete specifications, we estimate that the KeY proofs alone can be done in about 80 h.

The put method, together with the private method resize was the largest and most difficult, comprising about 1.2 million steps together. The size is caused mainly because the class invariant is large and must be proven in every proof branch of a return statement. To minimize the number of such branches, we aggressively used a branch merging technique [17]. For example, line 41 of put gives rise to three branches: $s + (s \ll 1) > len$ is false (branch 1), or it is true but resize returns false (branch 2) or true (branch 3). In branch 1 and branch 2 the heap is not modified, so we merged these branches. This prevents, for example, having to proving the class invariant twice.

Another valuable feature in KeY for put was the flexibility to verify loops by either unrolling the loop (with symbolic execution) or by supplying a loop invariant on a case-by-case basis. Observe that the body of the outer loop (line 26 is executed either just once (in case no resize is necessary) or twice (in case of a resize). To avoid having to write and use a (complex) loop invariant that complicates the proof, we exploited the feature of KeY to unroll the loop body instead. This is why there is no invariant for the outer loop.

5   Engineering Specifications Using Lightweight Analyses

Most of the time in a modular verification endeavor is spent on finding appropriate specifications, and we need to distinguish between two types of specification: While *property specifications* describe the exported guarantees one wants to verify, *auxiliary specifications* (like loop-invariants and contracts of helper methods) partition the verification condition into smaller obligations and guide tools to find proofs. In the present case study, coming up with both categories had challenges in store. To gain more confidence in the specifications and spot bugs early in the process, we applied two lightweight verification techniques.

5.1   Bounded Analysis for Auxiliary Specifications

Coming up with appropriate auxiliary specifications is a challenging task, because the specifications usually depend on each other in two directions: In modular verification, it is not possible to prove a method contract containing a method call without a specification of the called method. On the other hand, the inner method is difficult to specify while it is not clear what guarantees are needed at its call sites. It is thus very desirable to reduce these interdependencies and to step back from the design-by-contract paradigm for the inner method call. We achieved this by using a bounded analysis to check partially specified programs.

We use JJBMC [3] with which modular and bounded verification techniques can be combined: methods (and loops) with specifications are treated modularly (exploiting user-given method contracts and loop invariants to abstract from the program flow) while unspecified constructs can be formally treated using bounded verification (performing loop unrolling and method inlining to obtain a finite program to analyze), enabling a formal (albeit bounded) analysis of partially specified programs. The bounded analysis is parameterized by the maximum number $k \in \mathbb{N}$ of unwindings and unrollings to apply. For a too small value of k, specification violations may hence remain undiscovered by a bounded analysis.

The workflow to engineer auxiliary specifications is as follows: The user annotates a top-level API method m_0 with the desired property specification together with candidate class invariants (but leaves inner methods unspecified). They then run JJBMC to get feedback whether this specification is correct (within the set bound). If it is not, a concrete counterexample trace is produced and presented to the user who can use it for debugging. Once a suitable specification has been found, the user can continue engineering the specification for a method m_1 called by m_0. By continuously checking the bounded correctness of m_0 and the modular correctness of m_0 (wrt. the contract for m_1), the user hones in on an appropriate specification (strong enough for the call sites and weak enough to be provable) for m_1. The process then continues with the next nested method call, and also applies to (nested) loops. Using the bounded model checking analysis, we gained confidence in the specifications and avoided a few tedious refactorings otherwise needed for the proofs of the unbounded case.

As one example where this process helped us in the case study, reconsider the specification of `get` in Listing 1. In the first specification attempt, the conditions in line 7 missed the call to `maskNull`, making code and specification inconsistent. Using JJBMC we were able to spot and correct this flaw early on before the inner mechanisms of `get` had been looked at. We used this approach to come up with several parts of the specification, and while we do not have hard evidence, our subjective impression is that it allowed us to get to correct specifications faster than we would have without it. We spent about 0.14 person months to verify the `IdentityHashMap` with JJBMC.

5.2   Unit Tests for Property Specifications

Dynamic techniques that check whether specifications hold at run-time could be cheap to apply, provided those checks are generated automatically from the JML specifications. There are tools designed for this purpose: JMLUnitNG [18] aims to generate unit tests and OpenJML [6] is a general analysis framework that includes support for run-time assertion checking. However, our application of these tools to this case study was unsuccessful: the semantics of the source code and specifications proved to be too complex and intricate to load the `Identity-HashMap`. In particular, this triggered exceptions and we did not manage to get useful output of the tools (despite contacting the main developer of OpenJML).

Confronted with this problem, we instead manually wrote (ad-hoc) JUnit tests to perform checks on method contracts (both pre- and postconditions) and a test method for the class invariant that checks all clauses. We can then call the test method whenever the class invariant should hold. Since the class invariant accesses private fields such as `table`, we used Java Reflection (`Class.getDeclaredField(..)`) to read the values of these fields. We handled quantifiers in JML specifications with for-loops (all quantifiers are bounded over the integers in our case study, so they can be translated routinely to for-loops).

Conducting these tests helped us to gain confidence in our specifications and even uncovered some errors in early versions of it. However, there are two main limitations: first, since JUnit tests operate at the granularity of entire methods, internal specifications such as loop invariants and assignable clauses are difficult to cover. Secondly, the manual translation of the JML specifications could be inconsistent (e.g. due to a misunderstanding of the semantics of JML) with the actual specification. Finally, as we use unit tests to discover errors quickly, one should keep in mind that writing and maintaining the unit tests is very time-consuming. We spent about 0.5 person months to develop the unit test framework.

6   Discussion

6.1   Empirical Identification of Verification Challenges

To learn more about the particular challenges imposed by the verification of hash tables, we not only verified the `IdentityHashMap`, but also investigated the contributing factors for the complexity of hash table verification endeavors in KeY. We considered two families of hash table implementations with different

Table 2. Required number of rules applications for different hash table implementations. The dash "–" denotes a non-closed proof.

Method	Separate Chaining			Linear Probing		
	WI	NE	WE	WI	NE	WE
constructor	24,096	*0.90*	–	3,577	*1.06*	*1.04*
get	15,353	*1.26*	*1.02*	1,160	*1.35*	*3.32*
put	82,624	*2.72*	–	29,632	*1.63*	–
delete	32,060	*1.44*	–	15,290	*1.68*	–
hash	1,303	*1.10*	*2.80*	1,061	*1.37*	*7.03*
getIndex	3,460	*0.93*	*6.65*	44,216	*1.61*	*5.70*
addNewPair	58,964	–	–	385,191	–	–
total	217,860			480,127		

hashing paradigms. For each family, we provided three implementations with different complexity and abstraction levels and compared the effort needed to verify them using KeY. To make the results more comparable and not influenced by user input, we have run KeY fully automatically without user interaction. The specification has a similar degree of abstraction and follows similar lines as the one outlined in Sect. 4. By comparing the required number of proof steps for the different implementations we can draw conclusions about the complexity of the verification obligations and the strengths and weaknesses of the automated proof strategy in KeY.

The two compared hash collision resolution paradigms are *linear probing* and *separate chaining*. They differ in situations in which two different keys map to the same hash (index) into the hash map. Linear probing is used in the Identity-HashMap, as described in Sect. 3. Separate chaining is used in the HashMap class in the JDK. It allows storing multiple entries into one slot: each slot contains a bucket (i.e. a linear list) with all entries that are mapped by the hash function to the same index (slot). The collision resolution strategy affects the algorithms for insertion and lookup routines since these have to take conflicting keys with identical indices into account. The implementations of the two paradigms have quite different method contracts and in particular the class invariants capturing the properties of the hash structure differ considerably – with different challenges both for the specifier and the automatic verification engine.

The three variants implemented for each conflict resolution strategy mainly differ in the data types used for values and keys. In the first variant called With-Integers (WI), keys and values are of type int and the identity operator (==) is used to compare keys. The second variant is called NoEquals (NE), and keys are objects of a specialized immutable Key class, while values are arbitrary Objects, and it uses the identity operator (==) to compare keys, like the IdentityHash-Map does. The third variant is called WithEquals (WE) and is similar to NE, but uses the equals method to compare keys.

Table 2 shows the required effort to prove the respective method contracts correct. The numbers of the WI variants represent the absolute number of rule applications needed, whereas the other two variants (in italics) are stated as a ratio to the number in the WI column for the same method and hashing family. Thus the relative overhead between the family members can be seen more easily. The exact numbers of steps are not very important for the investigation, suffice it to say that the WI proof for addNewPair with more than 380,000 steps took 12 min to complete. The **hash** method computes the hash value of a key and **getIndex** returns the index of a key (if present). **addNewPair** inserts a new key-value pair and is called by **put**, when the key is not already in the hash table. Some proofs could not be finished (indicated as −) since the prover ran out of memory resources. Since the solver is designed to be deterministic, the runs are repeatable.

It can be observed that in most cases the complexity grows within a family between the variants from WI to NE and from NE to WE. The variants that introduce **equals** instead of == experience a vast increase in complexity for the central method **getIndex**. This can be explained by the fact that the built-in identity comparison is independent of the heap state (it only depends on the compared values) and is inherently transitive and symmetric. Such properties may (or may partially) be true for an **equals** implementation, but considerably more effort must be taken to show consequences when dealing with this more general form of equality. It can thus be safely said that one should use primitive values as keys for hash maps as often as possible for KeY.

Contrary to what one might expect, some numbers decrease for the more complex variants. This can be explained by the heuristic choices that are made by the KeY strategy. In some cases, good decisions are made earlier than in other cases, due to the presence/absence of certain trigger expressions.

6.2 Discovered Bugs and Recommendations

In this section, we discuss several issues that our analysis revealed.

Serialization. The **IdentityHashMap** supports serialization: writing a map to a stream (e.g. a file) with a **writeObject** method and reading a map from a stream with the **readObject** method. Effectively **readObject** acts as a constructor: it creates a map object, so it should ensure that this object satisfies the class invariant. To fill the map with serialized entries, **readObject** uses a **putForCreate** method that does not resize (for performance reasons) but allocates a table based on the size stored in the stream. Suppose an attacker serializes a map with a single empty entry (satisfying the requirement from the class invariant that there is an empty slot) to a file. The attacker can tamper with the file using a hex-editor to overwrite the empty slot with a key. A victim who deserializes this rogue map then inadvertently enters an infinite loop in **putForCreate**. We suggest solving this by checking in the code whether the map to deserialize satisfies the class invariant, and if not, throw an exception to prevent infinite loops or construction of a map object that breaks the class invariant.

put in JDK7u80. The binaries distributed by Oracle for JDK7 (an older but still widely used JDK) uses source code from an old JDK7u80 update[3]. The main difference between JDK7u80 and the **IdentityHashMap** in this paper (which is used in all newer JDK's and the later source-only updates to JDK7) is in the **put** method. The JDK7u80 version resizes *after* adding a new entry, rather than before (see Fig. 3), and there is no outer loop with a **continue** statement.

Suppose **put** is called on a map that is filled to the maximum capacity. The last empty spot in the table is first overwritten and only then **resize** throws an exception. So, the map is left in an inconsistent state: it breaks the class invariant. If a client then calls **get(k)** on a key **k** not stored in the map, an infinite loop

```
... // See Lst. 4, lines 27 − 35
tab[i] = k; tab[i + 1] = value;
if (++size >= threshold)
  resize(len);
  // len == 2 * current capacity.
return null;
```

Fig. 3. put(..) in JDK7u80

is triggered. In other words: this version of **put** breaks *failure atomicity*: put fails (as the table is full) so the operation should have been a no-op.

There is a way to fix this without resorting to **continue** statements: extract the code for the inner loop in **put**, **get**, etc., which searches for the index of a given key, or returns the index of its insertion point if the key is not present in the map, into a new private method **search(k)**. The duplicated code for the loop can then be eliminated from the various methods by calling **search**. In **put**, call resize before modifying the table. This may shuffle around the existing keys: the hashes are recalculated based on the new table length. If a resize occurred, call **search(k)** again to obtain the new insertion point for the key. Now the entries can be safely inserted at the index returned by **search**.

7   Conclusion

In this paper we specified and verified the core of the challenging, real-world implementation **IdentityHashMap** in KeY and discovered several issues. To speed up finding suitable specifications, we successfully leveraged model checking and unit testing. We extended our analysis with an investigation on the effect on the proof complexity in KeY of features and strategies used in other map implementations.

References

1. Ahrendt, W., Beckert, B., Bubel, R., Hähnle, R., Schmitt, P.H., Ulbrich, M. (eds.): Deductive Software Verification - The KeY Book - From Theory to Practice, Lecture Notes in Computer Science, vol. 10001. Springer, Cham (2016). https://doi.org/10.1007/978-3-319-49812-6
2. Beckert, B., Kirsten, M., Klamroth, J., Ulbrich, M.: Modular verification of JML contracts using bounded model checking. In: Margaria, T., Steffen, B. (eds.) ISoLA 2020. LNCS, vol. 12476, pp. 60–80. Springer, Cham (2020). https://doi.org/10.1007/978-3-030-61362-4_4

---

[3] http://hg.openjdk.java.net/jdk7u/jdk7u-dev/jdk/file/70e3553d9d6e/src/share/classes/java/util/IdentityHashMap.java.

3. Beckert, B., Kirsten, M., Klamroth, J., Ulbrich, M.: Modular verification of JML contracts using bounded model checking. In: Margaria, T., Steffen, B. (eds.) ISoLA 2020. LNCS, vol. 12476, pp. 60–80. Springer, Cham (2020). https://doi.org/10.1007/978-3-030-61362-4_4

4. Beckert, B., Schiffl, J., Schmitt, P.H., Ulbrich, M.: Proving JDK's dual pivot quicksort correct. In: Paskevich, A., Wies, T. (eds.) VSTTE 2017. LNCS, vol. 10712, pp. 35–48. Springer, Cham (2017). https://doi.org/10.1007/978-3-319-72308-2_3

5. de Boer, M., de Gow, S., Klamroth, J., Jung, C., Ulbrich, M., Weigl, A.: Artifacts of the formal specification and verification of JDK's identity hash map implementation, March 2022. https://doi.org/10.5281/zenodo.6415339

6. Cok, D.: OpenJML: Software verification for Java 7 using JML, OpenJDK, and Eclipse. In: Electronic Proceedings in Theoretical Computer Science, vol. 149, April 2014. https://doi.org/10.4204/EPTCS.149.8

7. Cok, D.R.: OpenJML: JML for Java 7 by extending openJDK. In: Bobaru, M., Havelund, K., Holzmann, G.J., Joshi, R. (eds.) NFM 2011. LNCS, vol. 6617, pp. 472–479. Springer, Heidelberg (2011). https://doi.org/10.1007/978-3-642-20398-5_35

8. Cordeiro, L., Kesseli, P., Kroening, D., Schrammel, P., Trtik, M.: JBMC: a bounded model checking tool for verifying Java bytecode. In: Chockler, H., Weissenbacher, G. (eds.) CAV 2018. LNCS, vol. 10981, pp. 183–190. Springer, Cham (2018). https://doi.org/10.1007/978-3-319-96145-3_10

9. Hatcliff, J., Leavens, G.T., Leino, K.R.M., Müller, P., Parkinson, M.J.: Behavioral interface specification languages. ACM Comput. Surv. 44(3), 16:1–16:58 (2012). https://doi.org/10.1145/2187671.2187678

10. Hiep, H.-D.A., Bian, J., de Boer, F.S., de Gouw, S.: History-based specification and verification of java collections in KeY. In: Dongol, B., Troubitsyna, E. (eds.) IFM 2020. LNCS, vol. 12546, pp. 199–217. Springer, Cham (2020). https://doi.org/10.1007/978-3-030-63461-2_11

11. Knüppel, A., Thüm, T., Pardylla, C., Schaefer, I.: Experience report on formally verifying parts of OpenJDK's API with KeY. In: F-IDE 2018: Formal Integrated Development Environment. EPTCS, vol. 284, pp. 53–70. OPA (2018). https://doi.org/10.4204/EPTCS.284.5

12. Knuth, D.E.: Notes on "open" addressing, July 1963. http://citeseerx.ist.psu.edu/viewdoc/summary?doi=10.1.1.56.4899

13. Leavens, G.T., et al.: JML Reference Manual (2008)

14. Meyer, B.: Applying "design by contract". Computer 25(10), 40–51 (1992). https://doi.org/10.1109/2.161279

15. Polikarpova, N., Tschannen, J., Furia, C.A.: A fully verified container library. In: Bjørner, N., de Boer, F. (eds.) FM 2015. LNCS, vol. 9109, pp. 414–434. Springer, Cham (2015). https://doi.org/10.1007/978-3-319-19249-9_26

16. Pottier, F.: Verifying a hash table and its iterators in higher-order separation logic. In: Bertot, Y., Vafeiadis, V. (eds.) Proceedings of the 6th ACM SIGPLAN Conference on Certified Programs and Proofs, CPP 2017, Paris, France, January 16–17, 2017. pp. 3–16. ACM (2017). https://doi.org/10.1145/3018610.3018624,https://doi.org/10.1145/3018610.3018624

17. Scheurer, D., Hähnle, R., Bubel, R.: A general lattice model for merging symbolic execution branches. In: Ogata, K., Lawford, M., Liu, S. (eds.) ICFEM 2016. LNCS, vol. 10009, pp. 57–73. Springer, Cham (2016). https://doi.org/10.1007/978-3-319-47846-3_5

18. Zimmerman, D.M., Nagmoti, R.: JMLUnit: the next generation. In: Beckert, B., Marché, C. (eds.) FoVeOOS 2010. LNCS, vol. 6528, pp. 183–197. Springer, Heidelberg (2011). https://doi.org/10.1007/978-3-642-18070-5_13

Reusing Predicate Precision
in Value Analysis

Marie-Christine Jakobs$^{(\boxtimes)}$

Technical University of Darmstadt, Department of Computer Science,
Darmstadt, Germany
jakobs@cs.tu-darmstadt.de

Abstract. Software verification allows one to examine the reliability of software. Thereby, analyses exchange information to become more effective, more efficient, or to eliminate false results and increase trust in the analysis result. One type of information that analyses provide are precisions, which describe an analysis' degree of abstraction (tracked predicates, etc.). So far, analyses mainly reuse their own precision to reverify a changed program. In contrast, we aim to reuse the precision of a predicate analysis within a value analysis. To this end, we propose 13 options to convert a predicate precision into a precision for value analysis. All options compute precisions with various degrees of abstraction and are broadly evaluated on three applications (cooperative verification, result validation, and regression verification). Also, we compare our options against using the coarsest and finest precision as well as a state-of-the-art approach for each application. Our evaluation reveals that coarser precisions work better for proof detection, while finer precisions perform better in alarm detection. Moreover, reusing a predicate precision in value analysis can be beneficial in cooperative verification and works well for validating and reverifying programs without property violations.

1 Introduction

Software plays a major role in our daily lives and we often expect our software to execute reliably. For safety critical software, reliable execution is even a necessity. Hence, reliability is important for a software's practicality and acceptance up to becoming a critical factor for the software's success. To ensure that a piece of software is reliable, one may verify certain of its properties. To this end, verification must (1) successfully check, i.e., prove or disprove, those software properties, (2) produce correct results, and (3) efficiently reverify new versions of the software. To accomplish all three needs, one may require cooperative verification, result validation, and regression verification techniques. Cooperative verification techniques, e.g., [11,18,20,40,49,57,58,83,89,90], combine the strengths of different approaches to become more effective. Result validation techniques,

This work was funded by the Hessian LOEWE initiative within the Software-Factory 4.0 project.

M. H. ter Beek and R. Monahan (Eds.): IFM 2022, LNCS 13274, pp. 63–85, 2022.
https://doi.org/10.1007/978-3-031-07727-2_5

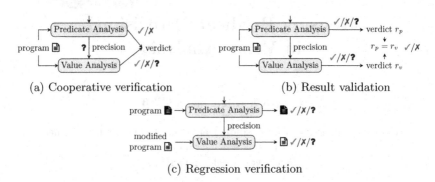

Fig. 1. Our applications for reusing a predicate precision in a value analysis

e.g., [15,16,39,45,53,61,75] target the trust in verification results. Instead of proving the correctness of a verification technique and its implementation, they use information provided by the verifier to validate its result, often using a different verifier. Regression verification techniques, e.g., [9,10,25,31,51,56,62,88,97,98], aim to speed up the reverification of a changed software.

Many techniques in cooperative verification, result validation, and regression verification exchange information, but most exchange techniques are only applicable in one of the three scenarios. Also, regression verification techniques typically exchange information between different runs of the same verification approach and not between different approaches, which hinders adapting regression verification to the latest development in software verification. Exceptions are the exchange of conditions [20,25] and the exchange of constraint satisfiability [97], which are both applied in cooperative verification and regression verification. Furthermore, CoVeriTest [24] recently adapted precision reuse [31], which was originally suggested to reverify a modified program with the same verification approach, to reuse predicate precisions obtained during test-case generation with predicate analysis in test-case generation with value analysis.

In this paper, we proceed to exchange precisions between predicate [28] and value analysis [30], two abstraction-based model checkers that automatically determine the precision (abstraction degree) required for program verification. We let the value analysis reuse a predicate precision in a sequential composition of predicate and value analysis (Fig. 1a), when validating results of the predicate analysis (Fig. 1b), or when changing from predicate to value analysis for the reverification of the modified program (Fig. 1c). In addition, we significantly extend the reuse suggested by CoVeriTest with 12 new reuse configurations that provide various options to adapt the reuse to the analyzed program.

Our extensive evaluation of the above applications (Fig. 1) reveals that CoVeriTest's reuse works well for programs meeting the properties of interest, but we require a different reuse configuration for programs violating a property of interest or sets of programs that contain both kinds of programs. Also, proof validation and regression verification work better when reusing the predicate precision than ignoring it or using a competing approach. While reusing the

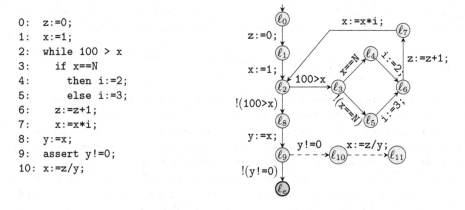

```
0:  z:=0;
1:  x:=1;
2:  while 100 > x
3:      if x==N
4:          then i:=2;
5:          else i:=3;
6:      z:=z+1;
7:      x:=x*i;
8:  y:=x;
9:  assert y!=0;
10: x:=z/y;
```

Fig. 2. Example program and its CFA representation

predicate precision is not always most effective, it often requires less verification effort, e.g., number of refinements or verification time, than its competitors.

2 Programs and Precisions

Programs. We model a program as a *control-flow automaton* (CFA) $P = (L, \ell_0, G, \ell_e)$. The set L represents the locations, i.e., the values of the program counter, $\ell_0 \in L$ reflects the initial location, and the set $G \subseteq L \times Ops \times L$ models the control flow plus the executed program instructions. For the sake of presentation, we restrict the set Ops of instructions to assume operations (boolean expressions *bexpr*) and assignments *var := expr*.[1] Finally, the location $\ell_e \in L$ is the error location, which the program must not reach to be correct.[2] Throughout the paper, we assume that the set $Var(expr)$ contains the variables occurring in (boolean) expression *expr* and that the set Var describes all program variables, i.e., it contains all variables that may occur in program instructions.

Figure 2 shows the program code and the CFA of our artificial example. We observe that assignments are transferred, while a condition of an assertion, if or while statement is translated into two assume edges (one per evaluation of the condition). Moreover, a violation of the assertion leads to the error location ℓ_e.

Next, we define a program's *syntactical paths*. A syntactical path of program P is finite, starts in P's initial location, and adheres to P's control flow.

$$synP((L, \ell_0, G, \ell_e)) := \left\{ g_0 \dots g_n \in G^+ \middle| \begin{array}{l} g_0 = (\ell_0, \cdot, \cdot) \wedge \forall 1 \leq i \leq n : \\ (g_{i-1} = (\cdot, \cdot, \ell_i) \implies g_i = (\ell_i, \cdot, \cdot)) \end{array} \right\}$$

Based on the syntactical program paths, we compute the subset G_{err} of all control-flow edges that occur on an error path, i.e., on a syntactical path that

---

[1] Our implementation supports C programs.

[2] Many safety properties can be encoded by the unreachability of an error location [61].

ends in the error location ℓ_e. We use the set G_{err} to focus the adaption of the predicate precision on the paths relevant for verification (solid paths in Fig. 2).

$$G_{\mathrm{err}}((L, \ell_0, G, \ell_e)) := \left\{ g \in G \middle| \begin{array}{l} \exists g_0 \ldots g_n \in synP((L, \ell_0, G, \ell_e)) : g_n = (\cdot, \cdot, \ell_e) \\ \wedge \exists 0 \leq i \leq n : g = g_i \end{array} \right\}$$

To retrieve additional relevant information for verification, our adaption also examines dependencies among variables. For example, we consider which variables are used to define a variable. Hence, we need to know which variables a control-flow edge defines and uses. A control-flow edge g *defines* variable v if its instruction is an assignment and v occurs on its left-hand side. In contrast, a control-flow edge g *uses* a variable v if its instruction is an assignment and v occurs on its right-hand side or its instruction is an assume operation in which v occurs. Then, the definitions (uses) of a control-flow edge g are all variables v that the edge defines (uses). Formally, this is stated as follows.

$$\mathrm{DEF}(g) := \left\{ \begin{array}{ll} \{v\} & \text{if } g = (\cdot, v := \cdot, \cdot) \\ \emptyset & \text{else} \end{array} \right.$$

$$\mathrm{USE}(g) := \left\{ \begin{array}{ll} Var(bexpr) & \text{if } g = (\cdot, bexpr, \cdot) \\ Var(expr) & \text{if } g = (\cdot, v := expr, \cdot) \end{array} \right.$$

Definitions and uses are associated with data-flow dependencies. In contrast, conditions of e.g. if and while statements, which are represented by assume operations in the CFA, guard the execution of certain control-flow edges and influence their executability. Hence, a control-flow edge g is *control dependent* on edge g' if the execution of g is guarded by g'. For example, the edge $(\ell_4, \mathtt{i:=2;}, \ell_6)$ in Fig. 2 is control dependent on the edges $(\ell_2, \mathtt{100>x}, \ell_3)$ and $(\ell_3, \mathtt{x==N}, \ell_4)$. To guard an edge g, the edge g' must describe an assume operation and each syntactical path to g must pass through g', i.e., g' dominates g. Formally, the edges that an edge g is control-dependent on in program P are defined as

$$CD(g, (L, \ell_0, G, \ell_e)) := \left\{ g' \in G \middle| \begin{array}{l} (\forall g_0 \ldots g_n \in synP((L, \ell_0, G, \ell_e)) : g_n = g \\ \implies \exists 0 \leq i < n : g_i = g') \wedge g' = (\cdot, bexpr, \cdot) \end{array} \right\}.$$

Precisions. Precisions specify the degree of abstraction for abstraction-based analyses. More concretely, abstraction-based analyses apply abstract interpretation [43] to compute an abstraction, i.e., an abstract model of the program. The analyses' abstract domain, e.g., interval, predicate, or value domain, fixes the type of abstraction, while the precision defines the abstraction degree of the abstract domain, i.e., the information (e.g., the set of predicates) that the analysis may use to compute the abstract model. In this paper, we are interested in the precisions of two analyses: predicate analysis and (explicit) value analysis.

The precision $\Pi_{\mathcal{P}}$ of a predicate analysis [28], named *predicate precision*, assigns to each program location a set of predicates (typically, properties or relations over program variables like $x > 0$ or $x < y$), which the predicate analysis can combine with boolean operators to compute the predicate abstraction at the respective location. Formally, a predicate precision is a function $\Pi_{\mathcal{P}} : L \to 2^{\Phi}$, where Φ denotes the set of all predicates. Note that similar to expressions, we use $Vars(p)$ to denote the variables occurring in predicate $p \in \Phi$.

The (value) precision $\Pi_\mathcal{V}$ of the value analysis [30] originally stores for each program location the variables that should be tracked, i.e., whose known values must not be abstracted by any value. Due to efficiency reasons, CPACHECKER's value analysis, which we consider, avoids such a location-based precision and uses a scope-based value precision that stores the variables that should be tracked throughout their scope. Hence, we formalize a value precision as $\Pi_\mathcal{V} \subseteq Var$.

Predicate and value analysis employ counterexample-guided abstraction refinement (CEGAR) [42] to compute a precision appropriate for checking a program's correctness. While any precision is sound, a too fine precision may be inefficient. Thus, CEGAR starts with an initial, coarse precision, e.g., no predicates or no tracked variables, and iteratively refines it. To speed up CEGAR, precision reuse [31] suggests to start with a precision from a previous verification (of an earlier version of the program), which is typically finer than the initial, coarse precision. While precision reuse exchanges precisions between the same analysis, we aim to reuse the predicate precision in the value analysis. Our approach uses the exchange format for predicate precisions defined by Beyer et al. [31], but it transforms the predicate precision into an initial value precision $\Pi_\mathcal{V}^0$, which becomes the initial precision for CEGAR. We discuss the transformation next.

3   From Predicate Precision to Initial Value Precision

To make the predicate precision reusable for the value analysis, our goal is to transform the predicate precision into a value precision. Hence, we aim to compute the set of initially tracked variables (i.e., the initial value precision $\Pi_\mathcal{V}^0$) based on information from the given predicate precision $\Pi_\mathcal{P}$. We compute $\Pi_\mathcal{V}^0$ using algorithm $\mathcal{P}2\mathcal{V}$ (see Algorithm 1). The algorithm gets as input a predicate precision, a program, and a configuration, while it outputs the initial value precision $\Pi_\mathcal{V}^0$. Its configuration is a tuple (`adapt`,`allEdges`,`controlDep`,`ineq`, `knownDefs`)$\in \mathbb{B}^5$ of five boolean options that determine which dependencies among variables in the program may be taken into account to compute the initial value precision. We explain the meaning of the options when describing the algorithm in detail.

Assuming that predicates in precision $\Pi_\mathcal{P}$ are relevant for verification[3], we deduce that values of variables that occur in a predicate of $\Pi_\mathcal{P}$ likely play an important role for verification. Thus, the value analysis should track these variables. The first line of algorithm $\mathcal{P}2\mathcal{V}$ takes this into account and always adds all variables occurring in a predicate of precision $\Pi_\mathcal{P}$ to the initial value precision. For instance given predicate precision $\Pi_\mathcal{P}^{ex}$ that assigns predicate $x > 0$ to location ℓ_2 and no predicate to any other location, line 1 computes $\Pi_\mathcal{V}^0 = \{x\}$.

The variables extracted in line 1 may be insufficient. Line 1 may miss variables relevant at certain locations because the predicate analysis we use performs

---

[3] In our scenarios, the predicates have been used for the (incomplete) verification of the same or a previous version of the program and therefore are likely relevant.

Algorithm 1. $\mathcal{P}2\mathcal{V}$ deriving an initial value precision from a predicate precision

Input: program $P = (L, \ell_0, G, \ell_e)$, predicate precision $\Pi_{\mathcal{P}}$, configuration config $\in \mathbb{B}^5$
Output: initial value precision $\Pi_{\mathcal{V}}^0$

1: $\Pi_{\mathcal{V}}^0 = \bigcup_{\ell \in dom(\Pi_{\mathcal{P}})} \bigcup_{p \in \Pi_{\mathcal{P}}(\ell)} Vars(p)$;
2: **if** config.adapt **then**
3:     **if** config.allEdges **then** $G_r := G$;
4:     **else** $G_r := G_{\mathrm{err}}(P)$;
5:     $V_{tbi} = \Pi_{\mathcal{V}}^0$;
6:     **while** $V_{tbi} \neq \emptyset$ **do**
7:         pop v from V_{tbi};
8:         $V_{\mathrm{add}} = \bigcup_{g \in G_r \wedge v \in \mathrm{DEF}(g)} \mathrm{USE}(g)$;
9:         **if** config.knownDefs **then**
10:           $V_{\mathrm{add}} = V_{\mathrm{add}} \cup \bigcup_{g \in G_r \wedge (\mathrm{USE}(g) \setminus \Pi_{\mathcal{V}}^0) = \emptyset \wedge v \in \mathrm{USE}(g)} \mathrm{DEF}(g)$;
11:         **if** config.controlDep **then**
12:           $V_{\mathrm{add}} = V_{\mathrm{add}} \cup$ trackable-dep$(v, P, \Pi_{\mathcal{V}}^0 \cup V_{\mathrm{add}}, G_r,$ config.ineq$)$;
13:         $V_{tbi} = V_{tbi} \cup (V_{\mathrm{add}} \setminus \Pi_{\mathcal{V}}^0)$; $\Pi_{\mathcal{V}}^0 = \Pi_{\mathcal{V}}^0 \cup V_{\mathrm{add}}$;
14: **return** $\Pi_{\mathcal{V}}^0$;

adjustable block encoding (ABE) [28] and only abstracts at and computes predicates for particular locations (loop heads). For instance, the predicate analysis succeeds to prove the correctness of our example program (Fig. 2) with precision $\Pi_{\mathcal{P}}^{\mathrm{ex}}$. However, the value analysis fails to prove the unreachability of the error location ℓ_e with precision $\Pi_{\mathcal{V}}^0 = \{x\}$ extracted at line 1. To succeed, it requires the value of y, which depends on x, which depends on i. To handle such dependencies between variables, we allow algorithm $\mathcal{P}2\mathcal{V}$ to adapt the set of variables extracted in line 1 when option adapt is set. The remaining options determine which dependencies to consider and influence the degree of abstraction (i.e., number of tracked variables), which determines the efficiency of the value analysis. For example, option allEdges configures whether $\mathcal{P}2\mathcal{V}$ considers all program edges (line 3) or only edges of error paths (line 4) when adapting.

During adaption, algorithm $\mathcal{P}2\mathcal{V}$ inspects every variable $v \in \Pi_{\mathcal{V}}^0$ once in lines 5–13. To this end, the set V_{tbi} maintains the variables of $\Pi_{\mathcal{V}}^0$ that still need to be inspected. During inspection of a variable v, algorithm $\mathcal{P}2\mathcal{V}$ identifies variables V_{add} that should be tracked, i.e., added to the initial value precision in line 13, because (1) variable v is tracked and (2) they are in a dependency relation with v that is considered by the given configuration. In the following paragraphs, we explain the details for computing V_{add}.

The value analysis can only realistically track a variable if it can compute its concrete value. In our example program (Fig. 2), we depend on variables i, y, and z to be able to always compute the value of variable x. When focusing on definitions of x on edges $g \in G_{\mathrm{err}}$ (solid edges) occurring on error paths, we only require variable i. Line 8 determines those variables when inspecting variable x in our example program either considering relevant edges $G_r = G$ or $G_r = G_{\mathrm{err}}$. More concretely, line 8 selects all relevant edges that define the currently inspected variable v and adds all variables to V_{add} that are used in one of those definitions of v. Hence, line 8 detects all variables required to compute the value of variable v on relevant edges. To ensure that values of tracked variables can be computed, we decided that the adaption always executes line 8.

Sometimes, it may be beneficial to track variables whose value one may compute based on already tracked variables. For instance, in our example we require the value of y to show the unreachability of the error location ℓ_e and we can compute the value of variable y when knowing the value of variable x. Since knowing the value of a variable at a particular location can already be beneficial for verification, we decided to add a variable to the initial precision if its value may be determined by at least one relevant edge. To determine those definable variables, line 10 collects the definitions of all relevant edges that only use tracked variables from $\Pi_\mathcal{V}^0$. Due to efficiency reasons and to exclude variables assigned constant values, line 10 only will collect a definition if it uses the currently inspected variable. Hence, for our example line 10 will add variable y when expecting variable x. Taking into account that not all variables whose value can be defined need to be tracked and tracking them may slow down the value analysis, algorithm $\mathcal{P}2\mathcal{V}$ adds variables whose value can be defined with the currently tracked variables only if option knownDefs is enabled (cf. lines 9–10).

To prove the unreachability of the error location ℓ_e in our example program (Fig. 2), the value analysis needs to show that condition !(y!=0) never evaluates to true, which requires tracking of variable y. In addition, the value analysis may infer variable values from equalities $(==, !=)$ in boolean conditions (assume operations), e.g., it derives y has value zero after assume operation y==0. Therefore, we may want to consider assume operation when adapting the set of extracted variables. Since equalities may be more valuable and tracking too many variables can become inefficient, we allow the user to configure via the option ineq whether the adaption should also consider inequalities (i.e., operators $<, \leq, \geq, >$). Nevertheless, we decided to restrict the adaption to (negated) assume operations of the form $var\ op_c\ expr$ and $expr\ op_c\ var$ with $op_c \in \{==, !=, <, \leq, \geq, >\}$ and $expr \in (Var \cup \mathbb{Z})$. First, the tool in which we integrate our approach translates complex boolean conditions into sequences of assume operations without binary boolean operators $(\&\&, \|)$ and multiple negations. Second, the tool can only derive values from assume operations like $var == expr$ or $expr == var$. Third, ignoring complex arithmetic expressions simplifies our approach. When inspecting a boolean expression (assume operation) of that form, our adaption adds var to the tracked variables if $expr$ is a constant or a variable already tracked. The following definition summarizes this.

$$\text{trackable-cond}(\Pi_\mathcal{V}^0, bexpr, \text{ineq}) :=$$
$$\left\{ v' \in Var \middle| \begin{array}{l} (bexpr \equiv v'\ op_c\ expr \vee bexpr \equiv expr\ op_c\ v' \\ \vee bexpr \equiv !(v'\ op_c\ expr) \vee bexpr \equiv !(expr\ op_c\ v')) \wedge \\ expr \in (\Pi_\mathcal{V}^0 \cup \mathbb{Z}) \wedge (op_c \in \{=, \neq\} \vee \text{ineq} \wedge op_c \in \{<, \leq, \geq, >\}) \end{array} \right\}$$

The previous definition describes which variables should be tracked for a relevant assume operation. Nevertheless, not all assume operations in a program are relevant to check the unreachability of the error location. Therefore, the adaption focuses on assume edges that are related to already tracked program behavior.

More concretely, our adaption only considers assume edges in the set G_r of relevant edges that control a definition of a variable already considered in the initial precision. However, control dependency is no guarantee for relevance of an assume edge. Hence, one may end up in tracking too many variables, which can result in an inefficient value analysis, when considering assume edges. Thus, one must enable option `controlDep` to derive initially tracked variables from assume edges (cf. lines 11–12). The following definition now formally states how to derive variables from assume edges for the currently inspected variable.

$$\texttt{trackable-dep}(v, P, \varPi_\mathcal{V}^0, G_r, \texttt{ineq}) :=$$
$$\bigcup_{g \in G_r \wedge v \in \mathrm{DEF}(g)} \bigcup_{(\cdot, bexpr, \cdot) \in \mathrm{CD}(g, P)} \texttt{trackable-cond}(\varPi_\mathcal{V}^0, bexpr, \texttt{ineq})$$

Next, we evaluate the options of Algorithm 1. Thereby, we use c_{no} to refer to `controlDep` =false as well as c_{eq} (c_{ineq}) to describe `controlDep`=true and `ineq`=false (=true).

4   Evaluation

In our evaluation, we aim to compare the different configurations of $\mathcal{P}2\mathcal{V}$ (Algorithm 1) on the three applications from Fig. 1. Also, we want to investigate whether our reuse approach is beneficial. To this end, we compare our reuse approach against the two extreme configurations of the initial value precision (track no or track all variables) and against one competing approach per application.

4.1   Experimental Setup

Analysis Configurations. We integrated Algorithm 1 into the software analysis framework CPACHECKER[4] [27], which supports predicate and value analysis as well as reading and writing of predicate precisions. Its predicate analysis [28] uses adjustable block encoding [28], only abstracts at loop heads, and computes the predicates with CEGAR [42] and lazy refinement [63] starting with $\varPi_\mathcal{P} = \emptyset$. Its value analysis [30] applies CEGAR with path prefix slicing [33] and refinement selection [32]. For our experiments, we use CPACHECKER revision 38247.

For all three applications (see Fig. 1), we study 15 *configurations to compute the initial value precision* $\varPi_\mathcal{V}^0$, namely all 13 options[5] to configure Algorithm 1 ($\mathcal{P}2\mathcal{V}$ configurations) plus configurations **no reuse** and **all vars** that do not run $\mathcal{P}2\mathcal{V}$ and use $\varPi_\mathcal{V}^0 = \emptyset$ (coarsest precision) and $\varPi_\mathcal{V}^0 = Var$ (track all variables).

For the cooperation and validation applications, $\mathcal{P}2\mathcal{V}$ reuses the predicate precision resulting from running the predicate analysis on the same program, while in regression verification $\mathcal{P}2\mathcal{V}$ uses the predicate precision that the predicate analysis produced when run on the previous version of the program. The cooperation setting runs a sequential combination of predicate and value analysis, in

---

[4] https://cpachecker.sosy-lab.org/
[5] Configurations `config` $= (\bot, \bot, \bot, \bot, \bot)$, `config` $= (\top, \cdot, \bot, \bot, \cdot)$, `config` $= (\top, \cdot, \top, \bot, \cdot)$, and `config` $= (\top, \cdot, \top, \top, \cdot)$, where $\cdot$ is either $\top$ (true) or $\bot$ (false).

which the predicate analysis is limited to at most 200 s of CPU time (its limit in SV-COMP 2021). In contrast, the validation and regression verification applications execute the predicate and the value analysis in separate runs.

Also, we compare the configurations of each application against one state-of-the-art approach. To this end, we compare our cooperation configurations against conditional model checking (CMC) [20], which also uses a combination of predicate and value analysis with a limit of 200 s for the predicate analysis. Moreover, we compare the validation configurations against witness validation [15, 16] using the value analysis as validator and check our regression verification configurations against reusing the predicate precision with the predicate analysis [31].

Programs. For the cooperation and validation applications, we consider the software verification benchmark[6] (tag sv-comp21), a common benchmark for the evaluation of verification approaches, which is also used by SV-COMP [13]. Since all our analyses support the `unreach-call` property, we select all programs from the ReachSafety categories. However, we exclude all programs from category `SoftwareSystems-uthash` since neither predicate nor value analysis can solve a single program in this category. In total, we get 7 615 programs.

The above benchmark is not appropriate for regression verification. Only a few of its tasks consider different versions of the same program. Hence for regression verification, we use the 4 193 programs from the precision reuse paper [31].[7]

Computing Resources. We run our experiments on machines with 33 GB of memory and an Intel Xeon E3-1230 v5 CPU with 8 processing units and a frequency of 3.4 GHz. The machines' operating system is an Ubuntu 20.04 with Linux kernel 5.4 and Java 11. Each run (a pair of an analysis configuration and a program) may use up to 4 processing units, 15 min of CPU time, and 15 GB of memory. We enforce those limits with BENCHEXEC [34] (version 3.8).

4.2   Experimental Results

Discussion of Cooperative Verification. To study the effect of reusing the predicate precision in cooperative verification, we study those programs that may reuse a predicate precision. These are all programs that are non-trivial for the value analysis, i.e., the value analysis requires at least one refinement, and that the predicate analysis cannot solve in 200 s in any of the configurations, but for which it provides a non-empty precision[8]. We get 1 017 incorrect programs (alarms) reaching the error location and 2 223 correct programs (proofs).

Table 1 shows for how many of the selected programs (row total) as well as for how many alarms and proofs CMC and the 15 configurations of $\Pi_\mathcal{V}^0$ report the expected result. For all other programs, those configurations do not report a result, e.g., timeout. Columns $\bigcup \mathcal{P}2\mathcal{V}$ and $\bigcup \Pi_\mathcal{V}^{0\leftrightarrows}$ show the number of programs for which at least one of the $\mathcal{P}2\mathcal{V}$ configurations (columns 2–14) and for which columns 1

---

[6] https://github.com/sosy-lab/sv-benchmarks/

[7] https://www.sosy-lab.org/research/cpa-reuse/supplementary-archive.zip

[8] Since we did not retrieve the temporary predicate precision, we checked that $\Pi_\mathcal{V}^0 \neq \emptyset$ if the value analysis with configuration `no adapt` $((\perp, \perp, \perp, \perp, \perp))$ reports a result.

Table 1. Number of relevant alarms and proofs correctly reported by a sequential combination of predicate and value analysis using either conditional model checking (CMC), one of the 15 configurations of $\Pi_{\mathcal{V}}^0$, the optimal $\mathcal{P}2\mathcal{V}$ configuration ($\bigcup\mathcal{P}2\mathcal{V}$), or the optimal choice ($\bigcup\Pi_{\mathcal{V}}^{0\rightleftharpoons}$) from no reuse and all vars

| | | | allEdges | | | | | | ¬ allEdges | | | | | | | | | |
| | | | ¬ knownDefs | | | knownDefs | | | ¬ knownDefs | | | knownDefs | | | all | $\bigcup$ | $\bigcup$ | |
correct	no reuse	no adapt	c_{no}	c_{eq}	c_{ineq}	c_{no}	c_{eq}	c_{ineq}	c_{no}	c_{eq}	c_{ineq}	c_{no}	c_{eq}	c_{ineq}	vars	$\mathcal{P}2\mathcal{V}$	$\Pi_{\mathcal{V}}^{0\rightleftharpoons}$	CMC
alarms	230	209	210	268	283	212	273	290	203	243	236	203	239	235	*291*	**297**	293	219
proofs	*331*	324	253	230	248	234	225	247	249	253	273	249	251	272	247	**384**	383	329
total	*561*	533	463	498	531	446	498	537	452	496	509	452	490	507	538	**681**	676	548

or 15 report the expected result. Also, we mark the best $\mathcal{P}2\mathcal{V}$ configuration (best Algorithm 1 configuration) in light gray, the best configuration of the initial precision $\Pi_{\mathcal{V}}^0$ in italics, and the best configuration overall in bold, blue.

First, let us study the results for sequential combinations using algorithm $\mathcal{P}2\mathcal{V}$ (columns 2–14). $\mathcal{P}2\mathcal{V}$ configurations that compute finer (larger) initial precisions $\Pi_{\mathcal{V}}^0$, i.e., enable more of $\mathcal{P}2\mathcal{V}$'s configuration options, e.g., allEdges or knownDefs, typically detect more alarms. The best configuration enables all options and computes the finest precision. We conclude that initially tracking more information is often better when detecting alarms because one avoids ruling out spurious counterexamples in costly CEGAR iterations. However, sometimes a fine, initial precision prevents the analysis from detecting a violation because it takes too long to explore another part of the state space. Hence, one can detect more alarms considering all $\mathcal{P}2\mathcal{V}$ configurations (column $\bigcup\mathcal{P}2\mathcal{V}$).

The best $\mathcal{P}2\mathcal{V}$ configuration for proof detection is no adapt, which computes the coarsest precision in $\mathcal{P}2\mathcal{V}$. In general, configurations that compute coarser initial precisions due to disabling allEdges or knownDefs often detect more proofs. However, deriving the maximal information from assume operations (c_{ineq} setting) seems to be better. We conclude that the value analysis must explore a small, but sufficient abstract state space to effectively prove program correctness. To this end, it may use a coarse precision or exclude infeasible paths, i.e., track variables of assume operations. Combining these alternatives may explain why the number of detectable proofs increases significantly in $\bigcup\mathcal{P}2\mathcal{V}$.

We do not know in advance whether a program violates its property. Thus, we require a configuration that detects alarms and proofs well. Looking at row total, we observe that it is mostly better to disable knownDefs, but enable allEdges. Also, c_{ineq} configurations are better than c_{eq} and c_{no}. Compromising on the initial precision level is typically better. Nevertheless, the best configuration is identical to the best configuration for alarm detection because enabling knownDefs makes a larger difference on alarm than on proof detection. Since the best alarm and proof detection technique differ severely, the detection capability increases significantly when choosing the best configuration per program (cf. column $\bigcup\mathcal{P}2\mathcal{V}$).

Comparing the best $\mathcal{P}2\mathcal{V}$ configuration with no reuse, all vars, and CMC, we observe that all vars detects slightly more alarms, while no reuse and

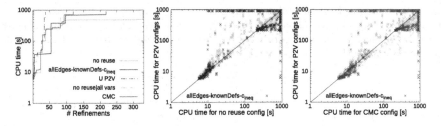

Fig. 3. Comparing maximal refinements per CPU time (left) and the CPU time of the $\mathcal{P}2\mathcal{V}$ configurations with **no reuse** (middle) and CMC (right)

CMC solve slightly more proofs and programs. However, when combining all $\mathcal{P}2\mathcal{V}$ configurations, $\mathcal{P}2\mathcal{V}$ outperforms its individual competitors and is slightly better than $\bigcup \Pi_{\mathcal{V}}^{0\leftrightarrows}$. While the $\mathcal{P}2\mathcal{V}$ configurations jointly solve 21 programs that neither **no reuse** nor **all vars** solve and 155 programs that CMC does not solve, CMC solves 22 programs that no $\mathcal{P}2\mathcal{V}$ configuration solves and **no reuse** plus **all vars** solve 16 programs not solvable by any $\mathcal{P}2\mathcal{V}$ configuration.

Now, let us study the verification effort. We start with the number of refinements. The quantile plot in Fig. 3 shows the maximal number of refinements x the value analysis uses when the respective sequential combination solves a program correctly in at most y seconds of CPU time. For programs that can be verified quickly, the best individual $\mathcal{P}2\mathcal{V}$ configuration (solid blue) requires fewer refinements than **no reuse** (orange) and CMC (violet) and after about 250 s it again requires fewer refinements than **no reuse**. Moreover, configuration $\bigcup \mathcal{P}2\mathcal{V}$ usually requires fewer refinements than its competitors. Also, when comparing the CPU times[9] of combinations using one of the single $\mathcal{P}2\mathcal{V}$ configurations (y-axis) with combinations using **no reuse** (left scatter plot in Fig. 3) and CMC (right scatter plot in Fig. 3), we observe that several points are in the lower right half, i.e., our approach is faster. A detailed comparison of the best $\mathcal{P}2\mathcal{V}$ configuration with **no reuse** and CMC (points in dark blue and violet) on the 421 (412) programs solved by our approach and **no reuse** (CMC) shows that our approach is faster than **no reuse** in 62% (263 of 421 programs) and faster than CMC in 82% (339 of 412 programs). The median and average speedups of **no adapt** are 1.01 and 1.14 for **no reuse** and 1.07 and 1.22 for CMC. However, when comparing $\bigcup \mathcal{P}2\mathcal{V}$ and $\bigcup \Pi_{\mathcal{V}}^{0\leftrightarrows}$ on the commonly solved tasks, $\bigcup \mathcal{P}2\mathcal{V}$ is only faster in 36% (239 of 660 programs) and its median and average speedups are 0.99 and 1.11.

Discussion of Result Validation. The predicate analysis disproved 1 034 and proved 2 061 programs. To study the effect of reusing the predicate precision, we select the 782 disproved programs (alarms) and 1 712 proved programs (proofs) for which the predicate analysis produced a precision[10] and that are non-trivial for the value analysis, i.e., the value analysis needs refinements.

---

[9] We use a CPU time limit of 900 s for all unsolved programs.

[10] We checked that the predicate analysis refined at least once and that $\Pi_{\mathcal{V}}^{0} \neq \emptyset$ if the value analysis with configuration **no adapt** $((\bot, \bot, \bot, \bot, \bot))$ reports a result.

Table 2. Number of relevant alarms and proofs generated by the predicate analysis and confirmed by witness validation (wv) with value analysis and by the value analysis using one of the 15 $\Pi_\mathcal{V}^0$ configurations, the optimal $\mathcal{P}2\mathcal{V}$ configuration ($\bigcup \mathcal{P}2\mathcal{V}$), or the optimal choice ($\bigcup \Pi_\mathcal{V}^{0\leftrightharpoons}$) from no reuse and all vars

confirmed	no reuse	no adapt	allEdges						¬ allEdges						all vars	$\bigcup \mathcal{P}2\mathcal{V}$	$\bigcup \Pi_\mathcal{V}^{0\leftrightharpoons}$	wv
			¬ knownDefs			knownDefs			¬ knownDefs			knownDefs						
			c_{no}	c_{eq}	c_{ineq}	c_{no}	c_{eq}	c_{ineq}	c_{no}	c_{eq}	c_{ineq}	c_{no}	c_{eq}	c_{ineq}				
alarms	306	309	299	399	460	306	445	468	306	356	359	302	349	350	474	476	476	**758**
proofs	1257	*1266*	1256	1253	1210	1253	1243	1200	1255	1258	1218	1254	1259	1217	1149	1314	**1321**	1138

Table 2 shows how many of the selected alarms and proofs witness validation (wv) and each of the 15 $\Pi_\mathcal{V}^0$ configurations of the value analysis confirm (i.e., find the alarm or proof). Similar to Table 1, columns $\bigcup \mathcal{P}2\mathcal{V}$ and $\bigcup \Pi_\mathcal{V}^{0\leftrightharpoons}$ aggregate columns 2–14 ($\mathcal{P}2\mathcal{V}$ configurations) and columns 1 and 15. Also, we use the same highlighting. Note that witness validation rejects 23 alarms and 318 proofs and does not report a result for the remaining programs. All other configurations either confirm the proof or alarm or do not report a result.

Since one knows whether one validates an alarm or proof, we study alarms and proofs separately. Looking at the confirmed alarms (first row), we notice that our approach confirms the largest number of alarms with the $\mathcal{P}2\mathcal{V}$ configuration that computes the largest set $\Pi_\mathcal{V}^0$ (i.e., all options set to true) and that configurations computing finer precisions, i.e., add more variables to $\Pi_\mathcal{V}^0$ e.g., enabling allEdges or knownDefs, confirm more alarms. For alarms, it is often better to track more variables and to avoid spending costs on CEGAR iterations. Hence, tracking all variables from the beginning (configuration all vars) is even better, but the difference fades away when selecting the optimal configuration per task (columns $\bigcup \mathcal{P}2\mathcal{V}$ and $\bigcup \Pi_\mathcal{V}^{0\leftrightharpoons}$). Nevertheless, it is best to perform witness validation that tracks all variables from the beginning and only explores a restricted state space. Inspecting the results in detail, we observe that configurations all vars, $\bigcup \Pi_\mathcal{V}^{0\leftrightharpoons}$, and witness validation confirm all except for two alarms that are confirmed by the best $\mathcal{P}2\mathcal{V}$ configuration. In addition, witness validation is always faster and all vars is faster for 82% (381 of 466) of the commonly confirmed alarms. Comparing $\bigcup \mathcal{P}2\mathcal{V}$ with $\bigcup \Pi_\mathcal{V}^{0\leftrightharpoons}$ looks similar.

In contrast, $\mathcal{P}2\mathcal{V}$ configurations that are coarser, e.g., disable allEdges or knownDefs, often validate proofs more effectively and configuration no adapt, in which $\mathcal{P}2\mathcal{V}$ computes the smallest set $\Pi_\mathcal{V}^0$, confirms the largest number of proofs of all studied validation approaches. However, combining different configurations increases the number of validated proofs by about 4 %. In total, the value analysis can validate 1 321 proofs when combining all 15 $\Pi_\mathcal{V}^0$ configurations.

Studying the validation effort for proofs, we will see that configuration no adapt often outperforms the two best competitors no reuse and witness validation. First, let us look at the number of refinements. The quantile plot in Fig. 4 shows the maximal number of refinements x an analysis requires to confirm a proof in at most y seconds of CPU time. We note that $\mathcal{P}2\mathcal{V}$ configuration no adapt ($\bigcup \mathcal{P}2\mathcal{V}$)

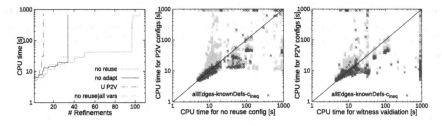

Fig. 4. For proof validation, comparing maximal refinements per CPU time (left) as well as the CPU time of $\mathcal{P}2\mathcal{V}$ configurations (value analysis plus Algorithm 1) with **no reuse** (middle) and witness validation (right)

requires fewer refinements than **no-reuse** ($\bigcup \Pi_{\mathcal{V}}^{0\leftrightarrows}$), while witness validation uses $\Pi_{\mathcal{V}}^0 = Var$, i.e., it cannot refine. Next, we compare the validation times. The left scatter plot in Fig. 4 compares the CPU times of the $\mathcal{P}2\mathcal{V}$ configurations (value analysis plus Algorithm 1) with the CPU times of configuration **no reuse**, while the right scatter plot compares them with witness validation. We use 900 s (maximal time limit) for all rejected and unconfirmed programs and highlight configuration **no adapt** in a darker color. We observe that several points are in the lower right half, i.e., configuration **no adapt** is faster. A detailed analysis of our results reveals that **no adapt** fails to confirm 24 proofs confirmed by **no reuse** and 49 confirmed by witness validation, but confirms 33 proofs that the configuration **no reuse** cannot confirm and 177 proofs that witness validation fails to confirm. Looking at the 1 089 proofs confirmed by **no adapt** and witness validation, we notice that configuration **no adapt** is faster for 59% of those proofs (639 of 1 089 proofs). Its median speedup is 1.04 and the average speedup is 1.42. Also, the **no adapt** configuration confirms 75% of the proofs (928 of 1 233 proofs) also confirmed by **no reuse** faster. The median speedup is 1.05 and the average speedup is 1.24. We conclude that **no adapt** profits from avoiding some CEGAR iterations, while its coarse initial abstraction still allows the value analysis to efficiently compute a sufficient abstraction.

Discussion of Regression Verification. Finally, we study the effect of reusing the predicate precision in regression verification. To this end, we choose those 2 715 programs that are non-trivial for the value analysis (i.e., require at least one refinement) and that have a previous version for which the predicate analysis produced a precision[11]. No chosen program violates its property and the previous versions typically differ in several hundred lines.

Table 3 shows how many of the chosen programs are correctly reverified by the value analysis using one of the 15 $\Pi_{\mathcal{V}}^0$ configurations or by the predicate analysis with precision reuse (column **reuse pred.**). Additionally, columns $\bigcup \mathcal{P}2\mathcal{V}$ and $\bigcup \Pi_{\mathcal{V}}^{0\leftrightarrows}$ show the number of programs correctly reverified by at least one of the

---

[11] We checked that the predicate analysis refined at least once and that $\Pi_{\mathcal{V}}^0 \neq \emptyset$ if the value analysis with configuration **no adapt** $((\bot, \bot, \bot, \bot, \bot))$ reports a result.

Table 3. Number of relevant, modified programs correctly reverified by the predicate analysis with precision reuse (**reuse pred.**) and by the value analysis when using one of the 15 $\Pi_\mathcal{V}^0$ configurations, the optimal $\mathcal{P}2\mathcal{V}$ configuration ($\bigcup \mathcal{P}2\mathcal{V}$), or the optimal choice ($\bigcup \Pi_\mathcal{V}^{0\leftrightarrows}$) from **no reuse** and **all vars**

			allEdges						¬ allEdges									
			¬ knownDefs			knownDefs			¬ knownDefs			knownDefs			all	$\bigcup$	$\bigcup$	reuse
correct	no reuse	no adapt	c_{no}	c_{eq}	c_{ineq}	c_{no}	c_{eq}	c_{ineq}	c_{no}	c_{eq}	c_{ineq}	c_{no}	c_{eq}	c_{ineq}	vars	$\mathcal{P}2\mathcal{V}$	$\Pi_\mathcal{V}^{0\leftrightarrows}$	pred.
proofs	*2708*	*2708*	1906	1733	1727	1906	1685	1682	1906	1906	1906	1906	1906	1907	2000	**2708**	**2708**	2401

Fig. 5. Comparing maximal refinements per CPU time (left) as well as the CPU time of $\mathcal{P}2\mathcal{V}$ configurations with **no reuse** (middle) and **reuse pred.** (right)

configurations in columns 2–14 ($\mathcal{P}2\mathcal{V}$ configurations) and by columns 1 and 15. For all other programs, no result is reported due to timeout, etc. As before, we mark the best configuration of $\mathcal{P}2\mathcal{V}$ in light gray, the best configuration of the initial precision $\Pi_\mathcal{V}^0$ in italics, and the best configuration overall in bold, blue.

Looking at Table 3, we once again notice that $\mathcal{P}2\mathcal{V}$ configurations that compute coarser precisions, i.e., disable some of the configuration options, typically prove correctness of more programs and, thus, perform better. Furthermore, once more configuration **no adapt** is the best configuration for $\mathcal{P}2\mathcal{V}$. In addition, we observe that **no adapt** solves more programs than **all vars** and **reuse pred.** and as many programs as **no reuse**. A detailed comparison reveals that **no adapt** and **no reuse** solve all programs that any other configuration solves.

Next, we compare the verification effort. First, let us consider the number of refinements. The quantile plot in Fig. 5 shows the maximal number of refinements x an analysis requires to correctly reverify a program in at most y seconds of CPU time. We observe that we require fewer refinements for configuration **no adapt** (blue) than for **no reuse** (orange), but only the predicate analysis with precision reuse (**reuse pred.**) never requires any refinements. Now, let us look at the verification times. We use 900 s (maximal time limit) for all unsolved programs. The left scatter plot in Fig. 5 compares the CPU times of all $\mathcal{P}2\mathcal{V}$ configurations with the CPU times of configuration **no reuse**, while the right scatter plot compares them with configuration **reuse pred.**. In both plots, our approach is faster for points in the lower right half and we highlight configuration **no adapt** in a darker color. Although some configurations of $\mathcal{P}2\mathcal{V}$ may perform worse than **reuse pred.**, the best configuration **no adapt** is mostly faster—it is only slower for two solved programs—and shows a median and average speedup of 1.39 and 4.39. One reason is that the value analysis is faster for the programs considered in the regression verification. Changing the analysis pays off. In addition, **no adapt** is slightly faster for 86% of the solved programs (2 331 of 2 708 programs) than **no reuse** (the default value analysis). The median and average speedup of **no adapt** over **no reuse** are 1.06 and 1.07. Saving refinements and never becoming more precise than **no reuse** pays off.

Threats to Validity. In cooperative verification, we generate the predicate precision in the sequential combination. Different $P2V$ configurations may use different precisions for the same program, which may invalidate our results for cooperative verification. We think getting different precisions is unlikely because the predicate analysis we use aims to be deterministic. Also, our results may not be valid for other applications or programs. We believe that a comparison with a competitor highly depends on the competitor. We already observe a difference between the applications when comparing against **no reuse**. In addition, we use a diverse benchmark for studying cooperative verification and result validation, but evaluate regression evaluation on correct Linux driver programs. Therefore, we expect that the results on cooperative verification and result validation more likely carry over to other programs and that the results for regression verification may not be valid on a different set of programs. Nevertheless, the insights on the configuration of $P2V$ (Algorithm 1) and the comparison against **all vars** are similar for all three applications and likely apply to other applications and programs. Finally, we require that the predicate analysis computes a non-empty predicate precision (otherwise our approach becomes identical to **no reuse**). Our results only apply to programs with loops that influence the program's property, i.e., programs for which the predicate analysis needs non-trivial abstractions.

5   Related Work

Originally, precisions are reused by the same analysis in context of regression verification [31]. We reuse the predicate precision in the value analysis for cooperative verification, result validation, and regression verification. In the following, we briefly discuss the related work in all three fields.

Cooperative Verification. Several verification tools apply different analyses using no cooperation [1,2,38,49,54,64,65,76] or select a suitable analysis from a set of analyses [2,14,50,83,96]. Further approaches split the verification effort among different analyses [20,23,26,29,40,41,46,47,52,54,89–91]. Also, several approaches testify alarms [1,38,39,45,48,49,53,72,82] to reduce the number of reported false alarms. To make verification more effective, analyses exchange information in sequential [5,22,66], alternating [3,11,24,55,57,60, 73,77,92,100], or parallel [18,21,44,58] combinations. Our approach exchanges the predicate precision in a sequential combination. Closest to our approach is CoVeriTest [24], which may exchange the predicate precision between predicate and value analysis during test generation, but only supports extraction (i.e., config.adapt $= \bot$).

Validating Verification Results. Witnesses [15,16] describe counterexamples or proofs in a standard format and allow validators [15–17,19,35,93] to perform a verifier-independent check of a verifier's result. Several cooperative verification approaches [1,38,39,45,48,49,53,72,82] testify counterexamples. In contrast, proof-carrying code (PCC) [75] aims at validating that a verifier proved a property. To this end, PCC generates and checks certificates, which contain some kind of proof. Many PCC approaches for abstraction-based analyses use a subset of the abstract states [4,6,12,67,70,84] as certificate. Other approaches [37,61,87] convert the abstract state space into a logic proof of program correctness. We use the abstraction degree (precision) computed by the predicate analysis to validate its proofs and alarms with a value analysis.

Regression Verification. Techniques that reverify a program after change range from functional equivalence checking [10,36,51,56,68,78–80,95] over updating the representation of the state space [9,62,71,86,88,94], or omitting the verification of unchanged program parts [25,81,98,99] to reusing (intermediate) results [7,8,59,74,97,101]. In our approach, we reuse the abstraction degree (precision). In contrast to existing techniques [31,85] that reuse the abstraction degree for regression verification, we exchange the abstraction degree between different analyses, i.e., the value analysis reuses the precision of the predicate analysis.

6   Conclusion

Software becomes more and more important in our daily routines while we require reliable software to experience smooth routines. Software verification allows us to analyze the reliability of software, but often needs to exchange information between different analyses to successfully inspect a software and its revisions.

In this paper, we focus on the exchange of precisions, which describe an analysis' degree of abstraction. Previously, analyses reused their own precisions in regression verification [31] and a value analysis may use the precision of a previous predicate analysis in cooperative test-case generation [24]. We extend the reuse of predicate precisions within a value analysis to three other applications: a sequential composition of predicate and value analysis, validating the results of a predicate analysis with a value analysis, and applying a value analysis to reverify a modified program whose prior version has been verified with a predicate analysis. To this end, we extend the transformation suggested by Beyer and Jakobs [24] with 12 additional options to convert a predicate precision into a precision for the value analysis. All options compute precisions with various degrees of abstraction. In addition, our new options consider the data- and control-flow of the analyzed program to also adapt the precision to the program.

In our extensive evaluation on thousands of programs, we compare our different options against each other, against using the coarsest and finest precision, as well as against a state-of-the-art approach. Our results show that configurations computing finer, more detailed precisions detect more alarms, while configurations computing coarser precisions typically detect more proofs. Nevertheless, only in one of the three applications we detect less proofs when using our coarsest reuse options instead of the coarsest precision. Moreover, on correct programs we outperform the competitors (using the coarsest precision, the finest precision, or a state-of-the-art approach) in two of three applications. In scenarios in which none of our reuse options outperforms all competitors, our approach correctly analyzes some programs that better approaches cannot solve and it analyzes many programs more efficiently, i.e., using fewer refinements or slightly less CPU time. Hence, reusing predicate precisions in value analysis is beneficial.

Data Availability Statement. All experimental data is made publicly available in a replication package [69].

References

1. Ádám, Z., Sallai, G., Hajdu, Á.: GAZER-THETA: LLVM-based verifier portfolio with BMC/CEGAR (Competition Contribution). In: Groote, J.F., Larsen, K.G. (eds.) TACAS 2021. LNCS, vol. 12652, pp. 433–437. Springer, Cham (2021). https://doi.org/10.1007/978-3-030-72013-1_27

2. Afzal, M., et al.: VeriAbs: Verification by abstraction and test generation. In: ASE, pp. 1138–1141. IEEE (2019). https://doi.org/10.1109/ASE.2019.00121

3. Albarghouthi, A., Gurfinkel, A., Chechik, M.: From under-approximations to over-approximations and back. In: Flanagan, C., König, B. (eds.) TACAS 2012. LNCS, vol. 7214, pp. 157–172. Springer, Heidelberg (2012). https://doi.org/10.1007/978-3-642-28756-5_12

4. Albert, E., Puebla, G., Hermenegildo, M.: Abstraction-carrying code. In: Baader, F., Voronkov, A. (eds.) LPAR 2005. LNCS (LNAI), vol. 3452, pp. 380–397. Springer, Heidelberg (2005). https://doi.org/10.1007/978-3-540-32275-7_25

5. Alhawi, O.M., Rocha, H., Gadelha, M.R., Cordeiro, L.C., de Lima Filho, E.B.: Verification and refutation of C programs based on k-induction and invariant inference. STTT **23**(2), 115–135 (2021). https://doi.org/10.1007/s10009-020-00564-1

6. Amme, W., Möller, M., Adler, P.: Data flow analysis as a general concept for the transport of verifiable program annotations. Electron. Notes Theor. Comput. Sci. **176**(3), 97–108 (2007). https://doi.org/10.1016/j.entcs.2006.06.019

7. Aquino, A., Bianchi, F.A., Chen, M., Denaro, G., Pezzè, M.: Reusing constraint proofs in program analysis. In: ISSTA, pp. 305–315. ACM (2015). https://doi.org/10.1145/2771783.2771802

8. Aquino, A., Denaro, G., Pezzè, M.: Heuristically matching solution spaces of arithmetic formulas to efficiently reuse solutions. In: ICSE, pp. 427–437. IEEE (2017). https://doi.org/10.1109/ICSE.2017.46

9. Arzt, S., Bodden, E.: Reviser: Efficiently updating IDE-/IFDS-based data-flow analyses in response to incremental program changes. In: ICSE, pp. 288–298. ACM (2014). https://doi.org/10.1145/2568225.2568243

10. Barthe, G., Crespo, J.M., Kunz, C.: Relational verification using product programs. In: Butler, M., Schulte, W. (eds.) FM 2011. LNCS, vol. 6664, pp. 200–214. Springer, Heidelberg (2011). https://doi.org/10.1007/978-3-642-21437-0_17

11. Beckman, N.E., Nori, A.V., Rajamani, S.K., Simmons, R.J.: Proofs from tests. In: ISSTA, pp. 3–14. ACM (2008). https://doi.org/10.1145/1390630.1390634

12. Besson, F., Jensen, T.P., Pichardie, D.: Proof-carrying code from certified abstract interpretation and fixpoint compression. Theor. Comput. Sci. **364**(3), 273–291 (2006). https://doi.org/10.1016/j.tcs.2006.08.012

13. Beyer, D.: Software verification: 10th comparative evaluation (SV-COMP 2021). In: Groote, J.F., Larsen, K.G. (eds.) TACAS 2021. LNCS, vol. 12652, pp. 401–422. Springer, Cham (2021). https://doi.org/10.1007/978-3-030-72013-1_24

14. Beyer, D., Dangl, M.: Strategy selection for software verification based on boolean features. In: Margaria, T., Steffen, B. (eds.) ISoLA 2018. LNCS, vol. 11245, pp. 144–159. Springer, Cham (2018). https://doi.org/10.1007/978-3-030-03421-4_11

15. Beyer, D., Dangl, M., Dietsch, D., Heizmann, M.: Correctness witnesses: exchanging verification results between verifiers. In: FSE, pp. 326–337. ACM (2016). https://doi.org/10.1145/2950290.2950351

16. Beyer, D., Dangl, M., Dietsch, D., Heizmann, M., Stahlbauer, A.: Witness validation and stepwise testification across software verifiers. In: FSE, pp. 721–733. ACM (2015). https://doi.org/10.1145/2786805.2786867

17. Beyer, D., Dangl, M., Lemberger, T., Tautschnig, M.: Tests from witnesses. In: Dubois, C., Wolff, B. (eds.) TAP 2018. LNCS, vol. 10889, pp. 3–23. Springer, Cham (2018). https://doi.org/10.1007/978-3-319-92994-1_1

18. Beyer, D., Dangl, M., Wendler, P.: Boosting k-induction with continuously-refined invariants. In: Kroening, D., Păsăreanu, C.S. (eds.) CAV 2015. LNCS, vol. 9206, pp. 622–640. Springer, Cham (2015). https://doi.org/10.1007/978-3-319-21690-4_42

19. Beyer, D., Friedberger, K.: Violation witnesses and result validation for multi-threaded programs. In: Margaria, T., Steffen, B. (eds.) ISoLA 2020. LNCS, vol. 12476, pp. 449–470. Springer, Cham (2020). https://doi.org/10.1007/978-3-030-61362-4_26

20. Beyer, D., Henzinger, T.A., Keremoglu, M.E., Wendler, P.: Conditional model checking: A technique to pass information between verifiers. In: FSE, pp. 57:1–57:11. ACM (2012). https://doi.org/10.1145/2393596.2393664

21. Beyer, D., Henzinger, T.A., Théoduloz, G.: Program analysis with dynamic precision adjustment. In: ASE, pp. 29–38. IEEE (2008). https://doi.org/10.1109/ASE.2008.13

22. Beyer, D., Holzer, A., Tautschnig, M., Veith, H.: Information reuse for multi-goal reachability analyses. In: Felleisen, M., Gardner, P. (eds.) ESOP 2013. LNCS, vol. 7792, pp. 472–491. Springer, Heidelberg (2013). https://doi.org/10.1007/978-3-642-37036-6_26

23. Beyer, D., Jakobs, M.-C.: FRED: Conditional model checking via reducers and folders. In: de Boer, F., Cerone, A. (eds.) SEFM 2020. LNCS, vol. 12310, pp. 113–132. Springer, Cham (2020). https://doi.org/10.1007/978-3-030-58768-0_7

24. Beyer, D., Jakobs, M.: Cooperative verifier-based testing with CoVeriTest. STTT **23**(3), 313–333 (2021). https://doi.org/10.1007/s10009-020-00587-8

25. Beyer, D., Jakobs, M.-C., Lemberger, T.: Difference verification with conditions. In: de Boer, F., Cerone, A. (eds.) SEFM 2020. LNCS, vol. 12310, pp. 133–154. Springer, Cham (2020). https://doi.org/10.1007/978-3-030-58768-0_8

26. Beyer, D., Jakobs, M., Lemberger, T., Wehrheim, H.: Reducer-based construction of conditional verifiers. In: ICSE, pp. 1182–1193. ACM (2018). https://doi.org/10.1145/3180155.3180259

27. Beyer, D., Keremoglu, M.E.: CPAChecker: A tool for configurable software verification. In: Gopalakrishnan, G., Qadeer, S. (eds.) CAV 2011. LNCS, vol. 6806, pp. 184–190. Springer, Heidelberg (2011). https://doi.org/10.1007/978-3-642-22110-1_16

28. Beyer, D., Keremoglu, M.E., Wendler, P.: Predicate abstraction with adjustable-block encoding. In: FMCAD, pp. 189–197. IEEE (2010). https://ieeexplore.ieee.org/document/5770949/

29. Beyer, D., Lemberger, T.: Conditional testing. In: Chen, Y.-F., Cheng, C.-H., Esparza, J. (eds.) ATVA 2019. LNCS, vol. 11781, pp. 189–208. Springer, Cham (2019). https://doi.org/10.1007/978-3-030-31784-3_11

30. Beyer, D., Löwe, S.: Explicit-state software model checking based on CEGAR and interpolation. In: Cortellessa, V., Varró, D. (eds.) FASE 2013. LNCS, vol. 7793, pp. 146–162. Springer, Heidelberg (2013). https://doi.org/10.1007/978-3-642-37057-1_11

31. Beyer, D., Löwe, S., Novikov, E., Stahlbauer, A., Wendler, P.: Precision reuse for efficient regression verification. In: FSE, pp. 389–399. ACM (2013). https://doi.org/10.1145/2491411.2491429

32. Beyer, D., Stefan, W.P.: Refinement selection. In: Fischer, B., Geldenhuys, J. (eds.) SPIN 2015. LNCS, vol. 9232, pp. 20–38. Springer, Cham (2015). https://doi.org/10.1007/978-3-319-23404-5_3

33. Beyer, D., Löwe, S., Wendler, P.: Sliced path prefixes: An effective method to enable refinement selection. In: Graf, S., Viswanathan, M. (eds.) FORTE 2015. LNCS, vol. 9039, pp. 228–243. Springer, Cham (2015). https://doi.org/10.1007/978-3-319-19195-9_15

34. Beyer, D., Löwe, S., Wendler, P.: Reliable benchmarking: Requirements and solutions. STTT **21**(1), 1–29 (2019). https://doi.org/10.1007/s10009-017-0469-y

35. Beyer, D., Spiessl, M.: MetaVal: Witness validation via verification. In: Lahiri, S.K., Wang, C. (eds.) CAV 2020. LNCS, vol. 12225, pp. 165–177. Springer, Cham (2020). https://doi.org/10.1007/978-3-030-53291-8_10

36. Böhme, M.D.S., Oliveira, B.C., Roychoudhury, A.: Partition-based regression verification. In: ICSE, pp. 302–311. IEEE (2013). https://doi.org/10.1109/ICSE.2013.6606576

37. Chaieb, A.: Proof-producing program analysis. In: Barkaoui, K., Cavalcanti, A., Cerone, A. (eds.) ICTAC 2006. LNCS, vol. 4281, pp. 287–301. Springer, Heidelberg (2006). https://doi.org/10.1007/11921240_20

38. Chalupa, M., Jašek, T., Novák, J., Řechtáčková, A., Šoková, V., Strejček, J.: Symbiotic 8: Beyond symbolic execution. In: Groote, J.F., Larsen, K.G. (eds.) TACAS 2021. LNCS, vol. 12652, pp. 453–457. Springer, Cham (2021). https://doi.org/10.1007/978-3-030-72013-1_31

39. Chebaro, O., Kosmatov, N., Giorgetti, A., Julliand, J.: Program slicing enhances a verification technique combining static and dynamic analysis. In: SAC, pp. 1284–1291. ACM (2012). https://doi.org/10.1145/2245276.2231980

40. Christakis, M., Müller, P., Wüstholz, V.: Collaborative verification and testing with explicit assumptions. In: Giannakopoulou, D., Méry, D. (eds.) FM 2012. LNCS, vol. 7436, pp. 132–146. Springer, Heidelberg (2012). https://doi.org/10.1007/978-3-642-32759-9_13

41. Christakis, M., Müller, P., Wüstholz, V.: Guiding dynamic symbolic execution toward unverified program executions. In: ICSE, pp. 144–155. ACM (2016). https://doi.org/10.1145/2884781.2884843

42. Clarke, E.M., Grumberg, O., Jha, S., Lu, Y., Veith, H.: Counterexample-guided abstraction refinement for symbolic model checking. J. ACM **50**(5), 752–794 (2003). http://doi.acm.org/10.1145/876638.876643

43. Cousot, P., Cousot, R.: Abstract interpretation: A unified lattice model for static analysis of programs by construction or approximation of fixpoints. In: POPL, pp. 238–252. ACM (1977). https://doi.org/10.1145/512950.512973

44. Cousot, P., et al.: Combination of abstractions in the ASTRÉE static analyzer. In: Okada, M., Satoh, I. (eds.) ASIAN 2006. LNCS, vol. 4435, pp. 272–300. Springer, Heidelberg (2007). https://doi.org/10.1007/978-3-540-77505-8_23
45. Csallner, C., Smaragdakis, Y.: Check 'n' crash: Combining static checking and testing. In: ICSE, pp. 422–431. ACM (2005). https://doi.org/10.1145/1062455.1062533
46. Czech, M., Jakobs, M.-C., Wehrheim, H.: Just test what you cannot verify! In: Egyed, A., Schaefer, I. (eds.) FASE 2015. LNCS, vol. 9033, pp. 100–114. Springer, Heidelberg (2015). https://doi.org/10.1007/978-3-662-46675-9_7
47. Daca, P., Gupta, A., Henzinger, T.A.: Abstraction-driven concolic testing. In: Jobstmann, B., Leino, K., Rustan, M.: (eds.) VMCAI 2016. LNCS, vol. 9583, pp. 328–347. Springer, Heidelberg (2016). https://doi.org/10.1007/978-3-662-49122-5_16
48. Dams, D.R., Namjoshi, K.S.: Orion: High-precision methods for static error analysis of C and C++ Programs. In: de Boer, F.S., Bonsangue, M.M., Graf, S., de Roever, W.-P. (eds.) FMCO 2005. LNCS, vol. 4111, pp. 138–160. Springer, Heidelberg (2006). https://doi.org/10.1007/11804192_7
49. Dangl, M., Löwe, S., Wendler, P.: CPACHECKER with support for recursive programs and floating-point arithmetic. In: Baier, C., Tinelli, C. (eds.) TACAS 2015. LNCS, vol. 9035, pp. 423–425. Springer, Heidelberg (2015). https://doi.org/10.1007/978-3-662-46681-0_34
50. Demyanova, Y., Pani, T., Veith, H., Zuleger, F.: Empirical software metrics for benchmarking of verification tools. In: Kroening, D., Păsăreanu, C.S. (eds.) CAV 2015. LNCS, vol. 9206, pp. 561–579. Springer, Cham (2015). https://doi.org/10.1007/978-3-319-21690-4_39
51. Felsing, D., Grebing, S., Klebanov, V., Rümmer, P., Ulbrich, M.: Automating regression verification. In: ASE, pp. 349–360. ACM (2014). https://doi.org/10.1145/2642937.2642987
52. Ferles, K., Wüstholz, V., Christakis, M., Dillig, I.: Failure-directed program trimming. In: FSE, pp. 174–185. ACM (2017). https://doi.org/10.1145/3106237.3106249
53. Ge, X., Taneja, K., Xie, T., Tillmann, N.: Dyta: Dynamic symbolic execution guided with static verification results. In: ICSE, pp. 992–994. ACM (2011). https://doi.org/10.1145/1985793.1985971
54. Gerrard, M.J., Dwyer, M.B.: ALPACA: A large portfolio-based alternating conditional analysis. In: ICSE, pp. 35–38. IEEE/ACM (2019). https://doi.org/10.1109/ICSE-Companion.2019.00032
55. Godefroid, P., Nori, A.V., Rajamani, S.K., Tetali, S.: Compositional may-must program analysis: Unleashing the power of alternation. In: POPL, pp. 43–56. ACM (2010). https://doi.org/10.1145/1706299.1706307
56. Godlin, B., Strichman, O.: Regression verification. In: DAC, pp. 466–471. ACM (2009). https://doi.org/10.1145/1629911.1630034
57. Gulavani, B.S., Henzinger, T.A., Kannan, Y., Nori, A.V., Rajamani, S.K.: SYNERGY: A new algorithm for property checking. In: FSE, pp. 117–127. ACM (2006). https://doi.org/10.1145/1181775.1181790
58. Haltermann, J., Wehrheim, H.: CoVEGI: Cooperative verification via externally generated invariants. In: Guerra, E., Stoelinga, M. (eds.) FASE 2021. LNCS, vol. 12649, pp. 108–129. Springer, Cham (2021). https://doi.org/10.1007/978-3-030-71500-7_6
59. He, F., Yu, Q., Cai, L.: Efficient summary reuse for software regression verification. TSE (2020). https://doi.org/10.1109/TSE.2020.3021477

60. Helm, D., Kübler, F., Reif, M., Eichberg, M., Mezini, M.: Modular collaborative program analysis in OPAL. In: FSE, pp. 184–196. ACM (2020), https://doi.org/10.1145/3368089.3409765
61. Henzinger, T.A., Necula, G.C., Jhala, R., Sutre, G., Majumdar, R., Weimer, W.: Temporal-safety proofs for systems code. In: Brinksma, E., Larsen, K.G. (eds.) CAV 2002. LNCS, vol. 2404, pp. 526–538. Springer, Heidelberg (2002). https://doi.org/10.1007/3-540-45657-0_45
62. Henzinger, T.A., Jhala, R., Majumdar, R., Sanvido, M.A.A.: Extreme model checking. In: Dershowitz, N. (ed.) Verification: Theory and Practice. LNCS, vol. 2772, pp. 332–358. Springer, Heidelberg (2003). https://doi.org/10.1007/978-3-540-39910-0_16
63. Henzinger, T.A., Jhala, R., Majumdar, R., Sutre, G.: Lazy abstraction. In: POPL, pp. 58–70. ACM (2002). https://doi.org/10.1145/503272.503279
64. Holík, L., Kotoun, M., Peringer, P., Soková, V., Trtík, M., Vojnar, T.: Predator shape analysis tool suite. In: HVC, pp. 202–209. LNCS 10028 (2016). https://doi.org/10.1007/978-3-319-49052-6_13
65. Holzmann, G.J., Joshi, R., Groce, A.: Swarm verification. In: ASE, pp. 1–6. IEEE (2008). https://doi.org/10.1109/ASE.2008.9
66. Inkumsah, K., Xie, T.: Improving structural testing of object-oriented programs via integrating evolutionary testing and symbolic execution. In: ASE, pp. 297–306. IEEE (2008). https://doi.org/10.1109/ASE.2008.40
67. Jakobs, M.-C.: Speed up configurable certificate validation by certificate reduction and partitioning. In: Calinescu, R., Rumpe, B. (eds.) SEFM 2015. LNCS, vol. 9276, pp. 159–174. Springer, Cham (2015). https://doi.org/10.1007/978-3-319-22969-0_12
68. Jakobs, M.: PEQcheck: Localized and context-aware checking of functional equivalence. In: FormaliSE, pp. 130–140. IEEE (2021). https://doi.ieeecomputersociety.org/10.1109/FormaliSE52586.2021.00019
69. Jakobs, M.: Replication package for article 'Reusing Predicate Precision in Value Analysis' In: iFM 2022 (2022). https://doi.org/10.5281/zenodo.5645043
70. Jakobs, M., Wehrheim, H.: Certification for configurable program analysis. In: SPIN, pp. 30–39. ACM (2014). https://doi.org/10.1145/2632362.2632372
71. Lauterburg, S., Sobeih, A., Marinov, D., Viswanathan, M.: Incremental state-space exploration for programs with dynamically allocated data. In: ICSE, pp. 291–300. ACM (2008). https://doi.org/10.1145/1368088.1368128
72. Li, K., Reichenbach, C., Csallner, C., Smaragdakis, Y.: Residual investigation: Predictive and precise bug detection. In: ISSTA, pp. 298–308. ACM (2012)
73. Majumdar, R., Sen, K.: Hybrid concolic testing. In: ICSE, pp. 416–426. IEEE (2007). https://doi.org/10.1109/ICSE.2007.41
74. Mudduluru, R., Ramanathan, M.K.: Efficient incremental static analysis using path abstraction. In: Gnesi, S., Rensink, A. (eds.) FASE 2014. LNCS, vol. 8411, pp. 125–139. Springer, Heidelberg (2014). https://doi.org/10.1007/978-3-642-54804-8_9
75. Necula, G.C.: Proof-carrying code. In: POPL, pp. 106–119. ACM (1997). https://doi.org/10.1145/263699.263712
76. Nguyen, T.L., Schrammel, P., Fischer, B., Torre, S.L., Parlato, G.: Parallel bug-finding in concurrent programs via reduced interleaving instances. In: ASE, pp. 753–764. IEEE (2017). https://doi.org/10.1109/ASE.2017.8115686
77. Noller, Y., Kersten, R., Pasareanu, C.S.: Badger: Complexity analysis with fuzzing and symbolic execution. In: ISSTA, pp. 322–332. ACM (2018). https://doi.org/10.1145/3213846.3213868

78. Noller, Y., Pasareanu, C.S., Böhme, M., Sun, Y., Nguyen, H.L., Grunske, L.: Hy-Diff: Hybrid differential software analysis. In: ICSE, pp. 1273–1285. ACM (2020). https://doi.org/10.1145/3377811.3380363

79. Palikareva, H., Kuchta, T., Cadar, C.: Shadow of a doubt: Testing for divergences between software versions. In: ICSE, pp. 1181–1192. ACM (2016). https://doi.org/10.1145/2884781.2884845

80. Person, S., Dwyer, M.B., Elbaum, S.G., Pasareanu, C.S.: Differential symbolic execution. In: FSE, pp. 226–237. ACM (2008). https://doi.org/10.1145/1453101.1453131

81. Person, S., Yang, G., Rungta, N., Khurshid, S.: Directed incremental symbolic execution. In: PLDI, pp. 504–515. ACM (2011). https://doi.org/10.1145/1993498.1993558

82. Post, H., Sinz, C., Kaiser, A., Gorges, T.: Reducing false positives by combining abstract interpretation and bounded model checking. In: ASE, pp. 188–197. IEEE (2008). https://doi.org/10.1109/ASE.2008.29

83. Richter, C., Hüllermeier, E., Jakobs, M., Wehrheim, H.: Algorithm selection for software validation based on graph kernels. JASE **27**(1), 153–186 (2020). https://doi.org/10.1007/s10515-020-00270-x

84. Rose, E.: Lightweight bytecode verification. JAR **31**(3–4), 303–334 (2003). https://doi.org/10.1023/B:JARS.0000021015.15794.82

85. Rothenberg, B.-C., Dietsch, D., Heizmann, M.: Incremental verification using trace abstraction. In: Podelski, A. (ed.) SAS 2018. LNCS, vol. 11002, pp. 364–382. Springer, Cham (2018). https://doi.org/10.1007/978-3-319-99725-4_22

86. Seidl, H., Erhard, J., Vogler, R.: Incremental abstract interpretation. In: Di Pierro, A., Malacaria, P., Nagarajan, R. (eds.) From Lambda Calculus to Cybersecurity Through Program Analysis. LNCS, vol. 12065, pp. 132–148. Springer, Cham (2020). https://doi.org/10.1007/978-3-030-41103-9_5

87. Seo, S., Yang, H., Yi, K.: Automatic construction of Hoare proofs from abstract interpretation results. In: Ohori, A. (ed.) APLAS 2003. LNCS, vol. 2895, pp. 230–245. Springer, Heidelberg (2003). https://doi.org/10.1007/978-3-540-40018-9_16

88. Sery, O., Fedyukovich, G., Sharygina, N.: Incremental upgrade checking by means of interpolation-based function summaries. In: FMCAD. pp. 114–121. FMCAD Inc. (2012). http://ieeexplore.ieee.org/document/6462563/

89. Sherman, E., Dwyer, M.B.: Structurally defined conditional data-flow static analysis. In: Beyer, D., Huisman, M. (eds.) TACAS 2018. LNCS, vol. 10806, pp. 249–265. Springer, Cham (2018). https://doi.org/10.1007/978-3-319-89963-3_15

90. Siddiqui, J.H., Khurshid, S.: Scaling symbolic execution using ranged analysis. In: Leavens, G.T., Dwyer, M.B. (eds.) SPLASH, pp. 523–536. ACM (2012). https://doi.org/10.1145/2384616.2384654

91. Staats, M., Pasareanu, C.S.: Parallel symbolic execution for structural test generation. In: ISSTA, pp. 183–194. ACM (2010). https://doi.org/10.1145/1831708.1831732

92. Stephens, N., et al.: Driller: Augmenting fuzzing through selective symbolic execution. In: NDSS. The Internet Society (2016)

93. Švejda, J., Berger, P., Katoen, J.-P.: Interpretation-based violation witness validation for C: NITWIT. In: Biere, A., Parker, D. (eds.) TACAS 2020. LNCS, vol. 12078, pp. 40–57. Springer, Cham (2020). https://doi.org/10.1007/978-3-030-45190-5_3

94. Szabó, T., Erdweg, S., Voelter, M.: IncA: A DSL for the definition of incremental program analyses. In: ASE, pp. 320–331. ACM (2016). https://doi.org/10.1145/2970276.2970298

95. Trostanetski, A., Grumberg, O., Kroening, D.: Modular demand-driven analysis of semantic difference for program versions. In: Ranzato, F. (ed.) SAS 2017. LNCS, vol. 10422, pp. 405–427. Springer, Cham (2017). https://doi.org/10.1007/978-3-319-66706-5_20

96. Tulsian, V., Kanade, A., Kumar, R., Lal, A., Nori, A.V.: MUX: Algorithm selection for software model checkers. In: MSR, pp. 132–141. ACM (2014). https://doi.org/10.1145/2597073.2597080

97. Visser, W., Geldenhuys, J., Dwyer, M.B.: Green: Reducing, reusing, and recycling constraints in program analysis. In: FSE, pp. 58:1–58:11. ACM (2012). https://doi.org/10.1145/2393596.2393665

98. Yang, G., Dwyer, M.B., Rothermel, G.: Regression model checking. In: ICSM, pp. 115–124. IEEE (2009). https://doi.org/10.1109/ICSM.2009.5306334

99. Yang, G., Păsăreanu, C.S., Khurshid, S.: Memoized symbolic execution. In: ISSTA, pp. 144–154. ACM (2012). https://doi.org/10.1145/2338965.2336771

100. Yorsh, G., Ball, T., Sagiv, M.: Testing, abstraction, theorem proving: Better together! In: ISSTA, pp. 145–156. ACM (2006). https://doi.org/10.1145/1146238.1146255

101. Yu, Q., He, F., Wang, B.: Incremental predicate analysis for regression verification. TOPLAS 4(OOPSLA), 184:1–184:25 (2020). https://doi.org/10.1145/3428252

Certified Verification of Relational Properties

Lionel Blatter[1], Nikolai Kosmatov[2,3](✉), Virgile Prevosto[2],
and Pascale Le Gall[4]

[1] Karlsruhe Institute of Technology, Karlsruhe, Germany
lionel.blatter@kit.edu
[2] Université Paris-Saclay, CEA, List, 91120 Palaiseau, France
{nikolai.kosmatov,virgile.prevosto}@cea.fr
[3] Thales Research and Technology, 91120 Palaiseau, France
[4] CentraleSupélec, Université Paris-Saclay, 91190 Gif-sur-Yvette, France
pascale.gall@centralesupelec.fr

Abstract. The use of function contracts to specify the behavior of
functions often remains limited to the scope of a single function call.
Relational properties link several function calls together within a single specification. They can express more advanced properties of a given
function, such as non-interference, continuity, or monotonicity. They can
also relate calls to different functions, for instance, to show that an optimized implementation is equivalent to its original counterpart. However,
relational properties cannot be expressed and verified directly in the traditional setting of modular deductive verification. Self-composition has
been proposed to overcome this limitation, but it requires complex transformations and additional separation hypotheses for real-life languages
with pointers. We propose a novel approach that is not based on code
transformation and avoids those drawbacks. It directly applies a verification condition generator to produce logical formulas that must be
verified to ensure a given relational property. The approach has been
fully formalized and proved sound in the CoQ proof assistant.

1 Introduction

Modular deductive verification [18] allows the user to prove that a function
respects its formal specification. More precisely, for a given function f, any individual call to f can be proved to respect the *contract* of f, that is, basically an
implication: if the given *precondition* is true before the call and the call terminates[1], the given *postcondition* is true after it. However, some kinds of properties

---

[1] Termination can be assumed (partial correctness) or proved separately (full correctness) in a well-known way [15]; for the purpose of this paper we can assume it.

Part of this work was funded by the AESC project supported by the Ministry of Science,
Research and Arts Baden-Württemberg (Ref: 33-7533.-9-10/20/1).

© Springer Nature Switzerland AG 2022
M. H. ter Beek and R. Monahan (Eds.): IFM 2022, LNCS 13274, pp. 86–105, 2022.
https://doi.org/10.1007/978-3-031-07727-2_6

are not easily reducible to a single function call. Indeed, it is frequently necessary to express a property that involves several functions or relates the results of several calls to the same function for different arguments. Such properties are known as *relational properties* [6].

//C program $\mathcal{C}_{sw1}$:	//Composed C program $\mathcal{C}_{sw3}$:	
`x3  = *x1;`	`x3_1  = *x1_1;`	$x_3 := *x_1;$
`*x1 = *x2;`	`*x1_1 = *x2_1;`	$\mathcal{C}_{sw1} \triangleq *x_1 := *x_2;$
`*x2 = x3;`	`*x2_1 = x3_1;`	$*x_2 := x_3;$
//C program $\mathcal{C}_{sw2}$:		
`*x1 = *x1 + *x2;`	`*x1_2 = *x1_2 + *x2_2;`	$*x_1 := *x_1 + *x_2;$
`*x2 = *x1 - *x2;`	`*x2_2 = *x1_2 - *x2_2;`	$\mathcal{C}_{sw2} \triangleq *x_2 := *x_1 - *x_2;$
`*x1 = *x1 - *x2;`	`*x1_2 = *x1_2 - *x2_2;`	$*x_1 := *x_1 - *x_2$

Fig. 1. Two C programs $\mathcal{C}_{sw1}$ and $\mathcal{C}_{sw2}$ swapping `*x1` and `*x2`, their composition $\mathcal{C}_{sw3}$, and their counterparts c_{sw1} and c_{sw2} in language $\mathcal{L}$ (defined below).

Examples of such relational properties include monotonicity (i.e. $x \leq y \Rightarrow f(x) \leq f(y)$), involving two calls, or transitivity ($cmp(x,y) \geq 0 \land cmp(y,z) \geq 0 \Rightarrow cmp(x,z) \geq 0$), involving three calls. In secure information flow [3], *non-interference* is also a relational property. Namely, given a partition of program variables between high-security variables and low-security variables, a program is said to be non-interferent if any two executions starting from states in which the low-security variables have the same initial values will end up in a final state where the low-security variables have the same values. In other words, high-security variables cannot interfere with low-security ones.

Relational properties can also relate calls to different functions. For instance, in the verification of voting rules [5], relational properties are used for defining specific properties (such as monotonicity, anonymity or consistency). Notably, applying the voting rule to a sequence of ballots and a permutation of the same sequence of ballots must lead to the same result, i.e. the order in which the ballots are passed to the voting function should not have any impact on the outcome.

Motivation. Lack of support for relational properties in verification tools was already faced by industrial users (e.g. in [8] for C programs). The usual way to deal with this limitation is to use *self-composition* [3,9,30], product program [2] or other self-composition optimizations [31]. Those techniques are based on code transformations that are relatively tedious and error-prone. Moreover, they are hardly applicable in practice to real-life programs with pointers like in C. Namely, self-composition requires that the compared executions operate on completely separated (i.e. disjoint) memory areas, which might be extremely difficult to ensure for complex programs with pointers.

Example 1 (Motivating Example). Figure 1 shows an example of two simple C programs performing a swap of the values referred to by pointers x1 and x2 (of type int*). Program $\mathcal{C}_{sw1}$ uses an auxiliary variable x3 (of type int), while $\mathcal{C}_{sw2}$ performs an in-place swap using arithmetic operations. As usual in that case, to work correctly, each of these programs needs some separation hypotheses: pointers x1 and x2 should be *separated* (that is, point to disjoint memory locations) and must not point to x1, x2 themselves and, for $\mathcal{C}_{sw1}$, to x3.

Consider a relational property, denoted $\mathcal{R}_{sw}$, stating that both programs, executed from two states in which each of *x1 and *x2 has the same value, will end up in two states also having the same values in these locations. To prove this relational property using self-composition, one typically has to generate a new C program $\mathcal{C}_{sw3}$ (see Fig. 1) composing $\mathcal{C}_{sw1}$ and $\mathcal{C}_{sw2}$. To avoid name conflicts, we rename their variables by adding, resp., suffixes "_1" and "_2". The relational property $\mathcal{R}_{sw}$ is then expressed by a contract of $\mathcal{C}_{sw3}$ with a precondition P and a postcondition Q. Obviously, both P and Q must include the equalities: *x1_1==*x1_2 and *x2_1==*x2_2, and P must also require the aforementioned separation hypotheses necessary for each function. But for programs with pointers and aliasing, this is not sufficient: the user also has to specify additional separation hypotheses between variables coming from the different programs, that is, in our example, that each of x1_1 and x2_1 is separated from each of x1_2 and x2_2. Without such hypotheses, a deductive verification tool cannot show, for example, that a modification of *x1_1 does not impact *x1_2 in the composed program $\mathcal{C}_{sw3}$, and is thus unable to deduce the required property. For real-life programs, such separation hypotheses can be hard to specify or generate. It can become even more complicated for programs with double or multiple indirections.   □

Approach. This paper proposes an alternative approach that is not based on code transformation or relational rules. It directly uses a verification condition generator (VCGen) to produce logical formulas to be verified (typically, with an automated prover) to ensure a given relational property. It requires no extra code processing (such as sequential composition of programs or variable renaming). Moreover, no additional separation hypotheses—in addition to those that are anyway needed for each function to work—are required. The locations of each program are separated by construction: each program has its own memory state. The language $\mathcal{L}$ considered in this work was chosen as a minimal language representative of the main issues relevant for relational property verification: it is a standard WHILE language enriched with annotations, procedures and pointers (see programs c_{sw1} and c_{sw2} in Fig. 1 for examples; we use a lower-case letter c for $\mathcal{L}$ programs and a capital letter $\mathcal{C}$ for C programs). Notably, the presence of dereferencing and address-of operations makes it representative of various aliasing problems with (possibly, multiple) pointer dereferences of a real-life language like C. We formalize the proposed approach and prove[2] its soundness in the COQ proof assistant [33]. Our COQ development contains about 3400 lines.

---

[2] The COQ development is at https://github.com/lyonel2017/Relational-Spec, where the version corresponding to this paper is tagged iFM2022.

Contributions. The contributions of this paper include:

- a COQ formalization and proof of soundness of recursive Hoare triple verification with a verification condition generator on a representative language with procedures and aliasing;
- a novel method for verifying relational properties using a verification condition generator, without relying on code transformation (such as self-composition) or making additional separation hypotheses in case of aliasing;
- a COQ formalization and proof of soundness of the proposed method of relational property verification for the considered language.

Outline. Section 2 introduces an imperative language $\mathcal{L}$ used in this work. Functional correctness is defined in Sect. 3, and relational properties in Sect. 4. Then, we prove the soundness of a VCGen in Sect. 5, and show how it can be soundly extended to verify relational properties in Sect. 6. Finally, we present related work in Sect. 7 and concluding remarks in Sect. 8.

2   Syntax and Semantics of the $\mathcal{L}$ Language

2.1   Notation for Locations, States, and Procedure Contracts

We denote by $\mathbb{N} = \{0, 1, 2, \dots\}$ the set of natural numbers, by $\mathbb{N}^* = \{1, 2, \dots\}$ the set of nonzero natural numbers, and by $\mathbb{B} = \{\text{True}, \text{False}\}$ the set of Boolean values. Let $\mathbb{X}$ be the set of program *locations* and $\mathbb{Y}$ the set of *program (procedure) names*, and let $x, x', x_1, \dots$ and $y, y', y_1, \dots$ denote metavariables ranging over those respective sets. We assume that there exists a bijective function $\mathbb{N} \to \mathbb{X}$, so that $\mathbb{X} = \{x_i \mid i \in \mathbb{N}\}$. Intuitively, we can see i as the *address* of location x_i.

Let Σ be the set of functions $\sigma : \mathbb{N} \to \mathbb{N}$, called *memory states*, and let $\sigma, \sigma', \sigma_1, \dots$ denote metavariables ranging over the set. A state σ maps a location to a value using its address: location x_i has value $\sigma(i)$.

We define the *update* operation of a memory state $set(\sigma, i, n)$, also denoted by $\sigma[i/n]$, as the memory state σ' mapping each address to the same value as σ, except for i, bound to n. Formally, $set(\sigma, i, n)$ is defined by the following rules:

$$\forall \sigma \in \Sigma, x_i \in \mathbb{X}, n \in \mathbb{N}, x_j \in \mathbb{X}. \ i = j \Rightarrow \sigma[i/n](j) = n, \tag{1}$$

$$\forall \sigma \in \Sigma, x_i \in \mathbb{X}, n \in \mathbb{N}, x_j \in \mathbb{X}. \ i \neq j \Rightarrow \sigma[i/n](j) = \sigma(j). \tag{2}$$

Let Ψ be the set of functions $\psi : \mathbb{Y} \to \mathbb{C}$, called *procedure environments*, mapping program names to commands (defined below), and let $\psi, \psi_1, \dots$ denote metavariables ranging over Ψ. We write $\text{body}_\psi(y)$ to refer to $\psi(y)$, the commands (or *body*) of procedure y for a given procedure environment ψ.

Assertions are predicates of arity one, taking as parameter a memory state and returning an equational first-order logic formula. Let metavariables $P, Q, \dots$ range over the set $\mathbb{A}$ of assertions. For instance, using λ-notation, assertion P assessing that location x_3 is bound to 2 can be defined by $P \triangleq \lambda\sigma.\sigma(3) = 2$. This form will be more convenient for relational properties (than e.g. $x_3 = 2$) as it makes explicit the memory states on which a property is evaluated.

Finally, we define the set Φ of *contract environments* $\phi : \mathbb{Y} \rightarrow \mathbb{A} \times \mathbb{A}$, and metavariables $\phi, \phi_1, ...$ to range over Φ. More precisely, ϕ maps a procedure name y to the associated (procedure) *contract* $\phi(y) = (\text{pre}_\phi(y), \text{post}_\phi(y))$, composed of a pre- and a postcondition for procedure y. As usual, a procedure contract will allow us to specify the behavior of a single procedure call, that is, if we start executing y in a memory state satisfying $\text{pre}_\phi(y)$, and the evaluation terminates, the final state satisfies $\text{post}_\phi(y)$.

$a ::= n$	natural const.
$\mid x$	location
$\mid * x$	dereference
$\mid \& x$	address
$\mid a_1 \; op_a \; a_2$	arithm. oper.

$b ::= true \mid false$	Boolean const.
$\mid a_1 \; op_b \; a_2$	comparison
$\mid b_1 \; op_l \; b_2 \mid \neg b_1$	logic oper.

$c ::= \textbf{skip}$	do nothing
$\mid x := a$	direct assignment
$\mid * x := a$	indirect assignment
$\mid c_1; c_2$	sequence
$\mid \textbf{assert}(P)$	assertion
$\mid \textbf{if } b \textbf{ then } \{c_1\} \textbf{ else } \{c_2\}$	condition
$\mid \textbf{while } b \textbf{ inv } P \textbf{ do } \{c_1\}$	loop
$\mid \textbf{call}(y)$	procedure call

Fig. 2. Syntax of arithmetic and Boolean expressions and commands in $\mathcal{L}$.

2.2   Syntax for Expressions and Commands

Let $\mathbb{E}_a$, $\mathbb{E}_b$ and $\mathbb{C}$ denote respectively the sets of arithmetic expressions, Boolean expressions and commands. We denote by $a, a_1, ...; b, b_1, ...$ and $c, c_1, ...$ metavariables ranging, respectively, over those sets. Syntax of arithmetic and Boolean expressions is given in Fig. 2. Constants are natural numbers or Boolean values. Expressions use standard arithmetic, comparison and logic binary operators, denoted respectively $op_a ::= \{+, \times, -\}$, $op_b ::= \{<=, =\}$, $op_l ::= \{\vee, \wedge\}$. Since we use natural values, the subtraction is bounded by 0, as in CoQ: if $n' > n$, the result of $n - n'$ is considered to be 0. Expressions also include locations, possibly with a dereference or address operators.

Figure 2 also presents the syntax of commands in $\mathcal{L}$. Sequences, skip and conditions are standard. An assignment can be done to a location directly or after a dereference. Recall that a location x_i contains as a value a natural number, say v, that can be seen in turn as the address of a location, namely x_v, so the assignment $*x_i := a$ writes the value of expression a to the location x_v, while the address operation $\& x_i$ computes the address i of x_i. An assertion command $\textbf{assert}(P)$ indicates that an assertion P should be valid at the point where the command occurs. The loop command $\textbf{while } b \textbf{ inv } P \textbf{ do } \{c_1\}$ is always annotated with an invariant P. As usual, this invariant should hold when we reach the command and be preserved by each loop step. Command $\textbf{call}(y)$ is a procedure call. All annotations (assertions, loop invariants and procedure contracts) will be ignored during the program execution and will be relevant only for program

$$c_{rec} \triangleq \begin{array}{l} x_1 := x_4; \\ x_2 := 0; \\ \mathbf{call}(y_1) \end{array} \qquad \psi = \left\{ y_1 \rightarrow \begin{array}{l} \mathbf{if}\ x_1 > 0\ \mathbf{then}\ \{ \\ \quad x_2 := x_2 + x_3; \\ \quad x_1 := x_1 - 1; \\ \quad \mathbf{call}(y_1) \\ \}\ \mathbf{else}\ \{ \\ \quad \mathbf{skip} \\ \} \end{array} ,\ \ldots \right\}$$

$$\phi = \left\{ y_1 \rightarrow \begin{pmatrix} \lambda\sigma.\sigma(2) = \sigma(3) \times (\sigma(4) - \sigma(1)) \wedge 0 \leq \sigma(1) \wedge \sigma(1) \leq \sigma(4), \\ \lambda\sigma.\sigma(2) = \sigma(3) \times \sigma(4) \end{pmatrix} ,\ \ldots \right\}.$$

Fig. 3. Example of an $\mathcal{L}$ program c_{rec} with its environments.

$$\xi_a\llbracket n \rrbracket \sigma \triangleq n \qquad \xi_a\llbracket x_i \rrbracket \sigma \triangleq \sigma(i) \qquad \xi_a\llbracket *x_i \rrbracket \sigma \triangleq \sigma(\sigma(i)) \qquad \xi_a\llbracket \&x_i \rrbracket \sigma \triangleq i$$

Fig. 4. Evaluation of expressions in $\mathcal{L}$ (selected rules).

verification in Sect. 5. Procedures do not have explicit parameters and return values (hence we use the term *procedure call* rather than *function call*). Instead, as in assembly code [22], parameters and return value(s) are shared implicitly between the caller and the callee through memory locations: the caller must put/read the right values at the right locations before/after the call. Finally, to avoid ambiguity, we delimit sequences of commands with { }.

Example 2. Figure 3 shows an example of a command c_{rec} and a procedure environment ψ where procedure y_1 points to a recursive command, called in c_{rec}. With the semantics of Sect. 2.3, from any initial state, the command will return a state in which $x_2 = x_3 \times x_4$. Procedure y_1 returns a state where $x_2 = x_3 \times x_4$ if the initial state satisfies $x_2 = x_3 \times (x_4 - x_1) \wedge 0 \leq x_1 \wedge x_1 \leq x_4$. This can be expressed by the contract environment ϕ given (in λ-notation) in Fig. 3. □

2.3 Operational Semantics

Evaluation of arithmetic and Boolean expressions in $\mathcal{L}$ is defined by functions ξ_a and ξ_b. Selected evaluation rules for arithmetic expressions are shown in Fig. 4. Operations $*x_i$ and $\&x_i$ have a semantics similar to the C language, i.e. dereferencing and address-of. Semantics of Boolean expressions is standard [36].

Based on these evaluation functions, we can define the operational semantics of commands in a given procedure environment ψ. Selected evaluation rules are shown in Fig. 5. As said above, both assertions and loop invariants can be seen as program annotations that do not influence the execution of the program itself. Hence, command $\mathbf{assert}(P)$ is equivalent to a skip. Likewise, loop invariant P has no influence on the semantics of $\mathbf{while}\ b\ \mathbf{inv}\ P\ \mathbf{do}\ \{c\}$.

We write $\Vdash \langle c, \sigma \rangle \xrightarrow{\psi} \sigma'$ to denote that $\langle c, \sigma \rangle \xrightarrow{\psi} \sigma'$ can be derived from the rules of Fig. 5. Our CoQ formalization, inspired by [29], provides a deep embedding of $\mathcal{L}$, with an associated parser, in files `Aexp.v`, `Bexp.v` and `Com.v`.

3   Functional Correctness

We define functional correctness in a similar way to the original *Hoare triple* definition [18], except that we also need a procedure environment ψ, leading to a quadruple denoted $\psi : \{P\}c\{Q\}$. We will however still refer by the term "Hoare triple" to the corresponding program property, formally defined as follows.

$$\langle \mathbf{assert}(P), \sigma \rangle \overset{\psi}{\to} \sigma \qquad \frac{\xi_a[\![a]\!]\sigma = n}{\langle x_i := a, \sigma \rangle \overset{\psi}{\to} \sigma[i/n]}$$

$$\frac{\xi_a[\![a]\!]\sigma = n}{\langle *x_i := a, \sigma \rangle \overset{\psi}{\to} \sigma[\sigma(i)/n]} \qquad \frac{\langle \mathrm{body}_\psi(y), \sigma_1 \rangle \overset{\psi}{\to} \sigma_2}{\langle \mathbf{call}(y), \sigma_1 \rangle \overset{\psi}{\to} \sigma_2}$$

Fig. 5. Operational semantics of commands in $\mathcal{L}$ (selected rules).

Definition 1 (Hoare triple). *Let c be a command, ψ a procedure environment, and P and Q two assertions. We define a Hoare triple $\psi : \{P\}c\{Q\}$ as follows:*

$$\psi : \{P\}c\{Q\} \triangleq \forall \sigma, \sigma' \in \Sigma. \ P(\sigma) \wedge (\Vdash \langle c, \sigma \rangle \overset{\psi}{\to} \sigma') \Rightarrow Q(\sigma').$$

Informally, our definition states that, for a given ψ, if a state σ satisfies P and the execution of c on σ terminates in a state σ', then σ' satisfies Q.

Next, we introduce notation $CV(\psi, \phi)$ to denote the fact that, for the given ϕ and ψ, every procedure satisfies its contract.

Definition 2 (Contract Validity). *Let ψ be a procedure environment and ϕ a contract environment. We define contract validity $CV(\psi, \phi)$ as follows:*

$$CV(\psi, \phi) \triangleq \forall y \in \mathbb{Y}. \ \psi : \{\mathrm{pre}_\phi(y)\}\boldsymbol{call}(y)\{\mathrm{post}_\phi(y)\}).$$

The notion of contract validity is at the heart of modular verification, since it allows assuming that the contracts of the callees are satisfied during the verification of a Hoare triple. More precisely, to state the validity of procedure contracts without assuming anything about their bodies in our formalization, we will consider an arbitrary choice of implementations ψ' of procedures that satisfy the contracts, like in assumption (3) in Lemma 1. This technical lemma, taken from [1, Equation (4.6)], gives an alternative criterion for validity of procedure contracts: if, under the assumption that the contracts in ϕ hold, we can prove for each procedure y that its body satisfies its contract, then the contracts are valid.

Lemma 1 (Adequacy of contracts). *Given a procedure environment ψ and a contract environment ϕ such that*

$$\forall \psi' \in \Psi. \ CV(\psi', \phi) \Rightarrow \forall y \in \mathbb{Y}, \psi' : \{\mathrm{pre}_\phi(y)\}\mathrm{body}_\psi(y)\{\mathrm{post}_\phi(y)\}, \qquad (3)$$

we have $CV(\psi, \phi)$.

Proof. Any given terminating execution traverses a finite number of procedure calls (over all procedures) that can be replaced by inlining the bodies a sufficient number of times. We first formalize a theory of k-inliners (that inline procedure bodies a finite number of times $k \geq 0$ and replace deeper calls by nonterminating loops) and prove their properties. Relying on this elegant theory, the proof of the lemma proceeds by induction on the number of procedure inlinings.   □

From that, we can establish the main result of this section. Theorem 1, taken from [1, Th. 4.2] states that $\psi : \{P\}c\{Q\}$ holds if assumption (3) holds and if the validity of contracts of ϕ for ψ implies the Hoare triple itself. This theorem is the basis for modular verification of Hoare Triples, as done for instance in Hoare Logic [18,36] or verification condition generation.

Theorem 1 (Recursion).   *Given a procedure environment ψ and a contract environment ϕ such that*

$$\forall \psi' \in \Psi.\ CV(\psi', \phi) \Rightarrow \forall y \in \mathbb{Y}, \psi' : \{\text{pre}_\phi(y)\}\text{body}_\psi(y)\{\text{post}_\phi(y)\},\ and$$
$$CV(\psi, \phi) \Rightarrow \psi : \{P\}c\{Q\},$$

we have $\psi : \{P\}c\{Q\}$.

Proof. By Lemma 1.   □

We refer the reader to the COQ development, more precisely the results `recursive_proc` and `recursive_hoare_triple` in file `Hoare_Triple.v` for complete proofs of Lemma 1 and Theorem 1 for $\mathcal{L}$. To the best of our knowledge, this is the first mechanized proof of these classical results.

An interesting corollary can be deduced from Theorem 1.

Corollary 1 (Procedure Recursion).   *Given a procedure environment ψ and a contract environment ϕ such that*

$$\forall \psi' \in \Psi.\ CV(\psi', \phi) \Rightarrow \forall y \in \mathbb{Y}, \psi' : \{\text{pre}_\phi(y)\}\text{body}_\psi(y)\{\text{post}_\phi(y)\},$$

we have $\forall y \in \mathbb{Y}.\ \psi : \{\text{pre}_\phi(y)\}\text{body}_\psi(y)\{\text{post}_\phi(y)\}$.

4   Relational Properties

Relational properties can be seen as an extension of Hoare triples. But, instead of linking one program with two properties, the pre- and postconditions, relational properties link n programs to two properties, called relational assertions. We define a *relational assertion* as a predicate taking a sequence of memory states and returning a first-order logic formula. We use metavariables $\widehat{P}, \widehat{Q}, ...$ to range over the set of relational assertions, denoted $\widehat{\mathbb{A}}$. As a simple example of a relational assertion, we might say that two states bind location x_3 to the same value. This would be stated as follows: $\lambda(\sigma_1, \sigma_2).\sigma_1(3) = \sigma_2(3)$.

A *relational property* is a property about n programs $c_1, ..., c_n$, stating that if each program c_i starts in a state σ_i and ends in a state σ_i' such that $\widehat{P}(\sigma_1, ..., \sigma_n)$

holds, then $\widehat{Q}(\sigma_1', ..., \sigma_n')$ holds, where $\widehat{P}$ and $\widehat{Q}$ are relational assertions over n memory states.

We formally define relational correctness similarly to functional correctness (cf. Definition 1), except that we now use sequences of memory states and commands of equal length. We denote by $(u_k)^n$ a sequence of elements $(u_k)_{k=1}^n = (u_1, ..., u_n)$, where k ranges from 1 to n. If $n \leq 0$, $(u_k)^n$ is the empty sequence denoted [ ].

$$\psi : \{\widehat{P}\} \, c_{sw1} \sim c_{sw2} \, \{\widehat{Q}\},$$

$$\widehat{P} \triangleq \lambda\sigma_1\sigma_2. \; \sigma_1(\sigma_1(1)) = \sigma_2(\sigma_2(1)) \wedge \sigma_1(\sigma_1(2)) = \sigma_2(\sigma_2(2)) \wedge$$
$$\sigma_1(1) \neq \sigma_1(2) \wedge \sigma_2(1) \neq \sigma_2(2) \wedge \sigma_1(1) > 3 \wedge \sigma_1(2) > 3 \wedge \sigma_2(1) > 2 \wedge \sigma_2(2) > 2,$$

$$\widehat{Q} \triangleq \lambda\sigma_1'\sigma_2'. \; \sigma_1'(\sigma_1'(1)) = \sigma_2'(\sigma_2'(1)) \wedge \sigma_1'(\sigma_1'(2)) = \sigma_2'(\sigma_2'(2)).$$

Fig. 6. A relational property for $\mathcal{L}$ programs c_{sw1} and c_{sw2} of Fig. 1.

Definition 3 (Relational Correctness). *Let ψ be a procedure environment, $(c_k)^n$ a sequence of n commands ($n \in \mathbb{N}^*$), and $\widehat{P}$ and $\widehat{Q}$ two relational assertions over n states. The relational correctness of $(c_k)^n$ with respect to $\widehat{P}$ and $\widehat{Q}$, denoted $\psi : \{\widehat{P}\}(c_k)^n\{\widehat{Q}\}$, is defined as follows:*

$$\psi : \{\widehat{P}\}(c_k)^n\{\widehat{Q}\} \triangleq$$
$$\forall(\sigma_k)^n, (\sigma'_k)^n. \; \widehat{P}((\sigma_k)^n) \wedge (\bigwedge_{i=1}^n \Vdash \langle c_i, \sigma_i \rangle \xrightarrow{\psi} \sigma'_i) \Rightarrow \widehat{Q}((\sigma'_k)^n).$$

This notation generalizes the one proposed by Benton [6] for relational properties linking two commands: $\psi : \{\widehat{P}\}c_1 \sim c_2\{\widehat{Q}\}$. As Benton's work mostly focused on comparing equivalent programs, using symbol $\sim$ was quite natural. In particular, Benton's work would not be practical for verification of relational properties with several calls such as transitivity mentioned in Sect. 1.

Example 3 (Relational property). Figure 6 formalizes the relational property $\mathcal{R}_{sw}$ for $\mathcal{L}$ programs c_{sw1} and c_{sw2} discussed in Example 1. Recall that $\mathcal{R}_{sw}$ (written in Fig. 6 in Benton's notation) states that both programs executed from two states named σ_1 and σ_2 having the same values in $*x_1$ and $*x_2$ will end up in two states σ_1' and σ_2' also having the same values in these locations. Notice that the initial state of each program needs separation hypotheses (cf. the second line of the definition of $\widehat{P}$). Namely, x_1 and x_2 must point to different locations and must not point to x_1, x_2 or, for c_{sw1}, to x_3 for the property to hold. This relational property is formalized in the COQ development in file Examples.v. □

5 Verification Condition Generation for Hoare Triples

A standard way [15] for verifying that a Hoare triple holds is to use a verification condition generator (VCGen). In this section, we formalize a VCGen for Hoare triples and show that it is correct, in the sense that if all verification conditions that it generates are valid, then the Hoare triple is valid according to Definition 1.

5.1 Verification Condition Generator

We have chosen to split the VCGen in three steps, as it is commonly done [23]:

- function $\mathcal{T}_c$ generates the main verification condition, expressing that the postcondition holds in the final state, assuming auxiliary annotations hold;
- function $\mathcal{T}_a$ generates auxiliary verification conditions stemming from assertions, loop invariants, and preconditions of called procedures;
- finally, function $\mathcal{T}_f$ generates verification conditions for the auxiliary procedures that are called by the main program, to ensure that their bodies respect their contracts.

$$\mathcal{T}_c[\![\mathbf{skip}]\!](\sigma, \phi, f) \triangleq \forall \sigma'. \sigma' = \sigma \Rightarrow f(\sigma')$$

$$\mathcal{T}_c[\![x_i := a]\!](\sigma, \phi, f) \triangleq \forall \sigma'. \sigma' = set(\sigma, i, \xi_a[\![a]\!]\sigma) \Rightarrow f(\sigma')$$

$$\mathcal{T}_c[\![*x_i := a]\!](\sigma, \phi, f) \triangleq \forall \sigma'. \sigma' = set(\sigma, \sigma(i), \xi_a[\![a]\!]\sigma) \Rightarrow f(\sigma')$$

$$\mathcal{T}_c[\![\mathbf{assert}(P)]\!](\sigma, \phi, f) \triangleq \forall \sigma'. \sigma' = \sigma \wedge P(\sigma) \Rightarrow f(\sigma')$$

$$\mathcal{T}_c[\![c_0; c_1]\!](\sigma, \phi, f) \triangleq \mathcal{T}_c[\![c_0]\!](\sigma, \phi, \lambda \sigma'. \mathcal{T}_c[\![c_1]\!](\sigma', \phi, f))$$

$$\mathcal{T}_c[\![\mathbf{if}\ b\ \mathbf{then}\ \{c_0\}\ \mathbf{else}\ \{c_1\}]\!](\sigma, \phi, f) \triangleq (\xi_b[\![b]\!]\sigma \Rightarrow \mathcal{T}_c[\![c_0]\!](\sigma, \phi, f)) \wedge$$
$$(\neg \xi_b[\![b]\!]\sigma \Rightarrow \mathcal{T}_c[\![c_1]\!](\sigma, \phi, f))$$

$$\mathcal{T}_c[\![\mathbf{call}(y)]\!](\sigma, \phi, f) \triangleq \mathrm{pre}_\phi(y)(\sigma) \Rightarrow (\forall \sigma'. \mathrm{post}_\phi(y)(\sigma') \Rightarrow f(\sigma'))$$

$$\mathcal{T}_c[\![\mathbf{while}\ b\ \mathbf{inv}\ inv\ \mathbf{do}\ \{c\}]\!](\sigma, \phi, f) \triangleq inv(\sigma) \Rightarrow$$
$$(\forall \sigma'. inv(\sigma') \wedge \neg(\xi_b[\![b]\!]\sigma') \Rightarrow f(\sigma'))$$

Fig. 7. Definition of function $\mathcal{T}_c$ generating the main verification condition.

Definition 4 (Function $\mathcal{T}_c$ generating the main verification condition).
Given a command c, a memory state σ representing the state before the command, a contract environment ϕ, and an assertion f, function $\mathcal{T}_c$ returns a formula defined by case analysis on c as shown in Fig. 7.

Assertion f represents the postcondition we want to verify after the command executed from state σ. For each command, except sequence and branch, a fresh memory state σ' is introduced and related to the current memory state σ. The new memory state is given as parameter to f. For **skip**, which does nothing, both states are identical. For assignments, σ' is simply the update of σ. An assertion introduces a hypothesis over σ but leaves it unchanged. For a sequence, we simply compose the conditions, that is, we check that the final state of c_0 is such that f will be verified after executing c_1. For a conditional, we check that if the condition evaluates to true, the *then* branch will ensure the postcondition, and that otherwise the *else* branch will ensure the postcondition. The rule for calls simply assumes that σ' verifies $\mathrm{post}_\phi(y)$. Finally, $\mathcal{T}_c$ assumes that, after a loop, σ' is a state where the loop condition is false and the loop invariant holds. As for an assertion, the callee's precondition and the loop invariant are just assumed to be true; function $\mathcal{T}_a$, defined below, generates the corresponding proof obligations.

Example 4. For $c \triangleq \mathbf{skip}; x_1 := 2$, and $f \triangleq \lambda\sigma.\ \sigma(1) = 2$, we have:

$$\mathcal{T}_c[\![c]\!](\sigma, \phi, f) \equiv \forall\sigma'_1.\sigma = \sigma'_1 \Rightarrow (\forall\sigma'_2.\sigma'_2 = set(\sigma'_1, 1, 2) \Rightarrow \sigma'_2(1) = 2).$$

$\square$

$$\mathcal{T}_a[\![\mathbf{skip}]\!](\sigma, \phi) \triangleq True$$
$$\mathcal{T}_a[\![x_i := a]\!](\sigma, \phi) \triangleq True$$
$$\mathcal{T}_a[\![*x_i := a]\!](\sigma, \phi) \triangleq True$$
$$\mathcal{T}_a[\![\mathbf{assert}(P)]\!](\sigma, \phi) \triangleq P(\sigma)$$
$$\mathcal{T}_a[\![c_0; c_1]\!](\sigma, \phi) \triangleq \mathcal{T}_a[\![c_0]\!](\sigma, \phi) \wedge$$
$$\mathcal{T}_c[\![c_0]\!](\sigma, \phi, \lambda\sigma'.(\mathcal{T}_a[\![c_1]\!](\sigma', \phi)))$$
$$\mathcal{T}_a[\![\mathbf{if}\ b\ \mathbf{then}\ \{c_0\}\ \mathbf{else}\ \{c_1\}]\!](\sigma, \phi) \triangleq \xi_b[\![b]\!]\sigma \Rightarrow \mathcal{T}_a[\![c_0]\!](\sigma, \phi) \wedge$$
$$\neg(\xi_b[\![b]\!]\sigma) \Rightarrow \mathcal{T}_a[\![c_1]\!](\sigma, \phi)$$
$$\mathcal{T}_a[\![\mathbf{call}(y)]\!](\sigma, \phi) \triangleq \mathrm{pre}_\phi(y)(\sigma)$$
$$\mathcal{T}_a[\![\mathbf{while}\ b\ \mathbf{inv}\ inv\ \mathbf{do}\ \{c\}]\!](\sigma, \phi) \triangleq inv(\sigma) \wedge$$
$$(\forall\sigma', inv(\sigma') \wedge \xi_b[\![b]\!]\sigma' \Rightarrow \mathcal{T}_a[\![c]\!](\sigma', \phi)) \wedge$$
$$(\forall\sigma', inv(\sigma') \wedge \xi_b[\![b]\!]\sigma' \Rightarrow \mathcal{T}_c[\![c]\!](\sigma', \phi, inv))$$

Fig. 8. Definition of function $\mathcal{T}_a$ generating auxiliary verification conditions.

Definition 5 (Function $\mathcal{T}_a$ generating the auxiliary verification conditions). *Given a command c, a memory state σ representing the state before the command, and a contract environment ϕ, function $\mathcal{T}_a$ returns a formula defined by case analysis on c as shown in Fig. 8.*

Basically, $\mathcal{T}_a$ collects all assertions, preconditions of called procedures, as well as invariant establishment and preservation, and lifts the corresponding formulas to constraints on the initial state σ through the use of $\mathcal{T}_c$.

Finally, we define the function for generating the conditions for verifying that the body of each procedure defined in ψ respects its contract defined in ϕ.

Definition 6 (Function $\mathcal{T}_f$ generating the procedure verification condition). *Given two environments ψ and ϕ, $\mathcal{T}_f$ returns the following formula:*

$$\mathcal{T}_f(\phi, \psi) \triangleq \forall y, \sigma. \; \mathrm{pre}_\phi(y)(\sigma) \Rightarrow \mathcal{T}_a[\![\mathrm{body}_\psi(y)]\!](\sigma, \phi) \wedge$$
$$\mathcal{T}_c[\![\mathrm{body}_\psi(y)]\!](\sigma, \phi, \mathrm{post}_\phi(y)).$$

The VCGen is defined in file `Vcg.v` of the COQ development. Interested readers will also find a proof (in file `Vcg_Opt.v`) of a VCGen optimization (not detailed here), which prevents the size of the generated formulas from becoming exponential in the number of conditions in the program [14], which is a classical problem for "naive" VCGens.

5.2 Hoare Triple Verification

We can now state the theorems establishing correctness of the VCGen. Their proof can be found in file `Correct.v` of the COQ development.

First, Lemma 2 shows that, under the assumption of the procedure contracts, a Hoare triple is valid if for all memory states satisfying the precondition, the main verification condition and the auxiliary verification conditions hold.

Lemma 2. *Assume the following two properties hold:*

$$\forall \sigma \in \Sigma, P(\sigma) \Rightarrow \mathcal{T}_a[\![c]\!](\sigma, \phi),$$
$$\forall \sigma \in \Sigma, P(\sigma) \Rightarrow \mathcal{T}_c[\![c]\!](\sigma, \phi, Q).$$

Then we have $CV(\psi, \phi) \Rightarrow \psi : \{P\}c\{Q\}$.

Proof. By structural induction over c. $\qquad\qquad\square$

Next, we prove in Lemma 3 that if $\mathcal{T}_f(\phi, \psi)$ holds, then for an arbitrary choice of implementations ψ' of procedures respecting the procedure contracts, the body of each procedure y respects its contract.

Lemma 3. *Assume that the formula $\mathcal{T}_f(\phi, \psi)$ is satisfied. Then we have*

$$\forall \psi' \in \Psi. \; CV(\psi', \phi) \Rightarrow \forall y \in \mathbb{Y}, \psi' : \{\mathrm{pre}_\phi(y)\}\mathrm{body}_\psi(y)\{\mathrm{post}_\phi(y)\}.$$

Proof. By Lemma 2. $\qquad\qquad\square$

Finally, we can establish the main theorem of this section, stating that the VCGen is correct with respect to our definition of Hoare triples.

Theorem 2 (Soundness of VCGen). *Assume that we have $\mathcal{T}_f(\phi, \psi)$ and*

$$\forall \sigma \in \Sigma, P(\sigma) \Rightarrow \mathcal{T}_a[\![c]\!](\sigma, \phi),$$
$$\forall \sigma \in \Sigma, P(\sigma) \Rightarrow \mathcal{T}_c[\![c]\!](\sigma, \phi, Q).$$

Then we have $\psi : \{P\}c\{Q\}$.

Proof. By Theorem 1 and Lemmas 2 and 3.   □

Example 5. Consider again the command c_{rec}, procedure environment ψ, and contract environment ϕ of Example 2 (presented in Fig. 3). We can apply Theorem 2 to prove its functional correctness expressed by the following Hoare triple:

$$\psi : \{\lambda\sigma.True\}\; c_{\text{rec}}\; \{\lambda\sigma.\sigma(2) = \sigma(4) \times \sigma(3)\}$$

(see command com_rec in file Examples.v).   □

6   Verification of Relational Properties

In this section, we propose a verification method for relational properties (defined in Sect. 4) using the VCGen defined in Sect. 5 (or, more generally, any VCGen respecting Theorem 2). First, we define the notation $\mathcal{T}_{cr}$ for the recursive call of function $\mathcal{T}_c$ on a sequence of commands and memory states:

Definition 7 (Function $\mathcal{T}_{cr}$). *Given a sequence of commands $(c_k)^n$ and a sequence of memory states $(\sigma_k)^n$, a contract environment ϕ and a predicate $\widehat{Q}$ over n states, function $\mathcal{T}_{cr}$ is defined by induction on n as follows.*

- *Basis: $n = 0$.*
$$\mathcal{T}_{cr}([\,],[\,],\phi,\widehat{Q}) \triangleq \widehat{Q}([\,]).$$

- *Inductive: $n \in \mathbb{N}^*$.*

$$\mathcal{T}_{cr}((c_k)^n,(\sigma_k)^n,\phi,\widehat{Q}) \triangleq$$
$$\mathcal{T}_c[\![c_n]\!](\sigma_n,\phi,\; \lambda\sigma'_n.\mathcal{T}_{cr}((c_k)^{n-1},(\sigma_k)^{n-1},\phi,\; \lambda(\sigma'_k)^{n-1}.\widehat{Q}((\sigma'_k)^n))).$$

Intuitively, for $n = 2$, $\mathcal{T}_{cr}$ gives the weakest relational condition that σ_1 and σ_2 must fulfill in order for $\widehat{Q}$ to hold after executing c_1 from σ_1 and c_2 from σ_2:
$\mathcal{T}_{cr}((c_1,c_2),(\sigma_1,\sigma_2),\phi,\widehat{Q}) \equiv \mathcal{T}_c[\![c_2]\!](\sigma_2,\phi,\; \lambda\sigma'_2.\mathcal{T}_c[\![c_1]\!](\sigma_1,\phi,\; \lambda\sigma'_1.\widehat{Q}(\sigma'_1,\sigma'_2))).$

Remark 1. Assume we have $n > 0$, a command c_n, a sequence of commands $(c_k)^{n-1}$, and a sequence of memory states $(\sigma_k)^{n-1}$. From Definition 1, it follows that

$$\forall\sigma_n,\sigma'_n.\; \widehat{P}((\sigma_k)^n) \wedge (\Vdash \langle c_n,\sigma_n \rangle \xrightarrow{\psi} \sigma'_n) \Rightarrow$$
$$\mathcal{T}_{cr}((c_k)^{n-1},(\sigma_k)^{n-1},\phi,\lambda(\sigma'_k)^{n-1}.\widehat{Q}((\sigma'_k)^n))$$

is equivalent to

$$\psi : \{\lambda\sigma_n.\widehat{P}((\sigma_k)^n)\}c_n\{\lambda\sigma'_n.\mathcal{T}_{cr}((c_k)^{n-1},(\sigma_k)^{n-1},\phi,\lambda(\sigma'_k)^{n-1}.\widehat{Q}((\sigma'_k)^n))\}.$$

Example 6 (Relational verification condition). In order to make things more concrete, we can go back to the relational property $\mathcal{R}_{\text{sw}}$ between two implementations c_{sw1} and c_{sw2} of swap defined in Example 1 and examine what would be the main verification condition generated by $\mathcal{T}_{cr}$. Let $\widehat{P}$ and $\widehat{Q}$ be defined as in

Example 3. In this particular case, we have $n = 2$, and ϕ is empty (since we do not have any function call), thus Definition 7 becomes:

$$\mathcal{T}_{cr}((c_{sw1}, c_{sw2}), (\sigma_1, \sigma_2), \emptyset, \widehat{Q}) = \mathcal{T}_c[\![c_{sw2}]\!](\sigma_2, \emptyset, \lambda\sigma_2'.\mathcal{T}_c[\![c_{sw1}]\!](\sigma_1, \emptyset, \lambda\sigma_1'.\widehat{Q}(\sigma_1', \sigma_2'))).$$

We thus start by applying $\mathcal{T}_c$ over c_{sw1}, to obtain, using the rules of Definition 4 for sequence and assignment, the following intermediate formula:

$$\mathcal{T}_{cr}((c_{sw1}, c_{sw2}), (\sigma_1, \sigma_2), \emptyset, \widehat{Q}) =$$
$$\mathcal{T}_c(c_{sw2}, \sigma_2, \emptyset,$$
$$\lambda\sigma_2'.\forall\sigma_3, \sigma_5, \sigma_7.$$
$$\sigma_3 = \sigma_1[3/\sigma_1(\sigma_1(1))] \Rightarrow$$
$$\sigma_5 = \sigma_3[\sigma_3(1)/\sigma_3(\sigma_3(2))] \Rightarrow$$
$$\sigma_7 = \sigma_5[\sigma_5(2)/\sigma_5(3)] \Rightarrow \widehat{Q}(\sigma_7, \sigma_2').$$

We can then do the same with c_{sw2} to obtain the final formula:

$$\mathcal{T}_{cr}((c_{sw1}, c_{sw2}), (\sigma_1, \sigma_2), \emptyset, \widehat{Q}) =$$
$$\forall(\sigma_k)^8.$$
$$\sigma_4 = \sigma_2[\sigma_2(1)/\sigma_2(\sigma_2(1)) + \sigma_2(\sigma_2(2))] \Rightarrow$$
$$\sigma_6 = \sigma_4[\sigma_4(2)/\sigma_4(\sigma_4(1)) - \sigma_4(\sigma_4(2))] \Rightarrow$$
$$\sigma_8 = \sigma_6[\sigma_6(1)/\sigma_6(\sigma_6(1)) - \sigma_6(\sigma_6(2))] \Rightarrow$$
$$\sigma_3 = \sigma_1[3/\sigma_1(\sigma_1(1))] \Rightarrow$$
$$\sigma_5 = \sigma_3[\sigma_3(1)/\sigma_3(\sigma_3(2))] \Rightarrow$$
$$\sigma_7 = \sigma_5[\sigma_5(2)/\sigma_5(3)] \Rightarrow \widehat{Q}(\sigma_7, \sigma_8).$$

Here, σ_k with odd (resp., even) indices result from $\mathcal{T}_c$ for c_{sw1} (resp., c_{sw2}).   □

We similarly define a notation for the auxiliary verification conditions for a sequence of n commands.

Definition 8 (Function $\mathcal{T}_{ar}$). *Given a sequence of commands $(c_k)^n$ and a sequence of memory states $(\sigma_k)^n$, we define function $\mathcal{T}_{ar}$ as follows:*

$$\mathcal{T}_{ar}((c_k)^n, (\sigma_k)^n, \phi) \triangleq \bigwedge_{i=1}^{n} \mathcal{T}_a[\![c_i]\!](\sigma_i, \phi).$$

Remark 2. For $n > 0$, it trivially follows from Definition 8 that:

$$\mathcal{T}_{ar}((c_k)^n, (\sigma_k)^n, \phi) \equiv \mathcal{T}_a[\![c_n]\!](\sigma_n, \phi) \wedge \mathcal{T}_{ar}((c_k)^{n-1}, (\sigma_k)^{n-1}, \phi).$$

Using functions $\mathcal{T}_{cr}$ and $\mathcal{T}_{ar}$, we can now give the main result of this paper: it states that the verification of relational properties using the VCGen is correct.

Theorem 3 (Soundness of relational VCGen). *For any sequence of commands* $(c_k)^n$, *contract environment* ϕ, *procedure environment* ψ, *and relational assertions over n states $\widehat{P}$ and $\widehat{Q}$, if the following three properties hold:*

$$\mathcal{T}_f(\phi, \psi), \tag{4}$$

$$\forall (\sigma_k)^n, \widehat{P}((\sigma_k)^n) \Rightarrow \mathcal{T}_{ar}((c_k)^n, (\sigma_k)^n, \phi), \tag{5}$$

$$\forall (\sigma_k)^n, \widehat{P}((\sigma_k)^n) \Rightarrow \mathcal{T}_{cr}((c_k)^n, (\sigma_k)^n, \phi, \widehat{Q}), \tag{6}$$

then we have $\psi : \{\widehat{P}\}(c_k)^n\{\widehat{Q}\}$.

In other words, a relational property is valid if all procedure contracts are valid, and, assuming the relational precondition holds, both the auxiliary verification conditions and the main relational verification condition hold. We give the main steps of the proof below. The corresponding COQ formalization is available in file `Rela.v`, and the COQ proof of Theorem 3 is in file `Correct_Rela.v`.

Proof. By induction on the length n of the sequence of commands $(c_k)^n$.

- Induction basis: $n = 0$. By Definition 3, our goal becomes:

$$\psi : \{\widehat{P}\}(c_k)^0\{\widehat{Q}\} \equiv \widehat{P}([\,]) \Rightarrow \widehat{Q}([\,]).$$

Indeed, by definition of $\mathcal{T}_{cr}$ and Hypothesis (6), $\widehat{P}([\,]) \Rightarrow \widehat{Q}([\,])$ holds.
- Induction step: assuming the result for n, we prove it for $n+1$. So, assume we have a sequence of commands $(c_k)^{n+1}$, relational assertions and environments respecting (4), (5), (6) (stated for sequences of $n + 1$ elements). We have to prove $\psi : \{\widehat{P}\}(c_k)^{n+1}\{\widehat{Q}\}$, which, by Definition 3, is equivalent to:

$$\forall (\sigma_k)^{n+1}, (\sigma'_k)^{n+1}. \; \widehat{P}((\sigma_k)^{n+1}) \wedge (\bigwedge_{i=1}^{n+1} \Vdash \langle c_i, \sigma_i \rangle \xrightarrow{\psi} \sigma'_i) \Rightarrow \widehat{Q}((\sigma'_k)^{n+1}). \tag{7}$$

First, we can deduce from Hypothesis (5) and Remark 2:

$$\forall (\sigma_k)^{n+1}, \widehat{P}((\sigma_k)^{n+1}) \Rightarrow \mathcal{T}_a[\![c_{n+1}]\!](\sigma_{n+1}, \phi), \tag{8}$$

$$\forall (\sigma_k)^{n+1}, \widehat{P}((\sigma_k)^{n+1}) \Rightarrow \mathcal{T}_{ar}((c_k)^n, (\sigma_k)^n, \phi). \tag{9}$$

By Hypothesis (6) and Definition 7, we have

$$\forall (\sigma_k)^{n+1}, \widehat{P}((\sigma_k)^{n+1}) \Rightarrow$$

$$\mathcal{T}_c[\![c_{n+1}]\!](\sigma_{n+1}, \phi, \lambda \sigma'_{n+1}.\mathcal{T}_{cr}((c_k)^n, (\sigma_k)^n, \phi, \lambda(\sigma'_k)^n.\widehat{Q}((\sigma_k)^{n+1}))). \tag{10}$$

Using (4), (8) and (10), we can now apply Theorem 2 (for an arbitrary subsequence $(\sigma_k)^n$, that we can thus put in an external universal quantifier) to obtain:

$$\forall(\sigma_k)^n.$$

$$\psi: \{\lambda\sigma_{n+1}.\widehat{P}((\sigma_k)^{n+1})\}c_{n+1}\{\lambda\sigma'_{n+1}.\mathcal{T}_{cr}((c_k)^n,(\sigma_k)^n,\phi,\lambda(\sigma'_k)^n.\widehat{Q}((\sigma'_k)^{n+1}))\}. \quad (11)$$

Using Remark 1 and by rearranging the quantifiers and implications, we can rewrite (11) into:

$$\forall\sigma_{n+1},\sigma'_{n+1}. \Vdash \langle c_{n+1},\sigma_{n+1}\rangle \xrightarrow{\psi} \sigma'_{n+1} \Rightarrow$$
$$\forall(\sigma_k)^n.\widehat{P}((\sigma_k)^{n+1}) \Rightarrow \mathcal{T}_{cr}((c_k)^n,(\sigma_k)^n,\phi,\lambda(\sigma'_k)^n.\widehat{Q}((\sigma'_k)^{n+1})). \quad (12)$$

For arbitrary states σ_{n+1} and σ'_{n+1} such that $\Vdash \langle c_{n+1},\sigma_{n+1}\rangle \xrightarrow{\psi} \sigma'_{n+1}$, using (4), (9) and (12), we can apply the induction hypothesis, and obtain:

$$\forall\sigma_{n+1},\sigma'_{n+1}. \Vdash \langle c_{n+1},\sigma_{n+1}\rangle \xrightarrow{\psi} \sigma'_{n+1} \Rightarrow$$
$$\psi: \{\lambda(\sigma_k)^n.\widehat{P}((\sigma_k)^{n+1})\}(c_k)^n\{\lambda(\sigma'_k)^n.\widehat{Q}((\sigma'_k)^{n+1})\}.$$

Finally, by Definition 3 and by rearranging the quantifiers, we deduce (7). $\square$

Example 7. The relational property of Example 3 is proven valid using the proposed technique based on Theorem 3 in file **Examples.v** of the CoQ development. For instance, (6) becomes $\forall\sigma_1,\sigma_2.\widehat{P}(\sigma_1,\sigma_2) \Rightarrow \mathcal{T}_{cr}((c_{sw1},c_{sw2}),(\sigma_1,\sigma_2),\emptyset,\widehat{Q})$, where the last expression was computed in Example 6. Such formulas—long for a manual proof—are well-treated by automatic solvers.

   Notice that in this example we do not need any code transformations or extra separation hypotheses in addition to those anyway needed for the swap functions while both programs manipulate the same locations x_1, x_2, and—even worse—the unknown locations pointed by them can be any locations x_i, $i > 3$.

$\square$

7   Related Work

Relational Property Verification. Significant work has been done on relational program verification (see [26,27] for a detailed state of the art). We discuss below some of the efforts the most closely related to our work.

   Various relational logics have been designed as extensions to Hoare Logic, such as Relational Hoare Logic [6] and Cartesian Hoare Logic [32]. As our approach, those logics consider for each command a set of associated memory states in the very rules of the system, thus avoiding additional separation assumptions. Limitations of these logics are often the absence of support for aliasing or a limited form of relational properties. For instance, Relational Hoare Logic supports only relational properties with two commands and Cartesian Hoare Logic supports only k-safety properties (relational properties on the same command). Our method has an advanced support of aliasing and supports a very general definition of relational properties, possibly between several dissimilar commands.

Self-composition [3,9,30] and its derivations [2,13,31] are well-known approaches to deal with relational properties. This is in particular due to their flexibility: self-composition methods can be applied as a preprocessing step to different verification approaches. For example, self-composition is used in combination with symbolic execution and model checking for verification of voting functions [5]. Other examples are the use of self-composition in combination with verification condition generation in the context of the Java language [12] or the C language [9,10]. In general, the support of aliasing of C programs in these last efforts is very limited due the problems mentioned earlier. Compared to these techniques, where self-composition is applied before the generation of verification conditions (and therefore requires taking care about separation of memory states of the considered programs), our method can be seen as relating the considered programs' semantics directly at the level of the verification conditions, where separation of their memory states is already ensured, thus avoiding the need to take care of this separation explicitly.

Finally, another advanced approach for relational verification is the translation of the relational problem into Horn clauses and their proof using constraint solving [21,34]. The benefit of constraint solving lies in the ability to automatically find relational invariants and complex self-composition derivations. Moreover, the translation of programs into Horn clauses, done by tools like REVE[3], results in formulas similar to those generated by our VCGen. Therefore, like our approach, relational verification with constraint solving requires no additional separation hypothesis in presence of aliasing.

Certified Verification Condition Generation. In a broad sense, this work continues previous efforts in formalization and mechanized proof of program language semantics, analyzers and compilers, such as [7,11,17,19,20,24,25,28,29,35]. Generation of certificates (in Isabelle) for the BOOGIE verifier is presented in [28]. The certified deductive verification tool WhyCert [17] comes with a similar soundness result for its verification condition generator. Its formalization follows an alternative proof approach, based on co-induction, while our proof relies on induction. WhyCert is syntactically closer to the C language and the ACSL specification language [4], while our proof uses a simplified language, but with a richer aliasing model. Furthermore, we provide a formalization and a soundness proof for relational verification, which was not considered in WhyCert or in [28].

To the best of our knowledge, the present work is the first proposal of relational property verification based on verification condition generation realized for a representative language with procedure calls and aliases with a full mechanized formalization and proof of soundness in COQ.

8   Conclusion

We have presented in this paper a method for verifying relational properties using a verification condition generator, without relying on code transformations

---

[3] https://formal.kastel.kit.edu/projects/improve/reve/.

(such as self-composition) or making additional separation hypotheses in case of aliasing. This method has been fully formalized in CoQ, and the soundness of recursive Hoare triple verification using a verification condition generator (itself formally proved correct) for a simple language with procedure calls and aliasing has been formally established. Our formalization is well-adapted for proving possible optimizations of a VCGen and for using optimized VCGen versions for relational property verification.

This work sets up a basis for the formalization of modular verification of relational properties using verification condition generation. We plan to extend it with more features such as the possibility to refer to the values of variables before a function call in the postcondition (in order to relate them to the values after the call) and the capacity to rely on relational properties during the proof of other properties. Future work also includes an implementation of this technique inside a tool like RPP [9] in order to integrate it with SMT solvers and to evaluate it on benchmarks. The final objective would be to obtain a system similar to the verification of Hoare triples, namely, having relational procedure contracts, relational assertions, and relational invariants. Currently, for relational properties, product programs [2] or other self-composition optimizations [31] are the standard approach to deal with complex loop constructions. We expect that user-provided coupling invariants and loop properties can avoid having to rely on code transformation methods. Moreover, we expect termination and co-termination [16,34] to be used to extend the modularity of relational contracts.

References

1. Apt, K., de Boer, F., Olderog, E.: Verification of Sequential and Concurrent Programs. Texts in Computer Science, Springer, London (2009). https://doi.org/10.1007/978-1-84882-745-5

2. Barthe, G., Crespo, J.M., Kunz, C.: Relational verification using product programs. In: Butler, M., Schulte, W. (eds.) FM 2011. LNCS, vol. 6664, pp. 200–214. Springer, Heidelberg (2011). https://doi.org/10.1007/978-3-642-21437-0_17

3. Barthe, G., D'Argenio, P.R., Rezk, T.: Secure information flow by self-composition. J. Math. Struct. Comput. Sci. 21(6), 1207–1252 (2011). https://doi.org/10.1017/S0960129511000193

4. Baudin, P., et al.: ACSL: ANSI/ISO C Specification Language (2021). https://frama-c.com/html/acsl.html

5. Beckert, B., Bormer, T., Kirsten, M., Neuber, T., Ulbrich, M.: Automated verification for functional and relational properties of voting rules. In: Proceedings of the 6th International Workshop on Computational Social Choice (COMSOC 2016) (2016)

6. Benton, N.: Simple relational correctness proofs for static analyses and program transformations. In: Proceedings of the 31st ACM SIGPLAN-SIGACT Symposium on of Programming Languages (POPL 2004), pp. 14–25. ACM (2004). https://doi.org/10.1145/964001.964003

7. Beringer, L., Appel, A.W.: Abstraction and subsumption in modular verification of C programs. In: ter Beek, M.H., McIver, A., Oliveira, J.N. (eds.) FM 2019. LNCS, vol. 11800, pp. 573–590. Springer, Cham (2019). https://doi.org/10.1007/978-3-030-30942-8_34

8. Bishop, P.G., Bloomfield, R.E., Cyra, L.: Combining testing and proof to gain high assurance in software: a case study. In: Proceedings of the 24th International Symposium on Software Reliability Engineering (ISSRE 2013), pp. 248–257. IEEE (2013). https://doi.org/10.1109/ISSRE.2013.6698924

9. Blatter, L., Kosmatov, N., Le Gall, P., Prevosto, V.: RPP: automatic proof of relational properties by self-composition. In: Legay, A., Margaria, T. (eds.) TACAS 2017. LNCS, vol. 10205, pp. 391–397. Springer, Heidelberg (2017). https://doi.org/10.1007/978-3-662-54577-5_22

10. Blatter, L., Kosmatov, N., Le Gall, P., Prevosto, V., Petiot, G.: Static and dynamic verification of relational properties on self-composed C code. In: Dubois, C., Wolff, B. (eds.) TAP 2018. LNCS, vol. 10889, pp. 44–62. Springer, Cham (2018). https://doi.org/10.1007/978-3-319-92994-1_3

11. Blazy, S., Maroneze, A., Pichardie, D.: Verified validation of program slicing. In: Proceedings of the 2015 Conference on Certified Programs and Proofs (CPP 2015), pp. 109–117. ACM (2015). https://doi.org/10.1145/2676724.2693169

12. Dufay, G., Felty, A., Matwin, S.: Privacy-sensitive information flow with JML. In: Nieuwenhuis, R. (ed.) CADE 2005. LNCS (LNAI), vol. 3632, pp. 116–130. Springer, Heidelberg (2005). https://doi.org/10.1007/11532231_9

13. Eilers, M., Müller, P., Hitz, S.: Modular product programs. In: Ahmed, A. (ed.) ESOP 2018. LNCS, vol. 10801, pp. 502–529. Springer, Cham (2018). https://doi.org/10.1007/978-3-319-89884-1_18

14. Flanagan, C., Saxe, J.B.: Avoiding exponential explosion: generating compact verification conditions. In: Proceedings of the 28th ACM SIGPLAN Symposium on Principles of Programming Languages (POPL 2001), pp. 193–205. ACM (2001). https://doi.org/10.1145/360204.360220

15. Floyd, R.W.: Assigning meanings to programs. In: Proceedings of Symposia in Applied Mathematics. Mathematical Aspects of Computer Science, vol. 19, pp. 19–32 (1967). https://doi.org/10.1090/psapm/019/0235771

16. Hawblitzel, C., Kawaguchi, M., Lahiri, S.K., Rebêlo, H.: Towards modularly comparing programs using automated theorem provers. In: Bonacina, M.P. (ed.) CADE 2013. LNCS (LNAI), vol. 7898, pp. 282–299. Springer, Heidelberg (2013). https://doi.org/10.1007/978-3-642-38574-2_20

17. Herms, P.: Certification of a tool chain for deductive program verification. Ph.D. thesis, Université Paris Sud - Paris XI, January 2013. https://tel.archives-ouvertes.fr/tel-00789543

18. Hoare, C.A.R.: An axiomatic basis for computer programming. Commun. ACM 12(10), 576–580 (1969). https://doi.org/10.1145/363235.363259

19. Jourdan, J., Laporte, V., Blazy, S., Leroy, X., Pichardie, D.: A formally-verified C static analyzer. In: Proceedings of the 42nd Annual ACM SIGPLAN-SIGACT Symposium on Principles of Programming Languages (POPL 2015), pp. 247–259. ACM (2015). https://doi.org/10.1145/2676726.2676966

20. Jung, R., Krebbers, R., Jourdan, J., Bizjak, A., Birkedal, L., Dreyer, D.: Iris from the ground up: a modular foundation for higher-order concurrent separation logic. J. Funct. Program. 28, e20 (2018). https://doi.org/10.1017/S0956796818000151

21. Kiefer, M., Klebanov, V., Ulbrich, M.: Relational program reasoning using compiler IR. J. Autom. Reason. 60(3), 337–363 (2017). https://doi.org/10.1007/s10817-017-9433-5

22. Kip, I.: Assembly Language for x86 Processors, 7th edn. Prentice Hall Press, Upper Saddle River (2014)

23. Kirchner, F., Kosmatov, N., Prevosto, V., Signoles, J., Yakobowski, B.: Frama-C: a software analysis perspective. Formal Aspects Comput. **27**(3), 573–609 (2015). https://doi.org/10.1007/s00165-014-0326-7
24. Krebbers, R., Leroy, X., Wiedijk, F.: Formal C semantics: CompCert and the C standard. In: Klein, G., Gamboa, R. (eds.) ITP 2014. LNCS, vol. 8558, pp. 543–548. Springer, Cham (2014). https://doi.org/10.1007/978-3-319-08970-6_36
25. Leroy, X., Blazy, S.: Formal verification of a C-like memory model and its uses for verifying program transformations. J. Autom. Reason. **41**(1), 1–31 (2008). https://doi.org/10.1007/s10817-008-9099-0
26. Maillard, K., Hritcu, C., Rivas, E., Van Muylder, A.: The next 700 relational program logics. In: Proceedings of the 47th ACM SIGPLAN Symposium on Principles of Programming Languages (POPL 2020), vol. 4, pp. 4:1–4:33 (2020). https://doi.org/10.1145/3371072
27. Naumann, D.A.: Thirty-seven years of relational Hoare logic: remarks on its principles and history. In: Margaria, T., Steffen, B. (eds.) ISoLA 2020. LNCS, vol. 12477, pp. 93–116. Springer, Cham (2020). https://doi.org/10.1007/978-3-030-61470-6_7
28. Parthasarathy, G., Müller, P., Summers, A.J.: Formally validating a practical verification condition generator. In: Silva, A., Leino, K.R.M. (eds.) CAV 2021. LNCS, vol. 12760, pp. 704–727. Springer, Cham (2021). https://doi.org/10.1007/978-3-030-81688-9_33
29. Pierce, B.C., et al.: Logical Foundations. Software Foundations series, vol. 1, Electronic Textbook (2018). http://www.cis.upenn.edu/~bcpierce/sf
30. Scheben, C., Schmitt, P.H.: Efficient self-composition for weakest precondition calculi. In: Jones, C., Pihlajasaari, P., Sun, J. (eds.) FM 2014. LNCS, vol. 8442, pp. 579–594. Springer, Cham (2014). https://doi.org/10.1007/978-3-319-06410-9_39
31. Shemer, R., Gurfinkel, A., Shoham, S., Vizel, Y.: Property directed self composition. In: Dillig, I., Tasiran, S. (eds.) CAV 2019. LNCS, vol. 11561, pp. 161–179. Springer, Cham (2019). https://doi.org/10.1007/978-3-030-25540-4_9
32. Sousa, M., Dillig, I.: Cartesian hoare logic for verifying k-safety properties. In: Proceedings of the 37th Conference on Programming Language Design and Implementation (PLDI 2016), pp. 57–69. ACM (2016). https://doi.org/10.1145/2908080.2908092
33. The Coq Development Team: The Coq Proof Assistant (2021). https://coq.inria.fr/
34. Unno, H., Terauchi, T., Koskinen, E.: Constraint-based relational verification. In: Silva, A., Leino, K.R.M. (eds.) CAV 2021. LNCS, vol. 12759, pp. 742–766. Springer, Cham (2021). https://doi.org/10.1007/978-3-030-81685-8_35
35. Wils, S., Jacobs, B.: Certifying C program correctness with respect to CompCert with VeriFast. CoRR abs/2110.11034 (2021). https://arxiv.org/abs/2110.11034
36. Winskel, G.: The Formal Semantics of Programming Languages - An Introduction. Foundation of Computing Series, MIT Press, Cambridge (1993)

B Method

Reachability Analysis and Simulation for Hybridised Event-B Models

Yamine Aït-Ameur[1], Sergiy Bogomolov[2], Guillaume Dupont[1],
Neeraj Kumar Singh[1], and Paulius Stankaitis[2(✉)]

[1] INPT–ENSEEIHT, 2 Rue Charles Camichel, Toulouse, France
{yamine,guillaume.dupont,nsingh}@enseeiht.fr
[2] School of Computing, Newcastle University, Newcastle upon Tyne, UK
{sergiy.bogomolov,paulius.stankaitis}@newcastle.ac.uk

Abstract. The development of cyber-physical systems has become one of the biggest challenges in the field of model-based system engineering. The difficulty stems from the complex nature of cyber-physical systems which have deeply intertwined physical processes, computation and networking system aspects. To provide the highest level of assurance, cyber-physical systems should be modelled and reasoned about at a system-level as their safety depends on a correct interaction between different subsystems. In this paper, we present a development framework of cyber-physical systems which is built upon a refinement and proof based modelling language - Event-B and its extension for modelling hybrid systems. To improve the level of automation in the deductive verification of the resulting hybridised Event-B models, the paper describes a novel approach of integrating reachability analysis in the proof process. Furthermore, to provide a more comprehensive cyber-physical system development and simulation-based validation, we describe mechanism for translating Event-B models of cyber-physical systems to Simulink. The process of applying our framework is evaluated by formally modelling and verifying a cyber-physical railway signalling system.

Keywords: Hybrid systems · Formal verification · Event-B ·
Reachability analysis · Simulink

1 Introduction

Cyber-physical systems (CPS) are complex computer-based systems which have closely intertwined physical processes, computation and networking system aspects. Because of their universal application, complexity and often safety-critical nature, one of the grand challenges in the field of model-based system engineering is their development and safety assurance. Firstly, their development and safety assurance difficulties arise from the need to model and reason at a system-level, as CPS safety depends on interactions between the different constituent subsystems [29]. Secondly, CPS generally exhibit discrete and continuous behaviours which are best captured by hybrid automata models that are notably difficult to formally reason about [4].

© Springer Nature Switzerland AG 2022
M. H. ter Beek and R. Monahan (Eds.): IFM 2022, LNCS 13274, pp. 109–128, 2022.
https://doi.org/10.1007/978-3-031-07727-2_7

In this paper, we propose an integrated framework for multifaceted design and analysis of cyber-physical systems. The integrated framework utilises the advantages of the refinement-based system development approach in order to address complexity, productivity and verification scalability challenges in designing cyber-physical systems. The proposed framework also enables modelling parts of the cyber-physical system at different abstraction levels while still making possible to formally reason about the system at a system-level (both challenges raised in [26]). Furthermore, the framework also provides a multifaceted CPS design by supporting simulation-based system analysis and validation.

The framework revolves around Event-B [1] as the pivot formal method, thus benefiting from its built-in *refinement* operation, which allows the designer to provide details step-by-step and in a correct-by-construction way. The Event-B method has been augmented with different continuous aspects to handle hybrid modelling [17], and is associated to formal design patterns to assist in designing CPS [15]. Verification of (hybridised) Event-B models is done by discharging proof obligations (POs) generated by Event-B using automatic or interactive provers. In the case of continuous behaviours, proof is often difficult due to the use of complex continuous structures (e.g. as shown in [5,9]).

To address this issue, the idea of the framework is to combine Event-B's deductive proof system with the use of reachability analysis tools – in our case, the JuliaReach toolbox [10] – to handle proof goals related to continuous aspects, for which the interactive prover is not well adapted. Concretely, such verification goals may be expressed as bounded-time reachability problems, and can be given to reachability tools in order to obtain properties on the given continuous dynamics, and in particular their feasibility/existence of solution. This process is similar to the use of SAT/SMT solvers in the proving process, but aimed at hybrid system verification. In addition, our framework is extended with the capability to encode hybrid models to a simulation tool (e.g., Matlab/Simulink [35]) in order to validate its specification, or to fine-tune its parameters. This is similar to how ProB [32] is used in discrete Event-B developments, with the limitation that ProB is unable to handle continuous dynamics.

The paper evaluates the integrated framework by formally modelling and proving safety of a cyber-physical railway signalling system. The system is made of trains, a hybrid system, which must stay within the issued safe travelling distance (model based on our previous work [41]). The other communicating subsystems are responsible for issuing safe travelling distances and managing railway infrastructure. Firstly, the evaluation demonstrates the effectiveness of the refinement-based framework in decomposing a complex cyber-physical system, thus reducing modelling and verification effort. Secondly, the evaluation demonstrates the benefits of integrating reachability analysis in automating proof-based verification of hybridised Event-B models.

Structure of this Article. Section 2 discusses the state-of-the-art in cyber physical system verification and validation. In Sect. 3, we describe the integrated framework we are proposing, including, an overall architecture and process. Section 4 provides preliminary information about the Event-B method and its extensions for capturing hybrid systems features. The preliminaries section also briefly describes reachability analysis and the JuliaReach tool as well as introduces the Simulink/Stateflow toolbox. In Sect. 5, we overview the cyber-physical railway signalling system we use to evaluate the proposed methodology while in Sect. 6 we describe its formal modelling and verification. Section 7 concludes the article, and describes future work.

2   The State-Of-The-Art in CPS V&V

In this section we discuss approaches which have integrated proof and state-exploration based verification and validation methods for cyber-physical and hybrid systems.

In [33], the authors proposed a method for mapping the informally defined execution semantics of hybrid Simulink model into formally defined semantics of differential dynamic logic (dL). This approach supports verification of hybrid Simulink models using the interactive theorem prover KeYMaera X, developed by Andre Platzer and his group, which supports dL [37]. This approach lacks a built-in refinement operation to model hybrid systems progressively. Moreover, there is no mechanism for simulating the hybrid system modelled using differential dynamic logic.

R. Banach proposed Hybrid Event-B [6] modelling and analysing hybrid systems. The core concepts are based on Event-B language supporting both continuous and discrete variables together for encoding differential equations. Several operators, such as *Solve*, *Comply*, machine interfaces and compositions, clock datatype, are introduced to handle differential equation. But, this approach is not tool supported. Formalizing hybrid systems with Event-B has been studied in [43]. The authors used Matlab to complement the Event-B modelling language by simulating examples with a set of correct and incorrect parameters. They model the discrete part of hybrid system in Event-B and they rely on Matlab Simulink for the continuous part. The differential equations are not explicitly formalised in the Event-B model and time progresses with fixed discrete jumps.

Lee et al. [31] proposed a hybrid system modelling framework, HyVisual, for modelling discrete and continuous aspects using graphical blocks based on Ptolemy II. The operational semantics of HyVisual is described in [30]. The key property of this framework is to support superdense time, signals are modelled as partial functions and continuous-time functions are defined as total function. In addition, this framework support animation as well as simulation to show evolution behaviour of hybrid systems. This approach is better for *a posteriori* model verification rather than design and development, as systems cannot be developed in a modular nor progressive way.

Vienna Development Method (VDM) [25] is a state-based formal method supporting model refinement via data reification and operation decomposition. It has been extended with the notion of time [44] and integrated into the cyberphysical system development framework based on the model exchange and cosimulation [28]. The primary goal of this work is simulation, but there is a lack of proof support as well as reachability analysis for the studied hybrid systems. Other well-known state and proof based formal modelling languages TLA+ [27] and Z [18] have been extended with real-time and hybrid modelling concepts.

Zou et al. [46] proposed an approach for verifying Simulink models by encoding them into hybrid CSP (HCSP)[24,45]. The formal verification of the HCSP model is supported by the Hybrid Hoare Logic (HHL) [34] prover based on Isabelle/HOL. This work is primarily concerned with the verification of Simulink models. There is no support for reachability analysis and there is no progressive modelling using refinement.

In [23], Isabelle/HOL theorem prover was used to address formal verification of ODE solvers. This work results in a formalisation of the mathematics required to reason about ODE properties and their resolution at the appropriate abstraction level. This enables the formalisation and verification of an ODE solver based on Runge-Kutta methods, and the computation of flow derivatives and Poincaré maps. The resulting proofs and certified algorithms are embedded in the HOL-ODE-Numerics tool. In [39], the authors proposed a framework to express homogeneous linear differential equation in the higher order theorem prover HOL4. They used several case studies to assess the proposed framework. In this framework, there is no support for simulation or animation to validate the modelled hybrid systems.

All the above discussed approaches face various challenges, such as a lack of formal design strategies based on abstraction or refinement for dealing with various aspects of hybrid systems, reachability analysis, and simulation analyses. Nonetheless, the main contribution of these studies and research is to address specific problems of hybrid systems, such as handling continuous and discrete behaviour, simulation and others. To our knowledge there is no unified framework that integrates formal modelling, refinement, reachability analysis, and simulation all together. Our work is the first integrated framework for modelling and designing cyber-physical systems using refinements, as well as performing proofs, reachability analysis and simulation.

3   Framework for CPS Design and Analysis

As we discussed in the previous section, several successful modelling, analysis, verification and validation approaches have been proposed. Each of them showed its efficiency in handling specific requirements for a design of safe cyber physical systems (e.g. formal modelling, reachability analysis, simulation, etc.). By integrating these techniques one would offer a unified framework supporting the design of cyber physical systems. In this paper, we propose a cyber physical system design and analysis framework which integrates three relevant modelling and verification techniques (framework is visualised in Fig. 1).

First, Event-B [1], in its hybridised version [15,17], supported by the Rodin platform [2] is set up to formalise a cyber physical system as a hybrid automaton. Refinement is used to decompose a high level specification into a detailed hybrid automata to be implemented (Fig. 1-(A)). Discharging the proof obligations associated to the intermediate models and to the refinement guarantees the

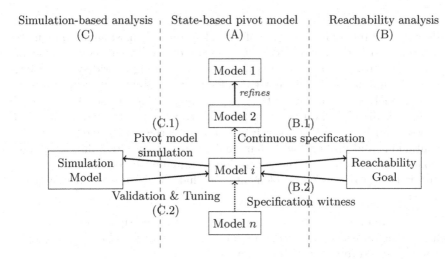

Fig. 1. The overview of the proposed design and analysis framework

correctness of these models. This refinement chain of Event-B models behaves as a pivot model and steers the development.

Throughout the development of the pivot Event-B model external analysis techniques may be invoked on the intermediate models in order to verify or validate specific model properties. These techniques would be selected with respect to their domain of efficiency. In addition to the external provers and model checkers invoked in the Rodin tool, hybrid system modelling requires two other fundamental analyses which are integrated in our framework:

- *Reachability analysis (Fig. 1-(B))* specifically applied for the hybrid automaton of the pivot model. In our case, it consists in guaranteeing that each continuous behaviour (continuous transition) reaches an end-state (represented by the feasibility proof obligation CFIS in hybridised Event-B presented in Sect. 4.1). While formal methods state this problem clearly in the discrete case, it is more complex in the continuous case. Indeed, a continuous behaviour is specified by a differential equation, and thus it is important to guarantee that there exists a solution of this equation fulfilling the system specification constraints. Reachability analysis tools are invoked for this purpose (Fig. 1-(B.1)) and in our framework the JuliaReach [10] toolbox is used. It is in charge of producing a family of solutions, if they exist, to the submitted differential equation and its constraints. These solutions are returned back to the pivot model (Fig. 1-(B.2)) as possible witnesses for the existentially quantified event parameters formalising possible solutions of the submitted differential equations manipulated in the pivot model.
- *Simulation-based analysis (Fig. 1-(C))* is used for simulating as well as validating the developed pivot model by performing simulation with a range of possible values for discrete and continuous states. The discrete and continuous components of the pivot model are transformed into the selected simulation

tool (i.e., Simulink [35]). Via simulation results analysis, we can validate the discrete and dynamic behaviour of hybrid systems. This simulation emulates the required behaviour based on the results of the formal models, allowing them to be used effectively to evaluate the developing hybrid system. Moreover, the simulation results may aid in identifying potential flaws in the developed model as well as tuning the range of input values for state variables. If an error is discovered during simulation, we can modify the pivot model. This process can be applied iteratively to obtain a correct pivot model satisfying continuous and discrete behaviour. In our case, we use Simulink for simulation analysis. Note that the generation of Simulink models is cost effective and it leads to a system implementation that can be used to deploy a real system.

In the remainder of this paper, we give a brief description of each of the techniques integrated to our framework and show how it is deployed on a complex case study issued from the railway domain.

4   Preliminaries

4.1   Event-B and Hybridised Event-B

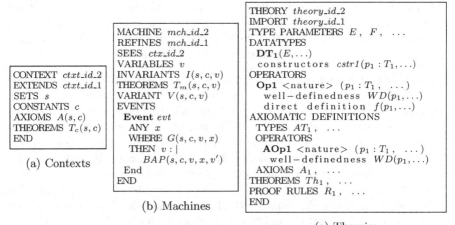

Listing 1.1. Event-B model structure

Event-B is a correct-by-construction formal method for system design [1]. An Event-B model consists of a *context* (Listing 1.1(a)) for the static part of the system, and *machines* (Listing 1.1(b)) for the dynamic part.

Formally, a system is modelled by *variables* representing its state, together with a set of *guarded events* describing their evolution, under the form of a predicate linking the previous and the new value of the variable, called *Before-After Predicate* (BAP). *Invariants* may be defined, i.e. predicates on the state that must be true at all time. Any system is associated to *proof obligations*, that must be discharged in order to ensure the system is correct, abides by its invariants, etc.

Event-B makes available the *refinement* operation, that allows to add details to a system step-by-step while ensuring it remains sound. This operation is the base of the correct-by-construction approach: starting with an abstract machine, close to specification, and introducing specific features at each refinement step.

Event-B's expression language is based on set theory and first order logic, making it very expressive, but lacking in higher-level structures. To overcome this, the theory extension has been proposed [11]. This extension enables the definition *theory components* (Listing 1.1(c)), and provides reusable and type-generic custom datatypes, operators (with expression or predicate nature), axioms, theorems and proof rules.

Hybridised Event-B. A methodology has been proposed to model hybrid systems in Event-B [16,17], inspired by Hybrid Event-B [6]. The idea is to embed continuous features (reals, differential equations) into Event-B using theories, and use that to model continuous behaviours, side by side with discrete behaviours.

Discrete and Continuous Variables. Discrete variables in Event-B models are associated with instantaneous, point-wise assignment, in the form of a Before-After Predicate (BAP). Continuous variables, on the other hand, represent a continuous behaviour on a time interval. For this reason, continuous variables are modelled using *functions of time*, and they are updated using the introduced *continuous before-after predicate* (CBAP) operator:

$$x_p :|_{t \to t'} \mathcal{P}(x_p, x_p') \And H \equiv [0, t[\lhd x_p' = [0, t[\lhd x_p \qquad (PP)$$
$$\land \mathcal{P}([0, t] \lhd x_p, [t, t'] \lhd x_p') \qquad (PR)$$
$$\land \forall t^* \in [t, t'], x_p(t^*) \in H \qquad (LI)$$

This operator modifies continuous variable x_p by appending a piece of function on interval $[t, t']$ while retaining its value on $[0, t]$, thereby preserving its "past" (past preservation, *PP*). The added piece is described using predicate $\mathcal{P}$ *PR*), and must remain in the given evolution domain or local invariant H (*LI*).

Modelling Hybrid Systems in Event-B. The base of the framework is the *generic pattern*, which generically encodes controller-plant loop hybrid systems. A particular hybrid system is designed by refining this generic pattern and providing specific details for each parameters (using witnesses).

```
MACHINE Generic
VARIABLES t, x_s, x_p
INVARIANTS
  inv_1 :  t ∈ ℝ⁺
  inv_2 :  x_s ∈ STATES
  inv_3 :  x_p ∈ ℝ ⇸ S
  inv_4 :  [0, t] ⊆ dom(x_p)
```

Listing 1.2. Generic pattern header

The generic pattern defines two variables (Listing 1.2): one for discrete/controller state (x_s) and one for continuous/plant state (x_p), which is a function of time, valued in state space S, usually a vector space (e.g. $\mathbb{R}^n, m \in \mathbb{N}$). It also define a read-only real variable for time (t), used for modelling and proving.

```
Sense
ANY  s ,  p
WHERE
  grd₁:   s ∈ ℙ1(STATES)
  grd₂:
          p ∈ ℙ(STATES × ℝ × S)
  grd₃:  (xs ↦ t ↦ xp(t)) ∈ p
THEN
  act₁:   xs :∈ s
END
```

(a) Sense event

```
Actuate
ANY  P ,  s ,  H ,  t′
WHERE
  grd₀:   t′ > t
  grd₁:   P ⊆ (ℝ⁺ ⇸ S) × (ℝ⁺ ⇸ S)
  grd₂:   Feasible([t, t′], xp, P, H)
  grd₃:   s ⊆ STATES ∧ xs ∈ s
  grd₄:   H ⊆ S ∧ xp(t) ∈ H
THEN
  act₁:   xp :|t→t′ P(xp, x′p) & H
END
```

(b) Actuate event

Listing 1.3. Generic pattern events

In addition, the model provides two types of events: discrete (controller) and continuous (plant). Sense (Listing 1.3a) is a discrete event, that models a change in the controller induced by the reading of a value from the plant. Actuate (Listing 1.3b) is a continuous event, that models the plant's behaviour, according to the controller, and using the CBAP operator previously defined.

These events are defined with *parameters* (ANY clause) that are instantiated using witnesses during refinement.

Proving Process. When using the generic pattern, POs are generated, ensuring its correct use. In particular, continuous events are associated to specific POs, relate to the use of the CBAP operator:

$$\Gamma \vdash \exists t' \cdot t' \in \mathbb{R}^+ \wedge t' > t \wedge \textbf{Feasible}([t, t'], x_p, \mathcal{P}, \mathcal{H}_{saf}) \tag{CFIS}$$

$$\Gamma, \mathcal{I}([0, t] \lhd x_p), CBAP(t, t', x_p, x'_p, \mathcal{P}, \mathcal{H}) \vdash \mathcal{I}([t, t'] \lhd x'_p) \tag{CINV}$$

Feasibility (CFIS) ensures that the continuous behaviour described in the CBAP operator is sound. This requires to prove that there exists a time t' for which the predicate $\mathcal{P}$ is feasible, i.e. there exists an x'_p defined on $[t, t']$ such that $\mathcal{P}(x_p, x'_p)$ holds.

Continuous invariant preservation (CINV) is a specialisation of invariant preservation; it ensures that, if x_p satisfies the invariant on $[0, t]$, then it also satisfies it on $[t, t']$.

4.2   Reachability Analysis and JuliaReach

Reachability analysis is a technique for computing all reachable states of dynamical systems starting from some initial states. The reachable set of states $\mathcal{R}_t$ at time t can be defined as a set containing all system's trajectories starting from some initial set, or formally:

$$\mathcal{R}_t(\mathcal{X}_0) = \{\varsigma(t, x_0, u) \mid x_0 \in \mathcal{X}_0, u(s) \in \mathcal{U}, \forall s \in [0, t]\} \tag{1}$$

where initial states $\mathcal{X}_0 \subseteq \mathbb{R}^n$, system's inputs $\mathcal{U} \subseteq \mathbb{R}^m$ and $\varsigma(t, x_0, u)$ is a unique solution of the dynamical system. More generally reachability analysis methods aim to construct a *conservative* flowpipe (2) which encompasses all possible reachable sets of a dynamical system for time period $[0, T]$.

$$\mathcal{R}_{[0,T]}(\mathcal{X}_0) = \bigcup_{t \in [0,T]} \mathcal{R}_t(\mathcal{X}_0) \tag{2}$$

Computing reachable states of a hybrid automaton requires computing *runs* of the hybrid system where a hybrid automaton run is an alternating N size sequence of trajectories and location jumps (see Section 5.2 in [3]). The reachability methods have been widely used in applications which range from a formal system verification to their synthesis [3]. Over the years, several reachability tools have been developed, for example, SpaceEx [19], Checkmate [13] or Flow* [12] just to name a few. Furthermore, to efficiently and accurately over-approximate reachable sets different convex and nonconvex set representations have been developed.

The JuliaReach toolbox [10] is a set of Julia[1] programming language [8] libraries developed for an efficient prototyping of set-based reachability algorithms. A particular advantage of JuliaReach is its Julia language implementation providing high-performance computation with an adequate compilation time [20]. The Reachability package of the toolbox contains algorithms for performing reachability analysis of continuous and hybrid systems, while LazySets library contains algorithms for operation with convex sets. Crucially for this work, JuliaReach supports nonconvex set representations (e.g. Taylor models) which are required for a more conservative approximation of nonlinear systems.

4.3 Simulink and Stateflow

Simulink [35] is a Matlab add-on product that provides a graphical environment for modelling, simulating, and analyzing complex dynamic systems. It is capable of modelling both linear and nonlinear systems in both continuous and sample time. It provides a graphical user interface (GUI) for designing complex models in the form of block diagrams. Simulink contains a comprehensive list of pre-defined libraries for dealing with various modelling constructs such as sinks, sources, linear and nonlinear components, and connectors. It also supports domain-specific toolboxes like neural networks, signal processing, HDL, and so on. All these blocks cooperate by data flow through connecting wires. A defined simulink model can be simulated using various parameters, which can also be

---

[1] Julia programming language website - https://julialang.org/.

updated on the fly. During the simulation run, the main results can be analyzed using scope and other display blocks.

Stateflow [36] is an interactive tool for simulating the behavior of reactive systems. The syntax of Stateflow is similar to Statecharts [21]. It also supports hierarchy (states can contain other states), concurrency (executes more than one state at the same time), and communication (broadcast mechanism for communicating between concurrent components). It also has more complex features such as inter level transitions, complex transitions through junctions, and event broadcasting. A Stateflow model is made up of a set of states linked together by arcs called transitions. A state can be decomposed into two types: 1) OR-states and 2) AND-states. Different types of actions can be carried out in a state in a sequential order. These actions are *entry, exit, during,* and *on event_name.* A transition is defined by a label, which can include event triggers, conditions, condition actions, and transition actions. A general format for a transition label can be represented as *event [condition] condition_action/transition_action* [40].

In our work, we use Stateflow to model discrete controller behaviour and Simulink blocks to model the plant model of a hybrid system.

5   Case Study: Railway Signalling System

In this section, we semi-formally describe a generalised cyber-physical railway signalling system which will be formally developed by using the proposed framework. The signalling system is comprised of trains, communication centres, interlocking boxes and field elements. The former are continuously communicated a safe distance they are allowed to travel, also known as the end of a movement authority (EoA). The speed controller of the train must ensure that at all times the train remains within the movement authority. The other sub-systems of the signalling system must ensure that the communicated EoA guarantees a safe train separation and prevents train derailment by passing over unlocked/moving railway track switches.

In the following sections, we first describe the hybrid rolling stock model which will be used to model train speed controller. Then, we briefly describe remaining railway signalling sub-systems, more specifically, their functionality and communication relation to other sub-systems.

5.1   Continuous Rolling Stock Model

A driver or an automated train operation system can only control a train engine power (tractive force) which eventually yields an acceleration. From Newton's second law we know that acceleration is proportional to a net force (tractive engines force) applied to the mass of that object. The train must also overcome a resistance force, which acts in the opposite direction to engines traction force and thus a total engines tractive force can be expressed as the difference between two forces. The total rolling stock resistance is comprised of the mechanical and air resistances, and commonly expressed as a second-order polynomial (Davis

Resistance equation $R_{tot.}(t)$ in Eq. 3), where A, B, C are fixed parameters and $v(t)$ is the speed of a train at time t [38].

$$\begin{cases} \dot{tv}(t) = f - (A + B \cdot tv(t) + C \cdot tv(t)^2) \\ \dot{tp}(t) = tv(t) \end{cases} \tag{3}$$

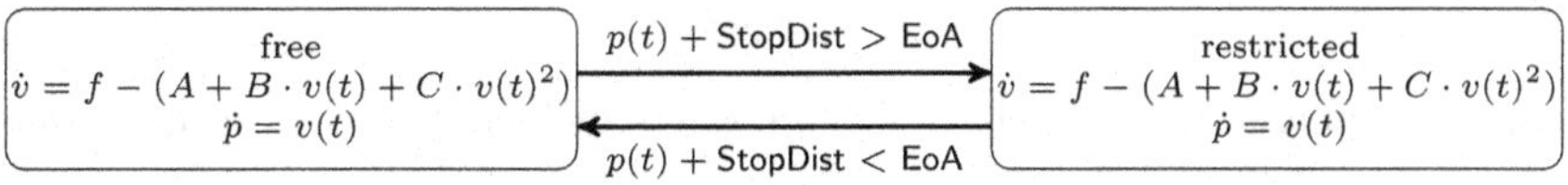

Fig. 2. Hybrid automaton model of rolling stock speed controller

The train speed controller we consider is continuously issued with the end of movement authority (EoA) which is updated discretely in the time by the communication centre. We assume that the speed controller is able to sense its distance to EoA and, in particular, determine if with a given current speed and acceleration it can stop before EoA. The stopping distance calculus is generally done by a complex algorithm on the on-board computer, whereas in our train model, we abstract the algorithm by a stopping distance function (*StopDist*) which takes the current acceleration and speed as parameters, and returns the distance needed by the train to stop, together with necessary assumptions, provided as axioms.

The train speed controller has two modes: free and restricted. If the stopping distance of the train is shorter than the EoA, then the train is said to be in a free mode and it can choose arbitrary values for f. Once the stopping distance of the train becomes shorter than the EoA, the train enters a restricted mode in which it is required to provide values for f such that it can stop before the EoA. The train speed controller hybrid automata model is visualised in Fig. 2.

5.2 Communication-Based Railway Signalling Model

We base our railway signalling model on the radio-based communication and in-cab signalling systems, which generally contain three sets of objects: trains, interlocking boxes and communication centres. On the infrastructure side, our railway model is made of railway tracks, which contain points that allow trains to switch tracks and block markers for marking a spatial beginning and ending of railway sections ($P1$ and $M_{1..3}$ in Fig. 3).

The objective of the railway signalling model is ensuring a safe spatial separation of trains and preventing train derailment by guaranteeing that only locked switches are crossed by train. Our signalling model is based on a moving-block signalling principle in which trains are issued the EoA up to the rear of the next train (e.g. $T3$ in Fig. 3) or up to next block marker which protects trains from moving over unlocked or incorrectly set points ($T2$ in Fig. 3). The system must also ensure that only a single train enters a *marked* junction section (area between $M_{1..3}$ in Fig. 3).

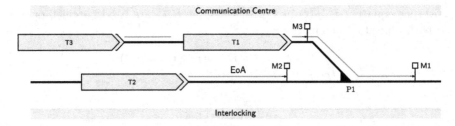

Fig. 3. An example of the cyber-physical railway signalling system with three trains

The communication centre is the one sub-system which issues rolling stock with EoA based on the information received from trains (e.g. position) and interlocking boxes (e.g. point locking and direction status). A centre contains and continuously updates an internal railway network map with junction locations (also their status: free or locked) and rolling stock positions.

6   Case Study: Formal Development

This section overviews the process of applying formal development methodology to the railway signalling case study. In the following sections, we first describe the modelling and verification of the pivotal railway signalling system Event-B model, and then, discuss simulation of the train speed controller model.

6.1   Event-B Model Development and Verification

Modelling the railway signalling system starts by formally defining static information. Common properties of the train are gathered in the Train domain Event-B theory. This theory defines the coefficient a, b and c for a traction force of f, with initial condition $p(t_0) = p_0$ and $v(t_0) = v_0$. This equation corresponds to Eq. 3.

In addition to the train's dynamics, model-specific information are gathered in the TrainCtx Event-B context defining several constants of the system, as well as constraints on them. In particular, particular Davis coefficients (a, b, c), are given as well as some bounds on the train's traction power (f_{min}, f_{max}), plus a special value for the minimum traction power for deceleration (f_{dec_min}).

Furthermore, in this context we define the train stopping distance function StopDist as a function of the current speed and acceleration with associated function constraining axioms. Finally, we introduce train controller modes free_move and restricted_move by refining the STATES set with an enumerated set.

The model of the dynamic part of the railway signalling system, refines the generic hybridised Event-B model. Two refinement steps are defined. The first one models the speed controller where the end of the movement authority is regularly updated. At this refinement level, it is left abstract and under specified. We import theories defined in Train domain theory and static information

MACHINE TrainMach REFINES Generic
VARIABLES t, tp, tv, ta, f, EoA
INVARIANTS
$\ldots$

inv$_4$: $f_{min} \leq f \wedge f \leq f_{max}$
saf$_1$: $\forall t^* \cdot t^* \in [0, t] \Rightarrow tp(t^*) \leq$ EoA
saf$_2$: $\forall t^* \cdot t^* \in [0, t] \Rightarrow tv(t^*) \geq 0$

Listing 1.4. Train model header

from TrainCtx context model. Furthermore, we introduce several new events by instantiating generic events to capture the hybrid automata depicted in Fig. 2. Listing 1.4 presents the train model header featuring 5 variables in addition to time. The train itself is modelled using its position, speed and acceleration (tp, tv and ta respectively), as well as its traction power (f). Additionally, the end of authority is modelled by a real variable, EoA. Each variable is associated to a number of constraints (e.g. inv$_4$ in Listing 1.4), plus a gluing invariant that links the concrete and abstract continuous states. The safety and dynamics requirements, which were described in Sect. 5.1, were expressed as two invariants saf$_1$ and saf$_2$.

The Transition_restricted_move (see Listing 1.5) event models the change in the speed controller by adjusting trains traction effort when the train is in the restricted move mode. The event is guarded by a single predicate which enables the event if and only if the status variable x_s is set to restricted_move. To control train's speed we introduce Variable f denoting the traction force. It is modified by the action such that the stopping distance would not overshoot the end of the movement authority. Then, one must prove an open proof obligation that such traction force value can be found.

Transition_restricted_move
REFINES Transition
WHERE
    grd$_1$: $x_s =$ restricted_move
WITH
    s : $s = \{$restricted_move$\}$
THEN
    act$_1$: $f :|\ tp(t) +$ StopDist$(f' \mapsto tv(t)) \leq$ EoA
END

Listing 1.5. Example of Transition event: calculating traction power f in restricted mode

The Actuate_move event (see Listing 1.6) is the main continuous event of the model. It models the dynamics of the train, using the CBAP operator (see Sect. 4.1) together with the Davis equation defined in the Train theory. The proposed evolution domain ensures that 1) the train remains before the end of authority, and 2) the train's speed remains positive, in accordance with the system's safety invariants.

Actuate_move REFINES Actuate
ANY t'
WHERE
    grd_1 : $tp(t) + \mathsf{StopDist}(ta(t), tv(t)) \leq \mathsf{EoA}$
    grd_2 : $t < t'$
WITH ...
THEN
    act_1 : $ta, tv, tp :\sim_{t \to t'} \langle \dot{tv} = \dot{ta} = f - (a + btv + ctv^2), \dot{tp} = tv \rangle$
        $\&\ tp + \mathsf{StopDist}(ta, tv) \leq \mathsf{EoA} \wedge tv \geq 0$
END

Listing 1.6. Event updating train's plant (actuation)

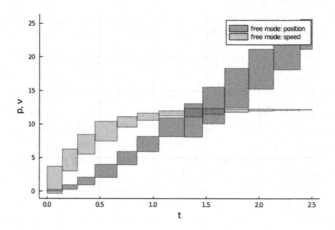

Fig. 4. Reachability analysis of the train speed controller in the free mode

To prove safety properties of the hybrid train speed controller, we rely on the verification technique (B.1). Firstly, we strengthen local invariants of the actuation event (see Listing 1.6) which in turn allows to automatically prove invariant preservation of invariants $saf_{1,2}$. The resulting $CBAP$ feasibility proof obligations requiring proof of solution existence, are translated to JuliaReach. Reachability analysis results of both modes are shown in Fig. 4. Table 1 (Speed Controller refinement step) provides statistics issued from proving speed controller model. In total, 55 proof obligations were generated at this refinement level and with reachability analysis additional 12 proofs were *automated* (8 feasibility and 4 invariant preservation proof obligations).

The second refinement step extends TrainMach machine by introducing other signalling sub-systems: interlocking, communication centres and field elements and their communication protocol. At this step, we are interested in proving safety of the cyber-physical railway signalling system, more specifically, proving that the issued EoA ensures safe rolling stock separation and prevents derailment. Based on Event-B communication modelling patterns [42] new events and variables are introduced to model message channels and capture message exchanges between different sub-systems.

The model was proved correct by discharging all the proof obligations. Corresponding proofs statistics are summarised in Table 1. As proof obligations were mostly related to discrete behaviour, the available automated theorem proving tools (e.g. [14,22]) were able to discharge the majority of them automatically. Observe that the already proven proof obligations of the first refinement model are preserved thanks to the introduced gluing invariant linking first and second refinement models.

Table 1. Proof statistics of the cyber physical railway signalling Event-B model (PO Type: WD - well-definedness, GRD - guard strengthening, INV - invariant preservation, FIS - feasibility and SIM - simulation [1]). The number in the brackets indicates the number of proof obligations when reachability analysis was used to discharge feasibility vproof obligations.

Refinement	PO Type	|POs|	Auto.	Inter.	Refinement	|POs|	Auto.	Inter.
Speed		55	36 (8)	19 (7)	**Comms.**	85	71	14
Controller	WD	12	12	0	**Model**	31	31	0
Model	GRD	11	11	0		12	7	5
	INV	18	10 (14)	8 (4)		42	33	9
	FIS	8	0 (8)	8 (0)		0	0	0
	SIM	6	3	3		0	0	0

6.2   Train Model Simulation and Validation

We describe the Simulink/Stateflow model translated from the train's hybridised Event-B model. Discrete and continuous parts of the train model are generated in form of Stateflow block and a user defined matlab function block, respectively. The Stateflow model contains two modes: *restricted* and *free*. These modes can be switched between based on various parameters such as end of authority (EoA), stopping distance (SD), engine power (f), position (p) and speed (v). Several Matlab functions are defined within the Stateflow model to calculate EoA, engine power and SD. For calculating SD, we use the Eq. 4, where U is the speed of the train when the break command was issued; a is the acceleration provided by the braking system; b is the acceleration provided by gravity; and t_d is the train's brake delay time [7].

$$SD = -(U + b * t_d)^2/2(a + b) - U * t_d - b * t_d^2/2 \qquad (4)$$

In each state, we use the *entry* and *during* actions to update the concrete variables. Similarly to Event-B models, the *restricted* mode is chosen as an initial state in the Stateflow model. The dynamic part of the train model is represented by a user defined matlab block in which we encoded the Davis equation 3 to calculate the train's acceleration, speed and position. The output of this Simulink block are connected as input to the Stateflow model. We use two scopes to display the train's position and speed. A step block is connected to the Stateflow model as input to define the power engine (f).

The train simulation results show the evolution of the train position and speed in Fig. 5. For this simulation, we use the standard coefficients for the Davis equation collected from [38], to simulate the dynamic behaviour of TGV. Moreover, we use a range of values for different parameters to analyse the dynamic behaviour of the train system. We simulate the train model using other standard passenger train coefficients to test scalability and coverage of other classes of trains. The train simulation results ensures the correctness of train dynamic behaviour as well as animation allows to validate the abstract functions of the hybrid train model.

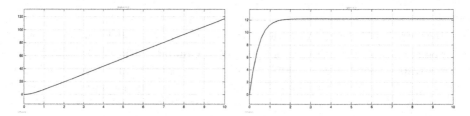

Fig. 5. TGV train simulation (engine power $f_{max} = 50$, Davis equation coefficients for TGV: $a = 25$, $b = 1.188$ and $c = 0.0703728$, moving authority (MA) $= 10$, time delay $t_d = 2$ s.

7   Conclusions and Future Work

In this paper, we presented a refinement-based development methodology of cyber-physical systems. The evaluation has shown that by integrating reachability analysis and system simulation techniques into the hybrid Event-B framework, the methodology provides a rigorous and comprehensive formal system development approach. Furthermore, the multifaceted methodology also addresses a major problem of proof automation of hybridised Event-B models by integrating automatic reachability analysis into the proof process.

In future work, we foremost would like to facilitate an automatic and certified translation of Event-B models to Simulink and JuliaReach. But crucially, in the future work, we would like to further explore synergies between proof and reachability analysis in automating deductive system verification and code generation.

Acknowledgements. This work was partially supported by the Air Force Office of Scientific Research under award no. FA2386-17-1-4065. Any opinions, findings, and conclusions or recommendations expressed in this material are those of the authors and do not necessarily reflect the views of the United States Air Force. This work is also supported by the DISCONT project of the French National Research Agency (ANR-17-CE25-0005, The DISCONT Project, https://discont.loria.fr).

References

1. Abrial, J.R.: Modeling in Event-B: System and Software Engineering. Cambridge University Press, New York (2013)
2. Abrial, J.R., Butler, M., Hallerstede, S., Hoang, T.S., Mehta, F., Voisin, L.: Rodin: an open toolset for modelling and reasoning in Event-B. Int. J. Softw. Tools Technol. Transf. **12**(6), 447–466 (2010)
3. Althoff, M., Frehse, G., Girard, A.: Set propagation techniques for reachability analysis. Ann. Rev. Control Robot. Autonom. Syst. **4**(1), 369–395 (2021). https://doi.org/10.1146/annurev-control-071420-081941
4. Alur, R.: Formal verification of hybrid systems. In: Proceedings of the Ninth ACM International Conference on Embedded Software, pp. 273–278. EMSOFT 2011, ACM, New York, NY, USA (2011). https://doi.org/10.1145/2038642.2038685
5. Babin, G., Aït-Ameur, Y., Nakajima, S., Pantel, M.: Refinement and proof based development of systems characterized by continuous functions. In: Li, X., Liu, Z., Yi, W. (eds.) Dependable Software Engineering: Theories, Tools, and Applications, pp. 55–70. Springer International Publishing, Cham (2015)
6. Banach, R., Butler, M., Qin, S., Verma, N., Zhu, H.: Core hybrid event-b I: single hybrid event-b machines. Sci. Comput. Program. **105**, 92–123 (2015)
7. Barney, D., Haley, D., Nikandros, G.: Calculating train braking distance. In: Proceedings of the Sixth Australian Workshop on Safety Critical Systems and Software - Volume 3, pp. 23–29. SCS 2001, Australian Computer Society Inc., AUS (2001)
8. Bezanson, J., Edelman, A., Karpinski, S., Shah, V.B.: Julia: a fresh approach to numerical computing. SIAM Rev. **59**(1), 65–98 (2017). https://doi.org/10.1137/141000671
9. Bogdiukiewicz, C., et al.: Formal development of policing functions for intelligent systems. In: 2017 IEEE 28th International Symposium on Software Reliability Engineering (ISSRE), pp. 194–204 (2017). https://doi.org/10.1109/ISSRE.2017.40
10. Bogomolov, S., Forets, M., Frehse, G., Potomkin, K., Schilling, C.: JuliaReach: a toolbox for set-based reachability. In: Proceedings of the 22nd ACM International Conference on Hybrid Systems: Computation and Control, pp. 39–44. HSCC 2019, Association for Computing Machinery, New York, NY, USA (2019). https://doi.org/10.1145/3302504.3311804
11. Butler, M., Maamria, I.: Practical theory extension in Event-B. In: Liu, Z., Woodcock, J., Zhu, H. (eds.) Theories of Programming and Formal Methods. LNCS, vol. 8051, pp. 67–81. Springer, Heidelberg (2013). https://doi.org/10.1007/978-3-642-39698-4_5
12. Chen, X., Ábrahám, E., Sankaranarayanan, S.: Flow*: an analyzer for non-linear hybrid systems. In: Sharygina, N., Veith, H. (eds.) CAV 2013. LNCS, vol. 8044, pp. 258–263. Springer, Heidelberg (2013). https://doi.org/10.1007/978-3-642-39799-8_18

13. Chutinan, A., Krogh, B.H.: Verification of polyhedral-invariant hybrid automata using polygonal flow pipe approximations. In: Vaandrager, F.W., van Schuppen, J.H. (eds.) HSCC 1999. LNCS, vol. 1569, pp. 76–90. Springer, Heidelberg (1999). https://doi.org/10.1007/3-540-48983-5_10

14. Déharbe, D., Fontaine, P., Guyot, Y., Voisin, L.: Integrating SMT solvers in Rodin. Sci. Comput. Program. **94**(P2), 130–143 (2014)

15. Dupont, G., Aït-Ameur, Y., Pantel, M., Singh, N.K.: An Event-B based generic framework for hybrid systems formal modelling. In: Dongol, B., Troubitsyna, E. (eds.) IFM 2020. LNCS, vol. 12546, pp. 82–102. Springer, Cham (2020). https://doi.org/10.1007/978-3-030-63461-2_5

16. Dupont, G., Aït-Ameur, Y., Pantel, M., Singh, N.K.: Proof-based approach to hybrid systems development: dynamic logic and Event-B. In: Butler, M., Raschke, A., Hoang, T.S., Reichl, K. (eds.) ABZ 2018. LNCS, vol. 10817, pp. 155–170. Springer, Cham (2018). https://doi.org/10.1007/978-3-319-91271-4_11

17. Dupont, G., Ait-Ameur, Y., Singh, N.K., Pantel, M.: Event-B hybridation: A proof and refinement-based framework for modelling hybrid systems. ACM Trans. Embed. Comput. Syst. **20**(4), 1–37 (2021). https://doi.org/10.1145/3448270

18. Fidge, C.J.: Specification and verification of real-time behaviour using Z and RTL. In: Vytopil, J. (ed.) FTRTFT 1992. LNCS, vol. 571, pp. 393–409. Springer, Heidelberg (1992). https://doi.org/10.1007/3-540-55092-5_22

19. Frehse, G., et al.: SpaceEx: scalable verification of hybrid systems. In: Gopalakrishnan, G., Qadeer, S. (eds.) CAV 2011. LNCS, vol. 6806, pp. 379–395. Springer, Heidelberg (2011). https://doi.org/10.1007/978-3-642-22110-1_30

20. Geretti, L., et al.: ARCH-COMP20 category report: continuous and hybrid systems with nonlinear dynamics. In: Frehse, G., Althoff, M. (eds.) ARCH 2020. 7th International Workshop on Applied Verification of Continuous and Hybrid Systems (ARCH20). EPiC Series in Computing, vol. 74, pp. 49–75. EasyChair (2020). https://doi.org/10.29007/zkf6

21. Harel, D.: Statecharts: a visual formalism for complex systems. Sci. Comput. Program. **8**(3), 231–274 (1987). https://doi.org/10.1016/0167-6423(87)90035-9

22. Iliasov, A., Stankaitis, P., Adjepon-Yamoah, D., Romanovsky, A.: Rodin platform why3 plug-in. In: Butler, M., Schewe, K.-D., Mashkoor, A., Biro, M. (eds.) ABZ 2016. LNCS, vol. 9675, pp. 275–281. Springer, Cham (2016). https://doi.org/10.1007/978-3-319-33600-8_21

23. Immler, F.: Verified reachability analysis of continuous systems. In: Baier, C., Tinelli, C. (eds.) TACAS 2015. LNCS, vol. 9035, pp. 37–51. Springer, Heidelberg (2015). https://doi.org/10.1007/978-3-662-46681-0_3

24. Jifeng, H.: A classical mind. chap. In: From CSP to Hybrid Systems, pp. 171–189. Prentice Hall International (UK) Ltd. (1994)

25. Jones, C.B.: Systematic Software Development Using VDM, 2nd edn. Prentice-Hall Inc., USA (1990)

26. Kim, K.D., Kumar, P.R.: Cyber-physical systems: a perspective at the centennial. In: Proceedings of the IEEE 100 (Special Centennial Issue), pp. 1287–1308, May 2012. https://doi.org/10.1109/JPROC.2012.2189792

27. Lamport, L.: Hybrid systems in TLA$^+$. In: Grossman, R.L., Nerode, A., Ravn, A.P., Rischel, H. (eds.) HS 1991-1992. LNCS, vol. 736, pp. 77–102. Springer, Heidelberg (1993). https://doi.org/10.1007/3-540-57318-6_25

28. Larsen, P.G., et al.: Integrated tool chain for model-based design of cyber-physical systems: the INTO-CPS project. In: 2016 2nd International Workshop on Modelling, Analysis, and Control of Complex CPS (CPS Data), pp. 1–6 (2016). https://doi.org/10.1109/CPSData.2016.7496424

29. Lee, E.A.: Cyber physical systems: design challenges. In: 2008 11th IEEE International Symposium on Object Oriented Real-Time Distributed Computing (ISORC), pp. 363–369. IEEE (2008)
30. Lee, E.A., Zheng, H.: Operational semantics of hybrid systems. In: Hybrid Systems: Computation and Control, 8th International Workshop, HSCC 2005, Zurich, Switzerland, March 9–11, 2005, Proceedings, pp. 25–53 (2005). https://doi.org/10.1007/978-3-540-31954-2_2
31. Lee, E.A., Zheng, H.: HyVisual: a hybrid system modeling framework based on Ptolemy II. IFAC Proc. Vol. **39**(5), 270–271 (2006). https://doi.org/10.3182/20060607-3-IT-3902.00050
32. Leuschel, M., Butler, M.: ProB: a model checker for B. In: Araki, K., Gnesi, S., Mandrioli, D. (eds.) FME 2003. LNCS, vol. 2805, pp. 855–874. Springer, Heidelberg (2003). https://doi.org/10.1007/978-3-540-45236-2_46
33. Liebrenz, T., Herber, P., Glesner, S.: Deductive Verification of Hybrid Control Systems Modeled in Simulink with KeYmaera X. In: Sun, J., Sun, M. (eds.) ICFEM 2018. LNCS, vol. 11232, pp. 89–105. Springer, Cham (2018). https://doi.org/10.1007/978-3-030-02450-5_6
34. Liu, J., et al.: A calculus for hybrid CSP. In: Ueda, K. (ed.) APLAS 2010. LNCS, vol. 6461, pp. 1–15. Springer, Heidelberg (2010). https://doi.org/10.1007/978-3-642-17164-2_1
35. MathWorks, T.: Simulink user's guide (2021)
36. MathWorks, T.: Stateflow user's guide (2021)
37. Platzer, A., Quesel, J.-D.: KeYmaera: a hybrid theorem prover for hybrid systems (system description). In: Armando, A., Baumgartner, P., Dowek, G. (eds.) IJCAR 2008. LNCS (LNAI), vol. 5195, pp. 171–178. Springer, Heidelberg (2008). https://doi.org/10.1007/978-3-540-71070-7_15
38. Rochard, B.P., Schmid, F.: A review of methods to measure and calculate train resistances. Proc. Inst. Mech. Eng. Part F J. Rail Rapid Transit. **214**(4), 185–199 (2000). https://doi.org/10.1243/0954409001531306
39. Sanwal, M.U., Hasan, O.: Formally analyzing continuous aspects of cyber-physical systems modeled by homogeneous linear differential equations. In: Berger, C., Mousavi, M.R. (eds.) CyPhy 2015. LNCS, vol. 9361, pp. 132–146. Springer, Cham (2015). https://doi.org/10.1007/978-3-319-25141-7_10
40. Singh, N.K., Lawford, M., Maibaum, T.S.E., Wassyng, A.: Stateflow to tabular expressions. In: Proceedings of the Sixth International Symposium on Information and Communication Technology, pp. 312–319. SoICT 2015, Association for Computing Machinery, New York, NY, USA (2015). https://doi.org/10.1145/2833258.2833285
41. Stankaitis, P., Dupont, G., Singh, N.K., Ait-Ameur, Y., Iliasov, A., Romanovsky, A.: Modelling hybrid train speed controller using proof and refinement. In: 2019 24th International Conference on Engineering of Complex Computer Systems (ICECCS), pp. 107–113 (2019). https://doi.org/10.1109/ICECCS.2019.00019
42. Stankaitis, P., Iliasov, A., Ameur, Y.A., Kobayashi, T., Ishikawa, F., Romanovsky, A.: A refinement based method for developing distributed protocols. In: IEEE 19th International Symposium on High Assurance Systems Engineering (HASE), pp. 90–97 (2019)
43. Su, W., Abrial, J.-R.: Aircraft landing gear system: approaches with event-b to the modeling of an industrial system. In: Boniol, F., Wiels, V., Ait Ameur, Y., Schewe, K.-D. (eds.) ABZ 2014. CCIS, vol. 433, pp. 19–35. Springer, Cham (2014). https://doi.org/10.1007/978-3-319-07512-9_2

44. Verhoef, M., Larsen, P.G., Hooman, J.: Modeling and validating distributed embedded real-time systems with VDM++. In: Misra, J., Nipkow, T., Sekerinski, E. (eds.) FM 2006. LNCS, vol. 4085, pp. 147–162. Springer, Heidelberg (2006). https://doi.org/10.1007/11813040_11
45. Chaochen, Z., Ji, W., Ravn, A.P.: A formal description of hybrid systems. In: Alur, R., Henzinger, T.A., Sontag, E.D. (eds.) HS 1995. LNCS, vol. 1066, pp. 511–530. Springer, Heidelberg (1996). https://doi.org/10.1007/BFb0020972
46. Zou, L., Zhan, N., Wang, S., Fränzle, M.: Formal verification of Simulink/Stateflow diagrams. In: Automated Technology for Verification and Analysis - 13th International Symposium, ATVA 2015, Shanghai, China, 12–15 October 2015, Proceedings, pp. 464–481 (2015). https://doi.org/10.1007/978-3-319-24953-7_33

Operation Caching and State Compression for Model Checking of High-Level Models
How to Have Your Cake and Eat It

Michael Leuschel[(✉)]

Institut für Informatik, Universität Düsseldorf, Universitätsstr. 1,
40225 Düsseldorf, Germany
michael.leuschel@hhu.de

Abstract. A lot of techniques try to improve the performance of explicit state model checking. Some techniques, like partial order reduction, are hard to apply effectively to high-level models, while others, like symmetry reduction, rarely apply to more complex real-life models. In this paper we present two techniques—state compression and operation caching—that are applicable to a wide range of models. These techniques were implemented in the ProB model checker and are available for B, Event-B, TLA+, Z and CSP∥B models. The combination of both techniques is surprisingly effective, reducing both memory consumption and runtimes on a set of benchmark programs. The techniques were inspired by the success of previous work integrating LTSMin and ProB. Earlier attempts of integrating the LTSMin techniques directly into ProB (to overcome limitations of the LTSMin integration) were not successful. Similarly, earlier attempts of making the LTSMin integration available to a wider range of models (e.g., combined CSP∥B models) were also not fruitful.

1 Introduction

PROB [22] is a constraint solver and model checker for high-level formal specifications. It supports B [1] and Event-B [2], but also related high-level formalisms such as TLA+ and Z. It can also be used for CSP∥B specifications [27].

In this article we focus on explicit state model checking [13], where individual states are explicitly constructed and individually checked and processed. Compared to model checkers for low-level specifications languages like Spin [12], the overhead for dealing with individual states in PROB is much higher due to the high-level nature of the models. On the other hand, (sometimes) the state space of a high-level model can be relatively small compared to that of an equivalent lower level model (cf. [21]). Via its mixed search strategy, PROB can also be beneficial for finding errors in very large or even infinite state spaces. Furthermore, model checking is often used as a debugging tool and not a verification tool in B: exhaustive verification in B can be performed via proof which scales to infinite state spaces (provided the right invariants are found).

Still, for many practical applications state explosion is a problem and improved model checking performance would be highly beneficial. Hence, over

© Springer Nature Switzerland AG 2022
M. H. ter Beek and R. Monahan (Eds.): IFM 2022, LNCS 13274, pp. 129–145, 2022.
https://doi.org/10.1007/978-3-031-07727-2_8

the years quite a few attempts have been made to improve the model checking performance of PROB, ranging from symmetry reduction to partial order reduction. We have also developed two alternate model checking backends based on TLC and LTSMin.

There are not that many model checkers for high-level languages, but TLC [29] is one of them. In [10] we developed a translation from B to TLA+ to be able to use TLC. TLC only has limited constraint solving capabilities, but is very efficient for those specifications that do not require constraint solving. In other work [4,18] we have made use of the generic LTSMin [16] model checking engine, whose C language interface we used to link it up with the PROB interpreter.

The integration with LTSMin can lead to a dramatic reduction in the model checking time, especially for specifications which consist of operations which only inspect and modify a small part of the variables. LTSMin, however, also has a few practical limitations: it does not use proof information [5], it is not suited for CSP‖B models (and attempts to solve this limitation have not been fruitful thus far), LTSMin is hard to install for end-users and the generated state space is not available for other PROB features (e.g., state space projection or coverage). For some models with larger individual states, the performance drops sharply.

The idea of this paper is to implement the most important aspects of LTSMin directly in PROB, thereby addressing all of the above limitations. Indeed, we believe that one of the most important improvements in [18] came from operation caching. In [18] we already mentioned first attempts at replicating the caching in PROB itself. But at that time, the experiments were discouraging. In this article we return to this issue, and show that with an improved implementation, we have managed to port the operation caching algorithm to Prolog and PROB. The breakthrough came via combining operation caching with state compression, and ensuring that the implementation performs compression and hashing of states incrementally. For several real-life industrial models, the new algorithm provides an order of magnitude improvement, both compared to PROB alone and the LTSMin integration. For some examples from [18] we do not attain the full performance of LTSMin yet, but our technique still considerably improves the performance, while providing many additional features not available with LTSMin (such as state space inspection and visualization).

2   Current State of Model Checking for B

2.1   Prolog Default Model Checker

The existing PROB default model checking backend stores the state space in memory as Prolog facts. These facts are indexed by the hash of the stored state. This allows to quickly determine whether a state already exists in the state space. The hash value is computed using a combination of two SICStus Prolog hash functions. With this combination, collisions are very rare.[1]

---

[1] Collisions, however, do not lead to unsoundness, as full states need to be compared for a successful lookup.

The Prolog database enables some quite unique features of PROB: model checking can be stopped and resumed at any point, and the state space can be inspected at any point. For example, one can obtain coverage information about the variables or transitions. In particular, it can be useful to obtain the minimal and maximal values of the variables. This can help the user understand why a state space becomes surprisingly large.[2] It is also useful to know which operations/events have not yet been covered; sometimes obtaining this coverage information is an essential verification aspect, to ensure that every transition in a formal model is feasible. For test-case generation it can be useful to instruct the model checker to stop when full coverage has been reached. Other useful debugging tools are projection diagrams [20], which project the state space onto a user-provided formula.

The operational semantics to compute the state space for all specification languages is specified in Prolog; Prolog being a convenient language for specifying denotational and operational semantics. As such, PROB provides the only "native" support for combined CSP and B specifications. (All other approaches like csp2b work by compiling a subset of one formalism to the other.)

The LTL model checker is written in C, but accesses the Prolog state space (and drives its construction on the fly). There is also a Prolog LTL model checker for safety properties and a Prolog CTL model checker. LTL and CTL checking can be performed interactively after the state space has been computed. PROB can also perform proof-directed model checking [5]: the model checker uses the Rodin proof information and the read-write matrix to avoid checking invariants that are guaranteed to be preserved by executed events or operations.

2.2 TLC Backend

TLC [29] is an efficient explicit state model checker for TLA+. It can be used as a backend [10] for PROB, by translating a subset of B to TLA+, and translating TLC's counter examples back to B.

When applicable, TLC can provide a very effective model checking backend, in particular for lower-level models. Here is a short summary of the key differences with PROB's default model checker:

- TLC can store states on disk and can be effectively parallelized,
- hash collisions are unlikely but possible and are not detected (then resulting in incomplete checking of the state space),
- B models may have to be rewritten for TLC (so that no constraint solving is required and identifiers are finitely enumerated in the right order),
- there is no support for Event-B and many classical B constructs are not supported (machine inclusion, operation calls, sequential composition, refinement, ...),
- counter example traces are replayed by PROB, but there is no access to the full state space.

---

[2] For example, for the drone model from [25] which we use later in the experiments, this feature was essential to detect an unbounded queue variable, and then put an upper bound on that queue for model checking.

2.3 LTSMin Backend

LTSMin [16] is another efficient model checker, which can target multiple languages via its Partitioned Next-State Interface (PINS). PROB can be integrated with LTSMin via this interface for symbolic model checking [4] and explicit state model checking [18]. The latter is more useful in practice, as it can generate counter-example traces. Compared to PROB's default model checker this backend

- provides a fast model checking engine implemented in C with partial order support and an optimisation called "local transition caching" [7], similar to our operation caching developed in this paper,[3]
- cannot currently check invariants and deadlocks at the same time,
- works with most languages supported by PROB, but the operation caching is not working for CSP∥B models,
- has no proof-directed support [5], particularly important for Rodin models,
- has no Windows support, and generates occasional segmentation faults,
- its support activity in general has been reduced (the latest release 3.0.2 dates from July 2018),
- models do not have to be rewritten for LTSMin (as the PROB interpreter is used),
- counter example traces are replayed by PROB, but there is no access to the full state space.

The main speedup of LTSMin seems to come from operation caching; partial order reduction is seldom of use and most of the time even detrimental. In this paper we try and integrate the operation caching technique into the PROB model checker directly. Our hope is to gain its performance benefits, while keeping the advantages of PROB's model checker and make it available to more specification languages like CSP∥B. Before providing a formal account of operation caching in Sect. 4, we first present a few other optimisations which will later turn out to be important in practice.

3 Compression and Other Improvements

3.1 Timeouts

PROB uses timeouts when evaluating invariants or computing the effect of an operation. This means that, even when part of the model is too complex to animate, a user can still inspect the other parts of the model.

The timeout mechanism, however, also induces a runtime overhead. This overhead is more noticeable for lower-level models with many events (a timer is started for every distinct event/operation of the model). We later realised that part of the speedups reported in [4,18] were due to the fact that the LTSMin backend did not use this time-out mechanism. It is now possible to disable timeouts using the `-disable-time-out` flag of probcli.

---

[3] Note, however, that local transition caching is not formally described in [7,16].

3.2   Reducing Stored Transitions

Some B models have a large number of events and thus also often a large number of transitions. Often, many transitions lead to an already explored state in the state space. In some settings, e.g., when performing invariant checking, these transitions are not relevant and just consume memory. To address this issue we have added a new model checking flag: when setting the preference SAFETY_MODEL_CHECK to true PROB will only store one incoming transition per state, so that a counter example can still be generated.

3.3   State Compression

A state of a B machine can consist of a mixture of variables and constants. PROB stores constants separately from variables: a stored state contains a reference to a constant valuation together with the variable values. When constants are large, PROB is then more (memory) efficient than TLC. Typically the LTSMin backend also slows down in that setting, because constants are also re-transferred between PROB and LTSMin.

Generally, PROB has a dedicated module to pack and unpack states for storage. It uses specialized Prolog functors to compress common data structures. Furthermore, B strings are encoded as Prolog atoms and as such the string content is stored only once.

An important data structure in B is the set. Here, PROB's solver uses balanced AVL-trees, enabling an efficient implementation of a variety of relation and function operators. For storage, however, these trees are not optimal. First, they have to be normalised (to ensure that a set representation is canonical). Second, they take up more memory and PROB thus provides a variety of alternate encodings when storing a set. By default, AVL-trees are flattened into a list before storing. Furthermore, when PROB's COMPRESSION preference is true the following techniques are also applied:

- sets of enumerated values are represented using a bit-vector encoding, i.e., as a Prolog integer,
- similarly finite total functions mapping to BOOL are represented as bit-vectors for storage,
- finally sets of values can be stored in a separate table, allowing reuse of the set value between multiple states and multiple variables (of the same type).

As we will see later in Sect. 5, this compression reduces memory consumption. On some models this may lead to a reduction in runtime (due to reduced swapping and more efficient state hashing), but the overhead of compression can also lead to slowdown. However, in the context of operation caching described in the next section, compression reduces both memory and runtime.

4 Operation Caching

In this section we suppose some familiarity with the B method. We will use the classical B machine in Listing 1.1 as running example. The model uses the ASCII notation, where <: stands for $\subseteq$. The exposition below is not specific to classical B and is also applicable to Event-B or TLA+, suitably replacing the name "operation" by "event" or "action" respectively.

A *state* s of a B machine consists of values for all its variables and constants. Formally, we view a state as a total function mapping identifiers to values. The initial state of Listing 1.1 is thus $\{books \mapsto \varnothing, cust \mapsto \varnothing, onloan \mapsto \varnothing\}$. Basic values in B are integers, booleans, strings and user-defined values. Sets, pairs and records make up complex values in B and can be arbitrarily nested.

An *update* is simply a partial function mapping identifiers to values. We denote applying an update δ to a state s by $s\delta$.[4]

```
1   MACHINE LibrarySimple
2   SETS
3     BOOKS={b1,b2}; CUSTOMERS = {c1}
4   VARIABLES books, cust, onloan
5   INVARIANT
6     books <: BOOKS &
7     cust <: CUSTOMERS &
8     onloan : books +-> cust
9   INITIALISATION books,cust,onloan := {},{},{}
10  OPERATIONS
11    AddBook(b) = SELECT b /: books THEN books := books \/ {b} END;
12    AddCust(c) = SELECT c /: cust THEN cust := cust \/ {c} END;
13    DelBook(b) = SELECT b:books & b /: dom(onloan) THEN books := books \ {b}
            END;
14    BorrowBook(c,b) = SELECT b:books & c:cust & b /: dom(onloan) THEN
15        onloan(b) := c
16    END;
17    ReturnBook(b) = SELECT b : dom(onloan) THEN onloan := {b} <<| onloan END
18  END
```

Listing 1.1. Running Library Example (<: stands for $\subseteq$, : stands for $\in$, /: for $\notin$, \/ for $\cup$, & for $\wedge$, +-> for partial function, and <<| for domain subtraction)

We denote the fact that an operation op with parameters α is *enabled* in a state s by $op(\alpha) \in en(s)$. If the execution of such an enabled operation in s can lead to a new state s' we write: $s \xrightarrow{op(\alpha)} s'$. As B operations can be non-deterministic $\xrightarrow{op(\alpha)}$ is a relation.

Example 1. For Listing 1.1 we have $s_0 \xrightarrow{AddBook(b1)} s_1$, where s_0 is the initial state of the machine (cf. above) and $s_1 = \{books \mapsto \{b1\}, cust \mapsto \varnothing, onloan \mapsto \varnothing\}$. We also have that $s_1 = s_0\delta$ for the update $\delta = \{books \mapsto \{b1\}\}$.

Below we need to reason about the identifiers read and variables written by an operation. Formally, $reads(Op)$ is the set of variables or constants read in the entire operation Op, $reads_{grd}(Op)$ is the set of variables or constants read

---

[4] This corresponds almost to B override operator, except that variables can have different types.

in the guard and $writes(Op)$ is the set of variables (potentially) written by the operation Op. Note that $reads_{grd}(Op) \subseteq reads(Op)$.

We define the domain restriction operator $\lhd$ as applied to states: $D \lhd s = \{x \mapsto V \mid x \in D \land x \mapsto V \in s\}$.

Example 2. In Listing 1.1 we have $reads(AddBook) = reads_{grd}(AddBook) = writes(AddBook) = \{books\}$. We have that $writes(AddBook) \lhd s_1 = \{books \mapsto \{b1\}\}$.

We now establish a few important properties about the read-write informations of operations. The first lemma allows us to draw conclusions about enabledness of operations:

Lemma 1. *Let x be a variable or constant and V a possible value for x. If $x \notin reads_{grd}(o)$ then $o(\alpha) \in en(s) \Leftrightarrow o(\alpha) \in en(s\{x \mapsto V\})$.*

Next we examine the effect of variables which are not read on the entire execution of an operation.[5]

Lemma 2. *Let x be a variable or constant and V a possible value for x. Let o be an operation such that $x \notin reads(o)$.*
If $x \notin writes(o)$ then

$$s \xrightarrow{op(\alpha)} s' \Leftrightarrow s\{x \mapsto V\} \xrightarrow{op(\alpha)} s'\{x \mapsto V\}.$$

If $x \in writes(o)$ then

$$s \xrightarrow{op(\alpha)} s' \Leftrightarrow s\{x \mapsto V\} \xrightarrow{op(\alpha)} s'.$$

Note that some operations only conditionally write a variable x, in which case x is also considered to be read! Take for example an operation o with body IF cust={} THEN books := {b1} END. Here it is vital that $books \in reads(o)$; otherwise part 2 of Lemma 2 would not hold for $x = books$. The fact that $books \in reads(o)$ is more obvious if we rewrite the operation into the equivalent: IF cust={} THEN books := {b1} ELSE books := books END.

The next result can be proven by repeated application of the above Lemma 2. It allows us to capture the effect of an operation on one state via its updates Δ and apply them safely to other states:

Lemma 3. *Let $x_1, \ldots, x_k$ be variables or constants with $x_i \notin reads(o)$. Let $\delta = \{x_1 \mapsto V_1, \ldots, x_k \mapsto V_k\}$ be an update. We define $\Delta(s', o) = writes(o) \lhd s'$ for which the following holds:*

$$s \xrightarrow{op(\alpha)} s' \Leftrightarrow s\delta \xrightarrow{op(\alpha)} (s\delta)\Delta(s', o).$$

---

[5] This lemma could actually also serve as a semantic definition of $reads(Op)$ and $writes(Op)$.

Example 3. In Example 1 we had $s_0 \xrightarrow{AddBook(b1)} s_1$. We have $\Delta(s_1, AddBook)$ = $\{books \mapsto \{b1\}\}$. Take $s_2 = \{books \mapsto \varnothing, cust \mapsto \{c1\}, onloan \mapsto \varnothing\}$. For $\delta = \{cust \mapsto \{c1\}\}$ we have $s_2 = s_0\delta$. Hence we can apply Lemma 3 to determine without computation that $s_2 \xrightarrow{AddBook(b1)} s_2\Delta(s_1, AddBook) = \{books \mapsto \{b1\}, cust \mapsto \{c1\}, onloan \mapsto \varnothing\}$. These two transitions are illustrated in Fig. 1.

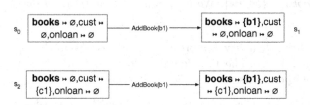

Fig. 1. Two transitions for AddBook from Listing 1.1

Lemma 3 is the foundation of our operation caching algorithm. The idea is to store updates $\Delta(s', o)$ and then safely apply them to any new state $s\delta$ where the read variables have not changed. So, instead of recomputing the effect of o, we simply re-apply the cached updates.

This idea is presented in Algorithm 1; it shows how to compute the effect of cached operations. Operations which read all variables (such as BorrowBook in Listing 1.1) are not cached. The cached updates are stored for each cached operation in a table $Cache_{op}$. This table can also be viewed as a projected state space, showing only the transitions involving op and only showing the variables in $reads(op)$. This is illustrated in Fig. 2; every $Cache_{op}$ is a projection of the full state space. The two transitions of the full state space shown in Fig. 1 can be reconstructed from a single AddBook transition in Fig. 2.

Algorithm 1 also contains a further improvement, by examining $reads_{grd}(op)$ to avoid computing operations which are guaranteed to be disabled by Lemma 1. This improvement is only applied if $reads_{grd}(op) \subset reads(op)$.

Below is a short summary of the transitions stored in $Cache_{op}$ as compared to the full state space with 14 states. (BorrowBook is not projected as it requires all variables.) Even for this very small example there is a reduction in the amount of work. For AddBook regular model checking computes the operation 14 times resulting in 10 transitions. With operation caching we only compute the operation AddBook 4 times resulting in 4 transitions.

Operation	Full	Projected		
	Transitions	Transitions	States	Variables
AddBook	10	4	4	1
AddCust	4	1	2	1
DelBook	10	6	9	2
ReturnBook	6	4	4	1

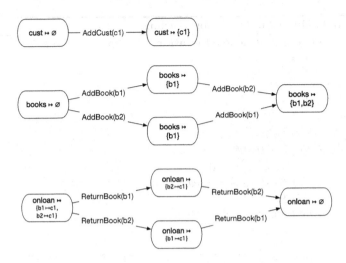

Fig. 2. Projected state space ($Cache_{op}$) for three cached operations of Listing 1.1

In the next section we examine whether this theoretical advantage "on paper" also materializes in practice. As mentioned in the introduction, this was not the case for earlier implementations of this algorithm. Indeed, Algorithm 1 does not address some of the practical issues that were relevant for performance.

To determine $s_{proj} \in dom(Cache_{op})$, the implementation hashes the value of s_{proj} and first checks whether the hash is new. If not, only then the full values in s_{proj} are compared.[6] The same is true for the check $\neg Fails_{op}(s_{grd})$.

Now comes an interesting interplay with state compression: if compression is enabled, the new implementation computes the hash not on the original values but on the compressed values, which are typically much smaller. Furthermore, for performance it is essential to perform compression and hashing incrementally, e.g., reusing compressed values from predecessor states and sharing compressed values between cached operations. Finally, the treatment of constants is also important to avoid re-compressing and re-hashing them at every step.

5 Experiments

One of our goals was to achieve the improvements of the LTSMin backend in [18] purely within ProB's model checker. We have hence chosen benchmarks from the previous articles [4,18] of the LTSMin backend. We have also added a few benchmarks from the evaluation [10] of the TLC backend. We have only included benchmarks with runtimes of at least a second (for the default model checker). We have also added a few new benchmarks from recent applications of ProB (a CSP‖B Interlocking, an ABZ'2020 automotive model, a GPU scheduler from Meeduse, a drone model using UML-B and a railway demonstrator from

---

[6] I.e., hash collisions reduce performance but do not affect correctness.

Algorithm 1. Outline of Operation Caching.

1: **procedure ComputeCachedOperation**(operation op, state s)
2:     $s_{proj} \leftarrow reads(op) \lhd s$
3:     **if** $s_{proj} \in dom(Cache_{op})$ **then**
4:         **for** $(\alpha, \delta) \in Cache_{op}(s_{proj})$ **do**
5:             **yield** $(\alpha, state\delta)$
6:     **else**
7:         $s_{grd} \leftarrow reads_{grd}(op) \lhd s$
8:         **if** $\neg Fails_{op}(s_{grd})$ **then**
9:             **for** s' s.t. $s \xrightarrow{op(\alpha)} s'$ **do**
10:                 $Cache_{op}(s_{proj}) \leftarrow Cache_{op}(s_{proj}) \cup \{(\alpha, \Delta(op, s'))\}$
11:                 **yield** (α, s')
12:             **if** no transition yielded **then**
13:                 $Fails_{op}(s_{grd}) \leftarrow true$

4SecuRail). For the latter two we have added scope predicates to restrict the state space (so that the benchmarks run in reasonable time).

All benchmark models and a script to execute the experiments below can be found in an artefact available at https://doi.org/10.5281/zenodo.6416981. Table 1 contains the list of benchmark models with some statistics. In order, we have a railway interlocking CSP‖B model [15], a Volvo cruise controller B model used in [4,10], a GSM model from [6] used in [10], an ABZ'20 case study model [24], GPU scheduler Meeduse model [14], a model of insertion sort adapted from [26],[7] two artificial benchmarks with large constants (used to benchmark PROB and uncover performance bottlenecks of operation caching), a drone model [25] generated from scxml via UML-B to Event-B, Abrial's interlocking model [2] for smaller topology with hand-coded partial-order reduction, a railway model of a demonstrator developed by 4SecuRail [3], a ABZ landing gear case study (used in [4]), a library information system model [9] (used in [10]) rether protocol and Simpson four slot models used in [18], a Nokia nota model used in [4], a CAN Bus model by Colley (used in [4,10,18]).

The tests were run using PROB 1.12.0-beta1 (b0e6595a09) on macOS 12.3.1 on a MacBook Pro (13" 2019, 2.8 GHz Quad-Core Intel Core i7).[8] All times are the total walltime (i.e., time including garbage collection and time spent in non-Prolog code). PROB's runtimes are the average of three runs.

The experiments were conducted using the command-line version probcli using the -bench-csv flag to write statistics to a CSV file. All experiments in the tables were conducting invariant checking using the -p SAFETY_MODEL_CHECK

---

[7] The figures in Table 7 of [26] are wrong, however. Insertion sort is quadratic and the reported timings are almost constant.

[8] This version is also available as a separate artefact https://doi.org/10.5281/zenodo.6415347.

Table 1. Overview of the benchmark models (†: scope predicate provided to restrict state space)

Model	Kind	Operations	Vars + Csts	Invariants	States	Transitions
interlocking [15]	CSP‖B	10	31	10	341	739
Cruise	B	26	15	25	1361	26149
GSM [6]	B	6	14	15	1850	53594
Pitman [24]	B	31	20	17	2096	16472
gpuScheduler [14]	B	31	8	7	3180	26054
sort100 [26]	B	4	6	6	5052	5052
incremental1	B	3	5	2	9002	44993
incremental2	B	3	5	2	9002	44993
drone0 [25]	Event-B	15	21	4	† 21862	† 32394
Train1Lukas [2]	B	8	11	14	24637	55370
SecuRail	B	171	87	75	† 9566	† 28452
Ref5Switch [4]	Event-B	38	30	30	29861	184845
Library33 [9]	B	10	5	3	35544	372716
rether	Event-B	8	8	3	42254	381074
Simpson4Slot	B	9	13	10	46658	112754
nota	B	11	16	13	80719	1864373
CanBus	B	21	19	8	132600	340266

`TRUE` flag and `-disable-time-out` option (see Sect. 3.1). The experiments were run with various combinations of the following flags:

- compression "no" : default compression settings of PROB, corresponds to `-p COMPRESSION FALSE`
- compression "yes" : turns state compression on using `-p COMPRESSION TRUE`
- Caching "no" : default settings of PROB with no operation caching, corresponds to `-p OPERATION_REUSE FALSE`
- Caching "yes" : PROB with operation caching and guard-failure checking, corresponds to `-p OPERATION_REUSE full`
- Caching "partial" : PROB with operation caching but no guard-failure checking, corresponds to `-p OPERATION_REUSE TRUE`

Memory Consumption. Table 2 shows the memory consumption for five settings. As we can, turning compression on leads for some models to a considerable reduction of 13% on average and up to 81% for an artificial benchmark, and 46% reduction for the landing gear case study. Turning operation caching on increases the memory consumption by 10% on average and up to 85% for Abrial's interlocking. However, using compression and caching together leads to an overall *reduction* in memory usage, even though there are still some examples where memory usage increases (up to 32% for Abrial's interlocking). There are no significant difference between partial and full caching.

Runtimes. Table 3 contains the walltimes for the experiments in Table 2. (Note: the times do not include the time to startup PROB nor load the models.) We see

Table 2. Relative memory consumption of PROB model checking compared to no compression and no caching (smaller is better)

Compression	No		Yes	No	Yes	Yes
Caching	No		No	Yes	Yes	Partial
Model						
Interlocking	184.92 MB	1	0.92	1.01	0.93	0.93
Cruise	169.12 MB	1	1.00	1.00	1.00	1.00
GSM	170.43 MB	1	0.99	1.02	1.01	1.01
Pitman	170.80 MB	1	1.00	1.03	1.02	1.02
gpuScheduler	174.33 MB	1	0.99	1.14	1.08	1.08
sort100	203.12 MB	1	0.84	1.01	0.85	0.85
incremental1	174.06 MB	1	1.00	1.01	1.00	1.01
incremental2	894.11 MB	1	0.19	1.00	0.20	0.20
drone0	199.04 MB	1	0.97	1.02	0.98	0.98
Train1Lukas	209.14 MB	1	0.92	1.85	1.32	1.28
SecuRail	197.59 MB	1	0.99	1.01	1.00	1.00
Ref5Switch	392.16 MB	1	0.54	1.01	0.54	0.54
Library33	223.15 MB	1	0.92	1.50	1.11	1.12
Rether	213.39 MB	1	0.96	1.05	0.99	1.00
Simpson4Slot	231.27 MB	1	0.90	1.01	0.91	0.91
Nota	352.57 MB	1	0.78	1.00	0.78	0.78
CanBus	329.87 MB	1	0.93	1.01	0.93	0.93
Average	264.06 MB	1	0.87	1.10	0.92	0.92
Geometric Mean		1	0.83	1.08	0.87	0.87

that turning compression on reduces model checking time slightly (4% on average). Caching reduces the model checking time significantly (by 52% on average, e.g. 90% for drone), and using caching with compression together reduces it further (by 56% on average and up to 90% for landing gear and drone). Using only partial compression is slightly worse on average, but beneficial for some models.

In summary, these Tables 2 and 3 show that we can have our cake and eat it: compression on its own increases runtime, caching on its own increases memory, adding compression to caching leads to even better runtime while resulting in an overall reduction in memory consumption.

Comparison with TLC and LTSMin. Table 4 contains a comparison of walltimes of the TLC and LTSMin backends as compared to PROB with operation caching and compression (Table 3).

Unfortunately, TLC cannot be applied to Event-B or CSP‖B models, nor to the SecuRail example because of the use of sequential composition. Also some rewrites of the models (e.g., CanBus) were necessary to be able to use TLC; these rewrites were not necessary for PROB or LTSMin. But when the TLC backend is applicable it is often still faster than PROB. It is slower when the size of the constants is considerable (incremental1 and 2 benchmarks), as TLC does not separate constants from variables. TLC also slows down when there is

Table 3. Relative walltimes of PROB model checking compared to no compression and no caching (smaller is better)

Compression	No		Yes	No	Yes	Yes	Yes
Caching	No		No	Yes	Partial	Yes	Yes
Model							Speedup
Interlocking	0.86 s	1	1.03	0.79	0.77	0.77	1.29
Cruise	0.80 s	1	1.01	0.44	0.39	0.40	2.47
GSM	1.37 s	1	1.07	0.37	0.35	0.36	2.77
Pitman	2.00 s	1	0.99	0.45	0.45	0.44	2.26
GpuScheduler	3.31 s	1	1.04	0.93	0.93	0.92	1.09
Sort100	0.64 s	1	1.04	1.11	0.91	0.94	1.06
Incremental1	573.00 s	1	1.05	0.00	0.00	0.00	906.64
Incremental2	573.74 s	1	1.04	0.02	0.00	0.00	347.23
drone0	24.46 s	1	1.00	0.10	0.10	0.10	10.00
Train1Lukas	29.64 s	1	1.00	0.42	0.40	0.40	2.49
SecuRail	10.28 s	1	1.05	0.73	0.58	0.64	1.57
Ref5Switch	56.85 s	1	1.07	0.19	0.10	0.10	9.80
Library33	43.93 s	1	1.02	0.74	0.74	0.74	1.36
Rether	19.18 s	1	1.03	0.25	0.24	0.24	4.08
Simpson4Slot	5.73 s	1	1.05	0.71	0.60	0.63	1.60
Nota	70.59 s	1	1.10	0.24	0.22	0.22	4.51
CanBus	25.91 s	1	1.03	0.58	0.47	0.51	1.96
Average		1	1.04	0.48	0.43	0.44	76.60
Geometric Mean		1	1.04	0.26	0.21	0.22	4.65

a large number of variables or constants. For the Cruise and GSM benchmarks PROB with operation caching is now faster than the TLC backend.

The LTSMin backend works in principle with all models, but a segmentation fault prevented using it for the first example and there is no support for scope predicates to restrict the state space. Table 4 shows that LTSMin can still be faster than PROB. However, in those cases the differences are much smaller than in [18]. E.g., [18] reported a speedup of 15.97 for rether, now we are down to a factor of 1.6. The best case for LTSMin is the nota example, which has very simple and regular structure. This example is maybe not typical of industrial models, but it shows that there is still scope for improving our operation caching algorithm (but may require incremental hashing, packing and bit fiddling at C level; see Sect. 6). For some larger examples, PROB with operation caching is now faster than LTSMin, e.g., more than 3 times faster for Abrial's interlocking. For the UML-B drone example LTSMin's algorithm seems to break down, possibly because the states are becoming too large. For the drone example we did run LTSMin without the scope predicate and obtained a rough estimate of the number of states processed (over 100 s for 2000 states).

In conclusion, operation caching and compression lead to significant performance improvements, completely staying within PROB's Prolog infrastructure, with hardly any disadvantage. TLC and LTSMin backends still have their uses,

Table 4. Relative walltimes of TLC and LTSMin backends compared to ProB with operation caching and compression, smaller is better (n/a: model not supported by TLC, †: scope predicate not supported)

Model	TLC	LTSMin
Interlocking	n/a	Segfault
Cruise	2.05	1.75
GSM	1.09	1.16
Pitman	0.37	2.26
GpuScheduler	0.10	1.84
Sort100	2.83	9.36
Incremental1	28.94	1.05
Incremental2	19.32	0.40
Drone0	n/a	† >50
Train1Lukas	0.42	2.94
SecuRail	n/a	†
Ref5Switch	n/a	0.14
Library33	0.11	2.23
rether	n/a	0.69
Simpson4Slot	0.43	0.20
Nota	0.32	0.06
CanBus	0.24	0.14

though, and can be beneficial when applicable. As some benchmarks show, there is scope to improve the operation caching implementation further.

6   Discussion and Conclusion

Partial Order Reduction. Operation caching is related to partial order reduction (POR). In contrast to POR, operation caching does not diminish the size of the state space, it only avoids computing certain edges. Its applicability conditions are, however, much more liberal than that of POR.

In fact, if two operations are independent operation caching can also derive independent caching tables ($Cache_{op}$). In Listing 1.1 the operation AddCust is syntactically independent of AddBook and operation caching computes independent projected state spaces (see Fig. 2). Within each projected state space POR might still be useful, e.g., for AddBook or ReturnBook in Fig. 2; but this would require POR to split an operation according to parameters (see [17]). Such a splitting could also be beneficial for operation caching. E.g., if we split the onloan variable into one variable per book, we could derive separate caching tables for ReturnBook(b1) and ReturnBook(b2).

Partial guard evaluation [8] is also somewhat related to operation caching. But its gains are modest, probably because it only affects the guard evaluations and like POR is dependent on precise static information.

State Compression. Spin [12] provides various compression techniques, such as collapse mode [11]. LTSMin [16], uses TreeDBS [19] for fixed length states.

PROB, however, needs to support variable length states. Possibly the recent DTREE approach [28] could be adapted for PROB states.

In future we could enable better sharing of subsets of B values amongst different variables. Another improvement would be to store only incremental updates to variables rather than full values of modified variables. For example, rather than storing $\{books \mapsto \{b1, b2\}\}$ in Fig. 2 for AddBook(b1), we would simply store $\{books \mapsto_\cup \{b1\}\}$. Similarly, for an action like $i := i + 1$ we could simply store $\{i \mapsto_+ 1\}$ and thus be independent of the current value of i. This would also make caching applicable to a larger set of projected states.

Various Improvements. As mentioned operation caching does not change the full state space. In future we could try and avoid storing the full state space explicitly; only implicitly by conjunction of projected state spaces of Fig. 2. Operation caching is also orthogonal to symmetry reduction [23]. Looking at Fig. 2 we can see that applying symmetry would also reduce the projected state spaces. Symmetry and operation caching are both applicable and do not interfere.

There are still various ways to fine tune the current Prolog implementation of Algorithm 1. In particular, we could share the hashing amongst different operations with the same or similar set $reads(Op)$.

Another important area is to devise a heuristic on when to automatically enable operation caching. Currently, Algorithm 1 is applied to an operation Op if at least one variable is projected away ($reads(Op) \subset Vars$). But this may not be enough to warrant the overhead of caching. Hence, an improved heuristic could take the number of read variables and their typing into account. Note that some variables are dependent; projecting away a dependent variable is not beneficial. Such problems could be detected in the fashion of a JIT compiler: after a warmup phase the model checker evaluates the effectiveness of caching and if the number of next state calls is similar to the number of states we stop caching the affected operation.

Conclusion. This work was motivated by achieving similar model checking improvements as with the LTSMin backend [18]. In Sect. 4.1 of [18] two early unsuccessful attempts were reported, one in Prolog and one in C. For the former hashing was too slow, for the latter the serialization overhead (to convert Prolog terms to C) was too costly. In this article we have developed a successful Prolog implementation, with incremental hashing and combined with state compression. Even though the development of the algorithm took considerable development effort, and is certainly not optimal yet, the result is already very satisfactory, yielding an order of magnitude improvements for several practical examples. The technique integrates well with all other features of PROB (e.g., coverage analyses or state space projection and visualisation) and can be applied to more formalisms such as CSP∥B. We have also provided a formal explanation and justification of the operation caching approach, and conducted an empirical evaluation. The latter has shown that we can have our cake and eat it too: state compression alone increases runtime, operation caching alone increases memory consumption, but combined compression and caching further improves runtime while leading to an overall reduction in memory consumption.

Acknowledgements. Many thanks for Colin Snook for providing me with the UML-B drone example and to anonymous referees for their useful feedback. I am also grateful to Philipp Körner and Fabian Vu for insightful discussions.

References

1. Abrial, J.-R.: The B-Book. Cambridge University Press, Cambridge (1996)
2. Abrial, J.-R.: Modeling in Event-B: System and Software Engineering. Cambridge University Press, Cambridge (2010)
3. Basile, D., et al.: Designing a demonstrator of formal methods for railways infrastructure managers. In: Margaria, T., Steffen, B. (eds.) ISoLA 2020. LNCS, vol. 12478, pp. 467–485. Springer, Cham (2020). https://doi.org/10.1007/978-3-030-61467-6_30
4. Bendisposto, J., et al.: Symbolic reachability analysis of B through PROB and LTSMIN. In: Ábrahám, E., Huisman, M. (eds.) IFM 2016. LNCS, vol. 9681, pp. 275–291. Springer, Cham (2016). https://doi.org/10.1007/978-3-319-33693-0_18
5. Bendisposto, J., Leuschel, M.: Proof assisted model checking for B. In: Breitman, K., Cavalcanti, A. (eds.) ICFEM 2009. LNCS, vol. 5885, pp. 504–520. Springer, Heidelberg (2009). https://doi.org/10.1007/978-3-642-10373-5_26
6. Bernard, E., Legeard, B., Luck, X., Peureux, F.: Generation of test sequences from formal specifications: GSM 11-11 standard case study. Softw. Pract. Exp. **34**(10), 915–948 (2004)
7. Blom, S., van de Pol, J., Weber, M.: LTSMIN: distributed and symbolic reachability. In: Touili, T., Cook, B., Jackson, P. (eds.) CAV 2010. LNCS, vol. 6174, pp. 354–359. Springer, Heidelberg (2010). https://doi.org/10.1007/978-3-642-14295-6_31
8. Dobrikov, I., Leuschel, M.: Enabling analysis for Event-B. Sci. Comput. Program. **158**, 81–99 (2018)
9. Frappier, M., Fraikin, B., Chossart, R., Chane-Yack-Fa, R., Ouenzar, M.: Comparison of model checking tools for information systems. In: Dong, J.S., Zhu, H. (eds.) ICFEM 2010. LNCS, vol. 6447, pp. 581–596. Springer, Heidelberg (2010). https://doi.org/10.1007/978-3-642-16901-4_38
10. Hansen, D., Leuschel, M.: Translating B to TLA$^+$ for validation with TLC. Sci. Comput. Program. **131**, 109–125 (2016)
11. Holzmann, G.J.: State compression in SPIN: recursive indexing and compression training runs. Technical report (1997)
12. Holzmann, G.J.: The model checker Spin. IEEE Trans. Softw. Eng. **23**(5), 279–295 (1997)
13. Holzmann, G.J.: Explicit-state model checking. In: Handbook of Model Checking, pp. 153–171. Springer, Cham (2018). https://doi.org/10.1007/978-3-319-10575-8_5
14. Idani, A.: Meeduse: a tool to build and run proved DSLs. In: Dongol, B., Troubitsyna, E. (eds.) IFM 2020. LNCS, vol. 12546, pp. 349–367. Springer, Cham (2020). https://doi.org/10.1007/978-3-030-63461-2_19
15. James, P., Moller, F., Nguyen, H.N., Roggenbach, M., Schneider, S.A., Treharne, H.: On modelling and verifying railway interlockings: tracking train lengths. Sci. Comput. Program. **96**, 315–336 (2014)

16. Kant, G., Laarman, A., Meijer, J., van de Pol, J., Blom, S., van Dijk, T.: LTSmin: high-performance language-independent model checking. In: Baier, C., Tinelli, C. (eds.) TACAS 2015. LNCS, vol. 9035, pp. 692–707. Springer, Heidelberg (2015). https://doi.org/10.1007/978-3-662-46681-0_61

17. Körner, P., Leuschel, M.: Towards practical partial order reduction for high-level formalisms (2022). (Submitted)

18. Körner, P., Leuschel, M., Meijer, J.: State-of-the-art model checking for B and event-B using PROB and LTSMIN. In: Furia, C.A., Winter, K. (eds.) IFM 2018. LNCS, vol. 11023, pp. 275–295. Springer, Cham (2018). https://doi.org/10.1007/978-3-319-98938-9_16

19. Laarman, A., van de Pol, J., Weber, M.: Parallel recursive state compression for free. In: Groce, A., Musuvathi, M. (eds.) SPIN 2011. LNCS, vol. 6823, pp. 38–56. Springer, Heidelberg (2011). https://doi.org/10.1007/978-3-642-22306-8_4

20. Ladenberger, L., Leuschel, M.: Mastering the visualization of larger state spaces with projection diagrams. In: Butler, M., Conchon, S., Zaïdi, F. (eds.) ICFEM 2015. LNCS, vol. 9407, pp. 153–169. Springer, Cham (2015). https://doi.org/10.1007/978-3-319-25423-4_10

21. Leuschel, M.: The high road to formal validation. In: Börger, E., Butler, M., Bowen, J.P., Boca, P. (eds.) ABZ 2008. LNCS, vol. 5238, pp. 4–23. Springer, Heidelberg (2008). https://doi.org/10.1007/978-3-540-87603-8_2

22. Leuschel, M., Butler, M.J.: ProB: an automated analysis toolset for the B method. STTT 10(2), 185–203 (2008)

23. Leuschel, M., Massart, T.: Efficient approximate verification of B via symmetry markers. Ann. Math. Artif. Intell. 59(1), 81–106 (2010)

24. Leuschel, M., Mutz, M., Werth, M.: Modelling and validating an automotive system in classical B and Event-B. In: Raschke, A., Méry, D., Houdek, F. (eds.) ABZ 2020. LNCS, vol. 12071, pp. 335–350. Springer, Cham (2020). https://doi.org/10.1007/978-3-030-48077-6_27

25. Morris, K., Snook, C., Hoang, T.S., Hulette, G., Armstrong, R., Butler, M.: Formal verification of run-to-completion style statecharts using event-B. In: Muccini, H., Avgeriou, P., Buhnova, B., Camara, J., Caporuscio, M., Franzago, M., Koziolek, A., Scandurra, P., Trubiani, C., Weyns, D., Zdun, U. (eds.) ECSA 2020. CCIS, vol. 1269, pp. 311–325. Springer, Cham (2020). https://doi.org/10.1007/978-3-030-59155-7_24

26. Rivera, V., Cataño, N., Wahls, T., Rueda, C.: Code generation for event-B. STTT 19(1), 31–52 (2017)

27. Treharne, H., Schneider, S.: How to drive a B machine. In: Bowen, J.P., Dunne, S., Galloway, A., King, S. (eds.) ZB 2000. LNCS, vol. 1878, pp. 188–208. Springer, Heidelberg (2000). https://doi.org/10.1007/3-540-44525-0_12

28. Berg, F.I.: Recursive variable-length state compression for multi-core software model checking. In: Dutle, A., Moscato, M.M., Titolo, L., Muñoz, C.A., Perez, I. (eds.) NFM 2021. LNCS, vol. 12673, pp. 340–357. Springer, Cham (2021). https://doi.org/10.1007/978-3-030-76384-8_21

29. Yu, Y., Manolios, P., Lamport, L.: Model checking TLA$^+$ specifications. In: Pierre, L., Kropf, T. (eds.) CHARME 1999. LNCS, vol. 1703, pp. 54–66. Springer, Heidelberg (1999). https://doi.org/10.1007/3-540-48153-2_6

Time

Conservative Time Discretization:
A Comparative Study

Marcelo Forets[1] and Christian Schilling[2]($\boxtimes$)

[1] DMA, CURE, Universidad de la República, Montevideo, Uruguay
[2] Aalborg University, Aalborg, Denmark
`christianms@cs.aau.dk`

Abstract. We present the first review of methods to overapproximate the set of reachable states of linear time-invariant systems subject to uncertain initial states and input signals *for short time horizons*. These methods are fundamental to state-of-the-art reachability algorithms for long time horizons, which proceed in two steps: First they use such a method to discretize the system for a short time horizon, and then they efficiently obtain a solution of the new discrete system for the long time horizon. Traditionally, both qualitative and quantitative comparison between different reachability algorithms has only considered the combination of both steps. In this paper we study the first step in isolation. We perform a variety of numerical experiments for six fundamental discretization methods from the literature. As we show, these methods have different trade-offs regarding accuracy and computational cost and, depending on the characteristics of the system, some methods may be preferred over others. We also discuss preprocessing steps to improve the results and efficient implementation strategies.

Keywords: Time discretization · Linear system · Reachability

1 Introduction

We study the fundamental problem of reachability for a system of linear differential equations. Given a set of initial states $\mathcal{X}_0 \subseteq \mathbb{R}^n$, we are interested in the set of states that can be reached by any trajectory up to some time horizon.

The classical analysis approach is numerical simulation, which has several drawbacks. First, one can only simulate finitely many trajectories, but a system has infinitely many trajectories. Second, a simulated trajectory is only available at finitely many discrete points in time. Third, even for these discrete points in time, a standard simulation is not guaranteed to be exact. For all these reasons, simulation may miss critical behaviors, which can lead to wrong conclusions.

In contrast, reachability algorithms construct a finite sequence of *sets* covering *all* possible *continuous* trajectories of the system. In general it is not possible to represent the exact set of reachable states, but for linear systems one can obtain arbitrary-precision approximations as a union of convex sets [6,28].

M. H. ter Beek and R. Monahan (Eds.): IFM 2022, LNCS 13274, pp. 149–167, 2022.
https://doi.org/10.1007/978-3-031-07727-2_9

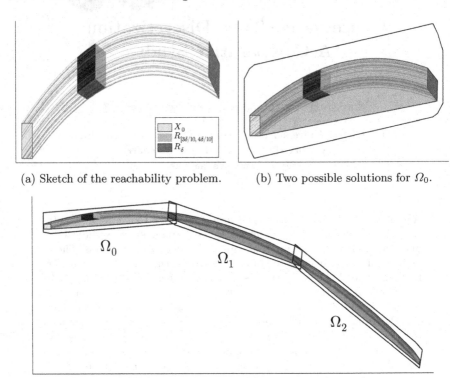

(a) Sketch of the reachability problem.   (b) Two possible solutions for Ω_0.

(c) First three steps of the iteration in a reachability algorithm.

Fig. 1. Left: Starting from the initial states $\mathcal{X}_0$ (yellow), we want to enclose the states reachable within $[0, \delta]$, $\mathcal{R}_{[0,\delta]}$, covering the random trajectories (magenta). **Right:** The purple set is the smallest convex solution for Ω_0. The blue set is a zonotope solution for Ω_0 computed with the method in [9]. **Bottom:** The first three sets of the discretized system computed by a reachability algorithm. (Color figure online)

The fundamental procedure behind all modern reachability algorithms [5] consists of two stages. In the first stage, the system is discretized, i.e., approximated by a discrete system. This requires to find a Euclidean set $\Omega_0 \subseteq \mathbb{R}^n$ that includes all states reachable starting from any initial state $x(0) \in \mathcal{X}_0$ up to a small time horizon δ, as illustrated in Fig. 1(a). Two possible solutions for Ω_0 are presented in Fig. 1(b). In the second stage, the set Ω_0 is propagated forward in time until the time horizon is reached, which is sketched in Fig. 1(c). Thus computing a precise Ω_0 is important for the precision of the overall result.

All state-of-the-art reachability tools such as CORA [3], the continuous version of Hylaa [12], HyPro [30], JuliaReach [13], and SpaceEx [21] follow this procedure of discretizing and computing an approximation Ω_0. Over the years, multiple methods to obtain such sets Ω_0 have been proposed [4,9,11,14,16,21,22,28]. These methods are tailored toward different set representations as a requirement of the second stage of the reachability algorithm. The two prevalent options are a concrete representation with a zonotope and a lazy representation based on the support function. Nevertheless, the different sets Ω_0 solve the same problem and can be partially interchanged between different algorithms. However, to our knowledge, these methods have never been compared to each other.

In this article we study different methods to compute Ω_0. We introduce this problem formally in the next section. Our study has these particular goals:

- Present the methods in a unified way (Sect. 3).
- Discuss potential gains of system transformations (Sect. 4).
- Discuss aspects of an efficient implementation (Sect. 5).
- Assess the effect of different system characteristics and evaluate the methods on different systems (Sect. 6).

An extended version of this paper is available in [18].

2   Problem Statement

In this work we study linear time-invariant (LTI) systems, which have the state-space form

$$\dot{x}(t) = Ax(t) + u(t), \tag{1}$$

where x is an n-dimensional state vector, $A \in \mathbb{R}^{n \times n}$ is the flow matrix, and u is a bounded but arbitrarily varying input signal that belongs to the input domain $\mathcal{U} \subseteq \mathbb{R}^n$, i.e., $u(t) \in \mathcal{U}$ for all $t \geq 0$. It is common to associate a linear map B with u in (1), but this map can be absorbed in $\mathcal{U}$ (via $\mathcal{U} \mapsto B\mathcal{U}$, which is no restriction in practice because common set representations for $\mathcal{U}$ such as zonotopes are closed under linear maps). An LTI system is homogeneous if $\mathcal{U} = \{0\}$ and heterogeneous otherwise. We consider initial-value problems for system (1) where the initial state $x(0) \in \mathbb{R}^n$ is taken from a set of initial states $\mathcal{X}_0 \subseteq \mathbb{R}^n$. The solution of (1) for a particular initial state x_0 and input signal u is the trajectory $\xi_{x_0,u}(t)$, which is a function of time. The set of solutions at time t is the set of reachable states

$$\mathcal{R}_t = \{\xi_{x_0,u}(t) : x_0 \in \mathcal{X}_0, u \in \mathcal{U}\}, \tag{2}$$

and we generalize this set to time intervals

$$\mathcal{R}_{[t_0,t_1]} = \{\xi_{x_0,u}(t) : x_0 \in \mathcal{X}_0, u \in \mathcal{U}, t \in [t_0,t_1]\}. \tag{3}$$

The time-bounded reachability problem asks to compute the set of reachable states $\mathcal{R}_{[0,T]}$ up to a time horizon T. Solving this problem exactly for LTI systems is generally not possible [26]. Hence an overapproximation $\Omega \supseteq \mathcal{R}_{[0,T]}$ is sought in practice. The common approach to compute the set Ω proceeds in two stages.

In the first stage, conservative time discretization is applied to compute a set Ω_0 with the property that it encloses the exact reachable states for an initial time interval $[0,\delta]$, i.e., $\Omega_0 \supseteq \mathcal{R}_{[0,\delta]}$; usually one chooses a small value for δ, much smaller than T. We illustrate two possible choices for Ω_0 in Fig. 1(b).

For efficiency reasons, in practice one restricts Ω_0 to convex sets. Under this restriction, the smallest set Ω_0 is the convex hull of $\mathcal{R}_{[0,\delta]}$ (purple set in Fig. 1(b)).

In a similar fashion to Ω_0, the second stage also requires a discretized input set $\mathcal{V}$, which encloses the trajectories of system (1) but starting from the origin ($x(0) = 0$), up to the time horizon δ. Since the set $\mathcal{U}$ is often assumed to have a simple shape, the computation of $\mathcal{V}$ is straightforward and mostly identical across the different discretization methods, and we do not discuss it further.

The second stage propagates the set Ω_0 through consecutive time intervals until reaching the time horizon T, which we sketch briefly because the technicalities are not of interest. The sequence of sets Ω_k, $k \geq 0$, is given by the following recurrence, where $\oplus$ denotes the Minkowski sum, $\mathcal{X} \oplus \mathcal{Y} = \{x+y : x \in \mathcal{X}, y \in \mathcal{Y}\}$:

$$\Omega_k = e^{A\delta k}\Omega_0 \oplus \bigoplus_{j=0}^{k-1} e^{A\delta j}\mathcal{V} \tag{4}$$

We finally define our approximation of the reachable states (see Fig. 1(c)) as

$$\Omega = \bigcup_{k=0} \Omega_k. \tag{5}$$

We note that state-of-the-art reachability algorithms for LTI systems are wrapping-free, i.e., they do not accumulate errors over time; as such, the precision of these algorithms is mainly determined by the precision of Ω_0 and $\mathcal{V}$.

The reader may wonder why reducing the problem of computing $\Omega \supseteq \mathcal{R}_{[0,T]}$ to the problem of computing $\Omega_0 \supseteq \mathcal{R}_{[0,\delta]}$, which is structurally equivalent, makes sense. It is important to remark that there are good convex approximation methods for small enough values of δ, but these methods fail for large values of δ (as we shall see later). While Ω_0 is convex, Ω is a union of convex sets (and thus typically not convex). We also note the analogy to numerical simulation methods, which may also require that the time step is small enough, for instance by the well-known Courant-Friedrichs-Lewy condition.

In summary, the fundamental problem that we study here is:

Problem 1. Given an LTI system and a time horizon δ, find a set $\Omega_0 \supseteq \mathcal{R}_{[0,\delta]}$.

3   Discretization Methods

In this section, after fixing some common notation and mentioning approaches for nonlinear systems, we introduce various methods to obtain a conservative discretization Ω_0 for solving Problem 1. The presentation follows the chronological order in which these methods have been proposed. The methods for computing Ω_0 we consider here assume that $\mathcal{X}_0$ and $\mathcal{U}$ are at least compact and convex. Under this condition it is known that $\mathcal{R}_t$ is also compact and convex for any t (unlike the sets $\mathcal{R}_{[t_1,t_2]}$). We end the section with pointers to related works outside the scope of this study.

3.1 Notation

In this article, when the norm of an operator is not specified, we assume a p-norm with $1 \leq p \leq \infty$. We denote the ball of radius ε in some p-norm and centered in the origin by $\mathcal{B}_\varepsilon$, and $\mathcal{B}_\varepsilon^p$ when the p-norm is relevant. Let $\mathcal{X}, \mathcal{Y} \subseteq \mathbb{R}^n$ be sets. The norm of $\mathcal{X}$ is defined as $\|\mathcal{X}\| = \sup_{x \in \mathcal{X}} \|x\|$. The symmetric interval hull of $\mathcal{X}$, written $\boxdot(\mathcal{X})$, is the smallest hyperrectangle that contains $\mathcal{X}$ and is centrally symmetric in the origin. We write $CH(\mathcal{X}, \mathcal{Y})$ to denote the convex hull of the union of $\mathcal{X}$ and $\mathcal{Y}$, and $\rho(d, \mathcal{X})$ to denote the support function of $\mathcal{X}$ along direction $d \in \mathbb{R}^n$ (see for instance [19] for a formal definition and examples). Given system (1), we define the state-transition matrix $\Phi = e^{A\delta}$ as the matrix exponential of $A\delta$. The following matrix function is also relevant:

$$\Phi_2(A, \delta) = \sum_{i=0}^{\infty} \frac{\delta^{i+2}}{(i+2)!} A^i. \tag{6}$$

If A is invertible, $\Phi_2(A, \delta) = A^{-2}(\Phi - I - A\delta)$. See Sect. 5.2 for the computation.

3.2 Methods for Nonlinear Systems

In principle, we can apply reachability algorithms for nonlinear systems to LTI systems as a special case. However, the methods developed specifically for LTI systems are much more precise and scalable. Hence we do not include nonlinear approaches in our study and only briefly mention some relevant works below.

A polyhedral enclosure Ω_0 can be computed for any dynamical system by choosing a set of normal directions $(d_i)_i$ and solving the corresponding optimization problems $\max_{t \in [0, \delta]} d_i^T x(t)$ [16]. This scheme relies on a sound optimizer and the run time depends on the number of directions and is difficult to predict. For LTI systems, the analytic expression of $x(t)$ can be used [27, Sect. 5.3].

The work in [10], describes how to deal with nondeterministic inputs for Lipschitz-continuous systems. If L is the Lipschitz constant, the reachable states of the heterogeneous system are contained in the bloated reachable states of the homogeneous system: $f_{heterog} \subseteq f_{homog} \oplus \mathcal{B}_\varepsilon$, where $\varepsilon = \frac{\|\mathcal{U}\|}{L}(e^{L\delta} - 1)$.

3.3 Common Structure of Methods for Linear Systems

Examining the different methods that we study in the remainder of this section, the following common structure emerges:

$$\Omega_0 = CH(\mathcal{X}_0, \Phi\mathcal{X}_0 \oplus \mathcal{H}) \oplus \mathcal{J}, \tag{7}$$

for suitable sets $\mathcal{H}$ and $\mathcal{J}$ (possibly empty). In short, the idea is to compute the convex hull between the reachable states at time 0 and at time δ, $\mathcal{X}_0$ and $\Phi\mathcal{X}_0$. That would suffice if the trajectories were just following straight lines. To correct for the curvature, the bloating terms $\mathcal{H}$ and $\mathcal{J}$ need to be added.

3.4 First-Order d/dt Method

The earliest work specifically designed for linear systems we are aware of was developed for the tool d/dt [11]. This work only considers homogeneous systems. The definition is

$$\Omega_0 = CH(\mathcal{X}_0, \Phi\mathcal{X}_0) \oplus \mathcal{B}_\varepsilon, \tag{8}$$

where

$$\varepsilon = \left(e^{\|A\|\delta} - 1 - \|A\|\delta\right)\|\mathcal{X}_0\| - \frac{3}{8}\|A\|^2\delta^2\|\mathcal{X}_0\|. \tag{9}$$

We note that the authors also claim that their method can be used to obtain an underapproximation, but this is not correct (see [18] for details).

3.5 First-Order Zonotope Method

The work in [22] computes a zonotope enclosure. The idea is to cover $CH(\mathcal{X}_0, \Phi\mathcal{X}_0)$ with a zonotope and then bloat with another zonotope (here: a ball in the infinity norm):

$$\Omega_0 = zonotope(CH(\mathcal{X}_0, \Phi\mathcal{X}_0)) \oplus \mathcal{B}_\varepsilon^\infty \tag{10}$$

where

$$\varepsilon = \left(e^{\|A\|_\infty\delta} - 1 - \|A\|_\infty\delta\right)\left(\|\mathcal{X}_0\|_\infty + \frac{\|\mathcal{U}\|_\infty}{\|A\|_\infty}\right) + \delta\|\mathcal{U}\|_\infty. \tag{11}$$

3.6 Correction-Hull Method

The method in [9] is designed for interval dynamics matrix A, which represents uncertain parameters and has the scalar matrix as a special case. The resulting set, a zonotope, is constructed from interval linear maps, which is described in [9, Theorem 4]. The approach is based on truncating the Taylor series at a chosen order p, and this order must satisfy the following inequality:

$$\alpha = \frac{\|A\|_\infty\delta}{p+2} < 1. \tag{12}$$

The method assumes that the input domain $\mathcal{U}$ contains the origin. If this is not the case, a simple transformation can bring the system to this form [2, Sect. 3.2.2], which we describe in Sect. 4.1. Then we have the following definitions:

$$\Omega_0 = CH(\mathcal{X}_0, \Phi\mathcal{X}_0) \oplus F_p\mathcal{X}_0 \oplus G_p\mathcal{U}, \tag{13}$$

where the correction matrices F and G are

$$F_p = E + \sum_{i=2}^{p}[\delta^i(i^{\frac{-i}{i-1}} - i^{\frac{-1}{i-1}}), 0]\frac{A^i}{i!} \tag{14}$$

and

$$G_p = E\delta + \sum_{i=0}^{p} \frac{A^i \delta^{i+1}}{(i+1)!}. \tag{15}$$

The remainder matrix E to bound $\sum_{i=p+1}^{\infty} A^i \delta^i / i!$ is a diagonal interval matrix based on results in [29]; here the assumption (12) is relevant to make the geometric series $\sum_i \alpha^i$ converge. Define

$$E = [-\varepsilon, \varepsilon]\mathbf{1} \tag{16}$$

where $\mathbf{1}$ is the $n \times n$ matrix filled with ones and

$$\varepsilon = \frac{(\|A\|_\infty \delta)^{p+1}}{(p+1)!} \frac{1}{1-\alpha}. \tag{17}$$

The method was later extended in [8] and in our implementation we use the remainder term E from that work instead.

3.7   First-Order Method

The method in [28] uses a first-order approximation similar to [22] in Sect. 3.5, but in contrast it is not restricted to zonotopes and the infinity norm:

$$\Omega_0 = CH(\mathcal{X}_0, \Phi\mathcal{X}_0 \oplus \delta\mathcal{U} \oplus \mathcal{B}_\varepsilon) \tag{18}$$

where

$$\varepsilon = \left(e^{\|A\|\delta} - 1 - \|A\|\delta \right) \left(\|\mathcal{X}_0\| + \frac{\|\mathcal{U}\|}{\|A\|} \right). \tag{19}$$

3.8   Forward-Backward Method

The approach in [21] describes an optimization procedure similar in spirit to the one discussed in Sect. 3.2 but specialized for LTI systems. Here one only needs to optimize over a quadratic function. First we define some auxiliary terms.

$$E_+ = \boxdot(\Phi_2(|A|, \delta) \boxdot (A^2 \mathcal{X}_0)) \tag{20}$$

$$E_- = \boxdot(\Phi_2(|A|, \delta) \boxdot (A^2 \Phi\mathcal{X}_0)) \tag{21}$$

$$E_\psi = \boxdot(\Phi_2(|A|, \delta) \boxdot (A\mathcal{U})) \tag{22}$$

$$\mathcal{Y}_\lambda = (1-\lambda)\mathcal{X}_0 \oplus \lambda\Phi\mathcal{X}_0 \oplus \lambda\delta\mathcal{U} \oplus (\lambda E_+ \cap (1-\lambda)E_-) \oplus \lambda^2 E_\psi$$

Here the term E_+ goes forward from $\mathcal{X}_0$ and the term E_- goes backward from $\Phi\mathcal{X}_0$, and it is sufficient to consider their intersection. The solution is then obtained by optimizing $\mathcal{Y}_\lambda$ (where the objective function is piecewise-linear for homogeneous systems and piecewise-quadratic for heterogeneous systems):

$$\Omega_0 = CH(\bigcup_{\lambda \in [0,1]} \mathcal{Y}_\lambda). \tag{23}$$

3.9 Forward-Only Method

The work in [14] uses a simplified version of (23) with only a forward approximation, which works without an optimization procedure. It can be seen that

$$CH(\bigcup_{\lambda \in [0,1]} \mathcal{Y}_\lambda) \subseteq CH(\mathcal{Y}_0, \mathcal{Y}_1 \oplus E_+) \tag{24}$$

and this method accordingly uses

$$\Omega_0 = CH(\mathcal{X}_0, \Phi\mathcal{X}_0 \oplus \delta\mathcal{U} \oplus E_\psi \oplus E_+), \tag{25}$$

where E_+ and E_ψ are defined in (20) and (22). Analogously one can define a "backward-only" method by using E_- instead of E_+.

3.10 Combining Methods

It should be noted that if Ω_0^a and Ω_0^b are two solutions to Problem 1, then their intersection $\Omega_0^a \cap \Omega_0^b$ is also a solution. (The dual statement holds for under-approximations and their unions.) It is hence possible to combine the different methods outlined above. This idea was used in [17] where the authors combined the "forward-only" method with the mentioned "backward-only" method; this method yields solutions that are closer to the "forward-backward" method than these methods individually but is more efficient than the latter.

3.11 Application to High-Dimensional Systems

The approach in [4] shows how to efficiently work with high-dimensional systems. The construction of Ω_0 is similar to the "correction-hull" method, including the focus on zonotopes as set representation. The difference is that the structure of the solution is rewritten to rely on matrices in the Krylov subspace. The idea is to compute two matrices W and H to approximate the effect of a vector v on the matrix exponential e^A without computing it:

$$e^A v \approx \|v\| W e^H e_1. \tag{26}$$

The matrix exponential e^H can be computed efficiently, and there exist estimates to bound the above approximation error [4].

In [17] the authors demonstrated that the "forward-only" method can also be efficiently implemented with Krylov techniques.

3.12 Application to Time-Varying Systems

Linear systems whose dynamics are time-varying due to uncertain parameters can be represented with interval matrices. This setting differs from the one in [9] from Sect. 3.6 where the system dynamics are uncertain but time-invariant. Methods based on zonotopes to handle such systems are presented in [2,7].

4   Problem Transformations

In this section we shortly explain possible transformations of system (1) to a normal form. These transformations are simple but yield interesting results.

For illustration, we use a simple harmonic oscillator with inputs f,

$$\ddot{y}(t) + \omega^2 y(t) = f, \tag{27}$$

where $\omega^2 = 4\pi$, $m = 1$ and $y(t)$ is the unknown. This problem can be associated with a spring-mass system, where $y(t)$ is the elongation of the spring at time t and ω is the natural frequency. Bringing Eq. (27) to the first-order form of Eq. (1) with the change of variables $x(t) = [y(t), \dot{y}(t)]^T$, we obtain

$$\dot{x}(t) = \begin{pmatrix} 0 & 1 \\ -4\pi & 0 \end{pmatrix} x(t) + \begin{pmatrix} 0 \\ f \end{pmatrix}. \tag{28}$$

4.1   Homogenization

The first transformation, which was used in [2, Sect. 3.2.2] for the "correction-hull" method (although with a different goal) and in [17], expresses some of the inputs' effect with a fresh state variable. For deterministic systems (i.e., where the input domain $\mathcal{U}$ is a singleton), this allows to completely eliminate the inputs. For proper nondeterministic systems, this extracts the "central" effect of the input signals into a state variable and only leaves the deviation from this central effect, effectively re-centering the input domain $\mathcal{U}$ in the origin. The transformation is motivated because $\mathcal{U}$ is treated rather pessimistically in the methods to compute Ω_0 (e.g., it may appear in the form of its norm $\|\mathcal{U}\|$).

We illustrate the issue in one dimension. For the p-norms considered here and any $a \in \mathbb{R}$ we have $\|a\| = \| - a\|$. Hence the norm of the singleton $\mathcal{U}_1 = \{a\}$ is equivalent to the norm of the proper interval $\mathcal{U}_2 = [-a, a]$. Thus Ω_0 is identical in both cases, but since it must cover the $\mathcal{U}_2$ case, with many more possible behaviors, it is coarse for $\mathcal{U}_1$ and large a.

Now suppose that the input domain $\mathcal{U}$ is centrally symmetric but not centered in the origin. The idea of the transformation is to shift $\mathcal{U}$ to the origin and add another state variable to account for this shift. Formally, assume a heterogeneous system (1), an initial set $\mathcal{X}_0$, and a domain $\mathcal{U}$ centered in a point $c \neq 0$. We define a new system $\dot{y}(t) = Cy(t) + u(t)$, where we have the block matrix

$$C = \begin{pmatrix} A & \frac{b}{\alpha} \\ 0 & 0 \end{pmatrix} \tag{29}$$

for some value $\alpha \neq 0$, $\mathcal{Y}_0 = \mathcal{X}_0 \times \{\alpha\}$ is the new initial set, and $\mathcal{U} \oplus \{-c\}$ is the new input domain. The parameter α can be used to trade off the impact in the norm of C (for methods where this term appears) and $\mathcal{Y}_0$. This transformation increases the state dimension n by one and removes the input dimension. The modification of the initial states (i.e., the construction of $\mathcal{Y}_0$ from $\mathcal{X}_0$) is efficient for typical

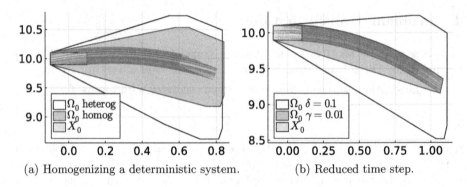

(a) Homogenizing a deterministic system.   (b) Reduced time step.

Fig. 2. Left: Several trajectories and the sets Ω_0 for a deterministic heterogeneous system (blue) and for the (projected) homogenized system (green). **Right:** Several trajectories and the sets Ω_0 obtained with a time step $\delta = 0.1$ (blue) and obtained by first computing the sets $\Omega'_0, \ldots, \Omega'_9$ with a time step $\gamma = 0.01$ (light gray, below the trajectories) and then computing the convex hull of their union (green). We use the "forward-only" method in all cases. (Color figure online)

set representations of $\mathcal{X}_0$. Likewise, projecting away the auxiliary dimension in the end is efficient for common set representations since this dimension is independent of all other dimensions and has the constant value 1.

It is easy to see that the set of trajectories of the latter system, after projecting away the auxiliary dimension, is equivalent to the set of trajectories of the original system. Yet, discretization methods typically yield more precise results for the latter system. We illustrate this claim in Fig. 2(a) for the deterministic harmonic oscillator. The effect for nondeterministic systems is similar [18].

4.2 Shrinking the Time Step

The time step δ has a large impact on the precision of Ω_0. Recall that Ω_0 is convex while $\mathcal{R}_{[0,\delta]}$ is generally not, so we have $\Omega_0 \supseteq CH(\mathcal{R}_{[0,\delta]}) \supseteq \mathcal{R}_{[0,\delta]}$. The gaps between these three sets grow with larger δ. Indeed, most methods have the property that they converge to $\mathcal{R}_{[0,\delta]}$ for $\delta \to 0$. The reason for not choosing a very small δ in practice is that the reachability algorithm requires $\lceil \frac{T}{\delta} \rceil$ steps to cover the time horizon T. Hence one needs to find a balance for δ: small enough to obtain a precise Ω_0 and large enough to be efficient later.

Observe that the gap between $CH(\mathcal{R}_{[0,\delta]})$ and $\mathcal{R}_{[0,\delta]}$ only depends on δ. Say that we fix δ to keep $\lceil \frac{T}{\delta} \rceil$ in a feasible range. The best we can do is minimize the gap between Ω_0 and $CH(\mathcal{R}_{[0,\delta]})$. We can achieve this by choosing a positive integer k and a smaller time step $\gamma = \delta/k$, computing the corresponding discretization Ω'_0 and propagating it (using some reachability algorithm) until time horizon δ, which yields sets $\Omega'_0, \ldots, \Omega'_{k-1}$, and finally constructing Ω_0 from their convex hull $CH(\Omega'_0 \cup \cdots \cup \Omega'_{k-1})$. We illustrate this idea in Fig. 2(b).

5   Efficient Implementation

As mentioned in Sect. 3.3, the different methods can be phrased in the structure of Eq. (7). Exceptions to this rule are the "first-order zonotope" method and the "forward-backward" method. The former applies an intermediate simplification to the CH, while the latter involves a CH in a continuous variable. In this section we describe how to operate with Eq. (7) numerically in an efficient way, even in high dimensions. We show example code for the set library LazySets.jl[1] [19]. If we allow for a post-processing operation, all the discretization methods can be cast into the same symbolic-numeric framework. In [18] we briefly describe the user interface for the implementation of the discretization methods available in the library ReachabilityAnalysis.jl[2].

5.1   The Concept of a Lazy Set

The key to an efficient implementation is lazy evaluation, that is, to *delay* computational effort until a result is needed. For example, we show how the "first-order d/dt" method from Sect. 3.4 can be implemented using LazySets, with the harmonic oscillator from Sect. 4 as running example. In this case, the sets $\mathcal{H}$ and $\mathcal{J}$ in Eq. (7) are the empty set and $\mathcal{B}_\varepsilon$, respectively. The following command defines the set Ω_0 as a lazy representation of Eq. (8).

```
1   # first - order  d / dt  method
2   julia>  Ω₀  =  CH( X₀ ,  Φ*X₀ )  ⊕  B
```

In other words, the lazy set operations (Minkowski sum, convex hull, and linear map) are not evaluated. The execution is instantaneous, while obtaining a concrete representation such as a polyhedron scales with the dimension of the sets. The operations are internally represented in the form of a tree as shown in the diagram on the right. Further operations such as the support function, conversion, and approximation can be efficiently applied to that symbolic representation [19].

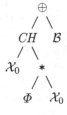

5.2   Computation of Matrix Functions

Some discretization methods require special matrix functions such as Φ_2 defined in Eq. (6). If A is not invertible, it can be obtained as the sub-matrix of the exponential of a higher-order matrix [21]. However, for large systems (typically $n > 2000$ depending on the sparsity pattern of A), such an approach can be prohibitively expensive. Instead, it is possible to use Krylov-subspace methods as discussed in Sect. 3.11, provided that we reformulate the problem as the

---

[1] See github.com/JuliaReach/LazySets.jl.

[2] See github.com/JuliaReach/ReachabilityAnalysis.jl.

Table 1. Average run times (in seconds) for different heat model instances.

Model instance	HEAT01	HEAT02	HEAT03	HEAT04
# Mesh points	5^3	10^3	20^3	50^3
Forward	0.134	23.6	–	–
Forward & Krylov	0.001	0.004	0.07	1.367

action of a matrix function over a direction. To illustrate this point, consider the "forward-only" from Sect. 3.9. Assume that the system is homogeneous and $\mathcal{X}_0$ is a hyperrectangle with center and radius vectors $c, r \in \mathbb{R}^n$ respectively. A priori, the Krylov method does not apply to Eq. (20) because Φ_2 is acting on the set $H_{in} := \square(A^2 \mathcal{X}_0)$. However, we observe that H_{in} is a hyperrectangle centered in the origin with radius $r_{in} = |A^2 c| + |A^2| r$. Therefore, it suffices to compute $|\Phi_2(|A|, \delta)| r_{in} = \Phi_2(|A|, \delta) r_{in}$ using Krylov methods.

As an application, we consider the discretized heat partial differential equation models. The model is obtained from a spatial discretization of a partial differential equation for heat transfer in three dimensions. Originally presented in [23] for two dimensions and later extended to three dimensions, it was used as a benchmark example for reachability analysis [5,12]. The model dimension is scalable and here we consider four different instances of increasing complexity, which are labeled HEAT0x, for grids of size $n \times n \times n$ mesh points, i.e., the associated ODEs are n^3-dimensional. The goal is to find the maximum temperature reached at the center of the spatially discretized domain, where one of its edges is initially heated. Since each mesh point corresponds to a given direction, it is sufficient to compute the support function along the center of the mesh. Furthermore, the set of initial states is a hyperrectangle contained in $[0,1]^3$ and the matrix A is hermitian.

We use Krylov subspace dimension $m = 30$ for instance HEAT01 and $m = 100$ for the rest (see [25] for details). A run-time comparison is presented in Table 1. The computation of the matrix exponential with the non-Krylov implementation runs out memory for the larger instances. The Krylov method additionally offers a significant speedup.

5.3   Simplification of the Set Representation

It is possible to post-process the set Ω_0 with another set that makes it easier to operate with in reachability algorithms. For example, an approximation with an axis-aligned box can be used. The main advantage of such a representation is that the support function can be computed efficiently. This is shown in the following comparison when computing the support function of Ω_0 resp. its box approximation along direction $d = (1,1)^T$. The box approximation of Ω_0 has approximately the same support value, but the computation is 13× faster.

```
1    julia> boxΩ₀ = box_approximation(Ω₀);
2
3    julia> d = [1.0, 1.0];
4
5    julia> ρ(d, Ω₀)
6    10.328776223585699
7
8    julia> ρ(d, boxΩ₀)
9    10.35390370135613
10
11   julia> @btime ρ($d, $Ω₀)
12   97.762 ns (1 allocation: 80 bytes)
13
14   julia> @btime ρ($d, $boxΩ₀)
15   7.209 ns (0 allocations: 0 bytes)
```

6   Experimental Evaluation

In this section we evaluate the discretization methods from Sect. 3 in two experiments.[3] In the first experiment, we visually compare the sets Ω_0 for variants of the harmonic oscillator (see Sect. 4). In the second experiment, we evaluate the methods on representative models while varying the time step δ. Next we describe the experimental setup, show the results, and finally discuss them.

6.1   Setup

We implemented the different methods (called here d/dt, Zonotope, Correction hull, First-order, Forward/backward, and Forward) in JuliaReach [13]. For matrix-exponential functionality we use [1]. For the correction-hull method we use the truncation order $p = 4$ (higher orders led to numerical errors for the biggest model). To plot results for the forward-backward method, one needs to choose a set of directions to evaluate the support function. In the plots we choose 30 uniform directions from the unit circle; we choose this high precision to show the theoretical power of the method, even if in practice this is rarely required. We obtained the results on a notebook with a 2.20 GHz CPU and 8 GB RAM.

6.2   Models

Two Degree of Freedom. We consider a two-degree-of-freedom model from [24, Chapt. 9]. The model has characteristics that are typical of large systems, containing both low-frequency and high-frequency components. It is given by

$$M\ddot{y}(t) + Ky(t) = 0, \qquad y(t) = [y_1(t), y_2(t)]^T \tag{30}$$

where the mass (M) and stiffness (K) matrices are respectively

$$M = \begin{pmatrix} m_1 & 0 \\ 0 & m_2 \end{pmatrix}, \qquad K = \begin{pmatrix} k_1 + k_2 & -k_2 \\ -k_2 & k_2 \end{pmatrix}. \tag{31}$$

---

[3] The scripts are available at [20].

Table 2. Average run times (in milliseconds) for the different methods.

Model	d/dt	Zonotope	Correction hull	First-order	Fwd/bwd	Forward
Oscillator	0.01	0.02	0.23	0.01	6.56	0.03
TDoF	0.03	0.05	0.51	0.01	6.17	0.06
ISS	–	32.99	4 701.20	25.93	657.80	476.96

Equation (30) is brought to first-order form of Eq. (1) by introducing the variable $x(t) = [y_1(t), y_2(t), \dot{y}_1(t), \dot{y}_2(t)]^T$, from which we obtain

$$\dot{x}(t) = Ax(t), \quad \text{where } A = \begin{pmatrix} 0 & 0 & 1 & 0 \\ 0 & 0 & 0 & 1 \\ -\frac{k_1+k_2}{m_1} & \frac{k_2}{m_1} & 0 & 0 \\ \frac{k_2}{m_2} & -\frac{k_2}{m_2} & 0 & 0 \end{pmatrix}. \tag{32}$$

The initial states are the box centered at $[1, 10, 0, 0]$ with radius $[0.1, 0.5, 0.5, 0.5]$. The numerical values for the parameters are $m_1 = m_2 = k_2 = 1$ and $k_1 = 10,000$.

ISS. The ISS (International Space Station) model was originally presented in [15] and later proposed as a benchmark example for order-reduction techniques [31] and reachability analysis [5]. It is a structural model of the component 1R (Russian service module) and models the vibration during the docking maneuver of a spacecraft. There are 270 state variables and three nondeterministic inputs. The matrices A and e^A are sparse ($>99\%$ sparsity) with $\|A\|_\infty \approx 3763$, $\|\mathcal{X}_0\|_\infty = 10^{-4}$, and $\|\mathcal{U}\|_\infty \approx 0.98$.

6.3 Visual Evaluation of Varying Parameters

We evaluate the methods on the harmonic oscillator for three different analysis and model parameters. In Fig. 3 we vary the step size δ. In Fig. 4 we vary the size of the initial set $\mathcal{X}_0$. In Fig. 5 we vary the size of the input domain $\mathcal{U}$. The plots also show a tight approximation of the true reachable states. For homogeneous systems, the analytic solution at time t can be computed ($e^{At}\mathcal{X}_0$) and we show several sets $\mathcal{R}_t$ (for uniformly chosen time points t from $[0, \delta]$) instead.

6.4 Quantitative Evaluation by Scaling δ

We run a quantitative analysis on the harmonic oscillator and two other models described in Sect. 6.2. The latter represent challenging model classes: The second model, a two-degree-of-freedom system, has a system matrix A of large norm; this shows the corresponding sensitivity of the methods. The third model, representing a docking maneuver at the International Space Station (ISS), is high-dimensional; this shows the scalability of the methods. For comparing the precision, we vary the time step δ and compute the support function $\rho(d, \Omega_0)$ of

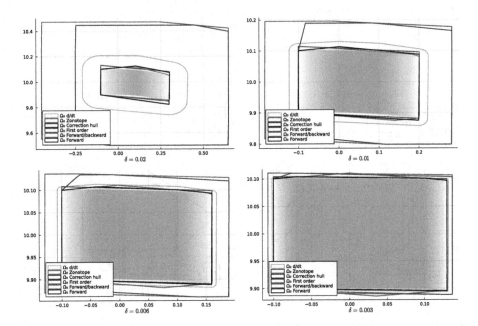

Fig. 3. The sets Ω_0 obtained with different methods for varying values of δ. In gray we show $\mathcal{R}_t$ for uniform $t \in [0, \delta]$.

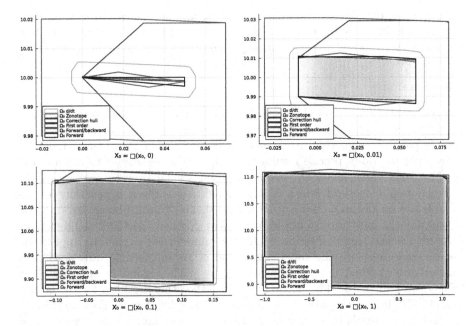

Fig. 4. The sets Ω_0 obtained with different methods for $\delta = 0.005$ and varying sets $\mathcal{X}_0$. In gray we show $\mathcal{R}_t$ for uniform $t \in [0, \delta]$.

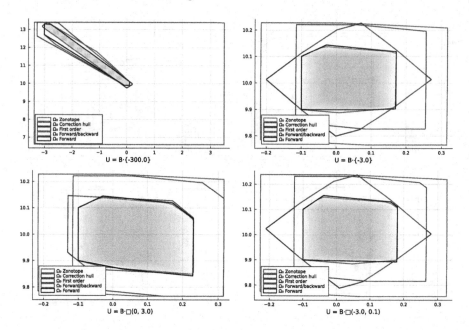

Fig. 5. The sets Ω_0 obtained with different methods for $\delta = 0.01$ and varying sets $\mathcal{U}$. In gray we show $\mathcal{R}_t$ for uniform $t \in [0, \delta]$.

the sets Ω_0 in direction $d = (1, \ldots, 1)^T$. The results are shown in Fig. 6. Average run times (which are independent of δ) are given in Table 2. Note that Ω_0 is computed lazily except for the "zonotope" and the "correction-hull" methods.

6.5   Summary

We generally observe that the first-oder methods (d/dt, Zonotope, First-order) yield coarser results and are more sensitive to the different model characteristics. In particular, for the two degree of freedom, a very small time step 10^{-5} is required to obtain precise results. This shows the sensitivity to the norm of A. The other three methods yield higher and similar precision, although the "correction-hull" method, which it is restricted to zonotopes, is generally incomparable (see for instance the first plot in Fig. 5). The "forward-backward" method is typically the most precise but also the most expensive method; recall that we computed a lazy representation of Ω_0 here and in a reachability application one needs to evaluate the support function of Ω_0 in multiple directions. The forward-only method is a simplification that yields a good compromise. The "correction-hull" method is much slower than the other methods for the largest model (ISS), but it computes a concrete zonotope. (Zonotopes enable an efficient "second stage" reachability analysis, which we ignore here.) Since this method is designed for interval matrices, it may be possible to devise a more efficient scalar variant.

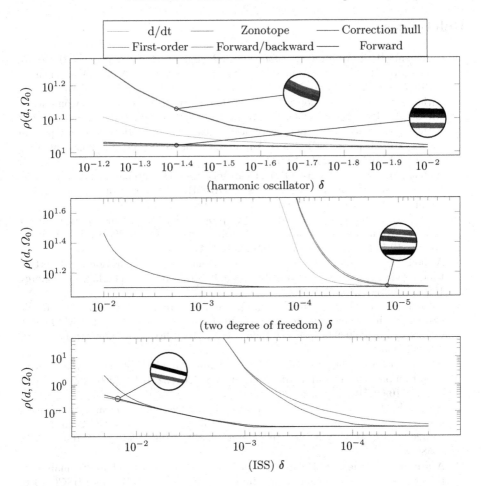

Fig. 6. Benchmark results with the graphs of $\rho(d, \Omega_0)$ (log axes). In the second plot, the methods "forward-backward" and "forward-only" yield identical results. In the third plot, the "d/dt" method is not applicable.

7 Conclusion

In this article we have studied six methods for conservative time discretization. We have discussed potential ways to improve their output in practice and how to efficiently implement them. Our empirical evaluation shows that the methods have different characteristics. In particular, methods based on a first-order approximation are generally less precise than the other methods. In the future we plan to perform a similar study of the full-fledged reachability algorithms using the insights gained in this study to use a precise discretization model.

Acknowledgments. This research was partly supported by DIREC - Digital Research Centre Denmark and the Villum Investigator Grant S4OS.

References

1. ExponentialUtilities.jl (2022). https://github.com/SciML/ExponentialUtilities.jl
2. Althoff, M.: Reachability Analysis and its Application to the Safety Assessment of Autonomous Cars. Ph.D. thesis, Technische Universität München (2010)
3. Althoff, M.: An introduction to CORA 2015. In: ARCH. EPiC Series in Computing, vol. 34, pp. 120–151. EasyChair (2015). https://doi.org/10.29007/zbkv
4. Althoff, M.: Reachability analysis of large linear systems with uncertain inputs in the Krylov subspace. IEEE Trans. Autom. Control **65**(2), 477–492 (2020). https://doi.org/10.1109/TAC.2019.2906432
5. Althoff, M., et al.: ARCH-COMP21 category report: continuous and hybrid systems with linear continuous dynamics. In: ARCH. EPiC Series in Computing, vol. 80, pp. 1–31. EasyChair (2021). https://doi.org/10.29007/lhbw
6. Althoff, M., Frehse, G., Girard, A.: Set propagation techniques for reachability analysis. Ann. Rev. Control Robot. Auton. Syst. **4**(1), 369–395 (2020). https://doi.org/10.1146/annurev-control-071420-081941
7. Althoff, M., Guernic, C.L., Krogh, B.H.: Reachable set computation for uncertain time-varying linear systems. In: HSCC, pp. 93–102. ACM (2011). https://doi.org/10.1145/1967701.1967717
8. Althoff, M., Krogh, B.H., Stursberg, O.: Analyzing reachability of linear dynamic systems with parametric uncertainties. In: Rauh, A., Auer, E. (eds.) MATHENGIN, vol. 3, pp. 69–94. Springer, Heidelberg (2011). https://doi.org/10.1007/978-3-642-15956-5_4
9. Althoff, M., Stursberg, O., Buss, M.: Reachability analysis of linear systems with uncertain parameters and inputs. In: CDC, pp. 726–732. IEEE (2007). https://doi.org/10.1109/CDC.2007.4434084
10. Asarin, E., Dang, T., Girard, A.: Reachability analysis of nonlinear systems using conservative approximation. In: Maler, O., Pnueli, A. (eds.) HSCC 2003. LNCS, vol. 2623, pp. 20–35. Springer, Heidelberg (2003). https://doi.org/10.1007/3-540-36580-X_5
11. Asarin, E., Bournez, O., Dang, T., Maler, O.: Approximate reachability analysis of piecewise-linear dynamical systems. In: Lynch, N., Krogh, B.H. (eds.) HSCC 2000. LNCS, vol. 1790, pp. 20–31. Springer, Heidelberg (2000). https://doi.org/10.1007/3-540-46430-1_6
12. Bak, S., Tran, H., Johnson, T.T.: Numerical verification of affine systems with up to a billion dimensions. In: HSCC, pp. 23–32. ACM (2019). https://doi.org/10.1145/3302504.3311792
13. Bogomolov, S., Forets, M., Frehse, G., Potomkin, K., Schilling, C.: Juliareach: a toolbox for set-based reachability. In: HSCC, pp. 39–44. ACM (2019). https://doi.org/10.1145/3302504.3311804
14. Bogomolov, S., Forets, M., Frehse, G., Viry, F., Podelski, A., Schilling, C.: Reach set approximation through decomposition with low-dimensional sets and high-dimensional matrices. In: HSCC, pp. 41–50. ACM (2018). https://doi.org/10.1145/3178126.3178128
15. Chahlaoui, Y., Van Dooren, P.: Benchmark examples for model reduction of linear time-invariant dynamical systems. In: Benner, P., Sorensen, D.C., Mehrmann, V. (eds.) Dimension Reduction of Large-Scale Systems. LNCSE, vol. 45, pp. 379–392. Springer, Heidelberg (2005). https://doi.org/10.1007/3-540-27909-1_24

16. Chutinan, A., Krogh, B.H.: Verification of polyhedral-invariant hybrid automata using polygonal flow pipe approximations. In: Vaandrager, F.W., van Schuppen, J.H. (eds.) HSCC 1999. LNCS, vol. 1569, pp. 76–90. Springer, Heidelberg (1999). https://doi.org/10.1007/3-540-48983-5_10

17. Forets, M., Caporale, D.F., Zerpa, J.M.P.: Combining set propagation with finite element methods for time integration in transient solid mechanics problems. Comput. Struct. **259** (2022). https://doi.org/10.1016/j.compstruc.2021.106699

18. Forets, M., Schilling, C.: Conservative time discretization: a comparative study. CoRR abs/2111.01454 (2021). https://arxiv.org/abs/2111.01454

19. Forets, M., Schilling, C.: LazySets.jl: scalable symbolic-numeric set computations. Proc. JuliaCon Conf. **1**(1), 11 (2021). https://doi.org/10.21105/jcon.00097

20. Forets, M., Schilling, C.: Package for repeatability evaluation (2022)

21. Frehse, G., et al.: SpaceEx: scalable verification of hybrid systems. In: Gopalakrishnan, G., Qadeer, S. (eds.) CAV 2011. LNCS, vol. 6806, pp. 379–395. Springer, Heidelberg (2011). https://doi.org/10.1007/978-3-642-22110-1_30

22. Girard, A.: Reachability of uncertain linear systems using zonotopes. In: Morari, M., Thiele, L. (eds.) HSCC 2005. LNCS, vol. 3414, pp. 291–305. Springer, Heidelberg (2005). https://doi.org/10.1007/978-3-540-31954-2_19

23. Han, Z., Krogh, B.H.: Reachability analysis of large-scale affine systems using low-dimensional polytopes. In: Hespanha, J.P., Tiwari, A. (eds.) HSCC 2006. LNCS, vol. 3927, pp. 287–301. Springer, Heidelberg (2006). https://doi.org/10.1007/11730637_23

24. Hughes, T.J.: The finite element method: linear static and dynamic finite element analysis. Courier Corporation (2012)

25. Koskela, A.: Approximating the matrix exponential of an advection-diffusion operator using the incomplete orthogonalization method. In: Abdulle, A., Deparis, S., Kressner, D., Nobile, F., Picasso, M. (eds.) ENUMATH 2013. LNCSE, vol. 103, pp. 345–353. Springer, Cham (2015). https://doi.org/10.1007/978-3-319-10705-9_34

26. Lafferriere, G., Pappas, G.J., Yovine, S.: Symbolic reachability computation for families of linear vector fields. J. Symb. Comput. **32**(3), 231–253 (2001). https://doi.org/10.1006/jsco.2001.0472

27. Le Guernic, C.: Reachability analysis of hybrid systems with linear continuous dynamics. Ph.D. thesis, Université Joseph-Fourier-Grenoble I (2009)

28. Le Guernic, C., Girard, A.: Reachability analysis of linear systems using support functions. Nonlinear Anal. Hybrid Syst. **4**(2), 250–262 (2010). https://doi.org/10.1016/j.nahs.2009.03.002

29. Liou, M.L.: A novel method of evaluating transient response. Proc. IEEE **54**(1), 20–23 (1966). https://doi.org/10.1109/proc.1966.4569

30. Schupp, S., Ábrahám, E., Makhlouf, I.B., Kowalewski, S.: Hypro: A C++ library of state set representations for hybrid systems reachability analysis. In: NFM. LNCS, vol. 10227, pp. 288–294 (2017). https://doi.org/10.1007/978-3-319-57288-8_20

31. Tran, H., Nguyen, L.V., Johnson, T.T.: Large-scale linear systems from order-reduction. In: ARCH. EPiC Series in Computing, vol. 43, pp. 60–67. EasyChair (2016). https://doi.org/10.29007/xk7x

Untangling the Graphs of Timed Automata to Decrease the Number of Clocks

Neda Saeedloei[1][(✉)] and Feliks Kluźniak[2]

[1] Towson University, Towson, USA
nsaeedloei@towson.edu
[2] LogicBlox, Atlanta, USA
feliks.kluzniak@logicblox.com

Abstract. For timed automata, the question of whether the number of clocks can be decreased without violating the semantics is known to be undecidable. It is, however, possible to obtain a number of clocks that is optimal, in a well-defined sense, for a timed automaton with a given graph and set of constraints. Such an optimal allocation of clocks can be improved further by changing the automaton's graph or its set of constraints. We address the first kind of change, and develop a novel method that may allow us to convert the automaton to one that requires fewer clocks, without changing its semantics.

1 Introduction

Timed automata [2] have been used as a standard formalism for specification and verification of real-time systems. Model checking [7] has been applied as an effective approach to formal verification of complex systems, including real-time systems. However, verification of a timed automaton can be computationally expensive, and the cost crucially depends on the number of clocks [3]. Although, for a given timed automaton, it is in general undecidable whether there exists a language-equivalent automaton with fewer clocks [10], the problem of decreasing the number of clocks of timed automata has been an active area of research [5,6,9,11,12]. The existing approaches for tackling the problem are based on either the syntactic form (e.g., [9,12]) or the semantics (e.g., [6,11]) of timed automata. Regardless of the particular approach—syntax or semantics based—the problem has been addressed mostly by constructing bisimilar timed automata [9,11].

In UPPAAL [6] a technique called "active clock reduction on the fly" is used during verification of timed automata [8]. This approach is semantic-based and works by identifying inactive clocks, i.e., clocks whose values do not matter in certain states. If two states differ only in the values of such variables, they are bisimilar, and therefore resetting these variables to a known value will make the two states identical, thus reducing the state space. (These results were later subsumed by those of Behrmann et al. [5], who reduce the state space—in a more general setting—by using a refined static analysis of the constraints.)

© Springer Nature Switzerland AG 2022
M. H. ter Beek and R. Monahan (Eds.): IFM 2022, LNCS 13274, pp. 168–187, 2022.
https://doi.org/10.1007/978-3-031-07727-2_10

Daws and Yovine [9] combine two methods for reducing the number of clocks. The first one is based on identifying the set of active clocks in each location of the automaton, and then applying a clock renaming to this set locally, to obtain a bisimilar automaton. The second method is based on equality between clocks: if two clocks are equal in a location, one is deleted. Their method will not always yield optimal results, as shown by Guha et al. [11].

The work of Guha et al. [11] is based on clock "zones" and constructing zone graphs. Given a timed automaton $\mathcal{A}$, their method constructs an automaton bisimilar to $\mathcal{A}$ that has the smallest number of clocks in the class of timed automata that are bisimilar to $\mathcal{A}$. It can be constructed in time that is doubly exponential in the number of clocks of $\mathcal{A}$. There is an exponential increase in the number of locations of the original automaton.

A more recent approach [12] is not based on constructing bisimilar timed automata, but on a compiler-like static flow analysis of a given automaton $\mathcal{A}$. This is made possible by abstracting from the particulars of the various constraints in $\mathcal{A}$ and considering an equivalence class of all automata that have the same graph and the same pattern of clock resets and uses. The resulting clock allocation is optimal *for that equivalence class*, in the sense that it is impossible to use a smaller number of clocks without violating the semantics of at least one member of the class (as long as all the members have their original graphs and constraints, modulo clock renaming). It turns out that this can be achieved when $\mathcal{A}$ belongs to TA_S: this is the class of automata that have at most one clock reset on any transition. Moreover, every clock has to be well-defined, i.e., on any path from the initial location to the use of a clock in a constraint, the clock is reset before it is used[1].

In the current paper we investigate what can be done by adopting the general approach of the cited work [12], but relaxing one of its assumptions: namely, that the underlying graph cannot be modified. We show that the graph of an automaton $\mathcal{A}$ can sometimes be "untangled" to decrease the number of clocks.

We present two original contributions. First, under the assumption that the original constraints in a timed automaton $\mathcal{A} \in TA_S$ cannot be changed, i.e., replaced by an equivalent set, we determine $\mathcal{A}$'s *real cost*. Intuitively, the real cost of $\mathcal{A}$ is the maximum of the smallest number of clocks that must be maintained on any path through the automaton. If the real cost of $\mathcal{A}$ is smaller than the number of clocks in an optimal clock allocation [12] for $\mathcal{A}$, then there is at least one language-equivalent automaton in TA_S that requires only as many clocks as the real cost of $\mathcal{A}$. By transforming $\mathcal{A}$ to such an automaton we improve the results obtained in the cited work [12]. This is our second contribution.

For example, the automaton on the left of Fig. 1 has two clocks, c_0 and c_1. It is not possible to lower the number of clocks of the automaton in its current form without violating its semantics. However, the real cost of this automaton

---

[1] This is a common-sense condition of a strictly technical nature. In the literature it is often assumed that all the clocks are implicitly reset to zero before the initial location: we would accommodate that by adding a sequence of extra epsilon transitions before the initial location, each such transition annotated by a reset.

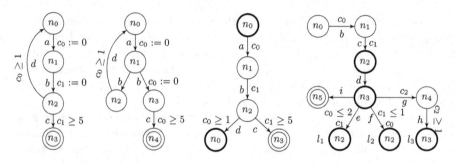

Fig. 1. Two equivalent automata   **Fig. 2.** Initial tree   **Fig. 3.** A tree

computed by our method is one. The automaton on the right of the figure is language-equivalent, but has only one clock.

2   Timed Automata

A *timed automaton* [2] is a tuple $\mathcal{A} = \langle \Sigma, Q, q_0, Q_f, C, T \rangle$, where Σ is a finite alphabet, Q is the (*finite*) set of locations, $q_0 \in Q$ is the initial location, $Q_f \subseteq Q$ is the set of final locations, C is a finite set of *clock* variables (clocks for short), and $T \subseteq Q \times Q \times \Sigma \times 2^C \times 2^{\Phi(C)}$ is the set of transitions. In each transition $(q, q', e, \lambda, \phi)$, λ is the set of clocks to be reset with the transition and $\phi \subset \Phi(C)$ is a set of clock constraints over C of the form $c \sim a$ (where $\sim \in \{\leq, <, \geq, >, =\}$, $c \in C$ and a is a constant in the set of rational numbers, $\mathbb{Q}$).

A *clock valuation* for C is a mapping from C to $\mathbb{R}^{\geq 0}$. ν *satisfies* a set of clock constraints ϕ over C iff every clock constraint in ϕ evaluates to true after each clock c is replaced with $\nu(c)$. For $\tau \in \mathbb{R}$, $\nu + \tau$ denotes the clock valuation which maps every clock c to the value $\nu(c) + \tau$. For $Y \subseteq C$, $[Y \mapsto \tau]\nu$ is the valuation which assigns τ to each $c \in Y$ and agrees with ν over the rest of the clocks.

A *timed word* over an alphabet Σ is a pair (σ, τ) where $\sigma = \sigma_1 \sigma_2...$ is a finite [1,4] or infinite [2] word over Σ and $\tau = \tau_1 \tau_2...$ is a finite or infinite sequence of (time) values such that (i) $\tau_i \in \mathbb{R}^{\geq 0}$, (ii) $\tau_i \leq \tau_{i+1}$ for all $i \geq 1$, and (iii) if the word is infinite, then for every $t \in \mathbb{R}^{\geq 0}$ there is some $i \geq 1$ such that $\tau_i > t$.

A run ρ of $\mathcal{A}$ over a timed word (σ, τ) is a sequence of the form $\langle q_0, \nu_0 \rangle \xrightarrow{\sigma_1}{\tau_1}$ $\langle q_1, \nu_1 \rangle \xrightarrow{\sigma_2}{\tau_2} \langle q_2, \nu_2 \rangle \xrightarrow{\sigma_3}{\tau_3} \ldots$, where for all $i \geq 0$, $q_i \in Q$ and ν_i is a clock valuation such that (i) $\nu_0(c) = 0$ for all clocks $c \in C$ and (ii) for every $i > 1$ there is a transition in T of the form $(q_{i-1}, q_i, \sigma_i, \lambda_i, \phi_i)$, such that $(\nu_{i-1} + \tau_i - \tau_{i-1})$ satisfies ϕ_i, and ν_i equals $[\lambda_i \mapsto 0](\nu_{i-1} + \tau_i - \tau_{i-1})$. The set $inf(\rho)$ consists of $q \in Q$ such that $q = q_i$ for infinitely many $i \geq 0$ in the run ρ.

A run over a finite timed word is *accepting* if it ends in a final location [4]. A run ρ over an infinite timed word is *accepting* iff $inf(\rho) \cap Q_f \neq \emptyset$ [2]. The *language* of $\mathcal{A}$, $L(\mathcal{A})$, is the set $\{(\sigma, \tau) \mid \mathcal{A} \text{ has an accepting run over } (\sigma, \tau)\}$.

3   Constructing a Better Automaton

A timed automaton belongs to the class TA_S if and only if for every transition $r = (q, q', e, \lambda, \phi)$, $|\lambda| \leq 1$ [12]. In the remainder of this paper we limit our attention to timed automata in TA_S. Moreover, we assume that $\mathcal{A} \in TA_S$ satisfies the following properties:

- In the graph of $\mathcal{A}$ there is a path from the initial location to every other location, and from every location to a final location.[2]
- Every clock c in $\mathcal{A}$ is *well-defined*: if c occurs in a constraint on transition r, then c must be reset on every path from the initial location to r.

Given an automaton $\mathcal{A} \in TA_S$, we want to know whether it is possible to transform it to a language-equivalent automaton $\mathcal{A}'$ *by changing its underlying graph, but not its clock constraints*, in such a way that an optimal clock allocation [12] for $\mathcal{A}'$ would require fewer clocks than that for $\mathcal{A}$. We begin by first building a tree $\mathcal{T}^{\mathcal{A}}$ that represents the same semantics as $\mathcal{A}$, but in a way that is more convenient for our purposes. $\mathcal{T}^{\mathcal{A}}$ is then analyzed to determine whether the aforementioned automaton $\mathcal{A}'$ exists. If so, we transform $\mathcal{T}^{\mathcal{A}}$ to an equivalent tree $\mathcal{T}^{\mathcal{A}'}$, which can then be converted to the full automaton $\mathcal{A}'$ (i.e., possibly with cycles). Finally, optimal clock allocation [12] can be performed for $\mathcal{A}'$.

In the remainder of this paper the term "equivalence" will always denote language equivalence.

3.1   Building a Tree from a Timed Automaton

Given $\mathcal{A}$, we build a tree $\mathcal{T}^{\mathcal{A}}$ that is a somewhat more direct representation of the paths in the graph of $\mathcal{A}$. Specifically, the root of $\mathcal{T}^{\mathcal{A}}$ is a copy of the initial location of $\mathcal{A}$. For every acyclic path of $\mathcal{A}$ that begins in the initial location there is an identical path in $\mathcal{T}^{\mathcal{A}}$ that begins at the root. If $\mathcal{A}$ includes cycles, we must make sure that $\mathcal{T}^{\mathcal{A}}$ is finite and that it is equivalent to $\mathcal{A}$. We do so by extending the tree with the remaining transitions and associating "looping leaves" with "looping ancestors".

The general idea can be illustrated by an example. Consider the original automaton of Fig. 1: n_0 is the initial location and n_3, enclosed in double circles, is the only final location. The corresponding tree is shown in Fig. 2 (we omit ":=0" from clock resets). The node and the leaf that are labeled with n_0 in the tree are the "looping ancestor" and the "looping leaf" : they both correspond to the same location in the original automaton. After we perform our transformations, the final automaton will be built by "unifying" looping leaves with the corresponding looping ancestors, thus re-introducing cycles into the graph.

Let $\mathcal{A} = \langle \Sigma, Q, q_0, Q_f, \mathcal{C}, T \rangle$ be a given timed automaton. We assume that each location of $\mathcal{A}$ is associated with a unique label in $\mathcal{L}$. The initial tree for $\mathcal{A}$ is constructed by a simple function (which is not presented here). In the worst case

---

[2] If there is no path from a location l to a final location, then l can be removed without affecting the language of the automaton.

the size of the tree is exponentially greater than the size of the original graph (see Sect. 4).

We assume $\mathcal{T}^{\mathcal{A}} = \langle \Sigma, V, n_0, V_f, \mathcal{C}, R \rangle$ is the tree corresponding to $\mathcal{A}$. V is the set of nodes and R is the set of transitions. n_0 is the root of $\mathcal{T}^{\mathcal{A}}$ (it corresponds to q_0) and V_f is the set of final nodes in $\mathcal{T}^{\mathcal{A}}$. A location of $\mathcal{A}$ might correspond to a number of different nodes in $\mathcal{T}^{\mathcal{A}}$. All the nodes that correspond to a final location in $\mathcal{A}$ are final nodes in $\mathcal{T}^{\mathcal{A}}$.

As we build $\mathcal{T}^{\mathcal{A}}$, we associate most of its nodes with unique labels. However, each looping leaf will have the same label as its looping ancestor. $\mathcal{M}^{\mathcal{T}^{\mathcal{A}}} : V \to \mathcal{L}$ denotes the labeling function in $\mathcal{T}^{\mathcal{A}}$. We use the following auxiliary notation:

- if $r = (n_i, n_j, e, \lambda, \phi) \in R$, then $source(r) = n_i$, $target(r) = n_j$, $clock(r) = \lambda$ (recall that $\mathcal{A} \in TA_S$, so $|\lambda| \leq 1$) and $constraints(r) = \phi$;
- if $n \in V$, then $out(n) = \{r \mid source(r) = n\}$ and $in(n) = \{r \mid target(r) = n\}$;
- if $p = r_1 \ldots r_k$ is a path, then $origin(p) = source(r_1)$, $end(p) = target(r_k)$.

In our examples different transitions will often be associated with different events. This will allow us to refer to a transition by the name of its event.

Most of the definitions in the remainder of this subsection are either taken directly from our earlier work [12], or are customized for the case of trees.

Definition 1. *Given* $\mathcal{T}^{\mathcal{A}}$, *we introduce the following notions:*

- *Let* $r \in R$ *and let* $c \in \mathcal{C}$. *An occurrence of* c *in* $constraints(r)$ *is called a* use *of clock* c *on* r. *An occurrence of* c *in* $clock(r)$ *is called a* reset *of* c *on* r. *All the uses on a given transition precede the reset on that transition (if any).*
- *Let* p *be a path between the root and a leaf,* r *be a transition on* p *and* c *be used on* r. *The use of* c *is* well-defined *iff it is reset on some transition* r' *that appears before* r *on* p.
- *Let* n *be a leaf such that* $\mathcal{M}^{\mathcal{T}^{\mathcal{A}}}(n) = \mu$ *for some* $\mu \in \mathcal{L}$. n *is a* looping leaf *if there is a node* n_a *on the path from the root to* n *such that* $\mathcal{M}^{\mathcal{T}^{\mathcal{A}}}(n_a) = \mu$. *Then* n_a *is the* looping ancestor *of* n, *and the path between* n_a *and* n *is an* open cycle *whose origin is* n_a.
- *A path* p *is* complete *iff* $origin(p) = n_0$ *and* $end(p) \in V_f$.

A looping leaf has a unique looping ancestor. A final leaf might also be looping.

Figure 3 shows a tree corresponding to some automaton. The looping ancestors and looping leaves are drawn with thick lines, while the final node is drawn with a double circle. The path between n_0 and n_5 is complete. The node labeled with n_2 is the looping ancestor of the leaves labeled with n_2 (i.e., l_1 and l_2) and the two paths between n_2 and l_1 and between n_2 and l_2 are open cycles. The other open cycle is between the two nodes labeled with n_3.

Observation 1. $\mathcal{T}^{\mathcal{A}}$ *has the following properties:*

- *Let* p *be a path such that* $origin(p) = n_0$ *and* $end(p)$ *is a looping leaf. There is exactly one label* $\mu \in \mathcal{L}$ *that labels more than one node on* p. *Moreover, there are exactly two nodes* n *and* n_a *on* p *such that* $\mathcal{M}^{\mathcal{T}^{\mathcal{A}}}(n) = \mathcal{M}^{\mathcal{T}^{\mathcal{A}}}(n_a) = \mu$: *the looping leaf that terminates the path and its looping ancestor.*
- *On every transition all uses of clocks are well-defined.*

Henceforth whenever we refer to a tree, we assume it is obtained from a timed automaton that satisfies the assumptions spelled out at the beginning of Sect. 3.

Definition 2. *Let T^A be a tree with set R of transitions and set V of nodes.*

- *Function act_target : $R \to V$ maps transition r to target(r) if target(r) is not a looping leaf, and otherwise to the looping ancestor of target(r).*
- *A sequence of transitions $r_0 r_1 \ldots r_n$ in T^A is called a* graph-path *(g-path for short), if source(r_{i+1}) = act_target(r_i), for $0 \le i < n$.*

Intuitively, the "actual target" of a transition is its target in the final automaton, after the looping leaves are unified with their looping ancestors (thus making them identical).

A g-path of T^A corresponds to a path in A. For instance, in the tree of Fig. 2, *abda* is a g-path corresponding to path *abda* in the original automaton of Fig. 1.

Definition 3. *Let p be a g-path and c be a clock that has a use on a transition of p. The use is* made visible *by p if it is not preceded on p by a reset of c.*

For a given T^A we define the following functions:

- *used : $R \to 2^C$ maps transition r to the set $\{c \mid c$ has a use on $r\}$.*
- *visible : $R \to 2^C$, where $c \in$ visible(r) iff a use of c is made visible by some g-path that begins at r.*
- *born : $R \to 2^C$ maps transition r to a set of clocks that is either a singleton or the empty set. $c \in$ born(r) iff $c \in$ clock(r) and there is a g-path $r r_1 \ldots$ such that $c \in$ visible(r_1).*
- *needed : $R \to 2^C$ is defined by needed(r) = born(r) $\cup$ visible(r).*

If $c \in$ needed(r), we say that c is needed on r.

Notice that $visible(r) = (needed(r) \setminus born(r)) \cup used(r)$.

In the tree of Fig. 3, $born(b) = born(f) = \{c_0\}$, $born(c) = born(e) = \{c_1\}$ and $born(g) = \{c_2\}$. $visible(b) = visible(i) = \emptyset$, $visible(c) = visible(e) = \{c_0\}$, $visible(f) = \{c_1\}$, $visible(d) = visible(g) = \{c_0, c_1\}$, and $visible(h) = \{c_0, c_1, c_2\}$. Observe that c_0 and c_1 are needed not only on c, d, f and e, but also on g and h. This is because in the final automaton the leaf labeled with n_3 will be unified with its looping ancestor (the actual target of h) and both c_0 and c_1 will be needed on paths that begin at this looping ancestor: c_0 is used on transition e and c_1 is used on transition f.

In the final automaton, the clocks of T^A will be replaced by a new set of clocks whose size cannot be smaller than the value of $needed(r)$ for any transition r, with one exception: if there are two different clocks, c_i and c_j, such that c_i "dies" on r (i.e., the value of c_i is not used on any subsequent transitions), c_j is not used on r and $c_j \in born(r)$, then they both belong to $needed(r)$, but c_i and c_j can be assigned the same clock.

Definition 4. *Let T^A be a tree with set R of transitions. Function weight : $R \to \mathbb{N}$ maps r to $|needed(r)| - 1$ iff*

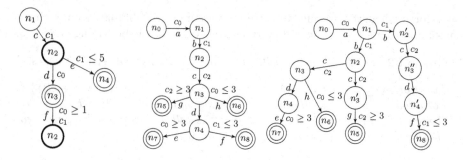

Fig. 4. A tree   **Fig. 5.** Two equivalent trees

- *there is a clock $c \in used(r)$ such that $\forall_{r' \in out(act\_target(r))}\ c \notin visible(r')$, and*
- *$born(r) \neq \emptyset \land born(r) \not\subset used(r)$.*

Otherwise $weight(r) = |needed(r)|$.

Intuitively, $weight(r)$ is the number of clocks that will have to be "alive" on r.

In the tree of Fig. 4 the weight of every transition is one. In particular, consider transition f: $c_0 \in used(f)$, $c_0 \notin visible(d)$ and $c_0 \notin visible(e)$ (where d and e are the outgoing transitions of the actual target of f), moreover, $born(f) = \{c_1\} \not\subset used(f) = \{c_0\}$, so $weight(f) = |needed(f)| - 1 = 1$.

Observation 2. *Let $\mathcal{T}^A$ be a tree with the set R of transitions. The number of clocks in an optimal clock allocation [12] for $\mathcal{T}^A$ is $\max\{weight(r) \mid r \in R\}$.*

We will say "the *cost* of an allocation" instead of "the number of clocks in a clock allocation".

3.2 Untangling Trees: An Overview

We begin this section with a motivating example. Consider the tree on the left of Fig. 5. Three clocks are used, and the weight of transition c is three: $weight(c) = |needed(c)| = |\{c_0, c_1, c_2\}|$. By Observation 2, an optimal allocation [12] for this tree would require three clocks. An equivalent tree is shown on the right of the figure: the weight of every transition is one, and therefore an optimal allocation would require only one clock.

The new tree is obtained by acting on the observation that there are four complete paths, each of which uses only one clock. By modifying the tree in such a way that the complete paths that use a clock are *untangled* from those that use other clocks, we effectively decrease the weight of each transition to one. This intuition will be formalised in what follows.

Definition 5. *Let $\mathcal{T}^A$ be a tree with root n_0 and n_f be a final node of $\mathcal{T}^A$. By $f\_tree(n_f)$ we denote the set of transitions of the maximal subtree of $\mathcal{T}^A$, rooted at n_0, such that each of its transitions can reach n_f via a g-path.*

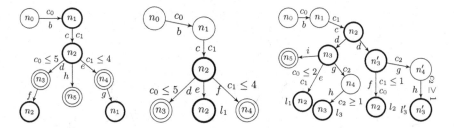

Fig. 6. Three f_trees   **Fig. 7.** A tree   **Fig. 8.** Untangled tree of Fig. 3

We will sometimes use the term f_tree to denote the underlying (sub)tree.

Each complete path in Fig. 5 is an f_tree. The tree of Fig. 3 is a single f_tree.

Observation 3. *Let m and n be two final nodes in T^A. $f\_tree(m) \subseteq f\_tree(n)$ iff there is a g-path from m to n. We say $f\_tree(m)$ is embedded in $f\_tree(n)$.*

In Fig. 6 $f\_tree(n_3) = f\_tree(n_4)$: they include all the transitions of the tree except for h. They are embedded in each other, and each is embedded in $f\_tree(n_5)$, which is the entire tree.

Given tree T^A corresponding to an automaton $A \in TA_S$, we are interested in transforming it into an equivalent "untangled" tree, whose transitions would weigh less: this tree would then require fewer clocks than T^A. One way of doing this is to make sure that f_trees that are not embedded in each other do not share any transitions. For instance, the tree on the left of Fig. 9 is such an untangled form of the tree of Fig. 7. Notice that to preserve the semantics of the original tree each f_tree must have access to the open cycle (with origin n_2). This is the reason for duplicating it at n'_2, the copy of n_2. The original tree requires two clocks, the untangled one requires only one.

Observation 4. *If a looping ancestor LA is duplicated during untangling, then all the open cycles that originate in LA must also be duplicated with it.*

It turns out that untangling within a *single* f_tree might also be beneficial. Figure 8 shows the untangled form of the tree of Fig. 3. Notice—again—the duplication of open cycles.

Definition 6. *An f_tree is fully untangled iff every node that has more than one outgoing transition is a looping ancestor, and each looping ancestor LA has at most one outgoing transition that does not belong to an open cycle originating in LA. A tree T^A is fully untangled iff (1) each of its f_trees is fully untangled and (2) if f_tree A is not embedded in f_tree B and vice versa, then the two share only the root node.*

Figure 10 shows a fully untangled f_tree which is also a fully untangled tree. The tree on the left of Fig. 9 is another fully untangled tree.

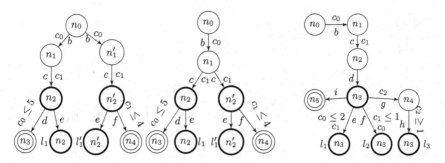

Fig. 9. Fully untangled and untangled trees of Fig. 7   **Fig. 10.** Impossible to untangle

A fully untangled tree shows the limits of what can be achieved. Our goal is to reach that limit by untangling as little as we can (compare the two equivalent trees of Fig. 9).

We will now present a semantics-preserving[3] untangling method that consists of two steps. In step one we analyse a tree T^A to determine whether it may have an untangled form for which the cost of an optimal clock allocation would be smaller than that for its original form. If this is the case then we proceed with step two: obtaining the untangled form of T^A.

3.3 Step One: Computing the Real Cost and Group Analysis

Definition 7. *The* real cost *of an f_tree is the cost of an optimal clock allocation for its fully untangled form (cf. Definition 6). The* real cost *of a tree T^A, denoted by real_ cost(T^A), is the maximum of the real costs of its f_trees.*

Recall that the cost of an optimal allocation is equal to the maximum weight of a transition (Observation 2). To determine the real cost of an f_tree one could untangle it fully and compute *needed* (and hence *weight*) by means of standard flow analysis with backward propagation (see, e.g., [12]).

Algorithm 1 simulates this by performing a backward traversal of the g-paths in the original f_tree, from the final node to the root, while carrying a "payload" that is the set of clocks whose uses are made visible by the g-path traversed (backwards) so far. When the traversal encounters a looping ancestor (i.e., an actual target of more than one transition) there is more than one possible route to take. Information about the alternative route(s) and the current payload is then pushed onto a stack, so that the traversal can later be resumed on the other route(s): this is similar to a standard backtracking search. A payload "seen" upon traversing a transition r is saved in a list associated with the target of r, so that r will not be traversed again with a payload that contains no new information: this is very much like the suppression of further propagation in data-flow analysis.

A slight complication is introduced by the fact that the open cycles that originate in the same looping ancestor cannot be separated from it without

---

[3] In the sense of language equivalence.

violating the semantics (Observation 4). This is dealt with by associating each looping ancestor LA with $cycle\_uses(LA)$, which is added to the payload whenever LA is passed. Intuitively, $cycle\_uses(LA)$ is the union of the sets of uses made visible by the open cycles that originate in LA. These sets are computed in advance, with at most one visit per transition. For the tree of Fig. 3 we have $cycle\_uses(n_2) = \{c_0, c_1\}$.

Each f_tree is analysed separately. If $f\_tree(m_f) \subseteq f\_tree(n_f)$, then it is enough to analyse $f\_tree(n_f)$: we say that m_f is *irrelevant*. If a final node m_f is on a path from the root to another final node, then we can treat m_f as irrelevant: the number of analysed f_trees will then not exceed the number of leaves.

Algorithm 1: Computing the real cost

Input   : A tree $T^{\mathcal{A}} = \langle E, V, n_0, V_f, C, R \rangle$
Output: $real\_cost(T^{\mathcal{A}})$.

$stack := [];$
$real\_cost := 0;$
foreach *relevant final node* $n_f \in V$ **do**
    foreach *node* $n \in V$ **do**
        $Seen(n) := \emptyset;$

    $try\_to\_push(n_f, \emptyset);$
    while *stack is not empty* **do**   /* Propagate */
        $(current\_node, payload) := stack.pop();$
        if *current_node is a looping ancestor* **then**
            $payload := payload \cup cycle\_uses(current\_node);$
            $real\_cost := \max(real\_cost, |payload|);$
            foreach *looping leaf* ll *of current_node* **do**
                $try\_to\_push(ll, payload);$

        if $current\_node \neq n_0$ **then**
            $r := in(current\_node); parent := source(r);$
            $payload := (payload \setminus clock(r)) \cup used(r);$
            $real\_cost := \max(real\_cost, |payload|);$
            $try\_to\_push(parent, payload);$

return $real\_cost$

Procedure try_to_push(a node *node*, a set of clocks *payload*)

---

if *there is no* $g \in Seen(node)$ *such that* $payload \subset g$ **then**
    $stack.push(\ (node, payload)\ );$
    foreach $g \in Seen(node)$ **do**
        if $g \subset payload$ **then**
            $Seen(node) := Seen(node) \setminus \{g\};$

    $Seen(node) := Seen(node) \cup \{payload\}$

Procedure computeCycleUses(tree T^A)

$cycle\_uses := \emptyset$;
foreach *looping ancestor* l_a *in* T^A **do**
  $\llcorner$ *ensureCycleUsesFor*(l_a);

Procedure ensureCycleUsesFor(node l_a)

if l_a *is not in domain of cycle_uses* **then**
  $\mid$ $s := \emptyset$;
  $\mid$ **foreach** *looping leaf ll of* l_a **do**
  $\mid$ $\llcorner$ $s := s \cup usesMadeVisible(ll, l_a)$;
  $\llcorner$ $cycle\_uses := cycle\_uses \cup \{(l_a, s)\}$;

Function usesMadeVisible(*node* n, *looping ancestor* l_a)

$uses := \emptyset$;
while $n \neq l_a$ **do**
  $\mid$ **if** n *is a looping ancestor* **then**
  $\mid$ $\mid$ *ensureCycleUsesFor*(n);
  $\mid$ $\llcorner$ $uses := uses \cup cycle\_uses(n)$;
  $\mid$ $trans := in(n)$;   /* there is only one */
  $\mid$ $uses := (uses \setminus clock(trans)) \cup used(trans)$;
  $\llcorner$ $n := source(trans)$;
return $uses$

Let V be the set of nodes, L be the set of leaves, and C be the set of clocks. The inner loop (for one f_tree) terminates after at most $|V| \cdot 2^{|C|}$ steps, since each step is accompanied by adding a new set to $Seen(n)$ (for some $n \in V$). The cost of each step is dominated by the check for membership in $Seen(n)$: at most $O(2^{|C|})$. So the total worst-case cost does not exceed $O(|L| \cdot |V| \cdot 2^{2 \cdot |C|})$, where $|C|$ cannot exceed the number of edges in the original graph (for automata in TA_S).

Theorem 1. *Algorithm 1 is correct. That is, given a tree T^A, it computes real_cost(T^A) in the sense of Definition 7.*[4]

After determining the real cost, we must find out whether profitable untangling is possible. To this end we perform *group analysis*, whose results will not only allow us to determine the weight of each transition, but also provide useful guidance in the process of untangling itself.

Definition 8. *A* group *is a set of clocks. An* l-group *is a pair consisting of the label of a leaf and a non-empty group. An l-group* (l, g) belongs *to a transition* r *if*

---

[4] An outline of the proof, too long to include here, is available from the authors.

1. *there is a (possibly empty) path from* $target(r)$ *to* l*; and*
2. *g is the greatest set such that for every* $c \in g$ *there is at least one (possibly empty) g-path p from* $target(r)$ *to a final node that passes through* l*, and (a)* c *is used on* r*, or (b) a use of* c *is made visible by* p*.*

In the example of Fig. 7 the l-groups that belong to transition c are $(n_3, \{c_0\})$, $(l_1, \{c_0, c_1\})$ and $(n_4, \{c_1\})$. If e had a use of c_1, then we would have $(n_3, \{c_0, c_1\})$ (because $cycle\_uses(n_2)$ would contain c_1).

The purpose of group analysis is to annotate each transition with all the l-groups that belong to it. This can be done by piggybacking on Algorithm 1 (see Algorithm 2). The payload is extended with information about the latest visited leaf, and at each visited transition the current payload is added to the annotations of that transition. In the worst case the number of visited transitions is multiplied by $|L|$.

Algorithm 2: Group analysis

Input   : A tree $T^A = \langle E, V, n_0, V_f, C, R \rangle$
Output: Transition annotations and $real\_cost(T^A)$.

$stack := [];$
$real\_cost := 0;$
foreach *transition* $r \in R$ **do**
  $\quad$ $annot(r) := \emptyset;$

foreach *relevant final node* $n_f \in V$ **do**
  $\quad$ **foreach** *node* $n \in V$ **do**
    $\quad\quad$ $Seen(n) := \emptyset;$
  $\quad$ $try\_to\_push(n_f, (n_f, \emptyset));$
  $\quad$ **while** *stack is not empty* **do**   /* Propagate: */
    $\quad\quad$ $(current\_node, (n, group)) := stack.pop();$
    $\quad\quad$ **if** *current_node is a looping ancestor* **then**
      $\quad\quad\quad$ $group := group \cup cycle\_uses(current\_node);$
      $\quad\quad\quad$ $real\_cost := max(real\_cost, |group|);$
      $\quad\quad\quad$ **foreach** *looping leaf* ll *of current_node* **do**
        $\quad\quad\quad\quad$ $try\_to\_push(ll, (ll, group));$

    $\quad\quad$ **if** *current_node* $\neq n_0$ **then**
      $\quad\quad\quad$ $r := in(current\_node); parent := source(r);$
      $\quad\quad\quad$ **if** *n is a leaf and group* $\neq \emptyset$ *and there is no g such that* $((n, g) \in annot(r) \wedge group \subset g)$ **then**
        $\quad\quad\quad\quad$ $augment((n, group), annot(r));$
      $\quad\quad\quad$ $group := (group \setminus clock(r)) \cup used(r);$
      $\quad\quad\quad$ $real\_cost := max(real\_cost, |group|);$
      $\quad\quad\quad$ $try\_to\_push(parent, (n, group));$

$return$ $annot, real\_cost$

Procedure try_to_push(*node*, $(n, group)$)

---

   if *there is no* $(n, g) \in Seen(node)$ *such that* $group \subset g$ **then**
      | *stack.push*($(node, (n, group))$);
      | *augment*($(n, group)$, *Seen(node)*);

Procedure augment($(n, group)$, *setOfPairs*)

---

   foreach *g such that* $((n, g) \in setOfPairs \land g \subset group)$ **do**
      | *setOfPairs* := *setOfPairs* \ $\{(n, g)\}$;
   setOfPairs := *setOfPairs* $\cup \{(n, group)\}$

After group analysis terminates, we can rearrange the annotations to produce the mapping, $\mathcal{M}_R : R \rightarrow 2^{2^V \times 2^C}$, which associates each transition r with a set of pairs of the form $(LS, group)$, where LS is a set of leaves such that, for each $l \in LS$, $(l, group)$ belongs to r. The union of all the groups in $\mathcal{M}_R(r)$ and $used(r)$ is $needed(r)$. For the tree of Fig. 3 we will obtain:

$$\mathcal{M}_R(b) = \{((\{n_5, l_1, l_2, l_3\}, \{c_0\}))\}, \qquad \mathcal{M}_R(c) = \{((\{n_5, l_1, l_2, l_3\}, \{c_0, c_1\}))\},$$
$$\mathcal{M}_R(d) = \{((\{l_1, l_3\}, \{c_0\}), (\{l_2, l_3\}, \{c_1\}))\}, \qquad \mathcal{M}_R(e) = \{((\{l_1\}, \{c_0, c_1\}))\},$$
$$\mathcal{M}_R(g) = \{((\{l_3\}, \{c_1, c_2\}), (\{l_3\}, \{c_0, c_2\}))\}, \qquad \mathcal{M}_R(f) = \{((\{l_2\}, \{c_0, c_1\}))\},$$
$$\mathcal{M}_R(h) = \{((\{l_3\}, \{c_1\}), (\{l_3\}, \{c_0\}))\}, \qquad \mathcal{M}_R(i) = \{\}.$$

The real cost is two. $needed(b) = \{c_0\}$, $needed(c) = needed(d) = needed(e) = needed(f) = \{c_0, c_1\}$, $needed(g) = needed(h) = \{c_0, c_1, c_2\}$, and $needed(i) = \{\}$.

3.4   Step Two: Untangling

Now that we have developed a method for computing the real cost of a tree, we return to our original problem. Given $\mathcal{T}^A$ with its real cost we want to know whether we must untangle the tree to achieve the real cost. If so, can we do it by producing a tree that is smaller than its fully untangled form?

To answer this question, we examine the transitions of $\mathcal{T}^A$ to see if there is a transition whose weight is greater than the tree's real cost. If there are such transitions, then $\mathcal{T}^A$ would require more clocks than the real cost (Observation 2). But for a sufficiently untangled form of $\mathcal{T}^A$ the cost will be the real cost.

Definition 9. *A transition r of tree $\mathcal{T}^A$ is* heavy *if* $weight(r) > real\_cost(\mathcal{T}^A)$.

For the tree of Fig. 3 $weight(g) = weight(h) = 3$, so both g and h are heavy transitions (remember that the real cost is 2). The tree of Fig. 10 is very similar to this one: n_2 is not a looping ancestor and all the non-final leaves (i.e., l_1, l_2 and l_3) are the looping leaves of n_3. The annotations on transitions are

$$\mathcal{M}_R(b) = \{(\{n_5, l_1, l_2, l_3\}, \{c_0\})\}, \quad \mathcal{M}_R(g) = \{(\{l_3\}, \{c_0, c_1, c_2\})\},$$
$$\mathcal{M}_R(c) = \mathcal{M}_R(d) = \{(\{n_5, l_1, l_2, l_3\}, \{c_0, c_1\})\}, \quad \mathcal{M}_R(h) = \{(\{l_3\}, \{c_0, c_1\})\},$$
$$\mathcal{M}_R(e) = \{(\{l_1\}, \{c_0, c_1\})\}, \quad \mathcal{M}_R(f) = \{(\{l_2\}, \{c_0, c_1\})\}, \quad \mathcal{M}_R(i) = \{\}.$$

The real cost is 3. There is no heavy transition: $weight(g) = weight(h) = 3$ and the weight of other transitions is at most 2. In fact, the tree is fully untangled.

The second step of our untangling method takes $\mathcal{T}^A$ with some heavy transitions, along with $real\_cost(\mathcal{T}^A)$, and returns the untangled form of the tree.

In Sect. 3.3 we showed the role of groups of clocks in computing the function *needed*. Next we show that l-groups also play an important role in the actual untangling: they are used to determine not only the paths that should be untangled, but also the nodes at which the untangling should begin and end (see Sects. 3.4.1 and 3.4.2). This is essential for ensuring that the number of nodes and transitions in the untangled tree stays reasonably low.

For simplicity of presentation and to help the reader's intuition we present this step in two phases. In the first phase we consider trees without open cycles, similar to the trees of Fig. 5. In the second phase we consider general trees.

3.4.1 Untangling Trees Without Open Cycles

If $\mathcal{T}^A$ does not include open cycles, then all its leaves are final. Moreover, if $\mathcal{T}^A$ has a heavy transition, then it must have at least two final leaves, and two f_trees (not embedded in each other). The heavy transition can become light only by separating parts of the appropriate f_trees from each other.

Observation 5. *Let $\mathcal{T}^A$ be a tree without open cycles, and let r be a heavy transition. Then there must exist two pairs (LS_1, g_1) and (LS_2, g_2) in $\mathcal{M}_R(r)$ such that $LS_1 \cap LS_2 = \emptyset$, $g_1 \nsubseteq g_2$ and $g_2 \nsubseteq g_1$.*

Procedure split(transition r, set of leaves *friends*, set of leaves *enemies*)

---

choose some $join \in joins(friends, enemies)$;
while $join \neq source(r)$ **do**
$\quad \lfloor \quad join := split\_join(friends, enemies, join);$

Function split_join(set of leaves *friends*, set of leaves *enemies*, a node *join*): a node

---

> **foreach** *transition* $r \in out(join)$ **do**
> > $(tfriends, tenemies) := refine\_leaves(friends, enemies, r)$;
> > **if** $tfriends \neq \emptyset \wedge tenemies \neq \emptyset$ **then**
> > > $split(r, friends, enemies)$;
>
> $friendlyTransitions := \emptyset$;
> **foreach** *transition* $r \in out(join)$ **do**
> > $(tfriends, tenemies) := refine\_leaves(friends, enemies, r)$;
> > **if** $tfriends \neq \emptyset \wedge tenemies = \emptyset$ **then**
> > > $friendlyTransitions := friendlyTransitions \cup \{r\}$;
>
> $otherTransitions := out(join) \setminus friendlyTransitions$;
> $join' := $ a copy of *join*;
> **foreach** *transition* $r \in otherTransitions$ **do**
> > $source(r) := join'$;
>
> $NewTrans := $ a copy of $in(join)$;
> $target(NewTrans) := join'$;
> update the annotations on $in(join)$ and $NewTrans$;
> return $source(in(join))$;

Function refine_leaves(set of leaves f, set of leaves e, a transition r): two sets of leaves

---

> $all\_leaves := \emptyset$;
> **foreach** $(LS, group) \in \mathcal{M}_R(r)$ **do**
> > $all\_leaves := all\_leaves \cup LS$;
>
> $tfriends := f \cap all\_leaves$;
> $tenemies := e \cap all\_leaves$;
> return $(tfriends, tenemies)$;

Definition 10. *Let e and f be two different leaves in $\mathcal{T}^A$. Then $join(e, f)$ is their nearest common ancestor (i.e., the one furthest from the root).*

Definition 11. *Let E and F be two disjoint sets of leaves in $\mathcal{T}^A$. We define $joins(E, F) = \{join(e, f) \mid e \in E \wedge f \in F\}$.*

Untangling $\mathcal{T}^A$ is performed by successively invoking procedure *split* on some heavy transition, until no heavy transitions are left. The order in which the heavy transitions are considered does not affect the correctness of the result.

The steps of the algorithm are illustrated by an example. Consider the tree on the left-hand side of Fig. 5. The tree requires three clocks in its current form, while its real cost is one. c is the heaviest transition: $weight(c) = 3$. b is the heavy transition that is closest to the root: $weight(b) = 2$. From group analysis we have $\mathcal{M}_R(b) = \{(\{n_6, n_7\}, \{c_0\}), (\{n_8\}, \{c_1\})\}$: this indicates that the paths ending at

n_6 and n_7 must be separated from the path ending at n_8. Equivalently, a part of $f\_tree(n_8)$ must be separated from $f\_tree(n_6)$ and $f\_tree(n_7)$. It is convenient to think of $\{n_6, n_7\}$ and $\{n_8\}$ as disjoint sets of *friends* and *enemies*.

The process begins by invoking $split(b, \{n_6, n_7\}, \{n_8\})$. Untangling can begin either at n_3 or at n_4: $joins(\{n_6, n_7\}, \{n_8\}) = \{n_3, n_4\}$. Suppose we begin at n_4 by invoking $split\_join(\{n_6, n_7\}, \{n_8\}, n_4)$. This duplicates n_4 and its incoming transition, in effect moving the join one node up: the new join is n_3.

Procedure *split_join* begins its task by examining all the outgoing transitions of the join. If one of them is a transition r for which $\mathcal{M}_R(r)$ includes two groups of leaves, LS_1 and LS_2, such that $friends \cap LS_1 \neq \emptyset$ and $enemies \cap LS_2 \neq \emptyset$ then $split(r, friends, enemies)$ is invoked recursively. Once all the outgoing paths of a join are untangled (if necessary) then the paths are divided into two sets: a set where the paths lead to leaves in *friends* and another one where the paths lead to leaves outside *friends*.

Transitions that begin the paths in the latter set are re-rooted in a new node, which is connected to the parent of the join. Annotations (i.e., sets of l-groups) on the transitions that lead from the parent to the old join and its new copy are updated to reflect the new situation: the join has thus been split.

This process continues until the source of the original heavy transition is reached. The heavy transition has then been split into two lighter ones.

3.4.2 Untangling General Trees

Untangling trees with open cycles requires extra care. In particular, when a looping ancestor n is being duplicated, we must make sure that *all* the nodes that were previously reachable from n, remain reachable from the copies of n. This is captured in Observation 4.

As we discussed in Sect. 3.4.1 a tree without cycles but with a heavy transition must include at least two f_trees that are not embedded in each other. This is not the case in the presence of cycles: it might be possible to reduce the weight of a transition by untangling within a single f_tree. Observe that in this case all the heavy transitions must reside in an open cycle. Figure 3 shows one such example: the entire tree is one f_tree. g and h are the heavy transitions with weight 3. $\mathcal{M}_R(g) = \mathcal{M}_R(h) = \{(\{l_3\}, \{c_1, c_2\}), (\{l_3\}, \{c_0, c_2\})\}$. The groups are separable, but associated with the same set of leaves, so there are no joins reachable from g and h where untangling can begin. However, this indicates that the incoming transition of the looping ancestor of l_3 (i.e., d), must be annotated with separable groups that contain c_0 and c_1. Indeed, $\mathcal{M}_R(d) = \{(\{l_1, l_3\}, \{c_0\}), (\{l_2, l_3\}, \{c_1\})\}$. Since $joins(l_1, l_2) = \{n_3\}$ we can begin untangling by duplicating n_3 and its incoming transition. This is enough to make both the heavy transitions lighter. The resulting tree is shown in Fig. 8: g and h on the left and on the right are now annotated with $\{(\{l_3\}, \{c_0, c_2\})\}$, and $\{(\{l_3'\}, \{c_1, c_2\})\}$, respectively.

We can now adjust our untangling method to account for open cycles. The main steps are as before: *split* is successively invoked on heavy transitions until no heavy transitions are left. There are two main extensions of the algorithm:

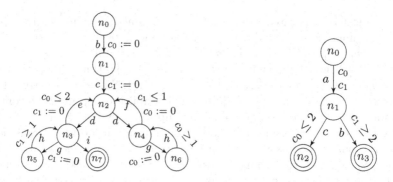

Fig. 11. The automaton for the tree of Fig. 8   **Fig. 12.** An automaton outside TA_S

- When a looping ancestor n is duplicated, we must make sure that all the open cycles originating at n are duplicated and attached to the copy of n.
- If a heavy transition r can be made lighter only by separating two groups that are associated with the same leaf l, then l is a looping leaf. Then untangling must begin with the incoming transition of the looping ancestor of l.

It is worth mentioning that if the root of a tree is also a looping ancestor, then the root is never split/duplicated by the algorithm: by the time the root is reached the current payload must have become empty (since all clocks are well-defined).

3.5 Obtaining the Final Automaton

The graph of the untangled $\mathcal{T}^A$ might not be the graph of the target automaton yet, if $\mathcal{T}^A$ includes open cycles. The open cycles must be replaced with actual cycles in order to obtain the graph of the final automaton. This step can be performed by a simple algorithm that unifies each looping leaf with its looping ancestor by removing the leaf and setting the target of its incoming transition to the looping ancestor. We use $\mathcal{G}^A$ to denote the resulting graph.

After obtaining the graph of the target automaton, we use the existing algorithm [12] to optimally allocate clocks in $\mathcal{G}^A$ to obtain the final automaton.

Figure 11 shows the final automaton for the tree of Fig. 8.

4   Implementation and Experimental Results

All our algorithms are implemented (in Python). The implementation has been applied to all the examples in the paper. We have also run a set of benchmarks consisting of timed automata that were generated randomly within the bounds of a set of parameters such as the number of locations and clocks.

Table 1 shows a selection of results from this set of benchmarks. These results suggest that our method can, indeed, be beneficial in practice.

In the course of our experiments we occasionally encountered very large initial trees. This occurred when the random graph became very complicated, with many nested cycles and converging paths. It is doubtful that such complication would arise in practice, i.e., in a timed automaton that is produced by humans and intended for human inspection.

Table 1. Experimental results

	$\mathcal{A}$			$\mathcal{T}^{\mathcal{A}}$	Untangled $\mathcal{T}^{\mathcal{A}}$	Optimal allocation	Real cost	Final automaton		
	$|Q|$	$|T|$	$|Q_f|$	nodes	nodes	$(\mathcal{A})$		$|Q|$	$|T|$	$|Q_f|$
1	11	11	3	12	16	7	4	15	15	3
2	15	19	3	38	46	7	3	39	45	16
3	11	11	3	12	17	6	3	16	16	3
4	21	33	3	190	194	6	3	123	193	32
5	17	20	3	21	34	5	3	28	33	4
6	16	20	4	22	29	5	2	27	28	4
7	12	14	3	15	21	5	2	19	20	3
8	12	14	2	16	25	4	2	22	24	4
9	16	23	3	39	41	3	2	28	40	5
10	7	9	2	11	12	3	2	8	11	4
11	8	11	2	14	17	3	1	14	16	6
12	7	9	2	11	13	2	1	10	12	4

5   Stepping Outside TA_S

After a few trivial modifications our method can be profitably applied to all automata that have well-defined clocks, i.e., also automata that have more than one reset per transition. We did not consider them here, because for such automata the notion of optimal clock allocation is problematic [12]. For a very simple example of the kind of difficulties that might arise, consider Fig. 12, which depicts both an automaton and its tree. Our method would reduce the number of clocks from two to one by duplicating node n_1 and transition a. But for this example the same result could be achieved just by *conflating* the two clocks, i.e., by replacing $c_1 \geq 2$ with $c_0 \geq 2$ on transition b. In other cases a similar improvement can be obtained by *splitting* a clock into two clocks [12]. In general, the two operations (conflation and splitting) make it computationally very difficult to obtain an allocation that is optimal (in the sense used here): for automata in TA_S there are no such operations, and a strictly optimal result is within reach.

6   Conclusions

We study the problem of minimizing the number of clocks for timed automata in the class TA_S [12]. For any automaton in TA_S there is at most one clock reset on any transition. Additionally, we assume that every clock is well-defined, i.e., it is reset before being used.

Given an automaton $\mathcal{A} \in TA_S$ with an optimal clock allocation ("optimal" in the sense of the cited work [12]) whose cost (i.e., number of clocks) is n, we compute the *real cost* of $\mathcal{A}$, i.e., the minimum of the costs of clock allocations for automata in $\mathcal{U}(\mathcal{A})$ (the set containing $\mathcal{A}$ and the language-equivalent automata that can be obtained by changing the graph of $\mathcal{A}$—via "untangling" its paths— but without changing the constraints). If the real cost of $\mathcal{A}$ is smaller than n, then we know that there is a non-empty set $S \subset \mathcal{U}(\mathcal{A})$ of automata for which the cost of an optimal clock allocation is the same as the real cost of $\mathcal{A}$. We present an algorithm that transforms $\mathcal{A}$ to an automaton in S.

References

1. Abdulla, P.A., Deneux, J., Ouaknine, J., Worrell, J.: Decidability and complexity results for timed automata via channel machines. In: Caires, L., Italiano, G.F., Monteiro, L., Palamidessi, C., Yung, M. (eds.) ICALP 2005. LNCS, vol. 3580, pp. 1089–1101. Springer, Heidelberg (2005). https://doi.org/10.1007/11523468_88
2. Alur, R., Dill, D.L.: A theory of timed automata. Theor. Comput. Sci. **126**(2), 183–235 (1994)
3. Alur, R., Madhusudan, P.: Decision problems for timed automata: a survey. In: Bernardo, M., Corradini, F. (eds.) SFM-RT 2004. LNCS, vol. 3185, pp. 1–24. Springer, Heidelberg (2004). https://doi.org/10.1007/978-3-540-30080-9_1
4. Baier, C., Bertrand, N., Bouyer, P., Brihaye, T.: When are timed automata determinizable? In: Albers, S., Marchetti-Spaccamela, A., Matias, Y., Nikoletseas, S., Thomas, W. (eds.) ICALP 2009. LNCS, vol. 5556, pp. 43–54. Springer, Heidelberg (2009). https://doi.org/10.1007/978-3-642-02930-1_4
5. Behrmann, G., Bouyer, P., Fleury, E., Larsen, K.G.: Static guard analysis in timed automata verification. In: Garavel, H., Hatcliff, J. (eds.) TACAS 2003. LNCS, vol. 2619, pp. 254–270. Springer, Heidelberg (2003). https://doi.org/10.1007/3-540-36577-X_18
6. Bengtsson, J., Larsen, K., Larsson, F., Pettersson, P., Yi, W.: UPPAAL—a tool suite for automatic verification of real-time systems. In: Alur, R., Henzinger, T.A., Sontag, E.D. (eds.) HS 1995. LNCS, vol. 1066, pp. 232–243. Springer, Heidelberg (1996). https://doi.org/10.1007/BFb0020949
7. Clarke, E.M., Jr., Grumberg, O., Peled, D.A.: Model Checking. MIT Press, Cambridge (1999)
8. Daws, C., Tripakis, S.: Model checking of real-time reachability properties using abstractions. In: Steffen, B. (ed.) TACAS 1998. LNCS, vol. 1384, pp. 313–329. Springer, Heidelberg (1998). https://doi.org/10.1007/BFb0054180
9. Daws, C., Yovine, S.: Reducing the number of clock variables of timed automata. In: Proceedings of the 17th IEEE Real-Time Systems Symposium (RTSS '96), December 4–6, 1996, Washington, DC, USA. pp. 73–81 (1996)). https://doi.org/10.1007/978-3-642-33365-1_12
10. Finkel, O.: Undecidable Problems About Timed Automata. CoRR abs/0712.1363 (2007)

11. Guha, S., Narayan, C., Arun-Kumar, S.: Reducing clocks in timed automata while preserving Bisimulation. In: Baldan, P., Gorla, D. (eds.) CONCUR 2014. LNCS, vol. 8704, pp. 527–543. Springer, Heidelberg (2014). https://doi.org/10.1007/978-3-662-44584-6_36
12. Saeedloei, N., Kluźniak, F.: Clock allocation in timed automata and graph colouring. In: Proceedings of the 21st International Conference on Hybrid Systems: Computation and Control (part of CPS Week), HSCC 2018, Porto, Portugal, 11–13 April 2018, pp. 71–80 (2018). http://doi.acm.org/10.1145/3178126.3178138

Probability

Probabilistic Model Checking of BPMN Processes at Runtime

Yliès Falcone, Gwen Salaün, and Ahang Zuo[✉]

Univ. Grenoble Alpes, CNRS, Grenoble INP, Inria, LIG, 38000 Grenoble, France
ahang.zuo@inria.fr

Abstract. Business Process Model and Notation (BPMN) is a standard business process modelling language that allows users to describe a set of structured tasks, which results in a service or product. Before running a BPMN process, the user often has no clear idea of the probability of executing some task or specific combination of tasks. This is, however, of prime importance for adjusting resources associated with tasks and thus optimising costs. In this paper, we define an approach to perform probabilistic model checking of BPMN models at runtime. To do so, we first transform the BPMN model into a Labelled Transition System (LTS). Then, by analysing the execution traces obtained when running multiple instances of the process, we can compute the probability of executing each transition in the LTS model, and thus generate a Probabilistic Transition System (PTS). Finally, we perform probabilistic model checking for verifying that the PTS model satisfies a given probabilistic property. This verification loop is applied periodically to update the results according to the execution of the process instances. All these steps are implemented in a tool chain, which was applied successfully to several realistic BPMN processes.

1 Introduction

A business process describes a set of structured tasks that follow a specific order and thus results in a product or service. The business process model and notation (BPMN), proposed by OMG, is the de facto standard for developing business processes [15]. BPMN relies on a graphical workflow-based notation that describes the structured tasks in a business process and the relationships between these tasks.

The BPMN standard was quickly adopted by industry and academia, even though several flaws were identified. One of them regards the lack of formal semantics. Several approaches proposed to use Petri nets or automata-based languages for filling this gap. Related to formal semantics, the lack of formal analysis techniques appeared as another weakness. The final goal is to provide (ideally automated) verification techniques and tools for ensuring that processes respect some functional and non-functional properties of interest (e.g. the absence of deadlocks, the execution of the process within a reasonable amount of time, the

© Springer Nature Switzerland AG 2022
M. H. ter Beek and R. Monahan (Eds.): IFM 2022, LNCS 13274, pp. 191–208, 2022.
https://doi.org/10.1007/978-3-031-07727-2_11

occupancy of resources, etc.). All these checks are particularly useful for optimising processes and thus reducing the costs associated with their execution.

In this paper, we tackle the problem of computing the probability of executing certain tasks or combination of tasks when running the processes. The
possibility of executing one task or another comes from the use of different kinds
of gateways in the BPMN process (e.g. exclusive gateways). These probabilities
are difficult to determine, especially when multiple instances of the process are
executed at the same time. In that case, since resources are necessary for executing some specific tasks, knowing these probabilities is of prime importance
for better adjusting the corresponding resources and thus converging to an optimal allocation of resources. It is worth noting that before executing the process
multiple times, the developer has often no clear idea regarding the probability of
executing some task or a specific sequence of tasks. Therefore, there is a need for
automated techniques that can compute (and update) at runtime these probabilities, thus allowing the verification of probabilistic properties (e.g. what is the
probability to execute task T? Is the probability to execute task T1 followed by
T2 higher than 40%?).

In this work, we define an approach to perform probabilistic model checking
of BPMN processes at runtime. To do so, we assume that a process is described
using an executable version of BPMN. The process can be executed multiple
times, each execution of the process is called an instance. Different instances
may perform different tasks in the process. Our approach first monitors these
executions to extract from the corresponding logs the probability of executing
each individual task. These probabilities are used to build a semantic model
of the BPMN process where these probabilities appear explicitly. This model
is called a Probabilistic Transition System (PTS). Then, given a probabilistic
property expressed in a dedicated temporal logic and this PTS, a probabilistic
model checker is called for verifying whether the property is true/false or for
computing the expected probability of that property. Note that this approach
is not applied once and for all, because more instances of the process can keep
executing including variations in terms of frequency of the executed tasks. Based
on these variations, the probability of each transition of the LTS evolves over
time. Therefore, the PTS is updated periodically, and the model checker is called
again. The result of our approach is thus not a single value, but a dynamic curve
indicating the evolution of the property evaluation over time.

To summarise, the main contributions of this work are as follows:

- Monitoring techniques for extracting at runtime relevant information about
  the execution of multiple instances of a process.
- Periodic computation of a Probabilistic Transition System by analysing execution logs resulting of the monitoring of the process.
- Integrated toolbox for probabilistic model checking of BPMN processes at
  runtime.
- Validation of our approach on a large set of realistic BPMN processes.

The remainder of this paper is organised as follows. In Sect. 2, we describe the
concepts and definitions used in the subsequent sections. In Sect. 3, we present

the approach in detail. Section 4 focuses on the tool support and the experiments performed for validation purposes. Section 5 describes related work. Finally, in Sect. 6, we present our conclusions and future work.

2 Models

In this section, we introduce the preliminary concepts.

BPMN. Business process model and notation (BPMN) is a workflow-based notation for describing business processes [15]. Originally, it was a modelling notation, but recent frameworks also allow the execution of such processes using a process automation engine or by translation to an executable language. The syntax of a BPMN process is given by a graph-based structure where vertices (or nodes) correspond to events, tasks and gateways, and edges (or flows) connect these nodes.

Figure 1 describes a fragment of the BPMN notation showing the main elements. Events include the initial/start event and the end event, which are used to initialise and terminate processes. We assume there is only one start event, and at least one end event. A task is an atomic activity containing only one incoming flow and one outgoing flow. Gateways are used to describe the control flow of the process. There are two patterns for each type of gateway: the split pattern and the merge pattern. The split pattern consists of a single incoming flow and multiple outgoing flows. The merge pattern consists of multiple incoming flows and a single outgoing flow. Several types of gateways are available, such as exclusive, parallel, and inclusive gateways. An exclusive gateway corresponds to a choice among several flows. A parallel gateway executes all possible flows at the same time. An inclusive gateway executes one or several flows. The choice of flows to execute in exclusive and inclusive gateways depends on the evaluation of data-based conditions.

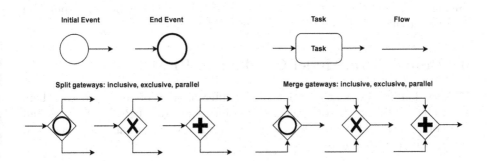

Fig. 1. Excerpt of the BPMN notation

In this paper, we consider multiple executions of a single process. Each execution is called an *instance* and is characterised by an identifier and the list of consecutive tasks executed by this process. We assume that a BPMN process cannot run infinitely and that each instance terminates at some point. Therefore, the list of tasks associated to an instance is always finite.

LTS. We use Labelled Transition Systems as a semantic model of BPMN processes, as described in [17,20,23].

Definition 1 (LTS). *A labelled transition system (LTS) is a tuple $\langle Q, \Sigma, q_{\mathrm{init}}, \Delta \rangle$ where: Q is a set of states; Σ is a finite set of labels/actions; $q_{\mathrm{init}} \in Q$ is the initial state; $\Delta \subseteq Q \times \Sigma \times Q$ is the transition relation.*

A transition $(q, a, q') \in \Delta$, written $q \xrightarrow{a} q'$, means that the system can move from state q to state q' by performing action a.

PTS. We also need a more expressive model than LTS because we want to associate transitions with probabilities. We therefore rely on Probabilistic Transition Systems [18], which is a probabilistic extension of the LTS model.

Definition 2 (PTS). *A probabilistic transition system (PTS) is a tuple $\langle S, A, s_{\mathrm{init}}, \delta, P \rangle$ such that $\langle S, A, s_{\mathrm{init}}, \delta \rangle$ is a labelled transition system as per Definition 1 and $P : \delta \to [0, 1]$ is the probability labelling function.*

$P(s \xrightarrow{a} s') \in [0, 1]$ is the probability for the system to move from state s to state s', performing action a. For each state s, the sum of the probabilities associated to its outgoing transitions is equal to 1, that is $\forall s \in S : \sum_{s' \in S} P(s, a, s') = 1$.

MCL. Model Checking Language (MCL) [21] is an action-based branching-time temporal logic suitable for expressing properties of concurrent systems. MCL is an extension of alternation-free μ-calculus [6] with regular expressions, data-based constructs, and fairness operators. We rely on MCL for describing probabilistic properties, using the following construct [19]: prob R is op [?] E end prob, where R is a regular formula on transition sequences, op is a comparison operator among "<", "≤", ">", "≥", "=", "<>", and E is a real number corresponding to a probability. MCL is interpreted over a PTS model.

3   Probabilistic Model Checking of BPMN

This section first gives an overview of the different steps of our approach. Then, we present with more details the solution for monitoring BPMN processes and the computation of a probabilistic model from the execution traces observed during the monitoring step.

3.1   Overview

Recall that before executing a process, it is unclear how often a certain task or combination of tasks are executed. This is of prime importance for adjusting the resources necessary for executing the tasks involved in a process. The goal of our approach is to analyse the multiple instances of a process at runtime to precisely measure the probabilities of executing the tasks involved in a process, and thus to evaluate automatically probabilistic properties on that process.

Our approach takes as input a BPMN process and a probabilistic property, and returns as output the verdict returned by the model checker. The verdict indicates whether the property holds on the system. Such a verdict is obtained by passing the process and the property to a model checker. This verdict is periodically updated, since the process keeps on executing, and our approach runs as long as there are new instances of the process completing. Figure 2 overviews the approach. First, we monitor and analyse the multiple instances resulting of the execution of the BPMN process. These instances are used to compute the probability of execution for each task. Then, these probabilities are added to the LTS semantic model obtained from the BPMN process, resulting in a PTS. Finally, we call a model checker to verify that the PTS satisfies the given probabilistic property. Since the process keeps running, the probability of each task and thus the PTS are periodically updated. The period is a parameter of the approach. Every time the PTS is updated, the model checker is called again. Let us now give a little more details on the three main parts of the approach.

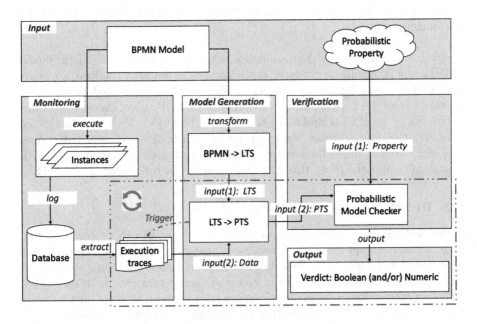

Fig. 2. Overview of the approach

Monitoring. The monitoring part focuses on the data streams generated by the execution of the BPMN process. A BPMN process may be executed multiple times, each of its executions produces an instance. Each time a new instance completes (meaning that the process has terminated), the information about that instance execution is stored into a database. We have implemented a technique for extracting from this database the events related to a set of instances that have completed, and we convert these events into execution traces (one trace per process instance). This extraction is applied periodically, where the period can be a duration (e.g. every hour) or a fixed number of completed instances (e.g. when 100 instances have completed).

Model Generation. The first step of this part is to generate an LTS from the BPMN process. This LTS stands as a semantic model, and exhibits all possible execution paths for the given process. There are several ways to transform BPMN to LTS. Here, we rely on an existing work, which proposes to first transform BPMN into the LNT (LOTOS New Technology) [10] process algebra. Since LNT operational semantics maps to LTS, the generation of that LTS is thus straightforward. Due to lack of space, the reader interested in more details regarding the transformation from BPMN to LTS can refer to [17,20,23]. Note that this transformation from BPMN to LTS is only computed once. In a second step, by analysing the execution traces built during the monitoring stage, we compute the probabilities of executing each task involved in the process, and add these probabilities to the LTS, which thus becomes a PTS. This PTS is updated periodically, every time a new set of execution traces is provided by the monitoring techniques.

Verification. This step of the approach takes as input a probabilistic model (PTS) and a probabilistic property, and computes as output a Boolean or numerical verdict depending on the property. This check is performed by using an existing model checker (the latest version of the CADP model checker [9] in this work). Since the PTS is updated periodically, the model checker is thus called whenever this update takes place. Therefore, the final result does not consist of a single value, but all successive values are gathered on a curve, which is dynamically updated every time the model checker is called with a new PTS.

3.2   BPMN Process Monitoring

In this section, we introduce monitoring techniques for BPMN processes at runtime. These techniques are useful because a process is usually not executed only once. Instead, a process can be executed multiple times. Each execution of the process is called an instance. An instance of the process can be in one of the following states: *initial* means that the instance is ready to start (one token in the start event), *running* means that the instance is currently executing and is not yet completed, *completed* means that all tokens have reached end events. Tokens are used to define the behaviour of a process. When a process instance is triggered, a token is added to the start node. The tokens move through nodes and flows of the process. When a token meets a split gateway (e.g. parallel gateway), it may be divided into multiple ones, depending on the type of split gateway. On the contrary, when multiple tokens meet a merge gateway (e.g. inclusive gateway), they are merged into a single token depending on the type of merge gateway. An identifier is used to characterise a specific instance, and this identifier is associated to all nodes (e.g. tasks) executed by this instance.

Monitoring techniques (see Fig. 3 for an overview) aim at analysing the information stored in a database, and extracting for each instance the corresponding execution trace. An execution trace corresponds to a list of tasks executed by this specific instance. The order of execution of these tasks is established by using timestamps at which each task is executed. These timestamps are computed by the process execution engine (Activiti [1] in this work), which relies on a global clock. The execution trace corresponding to a specific instance can be computed only when the instance is in its *completed* state.

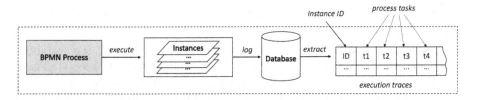

Fig. 3. Runtime monitoring of multiple executions of a BPMN process

Since new instances can execute at any time, we should extract execution traces periodically. There are several possible strategies that can be followed by taking into account different criteria. In this work, we propose to use one of the two following strategies:

- the time-based strategy means that the trace extraction is performed every fixed period of time;
- the instance-based strategy is based on the number of instances, and the trace extraction is triggered whenever the total number of new completed instances reaches a certain value.

It is worth noting that a hybrid strategy combining these two strategies is also an option, e.g. we extract traces whenever 100 instances have completed or every hour if after one hour less than 100 instances have completed. In addition, the choice of these different strategies may have a different impact on the actual results.

There are two similar algorithms for extracting execution traces depending on the strategy. We illustrate below with the algorithm relying on the time-based strategy. The first goal of this algorithm is to extract the relevant completed instances of this process from the database. These instances are then traversed in order to generate the corresponding execution traces.

Let us now go through the algorithm to give more details. Algorithm 1 describes the execution of the time-based extraction of execution traces. The inputs of the algorithm are the process identifier (*pid*), a timestamp (*ts*), and a time duration (td). This timestamp is the start time of the period to identify the new instances that have completed. The output is a set of execution traces ($\mathcal{T}$).

Algorithm 1. Algorithm for extracting execution traces

Inputs: A process ID (pid), a timestamp (ts), and a time duration (td)
Output: A set of execution traces ($\mathcal{T}$)
1: $\mathcal{I} := \emptyset$, $\mathcal{T} := \emptyset$
2: $\mathcal{I} := getInstances(pid)$
3: **for** each $I \in \mathcal{I}$ **do**
4:     **if** $I.hasEndEvent()$ and $ts < I.endts() \leq ts + td$ **then**
5:         $\mathcal{T} := \mathcal{T} \cup I.computeSortedTasks()$
    return $\mathcal{T}$

Algorithm 1 first connects to the database and retrieves all the instances corresponding to the process identifier by using function $getInstances()$. These instances are stored in variable $\mathcal{I}$. Each instance consists of the identifier of the instance and a set of tasks (lines 1 to 2). These instances are traversed to keep only those that have completed during the last period of time (presence of an end event and completion time lower than timestamp + duration, line 4). The resulting instances are all eligible instances. For each completed instance, function $computeSortedTasks()$ sorts the tasks using their completion times, and returns an execution trace consisting of the instance identifier and an ordered list of tasks (line 5). The algorithm finally returns the set of execution traces $\mathcal{T}$.

The time complexity of the algorithm is $\mathcal{O}(n \times m \times \log m)$, where n is the number of completed instances over a period, and m is the maximum number of tasks executed by an instance ($\mathcal{O}(m \times \log m)$ is the complexity of the timsort algorithm used for sorting tasks).

3.3   Transforming LTS into PTS

Given a BPMN process, we can generate its LTS semantic model using existing techniques such as [17,20,23]. The LTS model exhibits all possible execution paths of the input BPMN process. This generated model is non-deterministic, and it has only one final state[1]. In this section, we show how by analysing execution traces (one trace per instance) extracted during the monitoring of the process, we can extend this LTS with probabilities of execution for each transition included in this LTS model. These probabilities are added as annotations to the transitions of the LTS, which thus becomes a PTS.

Before explaining how we generate a PTS given an LTS and a set of execution traces, it is worth noting that, similarly to trace extraction, the PTS should be

---

[1] A final state is a state without outgoing transitions. If an LTS exhibits several final states, these states can be merged into a single one, resulting into an LTS strongly bisimilar [22] to the original one.

updated periodically as well due to the execution of multiple instances. Therefore, this part of the approach also relies on one of the two aforementioned strategies (time or instance-based strategy) for defining the period.

Algorithm 2 takes as input the LTS model corresponding to the BPMN process and a set of execution traces, and returns as output a PTS model. The main idea of the algorithm is to count the number of times each transition is executed using the information from the execution traces. This is achieved by associating a counter to each transition and by traversing the execution traces one after the other. Essentially, each time a task appears in an execution trace, we increment the counter of the corresponding transition. After traversing all execution traces, we compute the probability of executing each transition outgoing from a state by using the associated counter value. We augment the LTS model with these probabilities to obtain the PTS model.

Algorithm 2. Algorithm for transforming LTS into PTS

Inputs: LTS $= \langle Q, \Sigma, q_{\text{init}}, \Delta \rangle$, a finite set of execution traces $\mathcal{T} = \langle T_1, T_2, \ldots, T_n \rangle$
Output: PTS $= \langle S, A, s_{\text{init}}, \delta, P \rangle$
1:   $S := Q, A := \Sigma, s_{\text{init}} := q_{\text{init}}, \delta := \Delta$
2:   $Path := [\,], Fpaths := [\,], Bpaths := [\,], T_{\text{tasks}} := [\,]$ /* [ ] indicates an empty list */
3:   **for** each $(s, a, s') \in \Delta$ **do** $cnt((s, a, s')) := 0$
4:   **for** each $T \in \mathcal{T}$ **do**
5:       $\mathcal{Q}_{\text{current}} := \{q_{\text{init}}\}, \mathcal{Q}_{\text{next}} := \emptyset, \mathcal{Q}_{\text{pre}} := \emptyset, T_{\text{tasks}} := T.getTasks()$
6:       **for** each $task \in T_{\text{tasks}}$ **do**
7:           $q_{\text{succ}} := \{q' \in Q \mid \exists q \in \mathcal{Q}_{\text{current}}, (q, task, q') \in \Delta\}$
8:           **if** $task \neq T_{\text{tasks}}[T_{\text{tasks}}.length() - 1]$ **then**
9:               $\mathcal{Q}_{\text{next}} := q_{\text{succ}}, \mathcal{Q}_{\text{current}} := \mathcal{Q}_{\text{next}}$
10:          **else**
11:              $q_{\text{next}} := \{q \in Q \mid \exists q \in q_{\text{succ}} \text{ and } q \neq q', (q, task, q') \in \Delta\}$
12:              $\mathcal{Q}_{\text{next}} := q_{\text{succ}} \setminus q_{\text{next}}$
13:          **for** each $(q, task, q') \in \Delta, q \in \mathcal{Q}_{\text{current}}, q' \in \mathcal{Q}_{\text{next}}$ **do**
14:              $Fpaths.append((q, task, q'))$
15:      **for** each $task \in T_{\text{tasks}}.reverseOrder()$ **do**
16:          $\mathcal{Q}_{\text{pre}} := \{q \in Q \mid \exists q' \in \mathcal{Q}_{\text{next}}, (q, task, q') \in \Delta\}$
17:          **for** each $(q, task, q') \in \Delta, q \in \mathcal{Q}_{\text{pre}}, q' \in \mathcal{Q}_{\text{next}}$ **do**
18:              $Bpaths.append((q, task, q'))$
19:          $\mathcal{Q}_{\text{next}} := \mathcal{Q}_{\text{pre}}$
20:      $Path := Fpaths \cap Bpaths$
21:      **for** each $(s, a, s') \in Path$ **do** $cnt((s, a, s')) := cnt((s, a, s')) + 1$
22: $P := \{(s, a, s') \mapsto cnt((s, a, s')) / \sum_{q \in S, a' \in A, (s, a', q) \in \delta} cnt((s, a', q)) \mid (s, a, s') \in \delta\}$
     return $\langle S, A, s_{\text{init}}, \delta, P \rangle$

Let us now present with more details how this algorithm for generating the PTS model works. The PTS model is first initialised, and a counter (initialised to 0) is added to each transition of the LTS model (lines 1 to 3). The algorithm starts by traversing the set of execution traces $\mathcal{T}$. For each execution trace, the algorithm proceeds in three steps: (a) traversing the tasks of the execution trace, (b) finding the corresponding valid path into the LTS model, (c) increasing the value of the counters. As a final step, all execution traces are traversed for computing the probability of each transition. $\mathcal{Q}_{current}$ is the set of current states in the LTS during the traversal, $\mathcal{Q}_{next}$ is the set of successor states of a current state, and $\mathcal{Q}_{pre}$ is the set of predecessor states of a current state. We now present these steps with more details:

(a) *Traversing the tasks of the execution trace* (lines 5 to 14). Since the LTS may exhibit non-deterministic behaviours, this step (and the following one) computes the valid path in the LTS corresponding to an execution trace. This step relies on a forward traversal of the LTS (from initial state to final state). Each execution trace T consists of an identifier and a sequence of tasks T_{tasks}. For each trace, these tasks are handled one after the other, and by using transitions Δ, the successor states for each current state are obtained until all tasks of the current execution trace have been traversed. We use *Fpaths* (Forward-paths) to record the sequence of transitions in the LTS corresponding to the execution paths of the current execution trace.

(b) *Finding the corresponding valid path into the LTS model* (lines 15 to 20). This step relies on a backward traversal of the LTS (from final state to initial state). Therefore, we start by reversing the sequence of tasks for the current execution trace. By using this reversed list and the final state which is stored in the last $\mathcal{Q}_{next}$ of the previous step, we then traverse backwards to the initial state. We use *Bpaths* (Backward-paths) to record all the transitions from the final state to the initial state (lines 15 to 19). Next, we take the intersection of each element in *Fpaths* and *Bpaths*, and store the result in *Path*. This intersection operation eliminates the invalid paths, or more precisely the invalid transitions, in *Fpaths* and *Bpaths*. Thus, the *Path* variable finally stores all the transitions of the LTS model corresponding to the current execution trace (line 20).

(c) *Increasing the value of the counters* (line 21). The values of the counters for the transitions in *Path* are increased by 1.

(d) *Computing the probability of each transition* (line 22). The probability of each transition is computed. To do so, the value of each transition counter is divided by the total number of transitions with the same starting state.

When we have traversed all the execution traces, the algorithm finally returns the resulting PTS.

The time complexity of this algorithm is $\mathcal{O}(|\mathcal{T}| \times n \times |\Delta|)$, where $|\mathcal{T}|$ is the number of execution traces, n is the number of tasks in the longest trace, and $|\Delta|$ is the number of transitions in the LTS/PTS.

Figure 4 illustrates the execution of the algorithm. Figure 4(a) depicts the input of the algorithm: an LTS and a set of execution traces, where the number in the first column (e.g. 1003) is the identifier of the execution trace. In this example, we assume that State 2 is the end/final state of the LTS. Figure 4(b) depicts an example of traversing an execution trace, where the dashed lines

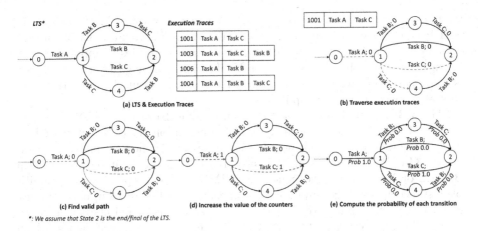

Fig. 4. Example describing the execution of the algorithm

indicate all possible transitions. Figure 4(c) depicts an example of filtering the invalid paths in it based on the paths obtained in the previous step, which is indicated by dotted lines. Dashed lines are used to represent the valid path. In this example, after the previous step, we get a total of two paths. One path contains two transitions of $(0 \xrightarrow{\text{Task A}} 1)$ and $(1 \xrightarrow{\text{Task C}} 4)$. The final state reached by this path is 4, which is not the final state of the LTS. Therefore, this path is invalid. For the other one, its final state is the final state of the LTS, and hence, this is a valid path. Figure 4(d) shows each relevant transition coming from the valid path (dashed lines) whose counter is incremented by 1. Figure 4(e) then describes the computation of the probability for each transition of the LTS. Finally, the PTS corresponding to the LTS extended with probabilities is returned.

4   Tool Support

In this section, we present the tool chain automating the different steps of our approach. We then illustrate the application of these tools to a case study, and end with additional experiments to evaluate performance of the tools on a set of realistic examples.

4.1   Tool

Figure 5 overviews the tool chain. First, we use the Activiti framework [1] for developing and executing BPMN processes. Activiti is a lightweight Java-centric open source tool. When running a BPMN process once or several times, all data related to these executions are stored into a MySQL database.

Beyond a BPMN process, the second input required by our approach is a probabilistic property. In this work, the property is specified using the MCL [21] temporal logic, which is one of the input languages of the CADP toolbox [9]. CADP is a toolbox for the design and verification of asynchronous concurrent systems. Note that the approach can take several properties as input, not just a single one. We also use the Script Verification Language [8] (SVL), which is convenient for automating all verification tasks, particularly when there are several properties given as input.

The VBPMN tool [17] is used for transforming BPMN into LTS. The generation of the PTS from the analysis of the execution traces is automated by a Python program we implemented. The property is then evaluated by calling the CADP probabilistic model checker [19]. As a result, it returns either a Boolean or Numerical value. Since the BPMN process keeps executing (multiple instances), the PTS is updated periodically according to an update strategy defined in Sect. 3. Whenever the PTS is updated, the model checker is called again. The final result is thus not a single value, but a series of values, which we represent as a curve (x: time or number of instances, y: verification result). This curve is drawn using Matplotlib, which is a plotting library for the Python programming language.

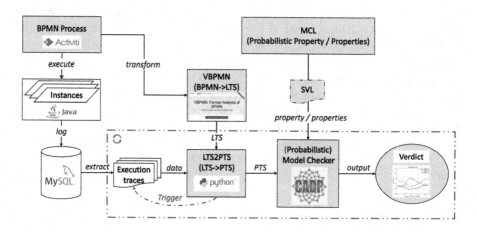

Fig. 5. Overview of the tool chain

4.2 Case Study

Let us illustrate our approach with the shipment process of a hardware retailer, which comes from [20]. This example, shown in Fig. 6, describes a realistic delivery process of goods. More precisely, this process starts when there are goods to be shipped (E1). Two tasks are then processed in parallel (PG1), one is the packaging of the goods (T7) and the other decides whether the goods require normal or special shipment (T1). Depending on that decision, a first option checks whether there is a need for additional insurance (T2), followed by the possibility to buy additional insurance (T4) and/or fill in a post label (T5).

A second option is to request quotes from carriers (T3), followed by the assignment of a carrier and preparation of the paperwork (T6). Before completing the whole process, the package is moved to a pick-up area.

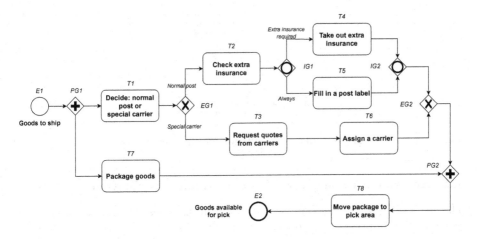

Fig. 6. BPMN shipment process of a hardware retailer

Probabilistic Property. For illustration purposes, we choose a property checking that the probability of executing task T4 after task T2 is less than 0.4. This is important because the choice of taking extra insurance (T4) comes with a cost, and if this decision is taken too often (e.g. more than four times out of ten), this may become a problem in terms of budget. This property is written in MCL as follows: prob true*. T2. true*. T4 is < ? 0.4 end prob. Since we use the '?' symbol, the model checker returns both a Boolean value (indicating whether the property is true or false) and a numerical value (indicating the probability to execute T4 after T2).

Simulation. We implemented a simulator in Java in charge of executing many instances of the BPMN process, varying the order and frequency of task executions in order to simulate a realistic operating environment. Figure 7 shows the Boolean and numerical results for a simulation consisting of 1400 instances, executed over a period of about 4 minutes, where the property is the one mentioned earlier. The update strategy used here relies on the number of completed instances. Every time there are ten completed instances, we compute again the execution probability of each transition of the LTS, generate a new PTS, and we call the model checker to obtain a new result. Figure 7 shows a variation of the truth and numerical values of the evaluated property over time. This is due to our simulator, which favours the execution of some specific tasks during some periods, resulting in the curve given in the figure.

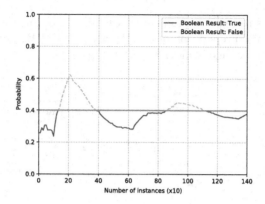

Fig. 7. Simulation results for the shipment process

4.3 Additional Experiments for Performance Evaluation

The goal of this section is to measure the execution times of the different steps of our approach in practice. To do so, we rely on a set of realistic BPMN processes found in existing papers and frameworks shown in Table 1. We used an Ubuntu OS laptop running on a 1.7 GHz Intel Core i5 processor with 8 GB of memory to carry out these experiments. Table 1 shows the results of these experiments. Each process is characterised by its size (number of tasks and gateways), the size of the generated PTS (number of states and transitions), and the execution time of each step is decomposed as follows:

(1) Time for transforming the BPMN process into an LTS (executed only once);
(2) Time for extracting a certain number of execution traces (100 in these experiments) from the database;
(3) Time for analysing these execution traces and for computing the PTS;
(4) Time for verifying the property on that PTS using the CADP model checker.

Let us now focus on the results presented in Table 1 for each step. The first step focuses on the transformation of the BPMN process to an LTS model. Table 1 shows this can be a time-consuming step compared to the other ones. This computation time depends on the structure of the BPMN process and increases with the number of parallel and inclusive gateways (in particular when they are nested). Rows 8 and 11 in the table illustrate this point. However, it is worth noting that this step of the approach is only executed once at the beginning, so this extra-time is not really a problem. The second step focuses on the computation time for connecting to the database and extracting a certain number of execution traces (100 in these experiments) from it. We can see that the computation time of this step is less than 0.5 s for all the examples in the table. The third step aims to analyse these execution traces, calculating the probabilities of each transition for building a PTS by annotating the previously computed LTS. The algorithm (and its complexity) for computing that PTS was presented in Sect. 3. According to our experiments, we can see that this time

Table 1. Experimental results for some case studies

No.	BPMN Process	Characteristics				PTS		Time (s)			
		Tasks	Gateways			States	Transitions	(1)	(2)	(3)	(4)
			Exclusive	Inclusive	Parallel						
1	Shipment [20]	8	2	2	2	18	38	15	0.32	0.61	1.45
2	Recruitment [7]	10	1	0	6	19	31	25	0.21	0.64	1.32
3	Shopping [17]	22	8	2	2	59	127	50	0.26	1.12	1.68
4	AccoutOpeningV2 [17]	15	3	2	2	20	33	31	0.25	0.71	0.84
5	Publish [17]	4	0	2	0	16	61	22	0.42	0.58	0.77
6	Car [17]	10	2	0	2	18	31	18	0.44	0.67	0.84
7	Online-Shop [17]	19	7	2	0	36	74	41	0.33	0.79	1.21
8	Multi-Inclusive [17]	9	0	6	0	47	194	42	0.23	2.32	1.39
9	Multi-Exclusive [17]	8	6	0	0	6	9	22	0.01	0.51	0.82
10	Multi-Parallel [17]	8	0	0	6	15	22	12	0.12	0.63	0.67
11	Multi-InclusiveV2 [17]	12	0	6	0	141	1201	78	0.25	4.29	1.58
12	Booking [17]	11	2	4	0	53	242	22	0.19	2.37	1.24

increases with the size of the LTS (number of transitions). It takes less than a second to compute this step for most examples and it is slightly longer for a few examples (about 4 s for example Multi-InclusiveV2 for instance). The final computation time corresponds to the verification of the PTS model by calling the probabilistic model checker. We can see in the table that it takes about 1 or 2 s for each example to make this computation.

To conclude, these experiments show that, except for the LTS computation that might be costly, the other steps of the approach are computed in a reasonable time for realistic processes. This shows that conducting probabilistic model checking of BPMN processes at runtime is feasible. Last but not least, the sum of the times observed for steps (2), (3) and (4) could be used to obtain a lower bound value to the period of time used by the time-based strategy. Indeed, this would not make sense to use as period a value that would be smaller than this lower bound.

5   Related Work

In this section, we overview some existing research efforts proposing probabilistic models and analysis for BPMN.

The approaches in [2,3] focus on the use of Bayesian networks to infer the relationship between different events. As an example, [3] introduces a BPMN normal form based on Activity Theory that can be used for representing the dynamics of a collective human activity from the perspective of a subject. This workflow is then transformed into a Causal Bayesian Network that can be used for modelling human behaviours and assessing human decisions.

The approach in [4] extends BPMN with time and probabilities. Specifically, the authors expect that a probability value is provided for each flow involved in an inclusive or exclusive split gateway. These BPMN processes are then transformed to rewriting logic and analysed using the Maude statistical model checker PVeStA. This work is extended in [5] to explicitly model and analyse resource allocation. This series of works allows one to compute at design time generic properties, such as average execution times, synchronisation times or resource usage, whereas the goal of this paper is to compute probabilistic properties at runtime by dynamically analysing the executions of multiple process instances.

The approach in [14] presents a framework for the automated restructuring of workflows that allows minimising the impact of errors on a production workflow. To do so, they rely on a subset of BPMN extended to include the tracking of real-valued quantities associated with the process (such as time, cost, temperature), and the modelling of probabilistic- or non-deterministic branching behaviour, and the introduction of error states. The main goal of this approach is to reduce the risk of production faults and restructure the production workflows for minimising such faults.

In [16,23], the authors first propose to give a formal semantics to BPMN via a transformation to Labelled Transition Systems (LTSs). This is achieved via a transformation to process algebra and use of existing compilers for automatically generating the LTS from the process algebraic specification. Once the LTS model is generated, model checking of functional properties is possible as well as comparison of processes using equivalence checking. This work does not provide any probabilistic model for BPMN nor any kind of quantitative analysis.

In [12,13], the authors present a framework for modelling and analysis of business workflows. These workflows are described with a subset of BPMN extended with probabilistic nondeterministic branching and general-purpose reward annotations. An algorithm translates such models into Markov decision processes (MDP) written in the syntax of the PRISM model checker. This enables quantitative analysis of business processes for properties such as transient/steady-state probabilities, reward-based properties, and best- and worst-case scenarios. These properties are verified using the PRISM model checker. This work supports design time analysis, but does not focus on the dynamic execution and runtime verification of processes.

Statistical model checking [11], which uses simulation and statistical methods, facilitates the generation of approximate results to quantitative model checking. Although it has a low memory requirement, the cost is expensive if high accuracy is required. In comparison, probabilistic model checking produces highly accurate results, despite the potential problem of state explosion.

6   Conclusion

We have presented a new approach that allows BPMN analysts to automatically carry out probabilistic model checking of BPMN processes at runtime. This approach takes as input an executable BPMN process and one (or several) probabilistic property. To evaluate this property, we build a probabilistic model

(PTS) by analysing the execution traces extracted from the multiple execution of this process. This analysis allows us to annotate the LTS semantic model corresponding to the BPMN process with probabilities, thus obtaining a PTS model. Finally, we can call the probabilistic model checker with the probabilistic model and the property. Since the process keeps executing, the probabilistic model is updated periodically and the model checker is called periodically as well. Therefore, we do not return a single value as a result but a curve displaying the successive truth or numerical values returned by the model checker. Our approach is fully automated by a tool chain consisting of existing and new tools. The tool chain was applied to several realistic examples for validation purposes.

As far as future work is concerned, we first plan to take advantage of the results computed by our approach to effectively adjust resource allocation depending on the runtime analysis results. This requires having an explicit description of resources associated with tasks and dynamically modifying the resource allocation with respect to the analysis results. A second perspective is to not only analyse properties at runtime, but predict the result of the evaluation of these properties in the near future. This would allow the anticipation of changes in the resource allocation for instance. This prediction can be achieved by relying on the computed probabilistic model or by using machine learning techniques.

Acknowledgements. This work was supported by the Région Auvergne-Rhône-Alpes within the *"Pack Ambition Recherche"* programme, the H2020-ECSEL-2018-IA call - Grant Agreement number 826276 (CPS4EU), the French ANR project ANR-20-CE39-0009 (SEVERITAS), and LabEx PERSYVAL-Lab (ANR-11-LABX-0025-01).

References

1. Activiti: open source business automation. https://www.activiti.org/. Accessed Dec 2021
2. Ceballos, H.G., Cantu, F.J.: Discovering causal relations in semantically-annotated probabilistic business process diagrams. In: Global Conference on Artificial Intelligence, GCAI, pp. 29–40 (2018)
3. Ceballos, H.G., Flores-Solorio, V., Garcia, J.P.: A probabilistic BPMN normal form to model and advise human activities. In: Baldoni, M., Baresi, L., Dastani, M. (eds.) EMAS 2015. LNCS (LNAI), vol. 9318, pp. 51–69. Springer, Cham (2015). https://doi.org/10.1007/978-3-319-26184-3_4
4. Durán, F., Rocha, C., Salaün, G.: Stochastic analysis of BPMN with time in rewriting logic. Sci. Comput. Program. **168**, 1–17 (2018)
5. Durán, F., Rocha, C., Salaün, G.: Analysis of resource allocation of BPMN processes. In: Yangui, S., Bouassida Rodriguez, I., Drira, K., Tari, Z. (eds.) ICSOC 2019. LNCS, vol. 11895, pp. 452–457. Springer, Cham (2019). https://doi.org/10.1007/978-3-030-33702-5_35
6. Emerson, E.A., Lei, C.L.: Efficient model checking in fragments of the propositional mu-calculus (extended abstract). In: LICS (1986)
7. Falcone, Y., Salaün, G., Zuo, A.: Semi-automated modelling of optimized BPMN processes. In: Proceedings of SCC 2021, pp. 425–430. IEEE (2021)

8. Garavel, H., Lang, F.: SVL: a scripting language for compositional verification. In: Kim, M., Chin, B., Kang, S., Lee, D. (eds.) Proceedings of FORTE 2001. IFIP Conference Proceedings, vol. 197, pp. 377–394. Kluwer (2001)

9. Garavel, H., Lang, F., Mateescu, R., Serwe, W.: CADP 2011: a toolbox for the construction and analysis of distributed processes. Int. J. Softw. Tools Technol. Transf. 15(2), 89–107 (2013). https://doi.org/10.1007/s10009-012-0244-z

10. Garavel, H., Lang, F., Serwe, W.: From LOTOS to LNT. In: Katoen, J.-P., Langerak, R., Rensink, A. (eds.) ModelEd, TestEd, TrustEd. LNCS, vol. 10500, pp. 3–26. Springer, Cham (2017). https://doi.org/10.1007/978-3-319-68270-9_1

11. Hérault, T., Lassaigne, R., Magniette, F., Peyronnet, S.: Approximate probabilistic model checking. In: Steffen, B., Levi, G. (eds.) VMCAI 2004. LNCS, vol. 2937, pp. 73–84. Springer, Heidelberg (2004). https://doi.org/10.1007/978-3-540-24622-0_8

12. Herbert, L., Sharp, R.: Precise quantitative analysis of probabilistic business process model and notation workflows. J. Comput. Inf. Sci. Eng. 13(1), 011007 (2013)

13. Herbert, L.T., Sharp, R.: Quantitative analysis of probabilistic BPMN workflows. In: International Design Engineering Technical Conferences and Computers and Information in Engineering Conference, vol. 45011, pp. 509–518. American Society of Mechanical Engineers (2012)

14. Herbert, L.T., Hansen, Z.N.L., Jacobsen, P.: Automated evolutionary restructuring of workflows to minimise errors via stochastic model checking. In: Probabilistic Safety Assessment and Management Conference 2014 (2014)

15. ISO/IEC: International standard 19510, information technology - business process model and notation (2013)

16. Krishna, A., Poizat, P., Salaün, G.: VBPMN: automated verification of BPMN processes (tool paper). In: Polikarpova, N., Schneider, S. (eds.) IFM 2017. LNCS, vol. 10510, pp. 323–331. Springer, Cham (2017). https://doi.org/10.1007/978-3-319-66845-1_21

17. Krishna, A., Poizat, P., Salaün, G.: Checking business process evolution. Sci. Comput. Program. 170, 1–26 (2019)

18. Larsen, K.G., Skou, A.: Bisimulation through probabilistic testing. Inf. Comput. 94(1), 1–28 (1991)

19. Mateescu, R., Requeno, J.I.: On-the-fly model checking for extended action-based probabilistic operators. Int. J. Softw. Tools Technol. Transfer 20(5), 563–587 (2018). https://doi.org/10.1007/s10009-018-0499-0

20. Mateescu, R., Salaün, G., Ye, L.: Quantifying the parallelism in BPMN processes using model checking. In: The 17th International ACM Sigsoft Symposium on Component-Based Software Engineering (CBSE 2014), Lille, France, June 2014

21. Mateescu, R., Thivolle, D.: A model checking language for concurrent value-passing systems. In: Cuellar, J., Maibaum, T., Sere, K. (eds.) FM 2008. LNCS, vol. 5014, pp. 148–164. Springer, Heidelberg (2008). https://doi.org/10.1007/978-3-540-68237-0_12

22. Milner, R.: Communication and Concurrency. Prentice Hall, Upper Saddle River (1989)

23. Poizat, P., Salaün, G., Krishna, A.: Checking business process evolution. In: Kouchnarenko, O., Khosravi, R. (eds.) FACS 2016. LNCS, vol. 10231, pp. 36–53. Springer, Cham (2017). https://doi.org/10.1007/978-3-319-57666-4_4

HyperPCTL Model Checking by Probabilistic Decomposition

Eshita Zaman[1]([✉]), Gianfranco Ciardo[1], Erika Ábrahám[2],
and Borzoo Bonakdarpour[3]

[1] Iowa State University, Ames, IA 50011, USA
{ezaman,ciardo}@iastate.edu
[2] RWTH Aachen University, 52062 Aachen, Germany
abraham@informatik.rwth-aachen.de
[3] Michigan State University, East Lansing, MI 48824, USA
borzoo@msu.edu

Abstract. *Probabilistic hyperproperties* describe system properties involving probability measures over multiple runs and have numerous applications in information-flow security. However, the poor scalability of existing model checking algorithms for probabilistic hyperproperties limits their use to small models. In this paper, we propose a model checking algorithm to verify discrete-time Markov chains (DTMC) against HyperPCTL formulas by integrating numerical solution techniques. Our algorithm is based on a *probabilistic decomposition* of the self-composed DTMC into variants of the underlying DTMC. Experimentally, we show that our algorithm significantly outperforms both a symbolic approach and the original approach based on brute-force self-composition.

1 Introduction

Important information-flow policies like noninterference [17] and observational determinism [26], or properties like fault tolerance and system robustness [25], service level agreements, and average response time cannot be expressed as single-trace properties. For such properties related to multiple execution traces, the theory of *hyperproperties* was introduced by Clarkson and Schneider in [9]. In non-probabilistic setting, various temporal logics have been proposed to express hyperproperties, e.g., HyperLTL and HyperCTL* [8] and A-HLTL [5]. These logics provide explicit and simultaneous quantification over multiple paths on LTL [21] and CTL* [14], respectively. HyperCTL* supports nested quantification over paths, while its syntactic fragment HyperLTL assumes formulas in *prenex* normal form. For these logics, several model checking tools have been developed to verify their formulas [6,10,16,19].

Probabilistic hyperproperties have been defined to formalize probabilistic relations between independent executions of systems with uncertainties. The temporal logic HyperPCTL [4], first proposed for discrete-time Markov chains (DTMCs) and later extended to Markov decision processes (MDPs) [3], allows quantification over states to relate executions starting in different states. The

© Springer Nature Switzerland AG 2022
M. H. ter Beek and R. Monahan (Eds.): IFM 2022, LNCS 13274, pp. 209–226, 2022.
https://doi.org/10.1007/978-3-031-07727-2_12

original HyperPCTL model checking algorithm [4] reduces the model checking problem for a formula with n state quantifiers to PCTL model checking on the n-ary self-composition (i.e., the composition of n copies) of the input DTMC. Another temporal logic, PHL, has been proposed in [11]. Both [4] and [11] proved that model checking probabilistic hyperproperties for MDPs is undecidable.

Recently, Wang et al. [23] introduced the temporal logic HyperPCTL*, which supports probabilistic quantification over explicit path variables, but evaluation of HyperPCTL* formulas has only been studied using statistical model checking. This and other statistical model checking approaches [23,24] have strong practical contributions but cannot provide exhaustive formal correctness guarantees.

HyperPCTL can express properties like probabilistic noninterference, differential privacy [13], and probabilistic causation [15]. For instance, *probabilistic noninterference* [22] requires the probability of each low-observable trace to be the same for all low-equivalent initial states, as illustrated by the following scheduling scenario [22], where threads t and t' execute the code

$$t : \textbf{while } h > 0 \textbf{ do } \{h \leftarrow h - 1\} \textbf{ endwhile}; \quad l \leftarrow 2; \qquad t' : l \leftarrow 1;$$

and are uniformly scheduled on a processor. If h is a *high-security* input and l is a *low-security* output, probabilistic noninterference requires the probability of observing $l = 1$ or $l = 2$ upon termination to be the same, regardless of the initial value of h. However, if this program is run multiple times for different values of h, the probability of observing $l = 2$ increases for larger values of h, thus an attacker gains knowledge about h's initial value by observing l's final value. The HyperPCTL probabilistic noninterference formula for this example,

$$\forall \sigma. \forall \sigma'. \left(h_\sigma \neq h_{\sigma'}\right) \Rightarrow \left(\mathbb{P}(\textsf{F}\,(l = 1)_\sigma) = \mathbb{P}(\textsf{F}\,(l = 1)_{\sigma'}) \;\wedge\; \mathbb{P}(\textsf{F}\,(l = 2)_\sigma) = \mathbb{P}(\textsf{F}\,(l = 2)_{\sigma'})\right),$$

requires the probability of observing $l = 1$ or $l = 2$ upon termination to be the same for every pair of initial states σ and σ' having different values for h. As mentioned above, the HyperPCTL model checking algorithm in [4] builds the n-ary self-composition of the input DTMC, thus it suffers from an exponential state-space growth in the number of quantifiers and cannot scale beyond small toy examples. The symbolic method in [3] remedies the problem to some extent, but it must still solve a constraint problem with a large number of variables.

In this paper, we propose a HyperPCTL model checking algorithm that integrates an efficient *numerical* technique that avoids building the self-composition. Our technique, based on *probabilistic decomposition*, computes (backward or forward) reachability probabilities for the states of DTMCs with size similar to that of the input DTMC, and is based on the fact that different traces involved in the self-composition are independent, except for evolving synchronously. In other words, the probability of a series of events in the self-composed DTMC is the product of the probabilities of events in the individual DTMCs, subject to enforcing that the number of steps is the same in these DTMCs. This numerical approach can be implemented by computing multiple probability vectors of size equal to the state space of the original DTMC. Unfortunately, not all probability calculations in a HyperPCTL formula can be decomposed independently;

sometimes we need to store or recompute the history of traces, which increases the runtime cost.

To the best of our knowledge, this is the first numerical approach for model checking the complete class of HyperPCTL formulas that can cope with models having significant state spaces. We have fully implemented our algorithm and we report experimental results through rigorous comparison with the existing techniques in [3,4]. Our experiments on multiple case studies on verification information-flow security policies (e.g., probabilistic noninterference, dining cryptographers, side-channel timing attack) and mission safety show that the proposed numerical approach outperforms the techniques in [3,4] by several orders of magnitude, while providing results with the same accuracy.

Organization. Section 2 presents preliminary concepts. Sections 3 and 4 introduce our novel decomposition-based technique. Section 5 provides an experimental evaluation on several case studies, and Sect. 6 concludes.

2 Preliminaries

We consider systems modeled as discrete-time Markov chains.

Definition 1. A *(labeled) discrete-time Markov chain (DTMC)* $\mathcal{M} = (\mathcal{S}, \mathbf{P}, \mathcal{A}, L)$ *has the following components:*

- *a finite nonempty set of* states $\mathcal{S}$*;*
- *a transition probability matrix* $\mathbf{P} : \mathcal{S} \times \mathcal{S} \to [0,1]$ *with* $\sum_{v' \in \mathcal{S}} \mathbf{P}(v, v') = 1$ *for all* $v \in \mathcal{S}$*;*
- *a set of* atomic propositions $\mathcal{A}$*;*
- *a function* $L : \mathcal{S} \to 2^{\mathcal{A}}$ *labeling each state with the propositions holding in it.*

Figure 1 shows an example DTMC. A *path* of a DTMC $\mathcal{M} = (\mathcal{S}, \mathbf{P}, \mathcal{A}, L)$ is an infinite sequence of states $\gamma = v_0 v_1 v_2 \cdots \in \mathcal{S}^\omega$ s.t. $\mathbf{P}(v_i, v_{i+1}) > 0$ for all $i \geq 0$. Let $\gamma[i]$ denote v_i and let $Paths^v(\mathcal{M})$ be the set of paths of $\mathcal{M}$ starting in v. The atomic propositions holding in a state, if any, are shown enclosed in braces; for example, a and b hold in state s_6.

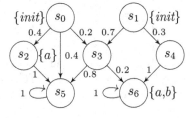

Fig. 1. A DTMC.

2.1 HyperPCTL Syntax

A HyperPCTL *quantified formula* ρ for DTMCs [4] is defined as follows:

$$\rho ::= \forall \sigma . \rho \mid \exists \sigma . \rho \mid \psi \qquad \psi ::= \mathbf{true} \mid a_\sigma \mid \psi \wedge \psi \mid \neg \psi \mid p \sim p$$
$$p ::= \mathbb{P}(\varphi) \mid f(p, \dots, p) \qquad \varphi ::= \mathsf{X} \psi \mid \psi \, \mathsf{U}^{[k_1, k_2]} \, \psi \mid \psi \, \mathsf{U}^{[k_1, \infty)} \, \psi$$

where σ is a *state variable* from a countably infinite set $\mathcal{V} = \{\sigma_1, \sigma_2, \dots\}$, ψ is a *state formula*, $a \in \mathcal{A}$ is an atomic proposition, $\sim \in \{<, \leq, =, \geq, >\}$, p is a *probability expression*, f is an n-ary measurable function (a constant if $n = 0$), φ is a *path formula*, and $k_1, k_2 \in \mathbb{N}$, with $k_1 \le k_2$. Besides standard syntactic sugar, we omit bound $[0, \infty)$, let $[k]$ denote interval $[k, k]$, and let $\mathsf{G}^{[k]}\psi \stackrel{\text{def}}{=} \psi \mathsf{U}^{[k+1]}\mathbf{true}$ and $\mathsf{F}^I\psi \stackrel{\text{def}}{=} \mathbf{true}\,\mathsf{U}^I\psi$, where I is a time interval. A HyperPCTL *formula* is a HyperPCTL quantified formula where each a_σ is in the scope of a quantifier for σ.

2.2 HyperPCTL Semantics

The semantics of HyperPCTL is based on the n-ary self-composition of a DTMC.

Definition 2. The *n-ary self-composition* of a DTMC $\mathcal{M} = (\mathcal{S}, \mathbf{P}, \mathcal{A}, L)$ is a DTMC $\mathcal{M}^n = (\mathcal{S}^n, \mathbf{P}^n, \mathcal{A}^n, L^n)$ where:

- $\mathcal{S}^n = \mathcal{S} \times \cdots \times \mathcal{S}$ is the n-ary Cartesian product of $\mathcal{S}$ with itself;
- $\mathbf{P}^n(v, v') = \prod_{i=1}^n \mathbf{P}(v_i, v'_i)$ for all $v = (v_1, ..., v_n) \in \mathcal{S}^n$ and $v' = (v'_1, ..., v'_n) \in \mathcal{S}^n$;
- $\mathcal{A}^n = \bigcup_{i=1}^n \mathcal{A}_i$, where $\mathcal{A}_i = \{a_i \mid a \in \mathcal{A}\}$ for $i \in \{1, ..., n\}$;
- $L^n(v) = \bigcup_{i=1}^n L_i(v_i)$ for $v = (v_1, ..., v_n) \in \mathcal{S}^n$, where $L_i(v_i) = \{a_i \mid a \in L(v_i)\}$.

Intuitively, $\mathcal{M}^n$ represents the DTMC decribing the synchronous evolution of n independent copies of $\mathcal{M}$.

The satisfaction of a HyperPCTL formula ρ by a DTMC $\mathcal{M} = (\mathcal{S}, \mathbf{P}, \mathcal{A}, L)$, written $\mathcal{M}, () \models \rho$, is defined recursively as follows, where $v = (v_1, \ldots, v_n) \in \mathcal{S}^n$ stores quantifier instantiations:

$$
\begin{aligned}
\mathcal{M}, v &\models \mathbf{true} \\
\mathcal{M}, v &\models a_i && \text{iff} && a \in L(v_i) \\
\mathcal{M}, v &\models \psi_1 \wedge \psi_2 && \text{iff} && \mathcal{M}, v \models \psi_1 \text{ and } \mathcal{M}, v \models \psi_2 \\
\mathcal{M}, v &\models \neg\psi && \text{iff} && \mathcal{M}, v \not\models \psi \\
\mathcal{M}, v &\models p_1 \sim p_2 && \text{iff} && [\![p_1]\!]_{\mathcal{M},v} \sim [\![p_2]\!]_{\mathcal{M},v} \\
\mathcal{M}, v &\models \forall\sigma.\psi && \text{iff} && \forall v_{n+1} \in \mathcal{S}.\ \mathcal{M}, (v_1, ..., v_n, v_{n+1}) \models \psi[\mathcal{A}_{n+1}/\mathcal{A}_\sigma] \\
\mathcal{M}, v &\models \exists\sigma.\psi && \text{iff} && \exists v_{n+1} \in \mathcal{S}.\ \mathcal{M}, (v_1, ..., v_n, v_{n+1}) \models \psi[\mathcal{A}_{n+1}/\mathcal{A}_\sigma] \\
[\![f(p, \ldots, p)]\!]_{\mathcal{M},v} &= f([\![p]\!]_{\mathcal{M},v}, ..., [\![p]\!]_{\mathcal{M},v}) \\
[\![\mathbb{P}(\varphi)]\!]_{\mathcal{M},v} &= \Pr\{\gamma \in Paths^v(\mathcal{M}^n) \mid \mathcal{M}, \gamma \models \varphi\}
\end{aligned}
$$

where ψ, ψ_1, and ψ_2 are HyperPCTL state formulas and $\psi[\mathcal{A}_{n+1}/\mathcal{A}_\sigma]$ replaces each free occurrence of a_σ in ψ with a_{n+1}, for each atomic proposition $a \in \mathcal{A}$. The satisfaction relation for HyperPCTL path formulas is defined as follows:

$$
\begin{aligned}
\mathcal{M}, \gamma &\models \mathsf{X}\psi && \text{iff } \mathcal{M}, \gamma[1] \models \psi \\
\mathcal{M}, \gamma &\models \psi_1 \mathsf{U}^{[k_1, k_2]}\psi_2 && \text{iff } \exists j \in [k_1, k_2].\Big(\mathcal{M}, \gamma[j] \models \psi_2 \wedge \forall i \in [0, j).\mathcal{M}, \gamma[i] \models \psi_1\Big) \\
\mathcal{M}, \gamma &\models \psi_1 \mathsf{U}^{[k_1, \infty)}\psi_2 && \text{iff } \exists j \ge k_1.\Big(\mathcal{M}, \gamma[j] \models \psi_2 \wedge \forall i \in [0, j).\mathcal{M}, \gamma[i] \models \psi_1\Big)
\end{aligned}
$$

where γ is a path of $\mathcal{M}^n$ for some $n \in \mathbb{N}_{>0}$, ψ, ψ_1, and ψ_2 are HyperPCTL state formulas, and $k_1, k_2 \in \mathbb{N}$ with $k_1 \le k_2$.

Example 1. Consider the DTMC $\mathcal{M}$ in Fig. 1 and the HyperPCTL formula

$$\psi = \forall \sigma_1. \forall \sigma_2. (init_1 \wedge init_2) \Rightarrow \mathbb{P}(\mathsf{F}a_1) = \mathbb{P}(\mathsf{F}a_2).$$

$\mathcal{M}$ satisfies ψ if, for all pairs of initial states (labeled by atomic proposition *init*), the probability to eventually reach a state satisfying a is the same, i.e., for each $(s_i, s_j) \in \mathcal{S}^2$ s.t. $init \in L(s_i)$ and $init \in L(s_j)$, we have $\mathcal{M}, (s_i, s_j) \models \mathbb{P}(\mathsf{F}a_1) = \mathbb{P}(\mathsf{F}a_2)$. The probability of reaching a from s_0 is $0.4 + (0.2 \cdot 0.2) = 0.44$ and the probability of reaching a from s_1 is $0.3 + (0.7 \cdot 0.2) = 0.44$. Hence, $\mathcal{M} \models \psi$.

3 A Probabilistic Decomposition Approach

The HyperPCTL semantics reduces the evaluation of a HyperPCTL formula with n (quantified) state variables on DTMC $\mathcal{M} = (\mathcal{S}, \mathbf{P}, \mathcal{A}, L)$ to the evaluation of a PCTL formula on the n-fold self-composition $\mathcal{M}^n$. However, this comes at the cost of exponentially higher space and time requirements, due to the state space being $\mathcal{S}^n$ instead of $\mathcal{S}$. We then propose a HyperPCTL formula evaluation approach that avoids self-composition and only requires solving DTMCs of size similar to that of $\mathcal{M}$. Its time complexity depends on the number and locations of state variables in $\mathbb{P}(\varphi)$ expressions. This section introduces the main idea for simpler but common cases where the time complexity is of the same order as the transient solution of the original DTMC $\mathcal{M}$, while Sect. 4 addresses the more complex (and computationally more expensive) cases. In the following, we let σ_i, for $i \geq 1$, denote state variables and symbols like a_i or b_i denote atomic propositions for the corresponding i^{th} DTMC in the self-composition.

The simplest subformulas $\mathbb{P}(\varphi)$ refer to only one quantified state variable:

$$\psi = \forall \sigma_1. \forall \sigma_2. (init_1 \wedge init_2) \Rightarrow \mathbb{P}(a_1 \cup b_1) = \mathbb{P}(a_2 \cup b_2)$$

states that the probability of being on a path of states satisfying a until reaching a state satisfying b is the same for all initial states. Obviously, self-composition is "overkill" in this case, as one could just compute the probabilities $\mathbb{P}(a_1 \cup b_1)$ starting from each initial state v_1, and simply check that they are equal. Indeed, we can determine that the model does *not* satisfy ψ as soon as we find two different initial states v_1 and v_2 in which $\mathbb{P}(a \cup b)$ evaluates to different probability values. As HyperPCTL can express this comparison of probabilities starting from different states but PCTL cannot, self-composition is theoretically needed but practically, and easily, avoidable in this case. For a numerical example, consider the DTMC in Fig. 1 and the HyperPCTL formula

$$\psi = \forall \sigma_1. \forall \sigma_2. (init_1 \wedge init_2) \Rightarrow \mathbb{P}(\mathsf{F}a_1) = \mathbb{P}(\mathsf{F}a_2).$$

Since a holds in states s_2 and s_6, make them absorbing, obtaining matrix $\mathbf{P}'$ and initialize $\pi^{[0]}$ accordingly (Fig. 2). Then, iteratively compute the backward probabilities [20] $\pi^{[k+1]} \leftarrow \mathbf{P}' \cdot \pi^{[k]}$ until convergence to $\pi^{[k^*]}$ at time $k = k^*$. The probabilities $\pi(\mathsf{F}^{[k^*]}a)[0]$ and $\pi(\mathsf{F}^{[k^*]}a)[1]$ of reaching a states from the initial states of $\mathcal{M}$, s_0 and s_1, are both 0.44, thus $\mathcal{M}$ satisfies ψ.

Probability expressions $\mathbb{P}(\varphi)$ with two state variables are more challenging:

$$\psi = \forall \sigma_1.\forall \sigma_2.(init_1 \wedge init_2) \Rightarrow \mathbb{P}(a_1 \cup b_2) \geq 0.8$$

states that, considering two copies of a DTMC, both starting execution in an initial state, the probability to move along states satisfying a in the first copy until we reach a state satisfying b in the second copy is at least 0.8. While this seems to inextricably tie the two DTMCs, we can avoid self-composition by observing that **copies of the DTMC in any self-composition interact only through their shared "clock"**. Thus, in this case, we can write

$$[\![\,\mathbb{P}(a_1 \cup b_2)\,]\!]_{\mathcal{M},v} = \sum_{k=0}^{\infty} [\![\,\mathbb{P}(\mathsf{G}^{[k-1]}a_1)\,]\!]_{\mathcal{M},v} \cdot [\![\,\mathbb{P}(\overline{b}_2 \cup {}^{[k]}b_2)\,]\!]_{\mathcal{M},v},$$

where $\mathsf{G}^{[k]}\psi$ means "ψ holds continuously during time $[0,k]$" and $\overline{\psi} \cup {}^{[k]}\psi$ means "ψ holds for the first time at time k"; also, in the following, we will slightly abuse notation and simply write "$\mathbb{P}(...)$" instead "$[\![\,\mathbb{P}(...)\,]\!]_{\mathcal{M},v}$". To compute $\mathbb{P}(a_1 \cup b_2)$ using this equality, define DTMC $\mathcal{M}'$ with transition probability matrix $\mathbf{P}'$ obtained from the original $\mathcal{M}$ by making all states *not* satisfying a absorbing by substituting their outgoing transitions with a self loop, so that $\mathcal{M}'$ cannot leave them. Then, for $k \in \mathbb{N}$, let $\pi(\mathsf{G}^{[k]}a)$ be vectors of size $|\mathcal{S}|$, defined as follows:

- for $k = -1$: $\pi(\mathsf{G}^{[-1]}a)[v] = 1$, for all $v \in \mathcal{S}$.
- for $k = 0$: $\pi(\mathsf{G}^{[0]}a)[v] = \delta_{a \in L(v)}$, i.e., 1 if $a \in L(v)$, 0 otherwise, for all $v \in \mathcal{S}$.
- for $k > 0$, use backward reachability: $\pi(\mathsf{G}^{[k]}a) = \mathbf{P}' \cdot \pi(\mathsf{G}^{[k-1]}a)$.

Thus, entry $\pi(\mathsf{G}^{[k]}a)[v]$ for $k \geq 0$ is the probability that the original DTMC $\mathcal{M}$ remains in states satisfying a for k steps if it was in state v at time 0.

Analogously, define DTMC $\mathcal{M}''$ with a *defective* transition probability matrix $\mathbf{P}''$ obtained from $\mathbf{P}$ by redirecting all outgoing transitions of any state satisfying b to a fresh absorbing state. Then, define

- for $k = 0$: $\pi(\overline{b} \cup {}^{[0]}b)[v] = \delta_{b \in L(v)}$, for all $v \in \mathcal{S}$.
- for $k > 0$, use backward reachability: $\pi(\overline{b} \cup {}^{[k]}b) = \mathbf{P}'' \cdot \pi(\overline{b} \cup {}^{[k-1]}b)$.

Thus, $\pi(\overline{b} \cup {}^{[k]}b)[v]$ is the probability that the original DTMC $\mathcal{M}$ enters a state satisfying b at step k for the first time if it was in state v at time 0.

Then, for any two states $v_1, v_2 \in \mathcal{S}$ of $\mathcal{M}$ and a "sufficiently large" value k^*, we can (under-)approximate the value of $\mathbb{P}(a_1 \cup b_2)$ in state $v = (v_1, v_2)$ of the 2-ary self-composition of $\mathcal{M}$ with the *truncated* sum

$$\mathbb{P}(a_1 \cup b_2) \approx \sum_{k=0}^{k^*} \pi(\mathsf{G}^{[k-1]}a)[v_1] \cdot \pi(\overline{b} \cup {}^{[k]}b)[v_2]. \tag{1}$$

Of course, bounded-until formulas involve a finite summation, so have no truncation error. For example, the following is an equality, not an approximation:

$$\mathbb{P}(a_1 \cup {}^{[0,t]}b_2) = \sum_{k=0}^{t} \mathbb{P}(\mathsf{G}^{[k-1]}a_1) \cdot \mathbb{P}(\overline{b}_2 \cup {}^{[k]}b_2).$$

Importantly, Eq. 1 is a *lower bound* of the exact value, since all the elements ignored by the partial sum are products of probabilities, thus non-negative. Moreover, (i) for any state v_1, the values $\pi(\mathsf{G}^{[k]}a)[v_1]$ are non-increasing in k, actually strictly decreasing unless v_1 reaches a recurrent class containing only states satisfying a (a recurrent class is a set of mutually reachable states that cannot be exited once entered, an absorbing state being a special case); and (ii) the values $\pi(\overline{b}\,\mathsf{U}^{[k]}b)[v_2]$ are instead not necessarily monotonic in k, but their sum $\Gamma_{k^*}[v_2] := \sum_{k=0}^{k^*}\pi(\overline{b}\,\mathsf{U}^{[k]}b)[v_2]$ is non-decreasing and upper-bounded by the probability $\Gamma[v_2]$ of eventually reaching a state satisfying b from v_2, a quantity we can compute. From (i) and (ii) we can then derive a practical stopping criterion, as they imply that the error when summing up to k^* is bounded by $\pi(\mathsf{G}^{[k^*-1]}a)[v_1] \cdot (\Gamma[v_2] - \Gamma_{k^*}[v_2])$, which in turn gives us the following *upper bound* on the desired value $\mathbb{P}(a_1 \cup b_2)$:

$$\left[\sum_{k=0}^{k^*}\pi(\mathsf{G}^{[k-1]}a)[v_1] \cdot \pi(\overline{b}\,\mathsf{U}^{[k]}b)[v_2]\right] + \pi(\mathsf{G}^{[k^*-1]}a)[v_1] \cdot \left(\Gamma[v_2] - \Gamma_{k^*}[v_2]\right). \quad (2)$$

This requires storing two additional vectors, Γ and Γ_{k^*}, a fair price to pay for a method that provides both a lower and an upper bound on the numerical result.

Considering now the efficiency of this computation, the described approach appears to require storing $2(k^* + 1)$ vectors of size $|\mathcal{S}|$, but this can be avoided in various ways. Let z be the number of initial states.

- Compute all the required vectors up to k^*, then approximate $\mathbb{P}(a_1 \cup b_2)$ using Eq. 1 for each of the z^2 pairs of initial states (v_1, v_2). This requires us to store $2(k^* + 1)|\mathcal{S}|$ floating point numbers, plus just one accumulator for $p_{v_1,v_2} = \mathbb{P}(a_1 \cup b_2)$, which can be discarded after comparing it with 0.8.
- Compute $\pi(\mathsf{G}^{[k-1]}a)$ and $\pi(\overline{b}\,\mathsf{U}^{[k]}b)$, add their contribution to $\mathbb{P}(a_1 \cup b_2)$ for each initial state pair (v_1, v_2), use them to compute $\pi(\mathsf{G}^{[k]}a)$ and $\pi(\overline{b}\,\mathsf{U}^{[k+1]}b)$, and then discard them. This requires storing only four vectors of size $|\mathcal{S}|$, but also all the z^2 accumulators $p_{(v_1,v_2)}$, one for each pair of initial states (v_1, v_2). The time complexity of this approach is the same as that of the first approach, so we could choose between them based on how large $2(k^*+1)|\mathcal{S}|$ is compared to $4|\mathcal{S}| + z^2$. If z is substantially smaller than $|\mathcal{S}|$, i.e., if there are only a few initial states, this second approach is preferable, especially since it is hard to know a priori how large k^* must be.
- A variant of the previous approach computes $p_{(v_1,v_2)}$ only for a subset of the z^2 initial state pairs, and repeats the entire computation, including that of the vectors $\pi(\mathsf{G}^{[k-1]}a)$ and $\pi(\overline{b}\,\mathsf{U}^{[k]}b)$, for the next subset of the initial state pairs, until all z^2 pairs have been considered (a time-memory tradeoff).
- In the limit, one can compute $\pi(\mathsf{G}^{[k-1]}a)[v_1]$ and $\pi(\overline{b}\,\mathsf{U}^{[k]}b)[v_2]$ for a single pair of initial states (v_1, v_2), in which case potentially more efficient *forward reachability probability* computations could be used (in forward reachability computations, $\pi^{[0]}$ is the initial probability vector of $\mathcal{M}'$ and $\pi^{[k]}$ is calculated iteratively as $\pi^{[k]} \leftarrow \pi^{[k-1]} \cdot \mathbf{P}'$). This requires z^2 such computations, thus is likely efficient only when z is small, although it would have the smallest memory requirements, just $4|\mathcal{S}|$ floating point numbers.

$$\mathbf{P} = \begin{pmatrix} 0 & 0 & .4 & .2 & 0 & .4 & 0 \\ 0 & 0 & 0 & .7 & .3 & 0 & 0 \\ 0 & 0 & 0 & 0 & 0 & 1 & 0 \\ 0 & 0 & 0 & 0 & 0 & .8 & .2 \\ 0 & 0 & 0 & 0 & 0 & 0 & 1 \\ 0 & 0 & 0 & 0 & 0 & 1 & 0 \\ 0 & 0 & 0 & 0 & 0 & 0 & 1 \end{pmatrix} \quad \mathbf{P}' = \begin{pmatrix} 0 & 0 & .4 & .2 & 0 & .4 & 0 \\ 0 & 0 & 0 & .7 & .3 & 0 & 0 \\ 0 & 0 & 1 & 0 & 0 & 0 & 0 \\ 0 & 0 & 0 & 0 & 0 & .8 & .2 \\ 0 & 0 & 0 & 0 & 0 & 0 & 1 \\ 0 & 0 & 0 & 0 & 0 & 1 & 0 \\ 0 & 0 & 0 & 0 & 0 & 0 & 1 \end{pmatrix} \quad \mathbf{P}'' = \begin{pmatrix} 0 & 0 & .4 & .2 & 0 & .4 & 0 \\ 0 & 0 & 0 & .7 & .3 & 0 & 0 \\ 0 & 0 & 0 & 0 & 0 & 1 & 0 \\ 0 & 0 & 0 & 0 & 0 & .8 & .2 \\ 0 & 0 & 0 & 0 & 0 & 0 & 1 \\ 0 & 0 & 0 & 0 & 0 & 1 & 0 \\ 0 & 0 & 0 & 0 & 0 & 0 & 0 \end{pmatrix}$$

$$\pi^{[0]} = \begin{pmatrix} 0 & 0 & 1 & 0 & 0 & 0 & 1 \end{pmatrix} \qquad \pi^{[k^*]} = \begin{pmatrix} .44 & .44 & 1 & .2 & 1 & 0 & 1 \end{pmatrix}$$

$$\pi(\overline{b}\,\mathsf{U}^{[0]}b) = \begin{pmatrix} 0 & 0 & 0 & 0 & 0 & 0 & 1 \end{pmatrix} \quad \pi(\overline{b}\,\mathsf{U}^{[1]}b) = \begin{pmatrix} 0 & 0 & 0 & .2 & 1 & 0 & 0 \end{pmatrix} \quad \pi(\overline{b}\,\mathsf{U}^{[2]}b) = \begin{pmatrix} .04 & .44 & 0 & 0 & 0 & 0 & 0 \end{pmatrix}$$

Fig. 2. Quantities computed by the probabilistic decomposition for our example.

Let's now instead evaluate the following formula on the same DTMC:

$$\psi = \forall \sigma_1.\forall \sigma_2.(init_1 \wedge init_2) \Rightarrow \mathbb{P}(\overline{a}_1 \,\mathsf{U}\, b_2) > 0.8.$$

Define the same transition probability matrix $\mathbf{P}'$ as above, where states not satisfying $\overline{a}$ (thus satisfying a) are now absorbing (the outgoing transition from state s_2 is redirected back to s_2, while state s_6 is already an absorbing state), and let $\mathbf{P}''$ be the defective transition probability matrix after zeroing rates from b states (again, as shown in Fig. 2).

After initializing $\pi(\overline{b}\,\mathsf{U}^{[0]}b)$, compute the probability of first reaching b at time 1, $\pi(\overline{b}\,\mathsf{U}^{[1]}b) = \mathbf{P}'' \cdot \pi(\overline{b}\,\mathsf{U}^{[0]}b)$, and time 2, $\pi(\overline{b}\,\mathsf{U}^{[2]}b) = \mathbf{P}'' \cdot \pi(\overline{b}\,\mathsf{U}^{[1]}b)$. Analogously, initialize $\pi(\mathsf{G}^{[-1]}\overline{a})$ and $\pi(\mathsf{G}^{[0]}\overline{a})$ and compute the probability of staying in $\overline{a}$ states for two time units, $\pi(\mathsf{G}^{[1]}\overline{a}) = \mathbf{P}' \cdot \pi(\mathsf{G}^{[0]}\overline{a})$. We need $\pi(\mathsf{G}^{[k-1]}\overline{a})$ and $\pi(\overline{b}\,\mathsf{U}^{[k]}b)$ only up to $k = 2$ because the DTMC has cycles only on the absorbing states, which are reached in at most two steps from s_0 and s_1. Then, the probability to satisfy $(\overline{a}_1 \,\mathsf{U}\, b_2)$ starting from (s_0, s_0) is computed to be 0.024, by summing $\pi(\mathsf{G}^{[-1]}\overline{a})[s_0] \cdot \pi(\overline{b}\,\mathsf{U}^{[0]}b)[s_0]$, $\pi(\mathsf{G}^{[0]}\overline{a})[s_0] \cdot \pi(\overline{b}\,\mathsf{U}^{[1]}b)[s_0]$, and $\pi(\mathsf{G}^{[1]}\overline{a})[s_0] \cdot \pi(\overline{b}\,\mathsf{U}^{[2]}b)[s_0]$, according to Eq. 1; similarly, the probabilities from the pairs of initial states (s_0, s_1), (s_1, s_0), and (s_1, s_1) are 0.264, 0.040, and 0.440, respectively. None of these probabilities exceed 0.8, so DTMC $\mathcal{M}$ does not satisfy the formula. Indeed, we could have already concluded that ψ is false after considering just the first pair of initial states (s_0, s_0), since the universal quantifiers in formula ψ require *all* possible pairs of initial states to satisfy the property; violation of the property by even just one pair of initial states is enough to decide the overall unsatisfiability of ψ and terminate the algorithm.

4 Probabilistically Dependent Markov Chains

A HyperPCTL formula with nested probability operators is evaluated "inside out", analogously to nested CTL formulas. For example, given the formula

$$\forall \sigma_1.\forall \sigma_2.(init_1 \wedge init_2) \Rightarrow \mathbb{P}(a_1 \,\mathsf{U}\, (\mathbb{P}(Fb_2) > 0.8)) > 0.9,$$

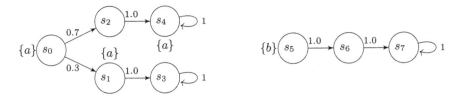

Fig. 3. A Markov chain illustrating the difficulty with $\mathbb{P}((a_1 \vee a_2) \cup b_3)$.

we evaluate $\mathbb{P}(Fb_2)$ first, using backward reachability probabilities in the DTMC $\mathcal{M}'$ obtained from the original DTMC $\mathcal{M}$ by making the b-states absorbing, as explained in Sect. 3. This gives us a size-$|\mathcal{S}|$ vector π of probabilities, which we can use to label all states v that satisfy $\pi[v] > 0.8$ with a fresh atomic proposition, say c. This way we have reduced the problem to a form handled in the previous section, namely checking the truth of formula

$$\forall \sigma_1.\forall \sigma_2.(init_1 \wedge init_2) \Rightarrow \mathbb{P}(a_1 \cup c_2) > 0.9.$$

Next, we tackle instead the more difficult cases where the logic operators combining propositions associated to different variables appearing in a $\mathbb{P}$ operator imply a *dependence* between the evolution of otherwise independent DTMCs.

For example the formula

$$\psi = \forall \sigma_1. \cdots . \forall \sigma_n. \mathbb{P}((a_1 \vee \cdots . \vee a_m) \cup (b_{m+1} \wedge \cdots \wedge b_n)) > 0.9 \qquad (3)$$

(for $n > m \geq 2$), asserts that, in the n-fold self-composition starting at $(\sigma_1, ..., \sigma_n)$, the probability that $\bigwedge_{m < i \leq n} b_i$ holds for the first time at some time k, while $\bigvee_{1 \leq i \leq m} a_i$ held at every time $h < k$, is greater than 0.9.

Even for $m = 2$ and $n = 3$, this case is difficult. Recall how the equality $\mathbb{P}(a_1 \cup b_2) = \sum_{k=0}^{\infty} \mathbb{P}(G^{[k-1]}a_1) \cdot \mathbb{P}(\overline{b_2} \cup {}^{[k]}b_2)$ allows us to compute $\mathbb{P}(a_1 \cup b_2)$ with two Markov chains of the same size as the original one, avoiding self-composition: we simply compute a pair of *independent* probability vectors for each time step k. Using the same approach, we rewrite probability $\mathbb{P}((a_1 \vee a_2) \cup b_3)$ as:

$$\mathbb{P}((a_1 \vee a_2) \cup b_3) = \sum_{k=0}^{\infty} \mathbb{P}(G^{[k-1]}(a_1 \vee a_2)) \cdot \mathbb{P}(\overline{b_3} \cup {}^{[k]}b_3).$$

However, the computation of $\mathbb{P}(G^{[k]}(a_1 \vee a_2))$ requires examining the *joint history* of a_1's and a_2's along the respective evolutions started at σ_1 and σ_2. To see why, consider Fig. 3 and assume that $\sigma_1 = s_0$ and $\sigma_2 = s_5$. At time $k = 0$, $\mathbb{P}(a_1 \vee a_2) = 1$ in state pair (s_0, s_5); at time $k = 1$, $\mathbb{P}(X(a_1 \vee a_2)) = 0.3$ since the probability of state pair (s_1, s_6) is 0.3, and a_1 holds in s_1; at time $k = 2$, $\mathbb{P}(X^{[2]}(a_1 \vee a_2)) = 0.7$ since the probability of state pair (s_4, s_7) is 0.7, and a_2 holds in s_4; however, $\mathbb{P}(G^{[2]}(a_1 \vee a_2)) = 0$ because if the composed DTMC is in state (s_1, s_6) at time $k = 1$, it cannot be in state (s_4, s_7) at time $k = 2$.

In other words, not satisfying a_1 at time k (in executions starting from σ_1) requires a_2 to be satisfied at time k (in executions starting from σ_2), thus knowledge of the first execution impacts our probabilistic assessment of the second one,

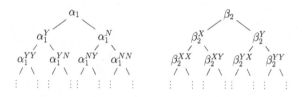

Fig. 4. Trees organizing the vectors needed to compute $\mathbb{P}(G^{[k]}(a_1 \vee a_2))$.

and vice versa, *independence is lost*: if a sequence $\delta \in (\{a_1, \overline{a_1}\} \times \{a_2, \overline{a_2}\})^k$ in the 2-fold self-composition satisfies $(a_1 \vee a_2)$ for the first k steps, the derived *sequence* $\delta_1 \in \{a_1, \overline{a_1}\}^k$ restricts the possible sequences $\delta_2 \in \{a_2, \overline{a_2}\}^k$, since $\delta_1[h] = \overline{a_1}$ implies $\delta_2[h] = a_2$, thus in turn affects the probability of a_2 holding at time $k + 1$.

We now show how to compute the desired result using size-$|\mathcal{S}|$ (possibly defective) probability vectors, but their number may be exponential in k^*. We use one *binary tree* to organize vectors α_1^δ, where $\delta \in \{Y, N\}^h$, for $h = 0, 1, ..., k^*$, and another for "matching" vectors $\beta_2^{\lambda(\delta)}$, where $\lambda(\delta)$ is the sequence obtained from δ by changing all Y's into X's and all N's into Y's (Fig. 4).

For $h = 0$, we initialize the entries of α_1 and β_2 to 0 except for $\alpha_1[\sigma_1] = 1$ and $\beta_2[\sigma_2] = 1$. Then, we compute further vectors using the recurrence

$$\alpha_1^{\delta Y}[v'] = \sum_{v \models a_1} \alpha_1^\delta[v] \cdot \mathbf{P}[v, v'] \qquad \alpha_1^{\delta N}[v'] = \sum_{v \not\models a_1} \alpha_1^\delta[v] \cdot \mathbf{P}[v, v']$$

$$\beta_2^{\lambda(\delta)X}[v'] = \sum_{v \in \mathcal{S}} \beta_2^{\lambda(\delta)}[v] \cdot \mathbf{P}[v, v'] \qquad \beta_2^{\lambda(\delta)Y}[v'] = \sum_{v \models a_2} \beta_2^{\lambda(\delta)}[v] \cdot \mathbf{P}[v, v'] .$$

The intuition behind the mapping λ is that, at any given time h, if a_1 holds (Y), a_2 may or may not hold (X) but, if a_1 does not hold (N), a_2 must hold (Y). This probabilistic *splitting* is similar to traditional *conditioning*, except that we do not normalize the vectors. Letting $||\cdot||$ indicate the 1-norm, at level h we have $\sum_{\delta \in \{Y,N\}^h} ||\alpha_1^\delta|| = 1$ (i.e., the sum of all α_1^δ vectors at level h is a full probability vector), while $||\beta_2^{X^h}|| = 1$ (i.e., $\beta_2^{X^h}$ is by itself a full probability vector) and, if $\lambda(\delta')$ is obtained from $\lambda(\delta)$ changing some X's into Y's, i.e., if δ' is obtained from δ by changing some Y's into N's, then $||\beta_2^{\lambda(\delta)}|| \geq ||\beta_2^{\lambda(\delta')}||$. The probability of continuously satisfying $a_1 \vee a_2$ during $[0, h]$ is then

$$\mathbb{P}(G^{[h]}(a_1 \vee a_2)) = \sum_{\delta \in \{Y,N\}^h} ||\alpha_1^\delta|| \cdot ||\beta_2^{\lambda(\delta)}||.$$

This approach can be generalized to a disjunction of m terms by defining $m - 1$ trees of vectors with nodes α_i^δ, for $i = 1, ..., m - 1$, $\delta \in \{Y, N\}^h$, and $h = 0, 1, ..., k$ (these are analogous to the tree for α_1^δ when $m = 2$) and one tree of vectors with nodes β_m^δ (analogous to the tree for β_2^δ when $m = 2$). Then, let $p_l^\delta = ||\alpha_l^\delta||$ and define $m - 1$ trees of *scalars* with nodes

$$p_{1:1}^\delta = p_1^\delta \quad \text{and, for } l = 2, ..., m - 1, \quad p_{1:l}^\delta = \sum_{\delta' \vee \delta'' = \delta} p_{1:l-1}^{\delta'} \cdot p_l^{\delta''},$$

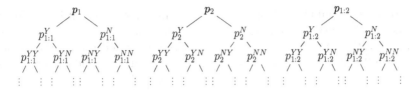

Fig. 5. Trees of scalars used for the disjunction of three or more terms.

where $\delta' \vee \delta''$ is the elementwise disjunction of same-length sequences, e.g. (Fig. 5)

$$p_{1:2}^{YY} = p_{1:1}^{NN} p_2^{YY} + p_{1:1}^{NY}(p_2^{YN} + p_2^{YY}) + p_{1:1}^{YN}(p_2^{NY} + p_2^{YY}) + p_{1:1}^{YY}\underbrace{(p_2^{NN} + p_2^{NY} + p_2^{YN} + p_2^{YY})}_{=1}$$
$$p_{1:2}^{YN} = p_{1:1}^{NN} \cdot p_2^{YN} + p_{1:1}^{YN}(p_2^{NN} + p_2^{YN})$$
$$p_{1:2}^{NY} = p_{1:1}^{NN} \cdot p_2^{NY} + p_{1:1}^{NY}(p_2^{NN} + p_2^{YN})$$
$$p_{1:2}^{NN} = p_{1:1}^{NN} \cdot p_2^{NN}$$

In other words, rather than considering all $2^m - 1$ combinations of $a_1, ..., a_m$ (and their negations) that satisfy $a_1 \vee \cdots \vee a_m$, we incrementally consider $a_1, ..., a_l$, so that $p_{1:l}^\delta$ is the probability of $a_1 \vee \cdots \vee a_l$ holding or not, according to the sequence δ, without detailing the individual value of each $a_1, ..., a_l$ that contributed to having $\delta[h] = Y$, while obviously none of them held at time h if $\delta[h] = N$.

Finally, we can compute $\mathbb{P}(\mathsf{G}^{[h]}(a_1 \vee \cdots \vee a_m)) = \sum_{\delta \in \{Y,N\}^h} p_{1:m-1}^\delta \cdot ||\beta_2^{\lambda(\delta)}||$. We conclude by observing that conjunctions to the right of an until operator present a similar difficulty, since computing the probability that $b_{m+1} \wedge \cdots \wedge b_n$ holds for the first time at time h requires to check that $\overline{b_{m+1}} \vee \cdots \vee \overline{b_n}$ held continuously during the interval $[0, h-1]$. Thus, in a sense, Eq. 3 is "a worst case" for our approach, while conjunctions on the left and disjunctions on the right of the until operator are much simpler because of the independence of DTMC executions in the n-fold semantics.

We now address the stopping criterion for our approach. If the HyperPCTL formula is a bounded-until with upper time bound t, or if the DTMC is acyclic and the maximum distance from the start nodes to the absorbing node(s) is t, or if, after time t, the DTMC can only visit states satisfying the same set of atomic propositions involved in the formula (a lucky but unlikely case), then we only need to perform at most t iterations.

Otherwise, we need to decide the level k^* at which to stop expanding the trees. Since the probability mass of the vectors α_i decreases exponentially with the level h as long as the DTMC keeps branching on a_1 and $\overline{a_1}$, the contribution of exploring additional levels eventually becomes negligible. Even better, we can use an A*-style search [18] to expand first tree nodes (vectors) with the highest probability mass. If the HyperPCTL formula is of the form $\mathbb{P}(\cdot) < C$ or $\mathbb{P}(\cdot) \geq C$, we can stop as soon as the accumulated probability reaches C (and determine that the formula is true or false, respectively). We observe that the difficulty of determining a stopping point is shared by the self-composition approach (which requires the same number k^* of iterations as our method), and it is well-known that the satisfiability problem for PCTL is undecidable.

However, there is a case where our probabilistic decomposition approach fails. Consider a 2-state DTMC $\mathcal{M}$ with states s_0 (satisfying $init$ and a) and s_1 (satisfying b), and $\mathbf{P}[s_0, s_1] = \mathbf{P}[s_1, s_0] = 1$, so that both states are periodic with period 2. The formula $\psi = \forall \sigma_1. \forall \sigma_2. (init_1 \wedge init_2) \Rightarrow \mathbb{P}(\mathsf{F}(a_1 \wedge b_2)) > 0.1$ is obviously false because, if the 2-fold self-composition $\mathcal{M}^2$ starts from (s_0, s_0), it can only alternate with (s_1, s_1), thus either a_1 or b_2 is satisfied at a given time, but not both. The self-composition approach detects this situation when exploring the transition probability matrix of $\mathcal{M}^2$. Our approach, instead, will compute sequences of probability vectors $[1, 0]$, $[0, 1]$, $[1, 0]$, ... attempting to find times when both a_1 and b_2 hold, but obviously never succeeding. While detecting such situation, is likely quite difficult (and may essentially be equivalent to examining the transition probability matrix of $\mathcal{M}^2$), a simple analysis of $\mathbf{P}$ can alert us that the DTMC has periodic states, thus the method *may* fail.

4.1   Time and Memory Complexity

We have seen how, for a disjunction of the form $a_1 \vee \cdots \vee a_m$, the number of (defective) size-$|\mathcal{S}|$ probability vectors to be computed grows exponentially in the truncation time k^* but only linearly in m. Since each probability vector of size $O(|\mathcal{S}|)$ is obtained from its parent through a multiplication with a matrix having no more nonzero entries than $\mathbf{P}$, the overall time complexity for our approach is $O(2^{k^*} \cdot \eta(\mathbf{P}) \cdot m)$, where $\eta(\mathbf{P})$ is the number of nonzeros in $\mathbf{P}$ (we assume the use of a sparse data structure in the common case where $\mathbf{P}$ has many zero entries). This should be compared with the time $O(k^* \cdot \eta(\mathbf{P})^m)$ required by self-composition, since self-composition also requires k^* iterations, but now each of them requires multiplying a probability vector of size $O(|\mathcal{S}|^m)$ with a transition probability matrix with $\eta(\mathbf{P})^m$ nonzeros. In practice, m is small, but $|\mathcal{S}|$ and $\eta(\mathbf{P})$ are large, thus our approach is faster up to moderate values of k^*.

More importantly, though, our approach will require substantially less memory, since not all vectors computed by our approach are needed at the same time. First of all, we can obviously build a tree of vectors α_l^δ at a time, and delete it before moving to the next tree, as long as we record the probability mass of these vectors in the tree of scalars p_l^δ. In fact, we do not even need to store all the vectors α_l^δ at the same time, as we can compute them in depth-first order, which requires to store only the vectors on a path from the root, without this requiring any duplicate work. Thus, the memory consumption due to vectors is just $k^* \cdot |\mathcal{S}|$. Considering instead the trees of scalars, it is easy to see that we can discard the trees for $p_{1:l-1}^\delta$ and for p_l^δ once we have computed the tree for $p_{1:l}^\delta$, so we only need to store simultaneously three trees of scalars, each requiring $2^{k+1} - 1$ scalars. Thus, the overall memory for our approach, including the storage for $\mathbf{P}$, is $O(\eta(\mathbf{P}) + k^* \cdot |\mathcal{S}| + 2^{k^*})$, independent of m. For self-composition, the memory requirements are $O(|\mathcal{S}|^m)$ if the transition probability matrix of $\mathcal{M}^m$ is not built explicitly but instead computed on-the-fly (a memory-time tradeoff), otherwise they are even worse, $O(\eta(\mathbf{P})^m)$.

5 Case Studies and Evaluation

We now describe a set of applications related to information flow security and mission safety. Table 1 shows the number of states and transitions in the corresponding DTMCs and the times (in seconds) to verify the respective Hyper-PCTL formulas, for three different solution approaches: our probabilistic decomposition implemented in C++ using the STORM [1] API, a prototype implementation of the *symbolic* approach of [3], and our Python implementation of self-composition [4]. "t/o" means runtime over 1 h; "o/m" means out-of-memory.

Probabilistic Noninterference. Considering the example described in the introduction, we compute the probability of l having the same value upon termination of the concurrent threads, for different initial values h_σ and $h_{\sigma'}$ of h. We use a non-uniform probabilistic scheduler, where the probability of scheduling thread t vs. t' is as specified in [2], and verify that, indeed, the value of h is not probabilistically disclosed by the value of the low observable output l.

Dining Cryptographers [7]. After finishing dinner, n cryptographers want to find out whether the NSA or one of them (but not which one) paid for the meal by executing this protocol: (1) each cryptographer flips a fair coin and shows it to the cryptographer on his right; (2) if a cryptographer did not pay, she/he announces whether her/his coin and the one she/he has been shown "agree" or "disagree"; (3) if a cryptographer paid, she/he announces the opposite: "disagree" if the coins agree, "agree" if they disagree. If n and the number of "agrees" a^i are both odd, or both even, then NSA paid, otherwise a cryptographer paid:

$$\forall \sigma. \forall \sigma'. \left(\bigvee_{i=1}^{n} pay_\sigma^i \right) \wedge \left(\bigvee_{i=1}^{n} pay_{\sigma'}^i \right) \Rightarrow \mathbb{P}\left(F(end_\sigma \wedge \bigoplus_{i=1}^{n} a_\sigma^i \right) = \mathbb{P}\left(F(end_{\sigma'} \wedge \bigoplus_{i=1}^{n} a_{\sigma'}^i \right).$$

Varying n from 3 to 10, we see that self-composition fails for $n \geq 5$.

Side-Channel Timing Attack. Generally speaking, a side channel timing attack may disclose a secret value to an attacker by observing the execution time of a function. For instance, the core of the RSA public-key encryption algorithm uses the modular exponentiation algorithm to compute a^b mod n, where a is the integer representing the plain text and b is the integer encryption key. With a poor implementation, b can be leaked through a probabilistic side channel timing attack because the two if branches in Fig. 6 can exhibit different timing behavior (lines 6–8). Using a uniform scheduler for parallel threads, an attacker thread can infer the

```
1  void mexp(){
2    c = 0; d = 1; i = k;
3    while (i >= 0){
4      i = i-1; c = c*2;
5      d = (d*d) % n;
6      if (b(i) = 1)
7        c = c+1;
8        d = (d*a) % n;
9    }
10 }
11 t = new Thread(mexp());
12 j = 0; m = 2 * k;
13 while (j < m & !t.stop)
14   j++;
```

Fig. 6. Modular exponentiation.

value of b by running in parallel to a modular exponentiation thread and iteratively incrementing a counter variable until the other thread terminates.

We model this system using a DTMC where the two `if` branches correspond to two different states. Upon termination, the probability of having the same counter value j should be equal for different bit configurations $b(i)$ of the key b. This can be formalized in HyperPCTL as:

$$\forall \sigma.\forall \sigma'.\Big(init_\sigma \wedge init_{\sigma'} \Big) \Rightarrow \bigwedge_{l=0}^{m} \Big(\mathbb{P}(\mathsf{F}(j=l)_\sigma) = \mathbb{P}(\mathsf{F}(j=l)_{\sigma'}) \Big).$$

To evaluate this property, we vary the number of encryption bits k from 1 to 5 and check whether the probability to reach the same counter value j depends on the choice of the encryption bits.

Triple Modular Redundancy. Fault tolerant systems use redundancy to ensure continuous operation. The following HyperPCTL formula for a TMR (Triple Modular Redundancy) system states that, with probability at least C, two or more of the three subsystems are "up" (atomic proposition a) at all times prior to reaching mission completion (atomic proposition b), where i^a and i^b denote the starting state for the portions of the DTMC modeling the failure time of one subsystem and the mission time, respectively:

$$\forall \sigma_1.\forall \sigma_2.\forall \sigma_3.\forall \sigma_4.(i_1^a \wedge i_2^a \wedge i_3^a \wedge i_4^b) \Rightarrow \mathbb{P}\Big((a_1 \wedge a_2) \vee (a_1 \wedge a_3) \vee (a_2 \wedge a_3) \vee (a_1 \wedge a_2 \wedge a_3) \, \mathsf{U} \, b_4\Big) \geq C.$$

The DTMC of Fig. 7 models the failure time distribution of a subsystem (on the left) and the mission time (on the right, assumed to be uniformly distributed between 1 and a maximum T, with $T = 3$ in the figure). Unlike the case of TMR with *repairable* subsystems, our subsystem remains "down" once it fails, thus the tree for the probability vectors α_i^δ, for $i = 1, 2, 3$, can only have sequences of the form $Y \cdots Y$ and $Y \cdots Y N \cdots N$ (in fact, we can stop expanding a sequence at the first N, i.e., at $Y \cdots Y N$). In other words, there is no need to compute an exponential number of vectors in this case, nor to store a full tree of scalars: our memory and time requirements are *linear* in k^* in this case.

Analysis of Results. As can be seen in Table 1, our numerical method significantly outperforms the brute-force method in [4] and the symbolic approach based on constraint solving in [3]. In most cases our verification time is in the order of milliseconds, while the alternative approaches easily require minutes. For the first case study, probabilistic non-interference, given a pair $(h_\sigma, h_{\sigma'})$ of values, each value of h is decremented until it reaches 0 Higher values of h add more states and transitions in the system model thus require more time to verify the hyperproperty. For the dining cryptographers, the state space grows so fast that both self-composition and symbolic verification approach run out of memory. For the side-channel timing attack, we increased the encryption key up to four bits, then we check whether the secret is leaked through the timing channel. Finally, the verification time for TMR is significantly higher using self-composition or the symbolic approach, as the former requires 4-ary self-composition and the latter requires to generate symbolic expressions for four copies of the model.

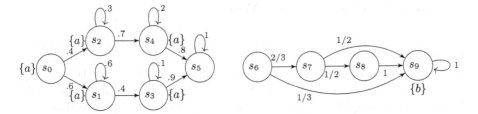

Fig. 7. Markov chain for the TMR system. The left portion model the failing distribution of a subsystem, the right one models the uniform $[0,3]$ distribution of the mission time. According to the HyperPCTL definition, the two portions form a single DTMC but, in practice, they could be considered separately.

Table 1. Experimental results for each choice of parameter model.

Parameters		States	Transitions	PD-based(s)	Symbolic(s)[3]	Self-composition(s)[4]
h_σ	$h_{\sigma'}$			Probabilistic noninterference		
0	1	22	28	0.003	0.008	0.055
0	5	46	60	0.003	0.011	0.723
0	10	76	100	0.006	0.018	0.918
0	15	106	140	0.005	0.051	1.986
3	5	64	84	0.005	0.027	0.995
4	8	88	116	0.004	0.078	2.031
8	14	148	196	0.026	0.043	5.129
N				Dining cryptographers		
	3	156	184	0.023	8.074	17.9
	4	475	550	0.027	159.011	6,965.8
	5	1,338	1,524	0.032	o/m	o/m
	6	3,577	4,018	0.073	o/m	o/m
	7	9,208	10,224	0.094	o/m	o/m
	10	135,157	146,410	0.271	o/m	o/m
m				Side-channel timing attack		
	1	24	42	0.006	0.020	0.48
	2	60	120	0.012	0.040	12.98
	3	112	238	0.016	1.010	134.68
	4	180	396	0.019	4.270	832.08
	5	264	594	0.025	6.370	t/o
T				TMR		
	10	17	32	0.06	118.39	1176.96
	11	18	34	0.11	180.37	1,797.29
	12	19	36	0.19	274.24	2,696.89
	13	20	38	0.36	402.63	3,922.58
	14	21	40	0.77	590.73	5,721.39
	15	22	42	2.99	837.59	8,175.37

6   Conclusion and Future Work

In recent years, much research has targeted new temporal logics to express hyper-properties, and different model checking algorithms have been proposed to verify them. However, none of them has defined efficient algorithms for HyperPCTL model checking. We proposed a numerical approach to model check HyperPCTL formulas based on a probabilistic decomposition of the self-composed DTMC into variants of the underlying DTMC, which requires truncation if time intervals are unbounded.

We stress that, for HyperPCTL, the DTMCs formally used in the self-composition differ only in their initial state, but our approach would apply even if they were completely different DTMCs, thus could have applications beyond HyperPCTL model checking. We showed that our proposed technique significantly outperforms existing algorithms through multiple case studies.

In the future, we plan to generalize our algorithm to MDPs, which is a substantially harder problem in terms of computation complexity. We are also planning to extend our numerical approach to verification of continuous-time Markov chains, by defining a CSL-style logic analogous to HyperPCTL. We also plan to include this new algorithm in our tool HyperProb [12].

References

1. STORM: a tool for the analysis of systems involving random or probabilistic phenomena. http://www.stormchecker.org/index.html
2. Ábrahám, E., Bartocci, E., Bonakdarpour, B., Dobe, O.: Parameter synthesis for probabilistic hyperproperties. In: Proceedings of the 23rd International Conference on Logic for Programming, Artificial Intelligence and Reasoning (LPAR), pp. 12–31 (2020)
3. Ábrahám, E., Bartocci, E., Bonakdarpour, B., Dobe, O.: Probabilistic hyperproperties with nondeterminism. In: Hung, D.V., Sokolsky, O. (eds.) ATVA 2020. LNCS, vol. 12302, pp. 518–534. Springer, Cham (2020). https://doi.org/10.1007/978-3-030-59152-6_29
4. Ábrahám, E., Bonakdarpour, B.: HyperPCTL: a temporal logic for probabilistic hyperproperties. In: McIver, A., Horvath, A. (eds.) QEST 2018. LNCS, vol. 11024, pp. 20–35. Springer, Cham (2018). https://doi.org/10.1007/978-3-319-99154-2_2
5. Baumeister, J., Coenen, N., Bonakdarpour, B., Finkbeiner, B., Sánchez, C.: A temporal logic for asynchronous hyperproperties. In: Silva, A., Leino, K.R.M. (eds.) CAV 2021. LNCS, vol. 12759, pp. 694–717. Springer, Cham (2021). https://doi.org/10.1007/978-3-030-81685-8_33
6. Bonakdarpour, B., Finkbeiner, B.: The complexity of monitoring hyperproperties. In: Proceedings of the 31st IEEE Computer Security Foundations Symposium, CSF, pp. 162–174 (2018)
7. Chaum, D.: Security without identification: transaction systems to make big brother obsolete. Commun. ACM 28(10), 1030–1044 (1985)

8. Clarkson, M.R., Finkbeiner, B., Koleini, M., Micinski, K.K., Rabe, M.N., Sánchez, C.: Temporal logics for hyperproperties. In: Abadi, M., Kremer, S. (eds.) POST 2014. LNCS, vol. 8414, pp. 265–284. Springer, Heidelberg (2014). https://doi.org/10.1007/978-3-642-54792-8_15

9. Clarkson, M.R., Schneider, F.B.: Hyperproperties. J. Comput. Secur. **18**(6), 1157–1210 (2010)

10. Coenen, N., Finkbeiner, B., Sánchez, C., Tentrup, L.: Verifying hyperliveness. In: Dillig, I., Tasiran, S. (eds.) CAV 2019. LNCS, vol. 11561, pp. 121–139. Springer, Cham (2019). https://doi.org/10.1007/978-3-030-25540-4_7

11. Dimitrova, R., Finkbeiner, B., Torfah, H.: Probabilistic hyperproperties of Markov decision processes. In: Hung, D.V., Sokolsky, O. (eds.) ATVA 2020. LNCS, vol. 12302, pp. 484–500. Springer, Cham (2020). https://doi.org/10.1007/978-3-030-59152-6_27

12. Dobe, O., Ábrahám, E., Bartocci, E., Bonakdarpour, B.: HYPERPROB: a model checker for probabilistic hyperproperties. In: Huisman, M., Pǎsǎreanu, C., Zhan, N. (eds.) FM 2021. LNCS, vol. 13047, pp. 657–666. Springer, Cham (2021). https://doi.org/10.1007/978-3-030-90870-6_35

13. Dwork, C., Roth, A.: The algorithmic foundations of differential privacy. Found. Trends Theor. Comput. Sci. **9**(3–4), 211–407 (2014)

14. Emerson, E.A., Halpern, J.Y.: "Sometimes" and "not never" revisited: on branching versus linear time temporal logic. J. ACM **33**(1), 151–178 (1986)

15. Fetzer, J.H. (ed.): Probability and Causality. Synthese Library, Springer, Dordrecht (1988). https://doi.org/10.1007/978-94-009-3997-4

16. Finkbeiner, B., Rabe, M.N., Sánchez, C.: Algorithms for model checking Hyper-LTL and HyperCTL*. In: Kroening, D., Pǎsǎreanu, C.S. (eds.) CAV 2015. LNCS, vol. 9206, pp. 30–48. Springer, Cham (2015). https://doi.org/10.1007/978-3-319-21690-4_3

17. Goguen, J.A., Meseguer, J.: Security policies and security models. In: IEEE Symposium on Security and Privacy, pp. 11–20 (1982)

18. Hart, P.E., Nilsson, N.J., Raphael, B.: A formal basis for the heuristic determination of minimum cost paths. IEEE Trans. Syst. Sci. Cybern. **4**(2), 100–107 (1968). https://doi.org/10.1109/TSSC.1968.300136

19. Hsu, T.-H., Sánchez, C., Bonakdarpour, B.: Bounded model checking for hyperproperties. In: Groote, J.F., Larsen, K.G. (eds.) TACAS 2021. LNCS, vol. 12651, pp. 94–112. Springer, Cham (2021). https://doi.org/10.1007/978-3-030-72016-2_6

20. Katoen, J.-P., Kwiatkowska, M., Norman, G., Parker, D.: Faster and symbolic CTMC model checking. In: de Alfaro, L., Gilmore, S. (eds.) PAPM-PROBMIV 2001. LNCS, vol. 2165, pp. 23–38. Springer, Heidelberg (2001). https://doi.org/10.1007/3-540-44804-7_2

21. Pnueli, A.: The temporal logic of programs. In: Symposium on Foundations of Computer Science (FOCS), pp. 46–57 (1977)

22. Smith, G.: Probabilistic noninterference through weak probabilistic bisimulation. In: Proceedings of the 16th IEEE Computer Security Foundations Workshop (CSF), pp. 3–13 (2003)

23. Wang, Y., Nalluri, S., Bonakdarpour, B., Pajic, M.: Statistical model checking for hyperproperties. In: Proceedings of the IEEE 34th Computer Security Foundations (CSF), pp. 1–16 (2021)

24. Wang, Y., Zarei, M., Bonakdarpour, B., Pajic, M.: Statistical verification of hyperproperties for cyber-physical systems. ACM Trans. Embed. Comput. Syst. **18**(5s), 92:1–92:23 (2019)

25. Wang, Y., Nalluri, S., Pajic, M.: Hyperproperties for robotics: planning via Hyper-LTL. In: International Conference on Robotics and Automation (ICRA), pp. 8011–8017 (2019)
26. Zdancewic, S., Myers, A.C.: Observational determinism for concurrent program security. In: Proceedings of the 16th IEEE Computer Security Foundations Workshop (CSFW), p. 29 (2003)

Learning and Synthesis

Learning Finite State Models from Recurrent Neural Networks

Edi Muškardin[1,2]([✉]) [ID], Bernhard K. Aichernig[2] [ID], Ingo Pill[1] [ID],
and Martin Tappler[1,2] [ID]

[1] Silicon Austria Labs, TU Graz - SAL DES Lab, Graz, Austria
[2] Institute of Software Technology, Graz University of Technology, Graz, Austria
edi.muskardin@silicon-austria.com

Abstract. Explaining and verifying the behavior of recurrent neural networks (RNNs) is an important step towards achieving confidence in machine learning. The extraction of finite state models, like deterministic automata, has been shown to be a promising concept for analyzing RNNs. In this paper, we apply a black-box approach based on active automata learning combined with model-guided conformance testing to learn finite state machines (FSMs) from RNNs. The technique efficiently infers a formal model of an RNN classifier's input-output behavior, regardless of its inner structure. In several experiments, we compare this approach to other state-of-the-art FSM extraction methods. By detecting imprecise generalizations in RNNs that other techniques miss, model-guided conformance testing learns FSMs that more accurately model the RNNs under examination. We demonstrate this by identifying counterexamples with this testing approach that falsifies wrong hypothesis models learned by other techniques. This entails that testing guided by learned automata can be a useful method for finding adversarial inputs, that is, inputs incorrectly classified due to improper generalization.

Keywords: Verifiable machine learning · Active automata learning · Finite state machines · Recurrent neural networks

1 Introduction

The impressive performance of artificial neural networks (ANNs) has made them an effective asset in our computing toolbox, and has been an enabler for innovative *intelligent* systems like autonomous vehicles. Prompted by their popularity, we have also seen significant advancements in their verification [11,15,31], which needs new concepts since ANNs differ significantly from traditional software (or hardware). Huang et al. [15], e.g., address robustness by checking for adversarial examples, i.e., misclassified inputs that are hardly distinguishable from similar correctly classified inputs and that can be used to fool an ANN.

So far, most verification research has been focusing on feed-forward neural networks that can be abstractly viewed as stateless mathematical functions.

© Springer Nature Switzerland AG 2022
M. H. ter Beek and R. Monahan (Eds.): IFM 2022, LNCS 13274, pp. 229–248, 2022.
https://doi.org/10.1007/978-3-031-07727-2_13

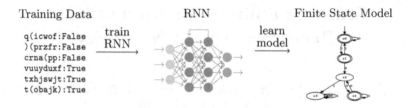

Fig. 1. The learning pipeline used in this paper.

In contrast, we analyze recurrent neural networks (RNNs) due to their ability to model sequential data which makes them well-suited for applications with stateful reactive behavior [1]. The connection between neural networks with recurrent connections and finite automata has already been studied by Kleene in the 1950s [18]. The ability of RNNs to learn regular languages prompted research on extracting formal models that explain the internal mechanisms underlying trained RNNs [26]. More recently, we have seen renewed interest in extracting finite-state models from RNNs [20,25,39]. Such models enable a manual inspection of RNN behavior on one hand, and the application of automated verification techniques like model checking on the other hand—both would be practically impossible otherwise.

Approaches based on active automata learning are promising techniques for learning concise, yet accurate finite-state models representing RNN behavior. In this paper, we will examine such approaches. First, we discuss how to learn finite-state models from RNNs by applying active automata learning to analyze their input-output behavior. In this context, we propose to apply model-guided conformance testing in combination with active automata learning, which is applicable in a black-box setting. We compare this approach with two other approaches based on active automata learning, which have been applied to extract FSMs from RNNs; one white-box [39] and one black-box approach [20]. Since models undoubtedly should faithfully model the system that they represent, we examine the accuracy of learning. We compare the three different approaches based on the properties of the learned models and of the learning process. In line with research in this area [20,25,39], we train RNNs on words sampled from regular languages that can be represented by small finite automata. Finite automata as ground truth enable a manual analysis, while following a black-box approach enables scaling to RNNs of different sizes and architectures.

Figure 1 illustrates the learning pipeline that we consider and that consists of training an RNN from labeled sequences and then learning a finite state model from the RNN. Active automata learning generally follows a black-box approach, where hypothesis models of an RNN's behavior are learned iteratively, by interaction through input stimuli and the observation of output behavior. With model-guided conformance testing, we aim to validate or falsify hypotheses. The results of our experiments in the scope of several benchmark models show that in comparison to a state-of-the-art white-box approach [39], model-guided conformance testing enables us to investigate more of an RNN's behavior. This, in turn, results in more complete models that can improve trust in an ANN. On the same benchmark models, we also compare to a black-box learning approach in the probably approximately correct (PAC) framework [33], similar to the approach proposed by Mayr and Yovine [20]. While PAC learning provides probabilistic guarantees, we highlight potential weaknesses of such guarantees that we discover with conformance testing. These guarantees essentially only hold under the conditions, i.e., interaction patterns that were used for model learning. As a result, learned models may provide little insight into the RNN's input-output behavior when facing unknown situations. This hinders using learned models to analyze the RNN's robustness in and generalization to such situations. We demonstrate that model-guided conformance testing can quickly generate interaction patterns that falsify learned models although they are probably approximately correct under different conditions.

Our main contributions comprise (1) the application of black-box model learning through active automata learning supported by coverage-guided conformance testing, (2) an implementation of this approach with AALPY [22], and (3) experiments comparing said approach to a state-of-the-art white-box approach [39] and a black-box approach similar to the one proposed in [20].

The rest of this paper is structured as follows. We introduce background knowledge in Sect. 2 and active automata learning from RNNs in Sect. 3. In Sect. 4, we present experimental results comparing the different learning approaches. We discuss related work in Sect. 5 and conclude the paper in Sect. 6.

2   Preliminaries

Recurrent Neural Networks. An ANN consists of computational units, called neurons, that are connected via weighted edges. The neurons are usually organized into ordered layers with a dedicated input layer, a dedicated output layer, and intermediate layers, called hidden layers. ANNs can abstractly be viewed as functions $f(\mathbf{x}) = \mathbf{y}$ mapping an n-dimensional real-valued input $\mathbf{x} \in \mathbb{R}^n$ to an m-dimensional real-valued output $\mathbf{y} \in \mathbb{R}^m$. We consider a specifc form of ANN, called RNNs, that can model sequential behavior through connections from one layer to itself or to a previous layer [42]. Through such connections, the output of an RNN depends not only on the current input, but on accumulated hidden state from computations involving inputs from previous time steps. This enables RNNs to model stateful reactive systems. The behavior of an RNN can be recursively defined as $f(\mathbf{x}_i, \mathbf{h}_i) = \mathbf{y}_i$ and $\mathbf{h}_i = g(\mathbf{x}_i, \mathbf{h}_{i-1})$, where $\mathbf{x}_i, \mathbf{y}_i, \mathbf{h}_i$ are the input, the output, and the hidden state vector at time step i, and $\mathbf{h}_0$ is the initial hidden state. There is a function f computing the RNN's output and a function g updating the RNN's state based on the current state and input.

In this paper, we generally view RNNs as acceptors that map sequences over a finite input alphabet I to Boolean values denoting acceptance. We represent both inputs and outputs via a one-hot encoding. Inputs are encoded as n-dimensional vectors, where n is the size of I. We further map every $i \in I$ to a distinct standard-basis vector in the n-dimensional input space of the RNN.

The Boolean outputs are encoded analogously. Training plain RNNs to learn long-term dependencies in data faces challenges [42], therefore we use long short-term memory (LSTM) [13] and gated recurrent unit (GRU) [6] networks. Like Weiss et al. [39], we define adversarial inputs as words misclassified by an RNN, not included in the training or validation data.

Automata Learning. We apply Angluin's L^* algorithm [4] to learn finite-state models. L^* is an active automata learning algorithm in the minimally adequate teacher (MAT) framework. Such learning algorithms infer automata by interaction with a teacher through queries. To illustrate L^*-based learning, suppose that we aim to learn a deterministic finite automaton (DFA) accepting an unknown regular language L over alphabet Σ. The learner starts by posing membership queries to the teacher. A membership query checks whether a word over Σ is in L. Once the learner has sufficient membership information to create a hypothesis DFA H, it performs an equivalence query. Such a query checks whether H accepts exactly L. In case of a positive response from the MAT, learning can be stopped with H as result. Otherwise, the teacher additionally provides a counterexample to equivalence, which is a word in the symmetric difference between L and the language accepted by H. The learner integrates the counterexample into its knowledge and starts a new learning round.

Test-Based Automata Learning. In theory, a teacher needs perfect knowledge of L in order to answer equivalence queries. However, in a black-box approach this assumption does not hold. The absence of exact equivalence queries is commonly approached by simulating such queries by randomly sampling words and asking membership queries [4,21]. We take a test-based view of black-box automata learning, where we implement membership queries and equivalence queries through testing of a system under learning (SUL), from which want to learn a model. This is a common approach in automata-learning-based testing and verification [2]. Rather than sampling words completely randomly for equivalence queries, we use conformance-testing techniques to select words (a single word w refers basically to a test case). To perform a membership query for w, we provide w to the SUL, and an equivalence query is implemented by a series of membership queries.

Conformance testing usually takes a specification model of a software system and generates test cases from this model to reveal non-conformance between model and system [9]. Here, we take a hypothesis model H and generate test cases to reveal non-equivalence between H and the SUL. In other words, we want to find words where H disagrees with the SUL. Note that we use equivalence as a conformance relation. When implementing equivalence queries via testing, automata learning may not find the true, correct automaton underlying the SUL due to the incompleteness of testing. Instead, learning will halt upon finding a hypothesis that is deemed to conform to the SUL. An important property of L^*-based learning is that the *learned hypothesis is the minimal automaton*, in terms of the number of states, that is consistent with the queried information [4]. This means that additional information in the form of counterexamples adds states. Hence, we can compare equivalence-query implementations based on the size of learned models. A larger model means that the corresponding equivalence-query implementation is better and found more counterexamples.

3 Automata Extraction from RNNs

In this section, we outline the methods we apply to learn automata from RNNs, focusing on test-based implementations. We start by discussing the testing of RNNs that enables test-based automata learning. Then, we cover the implementation of equivalence queries, an essential aspect of active automata learning. We conclude the section with research questions on the experimental comparison of active automata learning instantiated with different equivalence queries.

3.1 Test-Based Learning from RNNs

While techniques like LIME [27] work well to explain what neural-network-based classifiers do for individual examples, they are not well suited for modeling of RNN behavior as it would have to train a linear model for each variable-length sequence. As RNNs have an unbounded input space of sequences, active automata learning is well-suited to handle such input data and thus to extract models from the input-output behavior of RNNs. What is more, it provides a guidance for exploring this input space through membership queries and conformance testing provides guidance for exploration during equivalence queries.

Since we learn models from RNNs, we use the terms SUL and RNN interchangeably. To avoid confusion between automata learning and training of the RNNs, we will exclusively use the word learning in the context of automata learning and training in the context of RNNs. To execute a test case, we first reset the RNN's internal state to a fixed value and then perform a sequence of steps. Each step stimulates the RNN with an element of the input alphabet and observes an output on the output layer of the RNN. In the case of RNN acceptors, we observe Boolean values. If the RNN framework does not support the step-by-step creation of variable-length sequences, then the whole input sequence can be passed to the RNN, and the output associated with the whole input sequence can be obtained.

Until now we implicitly assumed that the SUL's behavior can be described by a regular language. However, RNNs are theoretically Turing-complete [29]. If we try to learn a DFA from an RNN modeling a non-regular language, learning may not halt, as equivalence queries may find infinitely many counterexamples. To counter such issues, we need to extend learning with a secondary stopping criterion in addition to positive results from equivalence queries. By stopping after a maximum number of learning rounds or upon reaching a maximum number of hypothesis states, we can learn automata accepting a regular approximation of a non-regular language modeled by an RNN. A similar approach has been coined *bounded L** [20]. Alternatively, we may limit the scope of the equivalence oracle to specific parts of the input space. This solution is appealing in a verification context. For example, a regular language describing a safety property could be

---

Algorithm 1. Random-W Equivalence Oracle

Input: # tests per state n, random walk length distribution μ, inputs I, hypothesis hyp, SUL
Output: counterexample or $\emptyset$
1: $E \leftarrow characterizationSet(hyp)$
2: **for all** $state \in hyp.states$ **do**
3:     $prefix \leftarrow shortestPathTo(state)$
4:     **for** $i \leftarrow 1$ **to** n **do**
5:         $lenMiddle \leftarrow geometricSample(\mu)$
6:         $middle \leftarrow choose(I^{lenMiddle})$ ▷ random uniform choice of random walk
7:         $suffix \leftarrow choose(E)$ ▷ random choice of characterization sequence
8:         $testCase \leftarrow prefix \cdot middle \cdot suffix$
9:         $reset(SUL, hyp)$ ▷ Start query from the initial state.
10:         **for** $index \leftarrow 1$ **to** $len(testCase)$ **do**
11:             $hypOutput = step(hyp, testCase[index])$
12:             $sulOutput = step(SUL, testCase[index])$
13:             **if** $hypOutput \neq sulOutput$ **then**
14:                 **return** $testCase[1 \ldots index]$
15: **return** $\emptyset$

---

used to learn a safe subset of an RNN's behavior. In Sect. 4.2, we present experiments with a context-free grammar, where we limit the scope of the equivalence queries by bounding the number of recursive rule expansions.

3.2 Equivalence Queries from a Practical Perspective

We distinguish three types of equivalence queries implemented via testing: (1) formally proving equivalence between hypothesis and SUL up to some bound, (2) pure random sampling, and (3) testing guided by models. Weiss et al. [39] follow an orthogonal approach, where they use information about the hidden state space of RNNs to implement equivalence queries.

Formally proving equivalence with the W-Method [7] in the context of RNNs faces inherent challenges. The W-Method can be used to prove the equivalence between the hypothesis and the SUL up to an assumed upper bound on the number of RNN states. However, to prove equivalence, the W-method performs an exponential (with respect to the difference between the maximum number of states and the current number of states in the hypothesis) number of test cases. This limits the applicability of the W-Method, and often it is not a feasible option in practice [14]. Furthermore, defining the maximum number of states for models extracted from RNNs is not practically possible.

Random sampling has been used to extract DFAs from RNNs in a testing context [3,14]. Random-sampling-based equivalence queries enable a probabilistic notion of correctness, known as probably approximately correct (PAC) learning [33]. More generally, PAC learning is possible with using a (potentially unknown) *fixed* distribution to sample words in order to simulate equivalence queries with membership queries [21]. In the PAC framework, the number of tests performed by a random-sampling-based equivalence query can be configured to ensure that the returned hypothesis is an ϵ-approximation of the correct hypothesis with a probability of at least $1 - \delta$ [21]. Here, an $\epsilon > 0$ bounds the generalization error, the expected number of examples incorrectly classified by the final hypothesis w.r.t. the sampling distribution D. To achieve such PAC guarantees, the number of tests performed by the tth equivalence query should be chosen according to

$$m_t = \frac{1}{\epsilon}(\log(\frac{1}{\delta}) + t\log(2)) \text{ [21]}. \tag{1}$$

Note that the PAC guarantees are relative to D, which may not reflect all inter-action patterns with the SUL. Hence, a PAC learned model may have an error rate higher than ϵ when used under interaction patterns that differ from D. Consequently, such models may be quickly falsified with other testing methods, as shown in Sect. 4.

Fixing a sampling distribution enables probabilistic guarantees, but ignores learned information that is available in form of the intermediate hypotheses. This may cause improper sampling of certain parts of SUL, leading to premature halting of the learning procedure. Such issues are most prominent in non-strongly connected automata, automata with sink states, and combination lock automata. Nonetheless, for many systems, random testing has proved efficient.

Model-guided equivalence oracles use the structure of the current hypothesis as a basis for test-case generation. A prominent example of a guided explo-ration equivalence oracle is the Random-W equivalence oracle [16], shown in Algorithm 1. Its test cases consist of three parts: a prefix leading to a state in the hypothesis, a random walk, and an element of the characterization set. Such test cases provide better transition and state coverage of the hypothesis and were used successfully in many domains [14]. Another example of a coverage-based equivalence oracle is discussed in Sect. 4.2. Other equivalence oracles such as hybrid ADS [30] could achieve results comparable to the ones found in Sect. 4.

When extracting automata from RNNs, a coverage-guided equivalence oracle may produce more accurate models than random sampling. Since the sampling distribution changes during the course of learning, PAC guarantees cannot be provided in the same way as for random sampling. However, coverage-guided testing uses the available information gained throughout learning. It assures bet-ter coverage than purely random testing, and its variations are especially suited for discovering hard-to-find cases of non-conformance. Purely random sampling-based equivalence oracles have been used to learn models of the RNN's behav-ior [20], but they often fail to find counterexamples or adversarial inputs [39]. These findings are consistent with our experimental evaluation presented in the following section.

A *white-box refinement-based* equivalence oracle was proposed by Weiss et al. [39]. They keep track of two hypotheses: One hypothesis H_1 is learned using Angluin's L^* and the other hypothesis H_2 is a finite abstraction of the RNN obtained by partitioning the RNN's state space, thus they follow a white-box approach. That is, the approach is based on knowledge about the internal struc-ture of the RNN under consideration.

The intuition behind the oracle is that H_1 and H_2 need to be equivalent in order for them to be equivalent to the RNN. Whenever H_1 and H_2 disagree on a sample s, the true classification label of s is queried from the RNN. If H_1 incorrectly classifies s, then s is returned as a counterexample to L^*. Otherwise, the partitioning used to construct H_2 is refined. While this approach can benefit from additional information encoded in the RNN's state space, it may also suffer from exactly that. Improper partitioning of the high-dimensional state space may cause counterexamples to be left undetected.

3.3 Research Questions

We have outlined approaches to implement equivalence oracles in active automata learning above. Despite their attractive theoretical properties, we disregard approaches like the W-method, as they are highly inefficient. In our experiments, we will analyze coverage-guided conformance testing, learning in the PAC framework, and learning with the refinement-based oracle proposed by Weiss et al. [39]. We use the size of learned models to measure which approach produces the model closest to the true model capturing the input-output behavior of the RNN. This is motivated by the fact that every counterexample detected by an equivalence query increases the hypothesis size. Hence, model size provides us with a measure of accuracy. Therefore our first research question is:

RQ1: Learning with which equivalence oracle creates the most accurate models?

Since different counterexamples may lead to the different intermediate hypotheses, the size of learned models alone is not an ideal measure of the effectiveness of equivalence oracles. A potential issue is that two learning approaches may learn two models with x and y states, respectively. Unless the larger value of x and y is equal to the number of states of true model underlying the RNN, there may be covered by one of the models but not by the other and vice versa. To compare equivalence oracles more directly, we take a model learned by one approach and try to find counterexamples with another approach. Put differently, we try to falsify a model that was deemed correct by a different approach. This leads us to the second research question:

RQ2: Can the most effective equivalence oracle according to RQ1 falsify models that were deemed correct by the other two equivalence-oracle implementations?

RQ2 essentially aims to strengthen the conclusions from RQ1. RQ1 compares learning where all approaches share the same initial starting conditions. In contrast, RQ2 focuses on the most effective approach when starting from the conditions (the final hypotheses) found at the termination of the less effective approaches. In cases of positive answers to RQ2, we will also examine the effort necessary to falsify a learned model. This can, for instance, be measured as the number of test cases required for falsification. Alternatively to checking the size of learned models, other approaches are possible too. For example, we could consider measures on the language accepted by learned models with respect to a ground truth that we know, like precision and recall [35]. Since we solely compare $L*$-based approaches and due to the properties of L^*, we opted to consider the number of states as an objective criterion.

4   Experiments on Learning Automata from RNNs

We experimentally evaluated active automata learning instantiated with three different equivalence queries. We examine (1) our proposed approach of model-guided conformance testing, (2) a white-box refinement-based equivalence oracle proposed by Weiss et al. [39], and (3) a black-box approach providing PAC guarantees similar to the one proposed by Mayr and Yovine [20], who additionally introduced bounds. In the remainder of this section, we will dub the latter approach as PAC sampling-based learning.

Benchmarks. Tomita grammars [32] and the balanced parentheses grammar [39] are common benchmarks in automata learning and RNN-related domains [19,20,24,36,39]. We will use them to evaluate model-learning performance.

RNN Training Setup. We used a consistent approach for training all RNNs. That is, while the type (LSTM, GRU) or size (number of hidden layers, size of each layer) might vary, the other parameters of the training setup were consistent for all our experiments. For obtaining a training data set, we randomly generated sequences of various length using an FSM representing the considered language. Accepted sequences (i.e., words in the language) were labeled *True*, while sequences not in this language were labeled *False*. Training and validation data was split in an 80:20 ratio. All RNNs were trained to 100% accuracy on the training and validation data sets.

Implementation. We implemented[1,2] our RNNs with DyNet [23] and we implemented automata learning and the equivalence oracles using AALPY v1.1.1 [22]. For the direct comparison with refinement-based learning we used the authors' original implementation[3]. All experiments were performed on a Dell Lattitude 5410 with an Intel Core i7-10610U processor, 8 GB of RAM running Windows 10 and using Python 3.6. All experiments were conducted on both types of supported RNNs (LSTM and GRU). Experiments were repeated multiple times to account for randomness found in the training and learning process. For each experiment a representative example was chosen such that it approximately corresponds to the average observed case.

4.1   Learning Models of RNNs Trained on Tomita Grammars

Before examining RQ1, let us illustrate learning models from RNNs for the example of the Tomita 3 grammar. Figure 2 depicts on the right a learning procedure, and on the left the DFA extracted from an RNN trained on a dataset generated for said grammar. This five-state DFA was extracted and returned as a final hypothesis by multiple white-box [19,39] and black-box [20] approaches. Furthermore, we see that the learned automaton is indeed the same as the DFA

---

[1] Source code, experiments, and interactive examples can be found at: https://github.com/DES-Lab/Extracting-FSM-From-RNNs.

[2] DOI of the artifact: https://doi.org/10.5281/zenodo.6412571.

[3] https://github.com/tech-srl/lstar_extraction.

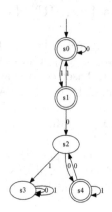
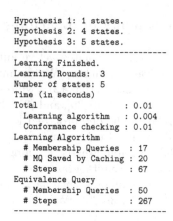

Fig. 2. DFA extraction process from RNN trained on Tomita 3 grammar.

Table 1. Comparison of refinement-based [39], PAC sampling-based [20] and model-guided learning. All GRU RNNs have 2 hidden layers with 50 nodes and were trained till 100% train and test set accuracy.

Tomita grammar	Refinement-based learning		PAC sampling-based learning		Model-guided learning	
	Cex. found	Model size	Cex. found	Model size	Cex. found	Model size
1	1	2	4	25	11	46
2	2	3	3	8	11	44
3	3	5	3	5	85	3945
4	1	4	1	4	1	4
5	3	5	6	32	115	4953
6	67	11975	6	318	121	15084
7	1	2	1	5	7	33

of the Tomita 3 grammar itself, which *would* indicate that the behavior of the RNN conforms to the ground truth.

Conformance testing guided by hypotheses, i.e., also guided by the model shown in Fig. 2, enables a deeper investigation of the RNN's behavior. While other approaches were not able to find any further counterexamples and concluded the learning process with reporting said DFA, by testing with the random-W method, we were able to find additional counterexamples. Since the DFA shown in the Fig. 2 is equivalent to that of the model learned by the RNN, it is important to note that such counterexamples thus reveal a faulty generalization by an RNN, i.e. they are adversarial inputs. By identifying such counterexamples, the model-guided conformance testing essentially falsifies the hypotheses returned by other approaches, such that a more detailed automaton can be learned. We observed that once a fault in the RNN generalization is found (i.e., an adversarial input), the size of learned automata increases substantially (for the example shown in Fig. 2, the next two hypotheses have 60 and 350 states).

The effectiveness of model-guided testing stems from the fact that it uses information gained throughout the automata-learning process. In contrast to random sampling, it revisits identified states and explores new paths from there to find new states.

Table 1 shows the results of our experiments performed towards answering RQ1. In the experiments, we compare all three learning approaches based on the size of learned models, which provides us with a measure of accuracy. In the table, we report the number of counterexamples isolated during the learning process as well as the final hypothesis' size. When conducting the model extraction experiments, we set a time limit of 500 s. Without such a time limit the learning process might not terminate if the RNN behavior cannot be captured by a regular language (see Sect. 3.1).

From the results we can conclude that model-guided learning creates larger automata than both refinement-based and PAC sampling-based learning, which can be explained by this approach finding more counterexamples. Recall that learned automata are minimal automata that are consistent with all queried information including all counterexamples. This means that the conformance-testing equivalence query finds more information and covers more of an RNN's input space. In fact, most models obtained via refinement-based learning conform to the ground truth models used for data generation. With PAC sampling-based learning and model-guided conformance testing, we were able to learn larger models. Hence, by using the black-box approaches we detected generalization issues that resulted in larger models that approximate the true input-output behavior underlying the examined RNNs more precisely.

For all 7 Tomita grammars, the RNNs generalized very accurately within the length bound of the training set. This in turn caused refinement-based learning to learn models that conform to the models used for generating the training data. It did so by finding all counterexamples that are not adversarial inputs. Such non-adversarial inputs are words misclassified by intermediate hypothesis automata, but classified correctly by the RNN. Additionally, the technique managed to find adversarial inputs only for the RNN trained on the Tomita 6 grammar. By performing extensive model-guided testing, we did not only find all non-adversarial counterexamples, but we also found adversarial inputs for all Tomita grammars except for Tomita 4. Finding all non-adversarial counterexamples means that we are able to learn an intermediate hypothesis that is equivalent to the ground truth, whereas adversarial inputs allow us to detect discrepancies between the RNN under considerations and the ground truth.

PAC sampling-based learning managed to find adversarial inputs for some RNNs, while for others it found only counterexamples that led to learning of the model that corresponds to the ground truth model. From the minimality of models learned with L^*, we can conclude that the models created by refinement-based learning and PAC sampling-based learning are incorrect, except for the Tomita 4 grammar. Note that they are incorrect in the setting of exact learning, while models created by PAC learning are *probably approximately correct*.

Algorithm 2. Transition-Focus Equivalence Oracle

Input: number of tests n, test length L, same state probability p, hypothesis hyp, SUL
Output: counterexample or $\emptyset$
1: **for** $i \leftarrow 1$ **to** n **do**
2:     $testCase \leftarrow \epsilon$ ▷ Initialize test case to empty sequence ϵ
3:     $state \leftarrow reset(SUL, hyp)$
4:     **for** $j \leftarrow 1$ **to** L **do**
5:         **if** $random \in [0, 1] < p$ **then**
6:             $input \leftarrow choose(sameStateTransitions(state))$
7:         **else**
8:             $input \leftarrow choose(diffStateTransitions(state))$
9:         $testCase \leftarrow testCase \cdot input$
10:         $hypState = step(hyp, input)$
11:         $sulState = step(SUL, input)$
12:         **if** $hypState.output \neq sulState.output$ **then**
13:             **return** $testCase$
14:         $state \leftarrow hypState$
15: **return** $\emptyset$

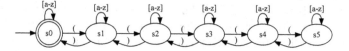

Fig. 3. DFA of the balanced parentheses grammar bound to the depth 5.

Based on these results, we can answer RQ1. Learning with model-guided conformance testing created the largest models and therefore the most accurate models. This means that the learned models are the closest to the RNNs from which they were learned.

Apart from the findings concerning the accuracy of learned finite state models, we discovered that generalization issues and overfitting impacts the automata interpretation of the language learned by RNNs. Our evaluation shows that even RNNs trained from a simple ground truth with only two states (Tomita 1), can lead to a finite state model with at least 46 states—due to generalization issues and overfitting. We generally observed that for well-trained networks finding counterexamples that are not adversarial inputs is less resource-intensive than finding generalization errors. To put this into perspective, it took usually several hundred test cases to find non-adversarial counterexamples, whereas the detection of the first adversarial input required up to 7000 test cases. It is important to note that finding subsequent adversarial inputs requires significantly fewer testing resources. This finding is explained in more detail in Sect. 4.2.

4.2   Learning Models of RNNs Trained on Balanced Parentheses

Balanced paraphrases is a context-free grammar that accepts sequences of characters where all opening parentheses have matching closing parentheses. Any or no characters can be found in between parentheses. As balanced parentheses form a context-free language, we create a regular subset from it and use it for data generation. E.g., the bounded parentheses model limited to a depth of 5 nested parentheses is shown in Fig. 3. We repeated the experiments on models

Table 2. Counterexamples obtained during the refinement-based [39] learning process and counterexamples falsifying the learned model via model-guided conformance testing.

Refinement-based Eq. oracle		Random-W Eq. oracle		Transition-focus Eq. oracle	
Counterexample	Time (s)	Counterexample	Time (s)	Counterexample	Time (s)
))	0.34	((ik()fa))	4.6	(((()((i)y)t))())	0.01
(())	0.16	((xvplzcmqzry()esp)sj)	4.3	(()(()())()pu)	0.02
–	–	((dkulbgh(ajczy)o)lax)	0.39	xs(()(())b)	0.01
		((i(h)dcaqgi)silnfg)	4.77	(y)k()((()v)m)	0.01
		(((uuldz)t)zc)	3.83	(cr(s)()(cu())(())h)	0.03
		(((fvtdjb)oeive)e)	1.16	a((j)))e)(((	0.02

with increasing depth of nested parentheses. Training and learning results were consistent irrespective of the balanced parentheses' nested depth. That is, the language learned by the RNN stayed mostly the same regardless of the depth that we tested.

We use experiments with this grammar as a basis for answering RQ2. For this purpose, we directly compare model-guided conformance testing, which produced the most accurate models, with the refinement-based and the PAC sampling-based learning. In contrast to Sect. 4.1, where we compared the entire extraction processes, we now focus on the falsification of the models obtained with the latter two approaches. That is, we applied refinement-based and PAC sampling-based learning to learn an automaton and use it as a basis for model-guided conformance testing.

In addition to RQ2, we want to briefly highlight how to integrate domain knowledge into the model-guided testing process. Knowledge about the structure of the balanced parentheses allows to develop a custom model-guided equivalence oracle especially suited for, but not limited to, this example. The *transition-focus* equivalence oracle is a model-guided equivalence oracle shown in Algorithm 2. The parameter p defines the focus of the test-case generation. E.g., a p value of 0.2 states that a newly chosen input will lead to a new hypothesis state 80% of the time and 20% of the time it will lead to the current state, i.e., correspond to a self loop in the hypothesis model. This equivalence oracle is especially suited for balanced parentheses, because only parentheses define transitions between states, whereas other inputs should lead to the same state. The transition-focus equivalence oracle generates test cases that explore the hypothesis structure primarily focusing on transitions between states. Compared to the random-W method, Algorithm 2 increases the probability of detecting a counterexample and potentially even an adversarial input.

Comparison with Refinement-Based Learning. Table 2 shows the counterexamples obtained during the complete refinement-based learning process and counterexamples found with two model-guided oracles that the white-box technique did not find. The random-W method was able to falsify the learned model and transition-focused testing increased the efficiency of falsification.

Table 3. Counterexamples obtained during learning with the PAC sampling-based oracle and counterexamples falsifying the learned model via model-guided testing.

PAC random word Eq. oracle		Random-W Eq. oracle		Transition-focus Eq. oracle	
Counterexample	# Tests	Counterexample	# Tests	Counterexample	# Tests
dnhugps)bch)	8	((gzbmcjin()weu))	15	((()p))	1
om(a(jvu))	2163	((qcss(sizx)uevu))	173	k(()(x(xv)))	4
–	–	((u()tysjxu))	157	(zz((t)))	14
		((isr(t)u))	354	((x(()(gh)())z))	5
		(((wdwv)onvu))	234	(t(v()))	9
		((aao()kgkfk))	61	((j()q))	11

This demonstrates that model-guided conformance testing can find additional counterexamples that falsify models created with refinement-based learning, leading to more precise model learning. Hence, we can provide a first positive answer to RQ2.

Furthermore, these experiments show that model-guided testing improves accuracy also for non-regular languages and domain knowledge further improves efficiency. The transition-focus oracle improved the efficiency of falsification significantly. The found counterexamples are often adversarial inputs revealing the RNN's generalization faults. This shows that model-guided testing can be used as a tool for finding adversarial inputs, even with incomplete models.

Comparison with PAC Learning. Now, we address RQ2 w.r.t. learning in the PAC framework, which has been used for analyzing RNNs by Mayr and Yovine [20]. We compare model-guided conformance testing and PAC sampling-based learning, by using the former approach to falsify a model learned by the latter approach. Finally, we will conclude with a discussion of PAC guarantees.

First, let us recap PAC-learning of automata. Equivalence queries are simulated through membership queries on words sampled according to a distribution D. By performing m_t membership queries for the tth equivalence query (see Eq. 1 for m_t), we learn a model with a generalization error of at most ϵ with a probability of at least $1 - \delta$ [21]. This requires the sampled words to be independently and identically distributed according to the *fixed* distribution D. As a result, testing guided by hypotheses does not directly permit PAC guarantees, since the distribution with which words are sampled changes throughout learning. For learning in the PAC framework, we fix a distribution for sampling at the beginning of learning. We sample input symbols according to a uniform distribution over the inputs and we choose the length of each test case according to a uniform distribution over the integer interval [4..20]. In every equivalence query, we perform m_t random tests with $\epsilon = 0.001$ and $\delta = 0.01$. Values of ϵ and δ were selected to ensure high PAC guarantees, providing the PAC sampling-based oracle with a high amount of testing resources. Note that we examine the number of test cases needed to find a counterexample, which may be lower than m_t, the maximum number of test cases executed by an equivalence query.

Table 4. Learning processes of PAC sampling-based and model-guided learning of an RNN trained on Tomita 3 grammar. The size of the current hypothesis and number of tests needed to falsify it are given for each round.

Learning round		1	2	3	4	5	6	7	8	9	10
PAC sampling-based learning	Hypothesis size	1	4	5	21	25	46	–			
	# Tests to Falsify	10	3	33929	20143	30111	–				
Model-guided learning	Hypothesis size	1	4	5	26	39	257	291	316	346	431
	# Tests to Falsify	4	5	1428	11	124	12	4	9	13	–

To answer RQ2, we perform the same experiments as above for refinement-based learning. We learn a model with the PAC sampling-based oracle and try to falsify it with model-guided testing. Table 3 shows results from these experiments. We can see that the PAC sampling-based learning managed to find only two counterexamples. This finding is consistent with the experiments presented by [39]. Even with the imprecise model learned with the PAC sampling-based oracle that found only two counterexamples, model-guided testing was able to quickly falsify said model. Hence, we can answer RQ2 positively. In Table 3, we can also see that it took a low number of test cases. It took on average only about 166 test cases to find additional counterexamples with the random-W method.

4.3 Analyzing RQ2 on the Tomita 3 Grammar

In further experiments, we compared model-guided learning with PAC-based learning when learning models from an RNN trained on the Tomita 3 grammar. Table 4 shows the results from these experiments. These experiments further demonstrate the advantage of exploiting the structure of the learned model during test-case generation. For both approaches, we observe that finding the first two counterexamples was equally fast, as those are the counterexamples leading to the creation of a model conforming to the ground truth. From that point onward, we notice significant differences between the two approaches. To falsify the ground truth model (learning round three) a substantial increase in testing resources is needed. We can observe that the process of finding subsequent counterexamples (adversarial inputs) by the PAC sampling oracle required significantly more test cases than its model-guided counterpart. Furthermore, the PAC sampling-based oracle was unable to find all counterexamples, terminating the learning in round 6 and returning 46-state model. An interesting observation can be made concerning the number of tests needed to falsify the hypothesis in the case of model-guided testing. To falsify the ground truth model, the random-W method required 1428 tests, while all subsequent equivalence queries returned a counterexample with a low amount of testing. This is due to the fact that once the counterexample falsifying the ground truth model is found, it is processed, which leads to an increase of the hypothesis size. This increased hypothesis encodes more knowledge about the structure of the system under learning, thus making the search for counterexamples easier. This observation confirms the need for exploiting the model structure in the test-case generation.

Finally, let us examine the guarantees provided by PAC learning. Note the meaning of the error-rate parameter ϵ in the PAC-based setting: random testing may also be able to falsify a learned model, but it would require on average at least $\frac{1}{\epsilon}$ tests. We see in Table 3 that model-guided testing requires between 11 and 354 tests for falsification, which is consistently lower than $\frac{1}{\epsilon} = 1000$. Hence, it tests the SUL more efficiently. Although PAC results in automata learning provide a quantification of correctness, such a quantification may result in a false sense of security. If the sampling distribution for simulating equivalence queries does not match usage patterns, PAC guarantees are not very useful. Hence, if expected usage patterns are not known, model-guided testing is preferable. This approach creates diverse data and it benefits from the knowledge gained during learning.

5   Related Work

Explaining the behavior of black-box systems [12] is a well-studied problem in computer science. In recent years, active automata learning approaches inferring the input-output behavior of RNNs have received much attention. Several white-box and black-box approaches were proposed. We focus on model learning from RNNs. The relationship between the internal state representation of RNNs and FSMs [10,24,37] is out of scope of this paper. Wang et al. [38] present an overview of rule-extraction-based verification for RNNs. A formal approach to explainable RNNs has been proposed by Ghosh and Neider [10], where they use linear temporal logic to explain RNN decision making.

Weiss et al. [39] proposed an L^*-based approach to extract automata from RNNs that encode their input-output behavior. The authors use a white-box equivalence oracle to learn binary classifiers as DFAs. Their equivalence oracle is based on the iteratively refined abstraction of an RNN's state space. We compared our approach to theirs in Sect. 4. In subsequent work, they also learned probabilistic automata [40] and a subset of context-free grammars [41] from RNNs. Another white-box approach has been proposed by Koul et al. [19]. They use a technique called *quantized bottleneck insertion* to extract Moore machines. Such models help them better understand the memory use in RNN-based control policies. Probably approximately correct black-box extraction of DFAs via Bounded-L^* and random testing has been presented by Mayr and Yovine [20]. They use a random sampling-based equivalence oracle with the number of samples chosen so as to achieve PAC learning [21,33]. We reasoned about the effectiveness of such an approach in Sect. 4. With our experiments, we found that the sampling distribution in the equivalence oracle is essential to learn complete models of RNNs. Khmelnitsky et al. propose a similar approach [17]. They use statistical model-checking to answer equivalence queries and formalize a property-directed verification method for RNNs. An algorithm for Angluin-style DFA learning from *binarized neural networks* over some input region has been presented by Shih et al. [28]. They use SAT solvers to answer equivalence queries. Dong. et al. [8] presented a white-box method for the extraction of probabilistic finite automata from RNNs. They achieve this through a symbolic encoding of the RNN's hidden state vectors and using a probabilistic learning algorithm that tries to recover the probability distribution of the symbolic data. Carr et al. [5] extracted a finite-state controller from an RNN via model learning. They demonstrate their technique by synthesizing policies for partially observable Markov decision processes.

6   Conclusion

We experimentally compared three approaches to actively learn automata capturing the input-output behavior of an RNN. Our experiments show that the choice of equivalence oracle greatly affects learning performance. They also show that using model-guided conformance testing leads to the most accurate learning. In direct comparisons, it managed to falsify models learned by two other approaches. Since it is a black-box testing approach, it does not require any knowledge of the RNN's internals. It exploits the structure of the current hypothesis obtained by the learning algorithm. The positive experimental results suggest that automata-learning-based testing is a promising method for efficiently finding adversarial inputs. These adversarial input could be used to extend the training data set such that they are correctly classified by the retained RNN.

In future work, we will examine the application of formal methods, more concretely automata learning, on RNNs and transformers [34] trained with high-dimensional input alphabets, as is often done in practice. To achieve this, we will apply methods, such as suitable dimensionality reduction techniques and clustering, to learn abstract automata. Furthermore, we will examine the hidden state space of RNNs trained on regular languages. By doing so, we hope to enable formal reasoning about the RNN's internal decision-making process.

The presented work demonstrates that model learning can play a role in explainable AI. Model-based conformance testing helps to raise the level of trust in RNN decision making, and learned models can be used as a basis for model checking and manual analysis.

Acknowledgments. This work has been supported by the "University SAL Labs" initiative of Silicon Austria Labs (SAL) and its Austrian partner universities for applied fundamental research for electronic based systems.

References

1. Aichernig, B.K., et al.: Learning a behavior model of hybrid systems through combining model-based testing and machine learning. In: Gaston, C., Kosmatov, N., Gall, P.L. (eds.) Testing Software and Systems - 31st IFIP WG 6.1 International Conference, ICTSS 2019, Paris, France, 15–17 October 2019, Proceedings. LNPSE, vol. 11812, pp. 3–21. Springer, Cham (2019). https://doi.org/10.1007/978-3-030-31280-0_1

2. Aichernig, B.K., Mostowski, W., Mousavi, M.R., Tappler, M., Taromirad, M.: Model learning and model-based testing. In: Bennaceur, A., Hähnle, R., Meinke, K. (eds.) Machine Learning for Dynamic Software Analysis: Potentials and Limits. LNCS, vol. 11026, pp. 74–100. Springer, Cham (2018). https://doi.org/10.1007/978-3-319-96562-8_3

3. Aichernig, B.K., Tappler, M., Wallner, F.: benchmarking combinations of learning and testing algorithms for active automata learning. In: Ahrendt, W., Wehrheim, H. (eds.) TAP 2020. LNCS, vol. 12165, pp. 3–22. Springer, Cham (2020). https://doi.org/10.1007/978-3-030-50995-8_1

4. Angluin, D.: Learning regular sets from queries and counterexamples. Inf. Comput. **75**(2), 87–106 (1987). https://doi.org/10.1016/0890-5401(87)90052-6

5. Carr, S., Jansen, N., Topcu, U.: Verifiable RNN-based policies for POMDPs under temporal logic constraints. In: Bessiere, C. (ed.) Proceedings of the Twenty-Ninth International Joint Conference on Artificial Intelligence, IJCAI 2020, pp. 4121–4127. ijcai.org (2020). https://doi.org/10.24963/ijcai.2020/570

6. Cho, K., van Merrienboer, B., Bahdanau, D., Bengio, Y.: On the properties of neural machine translation: Encoder-decoder approaches. CoRR abs/1409.1259 (2014). http://arxiv.org/abs/1409.1259

7. Chow, T.S.: Testing software design modeled by finite-state machines. IEEE Trans. Software Eng. **4**(3), 178–187 (1978). https://doi.org/10.1109/TSE.1978.231496

8. Dong, G., Wang, J., Sun, J., Zhang, Y., Wang, X., Dai, T., Dong, J.S., Wang, X.: Towards interpreting recurrent neural networks through probabilistic abstraction. In: 35th IEEE/ACM International Conference on Automated Software Engineering, ASE 2020, 21–25 September 2020, pp. 499–510. IEEE, Melbourne, Australia (2020). https://doi.org/10.1145/3324884.3416592

9. Gargantini, A.: 4 conformance testing. In: Broy, M., Jonsson, B., Katoen, J.-P., Leucker, M., Pretschner, A. (eds.) Model-Based Testing of Reactive Systems. LNCS, vol. 3472, pp. 87–111. Springer, Heidelberg (2005). https://doi.org/10.1007/11498490_5

10. Ghosh, B., Neider, D.: A formal language approach to explaining RNNs. CoRR abs/2006.07292 (2020). https://arxiv.org/abs/2006.07292

11. Gopinath, D., Katz, G., Pasareanu, C.S., Barrett, C.W.: Deepsafe: a data-driven approach for checking adversarial robustness in neural networks. CoRR abs/1710.00486 (2017). http://arxiv.org/abs/1710.00486

12. Guidotti, R., Monreale, A., Ruggieri, S., Turini, F., Giannotti, F., Pedreschi, D.: A survey of methods for explaining black box models. ACM Comput. Surv. **51**(5), 93:1–93:42 (2019). https://doi.org/10.1145/3236009

13. Hochreiter, S., Schmidhuber, J.: Long short-term memory. Neural Comput. **9**(8), 1735–1780 (1997). https://doi.org/10.1162/neco.1997.9.8.1735

14. Howar, F., Steffen, B., Merten, M.: From ZULU to RERS - lessons learned in the ZULU challenge. In: ISoLA 2010. LNCS, vol. 6415, pp. 687–704 (2010)

15. Huang, X., Kwiatkowska, M., Wang, S., Wu, M.: Safety verification of deep neural networks. In: Majumdar, R., Kunčak, V. (eds.) CAV 2017. LNCS, vol. 10426, pp. 3–29. Springer, Cham (2017). https://doi.org/10.1007/978-3-319-63387-9_1

16. Isberner, M., Howar, F., Steffen, B.: The open-source LearnLib. In: Kroening, D., Păsăreanu, C.S. (eds.) CAV 2015. LNCS, vol. 9206, pp. 487–495. Springer, Cham (2015). https://doi.org/10.1007/978-3-319-21690-4_32

17. Khmelnitsky, I., et al.: Property-directed verification and robustness certification of recurrent neural networks. In: Hou, Z., Ganesh, V. (eds.) ATVA 2021. LNCS, vol. 12971, pp. 364–380. Springer, Cham (2021). https://doi.org/10.1007/978-3-030-88885-5_24

18. Kleene, S.C.: Representation of Events in Nerve Nets and Finite Automata. RAND Corporation, Santa Monica, CA (1951)
19. Koul, A., Fern, A., Greydanus, S.: Learning finite state representations of recurrent policy networks. In: 7th International Conference on Learning Representations, ICLR 2019, 6–9 May 2019. OpenReview.net, New Orleans, LA, USA (2019). https://openreview.net/forum?id=S1gOpsCctm
20. Mayr, F., Yovine, S.: regular inference on artificial neural networks. In: Holzinger, A., Kieseberg, P., Tjoa, A.M., Weippl, E. (eds.) CD-MAKE 2018. LNCS, vol. 11015, pp. 350–369. Springer, Cham (2018). https://doi.org/10.1007/978-3-319-99740-7_25
21. Mohri, M., Rostamizadeh, A., Talwalkar, A.: Foundations of Machine Learning. The MIT Press (2012)
22. Muškardin, E., Aichernig, B.K., Pill, I., Pferscher, A., Tappler, M.: AALpy: an active automata learning library. In: Hou, Z., Ganesh, V. (eds.) ATVA 2021. LNCS, vol. 12971, pp. 67–73. Springer, Cham (2021). https://doi.org/10.1007/978-3-030-88885-5_5
23. Neubig, G., et al.: DyNet: The dynamic neural network toolkit. CoRR abs/1701.03980 (2017). http://arxiv.org/abs/1701.03980
24. Oliva, C., Lago-Fernández, L.F.: On the interpretation of recurrent neural networks as finite state machines. In: Tetko, I.V., Kurková, V., Karpov, P., Theis, F. (eds.) ICANN 2019. LNCS, vol. 11727, pp. 312–323. Springer, Cham (2019). https://doi.org/10.1007/978-3-030-30487-4_25
25. Oliva, C., Lago-Fernández, L.F.: Stability of internal states in recurrent neural networks trained on regular languages. Neurocomputing **452**, 212–223 (2021). https://doi.org/10.1016/j.neucom.2021.04.058
26. Omlin, C.W., Giles, C.L.: Extraction of rules from discrete-time recurrent neural networks. Neural Networks **9**(1), 41–52 (1996). https://doi.org/10.1016/0893-6080(95)00086-0
27. Ribeiro, M.T., Singh, S., Guestrin, C.: "why should I trust you?": explaining the predictions of any classifier. In: Krishnapuram, B., Shah, M., Smola, A.J., Aggarwal, C.C., Shen, D., Rastogi, R. (eds.) Proceedings of the 22nd ACM SIGKDD International Conference on Knowledge Discovery and Data Mining, 13–17 August 2016. pp. 1135–1144. ACM,San Francisco, CA, USA (2016). https://doi.org/10.1145/2939672.2939778
28. Shih, A., Darwiche, A., Choi, A.: Verifying binarized neural networks by angluin-style learning. In: Janota, M., Lynce, I. (eds.) SAT 2019. LNCS, vol. 11628, pp. 354–370. Springer, Cham (2019). https://doi.org/10.1007/978-3-030-24258-9_25
29. Siegelmann, H.T., Sontag, E.D.: Turing computability with neural nets. Appl. Math. Lett. **4**(6), 77–80 (1991). https://doi.org/10.1016/0893-9659(91)90080-F, https://www.sciencedirect.com/science/article/pii/089396599190080F
30. Smeenk, W., Moerman, J., Vaandrager, F., Jansen, D.N.: Applying automata learning to embedded control software. In: Butler, M., Conchon, S., Zaïdi, F. (eds.) ICFEM 2015. LNCS, vol. 9407, pp. 67–83. Springer, Cham (2015). https://doi.org/10.1007/978-3-319-25423-4_5
31. Sun, Y., Wu, M., Ruan, W., Huang, X., Kwiatkowska, M., Kroening, D.: Concolic testing for deep neural networks. In: Huchard, M., Kästner, C., Fraser, G. (eds.) Proceedings of the 33rd ACM/IEEE International Conference on Automated Software Engineering, ASE 2018, 3–7 September 2018, pp. 109–119. ACM, Montpellier, France (2018). https://doi.org/10.1145/3238147.3238172
32. Tomita, M.: Dynamic construction of finite automata from examples using hill-climbing. In: Conference of the Cognitive Science Society, pp. 105–108 (1982)

33. Valiant, L.G.: A theory of the learnable. Commun. ACM **27**(11), 1134–1142 (1984). https://doi.org/10.1145/1968.1972

34. Vaswani, A., Shazeer, N., Parmar, N., Uszkoreit, J., Jones, L., Gomez, A.N., Kaiser, L., Polosukhin, I.: Attention is all you need. In: Guyon, I., von Luxburg, U., Bengio, S., Wallach, H.M., Fergus, R., Vishwanathan, S.V.N., Garnett, R. (eds.) Advances in Neural Information Processing Systems 30: Annual Conference on Neural Information Processing Systems 2017, 4–9 December 2017, pp. 5998–6008. Long Beach, CA, USA 2017), https://proceedings.neurips.cc/paper/2017/hash/3f5ee243547dee91fbd053c1c4a845aa-Abstract.html

35. Walkinshaw, N., Bogdanov, K.: Automated comparison of state-based software models in terms of their language and structure. ACM Trans. Softw. Eng. Methodol. **22**(2), 13:1–13:37 (2013). https://doi.org/10.1145/2430545.2430549

36. Wang, C., Niepert, M.: State-regularized recurrent neural networks. In: Chaudhuri, K., Salakhutdinov, R. (eds.) Proceedings of the 36th International Conference on Machine Learning, ICML 2019, 9–15 June 2019. Proceedings of Machine Learning Research, vol. 97, pp. 6596–6606. PMLR,Long Beach, California, USA (2019). http://proceedings.mlr.press/v97/wang19j.html

37. Wang, Q., Zhang, K., II, A.G.O., Xing, X., Liu, X., Giles, C.L.: A comparison of rule extraction for different recurrent neural network models and grammatical complexity. CoRR abs/1801.05420 (2018). http://arxiv.org/abs/1801.05420

38. Wang, Q., Zhang, K., Liu, X., Giles, C.L.: Verification of recurrent neural networks through rule extraction. CoRR abs/1811.06029 (2018). http://arxiv.org/abs/1811.06029

39. Weiss, G., Goldberg, Y., Yahav, E.: Extracting automata from recurrent neural networks using queries and counterexamples. In: Dy, J.G., Krause, A. (eds.) Proceedings of the 35th International Conference on Machine Learning, ICML 2018, Stockholmsmässan, 10–15 July 2018. Proceedings of Machine Learning Research, vol. 80, pp. 5244–5253. PMLR, Stockholm, Sweden (2018). http://proceedings.mlr.press/v80/weiss18a.html

40. Weiss, G., Goldberg, Y., Yahav, E.: Learning deterministic weighted automata with queries and counterexamples. In: Wallach, H.M., Larochelle, H., Beygelzimer, A., d'Alché-Buc, F., Fox, E.B., Garnett, R. (eds.) Advances in Neural Information Processing Systems 32: Annual Conference on Neural Information Processing Systems 2019, NeurIPS 2019, 8–14 December 2019, pp. 8558–8569. Vancouver, BC, Canada (2019). https://proceedings.neurips.cc/paper/2019/hash/d3f93e7766e8e1b7ef66dfdd9a8be93b-Abstract.html

41. Yellin, D.M., Weiss, G.: Synthesizing context-free grammars from recurrent neural networks. In: TACAS 2021. LNCS, vol. 12651, pp. 351–369. Springer, Cham (2021). https://doi.org/10.1007/978-3-030-72016-2_19

42. Zachary Chase Lipton, John Berkowitz, C.E.: A critical review of recurrent neural networks for sequence learning. CoRR abs/1506.00019 (2015). http://arxiv.org/abs/1506.00019

Kaki: Concurrent Update Synthesis for Regular Policies via Petri Games

Nicklas S. Johansen, Lasse B. Kær, Andreas L. Madsen, Kristian Ø. Nielsen,
Jiří Srba^(✉), and Rasmus G. Tollund

Department of Computer Science, Aalborg University, Aalborg, Denmark
srba@cs.aau.dk

Abstract. Modern computer networks are becoming increasingly complex and for dependability reasons require frequent configuration changes. It is essential that forwarding policies are preserved not only before and after the configuration update but also at any moment during the inherently distributed execution of the update. We present Kaki, a Petri game based approach for automatic synthesis of switch batches that can be updated in parallel without violating a given (regular) forwarding policy like waypointing and service chaining. Kaki guarantees to find the minimum number of concurrent batches and it supports both splittable and nonsplittable flow forwarding. In order to achieve an optimal performance, we introduce two novel optimization techniques based on static analysis: decomposition into independent subproblems and identification of switches that can be collectively updated in the same batch. These techniques considerably improve the performance of our tool, relying on TAPAAL's verification engine for Petri games as its backend. Experiments on a large benchmark of real networks from the topology Zoo database demonstrate that Kaki outperforms the state-of-the-art tool FLIP as it provides shorter (and provably optimal) concurrent update sequences at similar runtime.

1 Introduction

Software defined networking (SDN) [7] delegates the control of a network's routing to the control plane, allowing for programmable control of the network and creating a higher degree of flexibility and efficiency. If a group of switches fail, a new routing of the network flows must be established in order to avoid sending packets to the failed switches, resulting ultimately in packet drops. While updating the routing in an SDN network, the network must preserve a number of policies like waypointing that requires that a given firewall (waypoint) must be visited before a packet in the network is delivered to its destination. The update synthesis problem [7] is to find an update sequence (ordering of switch updates) that preserves a given policy.

In order to reduce the time of the update process, it is of interest to update switches in parallel. However, due to the asynchronous nature of networks, attempting to update all switches concurrently may lead to transient policy

© Springer Nature Switzerland AG 2022
M. H. ter Beek and R. Monahan (Eds.): IFM 2022, LNCS 13274, pp. 249–267, 2022.
https://doi.org/10.1007/978-3-031-07727-2_14

violations before the update is completed. This raises the problem related to finding a concurrent update strategy (sequence of batches of switches that can be updated concurrently) while preserving a given forwarding policy during the update. We study the *concurrent update synthesis problem* and provide an efficient translation of the problem of finding an optimal (shortest) concurrent update sequence into Petri net games. Our translation, implemented in the tool Kaki, guarantees that we preserve a given forwarding policy, expressed as a regular language over the switches describing the sequences of all acceptable hops under the given policy.

Popular routing schemes like Equal-Cost-MultiPath (ECMP) [8] allow for switches to have multiple next hops that split a flow along several paths to its destination in order to account for traffic engineering like load balancing, using e.g. hash-based schemes [1]. In our translation approach, we support concurrent update synthesis taking into account such multiple forwarding (splittable flows) modelled using nondeterminism.

To solve the concurrent update synthesis problem, our framework, Kaki, translates a given network and its forwarding policy into a Petri game and synthetises a winning strategy for the controller using TAPAAL's Petri game engine [9,10]. Kaki guarantees to find a concurrent update sequence that is minimal in the number of batches. We provide two novel optimisation techniques based on static analysis of the network that reduce the complexity of solving a concurrent update synthesis problem, which is known to be NP-hard even if restricted only to the basic loop-freedom and waypointing properties [14]. The first optimisation, topological decomposition, effectively splits the network with its initial and final routing into two subproblems that can be solved independently and even in parallel. The second optimisation identifies collective update classes (sets of switches) that can always be updated in the same batch.

Finally, we conduct a thorough comparison of our tool against the state-of-the-art update synthesis tool FLIP [22] and another Petri game tool [4] (allowing though only for sequential updates). We benchmark on the set of 8759 realistic network topologies with various policies required by network operators. Kaki manages to solve almost as many problems as FLIP, however, in almost 9% of cases it synthesises a solution with a smaller number of batches than FLIP. When Kaki is specialized to produce only singleton batches and policies containing only reachability and single waypointing, it performs similarly as the Petri game approach from [4] that is also using TAPAAL verification engine as its backend but solves a simpler problem. This demonstrates that our more elaborate translation that supports concurrent updates does not create any considerable performance overhead when applied to the simpler setting.

Related Work. The update synthesis problem recently attracted lots of attention (see e.g. the recent overview [7]). State-of-the-art solutions/tools include NetSynth [17], FLIP [22], Snowcap [21] and a Petri game based approach [4].

The tool NetSynth [17] uses the generic LTL logic for policy specification but supports only the synthesis of sequential updates via incremental model checking. The authors in [4] argue that their tool outperforms NetSynth.

The update synthesis tool FLIP [22] supports general policies and moreover it allows to synthetise concurrent update sequences. Similarly to Kaki, it handles every flow independently but Kaki provides more advanced structural decomposition (that can be possibly applied also as a preprocessing step for FLIP). FLIP provides a faster synthesis compared to NetSynth (see [22]) but the tool's performance is negatively affected by more complicated forwarding policies. FLIP synthesises policy-preserving update sequences by constructing constraints that enforce precedence of switch updates, implying a partial order of updates and hence allowing FLIP to update switches concurrently. FLIP, contrary to our tool Kaki, does not guarantee to find the minimal number of batches and it sometimes reverts to an undesirable two-phase commit approach [20] via packet tagging, which is suboptimal as it doubles the expensive ternary content-addressable memory (TCAM) [13]. To the best of our knowledge, FLIP is the only tool supporting concurrent updates and we provide an extensive performance comparison of FLIP and Kaki.

A recent work introduces Snowcap [21], a generic update synthesis tool allowing for both soft and hard specifications. A hard specification specifies a forwarding policy, whereas the soft specification is a secondary objective that should be minimized. Snowcap uses LTL logic for the hard specification but it supports only sequential updates and hence is not included in our experiments.

Update synthesis problem via Petri games was recently studied in [4]. Our work generalizes this work in several dimensions. The translation in [4] considers only sequential updates and reduces the problem to a simplistic type of game with only two rounds and only one environmental transition. Our translation uses the full potential of Petri games with multiple rounds where the controller and environment switch turns—this allows us to encode the concurrent update synthesis problem. Like many others [15,16], the work in [4] fails to provide general forwarding policies and defines only a small set of predefined policies. Our tool, Kaki, solves the limitation by providing a regular language for the specification of forwarding policies and it is also the first tool that considers splittable flows with multiple (nondeterministic) forwarding.

Other recent works relying on the Petri net formalism include timing analysis for network updates [2] and verification of concurrent network updates against Flow-LTL specifications [6], however, both approaches focus solely on the analysis/verification part for a given update sequence and do not discuss how to synthesise such sequences.

2   Concurrent Update Synthesis

We shall now formally define a network, routing of a flow in a network, flow policy as well as the concurrent update synthesis problem.

A *network* is a directed graph $G = (V, E)$ where V is a finite set of *switches* (nodes) and $E \subseteq V \times V$ is a set of *links* (edges) such that $(s, s) \notin E$ for all $s \in V$. A *flow* in a network is a pair $\mathcal{F} = (S_I, S_F)$ of one or more initial (*ingress*) switches and one or more final (*egress*) switches where $\emptyset \neq S_I, S_F \subseteq$

V. A flow aims to forward packets such that a packet arriving to any of the
ingress switches eventually reaches one of the egress switches. Packet forwarding
is defined by network routing, specifying which links are used for forwarding of
packets. Given a network $G = (V, E)$ and a flow $\mathcal{F} = (S_I, S_F)$, a *routing* is a
function $R : V \to 2^V$ such that $s' \in R(s)$ implies that $(s, s') \in E$ for all $s \in V$,
and $R(s_f) = \emptyset$ for all $s_f \in S_F$. We write $s \to s'$ if $s' \in R(s)$, as an alternative
notation to denote the edges in the network that are used for packet forwarding
in the given flow.

Figure 1 shows a network example together with its routing. Note
that we allow nondeterministic forwarding as there may be defined multiple next-hops—this enables splitting of the traffic through several
paths for load balancing purposes.

We now define a trace in a
network as maximal sequence of
switches that can be observed when
forwarding a packet under a given
routing function. A *trace t* for a rout-

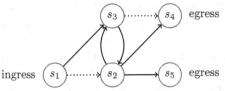

Fig. 1. Network and a routing function (dotted lines are links present in the network but
not used in the routing) where $R(s_1) = \{s_3\}$,
$R(s_2) = \{s_3, s_4, s_5\}$, $R(s_3) = \{s_2\}$ and
$R(s_4) = R(s_5) = \emptyset$.

ing R and a flow $\mathcal{F} = (S_I, S_F)$ is a finite or infinite sequence of switches starting
in an ingress switch $s_0 \in S_I$ where for the infinite case we have $t = s_0 s_1 \ldots$ where
$s_i \in R(s_{i-1})$ for $i \geq 1$, and for the finite case $t = s_0 s_1 \ldots s_n$ where $s_i \in R(s_{i-1})$
for $1 \leq i \leq n$ and $R(s_n) = \emptyset$ for the final switch in the sequence s_n. For a given
routing R and flow $\mathcal{F}$, we denote by $T(R, \mathcal{F})$ the set of all traces.

In our example from Fig. 1, the set $T(R, (\{s_1\}, \{s_4, s_5\}))$ contains e.g. the
traces $s_1 s_3 s_2 s_4$, $s_1 s_3 s_2 s_3 s_2 s_4$ as well as the infinite trace $s_1 (s_3 s_2)^\omega$ that exhibits
(undesirable) looping behaviour as the packets are never delivered to any of the
two egress switches.

2.1   Routing Policy

A routing policy specifies all allowed traces on which packets (in a given flow)
can travel. Given a network $G = (V, E)$, a *policy P* is a regular expression over V
describing a language $L(P) \subseteq V^*$. Given a routing R for a flow $\mathcal{F} = (S_I, S_F)$, a
policy P is *satisfied* by R if $T(R, \mathcal{F}) \subseteq L(P)$. Hence all possible traces allowed by
the routing must be in the language $L(P)$. As $L(P)$ contains only finite traces,
if the set $T(R, \mathcal{F})$ contains an infinite trace then it never satisfies the policy P.

Our policy language can define a number of standard routing policies for a
flow $\mathcal{F} = (S_I, S_F)$ in a network $G = (V, E)$.

- *Reachability* is expressed by the policy $(V \setminus S_F)^* S_F$. It ensures loop and
  blackhole freedom as it requires that an egress switch must always be reached.
- *Waypoint enforcement* requires that packets must visit a given waypoint
  switch $s_w \in V$ before they are delivered to an egress switch (where by our
  assumption the trace ends) and it is given by the policy $V^* s_w V^*$.

- *Alternative waypointing* specifies two waypoints s and s' such that at least one of them must be visited and it is given by the union of the waypoint enforcement regular languages for s and s', or alternatively by $V^*(s+s')V^*$.
- *Service chaining* requires that a given sequence of switches $s_1, s_2, \ldots, s_n$ must be visited in the given order and it is described by the policy $(V \setminus \{s_1, \cdots, s_n\})^* s_1 (V \setminus \{s_2, \cdots, s_n\})^* s_2 \cdots (V \setminus \{s_n\})^* s_n V^*$.
- *Conditional enforcement* is given by a pair of switches $s, s' \in V$ such that if s is visited then s' must also be visited and it is given by the policy $(V \setminus \{s\})^* + V^* s' V^*$.

Regular languages are closed under union and intersection, hence the standard policies can be combined using Boolean operations. As reachability is an essential property that we always want to satisfy, we shall assume that the reachability property is always assumed in any other routing policy.

In our translation, we represent a policy by an equivalent nondeterministic finite automaton (NFA) $A = (Q, V, \delta, q_0, F)$ where Q is a finite set of states, V is the alphabet equal to set of switches, $\delta : Q \times V \to 2^Q$ is the transition function, q_0 is the initial state and F is the set of final states. We extended the δ function to sequences of switches by $\delta(q, s_0 s_1 \ldots s_n) = \bigcup_{q' \in \delta(q, s_0)} \delta(q', s_1 \ldots s_n)$ in order to obtain all possible states after executing $s_0 s_1 \ldots s_n$. We define the language of A by $L(A) = \{w \in V^* \mid \delta(q_0, w) \cap F \neq \emptyset\}$. An NFA where $|\delta(q, s)| = 1$ for all $q \in Q$ and $s \in V$ is called a deterministic finite automaton (DFA). It is a standard result that NFA, DFA and regular expressions have the same expressive power (w.r.t. the generated languages).

2.2   Concurrent Update Synthesis Problem

Let R_i and R_f be the *initial* and *final* routing, respectively. We aim to update the switches in the network so that the packet forwarding is changed from the initial to the final routing. The goal of the concurrent update synthesis problem is to construct a sequence of nonempty sets of switches, called *batches*, such that when we update the switches from their initial to the final routing in every batch concurrently (while waiting so that all updates in the batch are finished before we update the next batch), a given routing policy is transiently preserved. Our aim is to synthesise an update sequence that is optimal, i.e. minimizes the number of batches.

During the update, only switches that actually change their forwarding function need to be updated. Given a network $G = (V, E)$, an initial routing R_i and a final routing R_f, the set of *update switches* is defined by $U = \{s \in V \mid R_i(s) \neq R_f(s)\}$. An *update* of a switch $s \in U$ changes its routing from $R_i(s)$ to $R_f(s)$.

Definition 1. Let $G = (V, E)$ be a network and let R and R_f be the current and final routing, respectively. An *update* of a switch $s \in U$ results in the updated routing R^s given by

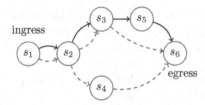

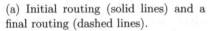

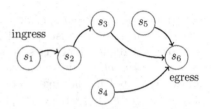

(a) Initial routing (solid lines) and a final routing (dashed lines).

(b) Intermediate routing after updating s_3 and s_4 in the first batch.

Fig. 2. Network with an optimal concurrent update sequence $\{s_3, s_4\}\{s_2, s_5\}$

$$
R^s(s') = \begin{cases} R(s') & \text{if } s \neq s' \\ R_f(s) & \text{if } s = s'. \end{cases}
$$

A *concurrent update sequence* $\omega = X_1 \ldots X_n \in (2^U \setminus \emptyset)^*$ is a sequence of nonempty batches of switches such that each update switch appears in exactly one batch of ω. As a network is a highly distributed system with asynchronous communication, even if all switches in the batch are commanded to start the update at the same time, in the actual execution of the batch the updates can be performed in any permutation of the batch. An *execution* $\pi = p_1 p_2 \cdots p_n \in U^*$ respecting a concurrent update sequence $\omega = X_1 \ldots X_n$ is the concatenation of permutations of each batch in ω such that $p_i \in perm(X_i)$ for all i, $1 \leq i \leq n$, where $perm(X_i)$ denotes the set of all permutations of switches in X_i.

Given a routing R and an execution $\pi = s_1 s_2 \cdots s_n$ where $s_i \in U$ for all i, $1 \leq i \leq n$, we inductively define the *updated routing* R^π by (i) $R^\varepsilon = R$ and (ii) $R^{s\pi} = (R^s)^\pi$ where $s \in U$ and ϵ is the empty execution. An *intermediate routing* is any routing $R^{\pi'}$ where π' is a prefix of π. We notice that for any given routing R and any two executions π, π' that respect a concurrent update sequence $\omega = X_1 \ldots X_m$, we have $R^\pi = R^{\pi'}$, whereas the sets of intermediate routings can be different.

Given an initial routing R_i and a final routing R_f for a flow (S_I, S_F), a concurrent update sequence ω where $R_i^\omega = R_f$ *satisfies a policy* P if R' satisfies P for all intermediate routings R' generated by any execution respecting ω.

Definition 2. The *concurrent update synthesis problem* (CUSP) is a 5-tuple $\mathcal{U} = (G, \mathcal{F}, R_i, R_f, P)$ where $G = (V, E)$ is a network, $\mathcal{F} = (S_I, S_F)$ is a flow, R_i is an initial routing, R_f is a final routing, and P is a routing policy that includes reachability i.e. $L(P) \subseteq L((V \setminus S_F)^* S_F)$. A *solution* to a CUSP is a concurrent update sequence ω such that $R_i^\omega = R_f$ where ω satisfies the policy P and the sequence is *optimal*, meaning that the number of batches, $|\omega|$, is minimal.

Consider an example in Fig. 2a where the initial routing is depicted in solid lines and the final one in dashed ones. We want to preserve the reachability policy between the ingress and egress switch. The set of update switches is $\{s_2, s_3, s_4, s_5\}$. Clearly, all update switches cannot be placed into one batch because the execution starting with the update of s_2 creates a possible blackhole at the switch s_4. Hence we need at least two batches and indeed the concurrent update sequence $\omega = \{s_3, s_4\}\{s_2, s_5\}$ satisfies the reachability policy. Any execution of the first batch preserves the reachability of the switch s_6 and brings us to the intermediate routing depicted in Fig. 2b. Any execution order of the second batch also preserves the reachability policy, implying that ω is an optimal concurrent update sequence.

3   Optimisation Techniques

Before we present the translation of CUSP problem to Petri games, we introduce two preprocessing techniques that allow us to reduce the size of the problem.

3.1   Topological Decomposition

The intuition of topological decomposition is to reduce the complexity of solving CUSP $\mathcal{U} = (G, \mathcal{F}, R_i, R_f, P)$ where $G = (V, E)$ by decomposing it into two smaller subproblems. In the rest of this section, we use the aggregated routing $R_c(s) = R_i(s) \cup R_f(s)$ for all $s \in V$ (also denoted by the relation $\rightarrow$) in order to consider only the relevant part of the network.

We can decompose our problem at a switch $s_D \in V$ if s_D splits the network into two independent networks and there is at most one possible NFA state that can be reached by following any path from any of the ingress switches to s_D, and the path has a continuation to some of the egress switches while reaching an accepting NFA state. By $\mathcal{Q}(s)$ we denote the set of all such possible NFA states for a switch s. Algorithm 1 computes the set $\mathcal{Q}(s)$ by iteratively relaxing edges, i.e. by forward propagating the potential NFA states and storing them in the function $\mathcal{Q}_f$ and in a backward manner it also computes NFA states that can reach a final state and stores them in $\mathcal{Q}_b$. An edge $s \rightarrow s'$ can be relaxed if it changes the value of $\mathcal{Q}_f(s')$ or $\mathcal{Q}_b(s)$ and the algorithm halts when no more edges can be relaxed.

Lemma 1. *Let $\mathcal{U} = (G, \mathcal{F}, R_i, R_f, P)$ be a CUSP where $\mathcal{F} = (S_I, S_F)$ is a flow and let (Q, V, δ, q_0, F) be an NFA describing its routing policy P. Algorithm 1 terminates and the resulting function $\mathcal{Q}$ has the property that $q \in \mathcal{Q}(s_i)$ iff there exists a trace $s_0 \ldots s_i \ldots s_n \in T(R_c, \mathcal{F})$ such that $s_0 \in S_I$, $s_n \in S_F$, $q \in \delta(q_0, s_0 \ldots s_i)$ and $\delta(q, s_{i+1} \ldots s_n) \cap F \neq \emptyset$.*

Let $\mathcal{U} = (G, \mathcal{F}, R_i, R_f, P)$ be a CUSP where $G = (V, E)$, $\mathcal{F} = (S_I, S_F)$ and where P is expressed by an equivalent NFA $A = (Q, V, \delta, q_0, F)$. A switch $s_D \in V$ is a *topological decomposition point* if $|\mathcal{Q}(s_D)| = 1$ and for all $s \in V \setminus \{s_D\}$ either (i) $s \rightarrow^* s_D$ and $s_D \not\rightarrow^* s$ or (ii) $s \not\rightarrow^* s_D$ and $s_D \rightarrow^* s$.

Let s_D be a decomposition point. We construct two CUSP subproblems $\mathcal{U}'$ and $\mathcal{U}''$, the first one containing the switches $V' = \{s \in V \mid s \rightarrow^* s_D\}$ and the latter one with switches $V'' = \{s \in V \mid s_D \rightarrow^* s\}$. Let $G[\overline{V}]$ be the induced subgraph of G restricted to the set of switches $\overline{V} \subseteq V$.

Algorithm 1: Potential NFA state set

input : A CUSP $\mathcal{U} = (G, \mathcal{F}, R_i, R_f, P)$ and NFA $A = (Q, V, \delta, q_0, F)$.
output: Function $\mathcal{Q} : V \to 2^Q$ of potential NFA states at a given switch.

1   $\mathcal{Q}_f(s) := \emptyset$ and $\mathcal{Q}_b(s) := \emptyset$ for all $s \in V$
2   $\mathcal{Q}_f(s_i) := \delta(q_0, s_i)$ for all $s_i \in S_I$
3   $\mathcal{Q}_b(s_f) := F$ for all $s_f \in S_F$

    // $s \to s'$ **can be relaxed if it changes** $\mathcal{Q}_f(s')$ **or** $\mathcal{Q}_b(s)$
4   **while** *there exists* $s \to s' \in R_c$ *that can be relaxed* **do**
5      $\mathcal{Q}_f(s') := \mathcal{Q}_f(s') \cup \bigcup_{q \in \mathcal{Q}_f(s)} \delta(q, s')$
6      $\mathcal{Q}_b(s) := \mathcal{Q}_b(s) \cup \{q \in Q \mid \delta(q, s') \cap \mathcal{Q}_b(s') \neq \emptyset\}$

7   **return** $\mathcal{Q}(s) := \mathcal{Q}_f(s) \cap \mathcal{Q}_b(s)$ for all $s \in V$

The first subproblem is given by $\mathcal{U}' = (G[V'], \mathcal{F}', R_i', R_f', P')$ where (i) $\mathcal{F}' = (S_I, \{s_D\})$, (ii) $R_i'(s) = R_i(s)$ and $R_f'(s) = R_f(s)$ for all $s \in V' \setminus \{s_D\}$ and $R_i'(s_D) = R_f'(s_D) = \emptyset$, and (iii) $L(P') = L(A') \cap L((V' \setminus \{s_D\})^* s_D)$ where $A' = (Q, V, \delta, q_0, F')$ with $F' = \mathcal{Q}(s_D)$. In other words, the network and routing are projected to only include the switches from V' and the policy ensures that we must reach s_D as well as the potential NFA state of s_D.

The second subproblem is given by $\mathcal{U}'' = (G[V''], \mathcal{F}'', R_i'', R_f'', P'')$ where (i) $\mathcal{F}'' = (\{s_D\}, S_F)$, (ii) $R_i''(s) = R_i(s)$ and $R_f''(s) = R_f(s)$ for all $s \in V''$, and (iii) $L(P'') = L(A'')$ where $A'' = (Q, V, \delta, q_0', F)$ and $\{q_0'\} = \mathcal{Q}(s_D)$. The policy of the second subproblem ensures that starting from the potential NFA state q_0' for the switch s_D, a final state of the original policy can be reached.

We can now realise that a solution to $\mathcal{U}$ implies the existence of solutions to both $\mathcal{U}'$ and $\mathcal{U}''$.

Theorem 1. *If* $\omega = X_1 \dots X_n$ *is a solution to* $\mathcal{U}$ *then* $\omega' = (X_1 \cap V') \dots (X_n \cap V')$ *and* $\omega'' = (X_1 \cap V'') \dots (X_n \cap V'')$, *where empty batches are omitted, are solutions to* $\mathcal{U}'$ *and* $\mathcal{U}''$, *respectively.*

Even more importantly, from the optimal solutions of the subproblems, we can synthesise an optimal solution for the original problem.

Theorem 2. *Let* $\omega' = X_1' X_2' \dots X_j'$ *and* $\omega'' = X_1'' X_2'' \dots X_k''$ *be optimal solutions for* $\mathcal{U}'$ *and* $\mathcal{U}''$, *respectively. Then* $\omega = (X_1' \cup X_1'')(X_2' \cup X_2'') \dots (X_m' \cup X_m'')$ *where* $m = \max\{j, k\}$ *and where by conventions* $X_i' = \emptyset$ *for* $i > j$ *and* $X_i'' = \emptyset$ *for* $i > k$, *is an optimal solution to* $\mathcal{U}$.

Hence, if the original problem has a solution and can be decomposed into two subproblems, then these subproblems also have solutions and from the optimal solutions of the subproblems, we can construct an optimal solution for the original problem. Importantly, since the subproblems are themselves also CUSPs, they may be subject to further decompositions.

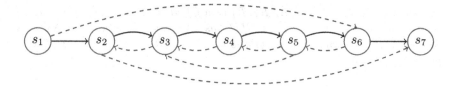

Fig. 3. Chain structure with initial (solid) and final (dashed) routings.

3.2 Collective Update Classes

We now present the notion of a *collective update class*, or simply *collective updates*, which is a set of switches that can be always updated in the same batch in an optimal concurrent update sequence. The switches in a collective update class can then be viewed only as a single switch, thus reducing the complexity of the synthesis by reducing the number of update switches.

The first class of collective updates is inspired by [4] where the authors realize that in case of sequential updates, update switches that are undefined in the initial routing can be always updated in the beginning of the update sequence and similarly update switches that should become undefined in the final routing can always be moved to the end of the update sequence. We generalize the proof of this observation also to concurrent update sequences.

Theorem 3. *Let* $\mathcal{U} = (G, \mathcal{F}, R_i, R_f, P)$ *be a CUSP. Let* $\aleph_i = \{s \in V \mid R_i(s) = \emptyset \wedge R_f(s) \neq \emptyset\}$ *and* $\aleph_f = \{s \in V \mid R_f(s) = \emptyset \wedge R_i(s) \neq \emptyset\}$. *If* $\mathcal{U}$ *is solvable then it has an optimal solution of the form* $X_1 \ldots X_n$ *where* $\aleph_i \subseteq X_1$ *and* $\aleph_f \subseteq X_n$.

In Fig. 3 we show another class of collective updates with a chain-like structure where the initial and final routings forward packets in opposite directions. We claim that the switches $\aleph_c = \{s_3, s_4, s_5\}$ can be always updated in the same batch because updating any switch in $\aleph_c$ introduces looping behaviour, as long as the intermediate routing is passing through the switches. Once the switches in $\aleph_c$ are not part of the intermediate routing, we can update all of them in the same batch without causing any forwarding issues. The notion of chain-reducible collective updates is formalized as follows.

Definition 3. *Let* $C \subseteq V$ *be a strongly connected component w.r.t.* $\rightarrow$ *such that* $|C| \geq 4$. *The triple* $(s_e, s_{e'}, C)$, *where* $s_e, s_{e'} \in C$, *is chain-reducible whenever (i) if* $s \in C \setminus \{s_e, s_{e'}\}$ *and* $s' \rightarrow s$ *then* $s' \in C$, *and (ii) if* $s \in C \setminus \{s_e, s_{e'}\}$ *and* $s \rightarrow s'$ *then* $s' \in C$, *and (iii) for every* $s \in C \setminus \{s_e, s_{e'}\}$ *if there exists a switch* $s' \in R_f(s)$ *then* $s' \rightarrow^* s$ *using only the initial routing or* $R_i(s') = \emptyset$.

The restriction $|C| \geq 4$ is included so that reduction in size can be achieved. Cases (i) and (ii) ensure that the switches in $C \setminus \{s_e, s_{e'}\}$ do not influence or are influenced by any of the switches not in C and can be part of a collective update. Case (iii) guarantees that updating a reachable switch $s \in C \setminus \{s_e, s_{e'}\}$ induces either a loop or a blackhole.

Theorem 4. *Let* $\mathcal{U} = (G, \mathcal{F}, R_i, R_f, P)$ *be a CUSP and let* $(s_e, s_{e'}, C)$ *be chain-reducible and let* $\aleph_c = C \setminus \{s_e, s_{e'}\}$. *If* $\mathcal{U}$ *has an optimal solution* $\omega = X_1 \ldots X_n$ *then there exists another optimal solution* $\omega' = X_1 \setminus \aleph_c \ldots X_k \cup \aleph_c \ldots X_n \setminus \aleph_c$ *for some* k, $1 \leq k \leq n$.

4   Translation to Petri Games

We shall first present the formalism of Petri games and then reduce the concurrent update synthesis problem to this model.

4.1   Petri Games

A Petri net is a mathematical model for distributed systems focusing on concurrency and asynchronicity (see [18]). A Petri game [4,10] is a 2-player game extension of Petri nets, splitting the transitions into controllable and environmental ones. We shall reduce the concurrent update synthesis problem to finding a winning strategy for the controller in a Petri game with a reachability objective.

A *Petri net* is a 4-tuple (P, T, W, M) where P is a finite set of places, T is a finite set of transitions such that $P \cap T = \emptyset$, $W : (P \times T) \cup (T \times P) \to \mathbb{N}^0$ is a weight function and $M : P \to \mathbb{N}^0$ is an initial marking that assigns a number of tokens to each place. We depict places as circles, transitions as rectangles and draw an arc (directed edge) between a transition t and place p if $W(t, p) > 0$, or place p and transition t if $W(p, t) > 0$. When an arc has no explicit weight annotation, we assume that it has the weight 1.

The semantics of a Petri net is given by a labeled transition system where states are Petri net markings and we write $M \xrightarrow{t} M'$ if $M(p) \geq W(p, t)$ for all $p \in P$ (the transition t is enabled in M) and $M'(p) = M(p) - W(p, t) + W(t, p)$.

Marking properties are given by a formula φ which is a Boolean combination of the atomic predicates of the form $p \bowtie n$ where $p \in P$, $\bowtie \in \{<, \leq, >, \geq, =, \neq\}$ and $n \in \mathbb{N}^0$. We write $M \models p \bowtie n$ iff $M(p) \bowtie n$ and extend this naturally to the Boolean combinators. We use the classical CTL operator AF and write $M \models AF\ \varphi$ if *(i)* $M \models \varphi$ or *(ii)* $M' \models AF\ \varphi$ for all M' such that $M \xrightarrow{t} M'$ for some $t \in T$, meaning that on any maximal firing sequence from M, the marking property φ must eventually hold.

A *Petri game* [4,10] is a two-player game extension of Petri nets where transitions are partitioned $T = T_{ctrl} \uplus T_{env}$ into two distinct sets of *controller* and *environment* transitions, respectively. During a play in the game, the environment has a priority over the controller in the decisions: the environment can always choose to fire its own fireable transition, or ask the controller to fire one of the controllable transitions. The goal of the controller is to find a strategy in order to satisfy a given $AF\ \varphi$ property whereas the environment tries to prevent this. Formally, a (controller) *strategy* is a partial function $\sigma : \mathcal{M}_N \rightharpoonup T$, where $\mathcal{M}_N$ is the set of all markings, that maps a marking to a fireable controllable transition (or it is undefined if no such transition exists). We write $M \xrightarrow{t}_\sigma M'$ if $M \xrightarrow{t} M'$ and

$t \in T_{env} \cup \{\sigma(M)\}$. A Petri game satisfies the reachability objective $AF\ \varphi$ if there exists a controller strategy σ such that the labelled transition system under the transition relation $\rightarrow_\sigma$ satisfies $AF\ \varphi$.

4.2   Translation Intuition

We now present the intuition for our translation from CUSP to Petri games. For a given CUSP instance, we compositionally construct a Petri game where the controller's goal is to select a valid concurrent update sequence and the environment aims to show that the controller's update sequence is invalid. The game has two phases: generation phase and verification phase.

The generation phase has two modes where the controller and environment switch turns in each mode. The controller proposes the next update batch (in a mode where only controller's transitions are enabled) and when finished, it gives the turn to the environment that sequializes the batch by creating an arbitrary permutation of the update switches in the batch (in this mode only environmental transitions are enabled). At any moment during the batch sequentialisation, the environment may decide to enter the second phase that is concerned with validation of the current intermediate routing.

The verification phase begins when the environment injects a packet (token) to the network and wishes to examine the currently generated intermediate routing. In this phase, one hop of the packet is simulated in the network according to the current switch configuration; in case of nondeterministic forwarding it is the environment that chooses the next switch. A hop in the network is followed by an update of the current state of a DFA that represents the routing policy. These two steps alternate, until (i) an egress switch is reached, (ii) the token ends in a blackhole (deadlock) or (iii) the packet forwarding forms a loop, which also makes the net execution to deadlock as soon as the same switch is visited the second time. The controller wins the game only in situation (i), providing that the currently reached state in the DFA is an accepting state.

The controller now has a winning strategy if and only if the CUSP problem has a solution. By restricting the number of available batches and using the bisection method, we can further identify an optimal concurrent update sequence.

4.3   Translation of Network Topology and Routings

Let $(G, \mathcal{F}, R_i, R_f, P)$ be a concurrent update synthesis problem where $G = (V, E)$ is a network and $\mathcal{F} = (S_I, S_F)$ is the considered flow. We now construct a Petri game $N(\mathcal{U}) = (P, T, W, M)$. This subsection describes the translation of the network and routings, next subsection deals with the policy translation.

Figure 4 shows the Petri game building components for translating the network and the routings. Environmental transitions are denoted by rectangles with a white fill-in and controller transitions are depicted in solid black; if a transition/place is framed by a dashed line then it is shared across the components.

Network Topology Component (Fig. 4a). This component represents the network and its current routing. For each $s \in V$, we create the shared places p_s and a

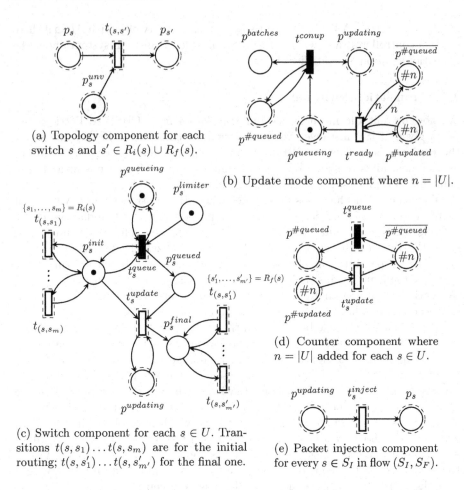

(a) Topology component for each switch s and $s' \in R_i(s) \cup R_f(s)$.

(b) Update mode component where $n = |U|$.

(c) Switch component for each $s \in U$. Transitions $t(s, s_1) \ldots t(s, s_m)$ are for the initial routing; $t(s, s'_1) \ldots t(s, s'_{m'})$ for the final one.

(d) Counter component where $n = |U|$ added for each $s \in U$.

(e) Packet injection component for every $s \in S_I$ in flow (S_I, S_F).

Fig. 4. Construction of Petri game components; U is the set of update switches

shared unvisited place p_s^{unv} with 1 token. The unvisited place tracks whether the switch has been visited and prevents looping. We use uncontrollable transitions so that the environment can decide how to traverse the network in case of nondeterminism. The switch component ensures that these transitions are only fireable in accordance with the current intermediate routing.

Update Mode Component (Figs. 4b and 4d). These components handle the bookkeeping of turns between the controller and the environment. A token present in the place $p^{queueing}$ enables the controller to queue updates into a current batch. Once the token is moved to the place $p^{updating}$, it enables the environment to schedule (in an arbitrary order) the updates from the batch. The dual places $p^{\#queued}$ and $\overline{p^{\#queued}}$ count how many switches have been queued in this batch and how many switches have not been queued, respectively. The place $p^{\#updated}$ is decremented for each update implemented by the environment. Hence the

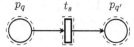

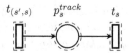

(a) Component for each DFA transition $q \xrightarrow{s} q'$; if $q = q_0$ then p_q gets a token.

(b) Tracking component for each already added transition $t_{(s',s)}$ and each switch $s \in V$; creates a new transition t_s.

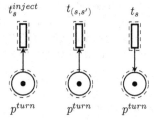

(c) Turn component for all created transitions t_s^{inject} and $t_{(s,s')}$ and t_s.

(d) Injection component for each $s \in S_I$ in the flow (S_I, S_F).

Fig. 5. Policy checking components

environment is forced to inject a token to the network, latest once all update switches are updated. Additionally, the number of produced batches is represented by the number of tokens in the place $p^{batches}$.

Switch Component (Fig. 4c). This component handles the queueing (by controller) and activation (by environment) of updates. For every $s \in V$ where $R_i(s) \neq R_f(s)$ we create a switch component. Let U be the set of all such update switches. Initially, we put one token in p_s^{init} (the switch forwards according to its initial routing) and $p_s^{limiter}$ (making sure that each switch can be queued only once). Once a switch is queued (by the controller transition t_s^{queue}) and updated (by the environment transition t_s^{update}), the token from p_s^{init} is moved into p_s^{final} and the switch is now forwarding according to the final routing function.

Packet Injection Component (Fig. 4e). The environment can at any moment during the sequentialisation mode use the transition t_s^{inject} to inject a packet into any of the ingress routers and enter the second verification phase.

4.4 Policy Translation

Given a CUSP $(G, \mathcal{F}, R_i, R_f, P)$, we now want to encode the policy P into the Petri game representation. We assume that P is represented by a DFA $A(P)$ such that $L(P) = L(A(P))$. We translate $A(P)$ into a Petri game so that DFA states/transitions are mapped into corresponding Petri net places/transitions which are connected to earlier defined Petri game for the topology and routing.

Figure 5 presents the components for the policy translation.

1. *DFA transition component (Fig. 5a).* This component creates places/ transitions for each DFA state/transition. Note that if a Petri game

transition is of the form t_s then it corresponds to a DFA-transition, contrary to transitions of the form $t_{(s,s')}$ that represent network topology links.

2. *Policy tracking component (Fig. 5b).* For all $s \in V$, we create the place p_s^{track} in order to track the current position of a packet in the network.

3. *Turn component (Fig. 5c).* The intuition here is that whenever the environment fires the topology transition $t_{(s,s')}$ then the DFA-component must match it by firing a DFA-transition $t_{s'}$. The token in the place p^{turn} means that it is the environment turn to challenge with a next hop in the network topology.

4. *DFA injection component (Fig. 5d).* For all inject transitions t_s^{inject} to the switch s, we add an arc to its tracking place p_s^{track}. This initiates the second phase of verification of the routing policy.

4.5 Reachability Objective and Translation Correctness

We finish by defining the reachability objective $C(k)$ for each positive number k that gives an upper bound on the maximum number of allowed batches (recall that F is the set of final DFA states): $C(k) = AF\ p^{batches} \leq k \wedge \bigvee_{q \in F} p_q = 1$.

The query expresses that all runs must use less than k batches and eventually end in an accepting DFA state. Note that since reachability is assumed as a part of the policy P and that the final switch has no further forwarding, there can be no next-hop in the network after the DFA gets to its final state.

The query can be iteratively verified (e.g. using the bisection method) while changing the value of k, until we find k such that $C(k)$ is true and $C(k-1)$ is false (which implies that also $C(\ell)$ is false for every $\ell < k - 1$). Then we know that the synthesised strategy is an optimal solution. If $C(k)$ is false for $k = |U|$ where U is the set of update switches then there exists no concurrent update sequence solving the CUSP. The correctness of the translation is summarized in the following theorem.

Theorem 5. *A concurrent update synthesis problem $\mathcal{U}$ has a solution with $k \geq 1$ or fewer batches if and only if there exists a winning strategy for the controller in the Petri game $N(\mathcal{U})$ for the query $C(k)$.*

Let us note that a winning strategy for the controlled in the Petri game can be directly translated to a concurrent update sequence. The firing of controllable transitions of the form t_s^{queue} indicates that the switch s should be scheduled in the current batch and the batches are separated from each other by the firings of the controllable transitions t^{conup}.

5   Experimental Evaluation

We implemented the translation approach and optimisation techniques in our tool Kaki. The tool is coded in Kotlin and compiled to JVM. It uses the Petri game engine of TAPAAL [3,9,10] as its backend for solving the Petri games. The source code of Kaki is publicly available on GitHub[1].

---

[1] https://github.com/Ragusaen/Kaki.

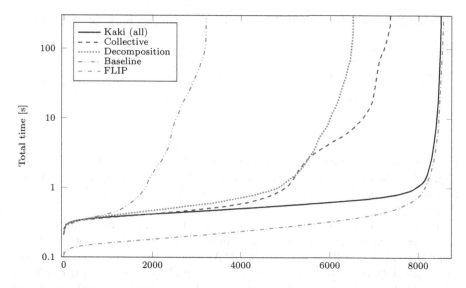

Fig. 6. Optimization techniques and FLIP comparison (y-axis is logarithmic)

We shall discuss the effect of our novel optimisation techniques and compare the performance of our tool to FLIP [22] as well as the tool for sequential update synthesis from [4], referred to as SEQ. We use the benchmark [5] of update synthesis problems from [4], based on 229 real-network topologies from the topology ZOO database [12]. The benchmark includes four update synthesis problems for reachability and single waypointing for each topology, totalling 916 problem instances. As Kaki and FLIP support a richer set of policies, we further extend this benchmark with additional policies for multiple waypointing, alternative waypointing and conditional enforcement, giving us 8759 instances of the concurrent update synthesis problem.

All experiments (each using a single core) are conducted on a compute-cluster running Ubuntu version 18.04.5 on an AMD Opteron(tm) Processor 6376 with a 1 GB memory limit and 5 min timeout. A reproducibility package is available in [11] and it includes executable files to run Kaki, pre-generated outputs that are used to produce the figures as well as the benchmark and related scripts.

5.1   Results

To compare the optimization techniques introduced in this paper, we include a baseline without any optimisation techniques, its extension with only topological decomposition technique and only collective update classes, and also the combination of both of them. Each method decides the existence of a solution for the concurrent update synthesis problem and in the positive case it also minimizes the number of batches. Figure 6 shows a cactus plot of the results where the problem instances on the x-axis are (for each method independently) sorted by

Table 1. Number of solved problems (suboptimal and tagging refers to FLIP)

	Reachability	1-wp	2-wp	4-wp	8-wp	1-alt-wp	2-alt-wp	4-alt-wp	1-cond-enf	2-cond-enf	All	Percentage
Total	856	916	916	844	647	916	916	916	916	916	8759	100.0%
Only Kaki	0	0	17	37	63	0	5	8	1	2	133	1.5%
Only FLIP	0	0	0	0	0	17	20	35	40	84	196	2.2%
Suboptimal	0	11	18	14	4	283	198	104	41	114	787	8.9%
Tagging	0	0	47	55	21	4	39	100	1	1	268	3.0%

the increasing synthesis time shown on y-axis. Both of the optimization techniques provide a significant improvement over the baseline and their combination is clearly beneficial as it solves 97% of the problems in the benchmark in less than 1 s.

In Fig. 6 we also show a cactus plot for FLIP on the full benchmark of concurrent update synthesis problems. As Kaki has to first generate the Petri game file and then call the external TAPAAL engine for solving the Petri game, there is an initial overhead that implies that the single-purpose tool FLIP is faster on the smaller and easy-to-solve instances of the problem that can be answered below 1 s. For the more difficult instances both Kaki and FLIP quickly time out and exhibit similar performance.

More importantly, FLIP does not always produce the minimal number of batches, which is critical for practical applications because updating a switch can cause forwarding instability for up to 0.4 s [19]. Hence minimizing the number of batches where switches can be updated in parallel significantly decreases the forwarding vulnerability (some networks in the benchmark have up to 700 switches). In fact, FLIP synthesises a strictly larger number of batches in 787 instances, compared to the minimum number of possible batches (that Kaki is guaranteed to find). The distribution of the solved problems for the different policies is shown in Table 1. Here we can also notice that FLIP uses the less desirable tag-and-match update strategy in 268 problem instances, even though there exists a concurrent update sequence as demonstrated by Kaki. In conclusion, Kaki has a slightly larger overhead on easy-to-solve instances but scales almost as well as FLIP, however, FLIP in almost 12% of cases does not find the optimal update sequence or reverts to the less desirable two-phase commit protocol.

Comparison with SEQ from [4] is more difficult as SEQ supports only reachability and single waypointing and computes only sequential updates (single switch per batch). When we restrict the benchmark to the subset of these policies and adapt our tool to produce sequential updates, we observe that Kaki's performance is in the worst case 0.06 s slower than SEQ when measuring the verification time required by the TAPAAL engine. We remark that SEQ solved all problems in under 0.55 s, except for two instances where it timed out while Kaki was able to solve both of them in under 0.1 s.

We also extended the benchmark with nondeterministic forwarding that models splittable flows (using the Equal-Cost-MultiPath (ECMP) protocol [8] that divides a flow along all shortest paths from an ingress to an egress switch). We observe that verifying the routing policies in this modified benchmark implies only a negligible (3.4% on the median instance) overhead in running time.

6   Conclusion

We presented Kaki, a tool for update synthesis that can deal with (i) concurrent updates, (ii) synthesises solutions with minimum number of batches, (iii) extends the existing approaches with nondeterministic forwarding and can hence model splittable flows, and (iv) verifies arbitrary (regular) routing policies. It extends the state-of-the-art approaches with respect to generality but given its efficient TAPAAL backend engine, it is also fast and provides more optimal solutions compared to the competing tool FLIP.

Kaki's performance is the result of its efficient translation in combination with optimizations techniques that allow us to reduce the complexity of the problem while preserving the optimality of its solutions. Kaki uses less than 1 s to solve 97% of all concurrent update synthesis problems for real network topologies and hence provides a practical approach to concurrent update synthesis.

Acknowledgments. We thank Peter G. Jensen for his help with executing the experiments and Anders Mariegaard for his assistance with setting up FLIP. This work was supported by DFF project QASNET.

References

1. Cao, Z., Wang, Z., Zegura, E.W.: Performance of hashing-based schemes for internet load balancing. In: Proceedings IEEE INFOCOM 2000, The Conference on Computer Communications, Nineteenth Annual Joint Conference of the IEEE Computer and Communications Societies, Reaching the Promised Land of Communications, Tel Aviv, Israel, 26–30 March 2000, pp. 332–341. IEEE Computer Society (2000). https://doi.org/10.1109/INFCOM.2000.832203
2. Christesen, N., Glavind, M., Schmid, S., Srba, J.: Latte: Improving the latency of transiently consistent network update schedules. In: IFIP PERFORMANCE 2020. Performance Evaluation Review, vol. 48, no. 3, pp. 14–26. ACM (2020)
3. David, A., Jacobsen, L., Jacobsen, M., Jørgensen, K.Y., Møller, M.H., Srba, J.: TAPAAL 2.0: integrated development environment for Timed-Arc Petri Nets. In: Flanagan, C., König, B. (eds.) TACAS 2012. LNCS, vol. 7214, pp. 492–497. Springer, Heidelberg (2012). https://doi.org/10.1007/978-3-642-28756-5_36
4. Didriksen, M., et al.: Automatic synthesis of transiently correct network updates via petri games. In: Buchs, D., Carmona, J. (eds.) PETRI NETS 2021. LNCS, vol. 12734, pp. 118–137. Springer, Cham (2021). https://doi.org/10.1007/978-3-030-76983-3_7
5. Didriksen, M., et al.: Artefact for: automatic synthesis of transiently correct network updates via petri games, February 2021. https://doi.org/10.5281/zenodo.4501982

6. Finkbeiner, B., Gieseking, M., Hecking-Harbusch, J., Olderog, E.-R.: ADAMMC: a model checker for petri nets with transits against flow-LTL. In: Lahiri, S.K., Wang, C. (eds.) CAV 2020. LNCS, vol. 12225, pp. 64–76. Springer, Cham (2020). https://doi.org/10.1007/978-3-030-53291-8_5

7. Foerster, K., Schmid, S., Vissicchio, S.: Survey of consistent software-defined network updates. IEEE Commun. Surv. Tutor. **21**(2), 1435–1461 (2019)

8. Hopps, C., et al.: Analysis of an equal-cost multi-path algorithm. Tech. rep., RFC 2992, November 2000

9. Jensen, J.F., Nielsen, T., Oestergaard, L.K., Srba, J.: TAPAAL and reachability analysis of P/T nets. In: Koutny, M., Desel, J., Kleijn, J. (eds.) Transactions on Petri Nets and Other Models of Concurrency XI. LNCS, vol. 9930, pp. 307–318. Springer, Heidelberg (2016). https://doi.org/10.1007/978-3-662-53401-4_16

10. Jensen, P., Larsen, K., Srba, J.: Real-time strategy synthesis for timed-arc Petri net games via discretization. In: Proceedings of the 23rd International SPIN Symposium on Model Checking of Software (SPIN'16). LNCS, vol. 9641, pp. 129–146. Springer-Verlag (2016)

11. Johansen, N., Kær, L., Madsen, A., Nielsen, K., Srba, J., Tollund, R.: Artefact for Kaki: Concurrent update synthesis for regular policies via Petri games (2022). https://doi.org/10.5281/zenodo.6379555

12. Knight, S., Nguyen, H.X., Falkner, N., Bowden, R.A., Roughan, M.: The internet topology zoo. IEEE J. Sel. Areas Commun. **29**(9), 1765–1775 (2011), https://doi.org/10.1109/JSAC.2011.111002

13. Liu, A.X., Meiners, C.R., Torng, E.: TCAM razor: a systematic approach towards minimizing packet classifiers in TCAMs. IEEE/ACM Trans. Netw. **18**(2), 490–500 (2010), http://doi.acm.org/10.1145/1816262.1816274

14. Ludwig, A., Dudycz, S., Rost, M., Schmid, S.: Transiently secure network updates. ACM SIGMETRICS Perform. Eval. Rev. **44**(1), 273–284 (2016)

15. Ludwig, A., Marcinkowski, J., Schmid, S.: Scheduling loop-free network updates: It's good to relax! In: Georgiou, C., Spirakis, P.G. (eds.) Proceedings of the 2015 ACM Symposium on Principles of Distributed Computing, PODC 2015, Donostia-San Sebastián, Spain, 21–23 July 2015. pp. 13–22. ACM (2015). https://doi.org/10.1145/2767386.2767412

16. Ludwig, A., Rost, M., Foucard, D., Schmid, S.: Good network updates for bad packets: waypoint enforcement beyond destination-based routing policies. In: Katz-Bassett, E., Heidemann, J.S., Godfrey, B., Feldmann, A. (eds.) Proceedings of the 13th ACM Workshop on Hot Topics in Networks, HotNets-XIII, Los Angeles, CA, USA, 27–28 October 2014. pp. 15:1–15:7. ACM (2014). https://doi.org/10.1145/2670518.2673873

17. McClurg, J., Hojjat, H., Černý, P., Foster, N.: Efficient synthesis of network updates. SIGPLAN Not. **50**(6), 196–207 (2015). https://doi.org/10.1145/2813885.2737980

18. Murata, T.: Petri nets: properties, analysis and applications. Proc. IEEE **77**(4), 541–580 (1989)

19. Pereíni, P., Kuzniar, M., Canini, M., Kostić, D.: ESPRES: transparent SDN update scheduling. In: Proceedings of the Third Workshop on Hot Topics in Software Defined Networking, pp. 73–78. HotSDN 2014, Association for Computing Machinery, New York, NY, USA (2014).https://doi.org/10.1145/2620728.2620747

20. Reitblatt, M., Foster, N., Rexford, J., Schlesinger, C., Walker, D.: Abstractions for network update. In: Eggert, L., Ott, J., Padmanabhan, V.N., Varghese, G. (eds.) ACM SIGCOMM 2012 Conference, Helsinki, Finland, pp. 323–334. ACM (2012)

21. Schneider, T., Birkner, R., Vanbever, L.: Snowcap: synthesizing network-wide configuration updates. In: Kuipers, F.A., Caesar, M.C. (eds.) ACM SIGCOMM 2021 Conference, Virtual Event, USA, 23–27 August 2021, pp. 33–49. ACM (2021). https://doi.org/10.1145/3452296.3472915
22. Vissicchio, S., Cittadini, L.: FLIP the (flow) table: fast lightweight policy-preserving SDN updates. In: 35th Annual IEEE International Conference on Computer Communications, INFOCOM 2016, San Francisco, CA, USA, 10–14 April 2016, pp. 1–9. IEEE (2016)

Security

Verified Password Generation
from Password Composition Policies

Miguel Grilo[1], João Campos[2], João F. Ferreira[2(✉)], José Bacelar Almeida[3],
and Alexandra Mendes[4]

[1] INESC TEC and IST, University of Lisbon, Lisbon, Portugal
[2] INESC-ID and IST, University of Lisbon, Lisbon, Portugal
joao@joaoff.com
[3] HASLab, INESC TEC and University of Minho, Braga, Portugal
[4] HASLab, INESC TEC and Faculty of Engineering, University of Porto,
Porto, Portugal

Abstract. Password managers (PMs) are important tools that enable
the use of stronger passwords, freeing users from the cognitive burden
of remembering them. Despite this, there are still many users who do
not fully trust PMs. In this paper, we focus on a feature that most PMs
offer that might impact the user's trust, which is the process of generating a random password. We present three of the most commonly
used algorithms and we propose a solution for a formally verified reference implementation of a password generation algorithm. We use Easy-
Crypt to specify and verify our reference implementation. In addition,
we present a proof-of-concept prototype that extends Bitwarden to only
generate compliant passwords, solving a frequent users' frustration with
PMs. This demonstrates that our formally verified component can be
integrated into an existing (and widely used) PM.

Keywords: Password manager · Random password generator ·
Formal verification · Security · EasyCrypt · Jasmin · Interactive
theorem proving · Verified compilation · Bitwarden

1 Introduction

To address many of the existing problems regarding password authentication [16,
22,28], security experts often recommend using password managers (PMs) for
storing and generating strong random passwords. Indeed, a key feature of PMs is
random password generation, since it helps prevent the use of weaker passwords
and password reuse [21]. Moreover, it provides users with a greater sense of
security [1], thus contributing to a wider adoption of PMs.

However, users frequently express concern and disapproval when PMs do
not generate passwords compliant [6,26] with the password composition policies
stipulated by the services they use [12]. Stajano et al. [25] argue that this problem
arises due to very restrictive password composition policies that services usually

© Springer Nature Switzerland AG 2022
M. H. ter Beek and R. Monahan (Eds.): IFM 2022, LNCS 13274, pp. 271–288, 2022.
https://doi.org/10.1007/978-3-031-07727-2_15

have [13]. These policies present a greater challenge to password managers since randomly generated passwords have a higher chance of being non-compliant with more restrictive policies.

This problem leads to frustrated users and can be an obstacle to the adoption of PMs. Therefore, it is important to ensure that the password generation component of a PM is reliable. In particular, it is desirable to guarantee that generated passwords (1) satisfy the requirements specified by the user (or service), and (2) are uniformly sampled from the universe induced by the password policy, thus guaranteeing unpredictability of the password generator. In this paper, we propose a formally verified reference implementation for a Random Password Generator (RPG) that addresses these two points. Our main contributions are:

1. We use EasyCrypt [7] to prove that all the passwords generated by our reference implementation satisfy the given password composition policy and that when the given policy is unsatisfiable, the implementation does not generate any password.
2. We formalize the security property stating that our reference implementation samples the set of passwords according to a uniform distribution, using the game-based approach for cryptographic security proofs [8,24]. This justifies the use of EasyCrypt, since we the need to reason about probability distributions.
3. We extend the open-source PM Bitwarden to (1) read Apple's Password Autofill Rules [5] and to (2) generate passwords using a Jasmin [2] implementation provably equivalent to our reference implementation. This case study is a proof-of-concept that integrates interactive theorem proving (EasyCrypt) and verified compilation (Jasmin) to solve an existing frustration with PMs generating non-compliant passwords. It also demonstrates that our formally verified component can be integrated into an existing (and widely used) PM[1]. Part of this extension was submitted to the Bitwarden team, who accepted it and will merge it into the product after a process of code review.

After reviewing current password generation algorithms in Sect. 2, we present our reference implementation and its verification in Sect. 3. In Sect. 4 we present the end-to-end case study and in Sect. 5 we discuss related work. We conclude the paper in Sect. 6, where we also discuss future work.

2   Current Password Generation Algorithms

In this section we present a brief description of widely-used password generation algorithms. We focus on the password generation algorithms of three PMs: Google Chrome's PM (v89.0.4364.1)[2], Bitwarden (v1.47.1)[3], and KeePass (v2.46)[4]. These were chosen because they are widely used and open-source, which allows us to access their source code and study them in detail.

---

[1] https://github.com/passcert-project/pw_generator_server.
[2] https://source.chromium.org/chromium/chromium/src/+/master:components.
[3] https://github.com/bitwarden.
[4] https://github.com/dlech/KeePass2.x.

2.1 Password Composition Policies

In general, PMs allow users to define password composition policies that the generated passwords must satisfy. These policies define the structure of the password, including its length and the different character classes that may be used. These policies are used to restrict the space of user-created passwords, thus precluding some that are easily guessed. Table 1 shows the policies that can be specified in the studied PMs. In the second row, the Alphabetic set in Chrome is the union of Lowercase Letters and Uppercase Letters. The set of Special Characters in Chrome and Bitwarden is {- _ . : !}, while in KeePass it is {! " # $ % & ' * + , . / : ; = ? @ \^ |}. The Brackets set in KeePass is {( ) { } [ ] ⟨⟩}. The Space, Minus, and Underline are the single element sets {␣}, {-}, and {_}, respectively.

Table 1. Available policy options a user can define.

	Chrome	Bitwarden	KeePass
Password length	1–200	5–128	1–30000
Available sets	Lowercase Letters Uppercase Letters Alphabetic Numbers Special Characters	Lowercase Letters Uppercase Letters Numbers Special Characters	Lowercase Letters Uppercase Letters Numbers Special Characters Brackets Space Minus Underline
Minimum and maximum occurrences of characters per set	Yes	Yes. Can only define minimum	No
Exclude similar characters	Yes {l o I O 0 1}	Yes {l I O 0 1}	Yes {l I O 0 1 |}
Define by hand a character set	No	No	Yes
Define by hand a character set to be excluded	No	No	Yes
Remove duplicates	No	No	Yes

2.2 Random Password Generation

The main idea of the surveyed algorithms is to generate random characters from the different character sets until the password length is fulfilled, taking also into consideration the minimum and maximum occurrences of characters per set. Chrome's algorithm starts by randomly generating characters from the sets which have the minimum number of occurrences defined. Then, it generates characters from the union of all sets which have not already reached their maximum number of occurrences. Lastly, it generates a permutation on the characters of the string, resulting in a random generated password. Bitwarden's algorithm is similar, but it makes the permutation before generating the characters. For example, it starts by creating a string like '*llunl*' to express that the first two characters are lowercase letters, followed by an uppercase letter, then a number, and finally a lowercase letter. Only then it generates the characters from the respective sets. KeePass does not support defining the minimum and maximum occurrences of characters per set, so the algorithm just randomly generates characters from the union of the sets defined in the policy.

String Permutation. Given the need to generate a random permutation of the characters of a string, Bitwarden and Chrome both implement an algorithm to do so. The basic idea for both PMs is the same, which is to randomly choose one character from the original string for each position of the new string.

Random Number Generator. The RPG needs to have an implementation of a Random Number Generator (RNG) that generates random numbers within a range of values. Chrome and KeePass use similar RNGs that generate numbers from 0 to an input *range*. Bitwarden's RNG allows generating numbers from an arbitrary minimum value up to an arbitrary maximum value, but it can trivially be reduced to the former approach. The main idea of these RNGs is (1) to rely on a random byte generator, (2) to perform some form of rejection sampling to ensure uniformly distributed values up to a given bound, and (3) finally reducing it to the required range.

The three PMs adopt different approaches regarding the source of random bytes: Chrome uses system calls depending on the operating system it is running, Bitwarden uses the NodeJS *randomBytes()* method, while KeePass defines its own random bytes generator based on ChaCha20. Because of these different strategies, *in this work we choose not to address the pseudo-random nature of the random byte generator—instead, we assume the existence of a mechanism allowing to sample bytes according to an uniform distribution*. Specifically, we assume an operation that uniformly samples 64-bit words, and then reason on the remaining steps towards the construction of an arbitrary integer range RNG.

3 Verified Password Generation

In this section, we present our reference implementation and the properties that we formally prove. We separate the specifications into an abstract overview, followed by a concrete one in EasyCrypt.

3.1 Reference Implementation

Abstract Overview. Based on the information presented in Sect. 2, we propose a reference implementation for an RPG which offers the following policy adjustments: (1) the user can define the password length (1–200); (2) the user can choose which sets to use (from Lowercase Letters, Uppercase Letters, Numbers, and Special Characters); (3) the user can define the minimum and maximum occurrences of characters per set. The restriction on the maximum length is the same as in Chrome's algorithm (also, we argue that 200 is a reasonable limit, since that arbitrary passwords with at least 16 characters seem to be hard to guess and considered secure [23]).

The pseudo-code of the proposed reference implementation is shown in Algorithm 1. The entry point is the procedure GENERATEPASSWORD, which receives as input a password composition *policy* and, if it is satisfiable, a password is generated and returned. Otherwise, a password is not generated and *null* is returned. The policy is satisfiable if the defined *length* is in the interval [1, 200], if all *min* values are non-negative, if all *max* values are greater or equal to the corresponding *min* value, if the sum of all *min* values is less or equal to *length*, and if the sum of all *max* values is greater or equal to *length*. If any of these conditions is not true, then no password is able to satisfy the policy.

To output a random generated password, the algorithm first randomly generates characters from the sets that have a *min* value greater than 0, and appends them to the *password* (initially an empty string). Then, it randomly generates characters from the union of all sets which have fewer occurrences of characters in *password* than their *max* value defined in the policy until the size of *password* becomes equal to the length defined in the policy. Finally, it generates a random permutation of the string, and returns it.

EasyCrypt Implementation. EasyCrypt [7] is an interactive framework for verifying the security of cryptographic constructions and protocols using a game-based approach [8,24]. EasyCrypt implements program logics for proving properties of imperative programs. Its main logics are Hoare Logic and Relational Hoare Logic. Relational Hoare Logic is essential in EasyCrypt, because it provides the ability to establish relations between programs, and how they affect memory values, which is fundamental in the game-based approach. Notice that we do not consider any cryptographic assumption—our use of EasyCrypt is rather justified on the need to reason about probability distributions (e.g. in reasoning on the RNG procedure, as explained above), alongside with more standard Hoare Logic reasoning used for proving correctness assertions.

To model our reference implementation in EasyCrypt, we need to be more precise regarding the types and methods of the algorithm. Figure 1 shows the definitions of the types used to reason about password generation. Instances of type **char** are integers (which can be directly mapped to the corresponding ASCII character), and both the types **password** and **charSet** are lists of **chars**. The type **policy** is a record type, with the necessary fields to specify a password composition policy. All this information is in a repository in GitHub[5], as well as some other previously explained definitions (e.g., satisfiability of a *policy*), theorems, and properties about these types.

---

[5] https://github.com/passcert-project/random-password-generator/blob/main/EC/
PasswordGenerationTh.eca.

Regarding the methods, it is easy to see how the abstract version of the reference implementation maps to the EasyCrypt implementation[6]. The main difference is when defining the *unionSet*. In the abstract implementation, we just say that this variable is the union of all sets such that their *max* values are greater than 0. In EasyCrypt we have the method `define_union_set` which implements this idea. To simplify the proofs, instead of decrementing the *max* value of a set after sampling a character from it, our algorithm has some extra variables (e.g., `lowercaseAvailable` for the Lowercase Set) which say how many characters we can still sample from the respective set. The method `define_union_set` receives these variables as arguments, and defines the union of the sets which we can still sample characters from.

```
type char = int.
type password = char list.
type charSet = char list.
type policy = {
  length : int;
  lowercaseMin : int;
  lowercaseMax : int;
  uppercaseMin : int;
  uppercaseMax : int;
  numbersMin : int;
  numbersMax : int;
  specialMin : int;
  specialMax : int
}.
```

Fig. 1. Type definitions

3.2   Formal Proofs

In this section we present the two main properties to be proved about our RPG: functional correctness and security.

Functional Correctness (Abstract). *We say that an RPG is functionally correct if generated passwords satisfy the input policy. This property guarantees that users will always get an output according to their expectations.*

We follow the standard approach of expressing correctness of the scheme by a probabilistic experiment that checks if the specification is fulfilled. Figure 2 shows the *Correctness* experiment, which is parameterized by an RPG implementation that, for any policy, outputs *true* if the RPG behaves according to the specification. Specifically, if the input policy is satisfiable, it checks if the password satisfies that policy. Otherwise, it returns whether it is equal to *None*. To simplify the reasoning around this property, when the policy is satisfiable, one can separate the proof into two steps: first we prove that the length defined in the policy is satisfied, and then

---

Correctness^{RPG}(*policy*)

---

if *policy* is *satisfiable*

    pwd ← *RPG*.generate_password(*policy*)

    return satisfiesPolicy(*policy*, *pwd*)

else

    return isNone(*pwd*)

fi

Fig. 2. Correctness experiment (abstract)

---

[6] https://github.com/passcert-project/random-password-generator/blob/main/EC/passCertRPG_ref.ec.

Algorithm 1. RPG Reference Implementation

1: **procedure** GENERATEPASSWORD($policy$)
2:      **if** $policy$ is $satisfiable$ **then**
3:          $pwLength \leftarrow policy.pwLength$
4:          $charSets \leftarrow policy.charSets$
5:          $password \leftarrow \varepsilon$
6:          **for all** $set \in charSets$ **do**
7:             **for** $i = 1, 2, \ldots, set.min$ **do**
8:                $char \leftarrow$ RANDOMCHARGENERATOR(set)
9:                $password \leftarrow password||char$
10:            **end for**
11:         **end for**
12:         **while** $len(password) < pwLength$ **do**
13:            $unionSet \leftarrow \bigcup_{set \in charSets} set$ such that $set.max > 0$
14:            $char \leftarrow$ RANDOMCHARGENERATOR($unionSet$)
15:            $password \leftarrow password||char$
16:         **end while**
17:         $password \leftarrow$ PERMUTATION($password$)
18:         **return** $password$
19:      **else**
20:         **return** $null$
21:      **end if**
22: **end procedure**
23:
24: **procedure** RANDOMCHARGENERATOR(set)
25:      $choice \leftarrow RNG(set.size)$
26:      $set.max \leftarrow set.max - 1$
27:      **return** $choice$
28: **end procedure**
29:
30: **procedure** PERMUTATION($string$)
31:      **for** $i = len(string) - 1, \ldots, 0$ **do**
32:         $j \leftarrow RNG(i)$
33:         $string[i], string[j] \leftarrow string[j], string[i]$
34:      **end for**
35:      **return** $string$
36: **end procedure**
37:
38: **procedure** RNG($range$)
39:      $maxValue \leftarrow (uint64.maxValue/range) * range - 1$
40:      **do**
41:         $value \leftarrow$ (uint64) GenerateRandomBytes
42:      **while** $value > maxValue$
43:      **return** $value$ mod $range$
44: **end procedure**

---

we prove that the different bounds of minimum and maximum occurrences per set are also satisfied.

Functional Correctness (EasyCrypt). In EasyCrypt, the correctness experiment is modelled as the module Correctness, shown in Fig. 3. It is parameterized by a password generator implementation (being RPG_T its signature), and has a single method main encoding the experiment. We note the use of password option for the output of the generate_password method, which extends the password type with the extra element None – is_some and is_none are predicates that query the constructor used in an optional value, and oget extracts a password from it (if available). The experiment simply executes the RPG and, depending on the satisfiability of the policy, either checks if the generated password satisfies it, or if it is equal to None. The EasyCrypt code is available online[7],[8].

```
module Correctness(RPG : RPG_T) = {
  proc main(policy:policy) : bool = {
    var pw : password option;
    var satisfied : bool;

    pw <@ RPG.generate_password(policy);
    if(satisfiablePolicy policy) {
      satisfied <- is_some pw /\ satisfiesPolicy policy (oget pw);
    }
    else {
      satisfied <- is_none pw;
    }

    return satisfied;
  }
}.
```

Fig. 3. Correctness procedure (Easycrypt)

The correctness property can be expressed in EasyCrypt as follows:

```
lemma rpg_correctness :
  Pr[Correctness(RPGRef).main : true ==> res] = 1%r.
```

[7] https://github.com/passcert-project/random-password-generator/blob/main/EC/passCertRPG_ref.ec.

[8] https://github.com/passcert-project/random-password-generator/blob/main/EC/RPGTh.eca.

It states that, running the correctness experiment (`main` method) of the
`Correctness` module instantiated with our RPG reference implementation, produces the output *true* with probability 1 (without any constraint on input policy). The proof of this lemma amounts essentially to prove termination of the
`main` method, while also proving that this method always returns *true*, independently on the policy given as input. These two properties can be expressed by
the two following lemmas, respectively:

```
lemma c_lossless :
    islossless Correctness(RPGRef).main.


lemma c_correct p:
    hoare[Correctness(RPGRef).main : policy = p ==> res].
```

The `islossless` assertion states that `Correctness(RPGRef).main` terminates with probability 1 for any input. Notice that this is indeed non-trivial,
as our RPG performs rejection sampling. Hence, we are not able to prove a
concrete bound for the number of iterations for the loop in the `RNG` procedure
(Algorithm 1), but we nevertheless establish that it eventually terminates (actually, in expected constant time).

The second lemma is an Hoare triple. In EasyCrypt an Hoare triple is written as `hoare [Command : Precondition ==> Postcondition]`. To prove this
Hoare triple, we need to prove that the `main` method outputs a password that
satisfies the input policy, in case it is satisfiable, and `None` if it is not satisfiable.
These ideas can be expressed with the following lemmas:

```
lemma rpg_correctness_sat_pcp_hl (p:policy) :
  hoare [ RPGRef.generate_password : policy = p /\
          satisfiablePolicy p
    ==>
          is_some res /\ satisfiesLength p (oget res)
                      /\ satisfiesBounds p (oget res)
      ].
```

and

```
lemma rpg_correctness_unsat_pcp_hl (p:policy) :
  hoare [ RPGRef.generate_password : policy = p /\
          !(satisfiablePolicy p)
    ==>
          res = None
      ].
```

The second lemma is trivial to prove, because the first thing our RPG implementation does is to check if the input policy is satisfiable. If it is not, our RPG
outputs `None`. As mentioned in Sect. 3.2, the first lemma can be proved by separately reasoning about the generated password satisfying the length defined in
the policy, and then about the different set bounds. This means that we should
first prove the lemmas:

```
lemma rpg_correctness_length_hl (p:policy) :
  hoare [ RPGRef.generate_password : policy = p /\
        satisfiablePolicy p
    ==>
        is_some res /\ satisfiesLength p (oget res)
        ].
```

and

```
lemma rpg_correctness_bounds_hl (p:policy) :
  hoare [ RPGRef.generate_password : policy = p /\
        satisfiablePolicy p
    ==>
        is_some res /\ satisfiesBounds p (oget res)
        ].
```

It is easy to see that we can combine these two lemmas to prove the lemma `rpg_correctness_sat_pcp_hl` since we can use `hoare [ C : P ==> Q1]` and `hoare [ C : P ==> Q2]`, to conclude `hoare [ C : P ==> Q1 /\ Q2]`. Using `rpg_correctness_sat_pcp_hl` and `rpg_correctness_unsat_pcp_hl`, we can prove the lemma `c_correct` using Hoare logic rules. With the lemmas `c_lossless` and `c_lossless` proved, we can combine them to finally prove our main lemma `rpg_correctness`, which ensures that our RPG implementation is correct.

Security (Abstract). *We say that an RPG is secure if, given any policy, the generated password has the same probability of being generated as any other possible password that satisfies that policy. In other words, the* `generate_password` *method samples the set of passwords that satisfy the policy according to a uniform distribution.* To prove this property we can use the game-based approach for cryptographic security proofs [8,24].

As shown abstractly in Fig. 4, we create a module called IdealRPG which, in case it receives as input a satisfiable policy, outputs a password sampled from the subset of passwords that satisfy the policy, according to a uniform distribution over that subset (here, sampling is denoted by the operator ←$).

If the policy is not satisfiable, it outputs *None*. In order to consider our implementation secure, we must show that any program (e.g., attacker) that has oracle access to the Ideal-RPG and our RPG can not distinguish whether it is interacting with one or the other.

To achieve this, we can use probabilistic relational Hoare Logic (pRHL) to show that

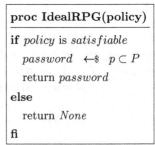

Fig. 4. Ideal RPG. p is the subset of the set of all possible passwords P that satisfy the given policy.

both modules' *generate_password* methods produce the same result (they have the same distribution over their output, given any input). We can avoid directly reasoning about the indistinguishability between these two modules, since their implementations are significantly different. By using the game-based approach, we can implement intermediate modules that are more closely related, thus breaking the proof into smaller steps that are easier to justify.

Security (EasyCrypt). To construct the IdealRPG module, we start by axiomatizing uniform distributions over the type of *passwords*:

```
op dpassword : password distr.
axiom dpassword_ll : is_lossless dpassword.
axiom dpassword_uni : is_uniform dpassword.
axiom dpassword_supp : forall p, p \in dpassword => validPassword p.
```

The operator *dpassword* is the declared distribution over the type *password*. The axioms defined are important properties about this distribution: (1) lossless means that it is a proper distribution (its probability mass function sums to one); (2) uniform means that all elements in its support have the same mass; (3) the support of the distribution is the set of all valid passwords (length and admissible chars). Here, validPassword p is true if p contains only valid characters (lowercase, uppercase, digits, and allowed symbols) and if its length is at most 200. This distribution can be used to construct the IdealRPG module that meets the requirements for our RPG security definition.

```
module IdealRPG = {
  proc generate_password(policy:policy) = {
    var pw;
    var out;
    if(satisfiablePolicy policy) {
      pw <$ dpassword \ (fun pass => !(satisfiesPolicy(policy pass)));
      out <- Some pw;
    } else {
      out <- None;
    }
    return out;
  }
}.
```

In this module, a password is sampled if the policy is satisfiable, otherwise outputs *None*. The sampling makes use of the axiomatized distribution over passwords, restricting its support by removing the passwords that do not satisfy the policy. Given these definitions, we can write the lemma that we need to prove to consider our RPG secure:

```
lemma rpg_security :
  equiv [IdealRPG.generate_password ~ RPGRef.generate_password :
    ={policy} ==> ={res} ].
```

This is a pRHL judgement which means that for all memories $m1$ and $m2$ (sets of variables of IdealRPG and RPGRef, respectively), if $= \{policy\}$ holds (the input *policy* has the same value in both memories), then the distribution on memories $dm1$ and $dm2$, obtained by running the respective methods from the initial memory, satisfy $= \{res\}$ (*res*, the output value, has the same mass in both distributions). If we prove this lemma for our RPG reference implementation, we prove that these methods produce the same distributions over their output, hence establishing security of the RPG reference implementation.

General Steps to Prove Security. To prove the security lemma stated above, we need to establish that the induced distribution from the execution of Real-RPG is uniform among all passwords satisfying the policy. It requires fairly detailed reasoning on the distribution level in EasyCrypt. The mechanised proof is work in progress; here, we present a proof sketch. The general structure of the argument follows the structure of Algorithm 1: (1) It starts by generating a password where each character class prescribed in the policy is placed in a specific position (what we have called policy-normalised password); (2) It randomly shuffles the password. The result follows from arguing that policy-normalised passwords are sampled according to a uniform distribution, and that the final shuffle allows to reach any possible password satisfying the policy. In the course of the formalisation of the above points, auxiliary results such as the correctness of the well-known probabilistic algorithm of rejection sampling (procedure RNG) and the *Fisher-Yates shuffle* algorithm (procedure PERMUTATION) have to be tackled.

4   Case Study: From Apple Password Rules to Verified Password Generation in Bitwarden

This section describes a proof-of-concept prototype that integrates a Jasmin [2] implementation provably equivalent to our reference implementation into a widely-used PM. In particular, we extend Bitwarden to (1) read Apple's Password Autofill Rules [5], which are password composition policies in a format defined by Apple, and (2) to generate compliant passwords using our Jasmin implementation.

The proof-of-concept offers a solution to the common problem of users being concerned and disappointed by the fact that passwords generated by the PM are often not compliant with the password composition policies stipulated by the websites they use [12]. One way to solve this problem is to, first, provide a domain specific language (DSL) that services can use to specify their required password composition policies, and, second, ensure that PMs use the DSL specifications in their password generation algorithms. There have been some proposals for this: Stajano et al. proposed the creation of HTML semantic labels [25] and Horsch et al. proposed the Password Policy Markup Language [18]. Oesch and Ruoti [20] recently reinforced this idea, suggesting that this type of annotations could help the users with using PMs, as well as increase the accuracy of the password

```
<rule> ::= (<required> | <allowed> | <length_reqs> | <max_consecutive>)*
<required> ::= "required: " <list_ids_classes> "; "
<allowed> ::= "allowed: " <list_ids_classes> "; "
<length_reqs> ::= "minlength: " <non_negative_integer> "; "
                | "maxlength: " <non_negative_integer> "; "
<max_consecutive> ::= "max-consecutive: " <non_negative_integer> "; "
<id_class> ::= (<identifier> | <character_class>)
<list_ids_classes> ::= <id_class> | <id_class> ", " <list_ids_classes>
<identifier> ::= "lower" | "upper" | "digits" | "special"
                | "ascii-printable" | "unicode"
<character_class> ::= "[" (<upper> | <lower> | <special> | <digit>)+ "]"
```

Fig. 5. Grammar used by Apple's password autofill rules.

generator. While investigating a way to achieve this with modern PMs, we found that Apple has also developed a DSL to express Password Autofill Rules [5]. The idea is to add a specification to the HTML code, in the form of annotations.

4.1 Apple's Password Autofill Rules

Apple's DSL is based on five properties—*required, allowed, max-consecutive, minlength, and maxlength*—and some identifiers that describe character classes—*upper, lower, digits, special, ascii-printable, and unicode*. These are the elements that allow the description of the password rules. It is also possible to specify a custom set of characters by surrounding it with square brackets (e.g., *[abcd]* denotes the lowercase letters from *a* to *d*). For example, to require a password with at least eight characters consisting of a mix of uppercase and lowercase letters, and at least one number, the following rule can be used:

```
required: upper; required: lower; required: digit; minlength: 8;
```

A more formal description of the grammar is shown in Fig. 5.

Properties Description. The *required* property is used when the restrictions must be followed by all generated passwords. The *allowed* property is used to specify a subset of allowed characters, i.e., it is used when a password is permitted to have a given character class, but it is not mandatory. If *allowed* is not included in the rule, all the *required* characters are permitted. If both properties are specified, the subspace of all *required* and *allowed* is permitted. If neither is specified, every ASCII character is permitted. The *max-consecutive* property represents the maximum length of a run of consecutive identical characters that can be present in the generated password, e.g., the sequence *aah* would be possible with *max-consecutive: 2*, but *aaah* would not. If multiple *max-consecutive* properties are specified, the value considered will be the minimum of them all. The *minlength* and *maxlength* properties denote the minimum and maximum number of characters, respectively, that a password can have to be accepted.

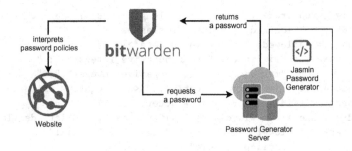

Fig. 6. Overview of proof-of-concept prototype

Both numbers need to be greater than 0 and ***minlength*** has to be at most ***maxlength***; otherwise, the default length of the PM will be used.

Identifiers. Next to the *allowed* or *required* properties, we can use any of the default ***identifiers***, which describe *conventional* character classes. The identifier ***upper*** describes the character class that includes all uppercase letters, i.e., *[A–Z]*; the identifier ***lower*** describes the character class that includes all lowercase letters, i.e., *[a–z]*; the ***digits*** identifier describes the character class that includes all digits, i.e., *[0–9]*; and the ***special*** identifier describes the character class that includes - ˜!@#$%^&*_+=´|(){}[:;"'<>,.?] and ＿. The identifiers ***ascii-printable*** and ***unicode*** describe the character classes that include all ASCII printable characters and all the unicode characters, respectively. Additionally, users of the DSL can choose to describe their custom character classes, e.g., *[aeiou]* is the character class that contains all the vowels, in lowercase.

4.2   Jasmin Password Generator

We coded our reference implementation in Jasmin [2], a framework for developing high-speed and high-assurance cryptographic software. The Jasmin programming language combines high-level and low-level constructs while guaranteeing verifiability of memory safety and constant-time security. The compiler transforms Jasmin programs into assembly, while preserving behavior, safety, and constant-time security of the source code. The Jasmin compiler is formally verified for correctness. We chose Jasmin because it is possible to automatically generate an EasyCrypt model from a Jasmin program. This ensures that when reasoning about the model, we are reasoning about the correspondent Jasmin program, making it possible to formally establish an equivalence between the Jasmin implementation and our reference implementation.

4.3   Integration with Bitwarden

An overview of our integration of the Jasmin password generator with the Bitwarden browser extension is shown in Fig. 6. We first extended Bitwarden to interpret Apple's Password Autofill Rules. We start by searching in the entire DOM for the HTML attribute *passwordrules*. When found, we parse its value. For this we used the official Apple's Javascript parser[9]. We then pass this information to the password generator component, using the browser's native messaging API. We also replaced the default password generator with our Jasmin password generator. Since in the context of the browser extension it is not possible to directly run local processes, we exposed our password generator as a RESTful service: the extension sends a POST request, with the body of the request containing the required password policy.

To demonstrate the impact of our proof-of-concept, we generated 20 test files, each one containing 1000 randomly generated passwords: 10 of these files were generated by Bitwarden's generator and the other 10 were generated by our Jasmin generator. Bitwarden's generator used its default settings—14-character password with uppercase characters, lowercase characters, and numbers. We used the following policy, which is actually used by British government services, according to a community-updated file in Apple's repo[10]:

```
minlength: 10; required: lower; required: upper; required: digit;
required: special;
```

We checked if the passwords generated by Bitwarden satisfy this policy. All passwords failed this test, since Bitwarden's default settings do not include symbols. This is an instance of the problem discussed above, regarding users' frustration with the generation of non-compliant passwords. We then used the same approach with our Jasmin generator and found that all passwords generated satisfy the policy.

Since our extension improves the usability of Bitwarden, we submitted the code that parses the password rules and passes them to the password generator to the Bitwarden team, who has internally approved our extension and will go through a code review process to get it ready to be merged[11].

5   Related Work

To the best of our knowledge, our work is the first to address formal verification of random password generators[12]. However, the area of formal verification of security and cryptographic software has attracted much interest in recent years. Regarding implementation correctness, HACL* [27] is a high-assurance cryptographic C library that has been formally verified against a readable mathematical specification in F*. Similarly, FiatCrypto [14] proposes a framework

---

[9] https://github.com/apple/password-manager-resources/blob/main/tools/ PasswordRulesParser.js.

[10] https://github.com/apple/password-manager-resources/blob/main/quirks/ password-rules.json.

[11] https://github.com/bitwarden/browser/pull/2047#issuecomment-978846599.

[12] A search on Google Scholar shows one relevant paper [17], which is the abstract of an informal talk delivered by our team.

written in Coq for deriving correct-by-construction C code. It has been deployed in Google's BoringSSL library which is used by Chrome and Android. Targeting directly assembly, Vale [9] builds on Microsoft's Dafny and Z3 SMT prover to verify annotated assembly code. Finally, the Jasmin framework [2], that we have adopted in our development, has been previously used to produce highly-efficient certified executable code [3], combining it with security proofs in an unified framework [4].

Regarding other uses of formal verification in the domain of password security, there is previous work on creating certified password composition policy enforcement software, implemented from within the Coq proof assistant and extracted to Haskell [15]. The extracted Haskell is then compiled into a pluggable authentication module readily usable from a real Linux system. Johnson et al. [19] also used Coq to model password composition policies and verify the immunity or vulnerability of 14 password composition policies to the password guessing attacks utilised by the Mirai and Conficker botnet worms. The Pass-Cert project[13] is exploring formal verification applied to password managers and aims to determine whether formal verification can increase users' confidence in PMs and thus increase their adoption [10,11].

6 Conclusion

We propose a formally verified reference implementation for a Random Password Generator. We prove that, given a password composition policy, generated passwords are compliant, and we formalize the property that the generator samples the set of passwords according to a uniform distribution. In addition, we present a proof-of-concept prototype that solves the identified frustration with PMs of generating non-compliant passwords and demonstrates that our formally verified component can be integrated into a widely used PM.

As future work, we plan to fully formalize the proof of security informally discussed in Sect. 3.2 and to further develop the proof-of-concept prototype so that other browser-based PMs can benefit from it. We might also add support for further password composition policies (e.g. policies that require characters from at least three different classes). While generally speaking strict password composition policies are preferable, these can still generate easily guessed passwords (e.g., a policy that enforces the use of all character classes may generate the easily guessed password "P@ssw0rd") [23]. So, it might also be interesting to formalize properties regarding password strength, which would guarantee that our RPG would only generate strong passwords (according to some metric).

Acknowledgments. This work was partially funded by the PassCert project, a CMU Portugal Exploratory Project funded by Fundação para a Ciência e Tecnologia (FCT), with reference CMU/TIC/0006/2019 and supported by national funds through FCT under project UIDB/50021/2020.

---

[13] PassCert project: https://passcert-project.github.io.

References

1. Alkaldi, N., Renaud, K.: Why do people adopt, or reject, smartphone password managers? In: 1st European Workshop on Usable Security-EuroUSEC 2016 (2016)
2. Almeida, J.B., et al.: Jasmin: high-assurance and high-speed cryptography. In: Proceedings of the 2017 ACM SIGSAC Conference on Computer and Communications Security, pp. 1807–1823 (2017)
3. Almeida, J.B., et al.: The last mile: high-assurance and high-speed cryptographic implementations. In: 2020 IEEE Symposium on Security and Privacy (SP) (2020)
4. Almeida, J.B., et al.: Machine-checked proofs for cryptographic standards: indifferentiability of sponge and secure high-assurance implementations of SHA-3. In: Proceedings of the 2019 ACM SIGSAC Conference on Computer and Communications Security (2019)
5. Apple. Customizing Password AutoFill Rules (2021). https://developer.apple.com/documentation/security/password_autofill/customizing_password_autofill_rules. Accessed 31 July 2021
6. Apple. Web sites won't accept Safari generated strong passwords due to dashes or other criteria (2021). https://discussions.apple.com/thread/251341081. Accessed 26 Oct 2021
7. Barthe, G., Dupressoir, F., Grégoire, B., Kunz, C., Schmidt, B., Strub, P.-Y.: EasyCrypt: a tutorial. In: Aldini, A., Lopez, J., Martinelli, F. (eds.) FOSAD 2012-2013. LNCS, vol. 8604, pp. 146–166. Springer, Cham (2014). https://doi.org/10.1007/978-3-319-10082-1_6
8. Bellare, M., Rogaway, P.: Code-based game-playing proofs and the security of triple encryption. IACR Cryptology ePrint Archive 2004/331 (2004)
9. Bond, B., et al.: Vale: verifying high-performance cryptographic assembly code. In: 26th USENIX Security Symposium, pp. 917–934 (2017)
10. Carreira, C., Ferreira, J.F., Mendes, A.: Towards improving the usability of password managers. In: INFORUM (2021)
11. Carreira, C., Ferreira, J.F., Mendes, A., Christin, N.: Exploring usable security to improve the impact of formal verification: a research agenda. In: First Workshop on Applicable Formal Methods (Co-Located with Formal Methods 2021) (2021)
12. Chiasson, S., van Oorschot, P.C., Biddle, R.: A usability study and critique of two password managers. In: USENIX Security Symposium, vol. 15, pp. 1–16 (2006)
13. EA. Password Does Not Meet Requirements (2021). https://web.archive.org/web/20210817105229/answers.ea.com/t5/EA-General-Questions/quot-Password-Does-Not-Meet-Requirements-quot/td-p/5744758. Accessed 26 Oct 2021
14. Erbsen, A., Philipoom, J., Gross, J., Sloan, R., Chlipala, A.: Simple high-level code for cryptographic arithmetic - with proofs, without compromises. In: 2019 IEEE Symposium on Security and Privacy, SP 2019, pp. 1202–1219. IEEE (2019)
15. Ferreira, J.F., Johnson, S.A., Mendes, A., Brooke, P.J.: Certified password quality. In: Polikarpova, N., Schneider, S. (eds.) IFM 2017. LNCS, vol. 10510, pp. 407–421. Springer, Cham (2017). https://doi.org/10.1007/978-3-319-66845-1_27
16. Florencio, D., Herley, C.: A large-scale study of web password habits. In: Proceedings of the 16th International Conference on World Wide Web, pp. 657–666 (2007)
17. Grilo, M., Ferreira, J.F., Almeida, J.B.: Towards formal verification of password generation algorithms used in password managers. arXiv preprint arXiv:2106.03626 (2021)

18. Horsch, M., Schlipf, M., Braun, J., Buchmann, J.: Password requirements markup language. In: Liu, J.K., Steinfeld, R. (eds.) ACISP 2016. LNCS, vol. 9722, pp. 426–439. Springer, Cham (2016). https://doi.org/10.1007/978-3-319-40253-6_26
19. Johnson, S., Ferreira, J.F., Mendes, A., Cordry, J.: Skeptic: automatic, justified and privacy-preserving password composition policy selection. In: Proceedings of the 15th ACM Asia Conference on Computer and Communications Security, pp. 101–115 (2020)
20. Oesch, S., Ruoti, S.: That was then, this is now: a security evaluation of password generation, storage, and autofill in browser-based password managers. In: USENIX Security Symposium (2020)
21. Pearman, S., Zhang, S.A., Bauer, L., Christin, N., Cranor, L.F.: Why people (don't) use password managers effectively. In: Fifteenth Symposium on Usable Privacy and Security (SOUPS 2019), pp. 319–338. USENIX Association, Santa Clara (2019)
22. Pereira, D., Ferreira, J.F., Mendes, A.: Evaluating the accuracy of password strength meters using off-the-shelf guessing attacks. In: 2020 IEEE International Symposium on Software Reliability Engineering Workshops (ISSREW), pp. 237–242. IEEE (2020)
23. Shay, R., et al.: Designing password policies for strength and usability. ACM Trans. Inf. Syst. Secur. (TISSEC) 18(4), 1–34 (2016)
24. Shoup, V.: Sequences of games: a tool for taming complexity in security proofs. IACR Cryptology ePrint Archive 2004/332 (2004)
25. Stajano, F., Spencer, M., Jenkinson, G., Stafford-Fraser, Q.: Password-manager friendly (PMF): semantic annotations to improve the effectiveness of password managers. In: Mjølsnes, S.F. (ed.) PASSWORDS 2014. LNCS, vol. 9393, pp. 61–73. Springer, Cham (2015). https://doi.org/10.1007/978-3-319-24192-0_4
26. TechNet. Can't create local user "Password does not meet password policy requirements" - but it does (2021). https://web.archive.org/web/20211026082725/. https://social.technet.microsoft.com/Forums/en-US/12b06881-ea1a-403d-aafb-99bbe7d4d1b0/cant-create-local-user-quotpassword-does-not-meet-password-policy-requirementsquot-but-it?forum=win10itprosecurity. Accessed 26 Oct 2021
27. Zinzindohoué, J.-K., Bhargavan, K., Protzenko, J., Beurdouche, B.: HACL*: a verified modern cryptographic library. In: Proceedings of the 2017 ACM SIGSAC Conference on Computer and Communications Security, CCS 2017, pp. 1789–1806. Association for Computing Machinery, New York (2017). ISBN: 9781450349468
28. Zuo, C., Lin, Z., Zhang, Y.: Why does your data leak? Uncovering the data leakage in cloud from mobile apps. In: 2019 IEEE Symposium on Security and Privacy (SP). IEEE (2019)

A Policy Language to Capture Compliance of Data Protection Requirements

Chinmayi Prabhu Baramashetru$^{(\boxtimes)}$, Silvia Lizeth Tapia Tarifa ,
Olaf Owe , and Nils Gruschka

Department of Informatics, University of Oslo, Oslo, Norway
{cpbarama,sltarifa,olaf,nilsgrus}@ifi.uio.no

Abstract. From the very outset of the digital era, the protection of personal data against unauthorized usage and distribution has been one of the most significant challenges in distributed services. For this reason, new regulations such as the European Union's the General Data Protection Regulation grant users tight control over their data that is handled by service providers. Compliance with such regulations can take expensive refitting of the existing systems and manual work. We propose a formal language that can define properties like informed consent, data subject rights, and the lawfulness to capture data protection requirements. The language is designed to abstract ownership information to make data dependencies explicit. We formalise a notion of policy compliance. This can be useful in service architecture with various actors who necessarily do not trust each other and may have conflicting interests.

1 Introduction

Nowadays, users knowingly or unknowingly provide their personal data to digital systems, e.g., online purchases, social media, surveillance cameras, digital IDs, etc. In data privacy, users are known as data subjects (DS) whose personal data is generally handled by service providers, who are known as data controllers (DC), for purposes beyond the user's vision. There are instances where service providers have traded personal data without explicit consent from the users [19,28]. To protect the human right to privacy, several data protection regulations such as the General Data Protection Regulation (GDPR) [10], California Consumer Privacy Act (CCPA) [23], and Health Insurance Portability and Accountability Act (HIPAA) [7] came into practice to primarily target different audiences. For instance, HIPAA in the United States mainly focuses on organizations, business associations, and their authority towards data handling. In contrast, the GDPR concentrates on end-users (data subjects) and makes it mandatory for organizations to grant the data subject rights such as "right to access" and "right to be forgotten" to endow users with significant control and power over their data. Non-compliance with the GDPR will result in fines up to 4% of annual turnover and there are many instances of severe fines for

ⓒ Springer Nature Switzerland AG 2022
M. H. ter Beek and R. Monahan (Eds.): IFM 2022, LNCS 13274, pp. 289–309, 2022.
https://doi.org/10.1007/978-3-031-07727-2_16

mishandling user's data [33]. Data protection regulations are mainly expressed in generic terms, and do not provide clear evidence of how they should be systematically implemented in distributed environments. Therefore providing useful ways to comply with the data protection requirements is an open research challenge. The situation becomes more critical with existing privacy policies. Users are often overwhelmed with lengthy and unclear privacy policies by the service provider and end up accepting broader consent without actually reading it.

We present a formal language that can capture data protection requirements. We envision using the language in a framework with systematic methods to enforce such requirements. The language can be used by both DSs and DCs to declare their policies. DCs can express their policies to propose the minimum conditions necessary to provide their services to customers. Furthermore, DS can use the same language to express their privacy preferences, can come to a negotiation, and can provide granular consent on data handling procedures. For instance, healthcare systems need user's personal information such as name, address, phone number as a minimum requirement for providing health services and both DSs and DCs should agree on these requirements.

In addition, every entity collecting personal data has to be compliant with legal regulations like the GDPR or the CCPA, where data subject's rights need to be exercised. How to incorporate compliance among stake-holders is an open question. Towards this direction, we define formal compliance checks in our language to make sure all parties with legal processing rights comply with each other. The language is designed to provide flexible granularity of policies, allowing user-centric selection and filtering of information to express preferences and exceptions in their policies. The main benefit of this language is keeping all the stakeholders in line with the current privacy preferences. For instance, data subjects cannot foresee all the possible purposes and entities that might need to use their data while agreeing to privacy policies. Several languages have been proposed in the state of art to address privacy policies. However, in Sect. 8, we discuss some of the advantages and limitations of these approaches. We draw our motivation from various previous results, expectations, and preferences and define a language that is flexible, expressive, and endowed with formal semantics.

Outline. In Sect. 2, we introduce the main legal requirements that we consider in our language. In Sect. 3, we define the language, and in Sect. 4, we define the underlying classification that is used in the language's attributes. In Sect. 5, we define policy compliance for the language. In Sect. 6, we present a proof of concept implementation using Maude [8]. In Sect. 7, we introduce a case study on a health wearable tracker. In Sect. 8, we analyze and compare the related work on privacy policy languages, and in Sect. 9 we conclude the paper.

2   Main Principles of the GDPR

There are currently 99 Articles in the GDPR to ensure data protection across EU members states. However in this section, we detail few principles which serve the sole purpose of the GDPR to ensure data protection by design and default.

Purpose Limitation: Art. 5 Sec 1(b) of the GDPR [10] states purpose limitation as *"Personal data shall be collected for specified, explicit and legitimate purposes and not further processed in a manner that is incompatible with those purposes; ... not be considered to be incompatible with the initial purposes"* This sentence can be interpreted in technical terms as, *purposes for which personal data is collected should be made explicit for Ds's, and data should not be further processed for any other purpose.* According to the purpose limitation, DCs are subjected to use personal data only for specific and well-defined purposes. This principle mainly focuses on imposing restrictions on systems collecting a vast amount of data for explicit and broadly classified purposes. For instance, sensor fusion [22] is a data processing technique that combines and integrates data from different sources, like Fitbit and health records, to infer future health damage. Under such conditions, sensor fusion data processing could use data analytics for purposes that are different from the initial ones.

Similarly, Art. 6 Sec 1(f) of the GDPR [10] states the legitimate reasons for processing data: *"Processing is necessary for the purposes of the legitimate interests pursued by the DC or by a third party, except where such interests are overridden by the interests or fundamental rights and freedoms of the DS's ... "* This statement can be interpreted as *the DC's operating purposes need to be subsumed in the DS's approved purposes.*

Conditions for Consent: Art. 6.1(a) specifies that DS's giving consent for processing his/her data for one or more purposes is vital for lawful processing. Under Art. 7 [10], the GDPR specifies various conditions for consent from DS's. Consent should be obtained freely before processing any form of personal data. The terms and conditions presented to receive consent from DS's should be clear, intelligible, and easy to understand. The GDPR also blueprints that DS's should be able to revoke their consent at any time and DC should facilitate this choice. If we translate this into a technical solution for service-oriented systems, any processing or collection of data should be attached to the respective consent from the users. Once the consent is withdrawn, the data should no longer be used for any processing. According to Art. 7, DC's should have a clear consent that states what kind of data is necessary for the offered services and what kind of data can be optional. In other words, privacy policies on pre-ticked boxes (e.g., third-party data sharing) will no longer be considered legitimate as it is not required to use their services. To comply with this, DC's need to collect consent in a more informed way, where users do not accept their consent on the fly because they want to avoid reading long and ambiguous privacy policies.

Data Subject Rights: The GDPR specifies a set of rights for DS's under Art. 15 – 21 that should be accommodated by any service provider while processing

DS's personal data. Art. 15 remarks that a *"data subject shall have the right to access to the purpose of processing categories of personal data, the recipients to whom personal data is disclosed or transferred, and the period for which the data will be stored."*. However, at the same time, Art.15 and recital 63 allows the DC's to limit the right to access based on conflicts and the freedom of others. Freedom of others focuses on intellectual property rights, privacy rights, and the interests of other DS's. These stipulations motivate to consider the crucial elements in a policy language to bring a fair balance between the interests of DC's and DS's. Regulations also indicate the necessity of fine-grained policies to restore the right to object to any form of processing of personal data at any time.

3   A Policy Language for Main Data Protection Principles

In this section, we present our policy language to meet the objectives of Sect. 2. We first define the attributes considered in our language and clarify why these attributes are vital in determining policies, we later provide its formalization.

Policy Attributes. We consider the following attributes for our language.

Entities. We define entities as identifiable organizations, organizational units or roles in an organization which have or can handle data. For instance, doctor or nurse are entities, but individuals in such categories (e.g., doctor Alice Anderson) are not entities. In this definition, both DCs and DSs can be included as part of the entities. If we have DCs declaring their policy requirements, they can mention DSs in such requirements. In our formalization, entities are classified using a taxonomy to facilitate fine-grained manipulation and to capture preferences and exceptions using selection and filtering of elements in such taxonomy. See Fig. 1 for an example of a graphical representation of an entity taxonomy.

Actions. We define actions as operations that provide fine-grained access of sensitive data along their whole data life-cycle. More specifically, we define the set $A = \{Use, Collect, Transfer, Store, Delete\}$ to capture the possible actions on protected data. Actions are mainly introduced to capture informed consent through system design, e.g., to capture data usage, data collection, and data transfer for specific purposes. These actions can be further refined in terms of read, write, and append accesses, where append only allows the addition of new information without being able to read it. In the future, we plan to express actions using such well-studied read and write accesses.

Purposes. We identify purposes as a key attribute to express constraints while handling sensitive data. Regulations such the GDPR and HIPAA [7] constantly indicate purpose restrictions to be incorporated in data handling. However, most of the frameworks do not give good support to represent purpose within the system design, as required by regulations. We design a language to capture fine-grained purposes using taxonomies (in the same way as we capture entities).

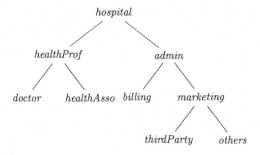

Fig. 1. Example of a tree with name *hcSysProf*, for the attribute entity.

Retention Time. This attribute is included to enforce the right to be forgotten under the GDPR. In our formalization, it is defined as a date in ISO format [15], capturing the date at which that data is no longer available for further manipulation. Currently, we define the retention time as a fixed date. In the future, we plan to include infinite retention time. In our language, retention time, purposes and actions go together to express data handling constrains over time.

Locations. This attribute expresses location constraints, and can be interpreted together with actions e.g., to capture storage location and restrict data migration by actions, i.e., transfer. We aim to capture locations at different granularity by using taxonomies (in the same way as we evaluate entities and purposes).

Policy Language. We now formally define a language to capture policy privacy requirements that we later use for compliance checks. The language uses:

- taxonomies τ to express hierarchical structures organizing elements. The language also defines a function $elem(\tau)$ that returns the elements in the leaves of a given taxonomy τ as a set. We use taxonomies τ_{ent}, τ_{pp}, and τ_{loc} to capture the attributes entity, purpose, and location. See Sect. 4, for further details of the formal definition of taxonomies.
- expressions in a given grammar Ψ to express selection and filtering of elements in a given τ (see Definition 4, in Sect. 4 for the formal syntax of the grammar), where the function $eval(e, \tau) \subseteq elem(\tau)$ returns the intended leaves in τ according to expression e. We use the grammars Ψ_{ent}, Ψ_{pp} and Ψ_{loc} that accept expressions for selecting and filtering elements in τ_{ent}, τ_{pp}, and τ_{loc}, respectively.
- a function $duration(d_i, d_j)$ that returns a natural number representing the number of days between the date values d_i and d_j.

We use the items above to define the language.

Definition 1 (Policy language). *Let us define a policy language as a set of policy entries $\overline{PE}$, where over-bar denotes set, and where each policy entry PE is a tuple (E, A, P, R, L) where the attributes E, A, P, R, L are defined as:*

- *E is an expression in the grammar Ψ_{ent}, such that $eval(E, \tau_{ent}) \subseteq elem(\tau_{ent})$ represents a set of entities in the leaves of τ_{ent}.*

Fig. 2. Example of a tree with name *hcSysPurp*, for the attribute purpose

- $A \subseteq \mathcal{A}$ represents the subset of actions that can be performed over data.
- P is an expression in the grammar Ψ_{pp}, such that $eval(P, \tau_{pp}) \subseteq elem(\tau_{pp})$ represents a set of purposes in the leaves of τ_{pp}.
- R is an expression in the format of a Date, capturing the expiration date for data retention, such that $duration(now, R)$ returns a natural number representing the retention time in days (letting now represent the current date).
- L is an expression in the grammar Ψ_{loc}, such that $eval(L, \tau_{loc}) \subseteq elem(\tau_{loc})$ represents a set of locations in the leaves of τ_{loc}.

We envision for the language to bring transparency between the stakeholders, it can be used by DSs to express their consent and obligations and DCs to declare their requirements for service provision. DSs declare their privacy policies and DCs should include such policies while operating on the user's sensitive data.

Example 1. Taxonomies in Figs. 1 and 2 are graphical representations for the attributes entity and a purpose, respectively. The taxonomy in Fig. 1 is capturing a classification of various professionals in a healthcare system, while the taxonomy in Fig. 2 is capturing a classification for the purposes of data manipulation in the healthcare domain. Assuming a taxonomy of countries, representing locations in the world, we can express a very coarse-grained policy entry for a user Alice as follows: (*hospital*, {*Collect, Store*}, *healthServ*, 21/02/2023, *Europe*), capturing that Alice allows a hospital organization to collect and store data for health care service purposes within Europe until February 21st, 2023. Similarly the more fine-grained policy entry (*healthProf*, {*Use*}, *treatm*, 01/01/2023, *Norway*) is capturing that Alice allows health care professionals to use her data for treatment purposes within Norway until January 1st, 2023.

4   Taxonomies as Tree Structures

To study the expressiveness of the language along with systematic compliance (see Sect. 5), we capture the semantics of expressions for selecting and filtering elements in the attributes entities, purposes and locations using taxonomies,

allowing to express preferences and exceptions, while defining policy requirements. We define taxonomies as *tree structures* with well-formedness properties.
We plan to investigate in the future what well-formedness properties can be
weakened to allow other sorts of classification, e.g., using Semantic Technology [14]. In the rest of this section, we present a formalization of tree structures.

Definition 2 (Tree Structures). *Let $\overline{\alpha}$ be a set of elements in some domain
language. We organize such elements into a tree structure. Let $\beta = \alpha_i \to \alpha_j$ be a
constructor of the tree, where α_i and α_j are two elements in $\overline{\alpha}$, and the relation
$\to$ indicate that α_i is the parent of α_j. Let $\overline{\beta}$ denote the set of constructors in
the tree. We define $\tau = (\overline{\alpha}, \alpha, \overline{\beta})$ to be a tree structure, where:*

- *$\alpha \in \overline{\alpha}$, is the root of the tree,*
- *$\forall \beta = \alpha_i \to \alpha_j$ s.t. $\beta \in \overline{\beta} \Rightarrow \alpha_i, \alpha_j \in \overline{\alpha}$,*
- *τ is well-formed, defined as,*
  $WF(\tau) = reachability(\tau) \wedge SingleParent(\tau) \wedge SingleNode(\tau)$, where
    *i) reachability(τ) denotes that all elements are reached from the root ele-
    ment,*
    ii) singleParent(τ) denotes that all elements have only one parent, and
    iii) singleNode(τ) denotes that each element appears only once in the tree.

Properties *reachability* and *singleParent* are needed to maintain the shape of a
tree (e.g., discard directed graphs with cycles), and *singleNode* is needed to rule
out ambiguities while classifying elements in the tree. Observe that a tree should
have at least one element, namely the root (e.g., $\tau_0 = (\{el\}, el, \emptyset)$).

Example 2. Figure 1 shows a graphical example of a tree structure for the
attribute entity. Following Definition 2, we can express the tree as follows:

$hcSysProf = (\{hospital, healthProf, admin, doctor, healthAsso, billing, marketing,$
$\quad thirdParty, others\}, hospital, \{hospital \to healthProf, hospital \to admin,$
$\quad healthProf \to doctor, healthProf \to healthAsso, admin \to billing,$
$\quad admin \to marketing, marketing \to thirdParty, marketing \to others\}).$

In this tree, the leaf elements are:

$elem(hcSysProf) = \{doctor, healthAsso, billing, thirdParty, others\}$

We can define the tree in Fig. 2 in a similar manner.

In our language for policy requirements, we envisage flexible granularity of
policy entries by allowing the selection and filtering of elements inside trees,
e.g., data controllers can express their *obligations/exceptions* by selecting and
filtering certain parts in the trees for the different attributes. We now extend
Definition 2 for pruned trees with phantom branches to capture the filtering of
elements.

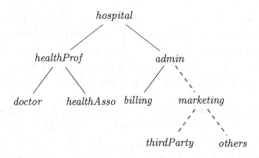

Fig. 3. Example of a pruned tree with name $hcSysProfPr$, for the attribute entity.

Definition 3 (Pruned trees). *A pruned tree is defined by a triple $(\overline{\alpha}, \alpha, \overline{\delta})$, denoted $\widehat{\tau}$, where $\overline{\delta}$ is a set of terms of the form $\alpha_i \not\rightarrow \alpha_j$ or $\alpha_i \rightarrow \alpha_j$, for $\alpha_i, \alpha_j \in \overline{\alpha}$. A pruned tree $(\overline{\alpha}, \alpha, \overline{\delta})$ is well-formed if it is a well-formed tree when replacing all occurrences of $\not\rightarrow$ by $\rightarrow$ in $\overline{\delta}$.*

Thus, $\not\rightarrow$ is a constructor for pruned trees, and the term $\alpha_i \not\rightarrow \alpha_j$ indicates that the sub-tree with root α_j is pruned in the tree. We extend $\mathrm{WF}(\widehat{\tau})$ and $elem(\widehat{\tau})$ accordingly. Observe that the trees in Definition 2 are a special case of pruned trees.

Example 3. Figure 3 shows an example of a pruned tree. Following Definition 3, we can express this pruned tree as follows:

$hcSysProfPr = (\{hospital, \ healthProf, \ admin, \ doctor, \ healthAsso, \ billing, \ marketing,$
    $thirdParty, \ others\}, \ hospital, \ \{hospital \rightarrow healthProf, \ hospital \rightarrow admin,$
    $healthProf \rightarrow doctor, \ healthProf \rightarrow healthAss, \ admin \rightarrow billing,$
    $admin \not\rightarrow marketing, \ marketing \rightarrow thirdParty, \ marketing \rightarrow others\}).$

In this pruned tree, the leaf elements are:

$elem(hcSysProfPr) = \{doctor, \ healthAsso, \ billing\}.$

Definition 4 (Filtering expressions over trees). *We define a grammar Ψ for selecting and filtering elements in well-formed pruned trees $\widehat{\tau}$. The grammar accepts the following expressions:*

$$e ::= \psi \mid e \backslash \psi$$

where ψ ranges over $\overline{\alpha}$. The expression ψ selects the sub-tree in $\widehat{\tau}$ that has as its root ψ, and it is well-formed if the sub-tree with root ψ is a sub-tree of $\widehat{\tau}$. The expression $e \backslash \psi$ is pruning the sub-tree with root ψ from a tree $\widehat{\tau}_0$ that is generated after the selection and pruning of $\widehat{\tau}$, according to the expression e, and it is well-formed if the sub-tree with root ψ is a sub-tree of $\widehat{\tau}_0$.

The evaluation of the expression $e \backslash \psi$ in $\widehat{\tau}$, will return a newly pruned tree $\widehat{\tau}'_0$, where the sub-tree with root ψ is pruned from $\widehat{\tau}_0$. Observe that due to the *singleNode* property, there is only one sub-tree with root ψ in $\widehat{\tau}$.

Example 4. The expression *healthProf* is a well-formed expression for the tree structure in Fig. 1. This expression selects the sub-tree with root *healthProf*, where the leaf elements are $\{doctor, healthAsso\}$. The expression *hospital\marketing* is a well-formed expression for the tree structure in Fig. 1, this expression will prune the sub-tree with root *marketing* as shown in Fig. 3.

Definition 5 (Evaluating filtering expressions in trees). *Let τ be a well-formed tree structure. Let e be a well-formed expression using a grammar Ψ. Let $\widehat{\tau}$ be the pruned tree generated after selecting and pruning in τ according to the expression e. We define the function $eval(e, \tau) = elem(\widehat{\tau})$.*

The function *eval* selects and/or filters the tree τ, according to the expression e and returns the leaf elements (in a set) after selection and filtering.

We can also express the evaluation of an expression $\alpha_1 \backslash \alpha_2 \backslash \alpha_3 \backslash \ldots$ over a tree by selecting the branch with root α_1, and then doing filtering by α_2, α_3 and so on, where the filtering operation over pruned trees can be defined as follows

$$
\begin{aligned}
filter(y, (\overline{\alpha}, \alpha, \overline{\delta} \cup (x \to y))) &= (\overline{\alpha}, \alpha, \overline{\delta} \cup (x \not\to y)) \\
filter(y, (\overline{\alpha}, \alpha, \overline{\delta})) &= (\overline{\alpha}, \alpha, \overline{\delta}) \qquad \textbf{[owise]}
\end{aligned}
$$

assuming an associative and commutative, pattern matching modulo for the set constructor $\cup$ and that the equation marked with **owise** only match when no other equation matches. We can similarly define a function $select(\alpha, \widehat{\tau})$ that returns the sub-tree in $\widehat{\tau}$ with root α.

Example 5. We use the tree *hcSysProf* and pruned tree *hcSysProfPr* in Fig. 1 and 3, respectively, to illustrate the function *eval*:

$eval(healthProf, hcSysProf) = elem(select(healthProf, hcSysProf))$ and
$elem(select(healthProf, hcSysProf)) = \{doctor, healthAsso\}$

$eval(hospital \backslash marketing, hcSysProf) = elem(hcSysProfPr) = \{doctor, healthAsso, billing\}$
where $hcSysProfPr = filter(marketing, select(hospital, hcSysProf))$.

Example 6. We now show how to express exceptions using trees in the policy language. Let us consider the trees in Figs. 1 and 2 for entities and purposes. Alice wants to express an exception in the context of these trees, i.e., *'She wants to block the **marketing** team from **transferring** her **data** for **marketing** purposes'*, the filtering operator helps in defining the exceptions as shown below:

$(hospital \backslash marketing, \{Transfer\}, healthServ \backslash marketing, 21/02/2023, Europe)$

Here the expression *hospital\marketing* is evaluated as in Example 5, returning {*doctor, healthAsso, billing*}. Similarly, *healthServ\marketing* is evaluated to {*gnrlTreatm, spclTreatm, billing, ITServ*}.

5   Policy Compliance

A major challenge in the existing multi-stakeholder service architecture is policy compliance. DSs and DCs are bound by service-level agreements, data usage agreements, and data protection agreements. There are also agreements shared between the DC and a data processor (DP) to ensure that processing is according to regulations and to the DSs interests, as stated in Art. (28) [10]. Agreements are usually expressed in natural language and a DS is often unaware of the agreements between DCs and DPs. This opens for opportunities, where stakeholders might tamper with the agreements to benefit their businesses. Hence, the language proposed in Sect. 3 can help to unambiguously capture the interpretations that the different stakeholders have for such agreements. In this section, we explore the support for systematic checks of compliance in a distributed setting, where a transitive and reflexive compliance relation $\sqsubseteq$ between sets of policies $\overline{PE}_{DP}$ for DP, $\overline{PE}_{DC}$ for DC and $\overline{PE}_{DS}$ for DS, is capturing the commonly unattended, however existing compliance relation between $\overline{PE}_{DP}$ and $\overline{PE}_{DS}$.

$$\overline{PE}_{DP} \sqsubseteq \overline{PE}_{DC} \sqsubseteq \overline{PE}_{DS}$$

We first check the compliance between two policy entries and compliance with a set of policy entries to finally define compliance between sets of policy entries. We use compliance between sets of policies to capture compliance between different stakeholders, as defined above. The idea behind the compliance between two policies is that the policy on the right-hand side should be able to subsume the policy on the left-hand side. For the trees defined in Sect. 4, this is straightforward. We use the function *eval* in Definition 5, to simplify compliance checks and work with sets instead of trees.

Definition 6 (Compliance between two policy entries).
Let $PE_i = (E_i, A_i, P_i, R_i, L_i)$ and $PE_j = (E_j, A_j, P_j, R_j, L_j)$ be policy entries. Let τ_{ent}, τ_{pp} and τ_{loc} be well-formed trees (see Definition 2) for entity, purpose and location, respectively. Let Ψ_{ent} be a grammar that accepts expressions E_i and E_j in τ_{ent} (see Definition 4). Similarly, let Ψ_{pp} be a grammar that accepts expression P_i and P_j in τ_{pp}, and Ψ_{loc} be a grammar that accepts expressions L_i and L_j in τ_{loc}. PE_i complies with PE_j, denoted by $PE_i \sqsubseteq PE_j$ if

$$eval(E_i, \tau_{ent}) \subseteq eval(E_j, \tau_{ent}) \ \wedge \ A_i \subseteq A_j \ \wedge \ eval(P_i, \tau_{pp}) \subseteq eval(P_j, \tau_{pp}) \ \wedge$$
$$duration(now, R_i) \leq duration(now, R_j) \ \wedge \ eval(L_i, \tau_{loc}) \subseteq eval(L_j, \tau_{loc}).$$

Example 7. Consider PE_1, PE_2, and PE_3 evaluated in the tree of Fig. 1 for entity, Fig. 2 for purpose and a tree for locations in the world, where

$PE_1 = (doctor\{Use, Store\},\ healthServ \backslash marketing \backslash admin,\ 2022\text{-}02\text{-}21,\ Europe)$
$PE_2 = (hospital \backslash admin,\ \{Use, Collect, Store\},\ treatm, 2024\text{-}02\text{-}21,\ Europe)$
$PE_3 = (doctor, \{Use, Transfer\},\ healthServ \backslash marketing \backslash billing, 2022\text{-}02\text{-}21, Europe)$

$PE_1 \sqsubseteq PE_2$ since,

- $eval(doctor, hcSysProf) \subseteq eval(hospital \backslash admin, hcSysProf)$, which reduces to $\{doctor\} \subseteq \{doctor, helathAsso\}$
- $\{Use, Store\} \subseteq \{Use, Collect, Store\}$
- $eval(healthServ \backslash marketing \backslash admin, hcSysPurp) \subseteq eval(treatm, hcSysPurp)$, which reduces to $\{gnrlTreatm, spclTreatm\} \subseteq \{gnrlTreatm, spclTreatm\}$
- $duration(now, 2022\text{-}02\text{-}21) \leq duration(now, 2024\text{-}02\text{-}21)$
- $eval(Europe, locWorld) \subseteq eval(Europe, locWorld)$

$PE_3 \not\sqsubseteq PE_2$ since the *Transfer* action is not allowed in the action set of PE_2 and $healthServ \backslash marketing \backslash billing$ evaluates to $\{gnrlTreatm, spclTreatm, ITserv\}$.

To lift this compliance relation to $PE \sqsubseteq \overline{PE}$ we distinguish two cases: (a) there is one entry on the right-hand side set which alone can give compliance, (b) we need to extend the policy set on the right-hand side with entries that combine other exiting entries (this subsumes the first case). We define two functions, a function that reduces policy entries with expressions into an intermediate representation, which we call *reduced policy entries* and a function that combines such entries and recursively extends the right-hand side set with all possible combinations of policies, until we reach a fixed point.

Definition 7 (Reduction function over policy entry).
Let $PE = (E, A, P, R, L)$ be a policy entry. Let τ_{ent}, τ_{pp} and τ_{loc} be well-formed trees capturing entities purposes and locations, respectively. We define a reduced policy entry $\mathcal{PE} = \mathcal{R}(PE)$ as a tuple that we obtain after evaluating each expression in PE, such that $\mathcal{R}(PE) = (eval(E, \tau_{ent}), A, eval(P, \tau_{pp}), duration(now, R), eval(L, \tau_{loc}))$. We define $\mathcal{PE}$ as well-formed if A is not empty, if each set returned by the eval function is not empty and if the number returned by the duration function is greater than zero.

We now define the same reduction function which takes sets of policy entries as input and returns a set of reduced policy entries, where all the elements are well-formed. Let $\overline{PE}$ be a set of policy entries. Let us define a reduction function $\mathcal{R}$ over $\overline{PE}$ such that, $\mathcal{R}(\overline{PE}) = \{\mathcal{R}(PE) | PE \in \overline{PE} \wedge \mathcal{R}(PE) \text{ is well-formed}\}$.

The reduction function over sets of policies discards reduced policy entries that are not well-formed, because such policies are not adding information, they are not expressing possible selections or exceptions. If the intention is to disallow some actions, then by not being included in the set, they are expressing exactly such intention.

Example 8. Consider the policy set $\overline{PE} = \{PE_4, PE_5, PE_6, PE_7\}$, where

$PE_4 = (healthAsso, \{Use\}, treatm, 2022\text{-}12\text{-}21, Europe)$
$PE_5 = (healthAsso, \{Use\}, admin, 2022\text{-}12\text{-}21, Europe)$
$PE_6 = (admin, \{Use\}, treatm, 2022\text{-}12\text{-}21, Europe)$
$PE_7 = (admin, \{Use\}, admin, 2022\text{-}12\text{-}21, Europe)$

Based on Definition 7, we apply the reduction function over $\overline{PE}$ to calculate a set of reduced policy entries $\overline{PE} = \mathcal{R}(\overline{PE})$ where, $\mathcal{R}(\overline{PE}) = \{\mathcal{PE}_1, \mathcal{PE}_2, \mathcal{PE}_3, \mathcal{PE}_4\}$, and

$\mathcal{PE}_1 = (\{healthAsso\}, \{Use\}, \{spclTreatm, gnrlTreatm\}, n, eur)$
$\mathcal{PE}_2 = (\{healthAsso\}, \{Use\}, \{billing, ITServ\}, n, eur)$
$\mathcal{PE}_3 = (\{billing, marketing, thirdParty, others\}, \{Use\}, \{spclTreatm, gnrlTreatm\}, n, eur)$
$\mathcal{PE}_4 = (\{billing, marketing, thirdParty, others\}, \{Use\}, \{billing, ITServ\}, n, eur))$

Here n and *eur* are variables representing a natural number greater than zero, and a set of countries in Europe, respectively.

Definition 8 (Closure function over policy entries). *Let $\overline{PE}$ be a set of policy entries. Let $\overline{PE_0} = \mathcal{R}(\overline{PE})$, we define a closure function $closure(\overline{PE_0})$ which returns a set $\overline{PE}$, calculated according to the following iterative steps:*

1. $\overline{PE} = \overline{PE_0} \cup \mathcal{C}(\overline{PE_0})$
2. *The combine function $\mathcal{C}(\overline{PE_0})$ returns a set of well-formed policy entries such that $\forall\, \mathcal{PE}_i, \mathcal{PE}_j \in \overline{PE_0}\,.\,\mathcal{C}(\mathcal{PE}_i, \mathcal{PE}_j)$, where*

$\mathcal{PE}_i = (\overline{\alpha}_{ent_i}, A_i, \overline{\alpha}_{pp_i}, n_i, \overline{\alpha}_{loc_i}), \mathcal{PE}_j = (\overline{\alpha}_{ent_j}, A_j, \overline{\alpha}_{pp_j}, n_i, \overline{\alpha}_{loc_j}), and$
$\mathcal{C}(\mathcal{PE}_i, \mathcal{PE}_j) = \overline{PE}_{\cup E} \cup \overline{PE}_{\cup A} \cup \overline{PE}_{\cup P} \cup \overline{PE}_{\cup R} \cup \overline{PE}_{\cup L}, and$

- $\overline{PE}_{\cup E} = (let\ PE = (\alpha_{ent_i} \cup \alpha_{ent_j},\ A_i \cap A_j,\ \alpha_{pp_i} \cap \alpha_{pp_j},\ R_r,\ \alpha_{loc_i} \cap \alpha_{loc_j})\ in$
  $if\ \alpha_{ent_i} \neq \alpha_{ent_j}\ and\ PE\ is\ well\text{-}formed\ and\ PE \not\sqsubseteq \overline{PE_0},\ then\ \{PE\}\ else\ \emptyset),$
- $\overline{PE}_{\cup A} = (let\ PE = (\alpha_{ent_i} \cap \alpha_{ent_j},\ A_i \cup A_j,\ \alpha_{pp_i} \cap \alpha_{pp_j},\ R_r,\ \alpha_{loc_i} \cap \alpha_{loc_j})\ in$
  $if\ A_i \neq A_j\ and\ PE\ is\ well\text{-}formed\ and\ PE \not\sqsubseteq \overline{PE_0},\ then\ \{PE\}\ else\ \emptyset),$
- $\overline{PE}_{\cup P} = (let\ PE = (\alpha_{ent_i} \cap \alpha_{ent_j},\ A_i \cap A_j,\ \alpha_{pp_i} \cup \alpha_{pp_j},\ R_r,\ \alpha_{loc_i} \cap \alpha_{loc_j})\ in$
  $if\ \alpha_{pp_i} \neq \alpha_{pp_j}\ and\ PE\ is\ well\text{-}formed\ and\ PE \not\sqsubseteq \overline{PE_0},\ then\ \{PE\}\ else\ \emptyset),$
- $\overline{PE}_{\cup R} = (let\ PE = (\alpha_{ent_i} \cap \alpha_{ent_j},\ A_i \cap A_j,\ \alpha_{pp_i} \cap \alpha_{pp_j},\ R_m,\ \alpha_{loc_i} \cap \alpha_{loc_j})$
  $in\ if\ n_i \neq n_j\ and\ PE\ is\ well\text{-}formed\ and\ PE \not\sqsubseteq \overline{PE_0},\ then\ \{PE\}\ else\ \emptyset),$
- $\overline{PE}_{\cup L} = (let\ PE = (\alpha_{ent_i} \cap \alpha_{ent_j},\ A_i \cap A_j,\ \alpha_{pp_i} \cap \alpha_{pp_j},\ R_r,\ \alpha_{loc_i} \cup \alpha_{loc_j})\ in$
  $if\ \alpha_{loc_i} \neq \alpha_{loc_j}\ and\ PE\ is\ well\text{-}formed\ and\ PE \not\sqsubseteq \overline{PE_0},\ then\ \{PE\}\ else\ \emptyset),$
  here the integer $R_r = min(n_i, n_j)$ and $R_m = max(n_i, n_j)$.
3. *if $\overline{PE_0} \cup \mathcal{C}(\overline{PE_0}) == \overline{PE_0}$ then return $\overline{PE}$, else $\overline{PE_0} = \overline{PE_0} \cup \mathcal{C}(\overline{PE_0})$ and go to step 1.*

The closure function uses a combine function that performs a union operation on one of the attributes in the tuple, while performing an intersection on other attributes, generating a set with at most five elements. This is done for each pair of elements in the set $\overline{\mathcal{PE}_0}$. Some of these elements are discarded if there exists already some other entry in $\overline{\mathcal{PE}_0}$ that subsumes the newly generated policy entries or if they are not well-formed.

Example 9. We extend Example 8 to illustrate the combine function on the set $\overline{\mathcal{PE}} = \{\mathcal{PE}_1, \mathcal{PE}_2, \mathcal{PE}_3, \mathcal{PE}_4\}$, where we can combine the entity attribute in $\mathcal{PE}_1, \mathcal{PE}_3$ and $\mathcal{PE}_2, \mathcal{PE}_4$ since they can produce the new policy entries $\mathcal{PE}_5$ and $\mathcal{PE}_6$, and we can combine the attribute purpose in $\mathcal{PE}_1, \mathcal{PE}_2$ and $\mathcal{PE}_3, \mathcal{PE}_4$ to produce $\mathcal{PE}_7$ and $\mathcal{PE}_8$.

$$\mathcal{PE}_5 = (\{healthAsso, billing, marketing, thirdParty, others\}, \{Use\},$$
$$\{spclTreatm, gnrlTreatm\}, n, eur)$$
$$\mathcal{PE}_6 = (\{healthAsso, billing, marketing, thirdParty, others\},$$
$$\{Use\}, \{billing, ITServ\}, n, eur)$$
$$\mathcal{PE}_7 = (\{healthAsso\}, \{Use\}, \{spclTreatm, gnrlTreatm, billing, ITServ\}, n, eur)$$
$$\mathcal{PE}_8 = (\{billing, marketing, thirdParty, others\}, \{Use\},$$
$$\{spclTreatm, gnrlTreatm, billing, ITServ\}, n, eur)\}$$

Since we don't have two distinct policies present in the policy set $\overline{\mathcal{PE}}$ where $A_i \neq A_j$, $n_i \neq n_j$, $\alpha_{\mathrm{loc}_i} \neq \alpha_{\mathrm{loc}_j}$, we have found all possible combinations in iteration number 1. Observe that a second iteration will not find new combinations. Thus, we have reached a fix point in one iteration.

We now define compliance with a policy set using the closure function and assuming an straightforward extension of compliance between a policy entry PE and a reduced policy entry $\mathcal{PE}$.

Definition 9 (Compliance with a policy set).
Let PE be a policy entry and $\overline{PE}$ be a set of policy entries.

$$PE \sqsubseteq \overline{PE} \text{ if } \exists \mathcal{PE} \in closure(\mathcal{R}(\overline{PE})) \,.\, PE \sqsubseteq \mathcal{PE}.$$

Example 10. We extend Example 9 to illustrate the compliance of three policy entries PE', PE'' and PE''' with $\overline{PE}$ where,

$$PE' = (hospital \backslash doctor, \{Use\}, treatm, 2022\text{-}10\text{-}21, Europe)$$
$$PE'' = (billing, \{Use\}, spclTreatm, 2022\text{-}10\text{-}21, Europe)$$
$$PE''' = (healthAsso, \{Use, Store\}, spclTreatm, 2022\text{-}10\text{-}21, Europe)$$

We have from Example 9,

$$closure(\mathcal{R}(\overline{PE})) = \{\mathcal{PE}_1, \mathcal{PE}_2, \mathcal{PE}_3, \mathcal{PE}_4, \mathcal{PE}_5, \mathcal{PE}_6, \mathcal{PE}_7, \mathcal{PE}_8\}.$$

```
***Compliance between two policy entries:
op _\C_ : Policy Policy ⟶ Bool .
ceq P1 \C P2  = true if entity(P1) subse entity(P2)
   /\ Actions(P1) subse Actions(P2) /\ purpose(P1) subse purpose(P2)
   /\ Ret(P1) ≤Ret(P2) /\ Loc(P1) subse Loc (P2) .
eq P1 \C P2  = false [owise] .

***Associative constructor for policy lists:
op _;_ : NePolicyList NePolicyList ⟶ NePolicyList [ctor assoc] .

***Compliance with a policy set:
op complyrule1 : Policy NePolicyList ⟶ Bool .
eq complyrule1(P1, P2 )  = if (P1 \C P2) then true else false fi .
eq complyrule1(P1, (P2 ; Ps))  = if (P1 \C P2) then
   true else complyrule1(P1 ,Ps ) fi .
eq complyrule1(P1, Ps )  = false [owise].

op totalCompl : NePolicyList NePolicyList ⟶ Bool .
eq totalCompl(P1,Ps1) = if complywithset(P1,Ps1) then
   true else false fi.
eq totalCompl((P1,,P2), Ps1) = if complywithset(P1, Ps1) and
   complywithset( P2, Ps1)  = true then true else false fi .
ceq totalCompl((P1,,P2,,Ps), Ps1)  = true if
   complywithset(P1, Ps1) =  true /\ complywithset(P2, Ps1) =  true
   /\ complywithset( Ps, Ps1)  = true .
eq totalCompl((P1,,P2,,Ps), Ps1)  = false [owise].
```

Fig. 4. Implementation of compliance rules in Maude

According to o Definition 9

$PE' \sqsubseteq \overline{PE}$, since $\mathcal{PE}_5 \in closure(\mathcal{R}(\overline{PE}))$ and $E' \sqsubseteq \mathcal{PE}_5$,
$PE'' \sqsubseteq \overline{PE}$, since $\mathcal{PE}_8 \in closure(\mathcal{R}(\overline{PE}))$ and $PE'' \sqsubseteq \mathcal{PE}_8$ and
$PE''' \not\sqsubseteq \overline{PE}$, since there isn't any $\mathcal{PE} \in closure(\mathcal{R}(\overline{PE}))$ that complies with PE'''.

We now lift Definition 9 to compliance between the two policy sets.

Definition 10 (Compliance between two policy sets).
Let $\overline{PE}_i$ and $\overline{PE}_j$ be two set of policy entries. $\overline{PE}_i$ complies with $\overline{PE}_j$, denoted as $\overline{PE}_i \sqsubseteq \overline{PE}_j$ if $\forall PE \in \overline{PE}_i . PE \sqsubseteq \overline{PE}_j$.

Example 11. Consider the policy set $\overline{PE} = \{PE_4, PE_5, PE_6, PE_7\}$ in Example 8 and consider PE' and PE'' in Example 10, where both PE' and PE'' complies with $closure(\mathcal{R}(\overline{PE}))$. Hence, $\{PE', PE''\} \sqsubseteq \{PE_4, PE_5, PE_6, PE_7\}$.

6   Proof of Concept Implementation

We have developed a proof of concept implementation in Maude [8], a rewriting logic system. Maude's formal framework allows us to build an executable implementation of the compliance checking using sorts, operations, terms t, and equations of the form **ceq** $t = t'$ **if** *cond* and **eq** $t = t'$, for conditional and non-conditional equations, respectively.

The proof of concept makes the checking of compliance executable. We implemented the structures (e.g., trees, pruned trees, policy entries, etc.) and functions (e.g., *elem, eval, reachability*, compliance $\sqsubseteq$, etc.) from Sects. 3–5. While structures are translated almost straightforward from the definitions, all functions other than constructors needed to be implemented. In this section we show a selected snippet in Fig. 4, implementing policy compliance, based on the compliance definitions. We present the code for our Definition 6 (compliance between policy entries), which is further used in implementing part of Definition 9 (where the equation `complyrule1` implements the base case) and finally checking compliance between two sets (with the equation `totalCompl`). Observe that our implementation explicitly checks the base case using `complyrule1` (the policy entry on the left-hand side complies with a distinct policy on the right-hand side) to make the computation more efficient, which is not explicitly consider in the compliance of Definition 9. The whole implementation in Maude, along with examples can be downloaded from https://github.com/Chinmayiprabhu/PL-ComplianceChecking-PoC-Maude-.git.

7 Case Study: Health Wearable

In this section, we introduce a case study to illustrate the use of policy language and compliance checking. In recent years, wearable technology has burgeoned, particularly fitness wearable and medical device trackers. As the underlying technology advances, many investors and manufacturers are producing advanced health wearables. The rise of this technology comes with an attached risk of breaching data privacy. Currently, EU medical devices regulations [17] clarify when wearables can be considered medical devices, where the software works in conjunction with the product. Even though prominent fitness device manufacturers like Fitbit and Apple claim that the user's health data will not be used for advertising, there have been instances [26] when third-party platforms exposed fitness tracking data to the world. We analyze part of the privacy policy of a health wearable company. Consider a DC, Ava bracelet [32], which produces a wrist band that measures skin temperature continuously during sleep and develops services that support women across their reproductive cycles. According to their privacy policy [5], " ... *When worn, the device collects data on key physiological parameters such as skin temperature, resting pulse, breathing rate, etc. (collectively 'Fertility Information' or 'FI') ...* **FI is then stored on servers operated by a third-party service provider on behalf of Ava.**" Additionally, Ava mentions "*... may partner with other companies who provide insurance and or benefit services. When those parties have a payment obligation for the device,* **Ava will transfer certain personally identifiable information (PII), excluding FI, to the partner for the exclusive purpose of payment processing.**" *and* "*... As part of our business activities, we may disclose your* **PII to third parties (as listed below) in Switzerland, the EU or**

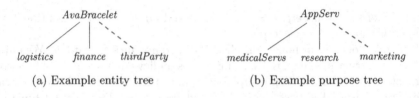

(a) Example entity tree   (b) Example purpose tree

Fig. 5. Tree structures of policy attributes entity and purpose

other countries for the purposes set out above and where appropriate." Let us now analyze these fragments of privacy requirements in the context of a user Alice. Let Alice be the DS and PE_1 be Alice's privacy preference.

$PE_1 = (AvaBracelet, \{ Use, Collect, Store, Transfer\}, medicalServs, 2024\text{-}02\text{-}21, Europe)$.

This policy can be expressed in natural language as follows: *Ava bracelet can use, collect, store and transfer Alice's data for the purpose of application services until 2024-02-21 only specified for the Europe region.*

For exceptions, Alice can extend her preferences in PE_2.

$PE_2 = (AvaBracelet\backslash thirdParty, \{ Transfer\}, AppServ\backslash marketing, 2024\text{-}02\text{-}21, Europe)$.

Expressed in natural language as: *All entities associated with Ava bracelet, except third parties, can transfer Alice's data for all the purpose of application services, except for marketing, until 2024-02-21 only specified for the Europe region.*

Figure 5 shows the filtered trees for both purposes and entities. Now both of Alice's policies are accumulated in the form of policy set $\overline{PE}_{Alice} = \{PE_1, PE_2\}$. Consider a data processor DP such as a logistics company who processes Alice's data on behalf of Ava bracelet. Using the various definitions of policy compliance in Sect. 5, we can check that Ava bracelet policies i.e., $\overline{PE}_{AvaBracelet}$, and the logistics company policies i.e., $\overline{PE}_{logistics}$ comply with $\overline{PE}_{Alice}$, for Alice to safely give her data to the logistics company, as shown in Fig. 6, even though her policy preferences are only agreed with Ava bracelet.

$$\overline{PE}_{logistics} \sqsubseteq \overline{PE}_{AvaBracelet} \sqsubseteq \overline{PE}_{Alice}$$

In a scenario where Alice's policy set is more restrictive than the policies of the DC Ava bracelet, the compliance check fails and the DS Alice is notified. In practice, Alice and Ava bracelet can initiate negotiations on minimum requirements. Negotiations are not further discussed in this paper. We plan to investigate such an extension in the future.

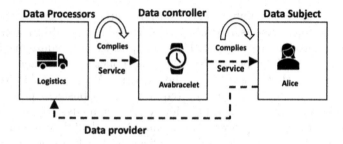

Fig. 6. Sample service model architecture for Ava bracelet

8   Analysis of Related Work

Privacy policy languages[1] are a widely explored area with many research contributions. P3P [9] was an initial attempt to define privacy policies with the intention to give users more control over their personal data on the web. P3P is complex and has not been used as a way of communication between distributed systems. Many languages similar to P3P have been proposed, some web-based, such XPref [1], APPEL [9] and fewer enterprise-based, such as E-P3P [4], EPAL [3]. However, they have not been thought to be combined with system execution. Languages like EPAL, P2U [16], and XACML [2] do not have a formal foundation with no guarantee of the correctness of properties [18]. Access control models like MAC, DAC, and RBAC [11] are mainly attribute-based models that associate policies with data-types and grant access to particular information, they fail to achieve the GDPR and focus on modeling the regulations rather than enhancing the awareness among DSs.

Gerl et al. [12] proposed a GDPR compliant policy language considering purpose, retention time, and user consent. However, it lacks several conditions and the centralized architecture makes it difficult to apply in a distributed environment. Previous work of one of the authors of this paper [29–31] develops a framework for the specification and analysis of privacy requirements via triples specifying access control, purpose, and consent, in asynchronously communicating distributed systems using static and run-time analysis to check compliance. Consent is given by a list of positive and negative policy entries, somewhat similar to selection and filtering. Location and retention are not considered. In contrast to the present work, it does not give an overall view of the resulting policy specification, something which is useful for users when viewing their preferences. Pardo et al. [24] proposed a privacy policy language that is designed to be used by both DCs (by defining their privacy rules) and DSs (to provide their consent). We take our motivation from this work and propose this double view as one of the characteristics to be considered in a privacy policy language.

---

[1] In this context, we consider privacy as a functionality of the modeling approach which should be complemented by appropriate security measures. Such security measures are not discussed in this paper.

Modeling privacy in distributed services has recently gained importance due to privacy regulations such as HIPAA, COPAA, and GLBA. Initiatives towards combining executable languages with privacy policies and requirements for the modeling and analysis of privacy specification, policies enforcement, and monitoring is an area that is starting to be explored. Witt *et al.* [27,34] present an approach to model check privacy requirements in business process models (BPM) using an extension of CTL. However, their analysis focuses on intra-process rather than inter-process. Hayati and Abadi [13] describe an approach to model and verify aspects of privacy policies with a focus on principles and purpose. Yang *et al.* [35,36] propose a programming model that allows programmers to separate privacy concerns from core program functionality. In a distributed setting, Myers and Liskov [21] propose a decentralized label model and its static analysis for the control of information flow in systems with mutual distrust and decentralized authority. However, their approach does not consider the GDPR compliance. Basin *et al.* [6] propose a methodology that relates a purpose with a business process to verify compliance for inter-process communication. An important outcome of this approach is the automatic generation of compliant privacy policies from business process models. Extended languages such as GeoXACML [20] use policies for location-based access control. However, they do not address other crucial requirements like purpose, retention, and transfer.

In summary, we noticed there is a lack of expressiveness in the languages and frameworks previously discussed. By looking at the previous work, there has been very little work in the state-of-the-art where languages are built to comply with legal regulations. We emphasize that the languages discussed in this section have complex structures. Our proposal in this paper aims to define a language that has fewer attributes and has the capacity to express wider preferences.

9   Conclusion and Future Work

This paper presents a flexible language with a formal foundation that can capture data protection requirements at different granularity. Currently, our language focuses on the main principles of the GDPR such as, informed consent, purpose limitation and data subject rights like the right to modify, access, and be forgotten. In the future, we plan to extend the language by including more vital principles from the GDPR. The main contribution of our work compared to earlier work is the increased expressiveness of the policy specification language due to taxonomies, which allows specifying different granularity of policies using selection and filtering over taxonomies. We consider this language as part of a work in progress framework, where compliance checking helps to establish trust within a service-oriented architecture with various actors, who do not necessarily have the same interests in mind. We plan to extend the framework to explore further static and run-time analysis for a core active object language, e.g., based on ABS [25]. In this paper, we assume that both DCs and DSs have already negotiated the minimum requirements before establishing a compliance environment. In the future, we plan to incorporate negotiation rules between DCs and DSs focusing on their conflicting interests. We also plan to explore compliance based on other classification frameworks for domain knowledge, e.g., Semantic Technology [14], where we would need to define compliance checks in open graphs.

References

1. Agrawal, R., Kiernan, J., Srikant, R., Xu, Y.: XPref: a preference language for P3P. Comput. Netw. **48**(5), 809–827 (2005)
2. Anderson, A., et al.: Extensible access control markup language (XACML) version 1.0. OASIS (2003)
3. Ashley, P., Hada, S., Karjoth, G., Powers, C., Schunter, M.: Enterprise privacy authorization language (EPAL). IBM Res. **30**, 31 (2003)
4. Ashley, P., Hada, S., Karjoth, G., Schunter, M.: E-P3P privacy policies and privacy authorization. In: Proceedings of the 2002 ACM Workshop on Privacy in the Electronic Society, pp. 103–109 (2002)
5. AvaWomen. Your privacy - avawomen. https://www.avawomen.com/privacy. Accessed 02 Jan 2022
6. Basin, D., Debois, S., Hildebrandt, T.: On purpose and by necessity: compliance under the GDPR. In: Meiklejohn, S., Sako, K. (eds.) FC 2018. LNCS, vol. 10957, pp. 20–37. Springer, Heidelberg (2018). https://doi.org/10.1007/978-3-662-58387-6_2
7. Centers for Medicare & Medicaid Services. The Health Insurance Portability and Accountability Act of 1996 (HIPAA) (1996). http://www.cms.hhs.gov/hipaa/
8. Clavel, M., et al.: All About Maude - A High-Performance Logical Framework. LNCS, vol. 4350. Springer, Heidelberg (2007). https://doi.org/10.1007/978-3-540-71999-1
9. Cranor, L.F.: P3P: making privacy policies more useful. IEEE Secur. Priv. **1**(6), 50–55 (2003)
10. European Parliament and Council: Regulation (EU) 2016/679 of the European parliament and of the council of 27 April 2016 on the protection of natural persons with regard to the processing of personal data and on the free movement of such data, and repealing directive 95/46/EC (general data protection regulation) (text with EEA relevance)
11. Ferraiolo, D., Cugini, J., Kuhn, D.R.: Role-based access control (RBAC): features and motivations. In: Proceedings of 11th Annual Computer Security Application Conference, pp. 241–248 (1995)
12. Gerl, A., Bennani, N., Kosch, H., Brunie, L.: LPL, towards a GDPR-compliant privacy language: formal definition and usage. In: Hameurlain, A., Wagner, R. (eds.) Transactions on Large-Scale Data- and Knowledge-Centered Systems XXXVII. LNCS, vol. 10940, pp. 41–80. Springer, Heidelberg (2018). https://doi.org/10.1007/978-3-662-57932-9_2
13. Hayati, K., Abadi, M.: Language-based enforcement of privacy policies. In: Martin, D., Serjantov, A. (eds.) PET 2004. LNCS, vol. 3424, pp. 302–313. Springer, Heidelberg (2005). https://doi.org/10.1007/11423409_19
14. Hitzler, P., Krötzsch, M., Rudolph, S.: Foundations of Semantic Web Technologies. Chapman and Hall/CRC Press, London (2010)

15. ISO.org. ISO - ISO 8601 - date and time format. https://www.iso.org/iso-8601-date-and-time-format.html. Accessed 28 Mar 2022

16. Iyilade, J., Vassileva, J.: P2u: a privacy policy specification language for secondary data sharing and usage. In: 2014 IEEE Security and Privacy Workshops, pp. 18–22. IEEE (2014)

17. Eur law. Eur-lex - 0199010385-20071011 - en - eur-lex. https://eur-lex.europa.eu/legal-content/EN/TXT/?uri=CELEX%3A01990L0385-20071011. Accessed 13 Apr 2022

18. Leicht, J., Heisel, M.: A survey on privacy policy languages: expressiveness concerning data protection regulations. In: 2019 12th CMI Conference on Cybersecurity and Privacy (CMI), pp. 1–6. IEEE (2019)

19. Lyon, D.: Surveillance, Snowden, and big data: capacities, consequences, critique. Big Data Soc. **1**(2), 2053951714541861 (2014)

20. Matheus, A., Herrmann, J.: Geospatial extensible access control markup language (GeoXACML). Open Geospatial Consortium Inc, OGC (2008)

21. Myers, A.C., Liskov, B.: Protecting privacy using the decentralized label model. ACM Trans. Softw. Eng. Methodol. **9**(4), 410–442 (2000)

22. Neubert, S., et al.: Multi-sensor-fusion approach for a data-science-oriented preventive health management system: concept and development of a decentralized data collection approach for heterogeneous data sources. Int. J. Telemed. App. **2019**, 1 (2019)

23. S. of California Department of Justice: California consumer privacy act (CCPA) | state of California - department of justice - office of the attorney general. https://oag.ca.gov/privacy/ccpa. Accessed 02 Oct 2022

24. Pardo, R., Le Métayer, D.: Analysis of privacy policies to enhance informed consent. In: Foley, S.N. (ed.) DBSec 2019. LNCS, vol. 11559, pp. 177–198. Springer, Cham (2019). https://doi.org/10.1007/978-3-030-22479-0_10

25. Schlatte, R., Johnsen, E.B., Kamburjan, E., Tapia Tarifa, S.L.: Modeling and analyzing resource-sensitive actors: a tutorial introduction. In: Damiani, F., Dardha, O. (eds.) COORDINATION 2021. LNCS, vol. 12717, pp. 3–19. Springer, Cham (2021). https://doi.org/10.1007/978-3-030-78142-2_1

26. Scott: Mass leak of fitness tracking data hits fitbit, apple, microsoft, google; 60 million records exposed by improperly configured third-party database - cpo magazine. https://www.cpomagazine.com/cyber-security/mass-leak-of-fitness-tracking-data-hits-fitbit-apple-microsoft-google-60-million-records-exposed-by-improperly-configured-third-party-database/. Accessed 02 Oct 2022

27. Speck, A., Witt, S., Feja, S., Feja, S., Pulvermüller, E.: Integrating validation techniques for process-based models. In: ENASE 2013 - Proceedings of the 8th International Conference on Evaluation of Novel Approaches to Software Engineering, Angers, France, 4–6 July 2013, pp. 246–253. SciTePress (2013)

28. New York Times: As Facebook raised a privacy wall, it carved an opening for tech giants - The Netherlands New York Times. https://www.nytimes.com/2018/12/18/technology/facebook-privacy.html. Accessed 02 Dec 2021

29. Tokas, S., Owe, O.: A formal framework for consent management. In: Gotsman, A., Sokolova, A. (eds.) FORTE 2020. LNCS, vol. 12136, pp. 169–186. Springer, Cham (2020). https://doi.org/10.1007/978-3-030-50086-3_10

30. Tokas, S., Owe, O., Ramezanifarkhani, T.: Language-based mechanisms for privacy-by-design. In: Friedewald, M., Önen, M., Lievens, E., Krenn, S., Fricker, S. (eds.) Privacy and Identity 2019. IAICT, vol. 576, pp. 142–158. Springer, Cham (2020). https://doi.org/10.1007/978-3-030-42504-3_10

31. Tokas, S., Owe, O., Ramezanifarkhani, T.: Static checking of GDPR-related privacy compliance for object-oriented distributed systems. J. Log. Algebr. Methods Program. **125**, 100733 (2022)
32. Ava Fertility Tracker: Ava fertility tracker - avawomen. https://www.avawomen.com/. Accessed 02 Jan 2022
33. G.E. Tracker. GDPR enforcement tracker - list of GDPR fines. https://www.enforcementtracker.com/. Accessed 02 Aug 2022
34. Witt, S., Feja, S., Speck, A.: Applying pattern-based graphical validation rules to business process models. In: Seventh IEEE International Conference on Software Testing, Verification and Validation, ICST 2014 Workshops Proceedings, pp. 274–283. IEEE Computer Society (2014)
35. Yang, J.: Preventing information leaks with policy-agnostic programming. Ph.D. thesis, Massachusetts Institute of Technology, Cambridge, MA, USA (2015)
36. Yang, J., Yessenov, K., Solar-Lezama, A.: A language for automatically enforcing privacy policies. In: Proceedings of the 39th ACM SIGPLAN-SIGACT Symposium on Principles of Programming Languages, POPL 2012, Philadelphia, Pennsylvania, USA, 22–28 January 2012, pp. 85–96. ACM (2012)

Static Analysis and Testing

Extending Data Flow Coverage to Test Constraint Refinements

Alexander Kolchin[(⊠)] ⓘ and Stepan Potiyenko

V.M. Glushkov Institute of Cybernetics NAS of Ukraine, Kyiv, Ukraine
kolchin_av@yahoo.com

Abstract. This paper presents a new data flow coverage criterion for a deeper analysis of possible refinements to the constraints on paths unfolding of software program's behavior. Such refinements represent a feasible chain of usages of the same variable without redefinitions in-between. An algorithm for reasonable chains selection is proposed.

Keywords: Testing · Coverage criteria · Data flow analysis

1 Introduction

The effectiveness of different types of test coverage is an important issue [1–4] in development, testing and maintenance of software systems used in the safety-critical domain; the development of effective test cases is a challenging task [5–7]. This paper is dedicated to applying data flow coverage criteria which is a popular white-box test case design strategy. It analyzes variables definitions and usages allowing to explore causal relationships, input-output dependencies etc. [6, 8–10].

Relying on the conventional data flow coverage criteria in industrial projects, we faced the problem of weak analysis of possible constraints refinements. The fact is that the existing criteria do not directly require a sub-path in which a value assigned at the def-point (like input signal or message parameter) to pass through a possible sequence of uses in conditions before reaching a use-point directly associated with the def-use pair. A conditional statement in such sequence is the usage itself, and therefore the corresponding def-use pair can be covered in a short stand-alone test case. Such strategy, however, leads to a decrease in the ability to detect faults [3–5] and may lose interesting scenarios, especially in cases where a def-point is an input parameter with arbitrary value, which becomes instantiated only after some conditionals whereas such instantiation itself does not play a role of a def-point in existing data flow coverage criteria. This work is aimed to extend data flow coverage with chains of usages to fill the gap.

2 Motivation Examples

This section describes three small examples, which are inspired by real-world testing problems in industrial systems. Typically, the validation of an input value being in some

M. H. ter Beek and R. Monahan (Eds.): IFM 2022, LNCS 13274, pp. 313–321, 2022.
https://doi.org/10.1007/978-3-031-07727-2_17

admissible region is required by software development standards; however, data flow coverage criteria are not specially adapted to test this requirement. There is still a small chance to catch the 'missed validation' defect – in case the input value would accidentally be selected outside of that admissible range, but relying on chance is not a systematic approach.

Example 1. Let us consider a small formal model described using the Event-B notation style. In the beginning, it has two requirements:

R1. **when**	R2. **when**
event = TURN_ON ∧	voltage < MIN_VOLTAGE
voltage >= MIN_VOLTAGE	**then**
then	machine := DISABLED
machine := ENABLED	report 'undervoltage'
report 'enabled'	**end**
end	

Here 'voltage' comes as an input with an arbitrary value. The main idea of the system is to control enabling/disabling of a certain machine depending on the voltage measurement. Later, after being additionally investigated, the model was enhanced with one more requirement:

```
R3. when
        voltage > MAX_VOLTAGE
    then
        machine := DISABLED
        report 'overvoltage'
    end
```

Adding new requirements is a typical situation in the development process; the problem of our model is that the previous requirements were not consistently updated (R1 still does not care about the overvoltage), and scenario R3->R1, while obviously unwanted, nevertheless is possible. Of course, this problem could be detected at the verification phase if an appropriate property was explicitly formulated, but the question is – what coverage type shall be used in order to obtain a test suite that is capable to reveal the problem? Neither applying the all-uses [9], nor MC/DC [11] can guarantee the desired test case.

Example 2. The more restrictive checks the input parameter has passed, the more options there are for selecting its specific values to be used as a test data. Example of a C program in Fig. 1 shows the way to exploit the data flow coverage tailoring to extend a test suite when the input parameter passes through a sequence of checks that refine its constraints.

```
1.   input(x, parity_check);
2.   if(x >= 0)
3.       print("non-negative");
4.   else
5.       print("negative");
6.   if(parity_check)
7.       if(x mod 2 != 0)
8.           print("odd");
9.       else
10.          print("even");
```

Fig. 1. Program with sign and parity checks

Note that test cases covering the sequence of conditions {4,7} and {4,9} (printing "negative", "even" and "negative", "odd") are not required by the all-uses adequate test suite (see Fig. 2). Notation [Def_loc:Use_loc]var is used to denote a def-use pair.

#	inputs	outputs	def-use pairs for x covered
1	(1,0)	"non-negative"	[1:2]x
2	(-1,0)	"negative"	[1:4]x
3	(1,1)	"non-negative", "odd"	[1:2]x, [1:7]x
4	(2,1)	"non-negative", "even"	[1:2]x, [1:9]x

Fig. 2. Test cases for the all-uses criterion (example #2)

Example 3. Another example shows the opposite problem. A test case guides some input value through its validation, but does not subsequently lead to its computational usage. Such an incoherence often occurs in automatically generated tests [3, 5]. Let us consider a code snippet described in Fig. 3. It includes a path like this: validation of x at line 4 and then return at line 10 before usage at line 11. This program has a fault – 'return Error' statement is missed after line 5, and therefore, the program can reach division-by-zero exception.

```
1.  input(x, y);
2.  if(x != 0)
3.      print("x != 0");
4.  else
5.      print("x = 0");
6.  if(y != 0)
7.      print("y != 0");
8.  else
9.      print("y = 0");
10.     return Error;
11. print (x/y + y/x);
```

Fig. 3. Program with division by zero faul

Figure 4 depicts the test suite produced to satisfy the all-uses criterion: in order to cover all def-use pairs it is sufficient to include only two tests. None of them catches the exception.

#	inputs	outputs	def-use pairs covered
1	(1,1)	"x != 0", "y != 0", 2	[1:2]x, [1:6]y, [1:11]x, [1:11]y
2	(0,0)	"x = 0", "y = 0", Error	[1:4]x, [1:8]y

Fig. 4. Test cases for the all-uses criterion (example #3)

3 Background

Let G = (C, E, s, f) be a flow graph of a program, where C – set of vertices, E – set of edges, s – the initial vertex, and f – the final vertex. Each variable occurrence is classified as being a definitional occurrence (i.e., where it is assigned with a new value), or a use occurrence (c-use type – in the right part of an assignment or in the parameter of an output signal; p-use type – in a predicate of a condition). A path on the graph G is a finite sequence of vertices $c_0, c_1,...,c_k$, where there exists an edge $(c_{i-1},c_i) \in E$ for all i, $(0 < i \leq k)$. A complete path is a path where $c_0 = s$ and $c_k = f$. Let v be a variable and $c \in C$. Then defs(c)/uses(c) denotes the set of all variables which are defined/used at vertex c respectively. A path $(n,c_1,...,c_k,m)$, $k \geq 1$, is called def-clear from vertex n to vertex m with respect to v if $v \notin defs(c_i)$ for all $1 \leq i \leq k$. A path p covers def-use pair $[D:U]v$ if $p = (s,D,q,U,f)$, where $D,U \in C$, $v \in defs(D)$, $v \in uses(U)$, and q is a def-clear path with respect to variable v. We will use DU to denote set of all def-use pairs. Test suite T satisfies the *all-uses* [9] criterion if for every vertex c and every variable $v \in defs(c)$, T includes a def-clear path w.r.t. v from c to all associated use-elements, meaning that each computation and condition affected by definition of v will be tested.

4   The Required k-Use Chains

Now let us introduce a notion of the required k-use chains coverage criterion.

Definition. A path p covers a k-use chain $[D:U_1:U_2:...:U_k]v$ if it covers all def-use pairs $[D:U_1]v$, $[D:U_2]v$, ... $[D:U_k]v$ in the given order. A test suite satisfies the required k-use chains criterion if it includes paths covering each chain from the predefined set.

For the first example, the scenario R3->R1 will be required to satisfy coverage of 2-use chain for vasriable voltage. The second example requires two more test cases additionally to the all-uses criterion on demand of the 2-use chains $[1:4:7]x$ and $[1:4:9]x$ covered by test inputs #5 and #6 respectively (see Fig. 5).

#	inputs	outputs	def-use pairs covered
1	(1,0)	"non-negative"	[1:2]x
2	(-1,0)	"negative"	[1:4]x
3	(1,1)	"non-negative", "odd"	[1:2]x, [1:7]x
4	(2,1)	"non-negative", "even"	[1:2]x, [1:9]x
5	(-1,1)	"negative", "odd"	[1:4]x, [1:7]x
6	(-2,1)	"negative", "even"	[1:4]x, [1:9]x

Fig. 5. Test cases for the k-uses criterion (example #2)

For the third example, Fig. 6. describes a test suite with one additional test input leading to the div-by-zero exception. It was generated to cover the 2-use chain $[1:4:11]x$.

Selecting the Chains. The problem of this approach is to identify the required set and the length of such k-use chains. Number of possible chains grows rapidly, and may become infinite in case of loops. One way to manage its size is to restrict those lengths to some reasonable value. Another approach is to extend the use-chain only if iteratively applying subsequent usage will indeed refine the value of the variable and skip if it does not. For example, after condition 'if(a == 2)' upcoming usage 'if(a > 0)' will not contribute to the chain. The chain can also break after the UNSAT-usage, e.g., after applying condition 'if(a == 2)' upcoming 'if(a < 0)' will terminate the chain (otherwise the chain will require a non-executable path).

#	inputs	outputs	def-use pairs covered
1	(1,1)	"x != 0", "y != 0", 2	[1:2]x, [1:6]y, [1:11]x, [1:11]y
2	(0,0)	"x = 0", "y = 0", Error	[1:4]x, [1:8]y
3	(0,1)	"x = 0", "y != 0", **Div-By-Zero**	[1:4]x, [1:6]y, [1:11]x, [1:11]y

Fig. 6. Test cases for the k-uses criterion (example #3)

Algorithm for the Required k-Use Chains Selection. The algorithm is presented in Fig. 7. It has two procedures **select_k_use_chains** and **continue_chain**. It essentially relies on SSA-form [12] (the algorithm assumes each variable to have a unique definition point) which allows identifying set of uses for each definition and on analysis of the control flow graph, which gives answers about the feasibility of continuing the chain.

The main procedure **select_k_use_chains** takes as inputs the name of a variable, its definition location and the maximum length of the required use-chains. Initially, the resulting set Req_chains is empty, formula F keeps restrictions (or just a specific value) set up at the definition point, and U_set is a set of all use-locations associated with the given definition. In case of loops, U_set can be extended to include the appropriate use-locations twice, distinguishing the first and iterative occurrences.

Procedure **continue_chain** recursively enumerates the use-locations (lines 13–31) increasing the length of the chain under construction and refines the constraints on the specified variable at each step (lines 21, 24 and 30). Line 17 prevents multiple consideration of a usage in one chain. Lines 19 and 26 together with their conditionals are needed to prevent going through infeasible paths. Usages of c-use type are processed at lines 20 and 21. If the p-use is not a comparison with a constant, and thus, the procedure can not reason about the satisfiability of the overall use-chain, then such a chain will be terminated by a recursive call with an empty u_set at line 24. Line 27 checks if the formula will be strengthened. If the new predicate will not actually refine the constraints already formed, then, for the reasons of test suite size, it will be skipped at line 28. The argument in favor of this rule is that a conventional test case concretization procedure, which is based on boundary checking, will not find any additional value for the test input in this case. The condition at line 15 is responsible for safely avoiding the generation of redundant combinations: indeed, a path covering an element implies covering all the elements included in the tree of its pre-dominators (the notion w< <u means that every path that reaches u goes through the vertex immediately preceding w), therefore, there is no need to consider u before considering w. In other cases, the recursion will terminate upon the chain length exceeds predefined maximum (lines 11–12) or u_set becomes empty. Lines 32 and 33 are responsible for storing the newly generated chain in Req_chains.

Let us consider the example of k-use chains generation for the program presented in Fig. 8. The only def-point for variable x is the input at line L1, thus we can assume **select_k_use_chains** (x, L1, 9) as an entry call.

```
01. proc select_k_use_chains(var, d_loc, k)
02. begin
03.    Req_chains := Ø;
04.    Let F = a constraint (or a value) defined for var at d_loc;
05.    Let U_set = a set of usage locations {u_loc∈C : [d_loc:u_loc]var∈DU};
06.    continue_chain(d_loc, F, U_set, [d_loc]var, 0, k);
07.    return Req_chains;
08. end

09. proc continue_chain(curr_loc, formula, u_set, [curr_chain]var, i, k)
10. begin
11.  if (i > k)
12.     return;
13.  for each u ∈ u_set do,
14.  begin
15.     if (∃w: w ∈ u_set ∧ w ∉ curr_chain ∧ w<<u)
16.        continue;
17.     remove u from u_set;
18.     if(u is unreachable from curr_loc)
19.        continue;
20.     if usage of var at u is of c-use type
21.        continue_chain(u, formula, u_set, [curr_chain: u]var, i+1, k);
22.     Let pred is a predicate over var at u for p-use type;
23.     if (pred is not a comparison of var with a constant)
24.        continue_chain(u, (formula ∧ pred), Ø, [curr_chain: u]var, i+1, k);
25.     if (UNSAT(formula ∧ pred))
26.        continue;
27.     if (i > 0 ∧ formula → formula ∧ pred)
28.        continue_chain(u, formula, u_set, [curr_chain]var, i, k);
29.     else
30.        continue_chain(u, (formula ∧ pred), u_set, [curr_chain: u]var, i+1, k);
31.  end
32.  if (i > 0 ∧ ¬(∃q: [curr_chain: [q]]var ∈ Req_chains))
33.     Req_chains := Req_chains ∪ [curr_chain]var;
34. end
```

Fig. 7. Algorithm for the required k-use chains selection

The formula F at line 04 of the selection algorithm is trivial ($-\infty < x < \infty$) since the definition itself does not apply restrictions. The set of usage locations U_set at line 05 consists of 9 elements: {L2, L4, L5, L7, L9, L11, L13, L15, L16}, so the potential number of k-use chains can be expressed as the sum of all permutations of each non-empty subset of U_set, i.e., $\sum_{i=1}^{9} \frac{9!}{(9-i)!} = 986409$. However, the number of test goals selected by the algorithm is only 5 (see Fig. 9). This reduction is achieved due to the rules that restrict the selection of chains. For example, after the usage at L2 only the usage at 17 is feasible: usages at L4, L5, L7 will not be included in the chain due to the

```
L1.    input(x);
L2.    if(x < 0)
L3.        print("less than 0");
L4.    else
L5.    if(x == 0)
L6.        print("equal to 0");
L7.    else if(x > 0)
L8.        print("more than 0");
L9.    if(x > 10)
L10.       print("more than 10");
L11.   else
L12.       print("no more than 10");
L13.   if(x > 20)
L14.       print("more than 20");
L15.   else
L16.       print("no more than 20");
L17.   print(x);
```

Fig. 8. Example of a program for k-use chains generation

#	k-use chains
1	[L1: L2: L17]x
2	[L1: L4: L5: L17]x
3	[L1: L4: L7: L9: L13: L17]x
4	[L1: L4: L7: L9: L15: L17]x
5	[L1: L4: L7: L11: L17]x

Fig. 9. The required k-use chains

#	val of x	achieved coverage of uses locations, associated with the definition of x at L1
1	-1	L2, L11, L15, L17
2	0	L4, L11, L15, L17
3	21	L4, L7, L9, L13, L17
4	11	L4, L7, L9, L15, L17
5	1	L4, L7, L11, L15, L17

Fig. 10. Test inputs and def-use coverage achieved

condition at line 18 (these locations are unreachable after L2); usages at L11, L15 – due to the condition at line 27 (formula will not be strengthened); usages at L9, L13 – due to the condition at line 25 (formula becomes unsatisfiable). Also note that the chain of usages can only start at L2 or L4 according to the condition at line 15 (reaching all other locations inevitably passes through L2 or L4). Figure 10 shows that in order to cover all def-use pairs it is sufficient to have only the first three test inputs, which represent the ranges $x < 0$, $x > 20$ and $x = 0$; the required k-use chains criterion additionally selects inputs from the ranges $10 < x \leq 20$ (test #4) and $0 < x \leq 10$ (test #5).

5   Related Work and Conclusions

Data flow coverage is extensively utilized to improve the efficiency of test suites [5–7, 13, 17]. Approaches [8–10, 15, 16] propose different kinds of def-use pairs, chains of pairs and paths examination. The required k-use chains criterion subsumes all-uses [9] and avoids redefinitions [16]. Combinations of conditions, produced on demand of the required k-use chains examined by test cases #5 and #6 for the second example and case #3 for the third, will be required neither by Laski and Korel [10] nor MC/DC criteria because the refinements to constraints are split into different conditionals. In a sense, our proposal resembles Ural and Hong 'dependence chain' [8] and Ntafos 'k-dr tuples' criterion [15], the main differences being that (1) the k-use chain has no redefinitions of the given variable in-between and it does not rely on control dependency between usages and (2) our approach to selecting the required k-use chains keeps the number of test goals manageable: in our practice, the maximum value of k reached 5, the average value is 2, and the total number of chains is comparable to the number of def-use pairs.

We have developed a prototype of the described method using algorithms [13, 14] adapted to generate test suites in accordance with the required k-use chains criterion, and provided experiments with several medium-sized formal models of different industrial systems. First results show that the required k-use chain coverage increases number of test goals (and correlatively the mutation score) by roughly 7–20% when compared to all-uses criterion. It is worth noting that in addition to the quantitative improvement, the resulting tests become more 'interesting' in their scenarios – they often describe a longer and coherent story; situations when two def-use pairs (with the same variable and definition location) which were initially covered by different test cases, fell into one test case, increasing the data cohesion score, were not unique. With regard to the problems in coverage-directed test generation [1, 3–5, 13, 18], our approach can be used as a supplement heuristic to guide test generation and increase the thoroughness of testing of the safety-critical parts of software.

References

1. Miranda, B., Bertolino, A.: Testing relative to usage scope: revisiting software coverage criteria. ACM Trans. Softw. Eng. Methodol. **29**(3), 18. 24p. (2020)
2. Lee, J., Kang, S., Pilsu, J.: Test coverage criteria for software product line testing: Systematic literature review. Inf. Softw. Techn. **122**, 106272 (2020)
3. Gay, G., Staats, M., Whalen, M., Heimdahl, M.: The risks of coverage-directed test case generation. IEEE Trans. Softw. Eng. **41**, 803–819 (2015)
4. Inozemtseva, L., Holmes, R.: Coverage is not strongly correlated with test suite effectiveness. In: Proceedings of ACM ICSE, pp. 435–445 (2015)
5. Kolchin, A., Potiyenko, S., Weigert, T.: Challenges for automated, model-based test scenario generation. Comm. Comput. Inf. Sci. **1078**, 182–194 (2019)
6. Su T., et al.: A survey on data-flow testing. ACM Comput. Surv. **50**, 35p (2017)
7. Sahoo, R.R., Ray, M.: Metaheuristic techniques for test case generation: a review. Research anthology on agile software. Softw. Dev. Test. 1043–1058 (2022)
8. Hong, H.S., Ural, H.: Dependence testing: extending data flow testing with control dependence. In: Khendek, F., Dssouli, R. (eds.) TestCom 2005. LNCS, vol. 3502, pp. 23–39. Springer, Heidelberg (2005). https://doi.org/10.1007/11430230_3
9. Rapps, S., Weyuker, E.: Data flow analysis techniques for test data selection. In: Proceedings of the International Conference of Software Engineering. pp. 272–277 (1982)
10. Laski, J., Korel, B.: A data flow oriented program testing strategy. IEEE Trans. Softw. Eng. **9**(3), 347–354 (1983)
11. Chilenski, J., Miller, S.: Applicability of modified condition/decision coverage to software testing. Softw. Eng. J. **7**(5), 193–200 (1994)
12. Static single assignment book (2018). https://pfalcon.github.io/ssabook/latest/book-full.pdf. Accessed 6 Apr 2022
13. Weigert, T., et al.: Generating test suites to validate legacy systems. In: Fonseca i Casas, P., Sancho, M.-R., Sherratt, E. (eds.) SAM 2019. LNCS, vol. 11753, pp. 3–23. Springer, Cham (2019). https://doi.org/10.1007/978-3-030-30690-8_1
14. Kolchin, A.: A novel algorithm for attacking path explosion in model-based test generation for data flow coverage. In: Proceedings of IEEE 1st International Conference on System Analysis and Intelligent Computing, SAIC. pp. 226–231 (2018)
15. Ntafos, S.: On required element testing. IEEE Trans. Softw. Eng. **10**, 795–803 (1984)
16. Kolchin, A., Potiyenko, S., Weigert, T.: Extending data flow coverage with redefinition analysis. In: Proceedings of the IEEE International Conference on Information and Digital Technologies. pp. 293–296 (2021)

17. Chaim, M.L., Baral, K., Offutt, J., Concilio, M.: Araujo, R.P.A.: Efficiently finding data flow subsumptions. In: Proceedings of 14th IEEE Conference on Software Testing, Verification and Validation (ICST). pp. 94–104 (2021)
18. Gal, R., Haber, E., Ibraheem, W., Irwin, B., Nevo, Z., Ziv, A.: Automatic scalable system for the coverage-directed generation (CDG) problem. In: Proceedings of Design, Automation & Test in Europe Conference & Exhibition (DATE), pp. 206–211 (2021)

Scalable Typestate Analysis
for Low-Latency Environments

Alen Arslanagić[1(✉)], Pavle Subotić[2], and Jorge A. Pérez[1]

[1] University of Groningen, Groningen, The Netherlands
a.arslanagic@rug.nl
[2] Microsoft, Belgrade, Serbia

Abstract. Static analyses based on *typestates* are important in certifying correctness of code contracts. Such analyses rely on Deterministic Finite Automata (DFAs) to specify properties of an object. We target the analysis of contracts in low-latency environments, where many useful contracts are impractical to codify as DFAs and/or the size of their associated DFAs leads to sub-par performance. To address this bottleneck, we present a *lightweight* typestate analyzer, based on an expressive specification language that can succinctly specify code contracts. By implementing it in the static analyzer INFER, we demonstrate considerable performance and usability benefits when compared to existing techniques. A central insight is to rely on a sub-class of DFAs with efficient *bit-vector* operations.

1 Introduction

Industrial-scale software is generally composed of multiple interacting components, which are typically produced separately. As a result, software integration is a major source of bugs [18]. Many integration bugs can be attributed to violations of *code contracts*. Because these contracts are implicit and informal in nature, the resulting bugs are particularly insidious. To address this problem, formal code contracts are an effective solution [12], because static analyzers can automatically check whether client code adheres to ascribed contracts.

Typestate is a fundamental concept in ensuring the correct use of contracts and APIs. A typestate refines the concept of a type: whereas a type denotes the valid operations on an object, a typestate denotes operations valid on an object in its *current program context* [20]. Typestate analysis is a technique used to enforce temporal code contracts. In object-oriented programs, where objects change state over time, typestates denote the valid sequences of method calls for a given object. The behavior of the object is prescribed by the collection of typestates, and each method call can potentially change the object's typestate.

Given this, it is natural for static typestate checkers, such as FUGUE [9], SAFE [23], and INFER's TOPL checker [2], to define the analysis property using Deterministic Finite Automata (DFAs). The abstract domain of the analysis is a set of states in the DFA; each operation on the object modifies the set of possible reachable states. If the set of abstract states contains an error state, then the

© Springer Nature Switzerland AG 2022
M. H. ter Beek and R. Monahan (Eds.): IFM 2022, LNCS 13274, pp. 322–340, 2022.
https://doi.org/10.1007/978-3-031-07727-2_18

analyzer warns the user that a code contract may be violated. Widely applicable and conceptually simple, DFAs are the de facto model in typestate analyses.

Here we target the analysis of realistic code contracts in low-latency environments such as, e.g., Integrated Development Environments (IDEs) [21,22]. In this context, to avoid noticeable disruptions in the users' workflow, the analysis should ideally run *under a second* [1]. However, relying on DFAs jeopardizes this goal, as it can lead to scalability issues. Consider, e.g., a class with n methods in which each method *enables* another one and then *disables* itself: the contract can lead to a DFA with 2^n states. Even with a small n, such a contract can be impractical to codify manually and will likely result in sub-par performance.

Interestingly, many practical contracts do not require a full DFA. In our enable/disable example, the method dependencies are *local* to a subset of methods: a enabling/disabling relation is established between pairs of methods. DFA-based approaches have a *whole class* expressivity; as a result, local method dependencies can impact transitions of unrelated methods. Thus, using DFAs for contracts that specify dependencies that are local to each method (or to a few methods) is redundant and/or prone to inefficient implementations. Based on this observation, we present a *lightweight* typestate analyzer for *locally dependent* code contracts in low-latency environments. It rests upon two insights:

1. *Allowed and disallowed sequences of method calls for objects can be succinctly specified without using DFAs.* To unburden the task of specifying typestates, we introduce *lightweight annotations* to specify *method dependencies* as annotations on methods. Lightweight annotations can specify code contracts for usage scenarios commonly encountered when using libraries such as File, Stream, Socket, etc. in considerably fewer lines of code than DFAs.
2. *A sub-class of DFAs suffices to express many useful code contracts.* To give semantics to lightweight annotations, we define *Bit-Vector Finite Automata (BFAs)*: a sub-class of DFAs whose analysis uses *bit-vector* operations. In many practical scenarios, BFAs suffice to capture information about the enabled and disabled methods at a given point. Because this information can be codified using bit-vectors, associated static analyses can be performed efficiently; in particular, our technique is not sensitive to the number of BFA states, which in turn ensures scalability with contract and program size.

We have implemented our lightweight typestate analysis in the industrial-strength static analyzer INFER [7]. Our analysis exhibits concrete usability and performance advantages and is expressive enough to encode many relevant typestate properties in the literature. On average, compared to state-of-the-art typestate analyses, our approach requires less annotations than DFA-based analyzers and does not exhibit slow-downs due to state increase. We summarise our contributions as follows:

- A specification language for typestates based on *lightweight annotations* (Sect. 2). Our language rests upon BFAs, a new sub-class of DFA based on bit-vectors.
- A lightweight analysis technique for code contracts, implemented in INFER (our artifact is available at [4]).[1]

---

[1] Our code is available at https://github.com/aalen9/lfa.git.

– Extensive evaluations for our lightweight analysis technique, which demonstrate considerable gains in performance and usability (Sect. 4).

2 Bit-Vector Typestate Analysis

2.1 Annotation Language

We introduce BFA specifications, which succinctly encode temporal properties by only describing *local method dependencies*, thus avoiding an explicit DFA specification. BFA specifications define code contracts by using atomic combinations of annotations '@Enable(n)' and '@Disable(n)', where n is a set of method names. Intuitively, '@Enable(n) m' asserts that invoking method m makes calling methods in n valid in a continuation. Dually, '@Disable(n) m' asserts that a call to m disables calls to all methods in n in the continuation. More concretely, we give semantics for BFA annotations by defining valid method sequences:

Definition 1 (Annotation Language). *Let* $C = \{m_0, \ldots, m_n\}$ *be a set of method names where each* $m_i \in C$ *is annotated by*

$$@Enable(E_i) \ @Disable(D_i) \ m_i$$

where $E_i \subseteq C$, $D_i \subseteq C$, *and* $E_i \cap D_i = \emptyset$. *Further, we have* $E_0 \cup D_0 = C$. *Let* $s = x_0, x_1, x_2, \ldots$ *be a method sequence where each* $x_i \in C$. *A sequence* s *is valid (w.r.t. annotations) if there is no substring* $s' = x_i, \ldots, x_k$ *of* s *such that* $x_k \in D_i$ *and* $x_k \notin E_j$, *for* $j \in \{i + 1, \ldots, k\}$.

The formal semantics for these specifications is given in Sect. 2.2. We note, if E_i or D_i is $\emptyset$ then we omit the corresponding annotation. Moreover, the BFA language can be used to derive other useful annotations defined as follows:

$$@EnableOnly(E_i) \ m_i \overset{\text{def}}{=} @Enable(E_i) \ @Disable(C \setminus E_i) \ m_i$$

$$@DisableOnly(D_i) \ m_i \overset{\text{def}}{=} @Disable(D_i) \ @Enable(C \setminus E_i) \ m_i$$

$$@EnableAll \ m_i \overset{\text{def}}{=} @Enable(C) \ m_i$$

This way, '@EnableOnly(E_i) m_i' asserts that a call to method m_i enables only calls to methods in E_i while disabling all other methods in C; '@DisableOnly(D_i) m_i' is defined dually. Finally, '@EnableAll m_i' asserts that a call to method m_i enables all methods in a class; '@DisableAll m_i' can be defined dually.

To illustrate the expressivity and usability of BFA annotations, we consider the SparseLU class from Eigen C++ library[2]. For brevity, we consider representative methods for a typestate specification (we also omit return types):

```
1   class SparseLU {
2       void analyzePattern(Mat a);
3       void factorize(Mat a);
4       void compute(Mat a);
5       void solve(Mat b);  }
```

---

[2] https://eigen.tuxfamily.org/dox/classEigen_1_1SparseLU.html

```
1    class SparseLU {                      class SparseLU {
2        states q0, q1, q2, q3;
3        @Pre(q0) @Post(q1)
4        @Pre(q3) @Post(q1)                    @EnableOnly(factorize)
5        void analyzePattern(Mat a);           void analyzePattern(Mat a);
6        @Pre(q1) @Post(q2)
7        @Pre(q3) @Post(q2)                     @EnableOnly(solve)
8        void factorize(Mat a);                void factorize(Mat a);
9        @Pre(q0) @Post(q2)
10       @Pre(q3) @Post(q2)                     @EnableOnly(solve)
11       void compute(Mat a);                  void compute(Mat a);
12       @Pre(q2) @Post(q3)
13       @Pre(q3)                              @EnableAll
14       void solve(Mat b); }                  void solve(Mat b);   }
```

Listing (1.1) SparseLU DFA Contract   **Listing (1.2)** SparseLU BFA Contract

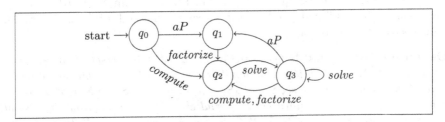

Fig. 1. SparseLU DFA

The `SparseLU` class implements a lower-upper (LU) decomposition of a sparse matrix. `Eigen`'s implementation uses assertions to dynamically check that: (i) `analyzePattern` is called prior to `factorize` and (ii) `factorize` or `compute` are called prior to `solve`. At a high-level, this contract tells us that `compute` (or `analyzePattern().factorize()`) prepares resources for invoking `solve`.

We notice that there are method call sequences that do not cause errors, but have redundant computations. For example, we can disallow consecutive calls to `compute` as in, e.g., sequences like '`compute().compute().solve()`' as the result of the first `compute` is never used. Further, `compute` is essentially implemented as '`analyzePattern().factorize()`'. Thus, it is also redundant to call `factorize` after `compute`. The DFA that substitutes dynamic checks and avoids redundancies is given in Fig. 1. Following the literature [9], this DFA can be annotated inside a class definition as in Listing 1.1. Here states are listed in the class header and transitions are specified by *@Pre* and *@Post* conditions on methods. However, this specification is too low-level and unreasonable for software engineers to annotate their APIs with, due to high annotation overheads.

In contrast, using BFA annotations the entire `SparseLU` class contract can be succinctly specified as in Listing 1.2. Here, the starting state is unspecified; it is determined by annotations. In fact, methods that are not *guarded* by other methods (like `solve` is guarded by `compute`) are enabled in the starting state. We remark that this can be overloaded by specifying annotations on the constructor method. We can specify the contract with only 4 annotations; the corresponding DFA requires 8 annotations and 4 states specified in the class header. We remark that a small change in local method dependencies by BFA annotations can result in a substantial change of the equivalent DFA. Let $\{m_1, m_2, m_3, \ldots, m_n\}$ be methods of some class with DFA associated (with states Q) in which m_1 and m_2 are enabled in each state of Q. Adding @Enable(m2) m1 doubles the number of states of the DFA as we need the set of states Q where m_2 is enabled in each state, but also states from Q with m_2 disabled in each state. Accordingly, transitions have to be duplicated for the new states and the remaining methods $(m_3, \ldots, m_n)$.

2.2 Bit-Vector Finite Automata

We define a class of DFAs, dubbed Bit-vector Finite Automata (BFA), that captures enabling/disabling dependencies between the methods of a class leveraging a bit-vector abstraction on typestates.

Definition 2 (Sets and Bit-vectors). *Let $\mathcal{B}^n$ denote the set of bit-vectors of length $n > 0$. We write $b, b', \ldots$ to denote elements of $\mathcal{B}^n$, with $b[i]$ denoting the i-th bit in b. Given a finite set S with $|S| = n$, every $A \subseteq S$ can be represented by a bit-vector $b_A \in \mathcal{B}^n$, obtained via the usual characteristic function. By a small abuse of notation, given sets $A, A' \subseteq S$, we may write $A \subseteq A'$ to denote the subset operation applied on b_A and $b_{A'}$ (and similarly for $\cup, \cap$).*

We first define a BFA per class. Let us write $\mathcal{C}$ to denote the finite set of all classes $c, c', \ldots$ under consideration. Given a $c \in \mathcal{C}$ with n methods, and assuming a total order on method names, we represent them by the set $\Sigma_c = \{m_1, \ldots, m_n\}$.

A BFA for a class with n methods considers states q_b, where, following Definition 2, the bit-vector $b_A \in \mathcal{B}^n$ denotes the set $A \subseteq \Sigma_c$ enabled at that point. We often write 'b' (and q_b) rather than 'b_A' (and 'q_{b_A}'), for simplicity. As we will see, the intent is that if $m_i \in b$ (resp. $m_i \notin b$), then the i-th method is enabled (resp. disabled) in q_b. Definition 3 will give a mapping from methods to triples of bit-vectors. Given $k > 0$, let us write 1^k (resp. 0^k) to denote a sequence of 1s (resp. 0s) of length k. The initial state of the BFA is then $q_{10^{n-1}}$, i.e., the state in which only the first method is enabled and all the other $n - 1$ methods are disabled.

Given a class c, we define its associated mapping $\mathcal{L}_c$ as follows:

Definition 3 (Mapping $\mathcal{L}_c$). *Given a class c, we define $\mathcal{L}_c$ as a mapping from methods to triples of subsets of Σ_c as follows*

$$\mathcal{L}_c : \Sigma_c \to \mathcal{P}(\Sigma_c) \times \mathcal{P}(\Sigma_c) \times \mathcal{P}(\Sigma_c)$$

Given $m_i \in \Sigma_c$, we shall write E_i, D_i and P_i to denote each of the elements of the triple $\mathcal{L}_c(m_i)$. The mapping $\mathcal{L}_c$ is induced by the annotations in class c: for each m_i, the sets E_i and D_i are explicit, and P_i is simply the singleton $\{m_i\}$.

In an BFA, transitions between states $q_b, q_{b'}, \cdots$ are determined by $\mathcal{L}_c$. Given $m_i \in \Sigma_c$, we have $j \in E_i$ if and only if the m_i enables m_j; similarly, $k \in D_i$ if and only if m_i disables m_k. A transition from q_b labeled by method m_i leads to state

$q_{b'}$, where b' is determined by $\mathcal{L}_c$ using b. Such a transition is defined only if a pre-condition for m_i is met in state q_b, i.e., $P \subseteq b$. In that case, $b' = (b \cup E_i) \setminus D_i$.

These intuitions should suffice to illustrate our approach and, in particular, the local nature of enabling and disabling dependencies between methods. The following definition makes them precise.

Definition 4 (BFA). *Given a* $c \in C$ *with* $n > 0$ *methods, a Bit-vector Finite Automaton (BFA) for* c *is defined as a tuple* $M = (Q, \Sigma_c, \delta, q_{10^{n-1}}, \mathcal{L}_c)$ *where:*

- Q *is a finite set of states* $q_{10^{n-1}}, q_b, q_{b'}, \ldots,$ *where* $b, b', \ldots \in \mathcal{B}^n$;
- $q_{10^{n-1}}$ *is the initial state;*
- $\Sigma_c = \{m_1, \ldots, m_n\}$ *is the alphabet (method identities);*
- $\mathcal{L}_c$ *is a BFA mapping (cf. Definition 3);*
- $\delta : Q \times \Sigma_c \to Q$ *is the transition function, where* $\delta(q_b, m_i) = q_{b'}$ *(with* $b' = (b \cup E_i) \setminus D_i$) *if* $P_i \subseteq b$, *and is undefined otherwise.*

We remark that in a BFA all states in Q *are accepting states.*

Example 1 (SparseLU). We give the BFA derived from the annotations in the SparseLU example (Listing 1.2). We associate indices to methods:

$$[0 : constructor, 1 : aP, 2 : compute, 3 : factorize, 4 : solve]$$

The constructor annotations are implicit: it enables methods that are not guarded by annotations on other methods (in this case, aP and $compute$). The mapping $\mathcal{L}_{\mathsf{SparseLU}}$ is as follows:

$$\mathcal{L}_{\mathsf{SparseLU}} = \{0 \mapsto (\{1, 2\}, \{\}, \{0\}),\ 1 \mapsto (\{3\}, \{1, 2, 4\}, \{1\}),$$
$$2 \mapsto (\{4\}, \{1, 2, 3\}, \{2\}),\ 3 \mapsto (\{4\}, \{1, 2, 3\}, \{3\}), 4 \mapsto (\{1, 2, 3\}, \{\}, \{4\})\}$$

The set of states is $Q = \{q_{1000}, q_{1100}, q_{0010}, q_{0001}, q_{1111}\}$ and the transition function δ is given by following nine transitions:

$$\delta(q_{1000}, constr) = q_{1100} \quad \delta(q_{1100}, aP) = q_{0010} \quad \delta(q_{1100}, compute) = q_{0010}$$
$$\delta(q_{0010}, factorize) = q_{0001} \quad \delta(q_{0001}, solve) = q_{1111} \quad \delta(q_{1111}, aP) = q_{0010}$$
$$\delta(q_{1111}, compute) = q_{0001} \quad \delta(q_{1111}, factorize) = q_{0001} \quad \delta(q_{1111}, solve) = q_{1111}$$

BFAs vs DFAs. First, we need define some convenient notations:

Definition 5 (Method sequences and concatenation). *We use* $\widetilde{m}$ *to denote a finite sequence of method names in* Σ. *Further, we use '·' to denote sequence concatenation, defined as expected.*

In the following theorem, we use $\hat{\delta}(q_b, \widetilde{m})$ to denote the extension of the one-step transition function $\delta(q_b, m_i)$ to a sequence of method calls (i.e., $\widetilde{m}$). BFAs determine a strict sub-class of DFAs. First, because all states in Q are accepting states, BFA cannot encode the *"must call"* property (cf. Sect. 5). Next, we define the *context-independency* property, satisfied by all BFAs but not by all DFAs:

Theorem 1 (Context-independency). *Let $M = (Q, \Sigma_c, \delta, q_{10^{n-1}}, \mathcal{L}_c)$ be a BFA. Also, let $L = \{\widetilde{m} : \hat{\delta}(q_{10^{n-1}}, \widetilde{m}) = q' \land q' \in Q\}$ be the language accepted by M. Then, for $m_n \in \Sigma_c$ we have*

1. If there is $\widetilde{p} \in L$ and $m_{n+1} \in \Sigma_c$ s.t. $\widetilde{p} \cdot m_{n+1} \notin L$ and $\widetilde{p} \cdot m_n \cdot m_{n+1} \in L$ then there is no $\widetilde{m} \in L$ s.t. $\widetilde{m} \cdot m_n \cdot m_{n+1} \notin L$.
2. If there is $\widetilde{p} \in L$ and $m_{n+1} \in \Sigma_c$ s.t. $\widetilde{p} \cdot m_{n+1} \in L$ and $\widetilde{p} \cdot m_n \cdot m_{n+1} \notin L$ then there is no $\widetilde{m} \in L$ s.t. $\widetilde{m} \cdot m_n \cdot m_{n+1} \in L$.

Proof. Directly by Definition 4. See [3] for details.

Informally, the above theorem tells that previous calls ($\widetilde{m}$) (*i.e.*, context) cannot impact the effect of a call to m_n to subsequent calls (m_{n+1}). That is, Item 1. (resp. Item 2.) tells that method m_n enables (resp. disables) the same set of methods in any context. For example, a DFA that disallows modifying a collection while iterating is not a BFA (as in Fig. 3 in [5]). Let *it* be a Java Iterator with its usual methods for collection c. For the illustration, we assume a single DFA relates the iterator and its collection methods. Then, the sequence 'it.hasNext;it.next;c.remove;it.hasNext' should not be allowed, although 'c.remove;it.hasNext' should be allowed. That is, c.remove disables it.hasNext *only if* it.hasNext is previously called. Thus, the effect of calling c.remove depends on the calls that precedes it.

BFAs Subsumption. Using BFAs, checking class subsumption boils down to usual set inclusion. Suppose M_1 and M_2 are BFAs for classes c_1 and c_2, with c_2 being the superclass of c_1. The class inheritance imposes an important question on how we check that c_1 is a proper refinement of c_2. In other words, c_1 must subsume c_2: any valid sequence of calls to methods of c_2 must also be valid for c_1. Using BFAs, we can verify this simply by checking annotations method-wise. We can check whether M_2 subsumes M_1 only by considering their respective annotation mappings $\mathcal{L}_{c_2}$ and $\mathcal{L}_{c_1}$. Then, we have $M_2 \succeq M_1$ iff for all $m_j \in \mathcal{L}_{c_1}$ we have $E_1 \subseteq E_2$, $D_1 \supseteq D_2$, and $P_1 \subseteq P_2$ where $\langle E_i, D_i, P_i \rangle = \mathcal{L}_{c_i}(m_j)$ for $i \in \{1, 2\}$.

3 Compositional Analysis Algorithm

Since BFAs can be ultimately encoded as bit-vectors, for the non-compositional case e.g., intra-procedural, standard data-flow analysis frameworks can be employed [15]. However, in the case of member objects methods being called, we present a compositional algorithm that is tailored for the INFER compositional static analysis framework. We motivate our compositional analysis technique with the example below.

Example 2. Let Foo be a class that has member lu of class SparseLU (cf. Listing 1.3). For each method of Foo that invokes methods on lu we compute a *symbolic summary* that denotes the effect of executing that method on types-tates of lu. To check against client code, a summary gives us: (i) a pre-condition

```
 1   class Foo {
 2     SparseLU lu; Matrix a;
 3     void setupLU1(Matrix b) {
 4       this.lu.compute(this.a);
 5       if (?) this.lu.solve(b); }
 6     void setupLU2() {
 7       this.lu.analyzePattern(this.a);
 8       this.lu.factorize(this.a); }
 9     void solve(Matrix b) {
10       this.lu.solve(b); } }
```

Listing (1.3) Class Foo using SparseLU

```
void wrongUseFoo() {
  Foo foo; Matrix b;
  foo.setupLU1();
  foo.setupLU2();
  foo.solve(b);
}
```

Listing (1.4) Client code for Foo

(i.e., which methods should be allowed before calling a procedure) and (ii) the effect on the *typestate* of an argument when returning from the procedure. A simple instance of a client is wrongUseFoo in Listing 1.4.

The central idea of our analysis is to accumulate enabling and disabling annotations. For this, the abstract domain maps object access paths to triplets from the definition of $\mathcal{L}_{\text{SparseLU}}$. A *transfer function* interprets method calls in this abstract state. We illustrate the transfer function, presenting how abstract state evolves as comments in the following code listing.

```
 1   void setupLU1(Matrix b) {
 2     // s1 = this.lu -> ({}, {}, {})
 3     this.lu.compute(this.a);
 4     // s2 = this.lu -> ({solve}, {aP, factorize, compute}, {compute})
 5     if (?) this.lu.solve(b); }
 6     // s3 = this.lu -> ({solve, aP, factorize, compute}, {}, {compute})
 7     // join s2 s3 = s4
 8     // s4 = sum1 = this.lu -> ({solve}, {aP, factorize, compute}, {compute})
```

At the procedure entry (line 2) we initialize the abstract state as a triplet with empty sets (s_1). Next, the abstract state is updated at the invocation of compute (line 3): we copy the corresponding tuple from $\mathcal{L}_{\text{SparseLU}}(\textit{compute})$ to obtain s_2 (line 4). Notice that compute is in the pre-condition set of s_2. Further, given the invocation of solve within the if-branch in line 5 we transfer s_2 to s_3 as follows: the enabling set of s_3 is the union of the enabling set from $\mathcal{L}_{\text{SparseLU}}(\textit{solve})$ and the enabling set of s_2 with the disabling set from $\mathcal{L}_{\text{SparseLU}}(\textit{solve})$ removed (i.e., an empty set here). Dually, the disabling set of s_3 is the union of the disabling set of $\mathcal{L}_{\text{SparseLU}}(\textit{solve})$ and the disabling set of s_1 with the enabling set of $\mathcal{L}_{\text{SparseLU}}(\textit{solve})$ removed. Here we do not have to add solve to the pre-condition set, as it is in the enabling set of s_2. Finally, we join the abstract states of two branches at line 7 (i.e., s_2 and s_3). Intuitively, join operates as follows: (i) a method is enabled only if it is enabled in both branches and not disabled in any branch; (ii) a method is disabled if it is disabled in either branch; (iii) a method called in either branch must be in the pre-condition (cf. Definition 6). Accordingly, in line 8 we obtain the final state s_4 which is also a summary for SetupLU1.

Now, we illustrate checking client code wrongUseFoo() with computed summaries:

```
 1   void wrongUseFoo() {
 2     Foo foo; Matrix b;
 3     // d1 = foo.lu -> ({aP, compute}, {solve, factorize}, {})
```

```
4    foo.setupLU1(); // apply sum1 to d1
5    // d2 = foo.lu -> ({solve}, {aP, factorize, compute}, {})
6    foo.setupLU2(); // apply sum2 = {this.lu -> ({solve}, {aP, factorize,
        compute}, {aP}) }
7    // warning! 'analyzePattern' is in pre of sum2, but not enabled in d2
8    foo.solve(b); }
```

Above, at line 2 the abstract state is initialized with annotations of constructor Foo. At the invocation of setupLU1() (line 4) we apply sum_1 in the same way as user-entered annotations are applied to transfer s_2 to s_3 above. Next, at line 6 we can see that aP is in the pre-condition set in the summary for setupLU2() (sum_2), computed similarly as sum_1, but not in the enabling set of the current abstract state d_2. Thus, a warning is raised: foo.lu set up by foo.setupLU1() is never used and overridden by foo.setupLU2().

Class Composition. In the above example, the allowed orderings of method calls to an object of class Foo are imposed by the contracts of its object members (SparseLU) and the implementation of its methods. In practice, a class can have multiple members with their own BFA contracts. For instance, class Bar can use two solvers SparseLU and SparseQR:

```
1    class Bar {
2      SparseLU lu; SparseQR qr; /* ... */ }
```

where class SparseQR has its own BFA contract. The implicit contract of Bar depends on contracts of both lu and qr. Moreover, a class as Bar can be a member of some other class. Thus, we refer to those classes as *composed* and to classes that have declared contracts (as SparseLU) as *base classes*.

Integrating Aliasing. Now, we discuss how *aliasing information* can be integrated with our technique. In Example 2 member lu of object foo can be aliased. Thus, we keep track of BFA triplets for all base members instead of constructing an explicit BFA contract for a composed class (e.g., Foo). Further, we would need to generalize an abstract state to a mapping of *alias sets* to BFA triplets. That is, the elements of abstract state would be $\{a_1, a_2, \ldots, a_n\} \mapsto \langle E, D, P \rangle$ where $\{a_1, a_2, \ldots, a_n\}$ is a set of access paths. For example, when invoking method setupLU1 we would need to apply its summary (sum_1) to triplets of each alias set that contains foo.lu as an element. Let $d_1 = \{S_1 \mapsto t_1, S_2 \mapsto t_2, \ldots\}$ be an abstract state where S_1 and S_2 are the only keys such that foo.lu $\in S_i$ for $i \in \{1, 2\}$ and t_1 and t_2 are some BFA triplets.

```
1    // d1 = S1 -> t1, S2 -> t2, ...
2    foo.setupLU1(); // apply sum1 = {this.lu -> t3}
3    // d2 = S1 -> apply t3 to t1, S2 -> apply t3 to t2, ...
```

Above, at line 2 we would need to update bindings of S_1 and S_2 (.resp) by applying an BFA triplet for this.foo from sum_1, that is t_3, to t_1 and t_2 (.resp). The resulting abstract state d_2 is given at line 4. We remark that if a procedure does not alter aliases, we can soundly compute and apply summaries, as shown above.

Algorithm. We formally define our analysis, which presupposes the control-flow graph (CFG) of a program. Let us write $\mathcal{AP}$ to denote the set of access paths.

Access paths model heap locations as paths used to access them: a program variable followed by a finite sequence of field accesses (e.g., $foo.a.b$). We use access paths as we want to explicitly track states of class members. The abstract domain, denoted $\mathbb{D}$, maps access paths $\mathcal{AP}$ to BFA triplets:

$$\mathbb{D} : \mathcal{AP} \to \bigcup_{c \in \mathcal{C}} Cod(\mathcal{L}_c)$$

As variables denoted by an access path in $\mathcal{AP}$ can be of any declared class $c \in \mathcal{C}$, the co-domain of $\mathbb{D}$ is the union of codomains of $\mathcal{L}_c$ for all classes in a program. We remark that $\mathbb{D}$ is sufficient for both checking and summary computation, as we will show in the remaining of the section.

Definition 6 (Join Operator). *We define* $\bigsqcup : Cod(\mathcal{L}_c) \times Cod(\mathcal{L}_c) \to Cod(\mathcal{L}_c)$ *as follows:* $\langle E_1, D_1, P_1 \rangle \sqcup \langle E_2, D_2, P_2 \rangle = \langle E_1 \cap E_2 \setminus (D_1 \cup D_2), \ D_1 \cup D_2, \ P_1 \cup P_2 \rangle$.

The join operator on $Cod(\mathcal{L}_c)$ is lifted to $\mathbb{D}$ by taking the union of un-matched entries in the mapping.

The compositional analysis is given in Algorithm 1. It expects a program's CFG and a series of contracts, expressed as BFAs annotation mappings (Definition 3). If the program violates the BFA contracts, a warning is raised. For the sake of clarity we only return a boolean indicating if a contract is violated (cf. Definition 8). In the actual implementation we provide more elaborate error reporting. The algorithm traverses the CFG nodes top-down. For each node v, it first collects information from its predecessors (denoted by $\mathsf{pred}(v)$) and joins them as σ (line 3). Then, the algorithm checks whether a method can be called in the given abstract state σ by predicate $\mathsf{guard}()$ (cf. Algorithm 2). If the precondition is met, then the $\mathsf{transfer}()$ function (cf. Algorithm 3) is called on a node. We assume a collection of BFA contracts (given as $\mathcal{L}_{c_1}, \ldots, \mathcal{L}_{c_k}$), which is input for Algorithm 1, is accessible in Algorithm 3 to avoid explicit passing. Now, we define some useful functions and predicates. For the algorithm, we require that the constructor disabling set is the complement of the enabling set:

Definition 7 (well_formed($\mathcal{L}_c$)). *Let c be a class, Σ methods set of class c, and $\mathcal{L}_c$. Then,* $\mathsf{well\_formed}(\mathcal{L}_c) = \mathbf{true}$ *iff* $\mathcal{L}_c(constr) = \langle E, \Sigma \setminus E, P \rangle$.

Definition 8 (warning($\cdot$)). *Let G be a CFG and $\mathcal{L}_1, \ldots, \mathcal{L}_k$ be a collection of BFAs. We define* $\mathsf{warning}(G, \mathcal{L}_1, \ldots, \mathcal{L}_k) = \mathbf{true}$ *if there is a path in G that violates some of $\mathcal{L}_i$ for $i \in \{1, \ldots, k\}$.*

Definition 9 (exit_node($\cdot$)). *Let v be a method call node. Then,* $\mathsf{exit\_node}(v)$ *denotes exit node w of a method body corresponding to v.*

Definition 10 (actual_arg($\cdot$)). *Let $v = Call-node[m_j(p_0 : b_0, \ldots, p_n : b_n)]$ be a call node where $p_0, \ldots, p_n$ are formal and $b_0, \ldots, b_n$ are actual arguments and let $p \in \mathcal{AP}$. We define* $\mathsf{actual\_arg}(p, v) = b_i$ *if $p = p_i$ for $i \in \{0, \ldots, n\}$, otherwise* $\mathsf{actual\_arg}(p, v) = p$.

For convinience, we use *dot notation* to access elements of BFA triplets:

Algorithm 1: BFA Compositional Analysis

Data: G : A program's CFG, a collection of BFA mappings: $\mathcal{L}_{c_1}, \ldots, \mathcal{L}_{c_k}$ over
classes $c_1, \ldots c_k$ such that $well\_formed(\mathcal{L}_{c_i})$ for $i \in \{1, \ldots, k\}$

Result: $warning(G, \mathcal{L}_{c_1}, \ldots, \mathcal{L}_{c_k})$

1 Initialize $NodeMap : Node \rightarrow \mathbb{D}$ as an empty map;
2 **foreach** v *in forward(G))* **do**
3 $\quad \sigma = \bigsqcup_{w \in pred(v)} w$;
4 $\quad$ **if** $guard(v, \sigma)$ **then** $NodeMap[v] := transfer(v, \sigma)$; **else return** *True*;
5 **return** *False*

Algorithm 2: Guard Predicate

Data: v : CFG node, σ : Domain
Result: False iff v is a method call that cannot be called in σ

1 **Procedure** $guard$ (v, σ)
2 $\quad$ **switch** v **do**
3 $\quad\quad$ **case** *Call-node[$m_j(p_0 : b_0, \ldots, p_n : b_n)$]* **do**
4 $\quad\quad\quad$ Let $w = exit\_node(v)$;
5 $\quad\quad\quad$ **for** $i \in \{0, \ldots, n\}$ **do**
6 $\quad\quad\quad\quad$ **if** $\sigma_w[p_i].P \cap \sigma[b_i].D \neq \emptyset$ **then return** *False*;
7 $\quad\quad\quad$ **return** *True*
8 $\quad\quad$ **otherwise do**
9 $\quad\quad\quad$ **return** *True*

Definition 11 (Dot notation for BFA triplets). *Let* $\sigma \in \mathbb{D}$ *and* $p \in \mathcal{AP}$.
Further, let $\sigma[p] = \langle E_\sigma, D_\sigma, P_\sigma \rangle$. *Then, we have* $\sigma[p].E = E_\sigma$, $\sigma[p].D = D_\sigma$, *and*
$\sigma[p].P = P_\sigma$.

Guard Predicate. Predicate guard(v, σ) checks whether a pre-condition for
method call node v in the abstract state σ is met (cf. Algorithm 2). We represent a call node as $m_j(p_0 : b_0, \ldots, p_n : b_n)$ where p_i are formal and b_i are
actual arguments (for $i \in \{0, \ldots, n\}$). Let σ_w be a post-state of an exit node of
method m_j. The pre-condition is met if for all b_i there are no elements in their
pre-condition set (i.e., the third element of $\sigma_w[b_i]$) that are also in disabling
set of the current abstract state $\sigma[b_i]$. For this predicate we need the property
$D = \Sigma_{c_i} \setminus E$, where Σ_{c_i} is a set of methods for class c_i. This is ensured by condition $well\_formed(\mathcal{L}_{c_i})$ (Definition 7) and by definition of transfer() (see below).

Transfer Function. The transfer function is given in Algorithm 3. It distin-
guishes between two types of CFG nodes:

Entry-node: (lines 3–6) This is a function entry node. For simplicity we
represent it as $m_j(p_0, \ldots, p_n)$ where m_j is a method name and $p_0, \ldots, p_n$ are
formal arguments. We assume p_0 is a reference to the receiver object (i.e., *this*).
If method m_j is defined in class c_i that has user-supplied annotations $\mathcal{L}_{c_i}$, in
line 5 we initialize the domain to the singleton map (*this* mapped to $\mathcal{L}_{c_i}(m_j)$).

Algorithm 3: Transfer Function

Data: v : CFG node, σ : Domain

Result: Output abstract state σ' : *Domain*

1 **Procedure** *transfer* (v, σ)

2   **switch** v **do**

3   **case** *Entry-node[$m_j(p_0, \ldots, p_n)$]* **do**

4   Let c_i be the class of method $m_j(p_0, \ldots, p_n)$;

5   **if** *There is $\mathcal{L}_{c_i}$* **then return** $\{this \mapsto \mathcal{L}_{c_i}(m_j)\}$;

6   **else return** *EmptyMap* ;

7   **case** *Call-node[$m_j(p_0 : b_0, \ldots, p_n : b_n)$]* **do**

8   Let σ_w be an abstract state of *exit_node(v)*;

9   Initialize $\sigma' := \sigma$;

10   **if** *this* not in σ' **then**

11   **for** *ap* in $dom(\sigma_w)$ **do**

12                $ap' = actual\_arg(ap\{b_0/\text{this}\}, v)$;

13   **if** ap' in $dom(\sigma)$ **then**

14                   $E' = (\sigma[ap'].E \cup \sigma_w[ap].E) \setminus \sigma_w[ap].D$;

15                   $D' = (\sigma[ap'].D \cup \sigma_w[ap].D) \setminus \sigma_w[ap].E$;

16                   $P' = \sigma[ap'].P \cup (\sigma_w[ap].P \setminus \sigma[ap'].E)$;

17                   $\sigma'[ap'] = \langle E', D', P' \rangle$;

18   **else**

19                   $\sigma'[ap'] := \sigma_w[ap]$;

20   **return** σ'

21   **otherwise do**

22   **return** σ

Otherwise, we return an empty map meaning that a summary has to be computed.

Call-node: (lines 7–20) We represent a call node as $m_j(p_0 : b_0, \ldots, p_n : b_n)$ where we assume actual arguments $b_0, \ldots, b_n$ are access paths for objects and b_0 represents a receiver object. The analysis is skipped if *this* is in the domain (line 10): this means the method has user-entered annotations. Otherwise, we transfer an abstract state for each argument b_i, but also for each *class member* whose state is updated by m_j. Thus, we consider all access paths in the domain of σ_w, that is $ap \in dom(\sigma_w)$ (line 11). We construct access path ap' given ap. We distinguish two cases: ap denotes (i) a member and (ii) a formal argument of m_j. By line 12 we handle both cases. In the former case we know ap has form $this.c_1.\ldots.c_n$. We construct ap' as ap with *this* substituted for b_0 (actual_arg$(\cdot)$ is the identity in this case, see Definition 10): e.g., if receiver b_0 is $this.a$ and ap is $this.c_1.\ldots.c_n$ then $ap' = this.a.c_1.\ldots.c_n$. In the latter case ap denotes formal argument p_i and actual_arg$(\cdot)$ returns corresponding actual argument b_i (as $p_i\{b_0/this\} = p_i$). Now, as ap' is determined we construct its BFA triplet. If ap' is not in the domain of σ (line 13) we copy a corresponding BFA triplet from σ_w (line 19). Otherwise, we transfer elements of an BFA triplet at $\sigma[ap']$ as follows. The resulting enabling set is obtained by (i) adding methods that m_j enables ($\sigma_w[ap].E$) to the current enabling set $\sigma[ap'].E$, and (ii) removing methods that m_j disables ($\sigma_w[ap].D$), from it. The disabling set D' is constructed in a complementary way. Finally, the pre-condition set $\sigma[ap'].P$ is expanded with elements of $\sigma_w[ap].P$ that are not in the enabling set $\sigma[ap'].E$. We remark that the property $D = \Sigma_{c_i} \setminus E$ is preserved by the definition of E' and D'. Transfer is the identity on σ for all other types of CFG nodes. We can see that for each method call we have constant number of bit-vector operations per argument. That is, BFA analysis is insensitive to the number of states, as a set of states is abstracted as a single set.

Note, in our implementation we use several features specific to INFER: (1) INFER's summaries which allow us to use a single domain for intra and inter procedural analysis; (2) scheduling on CFG top-down traversal which simplify the handling of branch statements. In principle, BFA can be implemented in other frameworks e.g., IFDS [19].

Correctness. In a BFA, we can abstract a set of states by the *intersection* of states in the set. That is, for $P \subseteq Q$ all method call sequences accepted by each state in P are also accepted by the state that is the intersection of bits of states in the set. Theorem 2 formalizes this property. First we need an auxiliary definition; let us write $Cod(\cdot)$ to denote the codomain of a mapping:

Definition 12 ($[\![\cdot]\!](\cdot)$). *Let* $\langle E, D, P \rangle \in Cod(\mathcal{L}_c)$ *and* $b \in \mathcal{B}^n$. *We define* $[\![\langle E, D, P\rangle]\!](b) = b'$ *where* $b' = (b \cup E) \setminus D$ *if* $P \subseteq b$, *and is undefined otherwise.*

Theorem 2 (BFA $\cap$-Property). *Let* $M = (Q, \Sigma_c, \delta, q_{10^n-1}, \mathcal{L}_c)$, $P \subseteq Q$, *and* $b_* = \bigcap_{q_b \in P} b$, *then*

1. *For* $m \in \Sigma_c$, *it holds:* $\delta(q_b, m)$ *is defined for all* $q_b \in P$ *iff* $\delta(q_{b_*}, m)$ *is defined.*
2. *Let* $\sigma = \mathcal{L}_c(m)$. *If* $P' = \{\delta(q_b, m) : q_b \in P\}$ *then* $\bigcap_{q_b \in P'} b = [\![\sigma]\!](b_*)$.

Proof. By induction on cardinality of P and Definition 4. See [3] for details.

Our BFA-based algorithm (Algorithm 1) interprets method call sequences in the abstract state and joins them (using join from Definition 6) following the control-flow of the program. Thus, we can prove its correctness by separately establishing: (1) the correctness of the interpretation of call sequences using a *declarative* representation of the transfer function (Definition 13) and (2) the soundness of join operator (Definition 6). For brevity, we consider a single program object, as method call sequences for distinct objects are analyzed independently. We define the *declarative* transfer function as follows:

Definition 13 (dtransfer$_c(\cdot)$). *Let* $c \in \mathcal{C}$ *be a class,* Σ_c *be a set of methods of* c, *and* $\mathcal{L}_c$ *be a BFA. Further, let* $m \in \Sigma_c$ *be a method,* $\langle E^m, D^m, P^m \rangle = \mathcal{L}_c(m)$, *and* $\langle E, D, P \rangle \in Cod(\mathcal{L}_c)$. *Then,*

$$\mathsf{dtransfer}_c(m, \langle E, D, P\rangle) = \langle E', D', P'\rangle$$

where $E' = (E \cup E^m) \setminus D^m$, $D' = (D \cup D^m) \setminus E^m$, *and* $P' = P \cup (P^m \setminus E)$, *if* $P^m \cap D = \emptyset$, *and is undefined otherwise. Let* $m_1, \ldots, m_n, m_{n+1}$ *be a method sequence and* $\phi = \langle E, D, P \rangle$, *then*

$$\mathsf{dtransfer}_c(m_1, \ldots, m_n, m_{n+1}, \phi) = \mathsf{dtransfer}_c(m_{n+1}, \mathsf{dtransfer}_c(m_1, \ldots, m_n, \phi))$$

Relying on Theorem 2, we state the soundness of join:

Theorem 3 (Soundness of $\sqcup$). *Let $q_b \in Q$ and $\phi_i = \langle E_i, D_i, P_i \rangle$ for $i \in \{1,2\}$. Then, $[\![\phi_1]\!](b) \cap [\![\phi_2]\!](b) = [\![\phi_1 \sqcup \phi_2]\!](b)$.*

Proof. By Definitions 6 and 12, and set laws. See [3] for details.

With these auxiliary notions in place, we show the correctness of the transfer function (i.e., summary computation that is specialized for the code checking):

Theorem 4 (Correctness of $\mathsf{dtransfer}_c(\cdot)$). *Let $M = (Q, \Sigma, \delta, q_{10^{n-1}}, \mathcal{L}_c)$. Let $q_b \in Q$ and $m_1 \ldots m_n \in \Sigma^*$. Then*

$$\mathsf{dtransfer}_c(m_1 \ldots m_n, \langle \emptyset, \emptyset, \emptyset, \rangle) = \langle E', D', P' \rangle \iff \hat{\delta}(q_b, m_1 \ldots m_n) = q_{b'}$$

where $b' = [\![\langle E', D', P' \rangle]\!](b)$.

Proof. By induction on the length of the method call sequence. See [3] for details.

4 Evaluation

We evaluate our technique to validate the following two claims:

Claim-I: Smaller annotation overhead. The BFA contract annotation overheads are smaller in terms of atomic annotations (e.g., @Post(...), @Enable(...)) than both competing analyses.

Claim-II: Improved scalability on large code and contracts. Our analysis scales better than the competing analyzers for our use case on two dimensions, namely, caller code size and contract size.

Experimental Setup. We used an Intel(R) Core(TM) i9-9880H CPU at 2.3 GHz with 16 GB of physical RAM running macOS 11.6 on the bare-metal. The experiments were conducted in isolation without virtualization so that runtime results are robust. All experiments shown here are run in single-thread for INFER 1.1.0 running with OCaml 4.11.1.

We implement two analyses in INFER, namely BFA and DFA, and use the default INFER typestate analysis TOPL as a baseline comparison. More in details: (1) BFA: The INFER implementation of the technique described in this paper. (2) DFA: A lightweight DFA-based typestate implementation based on an DFA-based analysis implemented in INFER. We translate BFA annotations to a minimal DFA and perform the analysis. (3) TOPL: An industrial typestate analyzer, implemented in INFER [2]. This typestate analysis is designed for high precision and not for low-latency environments. It uses PULSE, an INFER memory safety analysis, which provides it with alias information. We include it in our evaluation as a baseline state-of-the-art typestate analysis, i.e., an off-the-shelf industrial strength tool we could hypothetically use. We note our benchmarks do not require aliasing and in theory PULSE is not required.

We analyze a benchmark of 18 contracts that specify common patterns of locally dependent contract annotations for a class. Moreover, we auto-generate 122 client programs parametrized by lines of code, number of composed classes, if-branches, and loops. Note, the code is such that it does not invoke the need for aliasing (as we do not support it yet in our BFA implementation). Client programs follow the compositional patterns we described in Example 2; which can also be found in [13]. The annotations for BFA are manually specified; from them, we generate minimal DFAs representations in DFA annotation format and TOPL annotation format.

Our use case is to integrate static analyses in interactive IDEs e.g., Microsoft Visual Studio Code [21], so that code can be analyzed at coding time. For this reason, our use case requires low-latency execution of the static analysis. Our SLA is based on the RAIL user-centric performance model [1].

Usability Evaluation. Figure 2 outlines the key features of the 18 contracts we considered, called CR-1 – CR-18. In [3] we detail CR-4 as an example. For each contract, we specify the number of methods, the number of DFA states the contract corresponds to, and number of atomic annotation terms in BFA, DFA, and TOPL. An atomic annotation term is a standalone annotation in the given annotation language. We can observe that as the contract sizes increase in number of states, the annotation overhead for DFA and TOPL increase significantly. On the other hand, the annotation overhead for BFA remain largely constant wrt. state increase and increases rather proportionally with the number of methods in a contract. Observe that for contracts on classes with 4 or more methods, a manual specification using DFA or TOPL annotations becomes impractical. Overall, we validate Claim-I by the fact that BFA requires less annotation overhead on all of the contracts, making contract specification more practical.

Performance Evaluation. Recall that we distinguish between *base* and *composed* classes: the former have a user-entered contract, and the latter have contracts that are implicitly inferred based on those of their members (that could be either base or composed classes themselves). The total number of base classes in a composed class and contract size (i.e., the number of states in a minimal DFA that is a translation of a BFA contract) play the most significant roles in execution-time. In Fig. 3 we present a comparison of analyzer execution-times

Contract	#methods	#states	#BFA	#DFA	#TOPL	Contract	#methods	#states	#BFA	#DFA	#TOPL
CR-1	3	2	3	5	9	CR-10	10	85	18	568	1407
CR-2	3	3	5	5	14	CR-11	14	100	17	940	1884
CR-3	3	5	4	8	25	CR-12	14	1044	32	7766	20704
CR-4	5	5	5	10	24	CR-13	14	1628	21	13558	33740
CR-5	5	9	8	29	71	CR-14	14	2322	21	15529	47068
CR-6	5	14	9	36	116	CR-15	14	2644	24	26014	61846
CR-7	7	18	12	85	213	CR-16	16	3138	29	38345	88134
CR-8	7	30	10	120	323	CR-17	18	3638	23	39423	91120
CR-9	7	41	12	157	460	CR-18	18	4000	27	41092	101185

Fig. 2. Details of the 18 contracts in our evaluation.

(y-axis) with contract size (x-axis), where each line in the graph represents a different number of base classes composed in a given class (given in legends).

Comparing BFA Analysis Against DFA Analysis.   Figure 3a compares various class compositions (with contracts) specified in the legend, for client programs of 500-1K LoC. The DFA implementation sharply increases in execution-time as the number of states increases. The BFA implementation remains rather constant, always under the SLA of 1 s. Overall, BFA produces a geometric mean speedup over DFA of 5.52×. Figure 3b compares various class compositions for client programs of 15K LoC. Both implementations fail to meet the SLA; however, the BFA is close and exhibits constant behaviour regardless of the number of states in the contract. The DFA implementation is rather erratic, tending to sharply increase in execution-time as the number of states increases. Overall, BFA produces a geometric mean speedup over DFA of 1.5×.

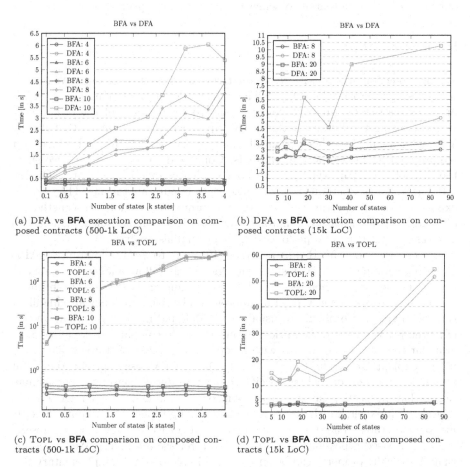

(a) DFA vs **BFA** execution comparison on composed contracts (500-1k LoC)

(b) DFA vs **BFA** execution comparison on composed contracts (15k LoC)

(c) Topl vs **BFA** comparison on composed contracts (500-1k LoC)

(d) Topl vs **BFA** comparison on composed contracts (15k LoC)

Fig. 3. Runtime comparisons. Each line represents a different number of base classes composed in a client code.

Comparing BFA-Based Analysis vs TOPL Typestate Implementations (Execution Time). Here again client programs do not require aliasing. Figure 3c compares various class compositions for client programs of 500-1K LoC. The TOPL implementation sharply increases in execution-time as the number of states increases, quickly missing the SLA. In contrast, the BFA implementation remains constant always under the SLA. Overall, BFA produces a geometric mean speedup over TOPL of 6.59×. Figure 3d compares various class compositions for client programs of 15K LoC. Both implementations fail to meet the SLA. The TOPL implementation remains constant until ~30 states and then rapidly increases in execution time. Overall, BFA produces a geometric mean speedup over TOPL of 287.86×.

Overall, we validate Claim-II by showing that our technique removes state as a factor of performance degradation at the expense of limited but suffice contract expressively. Even when using client programs of 15K LoC, we remain close to our SLA and with potential to achieve it with further optimizations.

5   Related Work

We focus on comparisons with restricted forms of typestate contracts. We refer to the typestate literature [6, 8, 9, 16, 20] for a more general treatment. The work [14] proposes restricted form of typestates tailored for use-case of the object construction using the builder pattern. This approach is restricted in that it only accumulates called methods in an abstract (monotonic) state, and it does not require aliasing for supported contracts. Compared to our approach, we share the idea of specifying typestate without explicitly mentioning states. On the other hand, their technique is less expressive than our annotations. They cannot express various properties we can (e.g., the property "cannot call a method"). Similarly, [11] defines heap-monotonic typestates where monotonicity can be seen as a restriction. It can be performed without an alias analysis.

Recent work on the RAPID analyzer [10] aims to verify cloud-based APIs usage. It combines *local* type-state with global value-flow analysis. Locality of type-state checking in their work is related to aliasing, not to type-state specification as in our work. Their type-state approach is DFA-based. They also highlight the state explosion problem for usual contracts found in practice, where the set of methods has to be invoked prior to some event. In comparison, we allow more granular contract specifications with a very large number of states while avoiding an explicit DFA. The FUGUE tool [8] allows DFA-based specifications, but also annotations for describing specific *resource protocols* contracts. These annotations have a *locality* flavor—annotations on one method do not refer to other methods. Moreover, we share the idea of specifying typestate without explicitly mentioning states. These additional annotations in FUGUE are more expressive than DFA-based typestates (e.g. "must call a release method"). We conjecture that "must call" property can be encoded as bit-vectors in a complementary way to our BFA approach. We leave this extension for future work.

Our annotations could be mimicked by having a local DFA attached to each method. In this case, the DFAs would have the same restrictions as our annotation language. We are not aware of prior work in this direction. We also note that while our technique is implemented in INFER using the algorithm in Sect. 2, the fact that we can translate typestates to bit-vectors allows typestate analysis for local contracts to be used in distributive dataflow frameworks, such as IFDS [19], without the need for modifying the framework for non-distributive domains [17].

6   Concluding Remarks

In this paper, we have tackled the problem of analyzing code contracts in low-latency environments by developing a novel lightweight typestate analysis. Our technique is based on BFAs, a sub-class of contracts that can be encoded as bit-vectors. We believe BFAs are a simple and effective abstraction, with substantial potential to be ported to other settings in which DFAs are normally used.

Acknowledgements. We are grateful to the anonymous reviewers for their constructive remarks. This work has been partially supported by the Dutch Research Council (NWO) under project No. 016.Vidi.189.046 (Unifying Correctness for Communicating Software).

References

1. RAIL model. https://web.dev/rail/. Accessed 30 Sep 2021
2. Infer TOPL (2021). https://fbinfer.com/docs/checker-topl/
3. Arslanagić, A., Subotić, P., Pérez, J.A.: Scalable Typestate Analysis for Low-Latency Environments (Extended Version). CoRR abs/2201.10627 (2022). https://arxiv.org/abs/2201.10627
4. Arslanagić, A., Subotić, P., Pérez, J.A.: LFA checker: scalable typestate analysis for low-latency environments (2022). https://doi.org/10.5281/zenodo.6393183
5. Bierhoff, K., Aldrich, J.: Modular typestate checking of aliased objects. In: Proceedings of the 22nd Annual ACM SIGPLAN Conference on Object-Oriented Programming Systems, Languages and Applications, pp. 301–320. OOPSLA 2007, Association for Computing Machinery, New York, NY, USA (2007). https://doi.org/10.1145/1297027.1297050
6. Bodden, E., Hendren, L.: The Clara framework for hybrid typestate analysis. Int. J. Softw. Tools Technol. Transf. **14**(3), 307–326 (2012)
7. Calcagno, C., Distefano, D.: Infer: an automatic program verifier for memory safety of C programs. In: Bobaru, M., Havelund, K., Holzmann, G.J., Joshi, R. (eds.) NFM 2011. LNCS, vol. 6617, pp. 459–465. Springer, Heidelberg (2011). https://doi.org/10.1007/978-3-642-20398-5_33
8. Deline, R., Fähndrich, M.: The fugue protocol checker: is your software baroque? Technical report MSR-TR-2004-07, Microsoft Research, April 2004
9. DeLine, R., Fähndrich, M.: Typestates for objects. In: Odersky, M. (ed.) ECOOP 2004. LNCS, vol. 3086, pp. 465–490. Springer, Heidelberg (2004). https://doi.org/10.1007/978-3-540-24851-4_21

10. Emmi, M., et al.: RAPID: checking API usage for the cloud in the cloud. In: Proceedings of the 29th ACM Joint Meeting on European Software Engineering Conference and Symposium on the Foundations of Software Engineering, pp. 1416–1426. ESEC/FSE 2021, Association for Computing Machinery, New York, NY, USA (2021). https://doi.org/10.1145/3468264.3473934
11. Fahndrich, M., Leino, R.: Heap monotonic typestate. In: Proceedings of the first International Workshop on Alias Confinement and Ownership (IWACO), July 2003. https://www.microsoft.com/en-us/research/publication/heap-monotonic-typestate/
12. Fähndrich, M., Logozzo, F.: Static contract checking with abstract interpretation. In: Beckert, B., Marché, C. (eds.) FoVeOOS 2010. LNCS, vol. 6528, pp. 10–30. Springer, Heidelberg (2011). https://doi.org/10.1007/978-3-642-18070-5_2
13. Jakobsen, M., Ravier, A., Dardha, O.: Papaya: global typestate analysis of aliased objects. In: 23rd International Symposium on Principles and Practice of Declarative Programming. PPDP 2021, Association for Computing Machinery, New York, NY, USA (2021). https://doi.org/10.1145/3479394.3479414
14. Kellogg, M., Ran, M., Sridharan, M., Schäf, M., Ernst, M.D.: Verifying object construction. In: ICSE 2020, Proceedings of the 42nd International Conference on Software Engineering. Seoul, Korea, May 2020
15. Khedker, U., Sanyal, A., Sathe, B.: Data Flow Analysis: Theory and Practice. CRC Press, Boca Raton (2017). https://books.google.rs/books?id=9PyrtgNBdg0C
16. Lam, P., Kuncak, V., Rinard, M.: Generalized typestate checking using set interfaces and pluggable analyses. SIGPLAN Not. **39**(3), 46–55 (2004). https://doi.org/10.1145/981009.981016
17. Naeem, N.A., Lhoták, O., Rodriguez, J.: Practical extensions to the IFDS algorithm. In: Gupta, R. (ed.) CC 2010. LNCS, vol. 6011, pp. 124–144. Springer, Heidelberg (2010). https://doi.org/10.1007/978-3-642-11970-5_8
18. Paul, R., Turzo, A.K., Bosu, A.: Why security defects go unnoticed during code reviews? A case-control study of the chromium OS project. In: 43rd IEEE/ACM International Conference on Software Engineering, ICSE 2021, Madrid, Spain, 22–30 May 2021, pp. 1373–1385. IEEE (2021). https://doi.org/10.1109/ICSE43902.2021.00124
19. Reps, T., Horwitz, S., Sagiv, M.: precise interprocedural dataflow analysis via graph reachability. In: Proceedings of the 22nd ACM SIGPLAN-SIGACT Symposium on Principles of Programming Languages, pp. 49–61. POPL 1995, Association for Computing Machinery, New York, NY, USA (1995). https://doi.org/10.1145/199448.199462
20. Strom, R.E., Yemini, S.: Typestate: a programming language concept for enhancing software reliability. IEEE Trans. Softw. Eng. **12**(1), 157–171 (1986). https://doi.org/10.1109/TSE.1986.6312929
21. Subotić, P., Milikić, L., Stojić, M.: A static analysis framework for data science notebooks. In: ICSE 2022: The 44th International Conference on Software Engineering, 21–29 May 2022
22. Szabó, T., Erdweg, S., Voelter, M.: IncA: a DSL for the definition of incremental program analyses. In: Proceedings of the 31st IEEE/ACM International Conference on Automated Software Engineering, pp. 320–331. ASE 2016, Association for Computing Machinery, New York, NY, USA (2016). https://doi.org/10.1145/2970276.2970298
23. Yahav, E., Fink, S.: The SAFE Experience, pp. 17–33. Springer, Heidelberg (2011). https://doi.org/10.1007/978-3-642-19823-6_3

PhD Symposium Presentations

Studying Users' Willingness to Use a Formally Verified Password Manager

Carolina Carreira[✉]

INESC-ID and IST, University of Lisbon, Lisbon, Portugal
carolina.carreira@tecnico.ulisboa.pt

Abstract. Password Managers (PMs) help users manage their passwords safely but many users do not trust them. To mitigate users' doubts, formal verification can be used. Formal verification can guarantee the absence of errors and make PMs more reliable. Nonetheless, the impact it has on the adoption of formally verified software is unknown. In previous work, we performed a preliminary user study which suggests that formal verification increases users' willingness to use PMs. However, a large-scale study is required to confirm our findings. As such we designed and plan to deploy a large-scale study to confirm our previous work and gather further insight on users' perceptions of formal verification in PMs.

Keywords: Usable security · Formal verification · Password manager

1 Introduction

While text passwords are one of the most used security mechanisms, users fail to use them effectively and safely [8,10,12,14]. To combat this, experts recommend the use of Password Managers (PMs) to help users generate and manage their passwords. However, their adoption is low as users do not trust PMs [13]. Formal verification can provide strong assurances, making software more reliable. Previous uses of formal verification in password security include the creation of certified password composition policy (PCP) enforcement software [3] and the use of Coq to model PCPs [6].

A formally verified PM that guarantees properties (e.g. on password generation [1,4,5]) was built in the context of the PassCert project[1]. Even though formal verification could help increase users' trust, we do not know the impact it effectively has on users. Therefore, we designed the first user-studies on users' perceptions of formal verification. Preliminary results from a first study suggest that formal verification has a positive impact on users' willingness to use PMs [1]. A second, larger-scale, study is now being designed.

Our main goals are to gather insights on users' perceptions of formal verification in PMs and to assess if formal verification has an impact on their willingness to use PMs.

---

[1] The PassCert project aims to build a formally verified PM and to investigate ways to effectively convey to users the formally verified properties. Project URL: https://passcert-project.github.io.

© Springer Nature Switzerland AG 2022
M. H. ter Beek and R. Monahan (Eds.): IFM 2022, LNCS 13274, pp. 343–346, 2022.
https://doi.org/10.1007/978-3-031-07727-2_19

2   Current Work

Our current work gathers conclusions from two studies on PMs and formal verification. This section briefly describes these two studies.

2.1   First Study

In the first small-scale study with 15 users, we compare a baseline PM (without formal verification) with a PM that includes visual aids (icons) to highlight formally verified features and brief explanations about them. Our goal was to gather preliminary insights on users' overall perception of formal verification in PMs. The emerging themes from the interviews were: (a) Users associated formal verification with security; (b) The use of formal verification may have increased some users' trust; (c) Users may be more willing to use a formally verified PM [1].

2.2   Second Study

To confirm the preliminary results obtained in the first study, we designed a large-scale study focused on the impact that formal verification has on PMs' users. Specifically, in this second study, we aim to answer:

RQ1. How does formal verification impact users' willingness to use PMs?
RQ2. What features would users like to see formally verified in a PM?
RQ3. Do users value the guarantees that formal verification can provide in PMs?

The design process of this study includes the use of techniques more adequate for large-scale surveys such as Likert scales and closed survey questions. To immerse users in the topic of a formally verified PMs we use vignette scenarios, which describe a protagonist faced with a realistic situation pertaining to the construct under consideration [7]. This study will be deployed in Prolific[2].

To answer RQ1 we present a scenario where we explain what is a PM and we ask users what factors impact their willingness to use a PM. Among these, we include formal verification. If users state that formal verification would affect their willingness to use a PM, we ask why. With this question, we hope to understand why users value (or not) the use of formal verification in PMs. The insights gathered here may provide relevant information about how users perceive formal verification in software and may be applied to other domains (e.g., Decentralized Finance Protocols [2]).

To answer RQ2 and RQ3 we begin by gathering all the common features of a PM (e.g. Password Generator and Clipboard clearing). For each of these, we present scenarios that represent the impact that formal verification can have on each feature. For example, for the Password Generator, the scenario is: "*Imagine that you are creating a new account on a website (e.g. twitter, facebook). To increase security, you ask the Password Manager to generate a password with 7*

---

[2] Prolific is a crowd-sourcing platform that enables large scale user studies by connecting research and users https://prolific.com.

characters and with at least 2 numbers. However, the password generated does not include any numbers." After each scenario, we ask users if that scenario would make them stop using a PM with a 5-point Likert agreement scale.

To minimize the introduction of biases, when designing these scenarios we: (a) remove mentions of formal verification; (b) randomize the order of the scenario descriptions; (c) remove jargon (e.g. "memory" and "encrypted"). By presenting the advantages of formal verification and excluding the term "formal verification" we aim to: (i) mitigate the Hawthorne effect[3] by hiding that the study is about formal verification; (ii) and better understand what specific advantages of formal verification users find important in PMs.

Another important concern is the sample of participants taking part in the study. To help characterize it we ask demographic questions (e.g., age, gender, and ethnicity) and questions specific to our study, including questions about users' previous experience with PMs.

Users' perceptions when using a product are influenced by their assumptions about it (e.g. previous experience or recommendations from friends can shape users trust in a website [11]). As we are studying the impact of formal verification, it is thus important to understand if users are familiar with the concept. With this goal in mind we ask questions about users' familiarity with the term "formal verification" and ask them to define it.

3   Conclusion and Impact

Investigating users' views of formal verification is largely unexplored. We hope to fill a gap in knowledge with the first large-scale user study on users' views of formal verification in PMs. Our work will provide insights on users' motivations and may be used to increase the adoption of PMs.

Correctly identifying where formal verification is valued by users will help understanding the priorities for future implementations of formally verified features in PMs. These insights may lead to: (i) the formally verification of features not yet formally verified; (ii) and, a higher adoption of PMs by matching the users' preferences with the software that is offered to them.

We also anticipate that our findings can be applied to other domains where formal verification is used. Learning about users' current perceptions of formal verification will enable us to address identified issues and misconceptions [2]. Moreover, our methodology can easily be replicated in other domains by adequately adapting the scenarios mentioned in Sect. 2.2.

Acknowledgments. I thank João F. Ferreira, Alexandra Mendes, Nicholas Christin, and Sarah Pearman for their valuable and constructive support. This work was partially funded by the PassCert project, a CMU Portugal Exploratory Project funded by Fundação para a Ciência e Tecnologia (FCT), with reference CMU/TIC/0006/2019 and supported by national funds through FCT under project UIDB/50021/2020.

---

[3] Hawthorne effect consists in users being inclined to agree with researchers [9].

References

1. Carreira, C., Ferreira, J.F., Mendes, A.: Towards improving the usability of password managers. InFORUM (2021)
2. Carreira, C., Ferreira, J.F., Mendes, A., Christin, N.: Exploring usable security to improve the impact of formal verification: a research agenda. In: First Workshop on Applicable Formal Methods (Co-located with Formal Methods 2021) (2021)
3. Ferreira, J.F., Johnson, S., Mendes, A., Brooke, P.: Certified password quality: a case study using Coq and Linux pluggable authentication modules. In: 13th International Conference on Integrated Formal Methods (2017)
4. Grilo, M., Campos, J., Ferreira, J.F., Mendes, A., Almeida, J.B.: Verified password generation from password composition policies. In: 17th International Conference on Integrated Formal Methods (2022)
5. Grilo, M., Ferreira, J.F., Almeida, J.B.: Towards formal verification of password generation algorithms used in password managers. arXiv:2106.03626 (2021)
6. Johnson, S., Ferreira, J.F., Mendes, A., Cordry, J.: Skeptic: automatic, justified and privacy-preserving password composition policy selection. In: 15th ACM Asia Conference on Computer and Communications Security (2020)
7. Lavrakas, P.J.: Encyclopedia of Survey Research Methods. Sage Publications, Thousand Oaks (2008)
8. Lyastani, S.G., Schilling, M., Fahl, S., Backes, M., Bugiel, S.: Better managed than memorized? Studying the impact of managers on password strength and reuse. In: 27th USENIX Security Symposium (USENIX Security 2018), pp. 203–220 (2018)
9. Merrett, F.: Reflections on the Hawthorne effect. Educ. Psychol. 26(1), 143–146 (2006). https://doi.org/10.1080/01443410500341080
10. Pearman, S., Zhang, S.A., Bauer, L., Christin, N., Cranor, L.F.: Why people (don't) use password managers effectively. In: Fifteenth Symposium on Usable Privacy and Security, pp. 319–338. USENIX Association, Santa Clara, CA (2019)
11. Seckler, M., Heinz, S., Forde, S., Tuch, A.N., Opwis, K.: Trust and distrust on the web: user experiences and website characteristics. Comput. Human Behav. 45, 39–50 (2015)
12. Shay, R., et al.: Can long passwords be secure and usable? In: Proceedings of the SIGCHI Conference on Human Factors in Computing Systems, pp. 2927–2936 (2014). https://doi.org/10.1145/2556288.2557377
13. Silver, D., Jana, S., Boneh, D., Chen, E., Jackson, C.: Password managers: attacks and defenses. In: 23rd USENIX Security Symposium, pp. 449–464 (2014)
14. Ur, B., et al.: "I Added '!' at the End to Make It Secure": observing password creation in the lab. In: Eleventh Symposium On Usable Privacy and Security, pp. 123–140 (2015)

Modeling Explanations in Autonomous Vehicles

Akhila Bairy[✉] [iD]

Department of Computing Science, Universität Oldenburg, Oldenburg, Germany
akhila.bairy@uni-oldenburg.de

Abstract. This research approach deals with rational methods for generating explanations provided by autonomous vehicles. The first part concerns a new model for generating explanation content. In the second part, we describe a method for providing explanations at time instants demanding less cognitive workload using game theory.

Keywords: Explanation · Autonomous vehicles · Conflict resolution · Game theory · SAT · Trust

1 Introduction

The autonomous vehicle (AV) vision includes the idea to reduce the number of accidents caused by human error during driving. However in order for AVs to establish themselves on the market, public acceptance of AVs is required. One way of increasing trust, and thus acceptance, is through situational awareness [10] by providing explanations of AV decisions and actions [2,4–6]. Several research approaches exist on providing an explanation [2,4]. In addition to the type of explanation, also its timing and relevance are crucial to ensure trust [2].

2 Related Work and Current Progress

There are two directions in which an explanation can flow. One is unidirectional explanation provided by the automated cyber physical systems (ACPS) to humans. For the ACPS to be accepted by people, they need to make accurate predictions and help the public to understand how they reached their predictions [5]. The other type of explanation is bidirectional debates to understand the AV's actions and its conflict resolution. Conflicts could be the incompatibility of goals between occupants, control systems in the car or supervisory control in each dynamic driving situation. An increase in conflicts would decrease the acceptance of the system. Current constraint solvers, such as Conflict Driven Clause Learning (CDCL) [7] and Craig Interpolation (CI) [8], achieve their results by exploiting

Supported by Research Training Group (RTG) "Social Embeddedness of Autonomous Cyber Physical Systems" (SEAS) at Universität Oldenburg.

M. H. ter Beek and R. Monahan (Eds.): IFM 2022, LNCS 13274, pp. 347–351, 2022.
https://doi.org/10.1007/978-3-031-07727-2_20

methods providing concise logical explanations of conflicts. Existing methods for conflict resolution are built on global introspection into the constraint problem. Our approach to tackling conflicts is a conflict resolution strategy using CI and propositional logic which utilises only the locally available variables.

To understand the need for this method, a real-world scenario is presented in Fig. 1. In Fig. 1a, cars allowed to exit the highway are highlighted in orange. The ego car shown in green is granted the right to bypass the traffic jam, leading to an expected arrival in one hour and 15 min. Here, the goals of individuals and the highway supervisory control would be non-conflicting. Figure 1b depicts a hypothetic further development of the situation, in which a medical emergency situation has occurred in a neighbouring car, which is then (Fig. 1c) signalled to the supervisory control system and the neighbouring cars. The supervisory control system now gives priority to this request by granting the corresponding car rights to bypass the traffic jam,

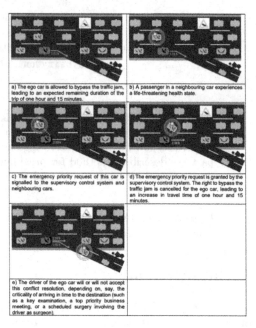

Fig. 1. Stylized traffic scenario

and simultaneously withdraws the right to bypass the traffic jam from the ego car (Fig. 1d). Now there exists a potential conflict between the goals of the ego car driver, of the supervisory system (prevent clogging of the side-road), and the car with the medical situation (quickly obtain medical support). Acceptance of the supervisory system's conflict resolution strategy by the driver in the ego car, and consequently future acceptance of the whole assistance system, will depend on factors such as the personal criticality level of reaching the destination in time (Fig. 1e).

$$\left.\begin{array}{ccc} A_1 \longrightarrow I_1 \longrightarrow B_1 \\ A_2 \longrightarrow I_2 \longrightarrow B_2 \\ \cdot \quad\quad \cdot \quad\quad \cdot \\ \cdot \quad\quad \cdot \quad\quad \cdot \\ \cdot \quad\quad \cdot \quad\quad \cdot \\ A_n \longrightarrow I_n \longrightarrow B_n \end{array}\right\} \Rightarrow \begin{array}{c} \vee A_i \\ \downarrow \\ I \\ \downarrow \\ \widehat{\wedge B_i} \\ B \end{array} \Rightarrow \begin{array}{c} I \\ \downarrow \\ I' \\ \downarrow \\ B \end{array}$$

Fig. 2. CI based model for explanation generation

Our model (Fig. 2) takes into consideration different scenarios and creates interpolants for each scenario. Then, all these interpolants are combined to get a new, simpler interpolant. This model is being implemented in iSAT [3]. According to CI [1], if there exists an implication $A \rightarrow B$ in some logic, then a Craig interpolant I is such that $A \rightarrow I$ and $I \rightarrow B$ are valid and I contains only the common variables of

A and B. Figure 2 is based on CI; $A_{1,2,..,n}$ and $B_{1,2,..,n}$ represent A-local and B-local symbols; $I_{1,2,..,n}$ represents the interpolants for these n scenarios. I is the combined interpolant. I' (interpolant of an interpolant) is the new simpler interpolant of I and it represents concise explanation extracted using locally available information.

The above mentioned method is helpful in conflict resolution. But there is more to an explanation than just conflict resolution. Explanations in AVs can be divided into two types: content and timing. The most commonly explored types in explanation content are: (1) what (2) why and (3) what + why [4]. There are also counterfactual explanations: "what if", which details alternatives and could be invaluable in situations where the occupant is called back for taking control, but very little research is done on this for AVs [9]. Explanation timing refers to the timing when an explanation is provided (before or after an event) [14]. Timing can also be based on the attention level/cognitive workload of the occupant; i.e., does the occupant have low or high workload? Shen et al., in their online survey with 38 different driving scenarios, found that attentive participants needed more explanation [11]. Explanations are not required in all scenarios [13]; they are required only in emergency or near-crash situations [11].

Our aim is to exploit reactive game theory to tweak explanation timing to minimise cognitive workload. Our approach to this uses a reactive game explanation mechanism with the AV and the occupant as the

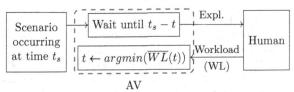

Fig. 3. Conceptual Expl. model using a reactive game

two players. Figure 3 shows a scenario occurring at time t_s. The AV waits until time $t_s - t$ to provide an explanation to the human. The induced cognitive workload (WL) of the human is measured and the explanation timing t is updated. This process repeats whenever the scenario is encountered, iteratively optimising the timing. The reactive game builds on the SEEV model [12], which is an attention model, to provide a stochastic dynamic model on when the occupant would start their own attention strategy (WL) scanning environmental conditions at corresponding cognitive effort. The explanation mechanism moves by the AV in the game represent decisions on whether and when to display an explanation. The explanation also induces cognitive cost, albeit lower cost than an attention shift. So, timely explanations may save overall accumulated cognitive cost by rendering an imminent attention superfluous. Untimely/redundant explanations do however increase overall cost. Construction of a winning strategy in such a game would thus provide a rational mechanism for deciding about explanation display and optimising their timing.

3 Conclusion and Future Work

This paper presents an overview of explanation generation models using SAT and game theory. The next step is to test SAT model on different scenarios and extend it to produce counterfactual explanations. The goals of this project are to generate explanations using the chosen strategy in a way that is understandable to the occupants in real-time and to improve the trust of the humans in AVs.

References

1. Craig, W.: Linear reasoning. a new form of the Herbrand-Gentzen theorem. J. Symb. Log. **22**(3), 250–268 (1957). https://doi.org/10.2307/2963593
2. Du, N., et al.: Look who's talking now: Implications of AV's explanations on driver's trust, AV preference, anxiety and mental workload. CoRR abs/1905.08878 (2019). http://arxiv.org/abs/1905.08878
3. Fränzle, M., Herde, C., Teige, T., Ratschan, S., Schubert, T.: Efficient solving of large non-linear arithmetic constraint systems with complex Boolean structure. J. Satisf. Boolean Model. Comput. **1**(3–4), 209–236 (2007). https://doi.org/10.3233/sat190012
4. Koo, J., Kwac, J., Ju, W., Steinert, M., Leifer, L., Nass, C.: Why did my car just do that? Explaining semi-autonomous driving actions to improve driver understanding, trust, and performance. Int. J. Interact. Des. Manuf. (IJIDeM) **9**(4), 269–275 (2014). https://doi.org/10.1007/s12008-014-0227-2
5. Koo, J., Shin, D., Steinert, M., Leifer, L.: Understanding driver responses to voice alerts of autonomous car operations. Int. J. Veh. Des. **70**(4), 377–392 (2016). https://doi.org/10.1504/IJVD.2016.076740
6. Körber, M., Prasch, L., Bengler, K.: Why do I have to drive now? Post hoc explanations of takeover requests. Hum. Factors **60**(3), 305–323 (2018). https://doi.org/10.1177/0018720817747730
7. Mahajan, Y.S., Fu, Z., Malik, S.: Zchaff2004: an efficient SAT solver. In: Hoos, H.H., Mitchell, D.G. (eds.) SAT 2004. LNCS, vol. 3542, pp. 360–375. Springer, Heidelberg (2005). https://doi.org/10.1007/11527695_27
8. McMillan, K.: Applications of Craig interpolation to model checking. In: Marcinkowski, J., Tarlecki, A. (eds.) CSL 2004. LNCS, vol. 3210, pp. 22–23. Springer, Heidelberg (2004). https://doi.org/10.1007/978-3-540-30124-0_3
9. Omeiza, D., Kollnig, K., Webb, H., Jirotka, M., Kunze, L.: Why not explain? Effects of explanations on human perceptions of autonomous driving. In: International IEEE Conference on Advanced Robotics and Its Social Impacts, pp. 194–199. IEEE (2021). https://doi.org/10.1109/ARSO51874.2021.9542835
10. Petersen, L., Robert, L., Yang, X.J., Tilbury, D.M.: Situational awareness, driver's trust in automated driving systems and secondary task performance. CoRR abs/1903.05251 (2019). http://arxiv.org/abs/1903.05251
11. Shen, Y., et al.: To explain or not to explain: a study on the necessity of explanations for autonomous vehicles. CoRR abs/2006.11684 (2020). https://arxiv.org/abs/2006.11684
12. Wickens, C., Helleberg, J., Goh, J., Xu, X., Horrey, W.: Pilot task management: testing an attentional expected value model of visual scanning. Savoy, IL, UIUC Institute of Aviation Technical report (2001)

13. Wiegand, G., Eiband, M., Haubelt, M., Hussmann, H.: "I'd like an explanation for that!" exploring reactions to unexpected autonomous driving. In: MobileHCI 2020: 22nd International Conference on HCI with Mobile Devices and Services, pp. 36:1–36:11. ACM (2020). https://doi.org/10.1145/3379503.3403554
14. Zhang, Q., Yang, X.J., Robert, L.P.: What and when to explain? A survey of the impact of explanation on attitudes toward adopting automated vehicles. IEEE Access **9**, 159533–159540 (2021). https://doi.org/10.1109/ACCESS.2021.3130489

A Requirements-Driven Methodology: Formal Modelling and Verification of an Aircraft Engine Controller

Oisín Sheridan$^{(\boxtimes)}$, Rosemary Monahan, and Matt Luckcuck

Department of Computer Science/Hamilton Institute,
Maynooth University, Maynooth, Ireland
`oisin.sheridan.2019@mumail.ie`

Abstract. The formal verification of software systems often requires the integration of multiple tools and techniques. To ensure the accuracy of any verification done and to ensure the applicability of formal methods to industrial use cases, traceability must be maintained throughout the process so that it is clear what the requirements for the system are and how they are fulfilled. We propose a three-phase methodology for formal verification with the aim of ensuring traceability, built around the Formal Requirements Elicitation Tool (FRET). Our current case study applies this methodology to the use of FRET, Simulink and Event-B for the verification of the software controller for a civilian aircraft engine.

Keywords: Software verification · Formal methods · FRET · Event-B

1 Overview

Despite the wide applicability of formal methods in industrial applications, particularly safety-critical domains such as aerospace, offshore oil and gas, and the nuclear industry, uptake of formal techniques in industry has historically been slow. To remedy this, the VALU3S project[1] aims to evaluate the state-of-the-art verification and validation (V&V) methods and tools and their application to a number of use cases across different sectors.

We have been working on the elicitation of formal requirements for a software controller using the Formal Requirements Elicitation Tool (FRET), an open source tool developed by NASA that allows requirements to be encoded in a structured natural-language called FRETISH [1]. These requirements can be automatically translated into other formalisms, and the use of FRET reduces ambiguity and simplifies the verification process.

---

[1] The VALU3S project: https://valu3s.eu/.

This research was funded by the European Union's Horizon 2020 research and innovation programme under the VALU3S project (grant No 876852), and by Enterprise Ireland (grant No IR20200054). The funders had no role in study design, data collection and analysis, decision to publish, or preparation of the manuscript.

© Springer Nature Switzerland AG 2022
M. H. ter Beek and R. Monahan (Eds.): IFM 2022, LNCS 13274, pp. 352–356, 2022.
https://doi.org/10.1007/978-3-031-07727-2_21

Our example application is a software controller for a civilian aircraft engine; the model of the controller in Simulink was provided by our industrial partner on the VALU3S project. The controller is a representative example of a Full Authority Digital Engine Control (FADEC), which is a software system monitoring and controlling everything about the engine, including thrust control, fuel control, health monitoring of the engine, and so on. The controller's high-level objectives are that it should continue to control the engine and respect specified operating limits in the presence of various sensor faults, perturbations of system parameters, and other low-probability hazards.

In this research, we address two main research questions:

1. Can we accurately support traceability of formalised requirements in the implementation of (safety-)critical systems using a combination of formal and non-formal methods?
2. How can we reuse diverse V&V artefacts (proofs, models, etc.) to modularise and simplify the software verification process?

We are interested in the integration of multiple software V&V techniques, to provide a framework for reasoning about the correctness of concrete software implementations with respect to their abstract software models, to provide and evaluate practical tool support for software engineers. To this end, we propose a three-phase methodology for the verification of software systems.

2   Three-Phase Methodology

Our workflow takes requirements in natural-language and a Simulink diagram as input, and enables the formal verification of the system's design against the requirements. In the case of our current use case, these requirements and Simulink model have been provided by our industrial partner on the VALU3S project. Our approach is split into three distinct phases, shown in Fig. 1. First, in Phase 1 we elicit and formalise the natural language requirements using FRET. Then we move on to formal verification either supported (Phase 2A) or guided (Phase 2B) by FRET. The 'FRET-Supported' toolchain uses FRET's built-in translation function to produce contracts in the CoCoSpec language that can be incorporated into a Simulink diagram.

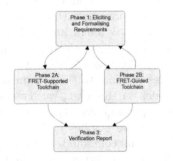

Fig. 1. High-Level Flowchart of our Methodology. After Phase 1 is complete, Phases 2A and 2B can occur in parallel. Phases 2A and 2B can both highlight deficiencies in the requirements, prompting a return to Phase 1.

The 'FRET-Guided' toolchain uses the formalised requirements to drive the (manual) translation into other formal methods as chosen by the verifier. Both verification phases can be applied in parallel. Finally, Phase 3 involves the assembly of a verification report to capture the verification results and traceability of requirements. The methodology is presented in full in [2]. A report on our experience using FRET is presented in [3].

3 'FRET-Guided' Modelling

The current focus of this PhD is on Phase 2B of our methodology, 'FRET-Guided' verification in Event-B. A flowchart of this phase is shown in Fig. 2.

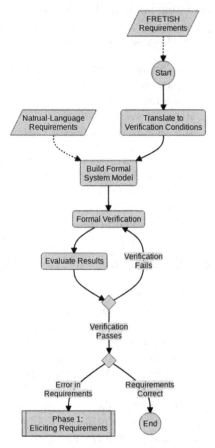

Rather than using a direct translation of the FRET requirements, the elicited semi-formal requirements and the Simulink model of the software controller are used to construct a formal model in the Event-B language, which can then be verified. Event-B is a set-theoretic modelling language that supports formal refinement [4]. Event-B has been used to verify models of cyber-physical systems, similar to our case study [5]. However, unlike this previous work, our goal is to model the behaviour of the entire engine control system, rather than using Event-B to model a particular self-contained algorithm. Work has also been done on using FRET as a basis for runtime monitoring with Copilot in [6], rather than theorem proving with Event-B.

Event-B offers an intuitive path to constructing a model of the Simulink diagram. We use a context to define variables external to the system we want to model; in this case, we have a composite input signal including operating limits for the engine (e.g. the shaft speed limit) and commands from the pilot (e.g. the desired thrust). Within the Event-B machine itself, we model the blocks from the system diagram as events where the guards are that the respective input variables have been set, and which then apply the specified function and set the variables representing their outputs. By using the Simulink block diagram as a

Fig. 2. Flowchart of Phase 2B: Verification guided by FRET requirements. The circular nodes are start and end points, the rectangular nodes are processes, the diamond nodes are decisions, and the rhomboid nodes are inputs or outputs.

basis and incorporating a consistent naming scheme to tie the events to their respective blocks, we can easily preserve traceability between the models.

Once the Simulink diagram has been adequately modelled, we can refine the Event-B model by incorporating the semi-formal FRETISH requirements as additional guards and invariants. If a conflict is found between the requirements and the existing model, we can return to the Simulink diagram to check whether this represents an error in the translation to Event-B or a failure of the diagram to meet the requirement in question. We may also find an error in the requirements themselves, prompting a return to the requirements elicitation phase.

4   Future Work

After modelling the system in Event-B, we will compare the verification process in Phase 2A and 2B of our methodology, investigating how both techniques can be utilised in parallel to reuse V&V artefacts to modularise and simplify the software verification process. We will also look into techniques to formally guarantee consistency in translation between models and ensure traceability in both directions, such as using institution theory to verify the translation or checking the Event-B model against the LTL specification using ProB.

Additionally, we are looking at ways to improve FRET with new functionality. Currently, FRET allows the user to define informal parent-child relationships between requirements, but we would like to expand this to support true formal refinement. This would be a great aid to both the requirements elicitation process and supporting traceability alongside other formalisms. We are also working on applying refactoring techniques to FRETISH requirements. Refactoring would minimise duplication of information across requirements, and so would streamline the elicitation process and remove opportunities for error. We discuss refactoring in full in [7].

References

1. Giannakopoulou, D., Pressburger, T., Mavridou, A., Schumann, J.: Generation of formal requirements from structured natural language. In: Madhavji, N., Pasquale, L., Ferrari, A., Gnesi, S. (eds.) REFSQ 2020. LNCS, vol. 12045, pp. 19–35. Springer, Cham (2020). https://doi.org/10.1007/978-3-030-44429-7_2
2. Luckcuck, M., Farrell, M., Sheridan, O., Monahan, R.: A methodology for developing a verifiable aircraft engine controller from formal requirements. In: IEEE Aerospace Conference (2022)
3. Farrell, M., Luckcuck, M., Sheridan, O., Monahan, R.: Fretting about requirements: formalised requirements for an aircraft engine controller. In: Gervasi, V., Vogelsang, A. (eds) Requirements Engineering: Foundation for Software Quality 2022. LNCS, vol. 13216, pp. 96–111. Springer, Cham (2022). https://doi.org/10.1007/978-3-030-98464-9_9
4. Abrial, J.-R.: Modeling in Event-B: System and Software Engineering. Cambridge University Press, Cambridge (2010)
5. Bourbouh, H., et al.: Integrating formal verification and assurance: an inspection rover case study. In: Dutle, A., Moscato, M.M., Titolo, L., Muñoz, C.A., Perez, I. (eds.) NFM 2021. LNCS, vol. 12673, pp. 53–71. Springer, Cham (2021). https://doi.org/10.1007/978-3-030-76384-8_4

6. Perez, I., Mavridou, A., Pressburger, T., Goodloe, A., Giannakopoulou, D.: Automated Translation of Natural Language Requirements to Runtime Monitors. In: Fisman, D., Rosu, G. (eds) Tools and Algorithms for the Construction and Analysis of Systems 2022. LNCS, vol. 13243, pp. 387–395. Springer, Cham (2022). https://doi.org/10.1007/978-3-030-99524-9_21
7. Farrell, M., Luckcuck, M., Sheridan, O., Monahan, R.: Towards Refactoring FRETish Requirements. (2022). https://arxiv.org/abs/2201.04531. (to appear)

A Dialogue Interface for Low Code Program Evolution

Luís Carvalho[✉]

NOVA LINCS - NOVA University of Lisbon, Lisbon, Portugal
la.carvalho@campus.fct.unl.pt

Abstract. Low code development platforms allow for the design, deployment, and maintenance of software applications through a graphical user interface which is targeted, primarily, at non-expert users. Despite the graphical interface being more accessible than plain text programming, the end user still needs to identify and put together the required building blocks to achieve the intended behavior, and this generally requires some basic knowledge of programming. To tackle this problem, I present an approach to low code programming by introducing a dialogue interface to such platforms.

A dialogue interface allows the user to write natural language instructions stating what they want in the application. The dialogue is mapped to an ontology representation. From these facts and the current state of the application, we infer a set of operations which must be applied to fulfill the user intent and reach the desired state ensuring that, at each interaction, we only apply the necessary operations.

1 Introduction

In this document, I propose an approach to designing a dialogue interface for program evolution, specifically targeting low code applications such as the Outsytems Platform [1]. In this setting, an application is typically described in terms of high-level components which can be manipulated graphically on the screen.

The core contribution of this work is a program synthesizer that takes natural language instructions regarding the development of a low code application as input, and generates the appropriate operations to satisfy those instructions. This involves having an abstract representation of the application state, as well as mapping the natural language sentences to ontology facts. The domain of those facts represents abstract application components such as actions (e.g. Show) and collections (e.g. MultiValue).

The approach presented in this document proposes to ensure that, given an abstract system representation of a low code application, and a set of ontology facts, we are able to infer which operations to apply in order to guarantee that the application will transition from its current state to the state intended from the natural language instructions. Consider the example of an application containing only a database entity products with attribute name. A user stating "I want to

M. H. ter Beek and R. Monahan (Eds.): IFM 2022, LNCS 13274, pp. 357–360, 2022.
https://doi.org/10.1007/978-3-031-07727-2_22

see a list of products with name and price in the Homepage" would result in applying 1) an operation to add the `price` attribute to the `products` entity; 2) an operation to create a screen called `Homepage`; and 3) an operation to create a table of `product` records with columns `name` and `price` in the `Homepage` screen. The design of this tool involves four critical aspects which are detailed in the following section.

2 Approach

Generate ontology facts from natural language instructions. The first step in the pipeline is to semantically represent a natural language utterance into an instruction ontology. The approach presented in [4] is used to map the user utterances to ontology facts. The authors define an ontology domain which models generic concepts for describing application components in low code platforms, such as the Outsytems Platform. If needed, the system can ask questions to the user to clarify the intended meaning of the user utterance. As an example, some of the concepts inferred from the interaction described in the Introduction, would be: `MultiValue(products)`, `Location(Homepage)`, `Show(products, Homepage)`, `IsComposedOf(produts, price)`.

Abstract system representation. The pipeline described here uses an abstract representation of an application in the style of [3]. An application comprises a set of entities (e.g. database tables), screens, database queries (associated with each screen), and template instances (e.g. a table of records or a record creation form). We infer the initial system representation from the current application state. To do so, we start by inferring which abstract components are present in the application. For instance, if the application already contains a database entity called `E` with a set of attributes `A`, then the initial system representation will contain `Entity(E, A)`. Finally, we also infer which ontology facts would yield such a representation. Following the same example, by inversion of rule (ENTITY), we can infer the fact `MultiValue(E)`. This allows the system representation to be manipulated by either our natural language tool or the low code platform in which the application is being developed.

Infer system components. From the total set of ontology facts (both from the dialogue and from the initial application state, as described in the previous paragraph) we can infer what abstract components will need to be present in the system to satisfy the user instructions. A simple rule-based inference system is used, partially shown in Fig. 1, which is then applied in a forward-chaining fashion. At this stage we infer, from the ontology facts, which entities, screens, queries, and templates will comprise the next state of the application. As an example, consider the sentence "I want to see a list of products in the Homepage.", and its corresponding ontology facts: `MultiValue(products)`, `Location(Homepage)`, `Show(products, Homepage)`. Then, from rules (ENTITY), (QUERY-ENT) and

$$\frac{MultiValue(E)}{Entity(E,\{\})}\;(\text{ENTITY}) \qquad \frac{Show(E,L)\quad Location(L)\,Entity(E,T)}{Query(N,L,\{\},\{E\},\{\},\{\})}\;(\text{QUERY-ENT})$$

$$\frac{\begin{array}{c} Show(E,L)\quad Location(L)\quad MultiValue(E) \\ Query(N,L,S,C,F,W)\quad E\in F \end{array}}{Template(List,k,L,Query(N,L,S,C,F,W))}\;(\text{TEMP-LIST})$$

Fig. 1. Inference rules for entities, queries, and list templates.

$$\frac{}{(S,Entity(E,T);Entity(E,T'),D)\;\xrightarrow{update}\;(S,Entity(E,T');D)}\;(\text{UPDATE-ENTITY})$$

Fig. 2. Transition rule for updating entities.

(TEMP-LIST) (Fig. 1), we can infer that the system will have a products entity, a query on the products table, and a template instance for that same query in the screen Homepage.

Compute system deltas and generate operations. The last stage of the pipeline involves computing the deltas between the system components that we infer and the existing components in the application, generating abstract operations for these deltas, and finally compiling them to a specific low code platform. For this, we use a labeled transition system. These are rules of the form $(S;D)\;\xrightarrow{label}\;(S';D')$, where S represents the current state of the system and D represents the components that are inferred from the user instructions. Each transition indicates what deltas need to be applied, and the label corresponds to the abstract operation that needs to be executed in order to obtain the desired state. Consider the previous example of an application with an existing products table with attribute name. If, from the user instructions, we infer the component $Entity(products,\{name,price\})$, then, by rule (UPDATE-ENTITY) (Fig. 2), we will generate an operation to update the entity.

3 Conclusions

We have developed a the tool that supports the development of simple web and mobile applications targeting the Outsystems Platform [1]. In this setting, we are able to create and update screens, queries, database tables and template instances (record list, detail form, and searchable list) [2] in an existing application. The prototype allows the input of natural language sentences which are ultimately compiled to operations in the Outsystems application model using the approach presented in this document. Future work involves adding support for nested data representations (e.g. one-to-many relationships), as well as static analysis to ensure the soundness of the labeled transition system, in particular ensuring that the operations are applied in a correct order, and a mechanism to identify and allow the upgrade between compatible template types (e.g. update a list of records to become a searchable list of records).

Acknowledgements. This work is supported by FCT/MCTES under Grant NOVA LINCS - UIDB/04516/2020 and GOLEM Lisboa-01-0247-Feder-045917.

References

1. Outsystems: The modern application development platform. https://www.outsystems.com/platform/
2. Hugo Lourenço, Carla Ferreira, J.C.S.: OSTRICH - a type-safe Template Language for Low-Code Development. In: 2021 ACM/IEEE 24th International Conference on Model Driven Engineering Languages and Systems (MODELS), pp. 216–226 (2021)
3. Jackson, D.: Alloy: a lightweight object modelling notation. ACM Trans. Softw. Eng. Methodol. (TOSEM) 11(2), 256–290 (2002)
4. Silva, J., Melo, D., Rodrigues, I., Seco, J., Ferreira, C., Parreira, J.: An ontology based task oriented dialogue. In: Proceedings of the 13th International Joint Conference on Knowledge Discovery, Knowledge Engineering and Knowledge Management - KEOD, pp. 96–107. INSTICC, SciTePress (2021)

Simple Dependent Types for OSTRICH

Joana Parreira[✉]

NOVA LINCS - NOVA University Lisbon, Lisbon, Portugal
jb.parreira@campus.fct.unl.pt

Abstract. The demand to develop more applications and in a faster way has been increasing over the years. Even non-experienced developers are jumping into the market thanks to low-code development platforms such as OutSystems. OSTRICH, a type-safe rich template language for the OutSystems platform, allows for the definition and instantiation of type-safe templates while ensuring a clear separation between compile-time and runtime computations. We formalise this two-stage language and introduce new features to the OSTRICH language, namely parametric polymorphism and a simplified form of dependent types. Such features enable instantiating the most commonly used OutSystems templates, reducing the knowledge required by the developer and easing the development process.

Keywords: Staged computation · Dependent types · Parametric polymorphism · Meta-programming · Low-code · Template

1 Introduction

With the increasing demand in the application development market, more inexperienced programmers started to build applications. Several metaprogramming tools and low-code development platforms emerged to aid software development [5–7].

OutSystems [5] is a low-code development platform with an intuitive visual interface that automatically manages several details about deployment, streamlining the development process. This platform contains reusable pre-built screens, such as lists, and dashboards, that aid and speed up the development of an application. So, for instance, if one were to build an application that lists elements on a screen, one could select a pre-built screen containing a list. However, such pre-built screens pose a problem: they contain temporary dummy data, meaning that developers must manually adjust them to their data to ensure that their application works as expected. Often, such adjustments require the developer to have a good understanding of programming basics. This contributes to a steeper learning curve, hindering the use and adoption of the platform.

That is the motivation behind the development of the OSTRICH language. OSTRICH is a rich type-safe template language for OutSystems [4]. This language supports the definition and instantiation of templates with input parameters. Templates, in this setting, are analogous to the previously mentioned pre-built screens, but their input parameters are the data to which the template

© Springer Nature Switzerland AG 2022
M. H. ter Beek and R. Monahan (Eds.): IFM 2022, LNCS 13274, pp. 361–364, 2022.
https://doi.org/10.1007/978-3-031-07727-2_23

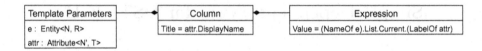

Fig. 1. Model fragment of a template definition and its expressions.

is applied. This language eases the developer's work by automatically adapting the template to the received parameters, thus avoiding time-consuming error-prone manual adjustments. The automated adjustments are defined by annotation nodes present in the language. These nodes contain expressions built during instantiation according to the template input parameters.

However, to create templates based on the most used pre-built screens, some templates require additional verifications and constraints regarding the input parameters [4]. To address this problem, we extend OSTRICH with new features. We introduce polymorphic functions and dependency between type declarations, allowing the definition of templates for more than half of the screen instantiations in OutSystems.

2   Approach

The OutSystems model comprises several user interface elements (tables, widgets, and others), database elements (entities and their attributes), and annotation elements. During template instantiation, the values of nodes' properties can be compile-time expressions, like the title of a column that depends on the name of an attribute (available at compile-time), or runtime expressions, like the values of an attribute's entity displayed in a table cell (only available at runtime). Figure 1 depicts an example of a template definition containing various nodes and both compile-time and runtime expressions.

We formalise OSTRICH, a language that guarantees that all template instantiations are valid and produce valid runtime expressions by ensuring phase distinction [1] to prevent dependencies between compile-time and runtime expressions; OSTRICH accomplishes this through staged computation [3,4,6,7].

That means it is a multi-stage language with a typechecking algorithm that reports both type and phase errors, thus ensuring that runtime and compile-time expressions are well-formed before execution. The algorithm (Algorithm 1) detects phase errors using a supplementary environment, *r-env*, that maps runtime variables to their types. This restricts the typing of runtime expressions so that they only enclose other runtime expressions and variables from *r-env*.

We can delve into Fig. 1, specifically the runtime expression:

$$(\texttt{NameOf } e).\textit{List}.\textit{Current}.(\texttt{LabelOf } attr)$$

Notice the variables *e* and *attr* are compile-time variables. When instantiated in compile-time with an entity `Product` and its attribute `Description`, for example, this expression evaluates to `Product` . *List* . *Current* . `Description`,

---

Algorithm 1. Typechecking algorithm (partial)

---

    input
        expression: Term   ▷ term expression to be typed
        c-env: Env   ▷ compile-time environment
        r-env: Env   ▷ runtime environment

1: **function** TYPEOF(expression, c-env, r-env)
2:    **match** expression **with**
3:       $x \mid x : \tau \in$ c-env $\triangleq \tau$
4:       $u \mid u : \tau \in$ r-env $\triangleq \texttt{Box}(\tau)$
5:       NameOf(M) $\mid$ TYPEOF(M, c-env, r-env) $= \texttt{Entity}(N, \tau) \triangleq$
6:          $\texttt{Box}(\{List : \{Current : \texttt{RecordAttr}(N)\}\})$
7:       LabelOf(M) $\mid$ TYPEOF(M, c-env, r-env) $= \texttt{Attribute}(N, \tau) \triangleq$
8:          $\texttt{Box}(\texttt{LabelAttr}(N, \tau))$
9:       box(M) $\mid$ TYPEOF(M, EMPTY, r-env) $= \tau \triangleq \texttt{Box}(\tau)$
10:       **let box** $u = M_1$ **in** $M_2 \mid$ TYPEOF(M_1, c-env, r-env) $= \texttt{Box}(\tau_1)$
11:              **and** TYPEOF(M_2, c-env, r-env $\cup \{u \mapsto \tau_1\}$) $= \tau_2 \triangleq \tau_2$
12:       $M_1 . M_2 \mid$ TYPEOF(M_1, c-env, r-env) $= \{L_i : \tau_i{}^{i \in 1..n}\}$
13:              **and** TYPEOF(M_2, c-env, r-env) $= L_j{}^{j \in 1..n} \triangleq \tau_j$
14:       $M_1 . M_2 \mid$ TYPEOF(M_1, c-env, r-env) $= \texttt{RecordAttr}(N)$
15:              **and** TYPEOF(M_2, c-env, r-env) $= \texttt{LabelAttr}(N', \tau)$
16:              **and** $N = N' \triangleq \tau$
17:    **end**

---

which is a runtime expression that may be later evaluated. Both NameOf and
LabelOf are compile-time built-in functions that receive compile-time arguments (e and *attr*) and evaluate as runtime expressions, thus securing the well-
formedness of the overall expression.

Inspired by [3], we delimit runtime expressions using a **box** constructor and
use the **let box** destructor to compose such expressions with other runtime
subexpressions. Hence, the previous expression example is written as follows:

$$\texttt{let box } name = \texttt{NameOf } e \texttt{ in}$$
$$\texttt{let box } label = \texttt{LabelOf } attr \texttt{ in}$$
$$\texttt{box}(name . List . Current . label)$$

Algorithm 1 shows part of the typechecking algorithm necessary for typing
this expression. Note, in line 9, that a boxed expression is typed solely according
to its runtime environment (the compile-time environment is empty). Also, the
let box sentence (lines 10 and 11) only accepts runtime expressions, as declared
by its first guard.

Often, some templates require the verification of dependencies between types
of parameters to ensure some relation between values. For instance, the template
depicted in Fig. 1 requires type dependency verification due to the aforementioned runtime expression. Within an entity, we can only access its attributes,
and therefore attr must be an attribute of entity e for the whole expression to
be well-typed. We ensure it through the entity and attribute types, the resulting

types of the functions NameOf (lines 5 and 6 of Algorithm 1) and LabelOf (lines 7 and 8), and the selection operation type represented as ".". (lines 12 and 13).

Besides, both functions (NameOf and LabelOf) are implemented as parametric polymorphic [2] functions, meaning they can be applied to different entities with different numbers and types of attributes while maintaining full-static type safety.

3   Conclusions

To summarise, in this work, we formalise a multi-stage language, OSTRICH, paired with some extensions, such as the abstraction of types and names, and dependencies between type declarations. These extensions help create more Out-Systems templates with increasing variety and possibilities, easing the application development process in this low-code development platform.

There is still plenty of room for improvement in future work by extending the restrictions and dependencies between parameters to allow for the instantiation of more complex templates. Additionally, the developer might want to customise a template after instantiating it. However, if the original template suffers an update, reapplying the new one might cause some conflicts to emerge. Keeping a log of the customisation progress allows instantiating the newly updated template and reapplying such customisations on the new instantiation, unless they do not produce type-safe results.

Acknowledgements. This work is supported by FCT/MCTES grants NOVA LINCS - UIDB/04516/2020 and GOLEM Lisboa-01-0247-Feder-045917.

References

1. Cardelli, L.: Phase Distinctions in Type Theory (1988)
2. Cardelli, L., Wegner, P.: On Understanding types, data abstraction, and polymorphism. ACM Comput. Surv. **17**(4), 471–523 (1985). https://doi.org/10.1145/6041.6042
3. Davies, R., Pfenning, F.: A modal analysis of staged computation. J. ACM **48**(3), 555–604 (2001). https://doi.org/10.1145/382780.382785
4. Lourenço, H., Ferreira, C., Seco, J.C.: OSTRICH - a type-safe template language for low-code development. In: ACM/IEEE 24th International Conference on Model Driven Engineering Languages and Systems, pp. 216–226 (2021). https://doi.org/10.1109/MODELS50736.2021.00030
5. OutSystems: Platform Overview (2021). https://www.outsystems.com/platform/
6. Sheard, T., Jones, S.P.: Template meta-programming for Haskell. In: Proceedings of the ACM SIGPLAN Workshop on Haskell, pp. 1–16. ACM (2002). https://doi.org/10.1145/581690.581691
7. Taha, W., Sheard, T.: MetaML and multi-stage programming with explicit annotations. Theoret. Comput. Sci. **248**, 211–242 (1999)

SNITCH: A Platform for Information Flow Control

Eduardo Geraldo(✉)

NOVA LINCS - NOVA University Lisbon, Lisbon, Portugal
e.geraldo@campus.fct.unl.pt

Abstract. Data confidentiality is critical. Existing approaches to data confidentiality often see their use restricted. To tackle the issue, we present a framework for hybrid value-dependent information flow control in low-level representations to boost the adoption of formal methods for certifying data confidentiality. We pair our framework with a concolic test generator to ensure significant coverage. We aim to support major frameworks such as Spring to ease the certification of web applications.

Keywords: Information flow control · Value-dependent labels · Hybrid analysis · Language-based security · Data confidentiality

1 Introduction

Due to increasing amounts of information traveling through the internet, data confidentiality has become a primary concern for users and companies. Those who neglect this property come under the prying eye of regulatory entities. Test-based certification is not enough to detect information leaks. Alternatives based on information flow control exist but have some issues; they are too restrictive, require significant specification effort, or lack expressiveness.

Information flow control [5] (IFC), the core of many tools, languages, and models [6–8,10], pairs security labels with sensitive data, posteriourly tracking them to ensure noninterference [4]. A central piece in IFC is the security lattice, a partially ordered set of labels with unique least upper and greatest lower bounds for every two labels. The lattice defines how information may flow in a program. Only entities with a label higher or equal in the lattice can, **directly** or **indirectly**, access information with a given label. **Direct/explicit flows** result from operations like assignments or sending data through channels, while **indirect/implicit flows** stem from programs' control structure, c.f. Fig. 1 and Fig. 2, respectively.Depending on the underlying techniques, information flow control mechanisms can be:

- **Static** [9,11] - Analyze programs' source or object code and enforce noninterference. These mechanisms require complete specification and tend to signal false leaks but work in a single passage and cause no overhead in systems.

Supported by FCT/MCTES under grants SFRH/BD/149043/2019 and NOVA LINCS - UIDB/04516/2020.

M. H. ter Beek and R. Monahan (Eds.): IFM 2022, LNCS 13274, pp. 365–368, 2022.
https://doi.org/10.1007/978-3-031-07727-2_24

```
var l //Low                        var l //Low
var h //High                       var h //High
l := h                             if h > 0 then l = 0 else l = 1
// leaks secret information        // can infer h through l
```

Fig. 1. Explicit leak.   **Fig. 2.** Implicit leak.

- **Dynamic** [1,2] - Rely on reference monitors to enforce flow policies. These mechanisms analyze executions and introduce some overhead. Dynamic IFC mechanisms avoid false leaks and accept incomplete specifications.
- **Hybrid** [12] - Combine static and dynamic mechanisms, minimizing the disadvantages of each IFC mechanism. Hybrid approaches reduce monitors' overhead and the number of tests required to ensure good code coverage, avoid false leaks, and enable gradual specification.

2 Approach

To encourage the adoption of formal verification techniques for data confidentiality, we propose an approach based on hybrid value-dependent information flow control to intermediate low-level code. Hybrid information flow control addresses the disadvantages of standalone static and dynamic mechanisms. Value-dependent security labels [7], i.e. security labels parameterized with runtime values, allow for finer-grained policies that better meet developers' needs. Targeting intermediate low-level code confers support to multiple high-level languages (e.g. Java, Kotlin, Clojure, and Scala all compile to bytecode), and allows for a more stable and easier to maintain solution. Furthermore, we aim to support the analysis of web applications using frameworks like Spring and supply a concolic test generation framework to feed the information flow monitor, that is, the dynamic component of our analysis.

Value-dependent labels (k) are user-defined security classes (SC) parameterized with fields (f), method parameters (p), return values (r), $\top$, or $\bot$:

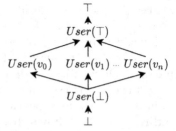

Label $k := SC(v)$
Values $v := f \mid p \mid r \mid \top \mid \bot$

$\top$ and $\bot$ act as least upper bound and greatest lower bound between arguments, cf. Fig. 3. Parametrizing labels allows for the allocation of new security compartments at run-time.

Fig. 3. Dependent lattice.

Label parametrization enhances the flexibility of policy definition mechanisms, allowing for richer policies while avoiding some pitfalls of regular labels. For instance, when analysing a system using regular security labels, one would define a label $User$ defining a single security compartment for all of the system's users, allowing for users to access other users' secret information. To avoid this with regular labels, one would need to know how many users a system would have, an unreasonable requirement in systems dealing with ever-growing user-bases. Using a value-dependent security label $User(\mathtt{id})$, we can define individual security compartments, one for each different user id (known only at runtime). Thus we can avoid unwanted accesses while maintaining a scalable lattice, like the one in Fig. 3, able to accommodate as many users as needed.

Following a hybrid approach, we rely both on a type system and a reference monitor to ensure programs' correctness. The type system works with abstract labels $(\widehat{k})$, as concrete security labels are known only at run-time. The type system also inlines the monitor in target programs, injecting only the necessary run-time checks. In Fig. 4 and Fig. 5 we present a fragment of our hybrid semantics, inspired on [3] where $\widehat{\Gamma}$ maps variables to labels, $\widehat{pc}$ is the computation's security label, x is a variable, and e an expression. Γ, pc, and k are the dynamic counterparts of $\widehat{\Gamma}$, $\widehat{pc}$, and $\widehat{k}$ respectively.

$$
\begin{array}{c}
[\![\text{S-VARIABLE-WRITE}]\!] \\
\dfrac{\widehat{\Gamma}(x) = \widehat{k}_1 \quad \widehat{\Gamma}, \widehat{pc} \vdash e \rightsquigarrow e' : \widehat{k}_2 \quad \widehat{pc} \sqsubseteq \widehat{k}_1 \quad \widehat{k}_3 = \widehat{pc} \sqcup \widehat{k}_2}{\widehat{pc} \vdash \{\widehat{\Gamma}\} x := e \rightsquigarrow x := e'\{\widehat{\Gamma}[x : \widehat{k}_3]\}}
\end{array}
\qquad
\begin{array}{c}
[\![\text{S-VARIABLE-WRITE-UNSAFE}]\!] \\
\dfrac{\widehat{\Gamma}(x) = \widehat{k}_1 \quad \widehat{\Gamma}, \widehat{pc} \vdash e \rightsquigarrow e' : \widehat{k}_2 \quad \widehat{pc} \sqsubseteq \widehat{k}_1 \downarrow \quad \widehat{k}_3 = \widehat{pc} \sqcup \widehat{k}_2}{\widehat{pc} \vdash \{\widehat{\Gamma}\} x := e \rightsquigarrow \|x := e'\|\{\widehat{\Gamma}[x : \widehat{k}_3]\}}
\end{array}
$$

Fig. 4. Type system semantics for assignments.

$$
\begin{array}{c}
[\![\text{D-VARIABLE-WRITE}]\!] \\
\dfrac{\Gamma(x) = v'^{k_1} \quad \Gamma \vdash e \Downarrow_{pc} v^{k_2} \dashv \Gamma'}{pc \vdash \{\Gamma\} \; x := e \; \{\Gamma'[x = v^{pc \sqcup k}]\}}
\end{array}
\qquad
\begin{array}{c}
[\![\text{D-VARIABLE-WRITE-GUARDED}]\!] \\
\dfrac{\Gamma(x) = v'^{k_1} \quad \Gamma \vdash e \Downarrow_{pc} v^{k_2} \dashv \Gamma' \quad pc \sqsubseteq k_1}{pc \vdash \{\Gamma\} \; \|x := e\| \; \{\Gamma'[x = v^{pc \sqcup k} : T]\}}
\end{array}
$$

Fig. 5. Monitor semantics for assignments.

The static semantic takes a $\widehat{\Gamma}$ and an instruction, rewriting the instruction if necessary and producing a $\widehat{\Gamma}'$ reflecting the changes associated with the instruction. According to the semantic in Fig. 4, an assignment has possible three outcomes: (1) by [S-VARIABLE-WRITE], the assignment is correct; (2) by [S-VARIABLE-WRITE-UNSAFE], the assignment is not correct nor incorrect, we need runtime checks; (3) no rule applies, the assignment is incorrect. Tracking the $\widehat{pc}$ allows to avoid implicit information leaks. Where purely static approaches may reject programs, our type system delegates the decision to the monitor as $pc \sqsubseteq k_1$ may hold at runtime.

The monitor evaluates statements or expressions under a certain pc performing verifications only where necessary. Hence, the semantics (Fig. 5) foresees two instruction types, safe and unsafe. The former ([D-VARIABLE-WRITE]) only propagates labels, while the latter ([D-VARIABLE-WRITE-GUARDED]) entails runtime checks ($pc \sqsubseteq k_1$). The monitor avoids false leaks and supports scarce specifications. Combining the type system with the monitor reduces the number of traces required and the overhead induced in target systems.

The test generation framework, still ongoing work, relies on concolic execution to generate inputs for program's under analysis; test required for the monitor to achieve good code coverage. Concolic test generation allows for a controlled exploration of untouched control flow paths without exponential memory consumption. By tweaking the test generation parameters, we can increase the coverage of monitored code executed while reducing the total number of tests.

3   Conclusion

To summarize, we propose an approach based on hybrid IFC; combining static and dynamic mechanisms reduces the downsides of each mechanism. Value-dependent security labels allow for richer and more detailed policies. We target low-level code, conferring our approach the ability to analyze programs in multiple mainstream languages. Finally, we aim to supply a concolic test generator to further automate program verification while obtaining better code coverage and, therefore, better guarantees of the absence of information leaks.

References

1. Arzt, S., et al.: Flowdroid: precise context, flow, field, object-sensitive and lifecycle-aware taint analysis for android apps, pp. 259–269. PLDI 2014 (2014)
2. Austin, T.H., Flanagan, C.: Efficient purely-dynamic information flow analysis. PLAS 2009 (2009)
3. Banerjee, A., Naumann, D.A.: Secure information flow and pointer confinement in a java-like language, p. 253. CSFW 2002 (2002)
4. Barthe, G., Rezk, T.: Non-interference for a JVM-like language, pp. 103–112. TLDI 2005 (2005)
5. Denning, D.E.: A lattice model of secure information flow. Commun. ACM **19**, 236–243 (1976)
6. Fennell, L., Thiemann, P.: Gradual security typing with references. In: CSF, pp. 224–239 (2013)
7. Lourenço, L., Caires, L.: Dependent information flow types. SIGPLAN Not, pp. 317–328 (2015)
8. Myers, A.C., Liskov, B.: Protecting privacy using the decentralized label model. ACM Trans. Softw. Eng. Methodol **19**, 410–442 (2000)
9. Myers, A.C., Zheng, L., Zdancewic, S., Chong, S., Nystrom, N.: Jif 3.0: Java information flow (2006). Accessed 15 Oct 2021
10. Polikarpova, N., Stefan, D., Yang, J., Itzhaky, S., Hance, T., Solar-Lezama, A.: Liquid information flow control. Lang. In: Proc. ACM Program (2020)
11. Simonet, V.: The Flow Caml System: Documentation and user's manual (2003). https://bit.ly/35E5lJ6. Accessed 15 Oct 2021
12. Toro, M., Garcia, R., Tanter, E.: Type-driven gradual security with references. ACM Trans. Program. Lang. Syst. **40**, 1–55 (2018)

Machine-Assisted Proofs for Institutions in Coq

Conor Reynolds$^{(\boxtimes)}$ ⓘ and Rosemary Monahan ⓘ

Department of Computer Science/Hamilton Institute, Maynooth University,
Maynooth, Ireland
`conor.reynolds@mu.ie`

Abstract. The theory of institutions provides an abstract mathematical framework for specifying logical systems and their semantic relationships. Institutions are based on category theory and have deep roots in a well-developed branch of algebraic specification. However, there are no machine-assisted proofs of correctness for institution-theoretic constructions, making them difficult to incorporate into mainstream formal methods. This paper provides an overview of our approach to formalizing the theory of institutions in the Coq proof assistant. We instantiate this framework with the institutions *FOPEQ* for first-order predicate logic and *EVT* for the Event-B specification language.

1 Introduction

The theory of institutions dates to Goguen and Burstall's 1984 paper [6] and the subsequent more detailed analysis in 1992 [7]. An institution is a mathematical realisation of the notion of "logical system" which does not commit to any one concrete system. The key insight is that many general results about logical systems do not depend in any interesting way on the details of those systems. In her PhD thesis, Marie Farrell [5] uses the theory of institutions to provide a semantics for the Event-B formal modelling method with an eye to addressing some drawbacks of the Event-B language—namely the lack of standardised modularisation constructs. *EVT* was shown in [5], on paper, to support such constructs.

Indeed, the theory of institutions has been applied to a wide variety of languages and formal methods: CLEAR [2], CSP [12], and UML [10] have been given an institution-theoretic semantics, to name a few. The HETS tool for heterogeneous specification [11] has the largest single repository of such institutions and their logical relationships, represented mainly by institution morphisms and comorphisms. The cost is that it can be difficult to set up a formalism in the theory of institutions, and to ensure that the encoding satisfies the constraints of that theory. Furthermore, there are, as far as we know, no machine-checked proofs that these constructions are correct. This research intends to address both problems.

Funded by the Irish Research Council (GOIPG/2019/4529).

M. H. ter Beek and R. Monahan (Eds.): IFM 2022, LNCS 13274, pp. 369–372, 2022.
https://doi.org/10.1007/978-3-031-07727-2_25

To this end, we built a framework in the Coq proof assistant [4] for interactive machine-assisted proofs for institutions. To date it has been instantiated to two institutions: the institution *FOPEQ* for first-order predicate logic and the institution *EVT* for Event-B. Many of the requirements and supporting proofs are novel and interesting, but some amount to little more than tedious bookkeeping; an interactive proof assistant such as Coq provides just enough automation to handle simple proofs, while allowing the user to step in and prove more complex results manually via Coq's sophisticated tactic language, if necessary.

Our framework relies on John Wiegley's category theory developments [14] and builds on the work done by Gunther, Gadea, and Pagano [8] formalizing multi-sorted universal algebra in Agda. We also note some other work in this direction in Coq by Capretta [3], and by Amato, Maggesi, Parton, and Brogi [1] which makes use of homotopy type theory. None go quite as far as defining institutions or instantiating first-order logic at the time of this writing; this is the first such formalization of which we are aware.

2   Mathematical Background and Contributions

An *institution* [6] consists of

- a category Sig of signatures;
- a sentence functor Sen : Sig → Set;
- a model functor Mod : Sig^{op} → Cat; and
- a semantic entailment relation $\models_\Sigma \subseteq |\mathsf{Mod}(\Sigma)| \times \mathsf{Sen}(\Sigma)$ for each $\Sigma \in \mathsf{Sig}$,

such that for any signature morphism $\sigma : \Sigma \to \Sigma'$, any sentence $\phi \in \mathsf{Sen}(\Sigma)$, and any model $M' \in \mathsf{Mod}(\Sigma')$, the *satisfaction condition* holds:

$$M' \models_{\Sigma'} \mathsf{Sen}(\sigma)(\phi) \quad \text{iff} \quad \mathsf{Mod}(\sigma)(M') \models_\Sigma \phi$$

ensuring that a change in signature induces a consistent change in the satisfaction of sentences by models.

The signature category Sig comprise the non-logical symbols of a logical system: data types, constants, functions, and so on. The sentence functor Sen explains how to build sentences over the non-logical symbols. The model functor Mod explains how to interpret the symbols in any given signature. The semantic entailment relation $\models$ explains how to decide if a sentence is true or false in a given model.

The institution *FOPEQ* can be defined briefly as follows: A first-order signature is a triple $\langle S, \mathscr{F}, \mathscr{P} \rangle$, where S is a set of sorts, $\mathscr{F}$ is a $(\mathsf{List}(S) \times S)$-indexed set of function symbols, and $\mathscr{P}$ is a $\mathsf{List}(S)$-indexed set of predicate symbols. The indices decide the arity and result sort of the symbols. A first-order model is a triple of functions interpreting the sorts as sets, the function symbols as set-functions, and the predicate symbols as predicates. First-order sentences are built from the logical symbols $=, \neg, \wedge, \vee, \rightarrow, \forall, \exists$, in the usual way; the semantics for first-order sentences are well known.

The institution EVT [5] provides a semantics for the Event-B formal method. It is used to model systems which can be abstractly represented as a discrete transition system. A transition in this framework is called an *event*, and is represented by a sequence of variable-update statements $x_i := T_i$, where x_i is a variable and T_i a term. In EVT this is rendered as an equation $x_i' = T_i$ in first-order logic, with T_i consisting of only unprimed variables. Primed variables represent the next state, and unprimed variables represent the current state. Hence EVT, at its core, can be thought of as $FOPEQ$ with state-variables—though of course modelling the full system requires us to be more specific.

We define both institutions fully in Coq and prove their satisfaction conditions. According to the `cloc` tool[1] we currently have over 3,000 significant lines of Coq developments. Around 1,200 of those are directly related to $FOPEQ$, with 500 directly related to EVT. The remainder comprise core modules common to both and further developments not discussed here. One thing is certainly clear: considerably less effort is required when one institution builds on another. Additionally, both institutions required for their development many reusable components which will aid in the construction of other concrete institutions and with proving their satisfaction conditions.

A major difficulty was deciding on a representation of first-order logic which is clear, concise, and which captures beyond doubt the mathematical structure being represented. Proofs involving indexed types in Coq are also notoriously difficult, but we suspect the difficulties to be uniform across most institutions. The lessons we have learned should be applicable to many other institutions— and could even be encoded into sophisticated automatic tactics.

3   Conclusions and Future Work

Having a formal framework for defining institutions continues to be useful in our own work. Indeed, we have already begun applying it to the problem of integrating linear-time temporal logic with Event-B, with a similar semantics to Hoang *et al.* [9]. Much work is already done in this direction, and we can say confidently that the guidance of the formal infrastructure has been invaluable. We hope in the future that this framework could facilitate wider adoption of the theory of institutions by alleviating some of the pain of constructing them.

We have also defined some institution-independent constructions, specifically modal and linear-time temporal logics over an arbitrary institution. We also have defined a very straightforward comorphism between $FOPEQ$ and EVT, an entailment system for $FOPEQ$, and a basic theory of derived signature morphisms and the term monad.

We intend in the future to show that both $FOPEQ$ and EVT have the amalgamation property [13], since model amalgamation is key for modularity. We also intend to add more concrete institutions to this framework, link them with institution (co)morphisms, and improve proof automation for institutions.

---

[1] https://github.com/AlDanial/cloc.

This work could also, in time, become a fully formal basis for the work already done for the HETS tool for heterogeneous specification.

References

1. Amato, G., Maggesi, M., Parton, M., Brogi, C.P.: Universal algebra in UniMath (2020). http://arxiv.org/abs/2007.04840
2. Burstall, R.M., Goguen, J.A.: The semantics of clear, a specification language. In: Bjøorner, D. (ed.) Abstract Software Specifications. LNCS, vol. 86, pp. 292–332. Springer, Heidelberg (1980). https://doi.org/10.1007/3-540-10007-5_41
3. Capretta, V.: Universal algebra in type theory. In: Bertot, Y., Dowek, G., Théry, L., Hirschowitz, A., Paulin, C. (eds.) TPHOLs 1999. LNCS, vol. 1690, pp. 131–148. Springer, Heidelberg (1999). https://doi.org/10.1007/3-540-48256-3_10. https://doi.org/10/fqj9bm
4. Coq Development Team: The Coq Proof Assistant (2022). https://coq.inria.fr/
5. Farrell, M.: Event-B in the Institutional Framework: Defining a Semantics, Modularisation Constructs and Interoperability for a Specification Language (2017). http://mural.maynoothuniversity.ie/9911/
6. Goguen, J.A., Burstall, R.M.: Introducing institutions. In: Clarke, E., Kozen, D. (eds.) Logic of Programs 1983. LNCS, vol. 164, pp. 221–256. Springer, Heidelberg (1984). https://doi.org/10.1007/3-540-12896-4_366. https://doi.org/10/dtcsqb
7. Goguen, J.A., Burstall, R.M.: Institutions: abstract model theory for specification and programming. J. ACM **39**(1), 95–146 (1992). https://doi.org/10/d9h9wf
8. Gunther, E., Gadea, A., Pagano, M.: Formalization of universal algebra in Agda. Electron. Notes Theor. Comput. Sci. **338**, 147–166 (2018). https://doi.org/10/gh36j7
9. Hoang, T.S., Schneider, S., Treharne, H., Williams, D.M.: Foundations for using linear temporal logic in Event-B refinement. Formal Aspects Comput. **28**(6), 909–935 (2016). https://doi.org/10.1007/s00165-016-0376-0. https://doi.org/10/f864wr
10. Knapp, A., Mossakowski, T., Roggenbach, M., Glauer, M.: An institution for simple UML state machines. In: Egyed, A., Schaefer, I. (eds.) FASE 2015. LNCS, vol. 9033, pp. 3–18. Springer, Heidelberg (2015). https://doi.org/10.1007/978-3-662-46675-9_1. https://doi.org/10/gjsjxn
11. Mossakowski, T., Maeder, C., Lüttich, K.: The heterogeneous tool set, HETS. In: Grumberg, O., Huth, M. (eds.) TACAS 2007. LNCS, vol. 4424, pp. 519–522. Springer, Heidelberg (2007). https://doi.org/10.1007/978-3-540-71209-1_40. https://doi.org/10/b9w795
12. Roggenbach, M.: CSP-CASL-a new integration of process algebra and algebraic specification. Theor. Comput. Sci. **354**(1), 42–71 (2006). https://doi.org/10/cwjgw4. http://www.sciencedirect.com/science/article/pii/S0304397505008534
13. Sannella, D., Tarlecki, A.: Foundations of Algebraic Specification and Formal Software Development. Monographs in Theoretical Computer Science. An EATCS Series, Springer, Heidelberg (2012). https://doi.org/10.1007/978-3-642-17336-3
14. Jwiegley: Jwiegley/category-theory (2014). https://github.com/jwiegley/category-theory

Author Index

Printed in the United States
by Baker & Taylor Publisher Services